Alaska

Ji

LONELY PLANET PUBLICATIONS
Melbourne • Oakland • London • Paris

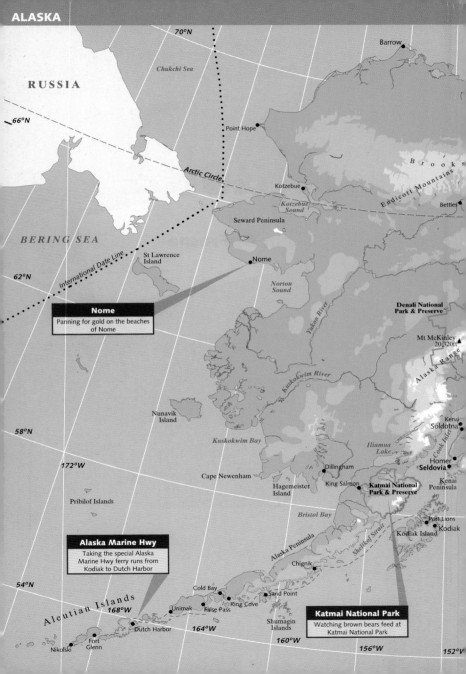

ALASKA

RUSSIA

Chukchi Sea

70°N

Barrow

66°N

Point Hope

Arctic Circle

Kotzebue

B r o o k s

Endicott Mountains

Bettles

Kotzebue Sound

Seward Peninsula

BERING SEA

International Date Line

St Lawrence Island

Nome

62°N

Norton Sound

Denali National Park & Preserve

Nome
Panning for gold on the beaches of Nome

Mt McKinley
20,320ft

Yukon River

Alaska Range

Nunavik Island

58°N

Kuskokwim River

Kenai
Soldotna

172°W

Kuskokwim Bay

Iliamna Lake

Homer
Seldovia

Dillingham

Kenai Peninsula

Cape Newenham

King Salmon

Katmai National Park & Preserve

Hagemeister Island

Cook Inlet

Pribilof Islands

Bristol Bay

Port Lions
Kodiak

Kodiak Island

Alaska Marine Hwy
Taking the special Alaska Marine Hwy ferry runs from Kodiak to Dutch Harbor

Alaska Peninsula

Shelikof Strait

Chignik

54°N

A l e u t i a n   I s l a n d s

168°W

Cold Bay

Sand Point

Katmai National Park
Watching brown bears feed at Katmai National Park

Unimak

False Pass

King Cove

164°W

Shumagin Islands

160°W

156°W

152°W

Nikolski

Fort Glenn

Dutch Harbor

Elevation

1600ft
1200ft
8000ft
4000ft
2000ft
Sea Level

ARCTIC OCEAN

Prudhoe Bay

Philip Smith Mountains

Range

Porcupine River

Northwest Territories

Chena Hot Springs
Soaking in the hot springs at
Chena Hot Springs Resort

Arctic Circle

Denali Park & Preserve
Viewing wildlife from the Denali
Park & Preserve shuttle

Yukon River

Circle

Livengood

White Mountains

Fairbanks

Chena Hot Springs

Eagle

Nenana

Healy

Delta
Junction

Alaska Hwy

Boundary

Yukon Territory

CANADA

Tok

Cantwell

Wrangell Mountains

Talkeetna

Talkeetna Mountains

Glennallen

Carmacks

Wasilla   Palmer

Anchorage   Valdez

Chugach Mountains

McCarthy

Haines Junction

Whitehorse

McCarthy
Visiting the Kennecott copper
mine ruins

**White Pass &
Yukon Route**
Riding the White Pass & Yukon
Route train from Skagway

Whittier

Prince
William
Sound

Cordova

Bering Glacier

Atlin

Seward

Kenai Fjords
National Park

Yakutat

Skagway

GULF OF
ALASKA

Haines

Glacier Bay
National Park
& Preserve

Gustavus

Juneau

Juneau
Viewing the Mendenhall Glacier

Admiralty
Island

British
Columbia

Cordova
Watching Childs Glacier calve

Sitka

Petersburg

Baranof
Island

Kupreanof
Island

Wrangell

Anchorage
Climbing Flattop Mtn to
view Mt McKinley

Alexander Archipelago

Prince of
Wales Island

Ketchikan

**Kenai Fjords
National Park**
Taking glacier and wildlife
cruises into Kenai Fjords
National Park

Dixon Entrance

PACIFIC OCEAN

148°W

144°W

140°W

136°W

132°W

0   150   300 km
0   100   200 miles

11

11

6

3

2

5

8   4

1

1

7

Alaska
6th edition – August 2000
First published – June 1983

Published by
Lonely Planet Publications Pty Ltd A.C.N. 005 607 983
192 Burwood Rd, Hawthorn, Victoria 3122, Australia

Lonely Planet Offices
Australia PO Box 617, Hawthorn, Victoria 3122
USA 150 Linden St, Oakland, CA 94607
UK 10a Spring Place, London NW5 3BH
France 1 rue du Dahomey, 75011 Paris

Photographs
Most of the images in this guide are available for licensing from
Lonely Planet Images.
email: lpi@lonelyplanet.com.au

Front cover photograph
Mt Redoubt from Sterling Hwy, Southcentral Alaska
(Randy Brandon/Alaska Stock)

ISBN 0 86442 754 9

text © Jim DuFresne 2000
maps © Lonely Planet 2000
photos © photographers as indicated 2000

Printed by The Bookmaker Pty Ltd
Printed in China

Contents

INTRODUCTION ... 11

FACTS ABOUT ALASKA ... 14

History 14
Geography 20
Geology 23
Climate &
the 24-Hour Day 24
Ecology & Environment .. 25
National Parks 26
Government & Politics ... 28
Economy 28
Population & People 30
Education 33
Arts 33
Society & Conduct 34
Religion 35

FACTS FOR THE VISITOR ... 36

Suggested Itineraries 36
Planning 36
Tourist Offices 39
Visas & Documents 40
Embassies & Consulates . 41
Customs 42
Money 42
Post & Communications . 45
Internet Resources 47
Books 48
Films & TV Shows 51
Newspapers & Magazines 52
Radio & TV 52
Photography & Video ... 52
Time 54
Electricity 54
Weights & Measures 54
Laundry 54
Health 54
Women Travelers 57
Gay & Lesbian Travelers . 57
Disabled Travelers 57
Senior Travelers 58
Travel With Children 58
Useful Organizations 58
Dangers & Annoyances .. 59
Legal Matters 61
Business Hours 61
Public Holidays &
Special Events 61
Courses 63
Work 63
Accommodations 65
Food 68
Drinks 69
Entertainment 69
Spectator Sports 70
Shopping 70

GETTING THERE & AWAY ... 72

Air 72
Land 78
Sea 82
Organized Tours 86

GETTING AROUND ... 88

Air 88
Bus 90
Train 92
Car 95
Bicycle 96
Boat 98
Local Transportation 99
Organized Tours 99

THE WILDERNESS ... 101

The Wilderness
Experience 101
Backpacking **110**
Chilkoot Trail 110
Resurrection Pass Trail . . 112
Russian Lakes Trail 114
Johnson Pass Trail 115
Coastal Trail 116
Chena Dome Trail 117
Pinnell Mountain Trail .. 119
White Mountains
Summit Trail 120
Denali National Park –
Mt Eielson Circuit 121
Deer Mountain Trail ... 124
Petersburg Lake Trail ... 125
Dan Moller Trail 126
Katmai National Park –
Valley of 10,000 Smokes 127
Wrangell-St Elias National
Park – Dixie Pass 129

2 Contents

Paddling 130
Misty Fjords
National Monument . . . 132
Tracy Arm 134
Cross Admiralty Island
Canoe Route 137

Hoonah to Tenakee
Springs Kayak Route . . . 138
Muir Inlet 139
Swanson River &
Swan Lake 140
Savonoski River Loop . . 142

Chena River 143
Beaver Creek 144
Other Activities **144**
Bicycling 146
Rock Climbing 147
Wilderness Fishing 144

FLORA & FAUNA OF ALASKA   148

Flora 149   Fauna 153

SOUTHEAST ALASKA   159

Ketchikan **161**
Around Ketchikan 169
Prince of Wales Island . . **174**
Craig 176
Klawock 176
Hydaburg 177
Thorne Bay 177
Wrangell **178**
Petersburg **185**
Around Petersburg 190
Sitka **191**

Secondary Ports **201**
Kake 201
Tenakee Springs 201
Hoonah 203
Pelican 204
Juneau **205**
Around Juneau 221
Admiralty Island **223**
Angoon 223
Pack Creek 224

Glacier Bay
National Park **225**
Gustavus 227
Bartlett Cove 228
Haines **229**
Around Haines 236
Skagway **238**
Around Skagway 246
Yakutat **247**
Around Yakutat 248

ANCHORAGE   249

South of Anchorage . . . **275**
Seward Highway 275
Girdwood 277

Portage 280
Portage Glacier 280
North of Anchorage . . . **281**

Palmer 284
Hatcher Pass 288

SOUTHCENTRAL ALASKA   290

Prince William Sound . . **290**
Cordova 292
Around Cordova 298
Valdez 300
Around Valdez 307
Columbia Glacier 308
Richardson Highway
to Mile 115 308
Wrangell-St Elias
National Park 310

Whittier 316
Kenai Peninsula **320**
Seward Highway 321
Seward 323
Kenai Fjords
National Park 331
Hope Highway 334
Sterling Highway
to Kenai NWR 336
Kenai NWR 337

Kenai 339
Captain Cook State
Recreation Area 341
Soldotna 341
Sterling Highway
to Homer 344
Homer 349
Kachemak Bay 358
Seldovia 361

SOUTHWEST ALASKA   365

Kodiak Island 368
Around Kodiak 376
Alaska Peninsula 378
King Salmon 378
Katmai National Park . . . 379

McNeil River State
Game Sanctuary 383
Lake Clark National Park . 384
Aleutian Islands 385
King Cove 386
Cold Bay 386

Unalaska &
Dutch Harbor 387
Bristol Bay 391
Dillingham 391
Wood-Tichik State Park . 392
Round Island 393

THE INTERIOR   395

George Parks Highway . 397
Wasilla 397
Big Lake 402
Nancy Lake State
Recreation Area 402
Willow 403
Talkeetna 404
Denali State Park 410
Broad Pass to Denali
National Park 411
Denali National Park . . . 413
North of Denali
National Park 426
Nenana 426

Ester 427
The Alcan 429
Tok 429
Tok to Delta Junction . . 431
Delta Junction 431
Richardson Highway . . . 433
Valdez to Delta Junction 434
Delta Junction
to Fairbanks 435
Denali Highway 436
Paxson to Tangle Lakes . 437
Tangle Lakes to Denali
National Park 438
Tok Cutoff 439

Nabesna Road 440
Chistochina &
Gakona Junction 441
Glenn Highway 441
Glennallen 441
Glennallen to Palmer . . . 442
Taylor Highway 444
Chicken 445
Fortymile River
Canoe Route 445
Walker Fork
to American Creek 445
Eagle 446

FAIRBANKS   450

Around Fairbanks 468
Chena Hot Springs Road 469

Steese Highway 471

Elliott Highway 474

THE BUSH   476

Western Alaska 478
Nome 478
Around Nome 485
Kotzebue 486

Arctic Alaska 489
Gates of the Arctic
National Park 492

Bettles 495
Barrow 495

GLOSSARY   500

ACKNOWLEDGMENTS   502

INDEX   510

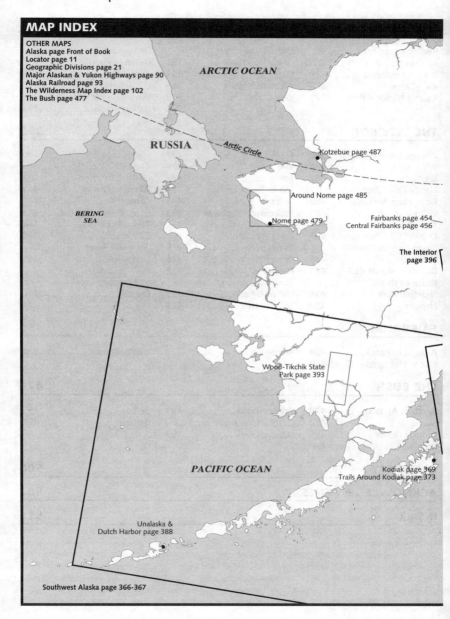

MAP INDEX

OTHER MAPS
Alaska page Front of Book
Locator page 11
Geographic Divisions page 21
Major Alaskan & Yukon Highways page 90
Alaska Railroad page 93
The Wilderness Map Index page 102
The Bush page 477

ARCTIC OCEAN

RUSSIA

Arctic Circle

Kotzebue page 487

BERING
SEA

Around Nome page 485

Nome page 479

Fairbanks page 454
Central Fairbanks page 456

The Interior
page 396

Wood-Tichik State
Park page 393

PACIFIC OCEAN

Kodiak page 369
Trails Around Kodiak page 373

Unalaska &
Dutch Harbor page 388

Southwest Alaska page 366-367

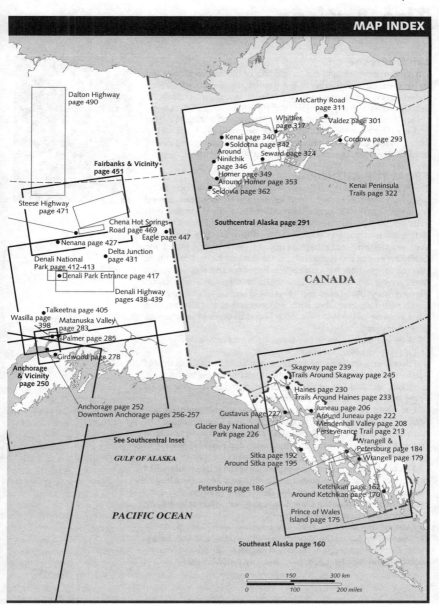

MAP INDEX

Dalton Highway page 490

McCarthy Road page 311

Whittier page 317

Valdez page 301

Cordova page 293

Kenai page 340

Soldotna page 342

Around Ninilchik page 346

Seward page 324

Fairbanks & Vicinity page 451

Homer page 349

Around Homer page 353

Seldovia page 362

Kenai Peninsula Trails page 322

Steese Highway page 471

Chena Hot Springs Road page 469

Eagle page 447

Nenana page 427

Delta Junction page 431

Denali National Park page 412-413

Denali Park Entrance page 417

Denali Highway pages 438-439

Southcentral Alaska page 291

CANADA

Talkeetna page 405

Wasilla page 398

Matanuska Valley page 283

Palmer page 285

Girdwood page 278

Anchorage & Vicinity page 250

Anchorage page 252

Downtown Anchorage pages 256-257

See Southcentral Inset

GULF OF ALASKA

Skagway page 239

Trails Around Skagway page 245

Haines page 230

Trails Around Haines page 233

Gustavus page 227

Juneau page 206

Around Juneau page 222

Glacier Bay National Park page 226

Mendenhall Valley page 208

Perseverance Trail page 213

Wrangell & Petersburg page 184

Sitka page 192

Around Sitka page 195

Wrangell page 179

Petersburg page 186

Ketchikan page 162

Around Ketchikan page 170

Prince of Wales Island page 175

PACIFIC OCEAN

Southeast Alaska page 160

0   150   300 km
0   100   200 miles

The Author

Jim DuFresne

Jim is a former sports and outdoors editor of the *Juneau Empire* and the first Alaskan sportswriter to win a national award from the Associated Press. He is presently a freelance writer, specializing in outdoor adventure and travel writing. He is the author of the Lonely Planet guidebooks *Tramping in New Zealand* and *Hiking in Alaska* and contributed a story about a death on an Alaskan raft trip to *Lonely Planet Unpacked*. His other books include wilderness guides to Isle Royale, Voyageurs and Glacier Bay National Parks.

FROM THE AUTHOR

The first time I researched Lonely Planet's Alaska guidebook, I was single and carefree. Now I'm married and the father of two, attend track meets and little league baseball games and am saddled with orthodontist bills. But I would be less than honest if I didn't say the sixth edition of this fine book was the most rewarding one I have ever worked on. That's because my 11-year-old son joined me briefly on one of my research trips. He climbed his first mountain, panned for gold on the Resurrection Pass Trail and was enthralled one evening when a dozen Dall sheep invaded our alpine camp. Through his youthful eyes and 11-year-old enthusiasm for anything that is new, I again realized what a special and overwhelming place Alaska can be to the first-time visitor – and to those of us who visit year after year

"Ever get tired of going to Alaska?" a friend once asked me.

"It's not possible," I replied.

I deeply appreciate all the assistance and accommodations my old Alaskan mates have provided during my many travels to the state, especially Jeff and Sue Sloss, Ken Leghorn and Susan Warner, Ed Fogel and Todd and Geri Hardesty.

I received considerable assistance from Karen Lundquist and Mandie Lewis of the Fairbanks Convention and Visitor Bureau, Ken Morris of the Anchorage Convention and Visitor Bureau and John Beiler of the Alaska Division of Tourism, Jon and Karin Nierenberg of Earthsong Lodge and Kathy Hedges of Chena Hot Springs Resort.

This book would not have been possible without the assistance of my editors and assorted bosses at Booth News Service – Meegan Holland, Dennis Tanner and Phil Moldenhauer – or Annette and the rest of the fine staff at the Clarkston post office, who make waiting in line one of the high points of my day.

Most of all I want to thank my traveling and hiking partners: Nadine Caisley, Samantha Thompson, Alistair Davidson, Bob Storey, Pattie Zwers, Brian Leigh, Ricardo and Rachel Miller, Martin McCaffery, Trish and Julia Finn and, of course, my son, Michael.

This Book

FROM THE PUBLISHER

This sixth edition of *Alaska* is a product of Lonely Planet's US office, in Oakland, California. Wade Fox and Valerie Sinzdak edited this book, with the help of senior editor Laura Harger, Kate Hoffman and Mariah Bear. Christine Lee proofed the text and maps, and Ken DellaPenta created the index.

Shelley Firth designed and laid out the book, with guidance from design manager Susan Rimerman. Rini Keagy designed the cover. Beca Lafore coordinated illustrations. Illustrations were drawn by Mark Butler, Hugh D'Andrade, Shelley Firth, Hayden Foell, Justin Marler, Anthony Phelan, Tamsin Wilson and Wendy Yanagihara.

Guphy, Patrick Phelan, Connie Lock, Sean Brandt, Annette Olson and Eric Thomsen drew the maps. Alex Guilbert and Tracey Croom edited the maps and oversaw the project. Tim Lohnes drew maps and provided much-needed technical support.

Foreword

ABOUT LONELY PLANET GUIDEBOOKS

The story begins with a classic travel adventure: Tony and Maureen Wheeler's 1972 journey across Europe and Asia to Australia. Useful information about the overland trail did not exist at that time, so Tony and Maureen published the first Lonely Planet guidebook to meet a growing need.

From a kitchen table, then from a tiny office in Melbourne (Australia), Lonely Planet has become the largest independent travel publisher in the world, an international company with offices in Melbourne, Oakland (USA), London (UK) and Paris (France).

Today Lonely Planet guidebooks cover the globe. There is an ever-growing list of books, and there's information in a variety of forms and media. Some things haven't changed. The main aim is still to help make it possible for adventurous travelers to get out there – to explore and better understand the world.

At Lonely Planet we believe travelers can make a positive contribution to the countries they visit – if they respect their host communities and spend their money wisely. Since 1986 a percentage of the income from each book has been donated to aid projects and human-rights campaigns.

Updates Lonely Planet thoroughly updates each guidebook as often as possible. This usually means there are around two years between editions, although for more unusual or more stable destinations the gap can be longer. Check the imprint page (following the color map at the beginning of the book) for publication dates.

Between editions, up-to-date information is available in two free newsletters – the paper *Planet Talk* and email *Comet* (to subscribe, contact any Lonely Planet office) – and on our website at www.lonelyplanet.com. The *Upgrades* section of the website covers a number of important and volatile destinations and is regularly updated by Lonely Planet authors. *Scoop* covers news and current affairs relevant to travelers. And, lastly, the *Thorn Tree* bulletin board and *Postcards* section of the site carry unverified, but fascinating, reports from travelers.

Correspondence The process of creating new editions begins with the letters, postcards and emails received from travelers. This correspondence often includes suggestions, criticisms and comments about the current editions. Interesting excerpts are immediately passed on via newsletters and the website, and everything goes to our authors to be verified when they're researching on the road. We're keen to get more feedback from organizations or individuals who represent communities visited by travelers.

Lonely Planet gathers information for everyone who's curious about the planet – and especially for those who explore it firsthand. Through guidebooks, phrasebooks, activity guides, maps, literature, newsletters, image library, TV series and website, we act as an information exchange for a worldwide community of travelers.

Research Authors aim to gather sufficient practical information to enable travelers to make informed choices and to make the mechanics of a journey run smoothly. They also research historical and cultural background to help enrich the travel experience and allow travelers to understand and respond appropriately to cultural and environmental issues.

Authors don't stay in every hotel because that would mean spending a couple of months in each medium-size city and, no, they don't eat at every restaurant because that would mean stretching belts beyond capacity. They do visit hotels and restaurants to check standards and prices, but feedback based on readers' direct experiences can be very helpful.

Many of our authors work undercover; others aren't so secretive. None of them accept freebies in exchange for positive write-ups. And none of our guidebooks contain any advertising.

Production Authors submit their raw manuscripts and maps to offices in Australia, the USA, the UK or France. Editors and cartographers – all experienced travelers themselves – then begin the process of assembling the pieces. When the book finally hits the shops, some things are already out of date, we start getting feedback from readers and the process begins again....

WARNING & REQUEST

Things change – prices go up, schedules change, good places go bad and bad places go bankrupt – nothing stays the same. So, if you find things better or worse, recently opened or long since closed, please tell us and help make the next edition even more accurate and useful. We genuinely value all the feedback we receive. Julie Young coordinates a well-traveled team that reads and acknowledges every letter, postcard and email and ensures that every morsel of information finds its way to the appropriate authors, editors and cartographers for verification.

Everyone who writes to us will find their name in the next edition of the appropriate guidebook. They will also receive the latest issue of *Planet Talk*, our quarterly printed newsletter, or *Comet*, our monthly email newsletter. Subscriptions to both newsletters are free. The very best contributions will be rewarded with a free guidebook.

Excerpts from your correspondence may appear in new editions of Lonely Planet guidebooks, the Lonely Planet website, *Planet Talk* or *Comet*, so please let us know if you *don't* want your letter published or your name acknowledged.

Send all correspondence to the Lonely Planet office closest to you:

Australia: PO Box 617, Hawthorn, Victoria 3122
USA: 150 Linden St, Oakland, CA 94607
UK: 10A Spring Place, London NW5 3BH
France: 1 rue du Dahomey, 75011 Paris

Or email us at: talk2us@lonelyplanet.com.au

For news, views and updates, see our website: www.lonelyplanet.com

HOW TO USE A LONELY PLANET GUIDEBOOK

The best way to use a Lonely Planet guidebook is any way you choose. At Lonely Planet, we believe the most memorable travel experiences are often those that are unexpected, and the finest discoveries are those you make yourself. Guidebooks are not intended to be used as if they provided a detailed set of infallible instructions!

Contents All Lonely Planet guidebooks follow the same format. The Facts about the Country chapters or sections give background information ranging from history to weather. Facts for the Visitor gives practical information on issues like visas and health. Getting There & Away gives a brief starting point for researching travel to and from the destination. Getting Around gives an overview of the transport options available when you arrive.

The peculiar demands of each destination determine how subsequent chapters are broken up, but some things remain constant. We always start with background, then proceed to sights, places to stay, places to eat, entertainment, getting there and away, and getting around information – in that order.

Heading Hierarchy Lonely Planet headings are used in a strict hierarchical structure that can be visualized as a set of Russian dolls. Each heading (and its following text) is encompassed by any preceding heading that is higher on the hierarchical ladder.

Entry Points We do not assume guidebooks will be read from beginning to end, but that people will dip into them. The traditional entry points are the list of contents and the index. In addition, however, some books have a complete list of maps and an index map illustrating map coverage.

There may also be a color map that shows highlights. These highlights are dealt with in greater detail later in the book, along with planning questions and suggested itineraries. Each chapter covering a geographical region usually begins with a locator map and another list of highlights. Once you find something of interest in a list of highlights, turn to the index.

Maps Maps play a crucial role in Lonely Planet guidebooks and include a huge amount of information. A legend is printed on the back page. We seek to have complete consistency between maps and text, and to have every important place in the text captured on a map. Map key numbers usually start in the top left corner.

Although inclusion in a guidebook usually implies a recommendation, we cannot list every good place. Exclusion does not necessarily imply criticism. In fact, there are a number of reasons why we might exclude a place – sometimes it is simply inappropriate to encourage an influx of travelers.

Introduction

It isn't the mountains, sparkling lakes or glaciers that draw travelers to Alaska every year but the magic in the land, an irresistible force that tugs on those who dream about the North Country. No area in the USA possesses the mystical pull that this land has. Alaska ignites the imaginations of people who live in the city but long to wander in the woods. Its mythical title, the Final Frontier, is as strong a lure today as it was in the past, when Alaska's promise of adventure and quick wealth brought the first invasion of miners to the state. Today, they have been replaced by travelers and backpackers, but the spirit of adventure is still the same.

Travelers, drawn to Alaska by its colorful reputation, are stunned by the grandeur of what they see. There are mountains, glaciers and rivers in other parts of North America, but few are on the same scale or as overpowering as those in Alaska. To see a brown bear rambling up the side of a mountain valley or to sit in a kayak and watch a 5-mile-wide glacier continually calve ice off its face are experiences of natural beauty that permanently change your way of thinking.

If nature's handiwork doesn't affect you, then the state's overwhelming size will. Everything in Alaska is big – that is, everything except its population. Alaska has only 609,311 residents, and almost half of them live in one city, Anchorage. Yet the state is huge. At 570,374 sq miles, it is a fifth the size of the USA; as big as England, France, Italy and Spain put together; bigger than the next three largest states in the USA combined; and 120 times larger than the US state of Rhode Island. There is just under a square

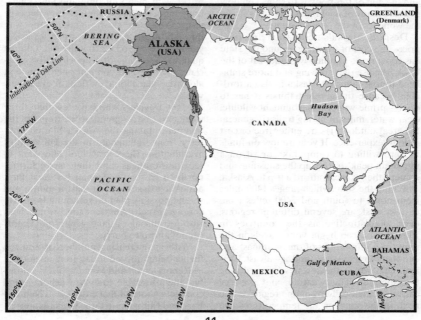

mile for every Alaskan resident. If New York City's Manhattan Island were populated to the same density, only 16 people would live there.

Alaska has the third longest river in North America, 17 of the country's 20 highest peaks and 5000 glaciers, including one glacier larger than Switzerland. The Arctic winters are one long night, and Arctic summers are one long day. In Alaska, you can still find king crabs that measure 3 feet from claw to claw, brown bears that stand over 12 feet tall and farmers who grow 70lb cabbages and 30lb turnips after a summer of 20-hour days.

Two things that have reached legendary proportions in Alaska are the state's mosquitoes and its prices. Traveler's tell tales of insects so large that campers have to beat them back with sticks and of plates of eggs, toast and potatoes costing $15 – myths spread by those who went home bug-bitten or penniless. For most people, a good bottle of bug dope will keep the mosquitoes away, and the aim of this book is to show you how to avoid many of the high prices and still see the wonders of the North Country.

Despite Alaska's reputation for high prices, the cost of traveling around the state has come more into line with the rest of the USA because of a growing and more stabilized tourist industry. Alaska is also affordable because the greatest things it has to offer – prime wilderness, abundant wildlife, clear water, miles of hiking trails (in general the great outdoors) – are either free or cost little to experience. If you are low on funds but are willing to camp, hike or sit on a mountain peak to soak up the sunshine and scenery, then you can afford a trip to Alaska.

Within the state, which ranges 1400 miles from north to south and 2400 miles from east to west, are several different regions, each as distinctive as the countries in Europe. You can begin your travels in the rainy, lush rain forests of the Southeast and end them in the Arctic tundra – a vast, treeless plain where the sun never sets during the summer. The weather and scenery change dramatically from one region to the next. In the summer, the temperatures can range from a cool 50°F in Glacier Bay to a sizzling 95°F on a hot August afternoon in Fairbanks. In some years, rainfall can measure less than 2 inches in areas north of the Arctic Circle or more than 300 inches at the little town of Port Walter in the Southeast. For the purpose of budget travel, Alaska has been divided into six regions in this book, with the main focus on the five areas that can be easily reached either by road or by the Alaska Marine Hwy ferries.

For all the expense and energy involved in getting to Alaska, don't make your trip a seven-day/six-night fling through five cities. To truly appreciate several regions of the state, or even one, visitors need to take the time to meet the people, hike the trails and view some of nature's most impressive features. You can drive or hitchhike from Anchorage to Fairbanks in a day, but in your hurry you will miss small and interesting towns like Talkeetna or outdoor opportunities like the canoe routes in the Nancy Lake State Recreational Area. Independent travel, with plenty of time and few obligations, has a distinct advantage over package tours. You can slowly make your way through the state, stopping when it pleases you and moving on when it doesn't. Often a quaint little village or seaport will be especially inviting, and you can pitch your tent along the beach for a few days, or even a few weeks.

Many travelers who have less than three weeks to spare spend it entirely in the Southeast, taking the Alaska Marine Hwy ferry from Bellingham in the US state of Washington. Those travelers who want to see the Southeast and then move farther north to Fairbanks, Denali National Park and Anchorage need at least a month and should possibly plan on returning from Anchorage by air. Any less time would be a rush job through a land where one simply cannot afford to hurry.

With an increasing number of nonstop flights being offered today from such cities as Reno, Detroit and Minneapolis, it's possible, and affordable, to fly to Anchorage and complete a tour of that city, Denali National Park and Fairbanks in three weeks. However,

Alaska's ever-increasing popularity has not only stabilized the tourist industry. It has also made Alaska a painfully crowded destination at times. Today, travelers are shocked to head into the Kenai Peninsula area and find campground after campground filled in July. Denali National Park can be a zoo in August, and finding a bed in towns like Valdez and Seward at the height of the tourist season is often a nearly impossible task. At times, the George Parks Hwy, between Anchorage and Fairbanks, is just an endless line of RVs heading south.

To avoid the crowds, pack in more days to escape farther off the beaten path, and make as many arrangements in advance of your trip as possible, especially if you plan to visit such popular areas as Denali or Katmai National Parks or hope to secure passage for your vehicle on the ferries. Not a day goes by during the summer without a motorist being stunned to find out in Valdez that a reservation is needed to transport a car to Whittier.

One last thing: for those who have seemingly been dreaming forever about Alaska, it's wise to start your trip at the beginning of the summer, in case you want to extend your stay another month, or even longer. One of the most common stories among residents is how somebody came to visit Alaska for six weeks and ended up staying six years. Once you are in Alaska, you'll find it a hard land to leave.

Facts about Alaska

HISTORY

Alaska's history is a strange series of spurts and sputters, booms and busts. Although today Alaska is viewed as a wilderness paradise and an endless source of raw materials, in the past it has often been regarded as a frozen wasteland, a suitable home only for Inuit and polar bears. When some natural resource has been uncovered, however, a short period of prosperity and exploitation followed: first with sea-otter skins; then gold, salmon and oil; and most recently, untouched wilderness. After each resource has been exhausted, some would say raped, the land slipped back into oblivion.

The First Alaskans

The first Alaskans migrated from Asia to North America between 30,000 and 40,000 years ago, during an ice age that lowered the sea level and created a 900-mile land bridge linking Siberia and Alaska. The nomadic groups who crossed the bridge were not bent

Captain James Cook

on exploration but on following the animal herds that provided them with food and clothing. Although many tribes wandered deep into North and South America, four ethnic groups – the Athabascans, Aleuts, Inuit and the coastal tribes of Tlingit and Haida – remained in Alaska and made the harsh wilderness their homeland.

The First Europeans

Thanks to the cold and stormy North Pacific, Alaska was one of the last places in the world to be mapped by Europeans. Because of this, several countries explored the region and then attempted to lay a claim to the land and its resources by establishing a fort or two. Spanish admiral Bartholeme de Fonte is credited by many with making the first trip into Alaskan waters when, in 1640, he sailed from Mexico up the western coast of North America to Alaska. There he explored a network of rivers looking for the Northwest Passage, a water route between the Pacific and Atlantic Oceans, before returning south.

The first written record of the state was made by Vitus Bering, a Danish navigator sailing for the Russian tsar. Bering's trip, in 1728, proved that America and Asia were two separate continents, and 13 years later, commanding the ship *St Peter,* he went ashore near Cordova, becoming the first European to set foot in Alaska. Bering and many of his crew died from scurvy during that journey, but his lieutenant (aboard the ship *St Paul*) sailed all the way to the site of present-day Sitka before turning around. Despite all the hardships, the survivors brought back fur pelts and tales of fabulous seal and otter colonies – Alaska's first boom was under way. Russian fur merchants wasted little time in overrunning the Aleutian Islands and quickly established a settlement on Kodiak Island. Chaos followed, as bands of Russian hunters robbed and murdered each other for furs while the peaceful Aleuts, living near the hunting grounds, were almost annihilated through disease and forced labor.

By the 1790s, Russia had organized the Russian-American Company to regulate the fur trade and ease the violent competition. However, tales of the enormous wealth to be gained in the Alaskan wildlife trade brought representatives of several other countries to the frigid waters. Spain claimed the entire western coast of North America, including Alaska, and sent several explorers to the Southeast region. These early visitors took boatloads of furs but left neither settlers nor forts, only a few Spanish place names.

The British arrived when Captain James Cook also began searching the area for the Northwest Passage. From Vancouver Island, Cook sailed north to Southcentral Alaska in 1778, anchoring at what is now Cook Inlet for a spell before continuing on to the Aleutian Islands, Bering Sea and even the Arctic Ocean. The French sent Jean-Françoise Galaup, comte de La Pérouse, who in 1786 made it as far as Lituya Bay on the southern coast of Alaska. The wicked tides within the long, narrow bay caught the exploration party off guard, capsizing three longboats, killing 21 sailors and discouraging the French from colonizing the area.

Cook's shipmate George Vancouver, returning on his own in the 1790s, finally charted the complicated waters of the Southeast's Inside Passage. Aboard his ship, HMS *Discovery,* Vancouver surveyed the coastline from California to Alaska's Panhandle, producing maps so accurate they were still being used a century later.

Having depleted the fur colonies in the Aleutians, Aleksandr Baranov, who headed the Russian-American Company, moved his territorial capital from Kodiak to Sitka in the Southeast. After ruthlessly subduing the Tlingit Indians with cannons and soldiers, Baranov built a stunning city, 'an American Paris in Alaska,' with the immense profits from furs. At one point, Baranov oversaw, or some would say ruled, a fur empire that stretched from Bristol Bay to Northern California. When the British began pushing north into Southeast Alaska, he built a second fort near the mouth of the Stikine

Aleksandr Baranov

River in 1834. That fort, which was named St Dionysius at the time, eventually evolved into the small lumbering and fishing town of Wrangell.

When a small trickle of US adventurers began to arrive, four nations had a foot in the Panhandle of Alaska: Spain, France, Britain and Russia. However, Spain and France were squeezed out of the area by the early 1800s, and the British were reduced to leasing selected areas from the Russians.

The Sale of Alaska

By the 1860s, the Russians found themselves badly overextended. Their involvement in Napoleon's European wars, a declining fur industry and the long lines of shipping between Sitka and the heartland of Russia were draining their national treasury. The country made several overtures to the USA for the sale of Alaska, and commercial fishing companies from the state of Washington pushed for the sale. The American Civil War delayed the negotiations, and it wasn't until 1867 that Secretary of State William H Seward, with extremely keen foresight, signed a treaty to purchase the state for $7.2 million – less than 2¢ an acre.

By then the US public was in an uproar over the purchase of the 'frozen wasteland.' Newspapers called it 'Seward's Ice Box' or 'Walrussia,' and one senator heatedly compared Alaska to a 'sucked orange,' as little was left of the rich fur trade.

On the Senate floor, the battle to ratify the treaty lasted six months before the sale was approved. On October 18, 1867, the formal transfer of Alaska to the Americans took place in Sitka, and nearby Wrangell, a town both the Russians and the British had controlled, changed flags for the third time in its short existence.

Alaska remained a lawless, unorganized territory for the next 20 years, with the US Army in charge at one point and the US Navy at another.

This great land, remote and inaccessible to all but a few hardy settlers, remained a dark, frozen mystery to most people. Eventually its riches were uncovered one by one. The first industry was hunting whales, which were mostly taken in the Southeast and later in the Bering Sea and the Arctic Ocean. Next, the phenomenal salmon runs were tapped, with the first canneries being built in 1878 at Klawock on Prince of Wales Island. Both industries brought a trickle of people and prosperity to Alaska.

Gold

What brought Alaska into the world limelight, however, was gold. The promise of quick riches and the adventure of the frontier became the most effective lure Alaska ever had. Gold was discovered in the Gastineau Channel in the 1880s, and the towns of Juneau and Douglas sprang up overnight, living off the very productive Treadwell and Alaska-Juneau Mines. Circle City, in the Interior, suddenly emerged in 1893, when gold was discovered in nearby Birch Creek. Three years later, one of the world's most colorful gold rushes took place in the Klondike region of Canada's Yukon Territory.

Often called 'the last grand adventure,' the Klondike gold rush occurred when the country and much of the world was suffering a severe recession. When the banner headline of the *Seattle Post-Intelligencer* bellowed 'GOLD! GOLD! GOLD! GOLD!' on July 17, 1897, thousands of people began quitting their jobs and selling their homes to finance a trip through Southeast Alaska to the newly created boomtown of Skagway. From this tent city, almost 30,000 prospectors tackled the steep Chilkoot Trail to Lake Bennett, where they built crude rafts to float the rest of the way to the goldfields; an equal number of people returned home along the route, broke and disillusioned.

The number of miners who made fortunes was small, but the tales and legends that emerged were endless. The Klondike stampede, though it only lasted from 1896 to the early 1900s, was Alaska's most colorful era and earned Alaska the reputation of being the country's last frontier.

Statehood

By the 1900s, the attention of the miners shifted from the Klondike to Nome, where gold was found on the beach, and then to Fairbanks, a boomtown that was born when Felix Pedro discovered gold 12 miles north of the area in 1902. The gold mines and the large Kennecott copper mines north of Cordova also stimulated the state's growth. Within three years of the Klondike stampede, according to the 1900 census, Alaska's population doubled to 63,592, including more than 30,000 nonindigenous people. Nome was the largest city in the territory that year, with 12,000 residents, but the capital was moved from Sitka to Juneau.

Gold and the sudden boom it created led Alaskans to clamor for more say in their future. The US Congress first gave them a nonvoting delegate to Washington in 1906 and then assisted them in setting up a territorial legislature that met at Juneau in 1913. Three years later, the territory submitted its first statehood bill to Congress. Statehood was set aside when many of Alaska's residents headed south for high-paying jobs that were created by WWI. Ironically, it took another war, WWII, to push Alaska firmly into the 20th century.

The USA experienced its only foreign invasion on home soil when the Japanese army attacked the Attu Islands and bombed Dutch Harbor in the Aleutian Islands during WWII. Congress and military leaders panicked and rushed to develop and protect the rest of Alaska. Large army and air-force bases were built throughout the state at places including Anchorage, Fairbanks, Sitka, Whittier and Kodiak, and thousands of military personnel were sent to Alaska. But the famous Alcan (also known as the Alaska Hwy) was the single most important project of the military buildup. The 1520-mile road was a major engineering feat and became the only overland link between Alaska and the rest of the USA.

At the time, Japan and Germany, allied with Italy, looked all but unbeatable, and Britain, the Soviet Union and the USA, the only countries with sufficient resources and armies to confront the aggressors, had but one common border – the Bering Strait, the narrow neck of water separating Alaska and Siberia. There was a need both to supply military hardware to Russia and to protect America's northwest flank, neither of which

could be accomplished by sea after Japan bombed Pearl Harbor in December 1941.

An overland route far enough inland to be out of range of airplanes carried by Japanese aircraft carriers was the obvious answer. The US Army Corps of Engineers were sent to build the wilderness route and used seven regiments, three of which were composed of African-American soldiers, to finish the project. The soldiers felled trees, put down gravel and built pontoon bridges at a breakneck pace. On October 25, 1942, after only eight months and 12 days, the Alcan was opened.

The road was built by the military, but Alaska's residents benefited, as the Alcan stimulated the development of Alaska's natural resources. The growth led to a drive for statehood, to fix what many felt was Alaska's '2nd-class citizenship.' Early in 1958, Congress approved a statehood act, which Alaskans quickly accepted, and on January 3, 1959, President Dwight Eisenhower proclaimed Alaska the USA's 49th state.

A Presidential Visit to Alaska

The first president to visit Alaska was Warren G. Harding, who arrived in Metlakatla aboard the USS *Henderson* on July 8, 1923. In the next two weeks, the president visited 11 Alaskan towns and participated in a variety of events and ceremonies. While passing the Taku Glacier near Juneau, gunners on his ship fired 5-inch shells into its face so Harding could watch an avalanche of ice fall into the sea. In Skagway, he became a member of the Arctic Brotherhood, promising 'never to mistreat a horse or dog.' And at Nenana, he pounded a golden spike into the train track to officially complete the Alaska Railroad.

Like most visitors to Alaska, Harding was overwhelmed with the land. Returning to Seattle afterwards, he spoke to a crowd of more than 60,000 people about the future of the territory, rejecting 'sudden exploitation' of its resources by outsiders for slow and planned development that would benefit local residents. He also noted that Southeast Alaska, where most Alaskans lived, was almost ready for statehood.

Unfortunately, the president, a smoker and heavy drinker despite Prohibition, slept poorly during his trip, due in part to Alaska's 20-hour days. He was visibly exhausted during his two-hour speech in Seattle and that evening complained of violent cramps. Harding was immediately placed on the presidential train and was rushed to San Francisco, where he died on August 3, only two weeks after leaving Alaska.

Harding's death was a major blow to Alaskans. Their chances of statehood floundered as the federal government became indifferent to the territory and then were lost when the stock market crashed in 1929 and Washington, DC, had more serious problems on its mind.

The Modern State

Alaska entered the 1960s full of promise, and then disaster struck: The most powerful earthquake ever recorded in North America (registering 9.2 on the Richter scale) hit Southcentral Alaska on Good Friday morning in 1964. More than 100 lives were lost, and damage was estimated at $500 million. In Anchorage, office buildings sank 10 feet into the ground, and houses slid more than 1200 feet off a bluff, into Knik Arm. A tidal wave virtually wiped out the community of Valdez. In Kodiak and Seward, 32 feet of the coastline slipped into the Gulf of Alaska, and Cordova lost its entire harbor as the sea rose 16 feet.

The earthquake left the newborn state in a shambles, but another gift from nature soon rushed Alaska to recovery and beyond.

Alaska's next boom took place in 1968, when Atlantic Richfield discovered massive oil deposits underneath Prudhoe Bay in the Arctic Ocean. The value of the oil doubled after the Arab oil embargo of 1973, but the oil couldn't be tapped until there was a pipeline to transport it to the warm-water port of Valdez. The pipeline, in turn, couldn't be built until the US Congress, which still administered most of the land, settled the intense controversy between industry, environmentalists and Native Alaskans with historical claims to the land.

The Alaska Native Claims Settlement Act of 1971 was an unprecedented piece of legislation that opened the way for a consortium of oil companies to undertake the construction of the 789-mile pipeline. The Trans-Alaska Pipeline took three years to

Alaskan Cuisine: Spam & Pilot Bread

Tucked away in the pantry of every Alaskan cabin for that midwinter siege, when the snow is past the windows and the temperature hits -50°F, is a can of Spam and a box of pilot bread. This is Alaskan cuisine at its best; food that never seems to spoil.

Pilot bread is a round, unleavened cracker that was first baked in New England in 1792, as a type of hardtack or ship's biscuit for sailors to take to sea. By 1920, a Seattle company was baking pilot bread and selling most of it to Alaska. Today, that company is Interbake, and 95% of the pilot bread it makes, or 2 million pounds annually, is still shipped to Alaska.

Why pilot bread? This unique cracker has no eggs or oil to make it go rancid and little water to make it mold. Officially, Interbake says pilot bread has a shelf life of six months. But Alaskans have been known to eat a 10-year-old box of the stuff and not only survive but not notice any difference in its texture or taste.

That's because pilot bread has no taste. It's as succulent as a bowl of sawdust and as appetizing as drywall, but it's always there for whenever hunger pains overwhelm an Alaskan's notion of fine cuisine.

Alaskans eat pilot bread with salmon (dried, pickled or sautéed), with melted cheese, spread with garlic butter or homemade salmonberry jam. You can toast pilot bread and sprinkle it with salt like a pretzel, fry it in bacon grease or layer it with sardines. By far the bulk of the pilot bread sold in the 49th state is consumed by Native Alaskans. They have long since learned that having tea and pilot bread after eating oily traditional foods such as whale blubber (muktuk) cuts the aftertaste and soothes the stomach.

But the best thing to put on pilot bread is Spam because – in the middle of a long cold spell when even the dogs won't go outside – Spam is probably the only other thing in the cupboard. That chopped-ham-in-a-can is such a favorite of Alaskans that the Alaska State Fair in Palmer stages a Spam recipe contest every year. One recent winner was Coconut Beer Batter Spam with Raspberry Horseradish Sauce, thick slices of Spam dipped in a mixture of beer and eggs, coated with shredded coconut and deep-fried.

build, cost more than $8 billion in 1977 dollars and, at the time, was the most expensive private construction project ever undertaken. At the peak of construction, the pipeline employed 28,000 people, doing '7-12s' (seven 12-hour shifts a week) and receiving weekly paychecks of more than $1500.

During the brief years of pipeline construction, Anchorage developed into a full-fledged, modern city, and Fairbanks burst at the seams as the transport center for much of the project. Along with four-digit weekly salaries, prices for basic items such as housing and food rose astronomically in Fairbanks, and some residents feel the prices never came down with the wages.

The oil began to flow on June 20, 1977, and for a decade or more, oil gave Alaska an economic base that was the envy of every other state, accounting for as much as 80% of state government revenue. In the explosive growth period of the mid-1980s, Alaskans enjoyed the highest per-capita income in the country. The state's budget was in the billions. Legislators in Juneau transformed Anchorage into a stunning city, with sports arenas, libraries and performing-arts centers, and virtually every bush town has a million-dollar school. From 1980 to 1986, this state of only a half-million residents generated revenue of $26 billion.

For most Alaskans, it was hard to see beyond the gleam of the oil dollar. Their first rude awakening came in 1986, when world oil prices dropped. Their second dose of reality was even harder to swallow. In March 1989, the *Exxon Valdez,* a 987-foot Exxon oil supertanker, rammed Bligh Reef a few hours out of the port of Valdez. The ship spilled almost 11 million gallons of North Slope crude into the bountiful waters of Prince William Sound. Alaskans and the rest of the country watched in horror as the spill quickly became far too large for booms to contain the oil, spreading 600 miles from the grounding site. Within months, miles of tainted coastline began to appear throughout the Gulf of Alaska as currents dispersed streamers of oil and tar balls. State residents were shocked as oil began to appear from

the glacier-carved cliffs of Kenai Fjords to the bird rookeries of Katmai National Park, and from lonely Cook Islet beaches to the salmon streams on Kodiak Island. The spill eventually contaminated 1567 miles of shoreline; scientists estimated between 300,000 and 645,000 birds were killed, and the 1013 sea otters found dead in the oil represented only 20% of the total killed.

Ironically, Valdez experienced another boom as the center of the cleanup effort, which employed 10,000 workers, 800 boats and 45 oil skimmers. But the best this highly paid army could do was scrape 364 miles of shoreline before the oncoming winter weather shut down the effort in September. Only 14% of the oil was ever recovered by the crews. The rest either evaporated, sank to the bottom of the sea or broke down into components and chemicals on the beaches or in the water. Exxon walked away from the country's worst oil spill, after agreeing to pay a $900 million settlement to the US and Alaska governments.

In the end, the oil, like resources exploited in the past, is simply running out. That pot of gold called Prudhoe Bay began its decline in production in 1989, and in 1995 alone, North Slope oil output decreased by more than 4%. Arco, the state's second largest employer, laid off almost a third of its 2350 employees in Alaska. Other related companies, which move the oil and maintain the Trans-Alaska Pipeline, also began to slash jobs. The end of the Cold War and the subsequent downsizing of the US military in the early 1990s was more economic bad news for Alaska. Fort Greely, Delta Junction's largest employer, was closed in 1994, with more Alaskan bases on the chopping block. Alaskan state revenues, once the envy of the governors of every other state in the country, went tumbling along with the declining oil royalties. In 1982, the Alaska state government enjoyed oil revenues of more than $3.5 billion. In 1999, when oil dropped below $9 a barrel, it received less than $1 billion. Such shortfalls have forced Governor Tony Knowles to slash services and programs in an attempt to balance the budget.

Many Alaskans see another North Slope oil field as the solution to their problems. Large mining projects are being pushed as Alaska faces its greatest debate – over the exploitation of its remaining wilderness. The issue first emerged when industry, conservationists and the government came head to head over a single paragraph in the Alaska Native Claims Settlement Act, known simply as 'd-2,' that called for the preservation of 80 million acres of Alaskan wilderness. To most residents, this paragraph evoked the issue of federal interference with the state's resources and future, resulting in a battle over how much land the US Congress would preserve, to what extent industries such as mining and logging would be allowed to develop, and what land permanent residents would be allowed to purchase. The fury over wilderness reached a climax when, on the eve of his departure from office in 1980, President Jimmy Carter signed the Alaska Lands Bill into law, setting aside 106 million acres for national parks and preserves with a single stroke of the pen.

The problems of managing the USA's remaining true wilderness areas are far from over, and presently the debate is centered on the Arctic National Wildlife Refuge (ANWR). Oil-company officials and Alaskan politicians in particular are pushing hard to open up this 1.5-million-acre refuge, one of the last great wilderness areas in the USA, to oil and gas drilling. A bill to open up the refuge in the US Congress, backed by President George Bush, was believed to be headed for passage when the *Exxon Valdez* ran aground in 1989. President Bill Clinton has since vowed to veto any bill opening up the ANWR to pipelines and oil rigs. But many Alaskans believe it's only a matter of time before the inevitable happens in a state where 80% of the revenue comes from the oil industry.

At the core of the dispute are issues of both 'locking up the land' and federal interference in the livelihood of Alaskans. Largely as the result of their remoteness, Alaskans have always been extremely independent, resenting anyone who traveled north with a book of rules and regulations.

To most Alaskans, Washington, DC, is a foreign capital.

Today's Alaskans tend to be young and relatively new to the state. They are individualistic in their lifestyles, following few outside trends and adhering only to what their environment dictates. They are lovers of the outdoors, though they don't always seem to take care of it, and generally extend a warm welcome to travelers. Occasionally you might run into an Alaskan who is boastfully loud, spinning and weaving tales of unbelievable feats while slapping you on the back. In this land of frontier fable, that's not being obnoxious – that's being colorful.

GEOGRAPHY
Southeast

Also known as the Panhandle, Southeast Alaska is a 500-mile coastal strip that extends from Dixon Entrance, north of Prince Rupert, to the Gulf of Alaska. In between are the hundreds of islands (including Prince of Wales Island, the third largest island in the USA) of the Alexander Archipelago and a narrow strip of coast separated from Canada's mainland by the glacier-filled Coast Mountains.

Winding through the middle of the region is the Inside Passage waterway, the lifeline for the isolated communities, as the rugged terrain prohibits road building. High annual rainfall and mild temperatures have turned the Southeast into rain forest broken up by majestic mountain ranges, glaciers and fjords that surpass those in Norway.

The Southeast area has many small fishing and lumber towns, and the larger communities of Ketchikan, Sitka and Juneau (the state capital, considered by many to be the most scenic city in Alaska). Other highlights of the region include the wilderness areas of Glacier Bay, Admiralty Island, Misty Fjord and Tracy Arm, and the White Pass & Yukon Route railroad, built in the days of the Klondike gold rush. Because the Alaska Marine Hwy connects the Southeast to Bellingham (USA) and Prince Rupert (Canada), this region is the cheapest area – and often the first area – for travelers to visit.

Anchorage

Because of the city's size and central location, Anchorage has to be viewed as a separate region, one that is passed through whether you want to deal with an urban area or not. At first glance, Anchorage appears to be like any other city – with billboards, rush-hour traffic, fast-food restaurants and what seem like hordes of people. Within this uncontrolled urban sprawl, however, is a city that in recent years has blossomed on the flow of oil money. While older cities in the Lower 48 often worry about decaying city centers, Anchorage has transformed its city center with such capital projects as a sports arena, a performing-arts center and 122 miles of bike paths.

Anchorage also has a feature most other cities don't have – wilderness at its doorstep. The nearby Chugach State Park, Turnagain and Knik Arms and the Matanuska Valley (home of softball-size radishes) make Anchorage an area worth spending a little time

in, if for no other reason than you'll have to arrive in, depart from or pass through it at some stage.

Southcentral

This region includes Prince William Sound, Kenai Peninsula and the most accessible portion of Wrangell-St Elias National Park, the largest national park in the US. Like the Southeast, much of Southcentral Alaska is a mixture of rugged mountains, glaciers, steep fjords and virgin forests. This mix of terrain has made Kenai Peninsula a superb recreational area for backpacking, fishing and boating, and Prince William Sound, home of Columbia Glacier, is a necca for kayakers and other adventurers.

The weather along the coastline can often be rainy and stormy, but the summers are usually mild and have their share of sunshine. The peninsula is served by road from Anchorage and by the Alaska Marine Hwy, which crosses Prince William Sound and

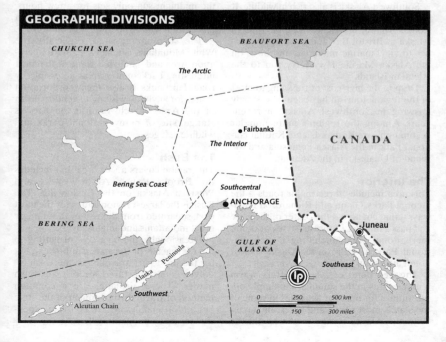

GEOGRAPHIC DIVISIONS

runs to Kodiak. In 1998, a new ship, M/V *Kennicott*, began making once-a-month runs between Juneau in the Southeast and Valdez in Prince William Sound.

Highlights of the region are the historical and charming towns of Homer, Seward, Cordova and Hope, and backpackers will find many opportunities for outdoor adventure in the wilderness areas of the Chugach National Forest, Kenai National Wildlife Refuge and the areas around Cordova and Valdez.

Southwest

Stretching 1500 miles, from Kodiak Island in the Gulf of Alaska to the international date line, Southwest Alaska is an island-studded region that includes the Aleutian Islands, the Alaska Peninsula and Bristol Bay. The region forms the northern rim of the Pacific Ocean's Ring of Fire and contains 46 active volcanoes, the greatest concentration anywhere in North America.

Southwest Alaska is also rich in wildlife. It boasts the largest bears in the world on Kodiak Island, the richest salmon runs in Alaska at Bristol Bay and great opportunities to view marine mammals and birds on the Alaska Marine Hwy ferry run to the Aleutian Islands.

Despite the high cost of traveling to most of the region, tourism has been on a steady upswing in Southwest Alaska in recent years. Among the region's more popular destinations are Kodiak Island, Katmai National Park in the Alaska Peninsula and the island of Unalaska in the Aleutians.

The Interior

This area includes three major roads – the George Parks, Glenn and Richardson Highways – that cut across the center of the state and pass a number of forests, state parks and recreational areas, including Denali National Park and Preserve, Alaska's most noted attraction.

The heartland of Alaska offers warm temperatures in the summer and ample opportunities for outdoor activities in some of the state's most scenic and accessible areas. With the Alaska Range to the north, the Wrangell and Chugach Mountains to the south and the Talkeetna Mountains cutting through the middle, the Interior has a rugged appearance matching that of either Southeast or Southcentral Alaska but without much of the rain and cloudy weather.

Fairbanks The boomtown of both the gold-rush days and the construction of the pipeline to Prudhoe Bay has settled down a little, but it still retains much of its colorful and hard-core Alaskan character. A quick trip through Fairbanks is often a disappointment to most travelers, as Alaska's second largest city is very spread out. Located in the flat valley floor formed by the Tanana and Chena Rivers, with the Alaska Range and Mt McKinley far off in the distance, Fairbanks lacks the dramatic setting many other areas offer. However, the true delights of this freewheeling frontier town are revealed if sufficient time is spent here. In the summer, the midnight sun only sets for a few hours, and Fairbanks can be an unusually warm place, often with temperatures of 80° to 90°F.

The surrounding area, especially the White Mountains, Chena River State Recreation Area and Circle has some of the most interesting backcountry areas accessible by road. Fairbanks is also the transportation center for anybody wishing to venture north of the Arctic Circle or into the Brooks Range, site of many national parks and wildlife refuges.

The Bush

This region covers a vast area that includes the Brooks Range, Arctic Alaska and Western Alaska on the Bering Sea. The Bush is the largest region and is, for the most part, separated from the rest of the state by great mountains and mighty rivers.

Occasionally, the high cost of getting to the far reaches of the state can be beat, but for the most part, traveling to the Bush involves small chartered aircraft, or 'bush planes.' These airplanes are a common method of travel through much of the state but, unfortunately, are prohibitively expensive for many budget travelers.

Except for the larger communities of Nome, Kotzebue and Barrow, independent travel in Bush villages is difficult unless you have a contact. If you have just stepped off a chartered airplane, the small and isolated villages may appear closed and unfriendly, and may have very limited facilities. For travelers who do make an effort to leave the roads, however, Bush Alaska offers a lifestyle that is rare in other areas of the USA and, for the most part, is unaffected by the state's booming summer tourist industry. The climate in the summer can range from a dry and chilly 40°F in the treeless and nightless Arctic tundra to the wet and fog of the considerably warmer Bering Sea coast, a flat land of lakes and slow-moving rivers.

GEOLOGY

Horizontally Alaska is spread over 586,000 sq miles, but vertically it is even more impressive, with elevations ranging from the Aleutian Trench, which lies 25,000 feet below the sea, to the highest mountain in North America, 20,320-ft Mount McKinley. This is a range of almost 9 miles.

Three impressive mountain systems arch across the state. The Coast Range sweeps along the southern edge of Alaska as a continuation of Washington State's Olympic Range and includes the St Elias Range and the Chugach and Kenai Mountains before dipping into the sea southwest of Kodiak Island. The Alaska and Aleutian Ranges parallel these mountains in the same arc, and the Brooks Range skirts the Arctic Circle. In between the Alaska Range and the Brooks Range is Interior Alaska, an immense plateau rippled by foothills, low mountains and great rivers. North of the Brooks Range is the North Slope, which gently descends to the Arctic Ocean.

In geologic time, the Alaskan landmass is relatively new and still very active. The result of plate tectonics, where the Pacific Plate (the ocean floor) drifts under the North American Plate, Alaska is the northern rim of the chain of Pacific Ocean volcanoes known as the Ring of Fire. The state is also the most seismically active region of North America. It's estimated that 10% of the world's earthquakes occur in Alaska. Almost half of the state is susceptible to an earthquake, and the town of Valdez on the Prince William Sound experiences a major one – 5.0 or higher on the Richter scale – almost annually. In 1964, Valdez was wiped out from the tsunamis produced by the Good Friday Earthquake. At 9.2 on the Richter scale this earthquake was the strongest ever recorded in North America.

Glaciers

Glaciers form whenever the snowfall in the mountains exceeds the rate of melting. As the snow builds up, it becomes a solid cap of ice that, because of gravity, flows like a frozen river. Because glacial ice absorbs all the colors of the spectrum except blue, which it reflects, glacial ice often appears blue. The more overcast the day, the bluer glacial ice appears. If it's raining on the day you are to view a glacier, rejoice; the blues will never be more intense.

Alaska is one of the few places in the world where active glaciation occurs on a grand scale. There are an estimated 100,000 glaciers in Alaska, covering 29,000 sq miles, or 5% of the state, and containing three-fourths of all its fresh water.

The largest glacier is the Bering Glacier, which stretches more than 100 miles, from the St Elias Range to the Gulf of Alaska. If you include the Bagley Ice Field, where the Bering Glacier begins, this glacial complex covers 2250 sq miles, making it larger than the state of Delaware. Just to the east is the Malaspina Glacier complex, which covers 2000 sq miles.

Tidewater glaciers calve (icebergs break off the glacier) directly into a body of water. The southernmost tidewater glacier in North America is the Le Conte Glacier, near Petersburg in the Southeast. La Perouse Glacier, in Glacier Bay National Park, is the only one that discharges icebergs directly into the Pacific Ocean. The largest collection of tidewater glaciers is in Prince William Sound, where 20 of them are active.

The longest tidewater glacier is Hubbard, which begins in Canada and stretches 76 miles to Russell Fjord near Yakutat. It might also be one of the most active. In 1986, Hubbard rapidly advanced across the fjord, reaching the shoreline on the other side. For most of the year, Russell Fjord was technically a lake, until the ice dam dramatically broke.

Active tidewater glaciers can be easily viewed from tour boats. The best places to go for such a day cruise are Glacier Bay National Park, Kenai Fjords National Park or Prince William Sound out of Whittier. Alaska's most popular roadside glaciers are Worthington (Richardson Hwy), Matanuska (Glenn Hwy), Exit (Seward Hwy), Portage (Seward Hwy) and Mendenhall Glaciers (off of the Glacier Hwy in Juneau).

CLIMATE & THE 24-HOUR DAY

It only makes sense that a place as large and diverse as Alaska would have a climate to match. The oceans surrounding 75% of the state, the mountainous terrain and the low angle of the sun give Alaska an extremely variable climate and daily weather that is famous for being unpredictable.

The Interior can top 90°F during the summer, yet six months later in the same region the temperature can drop to -60°F. Fort Yukon holds the state record for maximum temperature at 100°F in June

1915, yet it once recorded a temperature of -78°F in winter.

For the most part, Southeast and Southcentral Alaska have high rainfall and temperatures that only vary 40°F during the year. Anchorage, which is shielded by the Kenai Mountains, has an annual rainfall of 15 inches and average temperatures of 60° to 70°F from June to August. Juneau averages 57 inches of rain or snow annually, and Ketchikan gets 154 inches a year, most of which is rain, as the temperatures are extremely mild even in the winter.

Residents will tell you, however, that averages don't mean a thing. Some summers, it has rained just about every day, and there have been Aprils when every day has been sunny and dry. A good week in Southcentral and Southeast Alaska during the summer will include three sunny days, two overcast ones and two when you need to pull your rain gear out or duck for cover.

In the Interior and up around Fairbanks, precipitation is light, but temperatures can fluctuate by more than 100°F during the year. In summer, the average daytime temperature can range from 55° to 75°F, with a brief period in late July to early August when temperatures will top 80°F or even 90°F. At night, temperatures can drop sharply to 45°F

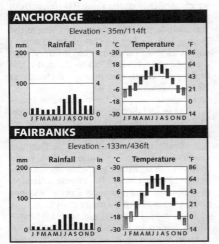

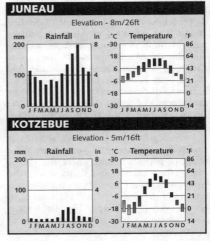

or even lower, and freak snowfalls can occur in the valleys during July or August, with the white stuff lasting a day or two.

The climate in the Bush varies. The region north of the Arctic Circle is cool most of the summer, with temperatures around 45°F, and annual rainfall is less than 4 inches. Other areas, such as Nome in Western Alaska or Dillingham in Southwest Alaska, aren't much warmer and tend to be foggy and rainy much of the summer.

In most of Alaska, summers are a beautiful mixture of long days and short nights, making the great outdoors even more appealing. At Point Barrow, Alaska's northernmost point, the sun never sets for 2½ months, from May to August. The longest day is on June 21 (the solstice), when the sun sets for only two hours in Fairbanks, for four hours in Anchorage and from five to six hours in the Southeast.

Even after the sun sets in late June and July, it is replaced not by night but by a dusk that still allows good visibility. The midnight sun allows residents and visitors to undertake activities at hours undreamed of in most other places – 6-mile hikes after dinner, bike rides at 10 pm or softball games at midnight. It also causes most people, even those with the best window shades, to wake up at 4 or 5 am.

No matter where you intend to travel or what you plan to do, bring protection against Alaska's climate. This should include warm clothing, rain gear and a covering if you are camping out. Alaska's weather is unpredictable and often changes when least expected. Don't be left out in the cold.

ECOLOGY & ENVIRONMENT

Due to Alaska's size and the huge tracts of remaining wilderness, its environmental concerns are not just regional conflicts but, more often than not, national debates. Whether to open up the coastal plain of the Arctic National Wildlife Refuge to oil drilling is just one of the prominent issues. Another heated controversy was the state's decision in the mid-1990s to embark on a program of 'wolf management' in a Connecticut-size chunk of spruce forests

and foothills south of Fairbanks. This is the home of the Fortymile caribou herd, whose numbers have bounced between 6,000 and 500,000 in the past century and have hovered around 20,000 since the early 1990s. In 1993, local hunters successfully urged the state to undertake the snaring and shooting of up to 80% of the wolves in the area, as a way to build up the herd. One state official even suggested that wolves could be killed more efficiently by using helicopters and automatic weapons. Outraged Alaskan environmentalists and national organizations like the Sierra Club turned the issue into a national debate, which led to a brief tourism boycott of Alaska. The program was permanently canceled in 1995, after photographs of a biologist repeatedly shooting wolves that had been trapped live appeared in papers across the country. The stormy issue, however, has not gone away. A citizen planning team studying the issue has recommended sterilizing wolves as a way to control their numbers. Environmentalists argue wolf control isn't necessary, because caribou herds naturally fluctuate in size. Meanwhile, impatient Fairbanks-area hunters have started a private bounty program on Fortymile wolves, offering trappers $400 per hide, twice the market value.

Other environmental concerns range from clear-cutting of the Tongass National Forest to overfishing by fleets of factory ships. In 1996, the Sierra Club announced a hard-line stance against commercial logging on federal lands, ensuring the battle over Alaska timber will rage on well into the 21st century. In the same year, Greenpeace launched a campaign to put factory trawlers out of business. Larger than football fields, these ships haul up hundreds of tons of fish in a single netting and are plundering the ecosystem, Greenpeace claims, in waters like the Bering Sea.

Perhaps the environmental issue that affects tourists the most is Alaska's desire to build roads. Politicians and pro-development Alaskans have been pushing for years to expand the state's meager system of highways. The issue came to climax in 1997, when Alaskan senator Ted Stevens tacked a rider onto a disaster-relief bill for flood-ravaged North Dakota. The rider would give Alaska the right to build roads through federal lands, including designated wilderness areas. Environmentalists promptly organized a campaign against what they dubbed the 'pave the parks' rider.

Stevens backed down, but road building remains a sensitive issue in Alaska. More pavement would provide low-cost transportation into remote areas of the state, which in turn would lower prices for everything from food to fuel, but roads threaten Alaska's most abundant resource, wilderness. The ability to escape the crowds and the fast pace of urbanization is not only a lifestyle in this state but often the main attraction for visitors. Once Alaska is bisected with highways, that ability is lost forever.

NATIONAL PARKS

One of the main attractions of Alaska is the 54 million acres administered by the National Park Service as national parks, national preserves and national monuments, by far the most national park land of any state in the USA. Much of the acreage is the result of the Alaska National Interest Lands Conservation Act of 1980, which created 10 new parks and upgraded the status of three others – Denali, Glacier Bay and Katmai – to national parks and preserves and substantially increased their size.

In 1997, Alaska's 15 national park units topped 2 million visitors for the first time, marking an 80% increase in visitors in the 10-year period since 1987. The most popular unit that year was Klondike Gold Rush National Historical Park, followed by Glacier Bay National Park and Preserve. Both units have experienced a jump in visitors in the 1990s, due primarily to an increased number of large cruise ships into Southeast Alaska. Other popular parks include Denali and Kenai Fjords National Park, in Seward, which recorded more than 300,000 visitors in 1997. The least crowded park is the Yukon-Charley Rivers National Preserve, northwest of Eagle, with just 1825 people visiting the area in 1997.

For information on all the parks before your trip, contact the Alaska Public Lands Information Center (☎ 907-271-2737), 605 W 4th St, Suite 105, Anchorage, AK 99501, or check the National Park Service website (www.nps.gov/parklists/ak.html).

Aniakchak National Monument and Preserve (☎ 906-246-3305, www.nps.gov/ania) PO Box 7, King Salmon, AK 99613. This 603,000-acre preserve is on the Alaska Peninsula and has no developed facilities. The main activities are wilderness backpacking and kayaking.

Bering Land Bridge National Preserve (☎ 907-443-2522, www.nps.gov/bela) PO Box 220, Nome, AK 99762. Located 100 miles north of Nome, this 2.7-million-acre unit is known for its lava fields, archaeological sites and migratory waterfowl.

Cape Krusenstern National Monument (☎ 907-442-8300, www.nps.gov/noaa) PO Box 1029, Kotzebue, AK 99752. This 660,000-acre unit has no developed facilities and attracts a small number of visitors interested in archaeological sites, birding and kayaking.

Denali National Park and Preserve (☎ 907-683-2290, www.nps.gov/dena) PO Box 9, Denali Park, AK 99755. Alaska's best-known park, Denali is a 6-million-acre unit in the heart of the Alaska Range. Well developed with facilities, the park features the highest peak in North America (Mt McKinley) and an abundance of wildlife.

Gates of the Arctic National Park and Preserve (☎ 907-456-0281, www.nps.gov/gaar) PO Box 74680, Fairbanks, AK 99707. Preserving a large slice of the Brooks Range is this 8.4-million-acre park above the Arctic Circle. Floating wild rivers, backpacking and climbing are the main activities in the park. Gates of the Arctic has no developed facilities but is well served by guiding companies and outfitters.

Glacier Bay National Park and Preserve (☎ 907-697-2232, www.nps.gov/glba) PO Box 140, Gustavus, AK 99826. Glacier Bay is a 3.2-million-acre park that includes 16 tidewater glaciers and some of the highest peaks in Southeast Alaska. Kayaking, whale watching and boat tours are the main activities.

Katmai National Park and Preserve (☎ 907-246-3305, www.nps.gov/katm) PO Box 7, King Salmon, AK 99613. This 4-million-acre park on the Alaska Peninsula is renowned for volcanoes, the Valley of 10,000 Smokes and giant brown bears. Kayaking, bear watching and wilderness backpacking are the most popular activities.

Kenai Fjords National Park (☎ 907-224-3175, www.nps.gov/kefj) PO Box 1727, Seward, AK 99664. The number of visitors has tripled in the past five years at this 580,000-acre park on the southeast corner of the Kenai Peninsula. Kenai Fjords is popular for glacier tours, whale watching and wilderness kayak trips.

Klondike Gold Rush National Historical Park (☎ 907-983-2921, www.nps.gov/klgo) PO Box 517, Skagway, AK 99840. This small unit covers only 2,271 acres but includes the historic gold rush town of Skagway and the American portion of the famous Chilkoot Trail that miners followed in 1898 to reach the Klondike goldfields.

Kobuk Valley National Park (☎ 907-442-8300, www.nps.gov/noaa) PO Box 1029, Kotzebue, AK 99752. Located 75 miles east of Kotzebue, this 1.7-million-acre Arctic park attracts a small number of visitors for river running and exploring the Great Kobuk Sand Dunes.

Lake Clark National Park and Preserve (☎ 907-271-3751, www.nps.gov/lacl) 4230 University Drive, Suite 311, Anchorage, AK 99508. Spreading across 4-million acres, Lake Clark is only a short flight from Anchorage,

making it a popular park for wilderness back-packing, fishing and river running.

Noatak National Preserve (☎ 907-442-8300, www.nps.gov/noaa) PO Box 1029, Kotzebue, AK 99752. Protecting much of the Noatak River, this 6.5-million-acre Arctic unit has no facilities but attracts visitors for river running and to witness the great caribou migrations in late summer and early fall.

Sitka National Historic Park (☎ 907-747-6281, www.nps.gov/sitk) PO Box 738, Sitka, AK 99835. Alaska's smallest unit at only 107 acres, this national historic park in Southeast Alaska is famous for its collection of totems.

Wrangell-St Elias National Park and Preserve (☎ 907-822-5235, www.nps.gov/wrst) PO Box 29, Glennallen, AK 99588. The largest unit in Alaska at 13.1 million acres, this park is a crossroads of mountains and includes the second highest peak in the USA (St Elias). Accessible by road, the park attracts back-packers, rafters and kayakers.

Yukon-Charley Rivers National Preserve (☎ 907-246-3305, www.nps.gov/yuch) PO Box 164, Eagle, AK 99738. Straddling the Yukon and Charley Rivers, this 2.5-million-acre park attracts a small number of river rafters and canoeists.

Who Owns the Land?

Alaska is the largest state in the USA, with 570,374 sq miles, yet it has just over 600,000 residents, giving it a population density of just over one person per sq mile. The national average is 76 persons per sq mile, and New Jersey, the most crowded state, has 1085 persons per sq mile. So there's lots of land for everybody in Alaska, right?

Well, not really. Two-thirds of the land in the state, or 379,369 sq miles, is owned by the federal government and set aside as national parks, wild rivers, designated wilderness areas and wildlife refuges. To put it in better perspective, there is a total of 1,034,375 sq miles of national parks, national forests, and Bureau of Land Management holdings in the USA, and a third this land is in Alaska.

The state of Alaska also owns its share of land, just over 162,500 sq miles, the result of its state-hood compact. The Alaska state park system alone totals over 4688 sq miles. The state park systems in the other 49 states total 14,375 sq miles. The Native corporations control another 68,750 sq miles, the result of the Alaska Native Claims Settlement Act that was passed in 1971 to pave the way for the Trans-Alaska Pipeline.

So, in the largest state in the US, less than 1% of the land (0.003), roughly 1760 sq miles, is in private, non-Native corporation ownership. Many Alaskans are demanding an opportunity to purchase, own and develop more of the state's acreage. On the other hand, the greatest, and some say last, true wilderness areas in the USA are protected for future generations to enjoy.

GOVERNMENT & POLITICS

The government sector in Alaska is very strong, especially in Juneau, the capital city. Statewide, one in every three people is paid for government work, and in Juneau an estimated two-thirds of the residents work for the federal, state or city government. The result is a lopsided pay scale, with few workers in the private sector having a salary comparable with government workers.

All this government is most obvious when the state legislature and its army of aides and advisers convene in Juneau for the annual session. From across Alaska, 40 state representatives and 20 state senators arrive and take up temporary residence in the city until April to draw up a budget, spend the oil money and pass bills. Potential legislation is then passed on to the governor, who either signs it into law or vetoes the measures. The best way to understand Alaska's state politics and its colorful history is to join one of the free tours offered at the Alaska State Capitol in Juneau.

Alaska, like three other states in the USA, has only one US state representative and two US senators, because of its small population. Local government consists of 1st-, 2nd- and 3rd-class boroughs and cities, along with hundreds of unincorporated villages, the category that most Bush communities fall into. Although the populations may be small, many cities and boroughs can be quite large in area. Juneau, with more than 3000 sq miles within its jurisdiction, is the largest city in the country, in area.

In 1998, Governor Tony Knowles was re-elected by a wide margin. Although the popular governor is a member of the Democratic political party, Alaskans often vote Republican, especially in presidential elections, and have grown more conservative in their attitudes since the 1970s.

ECONOMY

Alaska's economy, fueled by oil, is presently in a balancing act. The revenues from oil and gas still account for 80% of the gross state product annually, and Alaska is behind only Texas as the country's top oil producer, accounting for more than 25% of US production. But Prudhoe Bay, the largest oil field in North America, is drying up and not expected to have much of a life in the 21st century. Alaskans must deal with the increasing layoffs in the oil industry and also the dwindling of mineral royalties that paid for most of Alaska's government programs, from state parks to subsidized ferry travel. Thanks to North Slope crude, there are no state taxes in Alaska on income, sales or inheritance. But in the mid-1990s the state government was awash in red ink, forcing legislators to drastically reduce the budget by cutting programs, slapping user fees on parks and introducing new taxes. An income tax, sales tax or both appear inevitable after residents overwhelmingly voted no in 1999 on using the Permanent Fund to finance state government (see 'Alaska's Permanent Fund' boxed text).

Many experts believe that the Alaskan oil industry will turn the corner in the new millennium. Thanks to new technology, lower drilling costs and a cozy relationship with state government, it is now profitable to pump oil fields that in the past were bypassed as too costly. In 1988, the peak of North Slope production, two million barrels were being pumped per day, with 94% coming from either Prudhoe or Kuparuk fields. By 2001, experts predict that British Petroleum will still be producing 1.3 million barrels a day. The difference is that 32% of the oil will be coming from new wells in previously untapped fields. All this is good news for Alaskans and could keep the Arctic National Wildlife Refuge free from oil production.

Commercial fishing was once the second largest industry in the state. The Alaskan fleet contributes almost 25% of the country's annual catch, including nearly all canned salmon produced in the USA, but like the oil industry, commercial fishing has also faced troubling times and in the late 1990s slipped to third place behind tourism. The salmon fishery has been particularly depressed in recent years, due to decreasing runs and a glut on the world market that has led to dwindling prices. In 1998, Alaskan fishermen netted 130 million pounds of salmon that was

Alaska's Permanent Fund

Few things amaze visitors to Alaska more than being told that the state actually gives residents money every year just for living there. The annual checks date back to 1976, when Alaskans approved a constitutional amendment for the Alaska Permanent Fund, money set aside from a percentage of all mineral-lease royalties. Prudhoe Bay oil made this fund so lopsided that, in 1980, the state legislature created a Permanent Fund dividend payment program and, two years later, began handing out the interest from the fund. In 1999, the dividend amounted to more than $1,700 for every man, woman and child who lives in Alaska. For a family of four, that's almost $7000, or a trip to Hawaii in the middle of a long, dark winter.

The Permanent Fund now contains $26 billion and earns more than $1.5 billion in interest. If the fund was a Fortune 500 company, it would be in the top 5% for income earned, and after the year 2000, it will be earning more revenue for the state than Prudhoe Bay.

Unfortunately, as Prudhoe Bay oil dries up, so does the amount of money that is funneled into the state's general operating budget. Politicians have advocated capping or even reducing the annual dividend, in an effort to balance the budget, and in September of 1999, they put that question to Alaskans in a special election. State residents voted overwhelmingly, by more 80 percent, that in no way should their Permanent Fund checks be used to pay for state government.

Obviously once you start giving people money, it's nearly impossible – or sure political suicide – to ask them to give it back. Look for Alaska to institute either an income tax, statewide sales tax or both in the near future.

worth only $250 million, a far cry from the $700 million that the state's runs generated in 1988. Bristol Bay, the world's largest sockeye (red) salmon run, has been especially hard hit. The fishery produced a record 44 million pounds in 1995 but yielded only 12 million in 1998.

Even more startling are the decreased prices for salmon. Alaska now finds itself competing against huge government-subsidized salmon farming operations in places such as Norway, Chile and Scotland – and losing. In 1997, farmed-raised salmon and trout production topped 1.8 billion pounds and, for the first time ever, exceeded the total world harvest of wild salmon. Add to this the troubled economy in Japan, the biggest consumer of Alaskan salmon, and it's easy to see why prices have tumbled. A pink salmon that fetched 87¢ a pound in 1988 was worth only 5¢ a pound in 1996. The situation is so bad that one Alaskan lawmaker argued that commercial fishing is obsolete and that sports and subsistence fishermen should be given higher allocations in future salmon runs.

Balancing this bad economic news is the fact that tourism in Alaska is booming. Tourism is now the state's second largest industry; Alaska attracted a record 1.3 million visitors in 1997. Tourists spent $952 million in Alaska that year, a 40% increase since 1994, and generated 14,800 jobs, a workforce that is almost as large as the oil industry. The problem, however, is that while the average oil worker earned almost $7000 a month in 1996, the average hotel paycheck was only $2000.

Mining is also experiencing a resurgence in Alaska and is now the fastest-growing industry in the state. In 1997, mining provided 1,394 jobs, an increase of 30% from the year before. Although gold holds the lure of riches, zinc is actually the state's most valuable nonfuel mineral. Alaska is the top zinc-producing state in the country, with the Red Dog Mine, 90 miles north of Kotzebue, the largest such operation in the world.

Alaska is the only state that produces platinum and ranks second in the USA for gold production and third for silver. Near Fairbanks, the Fort Knox Gold Mine began

The Great Salmon War

The border between the USA and Canada is said to be the most peaceful one in the world. Maybe so, but not in the waters off Alaska and British Columbia, where what was dubbed the 'Great Salmon War' broke out in 1997.

The controversy began when the US-Canada Pacific Salmon Treaty talks stalled two years earlier, and accusations began to fly. The Canadians charge that Americans were stealing their fish. Alaskan and Washington state fishermen claimed the Canadians were fishing salmon into extinction. The struggle peaked in the summer of 1997, when Canadian fishermen used their boats to blockade the Alaskan ferry *Malaspina* for three days in Prince Rupert, leaving 300 passengers stranded on board. Canadians cheered. Alaskans called it 'a mild version of gunboat diplomacy' and immediately canceled the Prince Rupert route. In the heat of the battle, President Bill Clinton warned the Canadians to back off, and British Columbia's premier, Glen Clark, called Alaska a 'renegade' state and threatened to close an American military base.

There was much flag waving and even flag burning on both sides of the border, but the real problem is that the salmon themselves don't stop for customs. Fish that were hatched in British Columbian rivers migrate north into Alaskan waters, where American fishermen scoop them up before they have a chance to return to Canada. In protest, Canadian fishermen began netting more of the endangered American-born salmon migrating up from Washington state.

For almost a century, the two countries have had treaties allocating resources, but the wild salmon are slowly dying out. As fish farms in Chile, Norway and Scotland take over the market and push prices down, financially strapped fishermen in the Northwest will continue to fight over fewer salmon and make less for what they do catch.

operations in 1996 as the newest and biggest gold mine in the state. Near Juneau, the Greens Creek Mine reopened 1997, after closing in 1992 due to falling silver prices. Many other mines will begin operations in the near future. While the high-paying jobs that mining offers are attractive, the industry puts little in the state coffers. Mining contributes $2.6 million annually to the state treasury in taxes and royalties. Oil pumped in $2 billion in 1997.

Other industries include logging and, to a very small degree, commercial farming, which takes place almost exclusively in the Matanuska Valley around Palmer and the Tanana Valley between Fairbanks and Delta. These areas are home to the 70lb cabbages and softball-size radishes, but the top agricultural product for Alaskan farmers is milk.

POPULATION & PEOPLE

Alaska, the largest state in the USA, has the third smallest population and is the most sparsely populated state. Permanent residents, not including the large influx of seasonal workers in the fishing and tourist industries, number 609,311 in a state of 591,004 sq miles. There is almost a square mile for every resident in Alaska compared to 71.2 people per square mile in the rest of the USA. Alaska is actually even more sparsely populated when you consider that almost half of its population lives in the Anchorage area.

An estimated 30% of the state's population was born in Alaska. Of the rest, 25% has moved there in the last five years. The average resident is young (average age between 26 and 28 years), mobile and mostly from the US West Coast. Inuit and other indigenous groups make up only 15% of the total population, and ethnic groups of Japanese, Filipinos and African Americans represent less than 5%.

The five largest cities in Alaska are Anchorage (population 259,391), Fairbanks (population 31,697 in the city, 83,773 in the surrounding borough), Juneau (population

30,852), Sitka (population 8681) and Ketchikan (pop 8320, 13,961 in the surrounding borough).

Native Alaskans

Long before Bering's journeys to Alaska, other groups of people had made their way there and established a culture and lifestyle in one of the world's harshest environments. The first major invasion, which came across the land bridge from Asia, was by the Tlingits and the Haidas, who settled throughout the Southeast and British Columbia, and the Athabascans, a nomadic tribe which lived in the Interior. The other two major groups were the Aleuts of the Aleutian Islands and the Inuit (Eskimos) who settled on the coast of the Bering Sea and the Arctic Ocean; both groups are believed to have migrated only 3000 years ago but were well established by the time the Europeans arrived.

The Tlingit and Haida cultures were advanced; the tribes had permanent settlements, including large clan houses that housed related families. These tribes were noted for their excellent wood carving, particularly carved poles, called *totems*, which can still be seen today in most Southeast communities. The Tlingits were spread throughout the Southeast in large numbers and occasionally went as far south as Seattle in their large dugout canoes. Both groups had few problems gathering food, as fish and game were plentiful in the Southeast.

Life was not so easy for the Aleuts and the Inuit. With much colder winters and cooler summers, both groups had to develop a highly effective sea-hunting culture to sustain life in the harsh regions of Alaska. This was especially true for the Inuit, who could not have survived the winters without their skilled ice-hunting techniques. In the spring, armed with only jade-tipped harpoons, the Inuit, in skin-covered kayaks called *bidarkas* and *umiaks,* stalked and killed 60-ton bowhead whales.

The Aleuts were known for some of the finest basket weaving in North America, using the highly prized Attu grass of the Aleutian Islands. The Inuit were unsurpassed carvers of ivory, jade and soapstone; many support themselves today by continuing the art.

The indigenous people, despite their harsh environment, were numerous until non-Natives, particularly fur traders and whalers, brought guns, alcohol and disease that destroyed the Native Alaskans' delicate relationship with nature and wiped out entire villages. At one time, an estimated 20,000 Aleuts lived throughout the islands of the Aleutian chain. In only 50 years, the Russians reduced the Aleut population (mainly through deaths caused by forced labor) to less than 2000. The whalers who arrived at Inuit villages in the mid-19th century were similarly destructive, introducing alcohol that devastated the lifestyles of entire villages. Even when the 50th anniversary of the Alcan was celebrated in October 1992, many Native Alaskans and Canadians called the event a 'commemoration' and not a 'celebration,' due to the things that the highway brought (disease, alcohol and a cash economy) that further changed a nomadic lifestyle.

More than 85,000 indigenous people (half of whom are Inuit) live in Alaska. They are no longer tribal nomads but live in permanent villages ranging in size from less than 30 people to almost 4000 in Barrow, the largest center of indigenous people in Alaska.

Most indigenous people in the Bush still depend on some level of subsistence, but today their houses are constructed of modern materials and often heated by electricity or oil. Visitors are occasionally shocked when they fly hundreds of miles into a remote area only to see TV antennae sticking out of cabins, community satellite dishes, people drinking Coca-Cola or children listening to the latest pop songs on boom boxes.

All indigenous people received a boost in 1971, when Congress passed the Alaska Native Claims Settlement Act in an effort to allow oil companies to build a pipeline across the Natives' traditional lands. The act created the Alaska Native Fund and formed 13 regional corporations, controlled and adminis-

The Right to Subsist

One of the most explosive debates in Alaska is over subsistence, the right of rural residents to enjoy longer hunting seasons and bigger harvests of wild game, in an effort to maintain their traditional lifestyle. Until recently, most people living in Bush Alaska did not have access to stores or could not afford the high prices. Bush residents, particularly Native Alaskans, depended on a variety of game, from caribou and moose to salmon, walruses and bowhead whales, for protein, and the Bush residents needed to hunt whenever they could, because electricity was not always available to make freezing a method of food storage.

But subsistence is now a battle between the federal government and the state of Alaska. With the passage of the Alaska National Interest Lands Conservation Act in 1980, the federal government gave rural residents priority subsistence rights to fish and game, but in 1989, the Alaska Supreme Court ruled that the state constitution gives all residents equal access to game and fish. The controversy came to a boiling point at the end of 1999, when Department of Interior Secretary Bruce Babbitt said that the federal government would take over fishing regulations on federal lands unless the Alaskan legislature submitted a constitutional amendment for 'rural subsistence priority.' Throughout the year, Governor Tony Knowles and Native Alaskans battled sport hunting groups and urban Republicans in the legislature over the issue, but to no avail.

Partly at issue is Alaska's changing society. A growing number of Native Alaskans now live in nonrural areas. Should they still qualify as subsistence users? Native Alaskans say yes, arguing that subsistence hunting and fishing are fundamental to their culture and are a primary means of passing on traditions to their children. But as one Alaskan put it in the *Anchorage Daily News,* 'Why should someone in Barrow making $50,000 a year get subsistence rights and not someone in Palmer making $10,000 a year?'

Other Alaskans believe that only rural residents, whether they are Native or not, should get a priority. That would include first rights in times of shortage, because rural villagers often depend on wild game to survive. Rural subsistence priority, they say, 'is simply a matter of Alaskans looking out for one another.' But others call it 'discrimination by ZIP codes' and wonder what exactly is rural Alaska now that many villages have Internet connections and satellite dishes for better television reception.

Unable to settle this urban-rural, Native-non-Native split, on October 1, 1999, Alaska became the first state in which the federal government controls fish and game management on the majority of its land. Federal agencies such as the Bureau of Land Management and the National Park Service now dictate harvests and seasons for more than two-thirds of Alaska. This explosive issue, however, is far from being settled.

tered by the local tribes, that invested and developed the $900 million and 44 million acres received for their historical lands.

Today, all indigenous people hold stock in their village corporations and receive dividends when there's a profit. Although a few corporations floundered and lost money, others have done extremely well. The Arctic Slope Regional Corp, based in Barrow, has become the largest Alaskan-owned corporation in the state. The company, headed by Jacob Adams, an Inupiat whaling captain, has revenue of more than $460 million, thanks in part to the North Slope oil industry, which lies on its home turf.

Native Alaskans face serious challenges, however, as they enter the 21st century. Many live at or below the poverty level, as creating sustainable economic opportunities and jobs in small, isolated communities is especially difficult. Drug and alcohol abuse in rural Alaska is also rampant, leading to a high death rate. The rate of suicide for Native males is seven times higher than the national average, and it's estimated that one Native Alaskan dies every 12 days directly from alcohol abuse. This has led to a Native sobriety movement in recent years, and tempers have flared over whether communities should be dry or not. Dry communities are rarely dry; instead they usually have a thriving black market for liquor in which a $10 bottle of whiskey can sell for as much as $120. The alternative for 14 communities, including Barrow, Bethel and Kotzebue, is to be damp, allowing alcohol to be consumed but not sold. In such communities, the local government operates delivery centers where residents go to pick up alcohol orders, as a way to put at least some bootleggers out of business.

EDUCATION

Alaska has almost 500 public schools, offering education from kindergarten through 12th grade. The schools range in size from 2000-student high schools in Anchorage to one-teacher, one-room schools in the rural areas. Alaskan teachers are generally the highest paid in the country. Because of the remote nature of Alaska, however, any student can elect to study at home through a unique state-operated Centralized Correspondence School. This option has been available to Alaskans since 1939, and presently up to 3000 students a year are enrolled in the program.

The University of Alaska is the largest college in the state and maintains campuses at a half-dozen cities. The largest campuses are in Fairbanks and Anchorage, and the most scenic is in Juneau, where the school is on the banks of Auke Lake, with snow-capped mountains looming overhead.

ARTS
Native Art

Alaska's indigenous people are renowned for their traditional arts and crafts, primarily because of their ingenious use of local natural materials, which in the case of many groups, like the Inuit, were often limited. Roots, ivory tusks, birch bark, grasses and soapstone were used creatively to produce ceremonial regalia and other artwork.

Thanks to a flourishing arts market, prompted by the increased tourism to the state, Native Alaskan arts have become an important slice of the economy in many Bush communities. The Inupiat and Yupik Inuit, with the fewest resources to work with, made their objects out of sea-mammal parts; and their ivory carving and scrimshaw work is world renowned. Only Native Alaskans are allowed to possess unworked ivory, and they can only sell it after it is handcrafted. Other crafts produced by the Natives of Northern Alaska include hide and whale-bone masks, which often are sold for up to $1000.

The Aleuts of the Aleutian Islands are known for their bentwood hats and visors; the Athabascan Indians make decorative clothing with elaborate beadwork; and the Tlingit, Haida and Tsimshian of Southeast Alaska are among the carvers who ranged south into British Columbia and Washington and were responsible for the great totems and clan houses.

But perhaps no single item represents indigenous art better than Alaskan basketry. Each group produces stunning baskets in very distinctive styles, made solely from the materials at hand. Athabascans of the Interior weave baskets from willow roots or produce them from birch bark. The Tlingits use cedar bark; the Inuit use grasses and baleen, a glossy hard material that hangs in slats from the jaw of certain species of whales.

The Aleuts are perhaps the most renowned basket weavers. Using rye grass, which grows abundantly in the Aleutian Islands, the Aleuts are able to work the pliable and very tough material into tiny, intricately woven baskets. The three styles of Aleut baskets (Attu, Atka and Unalaska) are named after the islands on which they originated. These baskets carry a steep price whenever they are sold on the open market.

The best known examples of the Native Alaskan craft skills are the totems of Southeast Alaska. Although most tourists envision totems as freestanding poles, totemic art is also used on houses and other clan structures. Totem poles are carved from huge cedar trees and are used to preserve family history or make a statement about a clan. They invariably were raised during a potlatch, a ceremony in which a major event was held designed to draw clans from throughout the region. The totem was erected to commemorate the event. There probably isn't a community in Southeast Alaska without a totem or two. But Ketchikan has by far the most impressive collections of them, at both the Totem Heritage Center in town and Saxman Totem Park and Totem Bight State Park out of town.

Theater

Every port in Alaska that receives more than one cruise ship has a group of actors that first serve the local salmon bake and then perform a tongue-in-cheek, melodramatic play covering the history of their town. But the 49th state also has a serious – though small – theatrical community that writes, produces and performs plays. Perhaps the best-known stage in Alaska is Juneau's Perseverance Theater, which dates back to the mid-1970s. Among the plays it has produced is *How I Learned To Drive* in 1998. Written by playwright Paula Vogel while on sabbatical in Juneau, the play won the Pulitzer Prize the week before it began a month-long run in the city where it was conceived.

Serious theater can be found in several Alaskan communities as well. Haines hosts ActFest in April, when theatrical groups from around the state arrive for workshops, competition and performances. Anchorage has a number of performing groups, including the Alaska Dance Theatre, the Mainstage Theater at University of Alaska-Anchorage and the Off Center Playhouse at Cyrano's Books & Cafe, a coffee shop at D St.

The *Anchorage Daily News* is the only paper that makes an attempt to cover theater and the arts in Alaska. Every Sunday, in its Sun section, the ArtBeat, Creative Opportunities and Around Anchorage columns review and list performances and auditions around the state.

SOCIETY & CONDUCT
Traditional Culture

Despite the modernization of the Native Alaskans' lifestyles and the rapid advances of communications into what has been a remote region of the world, Natives still cling to their culture and practice traditional ceremonies. In recent years, there has even been a movement to resurrect Native languages before they are forever lost with the few elders that still speak them. Of the 20 Native languages, 16 are in danger of becoming extinct.

Perhaps the best-known Native ceremony is the potlatch, a village gathering to celebrate a major passage in a family's life. Usually the focal point of Native society, potlatches often involved the host family giving away most of its possessions in an effort to demonstrate wealth to the rest of the village. A funeral potlatch would result in the family giving away the deceased's worldly possessions. The USA and Canada outlawed potlatches in the 1880s, which resulted in a disintegration of all aspects of Native culture. That law was repealed in 1951.

The most commercialized Native custom is the blanket toss. Originally, groups of villagers would grab a walrus hide in a circle to form a trampoline. Then, a hunter standing on the hide would be tossed high in the air, to spot game on the flat, treeless terrain of the Arctic tundra. Depending on the number of people gripping the blanket, a hunter could be thrown 20 feet or higher. Today the ceremony is a popular one with tour-bus groups.

Travelers interested in experiencing a slice of Native culture should plan on attending the World Eskimo-Indian Olympics, held annually on the second-to-last weekend in July in Fairbanks. The four-day competition attracts several hundred Native athletes from Alaska and other circumpolar nations, who compete, usually dressed in authentic Native costumes, in such events as ear-weighted pull, knuckle hop, fish cutting,

The Inuit Culture of Snow

Alaska has numerous Native languages, but unfortunately, many are on the verge of extinction through lack of use. In recent years, there has been a move by many small Native villages to introduce bilingual education in their schools, in an attempt to keep their languages alive.

The most widely spoken Native language is that of the Inuit in the Arctic regions, but no place in Alaska will travelers with a command of English have trouble communicating. If, on the other hand, you plan to visit communities such as Barrow or Kotzebue, using a few Inuit words will undoubtedly result in a warm smile. The best two to master are *quyanak* (pronounced koy-ah-nuk), which means 'thank you,' and *quyanakpak* (coy-ah-nuk-puk), which means 'thank you very much.'

The most fascinating aspect of the Inuit language, however, is the language's numerous words for snow. Here are a few of many:

annui – falling snow
api – snow not yet touched by wind
det-thlok – snow so deep snowshoes are required
qali – snow that sticks to the branches of trees
saluma roaq – snow with a surface of very smooth and fine particles
siqoq – snow blowing along the ground
upsik – wind-beaten snow

blanket toss and dancing. For information write to World Eskimo-Indian Olympics, PO Box 2433, Fairbanks, AK 99707.

Dos & Don'ts

As with the indigenous people in any country, Native Alaskans deserve the respect of travelers, who basically are trespassing through the Natives' traditional homeland. Try to understand their culture and the delicate situation their society faces as it confronts the growing influence of modern society.

Don't just pick out a village and fly to it. It is wise to either have a contact there or travel with somebody who does. Although Native Alaskans, especially the Inuit, are very, very hospitable people, there can be much tension and suspicion of strangers in small, isolated Bush communities.

Also be conscious of the most widespread problem, the rip-off of Native arts, which have become extremely valuable and a lucrative business with tourists. Much of what is being passed on as authentic art has in reality been mass-produced in China, Taiwan or Bali. If you're considering purchasing Native art, try to search out a legitimate shop and look for the *Authentic Native Handicraft from Alaska* symbol (see Things to Buy in the Facts for the Visitor chapter). If the price of a soapstone carving seems too good to be true, it probably is.

RELIGION

For the most part, every religion that mainstream America practices in the Lower 48 can be found in Alaska. One of the most interesting religions, however, the Russian Orthodox Church, is the most enduring aspect of a unique period in Alaska's history. After Russian merchants and traders had decimated indigenous populations in the mid- to late 18th century, missionaries arrived as Russia's answer to the brutal subjugation. They managed to convert the indigenous people of Southwest, Southcentral and Southeast Alaska to a new religious belief. These beliefs are as strong today as they have ever been, and one only has to look at the familiar onion domes of the Russian Orthodox churches in communities such as Juneau, Sitka, Kodiak or Unalaska to realize this.

Facts for the Visitor

SUGGESTED ITINERARIES

The trip you take to Alaska depends on your time, money and how you like to travel. The mistake most people make is trying to see too much in too little time. Alaska is huge, and if your time is limited to less than three weeks, give serious consideration to exploring only one region of the state.

If travel by ferry appeals to you, a popular two-to-three-week adventure is to fly to Seattle and then cruise Southeast Alaska on the Alaska Marine Hwy ferry out of Bellingham, Washington, stopping at a handful of towns for a few days each. The same type of trip can be done on the ferry in Prince William Sound and could include stops at Homer and Seward on the Kenai Peninsula, as well as a stop at Kodiak Island.

Travel exclusively by train is also possible, by flying into Anchorage and then using the Alaska Railroad to see parts of the Kenai Peninsula to the south or to travel north to Denali National Park, Fairbanks and the towns in between.

I advocate seeing the state by car, even if you have no desire to drive the Alcan. For an excellent two-week trip, fly into Anchorage and rent a vehicle from one of the discount car-rental shops away from the airport. Subcompacts will cost $40 to $50 a day, with 100 free miles. A 10-day rental gives you 1000 free miles to play with, enough to thoroughly explore the Kenai Peninsula or drive the Glenn and Richardson Hwys loop to Valdez.

The classic Alaska trip begins in the Southeast and moves north into Anchorage, Denali National Park and Fairbanks, using a variety of public transportation. Plan at least a month for the trip, and more time if you are planning to undertake wilderness adventures along the way.

Finally, if you are bent on driving the Alcan, keep in mind that the Alaska Hwy is a trip in itself. The mistake most travelers make is to rush past the sights, parks and historic places found along this legendary highway on their way to Alaska. If that's the case, why drive it? For anybody coming from the Midwest or US East Coast, it's an eight- to 10-day drive just to reach Alaska by road. Plan at least five to six weeks for this type of trip, although two months is even better.

PLANNING
When to Go

Because most travelers like to avoid subzero temperatures, Alaska's traditional travel season has been from June through August, with the peak season from early July to mid-August, when visiting places like Denali National Park or the Kenai Peninsula can be a dismal experience due to crowds. An awful lot of tourists try to see Alaska in that very short period of time.

Consider traveling during part of the shoulder season. May and September offer not only mild weather but also a good chance for off-season discounts on accommodations and transportation. For the most part, the Alcan can be driven throughout September and early October without too much fear of being holed up by a three-day blizzard, but if you arrive early or stay late, just make sure you equip yourself for some cold, rainy weather.

Arriving in Alaska in late April is possible in the Southeast and the Kenai Peninsula, but in much of the Interior you could still be running into spring breakup, a time of slush and mud. Stay during October and you're guaranteed rain most of the time in the Southeast and Southcentral regions and snow in the Interior and Fairbanks.

In recent years, the state has been actively promoting winter travel in Alaska. Guiding companies that offer dogsled trips are on the increase, and downhill skiing is available at Anchorage's Alyeska Ski Resort. Even Fairbanks is now marketing winter travel to its frigid location in February, using the northern lights as the draw and avoiding mention of -50°F temperatures.

Alaska in April

Next to November and early December, April is often considered to be one of the worst times of the year to be traveling in Alaska. It's too late to go skiing, too early to start hiking and most of the state is in the middle of spring breakup, a time of melting rivers, dirty snowbanks and bottomless mud puddles.

Or is it? For people content with simply seeing the grandeur of Alaska, late April and early May can be a delightful time for exploring Anchorage and the Kenai Peninsula via a rental car. Pack your parka, because the weather can be cloudy and rainy at this time of the year, but you will also enjoy a few sunny days when the temperature easily breaks 50°F. The snow-laden mountains are never more beautiful than when they are framed by blue Alaskan sky. Depending on the previous winter, much of the Anchorage area and the Kenai Peninsula will be free of snow cover by late April, when the days are already long, with the sun not setting until 10 or 10:30 pm.

Alaska is also a bargain in April. You'll save considerably on airline tickets to the state. Once in Anchorage, you can pick up a subcompact from any of the discount car rental agencies for as little as $25 a day, whereas summer travelers will be paying close to $40. The price of motels and hotels is embarrassingly low. The 8th Avenue Hotel in Anchorage charges $130 for a single in the summer, $69 in April. The Kenai Princess Lodge, overlooking the Kenai River in Cooper Landing, will give you a private bungalow with a wood stove, a mountain view and an outdoor hot tub for $79 a night from March through May. In July, it's $175. You can discount anywhere from $20 to $40 for most room rates priced in this book during April.

Denali National Park is off limits unless you want to ski in, but in Kenai Fjords National Park the gray whale migration takes place in April. Kenai Fjords Tours, and other cruise-boat operators in Seward, offer two- to three-hour trips to spot the whales for $69. Other boat tours to spot wildlife can be arranged in Homer.

But the best reason to visit Alaska in April is to meet Alaskans themselves. You'll find locals more friendly and willing to chat with you than at almost any other time of the year. And why not? They have just endured another long, dark winter but are yet to be burned out by the approaching tourist season.

What Kind of Trip?

Independent travel to the 49th state is easy. In fact, it's easier than in most other states in the USA, thanks mainly to the booming tourist industry. Various forms of public transportation travel to practically every accessible corner of the state, even to Prudhoe Bay at the north end of the Dalton Hwy.

Package tours are offered by a variety of companies, and luxury cruise lines are the fastest-growing segment of Alaskan tourism. Most tours, however, are too limiting and too rushed to justify the high cost. Even if you only have a couple of weeks, you'll do better sticking to one region of the state and planning your own trip, the reason, no doubt, you purchased this book.

It's best to travel with somebody if possible, especially if you are planning to focus on wilderness adventures, hiking or backpacking. But every summer thousands of people arrive by themselves and then spend a good deal of time traveling solo throughout the state. It's just the spirit of adventure that Alaska evokes in all of us.

Maps

Unlike many places in the world, Alaska has no shortage of accurate maps, even if most of the state is still wilderness. In fact, the state will give you a map – free. When you call the Alaska Division of Tourism (☎ 907-465-2010), you can request a free state highway map on the recorded message, and a map will be mailed out in advance of your trip. In Alaska, every tourist office has free maps of its town and surrounding area.

Drivers often swear that *The Milepost* has the best set of road maps you can obtain for Alaska, but an even more detailed collection of maps can be found in the *Alaska Atlas & Gazetteer* published by DeLorme (☎ 800-227-1656), PO Box 298-7200, Freeport, ME 04032. This atlas contains more than 100 maps, covering the entire state, and includes some unique features, like an index of physical landmarks. The atlas's drawback, especially for backpackers and others living out of a suitcase, is its size – 11 by 15 inches. For the weight-conscious, the road maps in the free publications handed out at every visitor center are more than adequate to get from one town to the next.

For trekking in the backcountry and wilderness areas, the US Geological Survey (USGS) topographic maps are worth the $4-per-quad cost. USGS topographic maps come in a variety of scales, but hikers prefer the smallest scale of 1:63,360, with each inch equal to a mile. Canoers and other river runners can get away with the 1:250,000 map. The maps of Tongass and Chugach National Forests produced by the USFS will not do for any wilderness adventure, because these maps lack the detail that backpackers rely on.

USGS maps can be purchased at the Public Lands Information Centers in Anchorage, Tok and Fairbanks (see the regional chapters for addresses and phone numbers), but they tend to carry only the maps for their area of the state. Stop at the main USGS offices in Alaska, either in Fairbanks (Federal Building at 101 12th Ave) or Anchorage (Gambell Building on the Alaska Pacific University campus). They have topos and other maps that cover the complete state. You can also order maps in advance by writing for a free index of maps for Alaska from the USGS Western Distribution Branch (Denver Federal Center, PO Box 25286 Denver, CO 80225). The USGS also maintains a website (www.usgs.gov) that lists all the dealers who sell topos state-by-state, including Alaska.

Another source of excellent maps to the Alaska backcountry is Trails Illustrated (☎ 800-962-1643, www.trailsillustrated.com). The Colorado company has published a dozen maps to such areas as Kenai Fjords National Park, Admiralty Island and the Chilkoot Trail. The maps are printed on waterproof paper and cost $10 each.

What to Bring

Clothes With nights that freeze and days that fry, layering is the only way to dress for Alaskan summers without having to take a pair of shipping containers. It's an accepted fact in the North Country that several light layers of clothing are warmer than a single heavy layer. With layers, warm air trapped near the body acts as insulation against the cold. Layers are also easy to strip off when the midday sun begins to warm you up.

Instead of a heavy coat, pack a long-sleeved jersey or woolen sweater and a windbreaker or parka; they are easier to pack and more versatile for Alaska's many changes of weather. A woolen hat, mittens and socks are necessary items to fend off the cold night air, freak snowfalls or the chilly rain of the Southeast. Leave the umbrellas at home. Your parka is your protection against rain, wind or snow and, if you can afford it, should be made of a high-quality fabric that 'breathes.' If you plan to go on a lot of wilderness trips, then you should also pack along overpants. Gore-Tex is the best-known of the materials that breathe, but others are available. Such an outfit will cost $300 to $500, but for people who spend a great deal of time outdoors, it is a worthwhile investment.

The number of luxury restaurants, hotels and entertainment spots is growing in the large Alaskan cities, but for the most part, Alaska is still a land of jeans, hiking boots (or brown rubber boots in the Southeast) and woolen shirts – the acceptable attire for the majority of restaurants, bars and hotels throughout the state. If you are going to backpack around the north on a budget, there is no reason to take anything that isn't comfortable, functional in the harsh environment and easy to pack and wash.

Hiking Boots Most recreational hikers and backpackers today opt for the new light-weight nylon boots made by sporting-shoe companies like Nike, Vasque and Hi-Tech. These boots are lighter to pack and easier on the feet than leather boots, while providing the foot protection and ankle support needed on most trails and wilderness trips when carrying a medium-weight pack. Other hikers turn to leather boots when heavy loads must be shouldered or a trek involves off-trail hiking or scrambling over boulders or ridges or glacial streams. Normal tennis shoes are not enough for the trails but are handy to have as a change of footwear at night or for fording rivers and streams. All boots should either be waterproof or well greased.

Day-Hike Equipment Too often, visitors undertake day hikes with little or no equipment and then, three hours from the trail-head, get caught in bad weather, wearing only a flimsy cotton jacket. Along with your large, framed backpack, take a soft day pack or rucksack with you to Alaska. These small knapsacks are ideal for day hikes and should contain waterproof clothing, woolen mittens and hat, a knife, high-energy food (like chocolate), matches, a map and compass, a metal drinking cup and insect repellent.

Hikers should always carry a compass onto any trail and have some basic knowledge of how to use it correctly. You should also have the correct USGS map for the area in which you are planning to travel (see the Maps section earlier in this chapter for details).

Expedition Equipment For longer treks and adventures into the wilderness, back-packers should double-check their equipment before they leave home, rather than scurry around some small Alaskan town trying to locate a camp stove or a pair of glacier goggles. Most towns in Alaska will have at least one store with a wall full of camping supplies, but prices will be high and by mid- to late summer certain items will be out of stock.

You don't need to arrive with a complete line of the latest Gore-Tex, but then again, that $4.95 plastic rain suit probably won't last more than a few days in the woods. Bring functional and sturdy equipment to Alaska, and you will go home after a summer of wilderness adventures with much of your equipment intact.

Along with a tent (see the Accommodations section, later in this chapter), you need a sleeping bag. This is a good item to bring whether you plan on camping or not, as it is also very useful in hostels, on board the Alaska Marine Hwy ferry and in seedy hotels when you're not sure what's crawling in the mattress. There has been many an all-night discussion among backpackers on the qualities of down versus synthetic fibers. What can't be argued about, though, is down's tendency to clump when wet. In rainy Southeast and Southcentral Alaska, clumping means trouble during most wilderness trips. For a summer in Alaska, choose a three-season bag with a temperature range of -10°F to 40°F or close to that.

Also seriously consider bringing an insulated foam pad to sleep on. It will reduce much of the ground chill. In the Interior, you will often be sleeping just inches away from permafrost, permanently frozen ground. If you'll be spending a considerable amount of time sleeping in the wilderness, skip the foam and invest in a self-inflating sleeping pad, such as the Thermarest. It may cost $70 to $90, but once you're out there, you'll be glad you purchased it.

A reliable backpacker's stove will make life much simpler in the wilderness. Rain, strong winds and a lack of available wood will hamper your efforts to build a fire, and some preserves, like Denali National Park, don't even allow campfires in the backcountry.

Many brands of stove are sold today, but ones like MSR WhisperLite, which can be 'field repaired,' are the most dependable you can take along. Remember, you cannot carry white gas or other camp stove fuels on an airline flight, but just about every small town or park visitor center will stock stove fuel.

TOURIST OFFICES
The first place to write to while planning your adventure is the Alaska Division of

Tourism (☎ 907-465-2010, fax 907-465-2287), Dept 901, PO Box 110801, Juneau, AK 99811-0801, where you can request a copy of the *Alaska State Vacation Planner,* a 120-page annually updated magazine; a state highway map; and schedules for the Alaska Marine Hwy and the Alaska Railroad.

Travel information is easy to obtain once you are on the road, as almost every city, town and village has a tourist contact center, whether it is a visitor center, a chamber of commerce or a hut near the ferry dock. These places are good sources of free maps, information on local accommodations, and directions to the nearest campground or hiking trail.

For information on national parks, refuges and other public lands, contact the Alaska Public Lands Information Center (☎ 907-271-2599), 605 W 4th Ave, Anchorage, AK 99501. If you are planning to spend a considerable amount of time in Anchorage, contact the Anchorage Convention & Visitors Bureau (☎ 907-276-4118, fax 907-278-5559, www.anchorage.net), 524 W 4th Ave, Anchorage, AK 99501, to request its city guide, which is published twice a year.

VISAS & DOCUMENTS
Passport
If you are traveling to Alaska from overseas, you will need a passport. Only US and Canadian citizens can cross the borders to Alaska without one. Even they should carry valid identification, such as a driver's license and a voter registration card. Often a driver's license or a social security card alone is not enough to satisfy some customs officials.

Make sure your passport does not expire halfway through the trip, and if traveling with children, it's best to bring a photocopy of their birth certificates.

Visas
Overseas travelers also need at least one visa, possibly two. Obviously, a US visa is needed, but if you're taking either the Alcan or the Alaska Marine Hwy ferry from Prince Rupert in British Columbia, you will also need a Canadian visa. The Alcan begins

in Canada, requiring travelers to pass from the USA into Canada and back into the USA again.

Travelers from Western Europe and most Commonwealth nations do not need a Canadian visa and can get a six-month travel visa to the USA without too much paperwork or waiting. All visitors must have an onward or return ticket to enter the USA and sufficient funds to pass into Canada. Although there is no set amount that constitutes 'sufficient funds,' most customs officials suggest around $500, and anybody arriving at the Canadian border with less than $250 will most likely be turned back.

Vaccinations are not required for either country, and only people who have been on a farm during the previous 30 days will be detained by immigration officials.

A word of warning: Overseas travelers should be aware of the procedures to reenter the USA. Occasionally visitors get stuck in Canada because they had a single-entry visa into the USA and used it passing through the Lower 48. Canadian immigration officers often caution people whom they feel might have difficulty returning to the USA. Some information about visa or other requirements for entering the USA is available on the US Department of State home page (www.state.gov/index.html), which, among other things, lists foreign embassies and consulates in the US.

Travel Insurance
A travel insurance policy to cover theft, loss and medical problems is a good idea. Some policies offer lower and higher medical-expense options; the higher ones are chiefly for countries such as the USA, which have extremely high medical costs. A wide variety of policies are available, so check the small print.

Be sure that the policy does not exclude wilderness trekking, mountaineering, kayaking, white-water rafting or any other activities you might be participating in while traveling in Alaska, or you may have a difficult time settling a claim. It would also be prudent to be sure that the policy specifically covers helicopter evacuation, the most common way of reaching troubled backpackers in Alaska's wilderness areas.

You may prefer a policy that pays doctors or hospitals directly, rather than requiring you to pay on the spot and claim later. If you must claim later, make sure you keep all documentation. Some policies ask you to call back (reverse charges) to a center in your home country, where an immediate assessment of your problem is made.

Check that the policy covers ambulances or an emergency flight home.

Driver's License & Permits

Next to your passport, a picture driver's license is the best piece of identification you can carry. Most national driver's licenses are valid in Canada, or you can obtain an international driving permit before leaving home. If you plan to take a vehicle rented in the USA into Canada, make sure the rental company issues you a contract that stipulates the vehicle's use in Canada.

US citizens traveling extensively through Canada to reach Alaska should look into obtaining a Canadian Nonresident Interprovincial Motor Vehicle Liability Insurance Card. Such a card provides proof of insurance and can be obtained in the USA through insurance companies.

Hostel & Student Cards

Occasionally in Alaska, especially around the University of Alaska campuses in Anchorage and Fairbanks, student discounts are available, in which case your university identification or Hostelling International card is a handy thing to have. The hostel card is especially useful, as there are a growing number of businesses that feed off the Alaskan hostels (see the Accommodations section later in this chapter) by targeting such travelers with discounts.

In the USA, you can get a Hostelling International membership by contacting Hostelling International (☎ 202-783-6161), 733 15 St NW, Suite 840, Washington, DC 20005. Adult memberships are $25 a year, or $250 for a lifetime.

Seniors' Cards

The best card to carry is the one issued by the American Association of Retired Persons (AARP), which can be obtained for $8 if you're over the age of 50 (you don't even need to be retired) by contacting AARP at 601 E St NW, Washington, DC 20049; email the association at member@aarp.org or check its website (www.aarp.org).

Photocopies

All important documents (passport data page and visa page, credit cards, travel insurance policy, air/bus/train tickets, driver's license, etc) should be photocopied before you leave home. Leave one copy with someone at home and keep another with you, separate from the originals.

EMBASSIES & CONSULATES
US Embassies

The following is a list of US Embassies in other countries:

Australia (☎ 02-6214-5600) Moonah Place, Yaralumia ACT 2600

Canada (☎ 613-238-5335) 490 Sussex Drive, Ottawa, Ontario K1N 1GB

France (☎ 43-12-2222) 2 Ave Gabriel, 75008 Paris

Germany (☎ 30-832-9233) Neustädtische Kirchstrasse, 10117 Berlin

Japan (☎ 0990-5-26160) 10-5 Akasaka 1-Chome, Minato-ku, Tokyo 107-8420

Netherlands (☎ 70-310-9209) Lange Voorhout 102, 2514 EJ The Hague

New Zealand (☎ 644-472-2068) 29 Fitzherbert Terrace, Thorndon, Wellington

UK (☎ 171-499-9000) 24 Grosvenor Square, London W1A 1AE

Consulates in Alaska

There are no embassies in Alaska, but there are a dozen foreign consulates in Anchorage to assist overseas travelers with unusual problems. As a tourist, it's important to realize what your own consulate – the consulate of the country of which you are a citizen – can and can't do.

Generally speaking, it won't be much help in emergencies if the trouble you're in is remotely your own fault. Remember that you are bound by the laws of the country you are in. Your consulate will not be sympathetic if you end up in jail after committing a crime locally, even if such actions are legal in your own country.

In genuine emergencies you might get some assistance, but only if other channels have been exhausted. For example if you have all your money and documents stolen, it might assist in getting a new passport, but a loan for onward travel is out of the question.

Foreign consulates in Anchorage include the following:

Belgium (☎ 276-5617) 1031 W 4th Ave, Room 400, Anchorage, AK 99501-7502

Denmark (☎ 261-7600) 3111 C St, Suite 100, Anchorage, AK 99503-3915

Finland (☎ 279-6607) 1529 P St, Anchorage, AK 99501-4923

France (☎ 277-4770) 2605 Denali St, Suite 101, Anchorage, AK 99503

Germany (☎ 274-6537) 425 G St, Suite 650, Anchorage, AK 99501-2176

Italy (☎ 762-7664) 12840 Silver Spruce Drive, Anchorage, AK 99516-2603

Japan (☎ 279-8428) 550 W 7th Ave, Suite 701, Anchorage, AK 99501

Korea (☎ 561-5488) 101 W Benson Blvd, Suite 304 Anchorage, AK 99503-3997

Norway (☎ 279-6942) 203 W 15th Ave, Suite 105, Anchorage, AK 99501-5128

Sweden (☎ 265-2930) 301 W Northern Lights Blvd, Anchorage, AK 99503

UK (☎ 786-4848) 3211 Providence Drive, Room 362, Anchorage, AK 99508-4614

CUSTOMS

Travelers are allowed to bring all personal goods (including camping gear or hiking equipment) into the USA and Canada free of duty, along with food for two days and up to 50 cigars, 200 cigarettes and 40oz of liquor or wine.

There are no forms to fill out if you are a foreign visitor bringing a vehicle into Alaska, whether it is a bicycle, motorcycle or a car, nor are there forms for hunting rifles or fishing gear. Hunting rifles (handguns and automatic weapons are prohibited) must be registered in your own country, and you should bring proof of registration. There is no limit to the amount of money you can bring into Alaska, but anything over $5000 must be registered with customs officials.

Keep in mind that endangered-species laws prohibit transporting products made of bone, skin, fur, ivory, etc, through Canada without a permit. Import and export of such items into the USA is also prohibited. If you have any doubt about a gift or item you want to purchase, call the US Fish & Wildlife Service in Anchorage (☎ 907-786-3311).

Hunters and anglers who want to ship home their salmon, halibut or the rack of a caribou can easily do so. Most outfitters and guides will make the arrangements for you, including properly packaging the game. In the case of fish, most towns have a storage company that will hold your salmon or halibut in a freezer until you are ready to leave Alaska. When frozen, seafood can usually make the trip to any city in the Lower 48 without spoiling.

MONEY
Currency

All prices quoted in this book are in US dollars unless otherwise stated. The US dollar is divided into 100 cents (¢). Coins come in denominations of 1¢ (penny), 5¢ (nickel), 10¢ (dime), 25¢ (quarter) and the seldom seen 50¢ (half dollar). Quarters are the most commonly used coins in vending machines and parking meters, so it's handy to have a stash of them. Notes, commonly called bills, come in $1, $2, $5, $10, $20, $50 and $100 denominations – $2 bills are rare, but perfectly legal. There is also a $1 coin that the government has tried unsuccessfully to bring into mass circulation; you may get them as change from ticket and stamp machines. Be aware that they look similar to quarters.

Keep in mind that the Canadian system is also dollars and cents but is a separate currency and worth considerably less than American dollars.

Exchange Rates

The following currencies convert at these approximate rates:

country	unit		dollars
Australia	A$1	=	US$0.60
Canada	C$1	=	US$0.69
euro	€1	=	US$0.96
France	1FF	=	US$0.15
Germany	DM1	=	US$0.49
Japan	Yen100	=	US$0.93
New Zealand	NZ$1	=	US$0.48
UK	UK£1	=	US$1.57

Exchanging Money

The National Bank of Alaska (NBA) is the largest bank in the state with offices in most towns on the heavily traveled routes. The NBA can meet the needs of most visitors, including changing currency. Though opening hours vary from branch to branch, you can usually count on it being open 10 am to 3 pm Monday to Friday, with evening hours on Wednesday and Friday.

Cash Cash works. It may not be the safest way to carry funds, but nobody will hassle you when you purchase something with US dollars. Most businesses along the Alcan in Canada will also take US dollars, and to a lesser degree, many merchants in Alaska will accept Canadian money. Keep in mind, however, they often burn you on the exchange rate.

Traveler's Checks Other ways to carry your funds include the time-honored method of traveler's checks. The popular brands of US traveler's checks, such as American Express and VISA, are widely used around the state and will be readily cashed at any store, motel or bank in the major tourist areas of Alaska.

ATMs In 1995, the NBA embarked on a pilot program called Delivering Banking to Rural Alaska. Basically, it put an automatic teller machine (ATM) in Unalakleet, a small native village south of Nome on the Bering Sea. I suspect it won't be long until there's an ATM in every town and village in Alaska with more than 100 residents.

For this reason, you might also consider bringing your ATM card from home to access such machines in Alaska. Not only will you have easy access to your money, but you will save money. According to *Money Magazine,* using ATMs saves 3.5% when compared to exchanging traveler's checks. The NBA, which has offices throughout the state, is connected to both the Plus and Cirrus ATM networks. Chances are that any bank in the USA is connected to one or the other.

Credit Cards

There are probably some stores or hotels in some isolated Bush communities somewhere in Alaska that don't accept any type of credit card, but not many. Like in the rest of the USA, Alaskan merchants are ready and willing to accept just about all major credit cards. Visa and MasterCard are the most widely accepted cards, but American Express and Discovery are not far behind.

Tesoro is one of the most widespread chains of gasoline stations in Alaska and has its own form of plastic money. But practically all stations, Tesoro included, will accept one of the big four cards mentioned above.

In short, having some plastic money is good security for the unexpected on any major trip, and some travelers say it's now even better to take a credit card than haul a wad of traveler's checks.

International Transfers

You can also have money wired to Alaska from more than 100 countries through Western Union. Money transfers can also be sent and usually received in 15 minutes at any Western Union branch office in the state. If you're in Alaska, call ☎ 800-325-6000 to locate the nearest office and a complete list of services.

Bank Accounts

If you're spending several months in the state, anticipate working or think you might end up staying there for good, open an account at the NBA. With such an account, you will have access to your money at virtually every major town and village and 24 hours a day via ATMs. But keep in mind that you'll usually end up paying some banking fees.

Security

Due to a lack of large cities, Alaska is a relatively safe place in terms of carrying your money, credit cards and traveler's checks. Still, you want to be careful when moving through normally busy places like airport terminals. Don't flaunt your money when making a purchase, and avoid placing a wallet in your back pocket. Always keep some money stashed away in another location, in case you do lose your wallet or purse.

Costs

Alaskans use the same currency as the rest of the USA, American dollars, only they tend to use a little more of it. The state is traditionally known for having the highest cost of living in the country, though places like Southern California, San Francisco and New York City have caught up with Alaska, if not surpassed it. There are two reasons for the high prices in Alaska: the long distances needed to transport everything and the high cost of labor.

To buy a dozen eggs in Fairbanks will cost you more than in other parts of the USA (from around $1.50 to $1.90), but to walk into a cafe and have two eggs cooked and served is where the high prices slap you in the face like a July snowfall. In the restaurants, not only are the transport costs added to the price, but so are the high salaries of the chef, waitress and busboy who put the sunny-side-up plate of eggs on your table. Also keep in mind that tourism in Alaska has basically a three-month season. If the prices seem inflated, they have to be to cover the nine months when many restaurants, motels and other businesses are barely scraping by.

The trick to budget travel, or beating the high prices, is to either travel out of season or avoid the labor cost. If you just can't get yourself to take a vacation in Fairbanks in February, when it is -40°F, then try to avoid the labor cost. Buy your own food in a market and cook it at the hostel or campsite. Use public transport; sleep in campgrounds and enjoy your favorite brew around a campfire at night. It is the restaurants, bars,

hotels and taxi companies, with their inflated peak-season prices, that will quickly drain your money pouch.

A rule of thumb for Alaskan prices is that they are lowest in Ketchikan and increase gradually as you go north. Overall, the Southeast is generally cheaper than most places in the Interior or elsewhere because barge transport from Seattle (the supply center for the area) is only one to two days away. Anchorage, and to a lesser extent Fairbanks, are the exceptions to the rule, as they have competitive prices due to their large populations and business communities. Anchorage, which also receives most of its goods on oceangoing barges, can be extremely affordable if you live there, outrageous if you are a tourist. Gas prices often hover around $1.20 a gallon, and apples in a supermarket could cost less than 90¢ a pound. But it's hard to find a motel room under $80, and the price of other tourist-related services, such as taxis and restaurants, seems to be inflated as well.

When traveling in the Bush, on the other hand, be prepared for anything. The cost of fresh food, gasoline or lodging can be two or three times what it is anywhere else in the state. The Bush is where the tales of $25 breakfasts were conjured up, and in some isolated Bush villages, these stories might not be too mythical.

Outside of Anchorage, a loaf of bread will cost from $2 to $2.50, a can of tuna fish from 90¢ to $1.60, apples from $1.50 to $2 per pound and ground beef anywhere from $2 per pound in the large cities to over $4 per pound in outlying communities. Generally the cost of dairy products, even in Anchorage, will get you to swear off them forever, or at least until the end of your trip. A gallon of milk will be priced anywhere from $4 to over $5 (in Bettles it will cost $8). When buying fresh fruit and vegetables, take the time to inspect them closely, especially in small-town markets. It is not too uncommon to buy a stalk of celery and later discover the middle of it is spoiled.

The cost of gas here is surprisingly reasonable, far cheaper than it is in Canada. A gallon in Anchorage will cost anywhere from $1.25 to $1.35, and in many secondary cities, such as Seward and Valdez, gas will cost $1.50 or so. Only at some deserted stations will you pay more than $2.50 a gallon.

A single in the cheapest motels or hotels costs from $60 to $70 per night. Many state and federal campgrounds charge $6 per tent site, and privately owned campgrounds charge anywhere from $10 to $15 a night.

An inexpensive restaurant in Alaska is one where two people can have breakfast and coffee and leave a tip for under $15. For dinner, it's a challenge for two travelers to leave most restaurants, apart from fast-food chains, for under $25. If you need to obtain your main meal at a restaurant, look for the many places that now serve lunch buffets until late in the afternoon. Chinese restaurants (every major town has one) are good for this. Often until 3 pm you can enjoy an all-you-can-feed-on feast of fried rice, chow mein and egg rolls for around $8.

Tipping
Tipping in Alaska, like in the rest of the USA, is expected. The going rate for restaurants, hotels and taxi drivers is about 15%.

Taxes & Refunds
There is no national sales tax in the USA and no state sales tax in Alaska. But individual cities and boroughs are allowed to have a city tax. They might also have a bed tax, which is used to support local tourist bureaus. When both taxes are applied to your hotel bill, the price can raise anywhere from 4% to a whopping 11.5% in Ketchikan.

Canada does have a national sales tax called the Goods and Services Tax (GST), but travelers are often eligible for a rebate on certain purchases and short-term accommodations, like motel rooms. The purchase must be for a minimum of C$100 to qualify for the refund. Check with customs officials at the border for more information or refund forms.

POST & COMMUNICATIONS
Postal Rates
Postage rates increase every few years. At the time of writing, rates for 1st-class mail

within the USA are 33¢ for letters up to 1oz (22¢ for each additional ounce) and 20¢ for postcards.

International airmail rates (except to Canada and Mexico) are 60¢ for a ½oz letter, $1 for a 1oz letter and 40¢ for each additional ½oz. International postcard rates are 55¢. Letters to Canada are 48¢ for a ½oz letter, 55¢ for a 1oz letter and 45¢ for a postcard. Letters mailed to Mexico are 40¢ for a ½oz letter, 46¢ for a 1oz letter and 40¢ for a postcard. Aerograms are 60¢.

The cost for parcels airmailed anywhere within the USA is $3.20 for 2lb or less, increasing by $1 per lb up to $6.50 for 5lb. For heavier items, rates differ according to the distance mailed. Books, periodicals and computer disks can be sent by a cheaper 4th-class rate.

Sending & Receiving Mail
Planning to write home or to friends? Send your mail 1st class by sticking a 33¢ stamp on the envelope or by using a 50¢ aerogram for overseas destinations. For travelers, especially those from overseas, tripping through Canada into Alaska, it's best to wait until you're in the USA to mail home packages. Generally, you'll find the US postal service is half as expensive and twice as fast as its Canadian counterpart. Don't send packages from Alaska, however, since surface mail can take up to a month moving to or from Alaska.

To receive mail while traveling in Alaska, have it sent c/o General Delivery to a post office along your route. You can have mail sent to you care of General Delivery at any post office that has its own five-digit ZIP (postal) code. Mail is usually held for 10 days before it's returned to sender; you might request your correspondents to write 'hold for arrival' on their letters. Mail should be addressed like this:

Lucy Chang
c/o General Delivery
Caballo, NM 87931

Although everybody passes through Anchorage (ZIP code 99501), it's probably better to have mail sent to smaller towns like Juneau (99801), Ketchikan (99901), Seward (99664), Tok (99780) or Delta Junction (99737). Post offices are supposed to keep letters for 30 days before returning them, although smaller places may keep letters longer, especially if your letters have 'Please Hold Forever!!' written on the front in big red crayon. If you are planning to stay at hostels, theirs are the best addresses to leave with letter writers.

Telephone

Telephone area codes are simple in Alaska: the entire state shares 907, except Hyder, which uses 604.

Every little town and village in Alaska has public pay phones that you can use to call home if you have a phone card or a stack of quarters. There's a wide range of international and local phone cards. For local calls, you're usually better off with a local card. These cards are sold in amounts of $5, $10 and $20 and are available at airports, in many drugstores or at shipping companies like Mail Boxes Etc. The best way to make international calls is to first purchase a phone card. Lonely Planet's eKno Communication Card (see the insert at the back of this book) is aimed specifically at travelers and provides cheap international calls, a range of messaging services and free email. You can join online at www.ekno.lonelyplanet.com; to join by phone from the countries covered in this book, dial the relevant registration number. Once you have joined, to use eKno, dial the access number:

country	customer service	access numbers
Lower 48	800-707-0031	800-706-1333
Alaska	800-294-3676	800-318-7039
Canada	800-294-3676	800-808-5773

Fax

Facsimile machines, or 'fax' for short, are very common in Alaska. Within this book, the fax numbers of government offices or businesses are listed right after the phone number. Many lodges, hotels and print shops like Kinko's will also have fax machines for hire, charging a per page price to send or receive faxes.

Email & Internet Access

Traveling with a portable computer is a great way to stay in touch with life back home, but unless you know what you're doing, it's fraught with potential problems. If you plan to carry your notebook or palmtop computer with you, remember that the power supply voltage in the US and Canada may vary from that at home, risking damage to your equipment. The best investment is a universal AC adapter for your appliance, which will enable you to plug it in anywhere without frying the innards. You'll also need a plug adapter. Often it's easiest to buy these before you leave home.

Also, your PC card modem may or may not work once you leave your home country – and you won't know for sure until you try. The safest option is to buy a reputable 'global' modem before you leave home, or buy a local PC card modem if you're spending an extended time in the USA. Keep in mind that the telephone socket might be different from that at home, so ensure that you have at least a US RJ-11 telephone adapter that works with your modem. For more information on traveling with a portable computer, see www.teleadapt.com or www.warrior.com.

Major Internet service providers (ISPs) such as America Online (AOL; www.aol.com), CompuServe (www.compuserve.com) and IBM Net (www.ibm.net) have dial-in nodes throughout Alaska; it's best to download a list of the dial-in numbers before you leave home. If you access your Internet email account at home through a smaller ISP or your office or school network, your best option is either to open an account with a global ISP, like those mentioned above, or to rely on cybercafes and other public access points to collect your mail. A growing numbers of places throughout the state, including hostels, B&Bs and cybercafes, are also equipped to send and retrieve email. In most midsize towns, the best place to pick up email for free is the local library, which usually has one or two computers with Internet access.

If you do intend to rely on cybercafes, you'll need to carry three pieces of information with you to enable you to access your Internet mail account: your incoming (POP or IMAP) mail server name, your account name and your password. Your ISP or network supervisor will be able to give you these. Armed with this information, you should be able to access your Internet mail account from any Net-connected machine in the world, provided it runs some kind of email software (remember that Netscape and Internet Explorer both have mail modules). It pays to become familiar with the process for connecting before you leave home. A final option to collect mail through cybercafes is to open a free Web-based email account such as HotMail (www.hotmail.com) or Yahoo! Mail (mail.yahoo.com). You can then access your mail from anywhere in the world from any Net-connected machine running a standard Web browser.

INTERNET RESOURCES

Highly computer literate, extremely remote – Alaska was made for the Internet and electronic mail. Small, isolated schools in the Bush were some of the first in the country to get online in the classroom and use the Internet for a peek at the outside world.

As a traveler, you can access a great deal of information about the state if your computer at home is online. You can research your trip, hunt down bargain airfares, book hotels, check on weather conditions or chat with locals and other travelers about the best places to visit (or avoid!). There's no better place to start your Web explorations than at our own Lonely Planet website (www.lonelyplanet.com). You'll find succinct summaries on traveling to most places on Earth, postcards from other travelers and the Thorn Tree bulletin board, where you can ask questions before you go or dispense advice when you get back. You can also find travel news and updates to many of our most popular guidebooks, and the subWWWay section links you to the most

useful travel resources elsewhere on the Web.

Although many Alaskan Web pages are university and government sites, a large number are dedicated to travel in the state. The State of Alaska maintains a large website (www.state.ak.us/) that includes a link to its Division of Tourism, where you can use its vacation planner or click into a listing of more than 200 B&Bs. One of the most interesting features of the website is the Alaska Communities Online section, which has Web pages for more than 100 towns, from Anchorage to Eagle. The Alaska Tourism Marketing Council (www.travelalaska.com) maintains its own page with similar information.

The Alaskan Center website (alaskan.com/) features background on the state and bus, ferry, air and train schedules. The Alaskan Center also serves as a link to many other Web pages, including the Juneau Web, Alaskan Visitors and Information Center and the State of Alaska page. The Alaska Internet Travel Guide (www.AlaskaOne.com) includes lists of accommodations throughout the state, many guide companies and links to the Alaska Railroad, Alaska Marine Highway and bus companies such as Seward Bus Lines.

The National Park Service has a website (www.nps.gov/parklists/ak.html) for Alaskan parks. From a list of the national park units, you can click on the particular park you're interested in and its Web page will appear. The US Forest Service also maintains a website for the Alaska region (www.fs.fed.us/recreation/states/ak.html), allowing you to access information on trails, rustic cabins, fishing opportunities and wilderness areas in Tongass and Chugach National Forests. Other useful websites include the following:

www.alaskaair.com Alaska Airlines is the major airline that services the entire state.

www.AlaskaOne.com Alaska Internet Travel Guide is an excellent website for travelers and includes lists of accommodations throughout the state and links to the Alaska Railroad, Alaska Marine Hwy and bus companies.

www.akferry.com Alaska Marine Hwy posts its ferry schedules and allows you to book tickets.

www.akrr.com Alaska Railroad posts its schedules online.

www.anchorage.net Anchorage Convention & Visitors Bureau provides information on the city most visitors fly into when traveling to Alaska. You can request a city guide online.

www.adn.com Anchorage Daily News has an electronic edition that includes the latest news on Alaska and current weather.

www. nps.gov/dena Denali National Park posts up-to-date information on fees, shuttle bus and campground reservations and links to businesses outside the park.

www.nwa.com Northwest Air is the other major airline that services Anchorage and Fairbanks.

The travel sections of both AOL and CompuServe also have Alaskan message boards and chat rooms and are always popular. Be wary of the information posted, however. A great deal of what is posted is misleading or simply incorrect.

Other websites and email addresses will appear throughout this guidebook.

BOOKS
The following publications will aid travelers heading north to Alaska. Most books are published in different editions by different publishers in different countries. As a result, a book might be a hardcover rarity in one country and readily available in paperback in another. Fortunately, bookstores and libraries can search by title or author, so head to your local bookstore or library to find out about the availability of the following book recommendations.

Another alternative is to request a catalog from the Alaska Natural History Association (☎ 907-274-8440), ANHA, Mail Order Services, 605 W 4th Ave, Suite 85, Anchorage, AK 99501, which distributes more than 50 Alaskan titles. Most of the following books can also be ordered through Adventurous Traveler Bookstore (☎ 800-282-3963, www.AdventurousTraveler.com), PO Box 64769, Burlington, VT 05406-4769.

Lonely Planet Guides
Hiking in Alaska, by Jim DuFresne, is the Alaskan addition to the Lonely Planet trekking series. The book covers almost 50 trails around the state, with maps, day-by-day descriptions of the routes and information on getting to and from the trailheads. The treks range from day hikes to weeklong adventures, and they are scattered from Ketchikan to Fairbanks, including several routes in Denali National Park. Dozens of trails are also covered in every region of the state. The hikes mentioned in this Alaska guidebook are covered in greater detail in *Hiking in Alaska.*

Guidebooks
The Milepost, unquestionably the most popular travel guide, is put out every year. While it has good information, history and maps of Alaska and western Canada, its drawbacks include its large size – at eight by 11 inches, it is impossible to slip into the side pocket of a backpack – and that its listings of hotels, restaurants and other businesses are limited to advertisers.

The Alaska Wilderness Milepost used to be a slim section in *The Milepost* but is now the most comprehensive guide to Bush Alaska, the parts of Alaska that can't be reached by road. This *Milepost* covers more than 250 remote towns and villages in a much smaller format.

Adventuring in Alaska by Peggy Wayburn is a good general guidebook to the many new national parks, wildlife preserves and other remote regions of Alaska. It also contains excellent how-to information on undertaking wilderness expeditions in the state, whether the mode of travel is canoeing, kayaking or hiking.

Alaska's Southeast: Touring the Inside Passage by Sarah Eppenbach offers some of the most comprehensive accounts of the Southeast's history and culture, although it lacks detailed travel information.

Alaska's Wilderness Highway by Mike Jensen is a guide to traveling the Dalton Hwy, which climbs over the Brooks Range en route to Prudhoe Bay on the Arctic Sea. The book includes a history of the area, a primer for those driving the road and then a mile-by-mile description of the road itself.

Alaska's Parklands, The Complete Guide by Nancy Simmerman is the encyclopedia of

Alaskan wilderness, covering over 110 state and national parks and wilderness areas. It lacks detailed travel information and guides to individual canoe and hiking routes but does a thorough job of covering the scenery, location and activities available in each park or preserve.

Hiking Guides *55 Ways to the Wilderness in Southcentral Alaska,* by Helen Nienhueser and John Wolfe, is a hiking guide covering popular trails around the Kenai Peninsula, the Anchorage area and from Palmer to Valdez.

Juneau Trails (Alaska Natural History Association) is a bible for Juneau hikers, describing 26 trails around the capital city – perhaps the best area for hiking in Alaska. The guidebook includes basic maps, distances, rating of the trails and location of trailheads, along with brief descriptions of the route.

Sitka Trails (Alaska Natural History Association) is similar to *Juneau Trails* and covers 30 hiking trails around Sitka and its nearby coastline.

Petersburg Hiking Trails (USFS) is another trail guide for Southeast Alaska. The Petersburg booklet covers more than 20 trails and a handful of portages that kayakers would use when paddling Kuiu Island.

Discover Southeast Alaska with Pack and Paddle, by Margaret Piggott, a longtime guidebook to a dozen water routes and 58 trails of the Southeast, was out of print for years before the author finally updated the first edition in 1990. Its downfall is the weak, hand-drawn maps. Make sure you pack the topos.

Backcountry Companion for Denali National Park, by Jon Nierenberg, is a general guide to wilderness trekking in the popular national park. It's not a trail guide, but rather provides short synopses to each of Denali's backcountry zones to assist backpackers to pick the right area to travel in.

Katmai, by Jean Bodeau, is a general guide to Katmai National Park on the Alaska Peninsula. It will assist you in understanding this special park and help you arrange a trip here, but it won't necessarily

lead you through the Valley of 10,000 Smokes.

Chilkoot Pass, by Archie Satterfield, is a historical guide for hikers following Alaska's most famous gold rush trail. The book includes a mile-by-mile description of the trail and history and stories of every segment of the route that Klondike stampeders followed at the turn of the century.

Paddling Guides *The Kenai Canoe Trails,* by Daniel Quick, covers the Swanson River and Swan Lake canoe trails in the Kenai National Wildlife Refuge, although most paddlers don't need such an in-depth and expensive guide to an area that is so easily explored.

A Guide to Alaska's Kenai Fjords, by David Miller, is a coastal paddling guide to the Kenai Fjords National Park, with route descriptions and maps. The author provides an overview of the area and specific information about protected coves, hikes, fishing tips and protected areas for kayakers to arrange drop-offs and pickups.

Glacier Bay National Park: A Backcountry Guide to the Glaciers and Beyond, by Jim DuFresne, is a complete guide to Glacier Bay's backcountry. Along with introductory material on the park, the book contains information on kayak rentals, transport up the bay and detailed descriptions of water and land routes; maps are included.

Alaska Paddling Guide, by Jack Mosby & David Dapkus, is a statewide guide that covers 110 possible water trips, many having road access. Descriptions of the journeys are brief but practical, with information on access points, trip lengths and a rough map.

The Alaska River Guide, by Karen Jettmar, is the most complete river guide for Alaska, covering more than 100 possible trips with two or three pages of description each and a general map. The rivers range from the Chilkat in the Southeast to Colville on the Arctic slope.

Fast & Cold: A Guide to Alaska Whitewater, by Andrew Embick, is a companion to *The Alaska River Guide*. This book is dedicated to experienced white-water kayakers and rafters looking to enjoy the state's top rivers. The author covers 79 rivers and discusses difficulty, gradient, character of the trip and permits, among other topics.

General & History

Whether you love or hate James Michener as an author, just about everybody agrees that he leaves no stone unturned in writing about a place. He usually begins with the creation of the mountains and rivers, and 1000 pages later brings you to the present; his novel *Alaska* is no different. It's a bit wordy for my literary taste, but many others rave about the book.

Coming into the Country, by John McPhee, takes a mid-1970s look at Alaska in a book that is 600 pages shorter and considerably lighter than Michener's effort. McPhee's experiences included a kayak trip down the Kobuk River in the Brooks Range, living in the town of Eagle for a while and spending time in Juneau during the height of the capital move issue. All of the stories provide an excellent insight into the state and the kind of people who live there.

Mount McKinley: Icy Crown of North America, by Fred Beckey, is the history and lore of Alaska's tallest mountain and most popular natural attraction. Beckey, a climber himself, uses stories and a unique narrative style to bring the famed peak to life. He begins with the natural forces that created it, covers the fascinating race of the first successful attempt at the summit and looks at what climbers go through to climb Mt McKinley.

Authentic Alaska: Voices of Its Native Writers is part of the University of Nebraska Press's American Indian Lives series. The anthology is a collection of stories that provides an interesting portrait of Native Alaskan life in the Bush.

Alaska Almanac covers just about every topic imaginable, from what a potlatch is to the state's heaviest snowfall (974.4 inches).

Nature

Mammals of Alaska, edited by Penny Rennick, is a well-illustrated, concise and easy-to-carry guide that covers all of the mammals in the 49th state, from bears and beavers to marmots and lemmings. Each animal is discussed in a two-page mini-essay that includes habitat, range, eating habits and the best places for viewing.

Alaska Pocket Guides, by Alaska Northwest Books, are a series of slender pocket guidebooks to a variety of Alaskan species, including bears, birds, mammals, fish, mushrooms and wild plants. Each book includes color photos, natural history about the animals or plants and where to go for wildlife-viewing opportunities.

Roadside Geology of Alaska by Cathy Connor & Daniel O'Haire does an excellent job of covering the geology of Alaska you see from the road and explaining how it shaped the state's history and development. Every road and sea route is covered, even dead-end roads in the Southeast. Along the way you learn what happened during the Good Friday Earthquake and why miners turned up gold on the beaches of Nome – not dull reading by any means.

Alaska Wildlife Viewing Guide, by Michelle Sydeman and Annabell Lund, is a slender volume that briefly describes 68 places in the state to watch wildlife. The various sites were selected by state, federal and other wildlife experts in Alaska.

To ornithologists, Alaska is the ultimate destination. More than 400 species of birds have been spotted in the state, and the above guide has information on identification, distribution and habitat of 335 of them. Along with text, *Guide to the Birds of Alaska,* by Robert H Armstrong, contains color photographs of the species, drawings and a bird checklist.

A Guide to Alaskan Seabirds (Alaska Natural History Association) is a thin guide to the birds that thrive in coastal Alaska. It has excellent drawings for easy identification.

Alaska-Yukon Wild Flowers Guide, edited by Helen A. White, uses both illustrations and color photos to help you identify what's blooming.

Wildflowers along the Alaska Highway, written by Verna Pratt for the amateur botanist, has species keyed by color and includes 497 color photographs and a checklist for each 300-mile section of the road.

Wild, Edible & Poisonous Plants of Alaska, by Dr Christine Heller, is an excellent companion on any hike, as it contains both drawings, descriptions and color photos of Alaskan flora, including edible plants, berries and wildflowers.

Animal Tracks of Alaska, by Chris Stall, is a must for anybody who plans to do a fair amount of hiking or beachcombing in Alaska. You'll see wildlife tracks everywhere.

City Visitor Guides

Various large and small newspapers around the state put out special visitor guides at the beginning of the summer. All are filled with local history, information, things to do and trails to hike in the area where the newspaper circulates. Look for the free guides at restaurants, bars, hotels and tourist offices or write to the papers in advance:

Anchorage
Visitors Guide, Anchorage Daily News, PO Box 149001, Anchorage, AK 99514-9001

Fairbanks
Interior & Arctic Alaska Visitors' Guide, Fairbanks Daily News Miner, PO Box 70710, Fairbanks, AK 99707

Haines
Haines Sentinel, Chilkat Valley News, PO Box 630, Haines, AK 99827

Homer
Homer Tourist Guide, The Homer News, 3482 Landing St, Homer, AK 99603

Juneau
Juneau Guide, Juneau Empire, 3100 Channel Drive, Juneau, AK 99801-7814

Ketchikan
Ketchikan Visitors' Guide, Ketchikan Daily News, PO Box 7900, Ketchikan, AK 99901

Kodiak
Kodiak Visitors' Guide, Kodiak Daily Mirror, 1419 Selig St, Kodiak, AK 99615

Petersburg
Viking Visitor Guide, Petersburg Pilot, PO Box 930, Petersburg, AK 99833

Skagway
Skagway Alaskan, The Skagway News, PO Box 1898, Skagway, AK 99840

Sitka
All About Sitka, Sitka Daily Sentinel, PO Box 799, Sitka, AK 99835

Valdez
Valdez/Cordova Visitors' Guide, Valdez Vanguard, PO Box 157, Valdez, AK 99686

Wrangell
The Wrangell Guide, Wrangell Publishing Inc, PO Box 798, Wrangell, AK 99929

FILMS & TV SHOWS

Alaska is no stranger to Tinseltown. Over the years, the 49th state has been used as a cinematic backdrop for movies, television shows, documentaries and even television commercials. Among the feature films shot on location in Alaska include Disney's *White Fang* in Haines, *Star Trek VI: The Undiscovered Country,* which had a scene shot on Knik Glacier, and the opening sequence of *The Hunt for Red October* which was filmed in Resurrection Bay. *Limbo,* written and directed by John Sayles, was filmed in and around Juneau. The Alaska Film Office estimates that between 1990 and 1997 filmmakers pumped $30 million into Alaska's economy.

Television producers venture north as well, as episodes of several TV shows have been filmed in Alaska. Perhaps the most unusual was in 1997 when the buff beach babes of *Baywatch* – the most-watched television show in the world at the time – arrived. The episode was filmed in Southeast Alaska and included the lifeguards making 'frigid underwater rescues in the hostile, icy Alaskan environment full of icebergs, freezing winds and wildlife.' It was enough to make most Alaskans gag.

What really gave the state a boost was the TV show *Northern Exposure.* The Emmy-winning TV series was about a New York City doctor who had to repay the state of Alaska for financing his education by working in the fictional town of Cicely. Others in the cast played eccentric and free-spirited townspeople. The show was a hit in the mid-1990s, and some towns in Alaska, most notably Talkeetna, promoted themselves as the 'Cicely of Alaska.' Unfortunately, the TV series was canceled by CBS in the spring of 1995 and was never actually filmed in Alaska but rather the town of Roslyn in the state of Washington.

NEWSPAPERS & MAGAZINES

Alaska has more than 30 daily, weekly and trade newspapers, though most contain eight pages of local news, softball scores and advertising. The largest daily in the state, with a circulation of almost 61,000, is the *Anchorage Daily News,* a top-rate newspaper that captured the Pulitzer Prize in the l970s with its stories on the Trans-Alaska Pipeline.

The Sunday edition of the *Daily News* can make for particularly interesting reading, especially the Dispatch: look for the Alaska column, which features news from around the state, and the in-depth features in its *We Alaskans* magazine. The paper also has an Internet edition (www.adn.com) that includes articles on the state, weather reports and a list of entertainment events in the city.

The next biggest daily, and an equally outstanding publication, is the *Fairbanks Daily News Miner.* The largest paper in the Southeast is the *Juneau Empire.* The *Empire,* however, is owned by a rather detached company that is based in Georgia. The need for a local Juneau paper has given rise to *The Paper,* a new and highly entertaining weekly that began publication in Juneau in 1995. The *Seattle Post-Intelligencer* is flown into the Southeast daily, and the usual news magazines, *Time* and *Newsweek,* are available, though they are a week old by the time they reach the newsstand.

RADIO & TV

Because of its small, isolated communities, public broadcasting is more important to Alaska than almost any other state, but both the Alaska Public Radio Network and the Rural Alaska Television Network, which provides a mix of commercial and regional TV programs to the Bush, are under the knife due to the state's recent attempt to balance its budget. Still, if you are driving around the state, you'll find a wide range of radio stations, a lot of them playing country music. If possible, search for a public radio station like Homer's KBBI (AM 890). A daily staple for some radio stations is 'bush-lines,' messages passed to isolated residents on the airwaves. Bushlines provides an interesting glimpse of life in Alaska. Where else could you hear, 'Ben, meet me at the cabin Tuesday with a chainsaw and the dog,' on the radio but in rural Alaska.

PHOTOGRAPHY & VIDEO
Film & Equipment

The most cherished items you can take home from your trip are pictures and slides of Alaska's powerful scenery. Much of the state is a photographer's dream, and your shutter finger will be tempted by mountain and glacier panoramas, bustling waterfronts and the diverse wildlife encountered during paddling and hiking trips. Even if you have never toted a camera before, seriously consider taking one to Alaska.

A small, fixed-lens, point-and-shoot 35mm camera is OK for a summer of backpacking in the North Country. For a step up, however, purchase a 35mm camera with a built-in zoom lens. The Nikon Lite-Touch

---

Looking for Love in Alaska

There it was in the Sunday singles page of the *Anchorage Daily News*: 'Need a Woman!!! SWM, late 40s, with 30 sled dogs, looking for SWF to warm up the cabin and help feed the team.' Looking for love? If you're a woman, the odds are in your favor in Alaska. Of the 50 states in the USA, only in Alaska and Nevada do men outnumber women. Single men outnumbered single women 1.7 to one in Alaska. But it's estimated in some small communities, Skagway to name but one, that in the winter there are four or five single men to every single woman. The *Daily News*, meanwhile, prints an entire page of letters from 'desperately seeking' men every Sunday.

You can browse through the ads on the Internet (www.mva.com) or hear their message by calling ☎ 900-288-1870. Simply remember what one Alaskan woman said about men and love in the Last Frontier: 'The odds are good, but the goods are odd.'

110 is such a camera, providing a lens that zooms from a 38mm-wide angle to an 110mm telephoto. The camera is still compact and easy to use but will greatly increase your variety of shots.

If you want to get serious about photography, you need a full 35mm camera with a couple of interchangeable lenses and maybe even a second body. To photograph wildlife in its natural state, a 135mm or larger telephoto lens is needed to make the animal the main object in the picture. Any lens larger than 135mm will probably also require a tripod to eliminate camera shake, especially during low-light conditions. A wide-angle lens of 35mm, or better still 28mm, adds considerable dimension to scenic views, and a fast (f1.2 or f1.4) 50mm 'normal' lens will provide you with more opportunities for pictures during weak light. If you want simplicity, check out today's zoom lenses. They are much smaller and compact than they have been in the past and provide a sharpness that's more than acceptable to most amateur photographers. A zoom from 35mm to 105mm would be ideal. And keep in mind the rainy weather that you'll encounter on your trip; a waterproof camera bag is an excellent investment, especially if a great deal of your time will be spent in the woods.

Photographers find that Kodachrome ISO 64 or Fujichrome ISO 100 (older cameras and film refer to ASA, but the ASA number is the same as the ISO number) are the best all-around films for slides, especially when you're photographing glaciers or snowfields where the reflection off the ice and snow is strong. A few rolls of high-speed film (ISO 200 or 400) are handy for nature photography, as the majority of wildlife will be encountered at dusk and dawn, periods of low light. For print film, try to use Kodak Select series Royal Gold 100 or 200or Fujicolor 100.

Bring all your own film if possible; in the large Alaskan cities and towns, film will generally be priced around $9 to $11 for a roll of Kodachrome (36 exposures), and in smaller communities you may have a hard time finding the type of film you want.

Technical Tips

If you take enough shots, you're bound to end up with a few good ones, but here are a few tips to shooting better pictures in Alaska:

- Take time to compose your shots; don't just point and shoot. Experiment with different distances and angles – vertical, horizontal or from the ground shooting up.

- Get close to your subject and avoid what professional photographers call middle-distance shots; photos with too much foreground and clutter.

- Be aware that the best light for the most vivid colors is just after sunrise and before sunset. Shooting at midday, with its harsh light, is not as bad in Alaska as it would be in a place like Arizona, but you still want to take advantage of afternoon sunlight.

- If shadows are inevitable, make use of your flash (even in daytime) to brighten objects in the shade. You might also consider bracketing your photos, by reducing or adding to the exposure time over several frames, to ensure that one picture is at the right setting. Remember that film is cheap when compared to the cost of your trip to Alaska.

- Don't try to hold a camera for an exposure time longer than the focal length of your camera. If you're shooting with a 200mm lens, any exposure longer than 1/200 second will require a tripod. Consider purchasing a mini-tripod for the trip, one that will easily fit into a side pocket of a backpack but features a Velcro strap so you can attach the tripod to a tree for an extended exposure or self-portrait.

Video Systems

Overseas visitors who are thinking of purchasing videos should remember that the USA uses the National Television System Committee (NTSC) color TV standard. This system is not compatible with other standards used in Africa, Europe, Asia and Australasia unless it is converted, which can be expensive.

Airport Security

When flying to and around Alaska, pack your film in your carry-on luggage and have the airport security person visually inspect it. Security personnel at US airports are required by law to honor such requests and are usually very accommodating if you have the film out and ready. I've only met a handful who made me uncap all 48 rolls of film I was hauling along. Airport X-ray machines are supposed to be safe for film, but why take the chance? Remember the higher the film speed, the more susceptible the film is to damage by X rays.

TIME

With the exception of several Aleutian Island communities and Hyder, a small community on the Alaskan/British Columbian border, the entire state shares the same time zone, Alaska Time, which is one hour earlier than Pacific Standard Time – the zone in which Seattle, Washington, falls. When it is noon in Anchorage, it is 9 pm in London, 4 pm in New York and 7 am the following day in Melbourne, Australia.

ELECTRICITY

Voltage in Alaska is 110V – the same as everywhere else in the USA. The plugs have two (flat) or three (two flat, one round) pins. Plugs with three pins don't fit into a two-hole socket, but adapters are easy to buy at hardware or drugstores.

WEIGHTS & MEASURES

In the USA, distances are in feet, yards and miles. Three feet equal 1 yard (.914 meters); 1760 yards or 5280 feet equal 1 mile. Dry weights are in ounces (oz), pounds (lb) and tons (16oz are 1 pound; 2000lb are 1 ton), but liquid measures differ from dry measures. One pint equals 16 fluid oz; 2 pints equal 1 quart, a common measure for liquids like milk, which is also sold in half gallons (2 quarts) and gallons (4 quarts). The US gallon is about 20% less than the imperial gallon. Pints and quarts are also 20% less than the imperial measure. There is a conversion chart on the inside back cover of this book.

LAUNDRY

Virtually every town with more than 100 residents in Alaska has a Laundromat, the place to go to clean your clothes or take a shower. A small load of clothes is going to cost at least $3, plus you'll need another $1 to dry your clothes in the dryer. A shower and clean towel costs around $3. You'll find many hostels and a few motels also provide laundry facilities for a fee.

HEALTH
Predeparture Planning

Health Insurance The cost of health care in the USA is extremely high, and Alaska is no exception. A travel insurance policy to cover theft, lost tickets and medical problems is a good idea, especially in the USA, where some hospitals will refuse care without evidence of insurance. There are a wide variety of policies, and your travel agent will have recommendations. International student travel policies handled by STA Travel and other student travel organizations are usually a good value. Some policies offer lower and higher medical expenses options, but the higher one is chiefly for countries like the USA with extremely high medical costs. Check the fine print. (See Travel Insurance, earlier in this chapter, for more information.)

Water Purification

Tap water in Alaska is safe to drink, but you should purify surface water taken from lakes and streams that is to be used for cooking and drinking. The simplest way of purifying water is to boil it thoroughly. Technically, this means boiling it for 10 minutes. Remember that at high altitude water boils at a lower temperature, so germs are less likely to be killed.

If you cannot boil water, it can be treated chemically. Chlorine tablets (Puritabs, Steritabs or other brand names) will kill many pathogens but not those pathogens causing giardia and amoebic dysentery. Iodine is very effective in purifying water and is available in tablet form (such as Potable Aqua), but follow the directions carefully and remember that too much iodine can be harmful.

If you are trekking in the wilderness, all this can be handled easily by investing in a high-quality filter. Filters such as First Need or MSR's Waterworks are designed to take out whatever you shouldn't be drinking, including *Giardia lamblia* (see the following section). They cost between $45 and $80 and are well worth it.

Water from glacial rivers may appear murky, but you can drink it, if necessary, in small quantities. Don't drink too much, though. The murk is actually fine particles of silt scoured from the rock by the glacier, and drinking too much of it has been known to clog up internal plumbing.

Medical Problems & Treatment

Giardia Giardiasis, commonly known as giardia and sometimes called 'beaver fever,' is caused by an intestinal parasite *(Giardia lamblia)* present in contaminated water. The symptoms are stomach cramps; nausea; a bloated stomach; watery, foul-smelling diarrhea and frequent gas. Giardia can appear several weeks after you have been exposed to the parasite. The symptoms may disappear for a few days and then return; this can go on for several weeks. Metronidazole, known as Flagyl, or tinidazole, known as Fasigyn, are the recommended drugs for treatment.

Sunburn & Windburn Alaska has long hours of sunlight during the summer, and the sun's rays are even more intense when they are reflected off snow or water. Sunburn and windburn should be primary concerns for anyone planning to spend time trekking or paddling. The sun will burn you even if you feel cold and the wind will cause dehydration and skin chafing. Use a good sunscreen and a moisture cream on exposed skin, even on cloudy days. A hat provides added protection, and zinc oxide or some other barrier cream for your nose and lips is recommended for people spending any time on the ice or snow.

Reflection and glare off ice and snow can cause snow blindness, so high-protection sunglasses, known by many locals as 'glacier goggles,' should be considered essential for any sort of visit on or near glaciers.

Hypothermia Perhaps the most dangerous health threat in Alaska's Arctic regions is

---

Medical Kit

A small medical kit is a wise thing to carry, especially if you plan to venture away from populated areas. A possible kit list includes the following:

- ❑ Aspirin, acetaminophen or Panadol for pain or fever
- ❑ Antihistamine (such as Benadryl), which is useful as a decongestant for colds, for allergies, to ease itching from insect bites or stings, or to prevent motion sickness
- ❑ Kaolin preparation (Pepto-Bismol), Immodium or Lomotil for stomach upsets
- ❑ Rehydration mixture for treatment of severe diarrhea; this is particularly important if traveling with children.
- ❑ Antiseptic and antibiotic powder, or similar 'dry' spray for cuts and grazes
- ❑ Calamine lotion to ease irritation from bites or stings
- ❑ Bandages and Band-Aids for minor injuries
- ❑ Scissors, tweezers and a thermometer (mercury thermometers are prohibited by airlines)
- ❑ Cold and flu tablets and throat lozenges
- ❑ Pseudoephedrine hydrochloride (Sudafed) for flying with a cold, to avoid ear damage
- ❑ Insect repellent, sunscreen lotion, lip balm and water purification tablets

---

hypothermia. Hypothermia occurs when the body loses heat faster than it can produce it and the core temperature of the body falls. It is surprisingly easy to progress from very cold to dangerously cold due to a combination of wind, wet clothing, fatigue and hunger, even if the air temperature is above the freezing point.

Dress in layers for insulation – silk, wool and some of the new artificial fibers are all good insulating materials. A hat is important, as a lot of heat is lost through the head. A strong, waterproof outer layer is essential, as keeping dry is vital. Carry basic supplies, including food containing simple sugars to generate heat quickly and lots of fluid to drink.

Symptoms of hypothermia are exhaustion, numb skin (particularly toes and fingers), shivering, slurred speech, irrational or violent behavior, lethargy, stumbling, dizzy spells, muscle cramps and violent bursts of energy. Irrationality may take the form of sufferers claiming they are warm and trying to take off their clothes.

To treat hypothermia, first get the victim out of the wind and rain, remove the victim's clothing if it's wet and replace it with dry, warm clothing. Give the victim hot liquids – not alcohol – and some high-calorie, easily digestible food like chocolate, trail mix or energy bars. This should be enough for the early stages of hypothermia, but it may be necessary to place victims in warm sleeping bags and get in with them. Do not rub victims; instead allow them to slowly warm themselves.

Altitude Sickness Acute mountain sickness (AMS) occurs at high altitudes and can be fatal. In the thinner atmosphere of the high mountains, lack of oxygen causes many individuals to suffer headaches, nausea, nosebleeds, shortness of breath, physical weakness and other symptoms that can lead to very serious consequences, especially if combined with heat exhaustion, sunburn or hypothermia. There is no hard and fast rule as to how high is too high: AMS has been fatal at altitudes of 10,000 feet, although it is much more common above 11,500 feet. For mild cases, everyday painkillers such as aspirin will relieve symptoms until the body adapts. Avoid smoking, drinking alcohol, eating heavily or exercising strenuously. Most people recover within a few hours or days. If the symptoms persist, it is imperative to descend to lower elevations. The drugs acetazolamide (Diamox) and dexamethasone are recommended by some doctors for the prevention of AMS, but their use is controversial. They can reduce the symptoms, but they may also mask warning signs; severe and fatal AMS has occurred in people taking these drugs. In general, we do not recommend them for travelers. A number of other measures can prevent or minimize AMS:

- Ascend slowly. Have frequent rest days, spending two to three nights at each rise of 3000 feet. If you reach a high altitude by trekking, acclimatization takes place gradually, and you are less likely to be affected than if you fly directly to high altitude.

- It is always wise to sleep at a lower altitude than the greatest height reached during the day if possible. Also, once above 10,000 feet, care should be taken not to increase the sleeping altitude by more than 1000 feet per day.

- Drink extra fluids. The mountain air is dry and cold, and moisture is lost as you breathe. Evaporation of sweat may occur unnoticed and result in dehydration.

- Eat light, high-carbohydrate meals for more energy.

- Avoid alcohol as it may increase the risk of dehydration.

- Avoid sedatives.

Motion Sickness Since a great deal of travel in Alaska is done by boat and much of the overland travel is over rough, unsurfaced roads, motion sickness can be a real problem for those prone to it. Eating lightly before and during a trip will reduce the chances of motion sickness. If you are prone to motion sickness, try to find a place that minimizes disturbance – near the wing on aircrafts, close to midships on boats and near the center of buses. Fresh air or watching the horizon while on a boat usually helps; reading or cigarette smoke doesn't. Commercial motion-sickness preparations, which can cause drowsiness, have to be taken before the trip commences; when you're feeling sick it's too late. Ginger (available in a capsule) and peppermint (including mint-flavored sweets) are natural preventatives.

Rabies Rabies is found in Alaska, especially among small rodents such as squirrels and chipmunks in wilderness areas; it is caused by a bite or scratch from an infected animal. Any bite, scratch or even lick from a mammal should be cleaned immediately and thoroughly. Scrub with soap and running water and then clean with an alcohol or iodine solution. If there is any possibility that the animal is infected, medical help should be sought immediately.

Even if the animal is not rabid, all bites should be treated seriously, as they can become infected or can result in tetanus. A rabies vaccination is now available and should be considered if you are in a high-risk category – for instance, handling or working with animals.

HIV & AIDS HIV, the human immunodeficiency virus, develops into AIDS, acquired immune deficiency syndrome, which is a fatal disease. Any exposure to blood, blood products or body fluids may put an individual at risk. The disease is often transmitted through sexual contact, or via contaminated needles shared by intravenous drug users. Apart from abstinence from sex, the most effective preventative is always to practice safe sex by using condoms.

HIV/AIDS can also be spread by dirty needles – vaccinations, acupuncture, tattooing and body piercing can be potentially as dangerous as intravenous drug use if the equipment is not clean. If you do need an injection, ask to see the syringe unwrapped in front of you, or take a needle and syringe pack with you.

Fear of HIV infection should never preclude treatment for serious medical conditions. A good resource for help and information is the US Centers for Disease Control AIDS hotline (☎ 800-342-2437, 800-344-7432 in Spanish).

WOMEN TRAVELERS

Perfumes or scented cosmetics, including deodorants, should not be worn in areas where you are likely to encounter bears, as the smell will attract them. Women who are menstruating should also be cautious. Women should also be alert to the dangers of hitchhiking, especially when they are traveling alone – use common sense and don't be afraid to say no to lifts.

In general, women should feel safe traveling, hiking and camping in Alaska. The combination of a booming tourist industry, low crime rate and small towns and cities allow women to have fewer worries traveling without male companions in Alaska than in almost any other state in the USA.

Everyday Health

Normal body temperature is up to 37°C (98.6°F); more than 2°C (4°F) higher indicates a high fever. The normal adult pulse rate is 60 to 100 per minute (children 80 to 100, babies 100 to 140). As a general rule the pulse increases about 20 beats per minute for each 1°C (2°F) rise in fever.

Respiration (breathing) rate is also an indicator of illness. Count the number of breaths per minute: Between 12 and 20 is normal for adults and older children (up to 30 for younger children, 40 for babies). People with a high fever or serious respiratory illness breathe more quickly than normal. More than 40 shallow breaths a minute may indicate pneumonia.

GAY & LESBIAN TRAVELERS

There are gay people everywhere in the USA. Alaska is no exception. The gay community, however, is far smaller and much less open than in such cities as San Francisco or New York, and Alaskans in general are not as tolerant to the lifestyle. In 1993, debate over an Anchorage ordinance forbidding the city government or its contractors from discriminating against people because of sexual orientation became so heated that a delegation of church leaders made a public appeal for calm. The city assembly eventually repealed the measure, and in 1998 Alaska, along with Hawaii, passed a constitutional amendment banning same-sex marriages.

In Anchorage, the only city in Alaska with any real size, you have Identity, Inc, and its Gay & Lesbian Helpline (☎ 907-258-4777), a Gay & Lesbian Student Association at the University of Alaska campus and even openly gay dance bars, the Blue Moon Bar, at 530 E 5th Ave, and the Wave, at 3103 Spenard Rd. But none of the other cities have such an active gay community, and in rural Alaska, gay travelers should think twice before openly showing their sexual preference.

DISABLED TRAVELERS

Thanks to the American Disabilities Act, many state and federal parks are installing wheelchair-accessible sites and rest rooms in their campgrounds. You can call the Alaska Public Lands Information Center (☎ 907-271-2599) to receive a map and campground guide to such facilities. The Alaska Marine Hwy ferries, the Alaska Railroad, many bus services and cruise ships are also equipped with wheelchair lifts and ramps that make their facilities easier to access.

In advance of planning your trip, call Access Alaska (☎ 907-248-4777) for a free packet of tourist information on accessible services and sites within the state.

You might also consider Alaska Snail Trails (☎ 800-348-4532). This company offers 10-day tours for the mobility impaired on specially designed minibuses, including such popular attractions as Denali National Park and whale watching in Kenai National Park.

SENIOR TRAVELERS

Seniors, many in RVs or as cruise ship passengers, love Alaska. They can also receive discounts on admission to most museums, parks and other attractions, with an identification card such as the AARP card. What seniors will quickly discover, however, is the 10% discount at motels and the 'early bird dinner specials' at restaurants for seniors are not the widespread practices they are elsewhere in the USA. The reason is simple economics; the tourist season is too short and competition for rooms too high for most places to give seniors a discount.

TRAVEL WITH CHILDREN

Alaska is a great destination for children. Infant needs, such as disposable diapers and formula, are readily available in most cities, towns and villages. Children ages two through 11 years old receive a 50% discount on the Alaska Marine Hwy and infants travel free. The Alaska Railroad, bus companies and other forms of transportation also extend hefty discounts to kids – as do museums, national parks and other attractions that charge an entry fee.

If your family enjoys the outdoors, then Alaska can be a relatively affordable destination, once you have arrived. A campsite is cheap compared to a motel room, and activities as such hiking, backpacking and wildlife watching are free. Even fishing is free for children, as the state does not require anglers under the age of 16 years to purchase a fishing license.

The key to any Alaskan adventure is to match the hike or activity to your child's ability and level of endurance. Children lacking much outdoor experience might have a difficult time with a weeklong kayak trip in Glacier Bay or the Chena Dome Trail near Fairbanks. On the other hand, the easy Resurrection Pass Trail can be handled by most children, even those as young as six or seven, if their packs are light.

If your children are younger than five years old, and you still want to take them on a wilderness trip, consider a rental cabin in either Tongass or Chugach National Forest (see Accommodations). Most cabins are reached via a float plane, an exciting beginning to any adventure for a child, and allow you to bypass long hikes in or heavy backpacks, yet the cabins offer a remote location and often good opportunities to see wildlife or catch fish.

USEFUL ORGANIZATIONS

Tourism is booming in Alaska and is inevitably impacting the state's sensitive environment. Too many cruise ships in Glacier Bay, too many tour buses on the highways and too many people in wilderness areas like Denali National Park are having a negative effect on the land, the wildlife and Native cultures.

In 1992, the Alaska Wilderness Recreation and Tourism Association formed in an effort to balance tourism with 'environmentally sustainable economic growth.' Members of AWRTA are often tour companies and outfitters that are committed to responsible tourism and minimizing visitor impact. When looking for a guiding company, a charter operator or lodging, an AWRTA member should be given serious consideration. You can get a compete list of members by requesting the AWRTA's Alaska Adventure Sourcebook. Contact the AWRTA (☎ 907-463-3038), PO Box 22827, Juneau,

AK 99802, or check its website (www.alaska .net/~awtra).

There are a number of other useful organizations in Alaska; details follow.

Alaska Natural History Association

The Alaska Natural History Association (ANHA) promotes a better understanding of Alaska's natural, cultural and historical resources by working with the agencies that manage them. This group runs most of the bookstores in the national parks and another 30 located around the state. By joining the association (605 W 4th Ave, Suite 85, Anchorage, AK 99501), you can get a 10% discount on their books and on goods at Public Lands Information Centers that sell, among other things, USGS topos.

Arctic Bicycle Club

Alaska's largest bicycle club can provide information on mountain biking, racing, road routes and tours. Call their hot line (☎ 907-566-0177) for details on road conditions, mountain bike races and organized bike tours. You can also write to Arctic Bicycle Club at PO Box 140269, Anchorage, AK 99514, or check their website (arcticbike .alaska.net).

Mountaineering Club of Alaska

For information about scaling peaks or other climbs, contact this Anchorage-based club (☎ 907-272-1811) at PO Box 102037, Anchorage, AK 99501. If they cannot help you with your questions, they will know the outfitter who can.

National Audubon Society

For a local bird list or schedule of field trips during the summer, birders can contact the regional office in Anchorage (☎ 907-276-7034) at 308 G St, Suite 219, Anchorage, AK 99501-2134.

Sierra Club

The oldest and best known environmental group in the country today has a chapter in Anchorage (☎ 907-276-4048) at 241 E 5th Ave, Suite 205, Anchorage, AK 99501.

Southeast Alaska Conservation Council (SEACC)

This group is the environmental watchdog of Southeast Alaska. There would be a lot more clear cuts and strip mines without SEACC (☎ 907-586-6942, info@seacc.org). For more information, write to them at 419 6th St, Ste 328, Juneau, AK 99801, or check out the SEACC website (www.seacc.org).

The Wilderness Society

A national organization, the Wilderness Society lobbies for the preservation of the remaining wilderness areas in the USA. Contact its Alaska office (☎ 907-272-9453) at 430 W 7th Ave, Suite 205, Anchorage, AK 99501.

DANGERS & ANNOYANCES
Paralytic Shellfish Poisoning

In recent years, paralytic shellfish poisoning (PSP) has become a problem in Alaska. Since 1990, an average of eight people a year have become ill from eating untested shellfish, and in 1995 one Alaskan died from PSP. State officials warned people not to eat mussels, clams or snails gathered from unmonitored beaches in Alaska. PSP is possible anywhere in Alaska, and within 12 hours of consuming the infected shellfish, victims experience symptoms of tingling or numbness in the lips and tongue (which can spread to the fingers or toes), loss of muscle coordination, dizziness, weakness and drowsiness. To get an update on the PSP situation, or to find out which beaches in the state are safe to clam, call the Division of Environmental Health (☎ 907-465-5280).

Insects

Alaska is notorious for its biting insects. In the cities and towns you have few problems, but out in the woods you'll have to contend with a variety of insects, including mosquitoes, black flies, white-socks, no-see-ums and deer flies. Coastal areas, with their cool summers, have smaller numbers of insects than the Interior. Generally, camping on a beach where there is some breeze is better than pitching a tent in the woods. In the end, just accept the fact that you will be bitten.

Mosquitoes can often be the most bothersome pest. They emerge from hibernation before the snow has entirely melted away, peak in late June and are around until the first frost. You can combat mosquitoes by wearing light colors and a snug-fitting parka and by tucking the legs of your pants into your socks or boots.

The best protection by far is a high-potency insect repellent; the best contain a high percentage of Deet (diethyltoluamide), the active ingredient. A little bottle of Musk Oil or Cutters can cost $6 or $7 (they contain 100% Deet), but it's one of the best investments you will make.

Unfortunately, repellents are less effective, and some people say useless, against black flies and no-see-ums. Their season runs from June to August, and their bite is far more annoying. The tiny no-see-um bite is a prolonged prick, after which the surrounding skin becomes inflamed and itches intermittently for up to a week or more. Unlike the mosquito, these insects will crawl into your hair and under loose clothing in search of bare skin.

Thus, the best protections, and a fact of life in Alaska's backcountry, are long-sleeved shirts, socks that will allow you to tuck your pants into them and a snug cap or woolen hat. You also see many backcountry travelers packing head nets. They're not something you wear a lot, as it can drive you crazy looking through mesh all day, but when you really need one a head net is a lifesaver.

Other items you might consider are bug jackets and an after-bite medication. The mesh jackets are soaked in insect repellent and kept in a resealable plastic bag until needed. Some people say bug jackets are the only effective way to keep no-see-ums at bay. After-bite medications contain ammonia and are rubbed on; while this might drive away your tent partner, it does soothe the craving to scratch the assortment of bites on your arms and neck.

Bears

The fact is, as one ranger put it, 'no matter where you travel in Alaska, you'll never be far from a bear.' But too often travelers decide to skip a wilderness trip because they hear a local tell a few bear stories. Your own equipment and outdoor experience should determine whether you take a trek into the woods, not the possibility of meeting a bear on the trail. As the Alaska Department of Fish & Game points out, the probability of being injured by a bear is one-fiftieth the chance of being injured in a car accident on Alaskan highways.

The best way to avoid bears is to follow a few commonsense rules. Bears do not roam the backcountry looking for hikers to maul; bears only charge when they feel trapped, when a hiker comes between a sow and her cubs or when enticed by food. Sing or clap when traveling through thick bush, so you don't surprise a bear. That has happened, and usually the bear feels threatened and has no choice but to defend itself. Don't camp near bear food sources or in the middle of an obvious bear path. Stay away from thick berry patches, streams choked with salmon or beaches littered with bear scat.

Leave the pet at home; a frightened dog only runs back to its owner, and most dogs are no match for a bear. Set up the spot where you will cook and eat 30 to 50 yards away from your tent. In coastal areas, many backpackers eat in the tidal zone, knowing that when the high tide comes in all evidence of food will be washed away.

At night, try to place your food sacks 10 feet or more off the ground by hanging them in a tree, placing them on top of a tall boulder or putting them on the edge of a rock cliff. In a treeless, flat area, cover up the food sacks with rocks. A bear is not going to see the food bags, it's going to smell them. By packaging all food items in resealable plastic bags, you greatly reduce the animal's chances of getting a whiff of your next meal. Avoid odoriferous foods such as bacon or sardines, in areas with high concentrations of bears.

And please, don't take food into the tent at night. Don't even take toothpaste, hand lotion, suntan oils or anything with a smell. If a bear smells a human, it will leave; anything else might encourage it to investigate

If you do meet a bear on the trail, *do not* turn and run. Stop, make no sudden moves, and begin talking calmly to it. Bears have extremely poor eyesight, and speaking helps them understand that you are there. If it doesn't take off right away, back up slowly before turning around and leaving the area. A bear standing on its hind legs is not on the verge of charging; it's only trying to see you better. When a bear turns sideways or begins making a series of woofing sounds, it is only challenging you for space. Just back away slowly and leave. If the animal follows you, *stop* and hold your ground.

Most bear charges are bluffs, with the animal veering off at the last minute. Experienced backpackers handle a charge in different ways. Some people throw their packs 3 feet in front of them, which will often distract the bear long enough for the person to back away. Other backpackers fire a hand-held signal flare over the bear's head (but never at it) in an attempt to use the noise and sudden light to scare it away. If an encounter is imminent, drop into a fetal position, place your hands behind your neck and play dead. If a bear continues biting you after you have assumed a defensive posture, then you must fight back vigorously.

Some people carry guns to fend off bear charges. Shooting a charging bear is a skilled operation if you are a good shot, a foolish one if you are not. You must drop the bear with one or two shots, as a wounded bear is extremely dangerous.

Other people are turning to defensive aerosol sprays that contain red pepper extract. These sprays cost $40 to $50 each and have been used with some success for protection against bears. They are effective at a range of 6 to 8 yards but must be discharged downwind. If not, you will just disable yourself.

Be extremely careful in bear country, but don't let the bears' reputation keep you out of the woods.

LEGAL MATTERS

At one time, marijuana was technically legal in Alaska, when used in the privacy of the home. The legalization came about in 1975, after the state supreme court ruled that the health threat from marijuana was insufficient to warrant government intrusion on the privacy of residents. For 16 years, Alaskans showed their fierce individual character and distrust of government regulations, as Alaska was the only state in the country where you could legally smoke pot.

That all changed in 1991, when the voters approved a new drug law that made possession of small amounts of marijuana a misdemeanor punishable by up to 90 days in jail and a $1000 fine. The Alaska Civil Liberties Union has vowed to challenge the new law, and in 1998 Alaskans voted to legalize medical use of marijuana. Despite the lenient status of pot in Alaska, it is foolhardy for any visitor to carry it when hitchhiking or driving along the Alcan, as you have to pass through the close inspection of immigration officers at two borders. The use of other drugs is also against the law, resulting in severe penalties, especially for cocaine, which is heavily abused in Alaska.

Alcohol abuse is also a problem in Alaska, and if you are caught driving under the influence of alcohol (DWI) this can be a serious problem. The maximum penalty for a DWI is loss of your license, a $5000 fine and one year in jail. For most people with no prior record, a DWI usually results in a temporary loss of their driver's license, a $250 fine and 72 hours in jail.

BUSINESS HOURS

Banks and post offices in Alaska are generally open from 9 am to 5 pm Monday to Friday. Other business hours are variable, but many shops are open 9 am to 10 pm during the week, 10 am to 6 pm Saturday and noon to 5 pm Sunday.

PUBLIC HOLIDAYS & SPECIAL EVENTS

Alaskans do their fair share of celebrating, much of it during the summer. One of the biggest celebrations in the state is the summer solstice on June 21, the longest day of the year. Fairbanks holds the best community festival, with a variety of events including midnight baseball games (played without the use of artificial light) and hikes to local hills to view the midnight sun. Nome stages a weeklong Midnight Sun Festival, and Barrow stages a 'Sun will not set for 83 days' Festival. If you are in Anchorage or the Kenai Peninsula, head over to Moose Pass for its Summer Solstice Festival, where the barbecued chicken dinner alone is worth the trip.

Independence Day (July 4) is a popular holiday around the state. The larger communities of Ketchikan, Juneau, Anchorage and Fairbanks sponsor well-planned events. Perhaps even more enjoyable during this time of year is a visit to a small settlement such as Gustavus, Seldovia or McCarthy, where you cannot help but be swept along with the local residents in an afternoon of old-fashioned celebrating that usually ends with a square dance in the evening.

Salmon and halibut derbies that end with cash prizes for the heaviest fish caught are regular events around the coastal regions of Alaska, with Juneau and Seward having the largest. Although most travelers are ill-prepared to compete in such fishing contests, watching the boats returning to the marina with their catch makes for an interesting afternoon.

State fairs, though small compared to those in the Lower 48, are worth attending if for no other reason than to see what a 70lb cabbage, a 20lb stalk of celery or a 200lb pumpkin looks like. The fairs all take place in August and include the Alaska State Fair at Palmer, the Tanana Valley Fair at Fairbanks, the Southeast State Fair at Haines and smaller ones at Kodiak, Delta Junction and Ninilchik.

State & National Holidays

Public holidays for Alaskan residents include the following:

New Year's Day January 1
Martin Luther King Day Third Monday in January
Presidents' Day Third Monday in February
Seward's Day Last Monday in March
Easter Sunday in late March or early April
Memorial Day Last Monday in May

Independence Day July 4
Labor Day First Monday in September
Columbus Day Second Monday in October
Alaska Day October 18
Veterans' Day November 11
Thanksgiving Day Fourth Thursday in November
Christmas Day December 25

Special Events

The regional festivals and celebrations in Alaska include the following. For more information, see the regional chapters:

March
  Iditarod Trail Sled Dog Race – Anchorage to Nome
  Nenana Ice Classic Tripod Weekend – Nenana
April
  Piuraagiaqta Spring Festival – Barrow
  Garnet Festival – Wrangell
  Alaska Folk Festival – Juneau
  Tanner Crab Roundup – Unalaska
May
  Crab Festival – Kodiak
  Copper River Delta Shorebird Festival – Cordova
  Polar Bear Swim – Nome
  Little Norway Festival – Petersburg
  Kachemak Bay Shorebird Festival – Homer
June
  Alaska Renaissance Festival – Anchorage
  Nalukataq (Whaling Festival) – Barrow
  Summer Solstice, Great Tanana River Raft Classic – Fairbanks
  Summer Solstice Festival – Moose Pass
  Gold Rush Days – Juneau
  Midnight Sun Festival – Nome
  Summer Music Festival – Sitka
  All Alaska Logging Championships – Sitka
  Colony Days – Palmer
July
  Bear Paw Festival – Chugiak/Eagle
  Golden Days – Fairbanks
  Forest Faire – Girdwood
  Summer Festival – North Pole
  Soapy Smith's Wake – Skagway
  Progress Days – Soldotna
  Moose Dropping Festival – Talkeetna
  Kodiak Bear Country Music Festival – Kodiak
August
  Tanana Valley Fair – Fairbanks
  Southeast Alaska State Fair – Haines
  Blueberry Arts Festival – Ketchikan

St Herman's Pilgrimage – Kodiak
Kenai Peninsula State Fair – Ninilchik
Alaska State Fair – Palmer
Silver Salmon Derby – Seward

September
Equinox Marathon – Fairbanks
Taste of Homer – Homer
State Fair & Rodeo – Kodiak
Great Bathtub Race – Nome
Blueberry Festival – Seldovia
Trading Post Potato Festival – Willow

October
Oktoberfest – Fairbanks
Octoberfest and Arts Festival – Petersburg
Alaska Day Celebration – Sitka

COURSES

The three main campuses of University of Alaska, in Anchorage, Fairbanks and Juneau, serve more than 20,000 students and offer a variety of courses. The most interesting courses to visitors are in the Alaska Wilderness Studies (AWS) program, which utilizes the state's great parks, mountains and wilderness areas as its classrooms. University of Alaska Anchorage has the largest AWS selection, with classes ranging from mountaineering and rafting to beginning sea kayaking, dog mushing and advanced backpacking. Contact the Community and Technical College (☎ 907-786-4066) for more on the UAA's AWS program. You can also view the courses of all three campuses on the UA website (info.alaska.edu/).

Elderhostel

Elderhostel is a nonprofit organization that provides educational adventures and academic programs to older travelers, often senior citizens. Participants are 55 years or older and usually stay at college campuses when classes are out or in environmental study centers. Students take college-level courses that are taught by faculty members, but without homework, preparatory work, final exams or grades.

In short, you travel to the places that interest you, spend a few hours each day in the classroom learning the cultural or biological significance of the area and have the opportunity to join a number of extracurricular activities.

Alaska hosts a large number of Elderhostel programs each summer that are staged at a variety of places, including Sheldon Jackson College in Sitka, University of Alaska Fairbanks, Alaska Sealife Center in Seward and Denali National Park. The course titles include Alaska's Russian Connection, the Aleuts of the Pribilof Islands and the Natural History of Denali. Rates range from $520 to $1200. The fee includes accommodations, meals and classes. For more information contact Elderhostel (☎ 877-426-8056), 75 Federal St, Boston, MA 02110-1941, or check its website at www.elderhostel.org.

WORK

Opportunities for astronomical wages for jobs on the Trans-Alaska Pipeline and other high-paying employment are, unfortunately, either exaggerated or nonexistent today. Except for brief hiring booms, like during the Exxon oil spill cleanup, the cold reality is that Alaska usually has the highest unemployment rate in the country. In 1997, it averaged almost 7%, but in small towns and remote regions the rate was often in double digits.

Many summer travelers arrive think they will get work on a fishing boat, after hearing tales of earning $10,000 in six weeks by getting a percentage of the catch on a good boat. After discovering they lack the deckhand experience necessary for any kind of position on a fishing vessel, these people often end up cleaning salmon on the 'slime line' in a cannery for $7 to $11 per hour.

July is the month to be hanging around the harbors looking for a fishing boat desperate for help, and the best cities to be in are Kodiak, Cordova and Dillingham, where boats are based that work fish runs in Prince William Sound and Bristol Bay, or Ketchikan, Petersburg and Pelican, for boats that work the Southeast. Most canneries (many of which are based in the Seattle area) fill their summer employment needs during the winter. If you really want to work in a cannery instead of touring Alaska, contact them by February. Otherwise, just show up during the season and hope they are hiring. Finding work is possible, as most cannery positions don't require experience and burnout is common in this trade. Other summer employment in Alaska is possible, but be realistic about what you will be paid and look in the right places.

In the USA, workers are required to have a social security number, a birthright for anybody born in the country. If you're not a US citizen, you need to apply for a work visa from the US embassy in your home country before you leave. The type of visa varies depending on how long you're staying and the kind of work you plan to do. Generally, you need either a J-1 visa, which you can obtain by joining a visitor-exchange program, or a H-2B visa, which you get when being sponsored by a US employer. The latter is not easy to obtain (since the employer has to prove that no US citizen or permanent resident is available to do the job); the former is issued mostly to students for work in summer camps.

If you lack the proper documentation, then search out tourist-related businesses such as hotels, restaurants, bars and resorts that need additional short-term help to handle the sudden influx of customers. The smaller the business, the more likely the employer will be to pay you under the table. Other cash-paying jobs, whether housecleaning or stocking shelves, can sometimes be found by checking bulletin boards at hostels or the student unions at the various University of Alaska campuses. Be forewarned, however, that if you are a foreigner in the USA with a standard nonimmigrant visa, you are expressly forbidden to take paid work in the USA and will probably be deported if you are caught working illegally.

If you are a US citizen, finding some kind of work during the summer is usually not a problem. Retailing is booming in such cities as Anchorage, Fairbanks and Juneau, and in 1997, the wage for the retail trade ranged from $6 to $10 per hour. Tour companies also hire a large number of seasonal help in the form of bus drivers, raft guides, sales representatives and program coordinators. Companies you can contact in advance include the following:

Alaska Sightseeing (☎ 800-888-9378, www.cruisewest.com), 4th & Battery Building, Suite 700, Seattle, WA 98121-1438

Alaska Travel Adventures (☎ 907-789-0052), 9085 Glacier Hwy, Suite 301, Juneau, AK 99801

Alaska Wildland Adventures (☎ 907-783-2928), PO Box 389, Girdwood, AK 99587

Denali Park Resorts (☎ 907-279-2653), 241 W Ship Creek Ave, Anchorage, AK 99501

Gray Line of Alaska (☎ 907-277-5581, www.grayline.com), 745 W 4th Ave, Suite 200, Anchorage, AK 99501

Princess Tours (☎ 907-276-7711), 6441 Interstate Circle, Anchorage, AK 99518

You can also check out the websites of the USFS, Bureau of Land Management (BLM), US Fish and Wildlife Service and national parks (for addresses see Who Controls What in the Wilderness chapter), which hire a number of temporary workers during the summer. But be aware that these federal agencies, like many canneries, recruit their workers during the winter and have little if anything to offer someone passing through in June or July.

In short, those people whose sole interest is working for a summer in Alaska rather than traveling should begin looking for work the winter before. Start by contacting regional offices of the USFS, national parks or the chambers of commerce in fishing communities such as Petersburg, Kodiak or Cordova.

If you have access to the Internet, you can get a list and descriptions of job openings through the Alaska Department of Labor Job Bank (www.labor.state.ak.us). These positions are located throughout the state and include education requirements, salary and contract address. You can also post your resume on the same website. Finally the Alaska Employment Service (☎ 907-465-8900), PO Box 25509, Juneau, AK 99802-5509, can also assist you in finding a job in advance of arriving to Alaska.

Volunteer Work

The other option is volunteer work. Although you won't get a wage, you are often provided with room and board and get to work in a spectacular setting. Most volunteer positions are with federal or state agencies. The BLM uses almost 300 volunteers annually, people who do everything from office work and maintaining campgrounds to working on the famous Iditarod Trail. For more information on volunteer work with the BLM, begin making inquiries in the winter by writing to BLM-Alaska (Public Affairs, 222 W 7th Ave, Anchorage, AK 99513) or check its website (www.ak.blm.gov/).

The USFS maintains the largest volunteer program in the state, each year recruiting hundreds of people and providing their room and board and, at times, even transportation costs. A list of positions can be obtained from its website (www.fs.fed.us/recreation/states/ak.html), or you can make inquiries in the winter by writing to USFS (Pacific Northwest Region, Volunteer Coordinator, PO Box 3623, Portland, OR 97208). Also try contacting the individual area offices around the state (see the Wilderness chapter for addresses).

At state parks, summer volunteers fill many positions, ranging from trail crew members and research assistants to campground hosts. To receive a booklet on the positions, contact the Volunteer Coordinator, Alaska Division of Parks and Recreation (☎ 907-269-8708), 3601 C St, Suite 1200, Anchorage, AK 99503-5921.

You might also consider contacting the Student Conservation Association (SCA) during the winter. The nonprofit New Hampshire-based organization places more than 1000 college students and adults annually in expenses-paid internships that allow the volunteers to live and work with professionals in the conservation and natural resources field. Many of these positions are in Alaska. Contact the SCA (☎ 603-543-1700) at PO Box 550, Charlestown, NH 03603, or check its website (www.sca-inc.org).

ACCOMMODATIONS

When booking a room at a B&B, hotel, lodge or even the youth hostel, you will most likely be hit with a city tax and possibly a bed tax. Almost every town of any size in Alaska has a tax, and they can range from as low as 4% to the 9% city and bed tax added in Seward, or 11.5% in Ketchikan. Bed prices in this book do not include the taxes, but towns with the highest taxes are clearly noted.

Camping

Bring a tent. Then you will never be without inexpensive accommodations in Alaska. Alaska doesn't have cheap B&Bs like those in Europe, and the number of hostels is limited, but there are state, federal and private campgrounds from Ketchikan to Fairbanks. Nightly fees range from $6 for the walk-in Morino Campground in Denali National Park to $25 to park your 30-foot RV in some of the more deluxe private campgrounds. It is also a widely accepted practice among backpackers to just wander into the woods and find a spot to pitch a tent. With the exception of Anchorage, Fairbanks and a few cities, you can walk a mile or so from most towns and find yourself in an isolated wooded area.

Your tent should be light (under 5lb) and come complete with a good rain fly; if it has been on more than its fair share of trips, consider waterproofing the rain fly and tent floor before you leave for Alaska. Make sure the netting around the doors and windows is bugproof and will prevent you from turning into a nightly smorgasbord for mosquitoes. The new freestanding dome tents work best, as in many areas of the state the ground is rocky and difficult to sink a peg into.

USFS Cabins

Built and maintained by the US Forest Service, these cabins are scattered throughout the Tongass National Forest (practically the entire Southeast), the Chugach National Forest on the Kenai Peninsula and in Prince William Sound. For the most part, the cabins are rustic log cabins or A-frames with woodstoves, plywood bunks, pit toilets and often a rowboat if the cabins are on a lake. A few cabins can be reached by hiking, but for most a bush plane or chartered boat must drop you off and return for you. Staying in the cabins is an ideal way to sneak into the woods and separate yourself from the world without having to undertake rigorous back-country travel.

During the summer, the cabins are heavily used by both locals and travelers, and stays are limited to seven consecutive nights per party, or three days for hike-in cabins.

The cabins provide excellent shelter from bad weather, but you have to bring your own bedding (sleeping bag and ground pad), food and cooking gear, including a small back-packer's stove for when the woodpile is wet. Other items that come in handy are insect repellent, matches, candles, a water filter and a topographic map of the surrounding area.

Of the 190 USFS public-use cabins, almost 150 of them are in the Southeast and are accessible from Ketchikan, Petersburg, Juneau or Sitka. If you haven't made reservations but have a flexible schedule, it is still possible to rent a cabin. During the summer, USFS offices in the Southeast maintain lists of the cabins and dates still available. A few cabins are usually available for a couple of days in the middle of the week, although they will most likely be the remote ones requiring more flying time (and thus money) to reach.

In the regional chapters, a description of selected cabins is given under the names of towns they are most accessible from. These cabins are special because they can either be reached in 30 minutes or less by bush plane or have some intriguing feature nearby, such as natural hot springs or a glacier.

Reservations & Fees USFS cabins cost $25 to $40 per night to rent but can comfortably hold parties of six or more people. You can reserve the cabins 180 days in advance by calling the National Recreation Reservation Service (☎ 877-444-6777 or 518-885-3639 for international calls) or through its website (http://reserveusa.com). For a reservation less than 20 days in advance, you need a credit card to secure the booking. For dates more than 20 days out, you may use a credit card, money order or a cashier's check.

Once in Alaska, you can reserve the cabins through Forest Service visitor centers and district offices. Addresses and phone numbers for these offices are listed in the regional chapters.

Cabin Descriptions For a complete list and description of cabins, check out the Alaska Region website for the USFS (www.fs.fed.us/r10/) and then click on either Tongass or Chugach National Forest on the map.

For the Tongass National Forest, you can also write to the following USFS offices in Alaska, which will forward a booklet describing each cabin in its district, along with details about the surrounding terrain and the best way to travel to the cabin.

Forest Service Information Center (☎ 907-586-8751), 101 Egan Drive, Juneau, AK 99801

Southeast Alaska Visitor Center (☎ 907-228-6214, www.ktn.net/usfs/ketchikan/), 50 Main St, Ketchikan, AK 99901

The Chugach National Forest in Southcentral Alaska has 40 cabins, including seven along the Resurrection Trail and three on the Russian Lakes Trail. There are also a couple of cabins in the Cordova area that can be reached by foot, but the rest are accessible only by air or boat. For a complete list of cabins and for bookings in the Chugach National Forest, write to the following Alaska Public Lands Information Center or USFS district offices in Alaska:

Alaska Public Lands Information Center (☎ 907-271-2737), 605 W 4th Ave, Ste 105, Anchorage, AK 99501-5162

Cordova Ranger District (☎ 907-424-7661), PO Box 280, Cordova, AK 99574

Seward Ranger District (☎ 907-224-3374), PO Box 390, Seward, AK 99664

Other Cabins The BLM, US Fish and Wildlife Service and the Alaska Division of Parks also maintain rustic cabins in remote areas. There are 17 state parks and recreation areas with cabins, from Point Bridget in Juneau to Chena River near Fairbanks. State park cabins rent for $35 to $50 per night and are rented through any state park office or the DNR Public Information Center. For descriptions of cabins in advance, contact the

DNR Public Information Center (☎ 907-269-8400), 3601 C St, Suite 200, Anchorage, AK 99503-5929, or check its website (www.dnr .state.ak.us/parks/).

The BLM has nine cabins in the White Mountain National Recreational Area north of Fairbanks, and the USFWS has eight of them in the Kodiak National Wildlife Refuge on Kodiak Island. The cabins cost $20 a night. For BLM cabins, contact White Mountain National Recreation Area (☎ 907-474-2200, 800-437-7021), 1150 University Ave, Fairbanks, AK 99709-3899, or check out the BLM website (www.ak.blm .gov/WhiteMtns/). For the USFWS cabins, contact Kodiak National Wildlife Refuge (☎ 907-487-2600), 1390 Buskin River Rd, Kodiak, AK 99615.

Hostels

The Alaska Council of American Youth Hostels has 10 hostels scattered around the state that are stable, having been in operation for years at the same location. The mainstays of the system are the hostels in Anchorage, Juneau, Ketchikan, Delta Junction and Tok. The first hostel you check into is the best source of information on which hostels are open and which need reservations in advance. You should always plan on reserving your bed at Anchorage, Juneau and Ketchikan.

The hostels range from a huge house in Juneau (four blocks from the capitol building) with a common room with a fireplace, cooking facilities and showers to a church basement in Ketchikan. Perhaps the most important hostel for many budget travelers is the Anchorage International Hostel, which is now closer to the city center and the bus terminal.

The hostel fees are $10 for members for a one-night stay and $20 for nonmembers. Some hostels accept reservations and others don't; each hostel's particulars will be discussed later in this guide. Be aware that hosteling means separate male and female dormitories, house parents, chores assigned for each day you stay and curfews. Also, the hostels are closed during the day – even when it rains. The hostels are strict about

these and other rules. No smoking, drinking or illegal drugs are allowed. Still, hostels are the best bargains for accommodations in Alaska and the best place to meet other budget travelers and backpackers.

For more information on Alaska's hostels before you depart on your trip, write or call Hostelling International – Anchorage (☎ 907-276-3635 or 907-276-7772 for a machine message), 700 H St, Anchorage, AK 99501-3417.

Backpackers' Hostels Long overdue, Alaska finally has some offbeat hostels that offer cheap bunkroom accommodations but without all the rules and regulations of an official youth hostel. More than 20 backpacker hostels are scattered from Haines and Homer to Anchorage, the Denali Park area and Talkeetna. Fairbanks alone has six. More are sure to spring up in the near future.

B&Bs

It is now possible to stay in a B&B from Ketchikan to Anchorage, in Cordova, in Fairbanks, and as far away as Nome and Bethel. What was once a handful of private homes catering to travelers in the early 1980s is now a network of hundreds. One B&B owner estimated there are now more than 1000 B&Bs in Alaska, with several hundred in Anchorage alone.

For travelers who want nothing to do with a sleeping bag or tent, B&Bs can be an acceptable compromise between sleeping on the ground and high-priced motels and lodges. Some B&Bs are bargains, and most have rates below those of major hotels. Still, B&Bs are not cheap, and you should plan on spending anywhere from $60 to $100 per couple per night for a room.

Some B&Bs are in small, out-of-the-way communities such as Angoon, Gustavus, McCarthy or Talkeetna, where staying in a private home can be a unique and interesting experience. All recommend making reservations in advance, but it is often possible, in cities like Anchorage, Juneau and Fairbanks where there are many B&Bs, to obtain a bed the day you arrive by calling around. Many visitor centers now have sections devoted entirely to the B&Bs in their area and even courtesy phones for booking a room. Details about B&Bs will be covered in the regional chapters. You can also contact the following B&B reservation services to book rooms in advance of your trip:

Southeast Alaska
Bed & Breakfast Association of Alaska
(☎ 907-789-8822, www.wetpage.com/bbaaip),
PO Box 22800, Juneau, AK 99802
Ketchikan Reservation Service
(☎ 800-987-5337), 412 D-1 Loop Rd,
Ketchikan, AK 99901

Anchorage & Southcentral
Alaska Available (☎ 907-337-3414,
akavailable@juno.com), 1325 O St,
Anchorage, AK 99501
Alaska Private Lodging (☎ 907-258-1717,
apl@alaska.net), 704 W 2nd Ave, Anchorage,
AK 99520-0047; send $5 for a descriptive
directory
Alaska Sourdough B&B Association (☎ 907-
563-6244, aksbba@alaska.net), 889 Cardigan
Circle, Anchorage, AK 99503-7027

Matanuska Valley
Mat-Su Chapter of Bed and Breakfast
Association of Alaska (☎ 800-401-7444,
akhosts@alaska.net), PO Box 873507, Wasilla,
AK 99687-3507

Fairbanks
Fairbanks Bed & Breakfast (☎ 907-452-7700),
PO Box 73334, Fairbanks, AK 99707-3334

Roadhouses

Roadhouses, found along the highways, are another option. The authentic roadhouses that combine cabins with a large lodge/dining room are slowly being replaced by modern motels, but some places can still offer rustic cabins and sleep from two to four people for $50 to $70 per night. A few of the roadhouses, those with a roaring blaze in the stone fireplace and an owner who acts as chef, bartender and late-night storyteller, are charming. A classic roadhouse, one of the state's oldest, is located in Copper Center.

Hotels & Motels

Hotels and motels are the most expensive lodgings you can book. Although there are a few bargains, the average single room in an 'inexpensive' hotel costs $50 to $60, and a double costs $60 to $70 (these are the places down by the waterfront with shared bathrooms). Better hotels will even be close to $100 for a double, and Anchorage's best places exceed $200 per night.

The other problem with hotels and motels is that they tend to be full during much of the summer. Without being part of a tour or having advance reservations, you may have to search for an available bed in some cities. In small villages, you could be out of luck, as they may only have one or two places to choose from.

Wilderness Lodges

These are off the beaten path and usually require a bush plane or boat to reach them. The vast majority of places need advance booking and offer rustic cabins with saunas and ample opportunities to explore the nearby area by foot, canoe or kayak (they provide the boats). The lodges are designed for people who want to 'escape into the wilderness' without having to endure the 'hardship' of a tent, freeze-dried dinners or a small camp stove. The prices range from $150 to $250 per person per day and include all meals.

FOOD

The local supermarket will provide the cheapest food, whether you want to live on fruit and nuts or cook full meals at a hostel. The larger cities will have several markets that offer competitive prices and a good selection of fruit and vegetables during the summer.

While strolling down the aisles also keep an eye out for fresh Alaskan seafood, especially in Southeast and Southcentral markets. Local seafood is not cheap, but it is renowned throughout the country for its superb taste. The most common catches are king salmon steaks at $10 per pound, halibut fillets at $6 per pound, whole Dungeness crab at $4 to $5 per pound and prawns, which are large shrimp, at $9 to $10 per pound. The larger markets will also have halibut, smoked salmon and cooked king crab.

Alaska is no longer so remote that the US fast-food restaurants have not reached it. Back in the late 1970s, only Anchorage and Fairbanks had a McDonald's franchise. Now you can order a Big Mac in Ketchikan, Juneau and Kodiak, Homer and Eagle River, and other chains, such as Pizza Hut, Burger King, Wendy's and Taco Bell, are almost as widespread. Even Nome has a Burger King.

Much of the state, however, is safe from the fast-food invasion, and the smaller towns you pass through will offer only a local coffee shop or cafe. Breakfast, which many places serve all day, is the best bargain; a plate of eggs, toast and hash browns will cost from $5 to $7, and 75¢ to $1 will buy a cup of coffee.

An influx of Asian people immigrating to Alaska has resulted in most midsize towns having at least one Chinese restaurant, if not two. Some towns, like Homer (population 3900), support three. Many of these places have a lunch buffet that runs from 11 am to 3 pm or so and is an all-you-can-eat affair that costs $7 to $10. Eat a late lunch here, and you can make it through to breakfast the next morning.

One popular eating event during the summer in most of the state, but especially the Southeast, is the salmon bake. The salmon is caught locally, grilled, smothered with somebody's home-made barbecue sauce and often served all-you-can-eat-style. A dinner costs $15 to $20, but it is worth trying at least once. One of the best bakes is at Alaskaland in Fairbanks.

DRINKS
Coffee
The coffee craze that began in Seattle and the Northwest has extended into Alaska. Espresso shops are everywhere – even in towns as small as McCarthy you can find somebody with an espresso machine. Anchorage has dozens of these places.

Alcohol
The legal drinking age in Alaska is 21 years, and only the churches outnumber the bars. Except for 70 Native Alaskan towns that are dry (alcohol is prohibited) or that are damp (the sale of alcohol is prohibited), finding an open bar or liquor store is never very difficult. That and the long, dark winters explain why Alaska has the highest alcoholism rate in the USA, especially among the indigenous people. Bar hours vary, but there are always a few places that open their doors at 9 am and don't close until 5 am.

Bars in the larger cities vary in their decor, and many offer live entertainment, music and dancing. The bars in smaller towns are good places to have a brew and mingle with people from the fishing industry, loggers or other locals. All bars serve the usual US beer found in the Northwest (Miller, Rainier) and usually one or two places have that fine Canadian brew, which is darker and richer than US beer, costing around $4 for a 12oz bottle. Alaska also has a growing number of microbreweries, the largest being Juneau's Alaskan Brewing Co. Its Alaska Ambler is now seen all over the state and sold in stores for around $8 a six-pack.

ENTERTAINMENT
Theater
You won't find Broadway in Alaska – or stadium rock concerts – but the state does have a lively arts community that organizes events that are both affordable and well worth an evening out. Many theater groups feast on the summer tourists by offering plays that combine music, a little local history and a lot of comedy. These events are staged in bars, the Lions Clubs and hotels and generally range in admission price from $5 to $10 a show. The two shows not to be missed are the *Days of '98 Show* in Skagway and the show at Ester's Malamute Saloon.

Alaskan Bars
Alaskans work hard, play hard and, ultimately, drink hard. Their bars reflect that. Great Alaskan bars are saloons where an extensive menu might be peanuts, popcorn *and* pretzels, the floors are often covered by sawdust, the walls are decorated with an assortment of junk, including somebody's 50lb king salmon, and the clientele might include commercial fishers, loggers or a hard-bitten miner.

Here are eight classic Alaskan bars not to be missed:

Chilkoot Charlie's This is Anchorage's liveliest bar…and there are a lot of them in this city.

The Elbow Room A fishers' hangout in Unalaska that Playboy once named the 'most notorious bar in North America.'

Fairview Inn
This historic hotel in Talkeetna was built in 1923 as an overnight stop for the Alaska Railroad. Its bar was once the setting for a 'Women of Talkeetna' photo story in Playboy.

Howling Dog Saloon This is a rock & roll bar north of Fairbanks, where they play volleyball on outside courts all night long … without any lights.

Malamute Saloon Located just south of Fairbanks, this is the best place to tip a glass to the verses of Yukon poet Robert Service.

Red Dog Saloon This is Juneau's most famous drinking hole, but come late to miss the cruise-ship crowds snapping pictures.

Red Onion Saloon This former brothel now serves drinks in Skagway.

Salty Dawg Saloon The ramshackle lighthouse in Homer is now a great place to have a drink.

SPECTATOR SPORTS

The biggest spectator sport in Alaska is the Iditarod. The 1100-mile dogsled race from Anchorage to Nome is held in the first two weeks of March, when the temperatures are usually in the low teens and the snow coverage is good. In Anchorage, the start of the race at 4th Ave and E St is mostly ceremonial, as the 60-plus mushers run their teams only a few miles and then truck them up to Wasilla for the restart of the event. Still thousands of spectators come out in Anchorage for what is a lively weekend of events.

Not planning to come up to Alaska in March? Spectator sports in the summer are few, but there is the great American pastime of baseball, in the form of the Alaska League. Several towns, including Fairbanks, Anchorage and North Pole, sponsor these semipro teams of highly regarded college players trying to get a jump on the major leagues. Among the hall-of-famers who have played in Alaska are pitcher Tom Seaver and slugger Dave Winfield. See the regional chapters for where the teams play and when.

SHOPPING

Alaska abounds with gift shops, with items often much too tacky for my taste. Moose nuggets will be seen from one end of the state to the other, but even if they are varnished, you have to wonder who is going to wear earrings or a necklace made of the scat of an animal. More interesting, and much more affordable than gold-nugget jewelry, is what is commonly called Arctic opal. The blue and greenish stone was uncovered in the Wrangell Mountains in the late 1980s and now is set in silver in a variety of earrings, pins and other pieces.

Want a keepsake T-shirt or jacket? Avoid the gift shops in Anchorage and Fairbanks and head for the bookstores at the University of Alaska campuses, which have an interesting selection of clothing that you won't find anywhere else.

Authentic Native Alaskan carving, whether in ivory, jade or soapstone, is exquisite, highly prized and expensive. A 6-inch carving of soapstone, a soft stone that indigenous people in western Alaska carve and polish, runs from $150 to more than $300, depending on the carving and the detail. Jade and ivory will cost even more. When shopping for such artwork, be especially conscious of who you are purchasing it from. Non-Native art, sometimes carved in places as far away as Bali, is often passed off and priced as Native-produced. If you're considering investing in Native art, here is what you should know and do:

- Ask lots of questions. Is the product made in Alaska? Is it made by a Native artist? What is his or her name and where is he or she from? If you make a purchase, have the seller write the name and details on your receipt.
- Watch out for the wiggle words. Carvings may be labeled 'Alaska fossil ivory,' but just because the raw material is from Alaska it doesn't mean the work was done in the state.
- Look for the Silver Hand label. This state-run program is intended to guarantee that the tagged handicrafts are made by a Native Alaskan artist.

Just keep in mind that the Silver Hand is not widely used, and plenty of legitimate crafts do not display the Silver Hand.

- Be especially wary of soapstone carving. Almost all soapstone is imported; it is not a traditional material used by Native Alaskans. It is estimated that only 10% of the soapstone carvings in the state are made by Native artists, and the rest are made by Outsiders.

- Shop around and learn about the item you want to buy. Check out art books, museums or other collections for information. Purchasing Native Alaskan art is an investment that should not be taken lightly.

Getting There & Away

Many travelers from the Lower 48 mistakenly think that a trip to Alaska is like visiting another state of the USA. It isn't; getting to the North Country is as costly and complicated as traveling to a foreign country. Plan ahead and check around for the best possible deal, especially on airline flights.

If you're coming from the US mainland, there are three ways of getting to Alaska: by driving the Alcan (also known as the Alaska Hwy), taking a ferry or cruise up the Inside Passage waterway or flying in from a number of cities.

If you're coming from Asia or Europe, it's become harder to fly directly to Anchorage. Many international airlines, including British Airways and Japan Air Lines, have dropped their service to Anchorage. Now most international travelers come through the gateway cities of Seattle, Los Angeles, Detroit and Vancouver en route to Anchorage.

AIR

The quickest and easiest way to reach Alaska is to fly. A number of major US domestic carriers and a few international airlines offer regular service to Alaska, primarily to Anchorage International Airport. Unfortunately, thanks to the steady consolidation of the US airline industry in 1990s, ticket wars and travel promotions aren't nearly as common as they were during the height of airline deregulation in the 1970s. But in the all-important Seattle-to-Anchorage market, the 1995 demise of MarkAir, once the largest Alaska-based airline, created a void that the discount airlines Reno Air and America West soon filled, and the added competition has brought down the price of that ticket.

On intrastate routes, though, Alaska Airlines is now your only choice, which ultimately means higher prices. In the Southeast, Alaska Airlines has cornered the Anchorage-to-Juneau and Seattle-to-Juneau markets, ever since Delta Air Lines dropped its Juneau service in 1998.

Also in 1998, Northwest Airlines bought a controlling stake in Continental Airlines; American Airlines did the same with Reno Air the following year. Both Continental and Reno Air are important carriers to Alaska, and it remains to seen how these developments will affect ticket prices.

The only international airlines that serve Alaska from Asia are Aeroflot, China Airlines and Korean Air. Only Swissair offers a direct flight from Europe, with nonstop service from Zurich.

Airports & Airlines

The vast majority of visitors to Alaska fly into Anchorage International Airport, which handles 5 million passengers annually. Anchorage was once called the 'Air Crossroads of the World,' and practically every great foreign carrier made a stop here to refuel. But the introduction of new long-range jets led the international airlines to

Warning

The information in this chapter is particularly vulnerable to change: Prices for international travel are volatile, routes are introduced and canceled, schedules change, special deals come and go, and rules and visa requirements are amended. Airlines and governments seem to take a perverse pleasure in making price structures and regulations as complicated as possible. You should check directly with the airline or a travel agent to make sure you understand how a fare (and ticket you may buy) works. In addition, the travel industry is highly competitive and there are many lurks and perks.

The upshot of this is that you should get opinions, quotes and advice from as many airlines and travel agents as possible before you part with your hard-earned cash. The details given in this chapter should be regarded as pointers and are not a substitute for your own careful, up-to-date research.

begin dropping the Anchorage stopover in the mid-1980s.

Those few international flights that still come to Anchorage arrive at the north terminal; domestic flights arrive at the south terminal. A complimentary shuttle service runs between the two terminals and all parking lots. You'll find taxis and car rental companies at both terminals.

The airport has the usual services of any major center, including gift shops, restaurants, bars, pay phones, ATMs, currency exchange and baggage storage (ground level of south terminal; ☎ 907-266-2437) – $3 a day per bag.

Visitors flying into Southeast Alaska will arrive at the Ketchikan or Juneau airport. Both are extremely small facilities with only a handful of gates and one carrier – Alaska Airlines. A few visitors also fly directly from Seattle to the Fairbanks airport, which is bigger than the airports in Southeast Alaska but nowhere near the size of Anchorage International Airport.

The following airlines have scheduled services into and out of Anchorage. The phone numbers listed are either local Anchorage numbers or toll-free numbers good for anywhere in the USA and Canada.

Aeroflot (☎ 888-340-6400)
Website: www.aeroflot.com

Alaska Airlines (☎ 800-426-0333)
Website: www.alaskaair.com

America West Airlines (☎ 800-235-9292)
Website: www.americawest.com

Canada 3000 (☎ 877-658-3000)

China Airlines (☎ 800-227-5118)
Website: usa.china-airlines.com

Continental Airlines (☎ 800-525-0280)
Website: www.flycontinental.com

Delta Air Lines (☎ 800-221-1212)
Website: www.delta-air.com

ERA Aviation (☎ 800-426-0333)
Website: www.alaskaair.com

Korean Air (☎ 800-438-5000)
Website: www.koreanair.com

Northwest Airlines (☎ 800-225-2525)
Website: www.nwa.com

PenAir (☎ 800-448-4226)
Website: www.penair.com

Reeve Aleutian Airways (☎ 907-243-4700)
Website: www.reeveair.com

Reno Air (☎ 800-736-6247)
Website: www.renoair.com

TWA (☎ 800-221-2000)
Website: www.twa.com

United Airlines (☎ 800-241-6522)
Website: www.ual.com

Buying Tickets

Airfare Report once tracked down 58 different published fares for the same Northwest Airlines flight, with prices ranging from $129 to $629. Keep this in mind when purchasing a ticket. Even if you're using a travel agent, comparison shop to see who comes up with the best price. Ticket consolidators receive wholesale rates from airlines that fly to Alaska, including Reno Air and America West, then pass on the savings to travel agents.

Tickets fall into two groups: regular fares, which no budget traveler would ever be caught purchasing, and Advance Purchase Excursion (Apex), or 'Supersavers' as they are known domestically, which require 14- to 30-day advance reservations and limit your stay to a maximum number of days. The variety of prices results from an array of promotional gimmicks. US domestic airlines may offer a special price to passengers traveling on Tuesday and Wednesday – off-peak days for the airline industry – and most have off-season rates for travel to Alaska between December and May. Many airlines offer senior citizens and students a 10% discount, but you have to ask for it when booking the ticket.

'Nonrefundable' tickets are often the best deal. These are great if you make the flight, bad if you change your plans after you booked it. Airlines frequently charge penalties ($50 and up) for making any changes.

If you're traveling internationally, Round-the-World tickets allow you to fly on the combined routes of two or more airlines in one direction for a more economic journey around the globe. Several major airlines, including TWA and Continental, offer such tickets, but unfortunately Anchorage is not one of the possible stopovers.

Air Travel Glossary

Baggage Allowance This will be written on your ticket; you are usually allowed one 44lb item to go in the hold, plus one item of hand luggage. Some airlines that fly transpacific and transatlantic routes allow for two pieces of luggage (there are limits on their dimensions and weight).

Bumped Just because you have a confirmed seat doesn't mean you're going to get on the plane – see Overbooking.

Cancellation Penalties If you have to cancel or change an Apex or other discount ticket, there may be heavy penalties involved; insurance can sometimes be taken out against these penalties. Some airlines impose penalties on regular tickets as well, particularly against 'no-show' passengers.

Check In Airlines ask you to check in a certain time ahead of the flight departure (usually two hours on international flights). Be there early to avoid unforeseen delays. If you fail to check in on time and the flight is overbooked, the airline can cancel your booking and give your seat to somebody else.

Confirmation Having a ticket written out with the flight and date on it doesn't mean you have a seat until the agent has confirmed with the airline that your status is 'OK.' Prior to this confirmation, your status is 'on request.'

Consolidators Also known as bucket shops (UK), these are unbonded travel agencies specializing in discounted airline tickets.

Lost Tickets If you lose your airline ticket, an airline will usually treat it like a travelers' check and, after inquiries, issue you with a replacement. Legally, however, an airline is entitled to treat it like cash, so if you lose a ticket, it could be gone forever.

No-shows No-shows are passengers who fail to show up for their flight for whatever reason. Full-fare no shows are sometimes entitled to travel on a later flight. The rest of us are penalized (see Cancellation Penalties).

In recent years, the growth of Internet commerce has made it easier for travelers to seek out the lowest fares. Practically every major airline now has a website that allows you to check flight schedules, browse fares and purchase tickets with a credit card. Alaska Airlines and a number of other carriers entice customers with Internet specials – Alaska even has a special site for these offers (www.alaskair.com/webspecials/start.asp) – but these fares are pretty restrictive. When they're posted, you practically have to have your bags packed and be ready to leave within days. But if traveling on a whim suits you, the savings can be substantial, with roundtrip fares from Los Angeles to Anchorage for $239; from Boise, Idaho to Juneau for $279; or fares from Seattle to Fairbanks for $239.

While the Internet is a great way to comparison shop, you still might want to call the airline's toll-free numbers before booking the ticket. The sales representative will often know how to modify the ticket (and lower its price) by changing departure days or rerouting stopovers.

When you leave Alaska, there are no additional state or airport departure taxes to worry about, so a departure tax won't be added to the price of your airline ticket.

The USA

Domestic airfares are constantly moving up and down and will vary with the season, the days you want to travel, the length of stay and how rigid the ticket is in terms of changes and refunds after being purchased. Many tickets allow you to stay in Alaska for

Air Travel Glossary

Open Jaw Tickets These are return tickets that allow you to fly to one place and return from another, and travel between the two 'jaws' by any means of transport at your own expense. If available, this can save you backtracking to your arrival point.

Overbooking Airlines hate to fly with empty seats, and since every flight has some passengers who fail to show up (see No-shows), they often book more passengers than they have seats available. Usually, the excess passengers balance those who fail to show up, but occasionally somebody gets bumped. If this happens, guess who it is most likely to be? The passengers who check in late.

Reconfirmation You must contact the airline at least 72 hours prior to departure to 'reconfirm' that you intend to be on the flight. If you don't do this, the airline can delete your name from the passenger list and you could lose your seat.

Standby This is a discounted ticket where you only fly if there is a seat free at the last moment. Standby fares are usually only available at the airport, but sometimes may be handled by an airline's city office. To give yourself the best chance of getting on the flight, get there early and have your name placed on the waiting list. It's first come, first served.

Transferred Tickets Airline tickets cannot be transferred from one person to another. Travelers sometimes try to sell the return half of their ticket, but officials can ask you to prove that you are the person named on the ticket. This may not be checked on domestic flights, but on international flights, tickets are usually compared with passports.

Travel Periods Some officially discounted fares, Apex fares in particular, vary with the time of year. There is often a low (off-peak) season and a high (peak) season. Sometimes there's an intermediate or shoulder season as well. At peak times, when everyone wants to fly, both officially and unofficially discounted fares will be higher, or there may simply be no discounted tickets available. Usually the fare depends on your outward flight – if you depart in the high season and return in the low season, you pay the high-season fare.

---

three months to a year. Some only allow a stay of 21 days or less, which makes for a challenge when you're planning weeklong treks into the Alaskan wilderness.

The airfare to Alaska from most of the USA is far more affordable now than it was 15 years ago; occasionally, you can pick up a roundtrip ticket from the Midwest or East Coast to Anchorage for under $500. But most of those economy fares have tight restrictions, are for off-season travel or apply to a limited number of seats. Airlines don't offer economy fares during July, since the summer travel season in Alaska is short and demand for seats is high.

Seattle, Washington serves as the major hub for flights into Alaska. Alaska Airlines owns the lion's share of the market, with more than two dozen flights daily between Seattle and Anchorage, as well as direct flights to Ketchikan, Juneau and Fairbanks. Only Alaska Airlines and Reno Air offer daylight service to Anchorage.

A discount roundtrip fare between Seattle and Anchorage is now creeping toward $300. For the lowest possible fare, purchase your ticket 21 days in advance and book one of the red-eye flights that depart Seattle between 9 pm and 2 am and leave Anchorage between 12:45 am and 2 pm (Alaskan time) on the return leg. Alaska Airlines has five such flights daily; Reno Air, United, Delta and Continental also offer middle-of-the-night trips. Shop around and you might be able to pick up a ticket for $200 to $250.

An advance-purchase, roundtrip ticket between Seattle and Juneau on Alaska Airlines is $325. The Seattle-to-Fairbanks route costs $380 to $430. During the profitable summer season, you can add $100 to $150 for every stop you make along the way.

You can now book a nonstop flight to Anchorage from a number of other US cities, including San Francisco, Salt Lake City, Detroit, Minneapolis, Reno, Portland, Chicago and Los Angeles. Northwest Airlines flies nonstop between Minneapolis and Anchorage; advance-purchase tickets usually cost $600 to $700. A similar ticket from Detroit is $700 to $800. Delta Air Lines flies from Salt Lake City to Anchorage for a roundtrip fare of $696 and from Los Angeles for $300 to $400. United Airlines has two daily, nonstop flights from Chicago to Anchorage for $679 and similar flights from San Francisco for $454.

Continental Airlines offers a one-stop flight (with no change of planes) from Houston to Anchorage for $704 during the summer if booked 14 days in advance. TWA flies nonstop to Anchorage from St Louis daily during the summer for $575 roundtrip. From Boston, you can fly to Anchorage (with one or two stops) on Delta, United, Northwest or Continental, which often offers the lowest fare. Still, the price of a roundtrip, advance-purchase ticket usually exceeds $800.

Thanks to the arrival of Reno Air in Anchorage, there have been some bargain airfares to Alaska in recent years. Reno Air has offered roundtrip tickets from Reno for as low as $220, from Los Angeles for $320, from Las Vegas for $320 and from San Jose for $348. Also check out America West. The airline moved into the Alaska market in the mid-1990s with a $300 Phoenix-to-Anchorage nonstop flight but dropped out in 1997. In 1999, it was considering resuming service to the 49th state from its major hubs of Phoenix and Las Vegas.

Another strategy for saving money is to reserve a cheap flight to Seattle with such discount carriers as Southwest Airlines

Air Shipping a Bicycle

A bicycle is a handy thing to haul up to Alaska, especially if your itinerary includes a lot of travel on the state ferry system. If set up to carry your equipment, a bike will allow you to easily explore the many small ports the ferries connect and then in the evening ride out of the towns to stay at campgrounds that are usually cheaper and much more scenic than those found in the town centers.

You have to pay extra for shipping a bike on the airlines (Alaska Airlines charges $50 each way) but this is usually far cheaper than renting one a handful of times during a trip. In the few towns where you can rent a quality bicycle, you can expect to pay anywhere from $20 to $35 a day.

The first step to air-shipping your two-wheeler is to obtain a cardboard bike box. Most airlines will sell you one (Alaska Airlines charges $15), but you can usually get one free at your local bicycle shop. You will also need some bubble wrap, twine, duct tape and a small block of wood or a fork spacer.

Begin by removing and wrapping the seat and seatpost as a unit and then removing and wrapping both pedals. Open both brake quick releases and remove the handlebars and stem as a unit. Then remove the front wheel. Place the small block of wood or spacer between the front-fork dropouts and then rotate the fork so that it faces backward. You can protect the frame with the bubble wrap before placing the front wheel next to it and tying it in place. Align the handlebars-and-stem unit along the top tube with the stem inside the main frame triangle if you can, and then secure it with the twine. Wrap the rear derailleur where it is likely to contact the box as well as any loose parts (pedals, seat and seatpost, etc). You can secure the parts in the box below the down tube. Lower the bike into the box and make sure nothing is loose or rattling around.

Reinforce the outside of the box with the duct tape and make sure all previous addresses and shipping labels are blacked out. Finally, write your name and address all over the box. This is one piece of luggage you don't want to end up in Albuquerque instead of Anchorage.

(☎ 800-444-5660) or America West and then book a second ticket to Anchorage with a different airline. In 1999, Southwest was offering a special $99 one-way, cross-country fare.

In short, air travel is the best way to go if you plan to spend three weeks or less touring Alaska. But if you are planning to spend a month or more venturing through the state, you see more and pay less by combining the Alaska Marine Hwy ferry out of Bellingham, Washington, with a bus ride from Haines.

Canada
Canadian Airlines does not service Alaska but will fly you to Seattle, where you can pick up a domestic US carrier for the second leg of your journey. The roundtrip fare from Toronto to Seattle, for a ticket purchased 14 days in advance, is $351. Contact Canadian Airlines toll-free from Canada (☎ 800-665-1177) and from the USA (☎ 800-426-7000) or visit the website www.cdnair.ca.

You can also fly to Vancouver on Canadian Airlines and then take either an Alaska Airlines or Canada 3000 flight to Anchorage. Alaska Airlines charges $383 for the roundtrip ticket if purchased 21 days in advance. Another option is to fly to Whitehorse on Canadian Airlines and then jump on an Air North Flight headed for Juneau or Fairbanks. You can book that entire ticket through Canadian Airlines; a roundtrip flight to Juneau costs $500 to $536.

A roundtrip Air North flight from Whitehorse to Juneau is C$237; to Fairbanks, it's C$460. The Whitehorse-based airline also offers a Klondike Explorer Pass for C$654. This allows unlimited air travel for 21 days between the five cities Air North serves: Juneau, Whitehorse, Dawson City, Old Crow and Fairbanks. In Alaska, contact the airline at ☎ 800-764-0407; in northern British Columbia and the Yukon Territory, call ☎ 403-668-2228 for information.

Australia & New Zealand
In Australia, STA and Flight Centres are the major dealers in cheap airfares. They have branches in all the major cities. You can also contact the travel agents in the Yellow Pages. Qantas Airways has flights from Sydney to Los Angeles with direct connections on Alaska Airlines to Anchorage. A roundtrip, advance-purchase ticket starts at A$2741 and allows you to stay up to two months.

Air New Zealand has a similar agreement with Alaska Airlines. Most flights go through Los Angeles, where you pick up an Alaska Airlines flight. Such a roundtrip ticket is NZ$2986 if purchased seven days in advance and is good for up to two months of travel.

The UK
British Airways no longer flies into Anchorage. It does have nonstop flights from London (Heathrow) to Seattle, where you continue north on a domestic carrier. The roundtrip fare is UK£584; the ticket must be booked 21 days in advance, and your stay in the USA can't exceed 45 days.

Northwest has a London-to-Anchorage flight that begins at Gatwick Airport and changes planes in Detroit. A roundtrip economy fare is UK£635. Both Delta and United offer similar flights from Gatwick and Heathrow, respectively.

Continental Europe
The usual route to Anchorage from Europe is to head west with a stop in New York and then Seattle. From Paris, Continental offers a daily flight to Anchorage with a change of planes in Houston and an additional stop-over before reaching Alaska. A roundtrip fare, purchased 14 days in advance, is $1222. Northwest also has a daily Paris-to-Anchorage flight that changes planes in Detroit. The roundtrip fare is $1237, but the ticket must be booked 21 days in advance, can only be used in July and August and limits your stay in Alaska to 30 days. You also have to travel between Monday and Thursday.

Similar flights can be arranged from Frankfurt through Delta, Northwest and United. Northwest charges $1384 for a roundtrip ticket with a 21-day advance purchase; this allows you to stay up to three months. Travel must take place between Monday and Friday. Delta offers a similar ticket for $1376. Also, check Condor Airlines (www.condor.de), a carrier that began offering nonstop, semiweekly service between Anchorage and Frankfurt in 1999, with roundtrip fares around $1000. Balair/CTA, a division of Swissair, offers a nonstop Zurich-to-Anchorage flight every Wednesday from May through September for $1100 roundtrip.

Asia

In 1998, Northwest began a twice-weekly nonstop service between Anchorage and Tokyo during the summer. Otherwise, the daily flights from Tokyo to Anchorage fly into Seattle or Los Angeles first and then go on to Alaska.

Northwest flies into Seattle and onto Anchorage daily for a roundtrip fare of $2686. Delta offers daily flights that change at either Salt Lake City or Seattle; the roundtrip fare is $2700, with no requirements for length of stay.

Japan Air Lines has discontinued its service to Anchorage and does not fly into Seattle. On JAL, the best you can do is fly to San Francisco and then pick up an Alaska Airlines flight to Anchorage.

The daily service from Seoul to Anchorage is far cheaper than departing from Tokyo. United Airlines offers a daily flight with a change of planes at San Francisco. Or, you can fly nonstop four days a week with Korean Air. Its roundtrip fare is $1160 and requires only a four-day advance purchase.

There is also nonstop service between Taipei, Taiwan and Anchorage with China Air. United offers daily service from Taipei with a change of planes in San Francisco.

When booking a flight from Asia, remember that the fares of US-based airlines like Northwest and Delta fluctuate wildly with the rise and fall of the dollar against the yen.

LAND

What began in April 1942 as an unprecedented construction project during WWII ended eight months later as the first overland link between the Lower 48 and Alaska. Known formally as the Alaska-Canada Military Hwy, it's affectionately called the Alcan.

Today, the Alcan (also known as the Alaska Hwy) is a road through the vast wilderness of northwest Canada and Alaska, starting at Dawson Creek in British Columbia and ending at Delta Junction.

For those with the time, the Alcan is a unique way to travel north. The trip is an adventure in itself; the 1520-mile road is a legend among highways, and completing the journey along the Alcan is a feather in anyone's cap. Each summer, thousands of travelers enjoy the spectacular drive.

The Alcan is now entirely paved, and although sections of jarring potholes, frost heaves (the rippling effect of the pavement caused by freezing and thawing) and loose gravel still exist, the infamous rough conditions of 20 years ago no longer prevail. The era of lashing spare fuel cans to the side of the car because gasoline stations are 250 miles apart is also gone. Food, gas and lodging can be found every 20 to 50 miles along the highway, with 100 miles being the longest stretch between fuel stops.

There are several ways to get to the Alcan: you can begin in the US states of Washington, Idaho or Montana and pass through Edmonton or Jasper in Alberta or Prince George in British Columbia, Canada. There are also several ways of traveling the highway: bus, car or a combination of Alaska Marine Hwy ferry and bus.

Bus

A combination of buses will take you from Seattle via the Alcan to Anchorage, Fairbanks, Skagway or Haines for a moderate cost. There are no direct bus services from the Lower 48 to Alaska; travelers have to be patient, as services here are more limited than in the rest of the country. Be forewarned that a roundtrip ride on a bus from Seattle to Anchorage will end up costing you more than flying.

Greyhound On this major US bus company, the closest you can get to Alaska is Whitehorse in British Columbia, and this involves purchasing two tickets. You begin at the Seattle Greyhound station (☎ 206-628-5530, www.greyhound.com), on the corner of 8th Ave and Stewart St, where you can buy a one-way ticket to Vancouver for $20. The bus departs at least five times a day, more often if the demand is high during the summer. At Pacific Central Station on Main St in Vancouver, you switch to a Greyhound Lines of Canada bus for the rest of the journey, which includes a two-hour layover at Prince George and another at Dawson Creek in British Columbia. The Vancouver bus departs at 7:30 am daily except Saturday and arrives in Whitehorse at 4:30 am, 44 hours later – an epic journey that takes its toll. If you plan to continue your travels on an Alaska Direct bus and don't want to stay overnight in Whitehorse, you must catch the Monday morning bus from Vancouver.

The one-way fare from Vancouver to Whitehorse is C$298. For C$450, you can purchase a Canadian Pass that allows 30 days of travel within 40 days. When planning your trip, remember that most Greyhound special offers, such as Ameripass (unlimited travel for seven days), do not apply to Yukon or Alaska destinations.

There is also a more pleasant way to reach Alaska than spending two days on a Greyhound bus. Once in Vancouver, you can buy a ticket to Prince Rupert, where you can hop on a delightful Alaska Marine Hwy ferry. There are two buses a day, at 7:30 am and 8:30 pm, and they arrive in Prince Rupert some 20 hours later. The roundtrip fare is C$173. Contact Greyhound Lines of Canada (☎ 800-661-8747, www.greyhound.ca) for information.

Alaskon Express Once you've reached Whitehorse, you change to an Alaskon Express bus for the next leg of the journey. Gray Line of Alaska operates these buses from May to September, from either Westmark Whitehorse, at 2nd Ave and Steele St, or the Greyhound Bus Terminal at the north end of 2nd Ave.

Buses depart the Yukon capital for Anchorage on Tuesday, Thursday and Sunday at noon, stay overnight at Beaver Creek in the Yukon and then continue to Anchorage the next day, reaching the city at 7:30 pm. You can get off the bus earlier at Tok, Glennallen

or Palmer. On Monday, Wednesday and Saturday, buses depart Whitehorse at noon for Haines, reaching the Southeast Alaska town and ferry terminal port at 5:30 pm.

As a testimony to the popularity of the Chilkoot Trail, an Alaskon Express bus departs daily from Whitehorse at 4:30 pm for Skagway, stopping along the way to pick up backpackers coming off the popular trek.

You can also go overland to Fairbanks, something that was hard to do in the past. An Alaskon Express bus departs at noon on Tuesday, Thursday and Sunday for Fairbanks with a stopover in Beaver Creek. A nice thing about these buses is that you can flag them down along the road, which is good if you've been sitting around for most of the morning trying to thumb a ride out of a town like Haines Junction.

The one-way fare from Whitehorse to Anchorage is $195, to Fairbanks $165, to Haines $85 and to Skagway $56; these fares do not include lodging at Beaver Creek. In Whitehorse, call ☎ 867-667-2223 for current bus information. If you're still in the planning stages of your trip, contact Gray Line of Alaska (☎ 800-544-2206, fax 206-281-0621); by January, the company can provide schedules, departure times and rates for the following summer.

Alaska Direct Bus Line Much smaller and slightly cheaper than Gray Line's Alaskon Express is Alaska Direct Bus Line, based in Anchorage. On Tuesday, Friday and Sunday, an Alaska Direct bus departs Whitehorse at 7 am, reaching Tok around 3 pm. From there, you can continue on to Fairbanks or transfer to a bus for Anchorage.

The one-way fare from Whitehorse to Tok is $80, to Fairbanks $120 and Anchorage $145. In the USA, call Alaska Direct at ☎ 800-770-6652; in Whitehorse, call ☎ 867-668-4833. Make sure you call to find out where the pickup point is or if the company is even in business still.

Norline Coaches This Canadian bus company used to provide the final link between Whitehorse and Alaska but now the bus line runs between the Canadian towns of

Whitehorse and Dawson City. From June to September, buses depart from the Whitehorse bus terminal on Monday, Wednesday and Friday at 9 am and travel 335 miles to Dawson City, arriving at 3:30 pm. The bus then turns around and repeats the trip the same day. The one-way fare is C$68.

While many feel this is the more scenic and adventurous route into Alaska, there is no bus beyond Dawson City, and hitchhiking across the border through Chicken and down to Tok can mean a long wait at times. For current rates and schedules, call the Whitehorse Bus Terminal (☎ 867-668-3355), which handles information for Norline, Greyhound Lines of Canada and Alaska Direct.

Car

Without a doubt, driving your own car to Alaska allows you the most freedom. You can leave when you want, stop where you feel like it and pretty much make up your itinerary as you go along. It's not exactly cheap driving to Alaska, and that's not even considering the wear and tear and thousands of miles you'll put on your vehicle.

If you're contemplating this car trip, remember that the condition of your tires is most important. The Alcan may be paved, but it's constantly under repair, and stretches of frost heaves and potholes are common, especially on the Canadian side; worn tires don't last long here.

Even your spare – and you *must* have one – should be fairly new. You should also avoid the newer 'space-saver' spares and carry a full-size spare as your extra tire.

Replace windshield wipers before you depart and carry an extra set along with a gallon of solvent for the windshield-washer reservoir. Dust, dirt and mud make good visibility a constant battle while driving. Also bring a jack, wrenches and other assorted tools, spare hoses, fan belts and a quart of oil or two; even an extra headlight or air filter is not being too extreme. Carry them and hope you never have to use them.

Some travelers use an insect screen, some put plastic headlight covers or a wire-mesh screen over the headlights, and others place a rubber mat or piece of carpet between the gas tank and securing straps. These measures can protect the vehicle from the worst danger on the road – flying rocks that are kicked up by truck-and-trailer rigs passing you.

By far the worst problem on the Alcan and many other roads in Alaska and the Yukon is dust – that's why even on the hottest days you see most cars with their windows up. To control dust in an RV or trailer, reverse the roof vent on your rig so it faces forward. Then, keep it open a few inches while driving, creating air pressure inside to combat the incoming dust.

Those traveling the route in small or compact vehicles often face another problem – an overloaded car. Stuffing the trunk and the backseat and then lashing on a cartop carrier in order to take along extra boxes of macaroni-and-cheese dinners could do you in, miles from anywhere. It's been said that the biggest single cause of flat tires and broken suspension systems along the Alcan is an overloaded car.

Since almost 80% of the Alcan is in Canada, it's best to brush up on the metric system or have a conversion chart taped to the dashboard. On the Canada side, you'll find kilometer posts (as opposed to the mileposts found in Alaska) which are placed every 5km after the zero point in Dawson Creek. (With more than 1000 vehicles passing through Dawson Creek daily during the summer, it's the one place where you might want to book a room or a campsite in advance.) Most Alcan veterans say 300 miles a day is a good pace – one that will allow for plenty of stops to see the scenery or wildlife.

The best stretch? That's tough, but some will argue it's the 330 miles from Fort Nelson (British Columbia) to Watson Lake (Yukon). As you wind around hairpin turns, you'll enjoy panoramas of the Rocky Mountains and you'll stand a good chance of spotting wildlife, especially if you leave early in the morning.

It's always good to have Canadian currency or a major credit card on hand to purchase gasoline. One or two of the major gasoline credit cards will also come in handy, especially if you have a major breakdown. Along the way, Tourism Yukon operates a number of visitor reception centers that provide a wealth of information and maps for drivers. These include the following:

Watson Lake
(☎ 867-536-7469) Alaska Highway Interpretive Center, at the junction of the Alcan and Campbell St

Whitehorse
(☎ 867-667-2915) Visitor Center, downtown at 2nd St and Hanson Ave

Haines Junction
(☎ 867-634-2345) Visitor Center, at Kluane National Park Headquarters

Beaver Creek
(☎ 867-862-7321) Visitor Center, at Mile 1202 of the Alcan in the heart of Beaver Creek

Hitchhiking

Hitchhiking is probably more common in Alaska than it is in the rest of the USA, and more so on rural dirt roads like the McCarthy Rd and the Denali Hwy than on the major paved routes. But this doesn't mean it's a totally safe way of getting around. Hitchhiking is never entirely safe in any country in the world, and we don't recommend it. Travelers who decide to hitchhike should understand that they are taking a small but potentially serious risk. If you do choose to do this, you'll be safer if you travel in pairs and let someone know where you're planning to go. That said, if you're properly prepared and have sufficient time, thumbing the Alcan can be an easy way to see the country, meet people and save money.

The Alcan seems to inspire the pioneer spirit in travelers who drive it. Drivers are good about picking up hitchhikers, much better than those across the Lower 48 – the only problem is that there aren't as many of them. In places along the route, you may have to wait 30 minutes or longer before a car passes by. During the summer, the number of vehicles increases significantly, but if you're attempting the trip in early spring or late fall, be prepared to wait hours or even overnight at one of a handful of junctions along the way.

All hitchhikers should be patient and self-sufficient, with a tent, some food, water, warm clothing and a good book or two. Moving through the USA and southern Canada, you'll get the usual short and long rides from one city to the next. Once you make it to Dawson Creek, it will probably only take you one or two longer rides to reach your destination.

Any part of the Alcan can be slow, but some sections are notorious. The worst can be Haines Junction, the crossroads in the Yukon where southbound hitchhikers occasionally have to stay overnight before catching a ride to Haines in Southeast Alaska. Longer waits may also occur if you're heading home in late summer or early fall and thumbing out of Glennallen, Tok or Delta Junction back into Canada and the Lower 48. A sign with your destination on it helps, as does displaying your backpack, which tells drivers you're a summer traveler.

The hardest part of the trip for many is crossing the US-Canadian border. Canadian officials usually pull cars over if the passengers are not of the same nationality as the driver, and they will ask to see proof of sufficient funds. Anybody without pre-arranged transport is required to have $80 per day to travel through Canada or a total of $200 to $250.

The Canadians are not hassling hitchhikers when they do this; they're just making sure that visitors don't get stuck somewhere for a week because they've run out of money. On the way to Alaska, most travelers will have these funds; on the way back, however, it may be difficult if you're at the end of your trip and without money.

Three places to make contacts for a ride back to the Lower 48 are the Anchorage International Hostel; the Wood Center in the middle of the University of Alaska campus in Fairbanks, where there's a bulletin board for students offering or needing rides; and the Chamber of Commerce hospitality center in Tok, where the free coffee pulls in many drivers before they continue into Canada. If you're heading north, the bulletin board outside the tourist office in Dawson Creek is worth checking, as it often contains messages from people looking for somebody to help with fuel costs.

With luck, it can take you less than a week to hitchhike from Seattle to Fairbanks or Anchorage, but to be on the safe side, plan on the trip taking seven to eight days. The route from Seattle to Alaska is the most direct and sees the most traffic to Dawson Creek. This route involves hitchhiking along I-5 in Washington to the Canadian border, then on the Trans-Canada Hwy 1 to Cache Creek and finally on Hwy 97 north to Dawson Creek and the Alcan.

If you'd rather not hitchhike the entire Alcan, take the Alaska Marine Hwy ferry from Bellingham, Washington, to Haines and start hitchhiking from there; you'll cut the journey in half but still travel along the highway's most spectacular parts. Haines, however, is a town of about 1150 people, and traffic is light on the road to the Alcan at Haines Junction. It's best to hustle off the ferry and begin thumbing as vehicles unload, so you can catch a driver heading north. Or, seek out a lift while you're still on the boat by taping a notice outside the ship's cafeteria or showers.

AlaskaPass

A concept that has been hugely popular in Europe for years arrived in the North Country in 1989, when a small company in Haines (of all places) organized nine major carriers and offered an unlimited travel pass. AlaskaPass Inc, now with headquarters in Vashon, Washington, offers the only all-inclusive ground transportation pass that will get you from Washington through Canada into Alaska and even as far north as Dawson City in the Yukon for a set price.

The carriers include Alaska Marine Hwy, Greyhound Lines of Canada, Vancouver Island Coach Lines, British Columbia Rail, British Columbia Ferries, Alaskon Express, Norline Coaches and the Alaska Railroad.

After you purchase your pass, choosing the number of days you want to travel, you make your own reservations with the individual carriers. Each time you pick up a ticket, you simply show your AlaskaPass.

On the plus side, you can save money with such a pass. On the down side, you have to plan carefully to do so, and the pass does not include any air travel.

The passes are offered for either continuous or flexible travel, which allows travel on a number of days during a time period. The latter is a much better choice, as it leaves you time to enjoy an area or take side trips before moving on.

The eight-day pass is $499, but there's a $50 surcharge if you use it to board the Alaska Marine Hwy ferry in Bellingham. The longest is the 30-day pass at $949. Still better over the long haul is the 12/21-day pass (travel 12 out of 21 days) for $729 and the 21/45 for $999. There are discounts for children ages three to 11, and there's a cheaper off-season pass for travel between October and April.

You can purchase a pass ahead of time from most travel agents or directly from the company by calling ☎ 800-248-7598 or 0800-89-82-85 in Great Britain. You can also visit the website (www.alaskapass.com).

SEA
Ferry

As an alternative to the Alcan, you can travel the Southeast's Inside Passage, a waterway made up of thousands of islands, fjords and mountainous coastlines. To many, the Southeast is the most beautiful area in the state, and the Alaska Marine Hwy ferries are the country's best public transportation bargain.

With its leisurely pace, travel on the ferries is a delightful experience. The midnight sun is warm, and the possibility of sighting whales, bald eagles or sea lions keeps most travelers at the side of the ship. This is also an excellent way to meet other independent travelers heading for a summer in the North Country.

The ferries to Alaska begin at either Bellingham, Washington, or Prince Rupert in British Columbia and then continue on to Ketchikan in Alaska. Most ferries then depart for Wrangell, Petersburg, Sitka, Juneau, Haines and Skagway before heading back. A trip from Bellingham to Juneau takes 2½ to four days depending on the route. Most ferry terminals are a few miles out of town, and the short in-port time doesn't allow passengers to view the area without making a stopover.

If you intend to use the ferries to tour the Southeast, obtain a current schedule and keep it handy at all times. The ferries stop almost every day at larger centers like Juneau, but the smaller villages may only have one ferry every three or four days; many places won't have service at all.

Seven ships ply the waters of Southeast Alaska, but only the M/V *Columbia* sails the entire route from Bellingham to Skagway. The M/V *Matanuska*, M/V *Taku* and M/V *Kennicott* depart from Prince Rupert and reach Skagway before turning around.

The M/V *Kennicott* is the newest boat in the fleet and in 1998 began a special run from Southeast Alaska across the Gulf of Alaska to Seward. This marks the first time that the Southeast routes of the Alaska Marine Hwy ferry have been connected with a Southcentral portion that includes such ports as Homer, Valdez, Kodiak and Cordova. These trips are offered only once a month during the summer, departing Juneau and reaching Seward three days later. The one-way fare is $128. Because it allows travelers to skip the long haul over the Alcan, this sailing is extremely popular and should be booked before you arrive in Alaska.

The M/V *Malaspina* sails only North Lynn Canal during the summer, connecting Juneau with Haines and Skagway. The other two ships are smaller and serve out-of-the-way villages from Juneau or Ketchikan. In the summer, the M/V *Aurora* sails between Ketchikan, Metlakatla, Hollis and Hyder. The M/V *Le Conte* stops at Juneau, Hoonah, Angoon, Sitka, Kake, Tenakee Springs, Skagway, Haines and Petersburg; it makes a special run to Pelican once a month.

The large 'blue canoes' of the Alaska Marine Hwy are equipped with observation decks, food services, lounges and solariums with deck chairs. You can rent a stateroom for overnight trips, but most backpackers head straight for the solarium and sleep in one of the deck chairs or on the floor with a sleeping pad.

When boarding, it's best to scramble to the solarium and either stake out a lounge chair or at least an area on the floor. The solarium and observation deck are the best places to sleep, as the air is clean and the nighttime peace is unbroken. The other places to crash are the indoor lounges, which can be smoky, noisy or both.

On the long haul from Bellingham, backpackers are still allowed to pitch free-standing tents outside the solarium, and the ferry staff even designate the correct area for doing so. Bring duct tape to attach the tent to the floor, but remember that during a busy summer tents tend to take up more space than two people really need in an already crowded section of the ship.

Food on board is reasonably priced compared to what you will pay on shore, with breakfast and lunches costing around $4 to $6 and dinner $7 to $10. Still, it's cheaper to bring your own grub and eat it in the solarium or the cafeteria. Some backpackers bring their own tea bags, coffee or instant soup and then just purchase the cup of hot water. The pursers, however, do not allow any camp stoves to be used on board and are very strict about enforcing this.

The only thing cheaper than the food on board is the shower. Showers are free on all ferries except the M/V *Tustumena*, where they cost only 25¢ for 10 minutes. They're the best bargain you'll find in Alaska.

There is a tariff for carrying on bicycles or kayaks, but compared to the cost of bringing a car or motorcycle, it's very reasonable. The cost is only $41 to take what ferry officials call an 'alternative means of conveyance' from Bellingham to Haines. A bicycle can be a handy way to see at least part of a town without disembarking for a few days, while a summer (or even a lifetime) can be spent using the ferry system to hop from one wilderness kayak trip to another.

Above all else, when using the Alaska Marine Hwy system, check and double-check the departures of ferries once you have arrived in the Southeast. It's worth a phone call to the terminal to find out actual arrival and departure times; the ferries are notorious for being late or breaking down and having their departures canceled. It's something that happens every summer without fail.

Reservations The ferries are extremely popular during the peak season from June to August. You must make reservations if you want a cabin or vehicle space and if you're a walk-on passenger boarding at Bellingham. Space for summer sailings from Bellingham is often filled by April, forcing walk-on passengers to wait on standby for an available spot.

The Alaska Marine Hwy's reservation office will take written requests any time and telephone requests from the first working day of January for summer sailings. As telephone lines are jammed most of the time after the first day of the year, it's wise to send in a written or email request as soon as you can figure out your itinerary. When writing or faxing in the reservation, provide the port of embarkation; names and ages of all travelers; width, height and overall length of vehicle including trailers; mailing address; telephone numbers; alternative travel dates; and the date you will be leaving home.

The summer sailing schedule comes out in December; to obtain one, contact the Alaska Marine Hwy (☎ 907-465-3941), PO Box 25535, Juneau, AK 99802-5535. There are also toll-free telephone numbers (☎ 800-642-0066, 800-526-6731 from the Lower 48) to handle schedule requests, or you can view the schedule online at www.akferry.com.

Once you're ready to make a reservation, call the toll-free numbers, fax your request (fax 907-277-4829) or book your passage through the Alaska Marine Hwy website.

When you book a passage on the ferry, you must have an idea of what ports you want to visit along the route, with exact dates, before purchasing the ticket. Stopovers are not free; rather, tickets are priced on a port-to-port basis. From Bellingham to Haines, you can generally count on each stopover adding 2 percent to the fare.

Once on the boat, you can still arrange a stopover but will be charged an additional fee. If you plan to spend a good deal of time or the entire summer in the region, purchase a ticket to Juneau and then use that as your base, taking shorter trips to other towns on the M/V *Le Conte*. The fare for walk-on passengers from Bellingham to Haines is $244, while the ticket from Bellingham to Juneau is $226.

All fares listed in this book are for adults (ages 12 and older). Fares for children ages two to 11 are about half the price of an adult fare, and children under two travel free. The ferry system also offers 50% discount passes to both senior citizens and disabled persons. Both are restricted to travel between Alaskan ports when space is available and can be used only for the M/V *Le Conte*, M/V *Aurora*, M/V *Bartlett* and M/V *Tustumena*. Applications for a disabled pass must be filed in advance by writing to Alaska Marine Highway System Pass Desk, PO Box 25535, Juneau, AK 99802-5535.

Bellingham, Washington Bellingham is the southern terminus of the Alaska Marine Hwy and includes an information center, a ticket office, luggage lockers and an outdoor seating area with a nice view of Bellingham Bay and the surrounding hills. It's 10 minutes south of the Bellingham International Airport in the historic Fairhaven shopping district, 87 miles north of Seattle. From I-5, go west on Fairhaven Parkway (exit 250) for 1.1 miles and then turn right onto 12th St, where signs will direct you to the terminal at the end of Harris Ave.

Prince Rupert, British Columbia If the Alaska Marine Hwy ferries are full in Bellingham, one alternative is to begin your cruise in Seattle, utilizing two ferry systems before switching to the Alaska line in Prince Rupert, in Canada.

At Pier 69, off Alaskan Way in the heart of Seattle, catch the *Victoria Clipper* to Victoria on Vancouver Island. During the summer, boats depart at least four times daily – at 7:30, 8 and 8:30 am and 3:30 pm – for a trip that takes 2½ to three hours. The one-way fare for walk-on passengers is $58. For reservations, call ☎ 800-888-2535 from the USA.

Once you land on Vancouver Island, head north to Port Hardy and catch one of the BC Ferries to Prince Rupert. From this Canadian city, you have a much better chance of boarding the Alaska Marine Hwy ferry because there are three vessels that connect Prince Rupert to Southeast Alaska. Port Hardy can be reached by bus from Victoria on Laidlaw Coach Lines (☎ 800-318-0818 in Canada, 800-663-8390 in the USA), which leaves once a day at 6:15 am; the one-way fare is C$82. The bus depot is at 700 Douglas St, behind the Empress Hotel in the center of Victoria.

At Port Hardy, the BC Ferries dock is at Bear Cove, about 5 miles from town, but there is a shuttle van service from the Island Coach Line bus terminal on Main St. At Bear Cove, the *Queen of the North* departs at 7:30 am and reaches Prince Rupert at 10:30 pm and returns to Vancouver Island the next day, maintaining this every-other-day schedule from June to the end of September. The trip is scenic, and the daylight voyage takes 15 hours; the one-way fare for walk-on passengers is C$104. The same ship also makes a stop once a week at the isolated town of Bella Bella in British Columbia.

The easiest way to check current schedules or make reservations is to go to the BC Ferries website (bcferries.bc.ca). Schedules and reservations can also be obtained by calling or writing to BC Ferries (☎ 250-386-3431), 1112 Fort St, Victoria, British Columbia, Canada V8V 4V2. In British Columbia, there is a toll-free number (☎ 888-223-3779).

Once you reach Prince Rupert, the ferry fare to Haines is $122; to Juneau, it's $104.

Hyder If for some strange reason you can't catch an Alaska Marine Hwy ferry at Prince Rupert, there's a last alternative. Make your way east along the Yellowhead Hwy from Prince Rupert and then head north along the Cassiar Hwy. You travel 99 miles along the scenic Cassiar Hwy and then turn off at Kitwanga for Stewart. You can either hitchhike this route or catch a Greyhound bus to Kitwanga, basically the junction of Hwy 16 and Hwy 37, an hour's drive from the town of Terrace. At the Petro-Can Service Station, a Seaport Limousine Service bus (☎ 604-636-2622) stops by daily at 4 pm from Monday to Friday and will take you to Stewart for C$21. Across the border from Stewart is Hyder, a Southeast Alaska hamlet of about 100 people with cafes, bars and gift shops.

During the summer, the Alaska Marine Hwy ferry M/V *Aurora* departs from here on Tuesdays at 3:45 pm, bound for Ketchikan, where you can continue north on one of several other boats. The one-way fare from Hyder to Ketchikan is $40.

It's vital to double-check the departure time for the Hyder ferry, as it may leave on Pacific Time as opposed to Alaska Time.

Cruises

The biggest growth in Alaskan tourism during the past few years has been the number of cruise lines now sailing up the Inside Passage and beyond.

Nine lines deployed almost two dozen major cruise ships in Alaskan waters during the May-through-September season; these include the 1075-passenger *Rotterdam* and the 1590-passenger *Regal Princess*. There are also a dozen smaller vessels, which can hold 49 to 100 passengers each, sailing around the state.

Actually, an Alaskan cruise can be a real bargain with an early booking and a budget cabin. Two people sharing a cabin can often get a seven-day Alaskan cruise for about $800 to $900 a person if they book by February or March. That fee covers your food, lodging and transportation – not bad if you want to zip through a portion of Alaska in seven days. Just about everything else, including drinks on the boat, entertainment and onshore activities and tours will cost you extra.

If that's what you're looking for, contact a travel agent. Some of the popular large-vessel leaders of the Alaskan flotilla are:

Cunard Line (☎ 800-221-4770)
Norwegian Cruise Line (☎ 800-327-7030)
Princess Cruises (☎ 800-421-5522)
Regency Cruises (☎ 800-388-5500)

ORGANIZED TOURS

The land of the midnight sun is also the land of the package tour. Every cruise ship line and sightseeing company loves Alaska and its allure for travelers, especially older tourists with lots of disposable income but not a high sense of adventure.

Actually, package tours can often be the most affordable way to see a large chunk of Alaska if your needs include the better hotels in each town and a full breakfast every morning. Just keep in mind that they move quickly and rarely offer enough extra time to undertake such activities as a wilderness trek or a paddle into Glacier Bay National Park. A thumbnail sketch of just the largest tour companies follows.

Gray Line

You see this company so often throughout the state that it seems to practically own Alaska. Seattle-based Gray Line offers 19 package tours that begin in various cities, including Seattle, Vancouver and Anchorage. The All Alaska Air tour is an 11-day trip that includes Juneau, Anchorage, Denali National Park, Fairbanks and part of the Alcan for $2150 based on double occupancy.

A number of shorter Gray Line tours begin and end in Alaska, including the Denali/Prince William Sound Discovery, a seven-day tour from Anchorage that includes Fairbanks, Denali National Park and Columbia Glacier for $1275 per person. The Prince William Sound tour, a two-day bus and cruise-ship journey past the Columbia Glacier, costs $295 per person. Most of these intrastate tours are covered in detail in the regional chapters. If you're interested in a complete package tour, throw away this book and call Gray Line (☎ 800-628-2449) or check its website (www.grayline.com).

American Sightseeing

Another big player in Alaska, this company offers dozens of itineraries, including cruises/ tours out of Seattle and land tours that begin in Anchorage. A cruise on the company's *Spirit of Discovery* begins at $2055 during the peak season. The 11-day trip through Southeast Alaska leaves from Seattle, includes Glacier Bay National Park and ends in Alaska. The company's Prince William Sound & Denali National Park tour is a 10-day trip that includes Columbia Glacier, Denali National Park and Cordova for $2545. It begins and ends in Anchorage and doesn't include airfare to Alaska. Call American Sightseeing (☎ 800-426-7702) for more information.

Knightly Tours

This company offers budget package tours for independent travelers; in other words, you're not being herded around with a hundred others. Knightly makes all the reservations for you, from the Alaska Marine Hwy ferries to side tours with American Sightseeing to all your hotels along the way. A 12-day bed & breakfast, self-drive tour that includes roundtrip airfare from Seattle, a rental car for 10 days and a Southeast Alaska cruise is $2300 per person.

Knightly Tours also offers a varied selection of other tours that cover the state in a fashion that's similar to Gray Line. For a complete brochure, call ☎ 800-426-2123 or visit the website (www.knightlytours.com).

Green Tortoise

At the other end of the spectrum is Green Tortoise Alternative Travel, the company with recycled buses whose seats have been replaced with foam-covered platforms, sofas and dinettes.

When not sleeping on the bus during night drives, Green Tortoise groups use state and federal campgrounds and make an effort to include hiking, rafting and other outdoor activities on their itinerary. Food is not included in the fare, but bus travelers pool their funds to purchase goods in bulk and then prepare food in group cookouts.

On Green Tortoise tours, group interaction is a large part of the experience. Everybody pitches in during meal time, and spontaneous volleyball matches or Frisbee games are frequent activities during rest breaks. Beer and wine are allowed on the bus, and people are encouraged to bring musical instruments. Although passengers could be any age, the vast majority of tour members are in their 20s or early 30s.

This type of travel is not for everybody, especially if you suddenly discover you don't get along with half the people on the bus. Some readers have also complained about a general 'lack of organization' about the trips and 'dictatorial drivers.'

Still, there's no cheaper tour then Green Tortoise. The company runs a pair of four-week tours through Alaska in June and July. These include cruises through Southeast Alaska on the Alaska Marine Hwy ferry, with stops in the Yukon Territory, Fairbanks, Denali National Park, Kenai Peninsula, and a drive home on the Alcan. The bus can be picked up in San Francisco (California), Eugene and Portland (Oregon) or Seattle (Washington). The fare is $1500 per person plus $250 that covers food and admission fees into national parks.

For more information, write to Green Tortoise (☎ 415-821-0803, 800-867-8647), 494 Broadway, San Francisco, CA 94133.

Getting Around

Touring Alaska on a budget means not departing from the roads or not traveling in areas without a ferry dock. Travelers on a strict budget, however, shouldn't worry. Although the roads and the marine highway cover only a quarter of the state, this quarter includes the most popular regions of Alaska, with all the major attractions, parks and cities.

Even if there is a road to your destination, travel around Alaska is unlike travel in any other state in the country. The overwhelming distances between regions, and the fledgling public transportation system make getting around almost as hard as getting there. Any long visit to Alaska usually combines trips by car, bus, marine ferry, train and often a bush plane for journeys into the wilderness.

AIR
Domestic Air Services
As a general rule, if there is a regularly scheduled flight to your destination, it will be far cheaper than charter flights on the small airplanes known in Alaska as 'bush planes.' This is especially true if Alaska Airlines (☎ 800-426-0333, www.alaskaair.com) or its contract carrier, Horizon Air, fly where you want to go.

Alaska Airlines offers these roundtrip economy fares: Anchorage to Fairbanks $140 to $166, Juneau to Anchorage $225 to $260, Anchorage to Nome $352, Anchorage to Kodiak $186, Juneau to Cordova $255, Juneau to Sitka $101 and Juneau to Petersburg $160. Avoid one-way flights if you can; the fares are exorbitant.

Other domestic carriers include Era Aviation (☎ 800-866-8394, www.era-aviation.com), which connects Anchorage with Cordova, Seward, Kodiak and Homer; Reeve Aleutian Airways (☎ 800-544-2248, www.reeveair.com) and Peninsula Airways (☎ 800-448-4226), which cover Southwest Alaska and the Aleutian Islands; and Yute Air Alaska (☎ 907-543-3003), which services western Alaska from Bethel.

In Southeast Alaska, Taquan Air (☎ 888-388-1180, www.taquanair.com), a Ketchikan-based air carrier, has recently moved into the Juneau, Sitka and Petersburg markets. Taquan's AirPass ($299) offers you a week's worth of unlimited flights between those cities, as well as to the cities of Wrangell and Klawock.

Skipping the Alcan

Upon reaching Haines, many independent travelers continue their Alaskan adventure by heading north through Canada's Yukon Territory to the Alcan (Alaska Hwy). They drive, hitchhike or bus the famous highway to the state's interior, viewing Denali National Park and possibly Fairbanks before heading south towards Anchorage.

For travelers who were enchanted by the Southeast and the Alaska Marine Hwy and want to avoid the long days on the Alcan, there are two pleasant and cheaper alternatives from Juneau. For less than the price of a Haines-to-Anchorage bus ticket, you can fly one-way on Alaska Airlines from Juneau to Cordova ($130), another remote coastal fishing town. From Cordova you can jump on the southwest system of the Alaska Marine Hwy to explore Southcentral Alaska to the west.

The other alternative is to book passage on the monthly run of the M/V *Kennicott* from Juneau across the Gulf of Alaska to Valdez and then Seward. The special service began in 1998, the first time that the Southeast routes of the Alaska Marine Ferry have been connected with Southcentral portion. It's a three-day trip from Juneau to Seward, and one-way fare is $128.

Bush Planes

When you want to see more than the roadside attractions, you go to a dirt runway or small airfield outside town and climb into a bush plane. With 75% of the state not accessible by road, these small single-engine planes are the backbone of intrastate transport. They carry residents and supplies to desolate areas of the Bush, take anglers to some of the best fishing spots in the country and drop off backpackers in the middle of prime, untouched wilderness.

The person at the controls is a bush pilot, someone who might be fresh out of the US Air Force or somebody who arrived in Alaska 'way bee-fore statehood' and learned to fly by trial and error. A ride with such a local offers not only transportation to isolated areas and a scenic view of the state but also an earful of flying tales – some believable, some not.

Don't be alarmed when you hear that Alaska has the highest number of airplane crashes per capita in the country – it also has the largest percentage of pilots. One in every 58 residents has a license, and one resident in almost 60 owns a plane. That's six times more pilots and 16 times more planes per capita than any other state in the USA. Bush pilots are safe flyers who know their territory and its weather patterns; they don't want to go down any more than you do.

A ride in a bush plane is essential if you want to go beyond the common sights and see some of Alaska's most memorable scenery. In the larger cities of Anchorage, Fairbanks, Juneau and Ketchikan, it pays to check around before chartering. In most small towns and villages, however, you'll be lucky if there's a choice. For more information about air-taxi services, see the regional chapters; bush flights are listed under the town or area where they operate.

Bush aircraft include float planes that land and take off on water and beach-landers with oversized tires that can use rough gravel shorelines as air strips. Some aircraft may be equipped with skis to land on glaciers, sophisticated radar instruments for stormy areas like the Aleutian Islands

and boat racks to carry canoes or hard-shell kayaks.

Fares vary with the type of plane, its size, the number of passengers and the amount of flying time. On the average, a Cessna 185 that can carry three passengers and a limited amount of gear will cost up to $240 to charter for an hour of flying time. A Cessna 206, a slightly larger plane that will hold four passengers, costs up to $300, while a Beaver, capable of hauling five passengers with gear, averages $360 for an hour of flying time. When chartering a plane to drop you off at an isolated USFS cabin or a wilderness trail, you must pay for both the air time to your drop-off point and for the return to the departure point.

Before chartering your own plane, check out all the possibilities. Most air-taxi companies have regularly scheduled flights to small towns and villages in six to nine-seater aircraft with single-seat fares that are a fraction of the cost of chartering an entire plane. Others offer a 'mail flight' to small villages. These flights occur on a regular basis, with one or two seats available to travelers. Even when your destination is a USFS cabin or some wilderness spot, check with the local air-taxi companies. It's a common practice to match up a party departing from the cabin with another that's arriving, so that the air-charter costs can be split by filling the plane on both runs.

Booking a plane is easy and often can be done the day before departure or even at the last minute, if need be. Double-check all pickup times and places when flying to a wilderness area. Bush pilots fly over the pickup point and if you're not there, they usually return, call the USFS and still charge you for the flight.

When flying in and out of bays, fjords or coastal waterways, check the tides before determining your pickup time. It's best to schedule pickups and drop-offs at high tide or you may end up tramping a half mile through mud flats.

Always schedule extra days around a charter flight. It's not uncommon to be 'socked in' by weather for a day or two until a plane can fly in. Don't panic: they know you're there. Just think of the high school basketball team that flew to King Cove in the Aleutians for a weekend game in the 1960s – they were 'socked in' for a month before they could fly out again.

When traveling to small towns in the Bush, a scheduled flight or mail run is the cheapest way to go. Don't hesitate, however, to charter a flight to some desolate wilderness spot on your own; the best that Alaska has to offer is usually just a short flight away.

BUS

Regular bus services within Alaska are limited, but they are available between the larger towns and cities at reasonable rates. A trip by bus may be difficult to schedule, however, due to frequent turnover in the Alaska bus business. As one bus company goes under, another appears, so the phone numbers, schedules, rates and pickup points change drastically from one summer to the next. It pays to call ahead after arriving in Alaska to make sure that buses are still running to your destination.

The AlaskaPass offers discounts on bus, train and ferry transportation throughout the state. For more information, see Alaska-Pass in the Land section of the Getting There & Away chapter.

Alaskon Express

These Gray Line motorcoaches mainly serve travelers who need a ride along the last leg of the Alcan from Whitehorse in the Yukon to Haines, Skagway, Anchorage or Fairbanks (see Bus in the Land section of the Getting There & Away chapter). You can also travel from Anchorage to Glennallen ($60), from Anchorage to Seward ($40) or from Tok to Fairbanks ($69).

From Haines, Alaskon Express embarks on a two-day run to Anchorage every Tuesday, Thursday and Sunday at 8:45 am from mid-May to mid-September; the fare is $189,

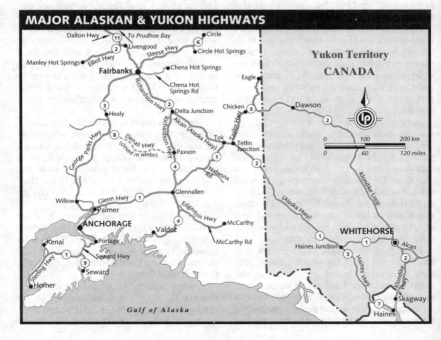

MAJOR ALASKAN & YUKON HIGHWAYS

not including overnight lodging at Beaver Creek. An Alaskon Express bus leaves for Skagway at 7:30 am on the same days, overnighting at Beaver Creek and reaching Anchorage at 7:30 pm. You can also travel the reverse routes.

For local passenger boarding points, departure times and phone numbers, see the regional chapters. Contact Gray Line of Alaska (☎ 800-544-2206), 300 Elliott Ave West, Seattle, WA 98119, to make advance reservations.

Alaska Direct Bus Line

Alaska Direct offers limited transportation from Anchorage to the rest of the state three times a week; the route ends in Whitehorse. On Sunday, Wednesday and Friday, a bus departs Anchorage at 6 am and reaches Whitehorse at midnight, passing through Palmer, Glennallen and Tok along the way. There is also daily van service to Skagway. The one-way fare from Anchorage to Glennallen is $37, to Whitehorse $145 and to Skagway $180.

A bus also departs Fairbanks on the same days at 9 am for a similar run to Whitehorse. The one-way fare from Fairbanks to Tok is $40; to Whitehorse, it's $120.

Buses stop at the major hotels in Anchorage, or you can board at the company office at 125 Oklahoma St on the north end of town. Call Alaska Direct Bus Line (☎ 907-277-6652, 800-770-6652) for more information.

Seward Bus Lines

This company provides services between Anchorage and Seward, with a bus leaving Seward daily at 9 am, reaching Anchorage at noon and then departing at 2:30 pm for the return run, which ends in Seward at 5:30 pm; the one-way fare is $30. Board these buses at 1915 Seward Hwy, just north of Seward, or at the company's Anchorage depot, 3339 Fairbanks St. Call ☎ 907-224-3608 for current schedules and rates.

Kachemak Bay Transit

This relatively new company has picked up the Anchorage-to-Homer route that Seward Bus Lines abandoned in the mid-1990s. A KBT van departs Homer between 6:30 and 8:30 am and then begins the return trip from Anchorage between 4 and 6 pm. Hey, this is Alaska, that's the best they can offer in the way of a schedule. The one-way fare between the two cities is $55. Call KBT (☎ 907-399-1378, 907-235-3795) for pickup points and other information.

Denali National Park Van Service

A number of small companies offer van transportation between Anchorage and Fairbanks with a stop at Denali National Park. At times, the drivers can be a little surly, but the regularity of the vans' arrivals and departures make this service an attractive option. Generally these companies offer the cheapest ride to the popular park and usually get you there well ahead of the train, an important consideration if you're hoping to arrange shuttle bus rides, campground sites or backpacking permits.

The best is Alaska Backpackers Shuttle (☎ 907-344-8775, 800-266-8625, abst@juno .com), which offers daily service along the Parks Hwy. The one-way fare from Anchorage to Denali National Park is $40; to Fairbanks, it's $65.

Parks Highway Express

This company began as a van service to Denali National Park, but in 1999 it expanded to offer service on the three major highways: Parks Hwy from Anchorage to Fairbanks, Glenn Hwy from Anchorage to Glennallen and Richardson Hwy from, Fairbanks to Valdez. Pickups and drop-offs are at popular hostels, and the fares are reasonable. You can go from Anchorage to Valdez for $110, Fairbanks to Valdez for $59, Fairbanks to Denali National Park for $25.

Parks Highway Express also offers the only bus pass in Alaska. The $145 pass buys you unlimited travel on any of the routes and is good for the entire travel season, from late May through early September. Contact Parks Highway Express (☎ 888-600-6001, info@alaskashuttle.com) or visit its website (www.alaskashuttle.com) for current schedules and fares.

TRAIN

In a state the size of Alaska, the logistics of building a railroad were overwhelming at the turn of the century; many private companies tried but failed, leading to federal government intervention in 1912. Three years later, construction began on a route from the tent city of Anchorage to the boomtown of Fairbanks. The line cut its way over what were thought to be impenetrable mountains, across raging rivers and through a wilderness as challenging as any construction crew had faced in the history of American railroading.

No wonder it took them eight years to build the Alaska Railroad. Today, it stretches 470 miles from Seward to Fairbanks and provides a good – though not cheap – means of transportation for travelers. The scenery on each route is spectacular. You'll save more money traveling by bus down the George Parks Hwy, but few travelers, even those counting their dimes, regret booking a seat on the Alaska Railroad and viewing one of the world's most pristine wilderness areas from the train's comfortable cars.

The AlaskaPass offers discounts on bus, train and ferry transportation throughout the state. For more information, see Alaska-Pass in the Land section of the Getting There & Away chapter.

Anchorage to Fairbanks

The Alaska Railroad operates a year-round service between Fairbanks and Anchorage, as well as summer services (from late May to mid-September) from Anchorage to Whittier on Prince William Sound and from Anchorage to Seward. Although the 114-mile trip down to Seward is a spectacular ride, unquestionably the most popular run is the 336-mile trip from Anchorage to Fairbanks with a stop at Denali National Park. Heading north, at Mile 279 the train passes within 46 miles of Mt McKinley, a stunning sight from the train's viewing domes on a clear day, and then slows down to cross the 918-foot bridge over Hurricane Gulch, one of the most spectacular views of the trip.

North of Denali National Park, the train hugs the side of the Nenana River Canyon, passes numerous views of the Alaska Range and crosses the 700-foot Mears Memorial Bridge (one of the longest single-span bridges in the world) over the Tanana River, 60 miles south of Fairbanks. Before the bridge was completed, this was the end of the line in both directions, as people and goods were then ferried across the river to waiting cars on the other bank.

From late May to mid-September, two express trains run daily between Anchorage and Fairbanks with stops at Wasilla, Talkeetna, Denali National Park and Nenana. The express trains are geared for out-of-state travelers, as they offer vista-dome cars, reclining seats and a full dining and beverage service. You can also take your own food and drink on board, which isn't a bad idea since dinner on the train can cost between $14 and $17.

The northbound train departs Anchorage daily at 8:15 am, reaching Denali National Park at 3:45 pm and Fairbanks at 8:15 pm. The southbound train departs Fairbanks at 8:15 am, arriving at Denali National Park at noon and Anchorage at 8:30 pm. The one-way fare from Anchorage to Denali National Park is $104; to Fairbanks, it's $154. A ticket from Fairbanks to Denali costs $54. During the railroad's 'Value Season' (from mid-May to early June and the second week of September), you'll save $18 on the Anchorage-to-Denali fare and $34 on the Anchorage-to-Fairbanks fare.

From mid-September to mid-May, the schedule changes to one train per week; it departs Anchorage at 8:30 am on Saturday and then leaves Fairbanks at 8:30 am on Sunday for the return trip.

The Alaska Railroad still makes a 'milk run,' in which a train stops at every town and can even be flagged down by backpackers, anglers and mountain climbers emerging from their treks at the railroad tracks. The run used to extend from Anchorage to Fairbanks but now stretches only from Talkeetna to Hurricane Gulch during the summer. Still, the trip takes you within view of Mt McKinley and into some remote areas of the state. It also allows you to mingle with more local residents than you would on the express train.

From May to October, this diesel train departs Talkeetna at 12:15 pm, reaches Hurricane Gulch at 2:15 pm and then turns around and arrives back at Talkeetna at 5:45 pm. The service is available Thursday through Sunday, and the one-way fare to Hurricane Gulch is $20. The rest of the year, the flag-stop service runs from Anchorage to Hurricane Gulch on the first Thursday of the month. The train departs Anchorage at 8:30 am, and a roundtrip ticket is $88.

There are a few things to keep in mind when traveling by train from Anchorage to Fairbanks. Arrive at the depot at least 15 minutes before departure, as the express trains leave on time. Sit on the east side of the train if you want to see the mileposts. The best scenery is on the west side from Anchorage to Denali National Park and on the east side north of there.

The windows in all carriages are big, but taking pictures through them is less than satisfactory due to their distorting curves and the dust that coats the glass. To avoid this, step outside to shoot photos on the platform between cars.

Finally, it pays to book early on this popular train; in Anchorage, call ☎ 907-265-2494. Before your trip, you can contact Alaska Railroad (☎ 800-544-0552, fax 907-265-2323, akrr@Alaska.net, www.akrr.com), PO Box 107500, Anchorage, AK 99510-7500.

Anchorage to Whittier

Alaska Railroad's newest service is an Anchorage-to-Whittier run with a stop in Girdwood. The train departs Anchorage daily at 9 am, reaches Whittier at 11:30 am and then departs at 5:45 pm for the return trip. The roundtrip fare is $52, and one-way is $26, making it a slightly better deal than purchasing van shuttle service to Portage and a Portage-to-Whittier ticket on the Alaska Railroad.

Even if you don't plan to take the Alaska Marine Hwy ferry across Prince William Sound, the trip to Whittier can be a fun day trip from Anchorage, as Whittier is a scenic and interesting town. The train ride itself is also interesting, since it includes two tunnels, one of which is 13,090 feet long.

Flagging a Train

In addition to catching the Alaska Railroad at designated stations, passengers may also 'flag' local trains anywhere along the track. Alaska Railroad officials claim this service is the only one of its kind in the USA. It offers wilderness access to summer visitors, and many residents flag trains to reach remote cabins and homesteads.

To flag a train, stand 25 feet outside the nearest rail with your gear. Wave a large piece of white cloth over your head until the engineer acknowledges you by sounding the train whistle. Stay away from the track until the train stops and the conductor opens the door and motions you to board.

For a unique adventure, try the flag-stop service between Talkeetna and Hurricane Gulch, a ride that includes stunning views of Mt McKinley if the Great One is showing herself. Either purchase a topographical map of the area and pick out a camping spot for the night or contact Zeroth's Cabin Rental (☎ 733-2499, talkaero@alaska.net). The isolated cabin is on Gold Creek in a mountainous setting north of Talkeetna and is reached by the flag-stop train. The cabin holds up to four people and costs $90 a night.

Rail service also connects Portage and Whittier during the summer. One run is timed to meet the arrivals and departures of the Alaska Hwy ferry M/V *Bartlett*, which crosses Prince William Sound to Valdez on a scenic cruise past the Columbia Glacier.

If you don't have a car, you'll have to take a van shuttle from Anchorage to Portage, since the train from Anchorage to Portage only runs once a day. Shuttle companies include Alaska Backpackers Shuttle (☎ 907-344-8775, 800-266-8625), which charges $20 one-way. To catch the ferry, you'll need to take the 1:20 pm train out of Portage to arrive in Whittier at 2 pm and board the M/V *Bartlett* by 2:45 pm. The train then departs Whittier at 3:15 pm. Reservations for the train and ferry are highly recommended, as this is a popular excursion.

The train makes several roundtrips daily; the roundtrip fare from Portage to Whittier is $20 per passenger and $100 for most cars, which includes driver fare.

There are four runs from Portage on Wednesday and Thursday (departing at 10:20 am and 1:20, 4:30 and 7:15 pm) and six trains during the rest of the week (departing at 7:30 and 10:20 am and 1:20, 4:40, 7:30 and 9:35 pm). Tickets can be purchased from conductors at Portage. Although you can't make reservations for the rail service between Anchorage and Whittier, passengers with confirmed ferry tickets enjoy priority boarding on the 1:20 pm train from Portage. Call (☎ 907-265-2607) for pre-recorded information about fares and schedules.

Anchorage to Seward

Some say the ride between Anchorage and Seward is one of the most spectacular train trips in the world, rivaling those in the Swiss Alps and the New Zealand train that climbs over Arthur's Pass in the Southern Alps. From Anchorage, the 114-mile trip begins by skirting the 60-mile-long Turnagain Arm on Cook Inlet, where travelers can study the bore tides. After leaving Portage, the train swings south, climbs over mountain passes, spans deep river gorges and comes within half a mile of three glaciers: Spencer, Bartlett and Trail. The trip ends in Seward, a quaint town surrounded by mountains on one side and Resurrection Bay on the other.

The service is offered daily from mid-May to early September, with a train departing Anchorage at 6:45 am and reaching Seward at 11:05 am. It departs Seward the same day at 6 pm and reaches Anchorage at 10:25 pm; the roundtrip fare is $86. In 1998 the Alaska Railroad added a baggage car to its Seward run, primarily to accommodate the growing number of kayaks and bicycles being hauled south.

White Pass & Yukon Route

The White Pass & Yukon Railroad, a historic narrow-gauge railroad, was built in 1898 to connect Skagway to Whitehorse. The first railroad to be built in Alaska, it was for a time the most northern line in North America.

The railroad was carved out of the rugged mountains by workers who had to be suspended by ropes from vertical cliffs in order to chip and blast the granite away. The route followed the 40-mile White Pass Trail from Skagway to Lake Bennett, where the miners would build rafts to float the rest of the way to Dawson City on the Yukon River. The line reached Whitehorse in 1900 and by then had made the Chilkoot Trail, a route miners hiked on foot, obsolete.

The railroad also played an important role in the construction of the Alcan during WWII. After that, it transported ore for mining companies in the Yukon Territory. In 1982, after world metal prices fell and the Canadian mines closed, operation of the White Pass & Yukon Railroad was suspended. But it has always been a popular tourist attraction, especially with travelers on big cruise ships, and in 1988 the railroad resumed limited service under the name White Pass & Yukon Route.

It's still the incredible ride it must have been for the Klondike miners. The White Pass & Yukon Railroad has one of the steepest grades in North America: it climbs from sea level in Skagway to 2885 feet at White Pass in only 20 miles. The mountain scenery is fantastic, the old narrow-gauge cars intriguing, and the trip is a must for anyone passing through Southeast Alaska.

The train operates from mid-May to late September and offers a one-day summit excursion and a scheduled through-service for travelers who actually want to use it as a means of transportation to Whitehorse and the Alcan. Northbound trains depart Skagway daily at 12:40 pm and arrive in Fraser at 2:40 pm; there, passengers transfer to buses, which arrive in Whitehorse at 5:45 pm (Pacific Time). Southbound buses depart from Whitehorse at 8 am (Pacific Time), and the train leaves Fraser at 10:20 am, arriving in Skagway at noon. The one-way fare from Skagway to Whitehorse is $95.

Given the historical allure of this train, reservations wouldn't be a bad idea. Before your trip, contact White Pass & Yukon Route (☎ 907-9832217, 800-343-7373, infor@whitepass.net, www.whitepassrailroad.com), PO Box 435, Skagway, AK 99840.

CAR
Rental & Purchase

Having your own car in Alaska, as in any other place, provides the freedom and flexibility that public transportation does not. Car rental, however, is a costly way for a single person to travel. But for two or more people, it can be an affordable way out of Anchorage, which has the best car rental rates by far. In Alaska, it isn't the charge per day for the rental but the charge per mile that makes it so expensive. Outside Anchorage and Fairbanks, drivers will find gas 20¢ to 30¢ per gallon more expensive than in the rest of the USA.

The Alaska tourist boom of the 1980s has produced a network of cheap car rental companies that offer rates considerably lower than those of national firms such as Avis, Hertz and National Car Rental. The largest of these is Practical Car Rental (also called Allstar in Alaska; ☎ 800-426-5243), which has offices in seven Alaskan towns but unfortunately not in Anchorage or Fairbanks. It does have branches in Ketchikan, Petersburg, Juneau, Wrangell and Sitka, as well as Klawock on Prince Wales Island. Its rates change from city to city, as its branches are independently owned, but most offices charge around $40 to $50 a day for a subcompact with 100 free miles.

Other companies include High Country Car Rental in Anchorage (☎ 907-562-8078, 888-685-1155), 512 W International Airport Rd, which has subcompacts for $40 a day during the summer. Before June and after August, the rates are considerably lower, sometimes only $30 a day. In Fairbanks, Rent-A-Wreck (☎ 907-452-1606) charges the same rates, with 150 free miles a day for a subcompact.

The downside of car rental is that some of these cars are occasionally stubborn about starting up right away, especially in the used models available through the cheaper rental companies. However, if there are three or four people splitting the cost, car rental is far less expensive than taking a bus and allows you total freedom to stop when you want.

All the used-car rental companies are listed in the regional chapters under the towns where they maintain offices. In Anchorage, you can also try Affordable Car Rental (☎ 907-243-3370), Airport Car Rentals (☎ 907-277-7662) or U-Save Car Rental (☎ 907-272-8728).

If you're planning on buying a car in Alaska, be forewarned: The winters are long and the environment is harsh, so used cars are not only expensive but more often than not rust buckets. Purchasing and selling a car for transportation is not a common practice in Alaska. The best place to obtain a used car is Anchorage; begin your search with the classified ads in the Sunday edition of the *Anchorage Daily News*. An even better – and undoubtedly cheaper – strategy is to purchase your car in the Lower 48 and drive it along the Alcan or put it on the ferry.

Motorhome Rental

Want to be a road hog? You can always rent a motorhome (also called a recreational vehicle), as many people do. RVers flock to the land of the midnight sun in numbers that are astounding. There are some roads, like the George Parks Hwy, that look like an endless stream of trailers, pop-ups and land cruisers.

More than a dozen companies, almost all of them based in Anchorage, will rent you a motorhome, ranging from 20 to 35 feet in length, that accommodates up to six people. The price can vary from $125 to $175 per day, but again you have to consider all the extra charges. Many places offer 100 free miles per day, then charge 15¢ to 25¢ per mile for any additional mileage.

You also have to pay for insurance and possibly even a 'housekeeping kit' – pots, pans and sheets. It's best to anticipate a daily fee between $150 and $200 and remember that full-hook-up campgrounds cost $15 to $20 a night. Still, when divided between four to six people, the cost comes to around $28 to $35 a day per person for both transportation and a bed – not a bad deal if you can round up several other people who want to share the same itinerary. Other costs include gasoline, food and campsites.

You have to reserve a motorhome four to five months in advance for the summer season. A few of the larger Anchorage rental companies are Great Alaskan Holidays (☎ 888-225-2752, 907-248-7777), which does not charge extra for housekeeping packages, cleaning or insurance and has 20-footers with prices that begin as low as $134 a day (plus 17¢ a mile for a rental of seven days or more); Alaska Motorhome Rentals (☎ 800-254-9929); Alaska Economy RVs (☎ 907-561-7723, mis@goalaska.com); and Clippership Motorhome Rentals (☎ 800-421-3456).

ABC Motorhome Rentals (☎ 800-421-7456, rvalaska@alaska.net) offers units that are totally self-contained, no hook-ups are needed as they are totally battery and propane operated. This means you can stay at small rustic and out-of-the-way places. A camper with a shower runs $150 a day.

BICYCLE

For those who want to bike it, Alaska offers a variety of cycling adventures on paved roads during long days with comfortably cool temperatures. Most cyclists hop on the Alaska Marine Hwy ferries, carrying their bikes on for an additional fee ranging from $7 to $42 for the longest run from Bellingham to Skagway.

From Haines, you can catch an Alaskon Express bus to Tok or Anchorage in the heart of Alaska. There is no charge for the bike, but be prepared to have it stored in the luggage compartment under the bus. You can also take your bike on Alaska Airlines for a $50 excess-baggage fee each way.

Summer cyclists have to take some extra precautions in Alaska. Few towns have comprehensively equipped bike shops, so it's wise to carry not only metric tools but also a tube repair kit, spare inner tubes, brake and shifter cables, spokes, brake pads and any other parts that might be needed during the trip.

Due to high rainfall, especially in the Southeast, waterproof saddle bags are useful, as are tire fenders. Rain gear is a must, and storing gear in resealable plastic bags within your saddlebags is advised. Carry warm clothing, mittens and a woolen hat, along with a tent and rain tarpaulin. It's not necessary to weigh yourself down with a lot of food, as you can easily restock on all major roads.

Some roads do not have much of a shoulder – the Seward Hwy between Anchorage and Girdwood, for example – so cyclists should utilize the sunlight hours when traffic is light to pedal in such areas.

Most cyclists avoid gravel, but biking the Alcan (an increasingly popular trip) does involve riding over some short gravel breaks in the paved asphalt. When riding along gravel roads, figure on making 50% to 70% of your normal distance and take spare inner tubes – flat tires will be a daily occurrence.

Mountain bikers, on the other hand, are in heaven on such gravel roads as the Denali Hwy in the Interior, the logging roads on Prince of Wales Island in the Southeast and the park road in Denali National Park. Mountain bikers are even pedaling the Dalton Hwy to Prudhoe Bay.

The Arctic Bicycle Club of Anchorage sponsors a wide variety of road-bike and mountain-bike tours during the summer. Call the club's information hot line (☎ 907-566-0177) for a recorded message of upcoming tours, or check its website (arcticbike .alaska.net).

You might also consider reading the *Alaska Bicycle Touring Guide* by Pete Praetorius and Alys Culhane, the first guide put together for touring Alaska on two wheels. It's been called the 'bicycling equivalent of *The Milepost*' for its thorough description of routes throughout the state, including two that go north of the Arctic Circle.

Another good book is *Mountain Bike Alaska*, by Richard Larson, a guide to 49 trails for mountain bikers. They range from the Denali Hwy and the Denali park road to many of the traditional hiking trails situated on the Kenai Peninsula.

Bicycle Routes
The following are the more common long-distance trips that can be undertaken by cyclists during the summer in Alaska.

Anchorage to Fairbanks This ride can be done comfortably in five to six days along the George Parks Hwy, and is 360 miles of generally flat road with scattered sections of rolling hills. Highlights are the impressive views of Mt McKinley and an interesting side trip into Denali National Park, where cyclists can extend their trip with a ride along the gravel park road. Keep in mind the stretch from Anchorage to Denali National Park is a busy road with heavy traffic most of the summer. To avoid this, many cyclists take the Alaska Railroad part of the way and then bike the rest; there is an excess-baggage charge for carrying your bicycle on the train.

Anchorage to the Kenai Peninsula There is an endless number of possible bike trips or combinations of biking and hiking adventures in the Kenai Peninsula. You can also utilize the Southwest runs of the Alaska Marine Hwy. A common trip is to cycle from Anchorage to Homer, take the ferry to Kodiak, then return via Seward and pedal back to Anchorage.

This is a seven- to 12-day trip, depending on how much time you spend in Homer and Kodiak; the distance by bike is 350 miles, with an additional 400 miles by ferry. Bikes can also be used to hop from one hiking trail to another in some of Alaska's most pleasant backcountry. Or, you can cycle to Portage, combine the rail and ferry transportation across Prince William Sound to Valdez and then head north. The Kenai Peninsula can also be a nightmare of heavy traffic for bikers, and the Seward Hwy from Anchorage to Girdwood is narrow, with a narrow shoulder in many places. The best bet is to begin with a bus or train trip at least to Portage.

Fairbanks to Valdez This is perhaps one of the most scenic, and one of the hardest, routes cyclists can undertake. The six- to seven-day trip follows the Richardson Hwy from Delta Junction to Glennallen and then goes onto Valdez – a total of 375 miles. It includes several hilly sections and tough climbs over Isabel Pass before Paxson, and

Thompson Pass at 2771 feet, 25 miles east of Valdez.

New brake pads are a must, along with rain gear and warm clothing, as the long ride downhill from Thompson Pass is often a cold and wet one. From Valdez, you can take a ferry across Prince William Sound and head back to Anchorage, or backtrack to the Glenn Hwy and eventually to Anchorage.

North Star Bicycle Route This 3400-mile ride is a summer-long adventure that begins in Missoula, Montana, and ends in Anchorage. Along the way you cross the Canadian Rockies, pick up the Alcan in British Columbia, pedal through the Yukon Territory and follow Alaskan highways from Tok to Anchorage.

Although the Alcan is now paved, miles of rough surface still exist due to construction work, making this a trip only for experienced cyclists looking for a grand adventure. The trip can be reduced significantly by either busing part of the route in Canada (see the Land section in the Getting There & Away chapter) or by utilizing the Alaska Marine Hwy from Bellingham. It is 446 miles from Haines to Tok, and 328 miles from Tok to Anchorage, a ride that can be done comfortably in five days.

Those interested in this route can contact Adventure Cycle Association (☎ 406-721-1776), PO Box 8308, Missoula, MT 59807, for information on maps and organized tours.

Rental & Purchase
The following cities and towns in Alaska have bike shops that sell bicycles and offer a good selection of spare parts. By the end of the summer, however, many shops are low on, or completely out of, certain spare parts.

Anchorage
  The Bicycle Shop (☎ 272-5219),
  1035 W Northern Lights Blvd
  Gary King Sporting Goods (☎ 279-7454),
  202 E Northern Lights Blvd
  REI Co-op (☎ 272-4565),
  1200 W Northern Lights Blvd

Fairbanks
  Beaver Sports (☎ 479-2494),
  2400 College Rd

Girdwood
  Girdwood Ski & Cycle (☎ 783-2453),
  Alyeska Access Rd
Juneau
  Adventure Sports (☎ 789-5696),
  8757 Glacier Hwy
  Mountain Gears (☎ 586-4327),
  210 N Franklin St
Kodiak
  58 Degrees North (☎ 486-6294),
  1231 Mill Bay Rd
Sitka
  Yellow Jersey Cycle Shop (☎ 747-6317),
  805 Halibut Point Rd
Skagway
  Sockeye Cycle (☎ 983-2851),
  5th Ave and Broadway St

You can rent a bike in a handful of areas, including Denali National Park. See the regional chapters for a list of rental shops.

BOAT
In the Southeast, the Alaska Marine Hwy ferries replace bus services and operate from Juneau or Ketchikan to Skagway, Haines, Hoonah, Tenakee Springs, Angoon, Sitka, Kake, Petersburg, Hyder and Hollis, with an occasional special run to the tiny fishing village of Pelican (see Ferry section of the Getting There & Away chapter for more details).

The Alaska Marine Hwy also offers services in Southcentral and Southwest Alaska, where the M/V Bartlett and the M/V Tustumena connect towns along Prince William Sound and the Gulf of Alaska.

Once a month during the summer, the M/V Kennicott sails from Juneau to Valdez and then on to Seward to connect the Southwest ferry with the Southeast line. You can also link the two systems by picking up an Alaska Airlines flight from Juneau to Cordova.

The M/V Bartlett sails from Cordova and Valdez to Whittier across Prince William Sound, passing the Columbia Glacier along the way. The M/V Tustumena calls at Seward, Homer and Seldovia on the Kenai Peninsula, Port Lions and Kodiak on Kodiak Island and Valdez on the eastern shore of Prince William Sound.

In 1993, the Alaska Marine Hwy instituted a direct service from Whittier to Cordova on the M/V *Bartlett*. From May to September, the ship leaves Whittier at 2:45 pm on Friday, reaching Cordova seven hours later. On Monday, the ship departs Cordova at 7 am and sails to Whittier. This makes the charming town of Cordova a nice three-day side trip from Anchorage.

Also in the summer, the M/V *Tustumena* makes a special run to Sand Point, King Cove, Cold Bay and Dutch Harbor at the end of the Alaska Peninsula. The trip is available five times (in mid-May, June, July, August and September) and takes six days roundtrip from Kodiak. It's clearly the cheapest way to see part of Alaska's stormy arm (see the Aleutian Islands section in the Southwest chapter).

Walk-on passengers can expect to pay the following fares for ferry travel along the Southwest routes: Valdez to Cordova $30; Valdez to Whittier $58; Valdez to Seward $58; Seward to Kodiak $54; Homer to Kodiak $48; Kodiak to Unalaska $202; Homer to Seldovia $18.

The AlaskaPass offers discounts on bus, train and ferry transportation throughout the state. For more information, see Alaska-Pass in the Land section of the Getting There & Away chapter.

LOCAL TRANSPORTATION

The vast majority of towns in Alaska are not large enough to require local transportation beyond taxicabs. The cities that are – Anchorage, Fairbanks, Juneau and Ketchikan – serve that need with a bus system. The largest and most important for travelers is Anchorage's People Mover, an excellent public bus system with reasonable fares ($1 per adult, 10¢ per transfer). See the regional chapters for more information about these systems.

ORGANIZED TOURS

As part of your trip to Alaska, you can join organized tours that begin and end within the state (as opposed to packaged tours that originate in Seattle or Vancouver). There are far too many to list here, but many of them

The Business of Ferrying

The Alaska Marine Hwy is not only an enjoyable way to travel; it's big business for the state. The nine vessels in the fleet travel 4000 miles of waterways, from Dutch Harbor to Ketchikan, visiting 30 communities. The ferries are responsible for bringing in one in every 12 visitors to Alaska, or about 60,000 people in a summer. Annually, the Alaska Marine Hwy pumps more than $150 million into the Alaskan economy by carrying more than 400,000 travelers and 100,000 vehicles.

are described in the Organized Tours sections of the regional chapters. For information about guided wilderness trips, see the Wilderness chapter.

Small Cruises

Unlike the 'Sheratons-at-Sea' that carry up to 3,000 passengers and have eight bars on board, these small ships handle less than 100 passengers. The result is a far more personal cruise, with an opportunity for close views of the beautiful scenery that drew you to Alaska in the first place. Small vessels can travel to confined areas like Misty Fjords National Monument and Le Conte Bay and stop at delightful towns like Petersburg, which is not equipped to handle the big ships.

One of the more interesting boats is the Glacier Bay Tours & Cruises' *Wilderness Adventure*. This 80-passenger ship features a bow ramp that allows passenger to disembark at remote shorelines for an afternoon of hiking and beachcombing away from the crowds. It also carries kayaks that can be launched right from the ship. Operating from Juneau, the *Wilderness Adventure* offers a six-night itinerary that includes Glacier Bay, Tracy Arm Fjord and Admiralty Island. Fares begin at $1700 per person. For reservations, contact Glacier Bay Tours & Cruises (☎ 800-451-5952), 520 Pike St, Suite 1400, Seattle, WA 98101.

Other companies that offer small overnight cruises are Alaska Sightseeing/Cruise West (☎ 800-888-9378), American Safari

Cruises (☎ 800-325-6722) and Alaska Yacht Cruises (☎ 206-780-0822).

Bicycle Tours

Alaskan Bicycle Adventures offer fully supported cycle tours across the state. These include lodging, meals, luggage transportation and even the bicycles. The company's most popular tour is a 450-mile, eight-day ride that includes the Parks, Richardson and Glenn Hwys and stops at Denali National Park, Fairbanks and Valdez. The cost is $2445 per person. Other tours offer an opportunity to hike, raft or sea kayak along the way.

Tours begin in Anchorage or Juneau. For reservations, contact Alaskan Bicycle Adventures (800-770-7242, bicycle@alaskabike .com, www.alaskabike.com), 907 E Dowling Rd, Suite 29, Anchorage, AK 99518.

The Backroads tour company offers similar bike tours but with shared accommodations and shared meals. Prices start at $1900 for an eight-day tour if you bring your own bike. Contact Backroads (☎ 800-462-2848), 801 Cedar St, Berkeley, CA 94710-1800, for information.

Camping Tours

CampAlaska uses vans and campgrounds to offer low-cost tours throughout the state. Along the way, activities might include scenic flights, hiking, rafting or glacier cruises. The company's Scout tour is a seven-day trip that includes Denali National Park, Valdez and the ferry across Prince William Sound. The cost is $725 per person plus $65 for food. Other tours are longer, and many involve passage on the Alaska Marine Hwy ferry. For reservations, contact CampAlaska (☎ 907-376-9438, 800-376-9439), PO Box 872247, Wasilla, AK 99687.

Other Land Tours

Road Runner offers small group tours, with travel in 13-passenger vans as opposed to buses. Road Runner groups sometimes camp and sometimes stay in hostels. The Alaska Grizzly tour is a two-week trip that begins in Anchorage and includes Kenai Peninsula, Fairbanks, Denali National Park and McCarthy. All accommodations are in hostels. The fare is $1000 per person plus $8 a day for food. Contact Road Runner (☎ 800-873-5872, fax 617-984-2045), 1050 Hancock St, Quincy, MA 02169, for more information.

Natural Habitat Adventures specializes in animal-watching adventures around the world, including several in Alaska. The trips offer an opportunity to photograph wildlife, which could include brown bears, moose, whales, sea lions, caribou and bald eagles. A 13-day tour that features whale watching in Glacier Bay, viewing giant brown bears at Katmai National Park and seeing other wildlife at Denali National Park is $4995. All tours include accommodations, but airfare to Anchorage is extra. For a catalog, call the company (☎ 303-449-3711, 800-543-8917 in the USA and Canada).

The Wilderness

Alaska is many things, but first and foremost it is the great outdoors; travelers go there for the mountains, the trails, the wildlife and the camping – the adventure. If retrieving the morning newspaper is all the fresh air you can handle, Alaska can be a dull place, but if you're a hiker, backpacker, kayaker or someone who likes scenic views, the North Country has two things for you – extensive wilderness areas and long days in which to enjoy them.

Compared to the cost of getting to Alaska, the cost of enjoying most of the backcountry is relatively low. Hiking is free, and even the most expensive camping fee is cheap compared to motels. Camping areas in Alaska range from places with cozy lounges and heated bathrooms to clearings outside of town.

The adventures available in Alaska vary as much; you can take a three-hour hike on a well-maintained trail that begins in downtown Juneau or a weeklong trek in Wrangell-St Elias National Park, where there are no trails at all.

The best way to enter the state's wilderness is to begin with a day hike the minute you step off the ferry or depart from the Alcan. After a taste of the woods, many travelers forgo the cities and spend the rest of their trip taking long-term adventures into the backcountry to make the most of Alaska's immense surroundings.

THE WILDERNESS EXPERIENCE

Alaska, which covers over 550,000 sq miles, is serviced by only 5000 miles of public highway. Most of the recent tourist boom is centered on these roads, and visitors tend to cling to them. Ironically, this causes the state, with all its space, to have its share of overcrowded parks and campgrounds. Residents of Alaska know this and tend to stay away from heavily touristed places like Denali National Park in the middle of summer. They also know how to escape into the backcountry – those wearing Sierra Club

T-shirts call it a 'wilderness experience'; others throw a backpack together and say they're 'going out the road for a spell.' It's all the same – a journey into the woods, away from the city, neighbors, TV and other signs of human existence. A week of nothing but nature in all its splendor is the greatest enjoyment Alaska can offer anyone.

You have to be careful on such adventures. In a true wilderness experience, you are completely on your own. But don't let the lack of communication with the civilized world prevent you from venturing away from the road. On an ideal trip, you won't meet another person outside your party, see a boat or hear the hum of a bush plane. In this perfect tranquillity, all the pressures of day-to-day living are cast aside, and you can begin to discover yourself in the natural setting. More enjoyment and satisfaction can be derived from a few days in the wilderness than from a three-week bus tour. Some people, once they enter the wilderness, never get it out of their blood.

The 23 trips described in this chapter are popular wilderness excursions – either maintained trails or natural paddling routes – that backpackers can do on their own, if they are properly equipped and have sufficient outdoor experience. Some trips cannot provide a true 'wilderness experience,' as they are too popular during the summer, but many are in isolated areas and offer a glimpse of pristine backcountry. Local hiking trails and camping areas are covered in the regional chapters.

Those people who didn't come to Alaska with the right gear or who lack camping knowledge can still escape into the woods and return safely. First, they can join a guided expedition, in which equipment, group organization and knowledge of the area are supplied. Guided expeditions, which cover the state, range from half a day to three weeks and cost between $150 and $175 per person per day (see the Guide Companies section of this chapter). Another way to sample the wilderness, without enduring a

THE WILDERNESS

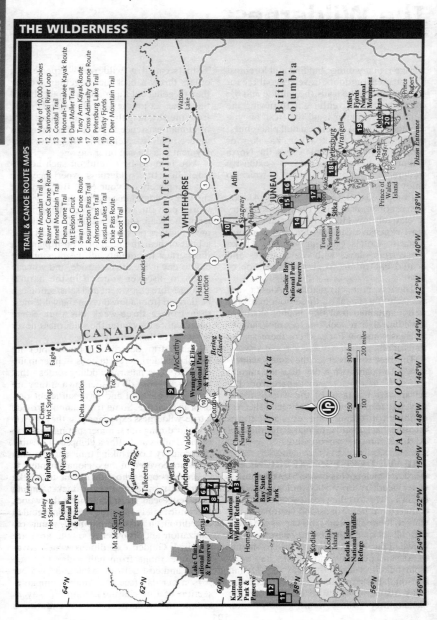

THE WILDERNESS

TRAIL & CANOE ROUTE MAPS

1 White Mountain Trail & Beaver Creek Canoe Route
2 Pinnell Mountain Trail
3 Chena Dome Trail
4 Mt Eielson Circuit
5 Swan Lake Canoe Route
6 Resurrection Pass Trail
7 Johnson Pass Trail
8 Russian Lakes Trail
9 Dixie Pass Route
10 Chilkoot Trail
11 Valley of 10,000 Smokes
12 Savonoski River Loop
13 Coastal Trail
14 Hoonah-Tenakee Kayak Route
15 Dan Moller Trail
16 Tracy Arm Kayak Route
17 Cross Admiralty Canoe Route
18 Petersburg Lake Trail
19 Misty Fjords
20 Deer Mountain Trail

20-mile hike or hiring the services of a tour guide, is to rent a Forest Service cabin (see the Accommodations section in the Facts for the Visitor chapter).

Who Controls What

With almost three-quarters of Alaska locked up by federal or state agencies, it's good to know who administers the land on which you want to hike. Almost all of the recreational areas, parks and forests, including the campgrounds and trails in them, are controlled by one of five agencies.

US Forest Service This federal bureau handles the Tongass and Chugach National Forests, which cover nearly all of the Southeast and the eastern Kenai Peninsula, including Prince William Sound. The US Forest Service (USFS) can provide detailed information on the 190 public-use cabins it maintains, along with hiking, kayaking, canoeing and other recreational opportunities in its domain. Most USFS campgrounds charge $6 to $16 per day, depending on the facilities, and have a 14-day limit. The addresses for the main USFS offices are given in the Accommodations section in the Facts for the Visitor chapter, but Craig, Wrangell, Hoonah and Yakutat also have small offices.

The Forest Service maintains a website for the Alaska region (www.fs.fed.us/recreation/states/ak.html), which has information on rustic cabins, access to trails, fishing opportunities and wilderness areas in Tongass and Chugach National Forests. If you think you'll be spending extended time in either area, check out this website while planning your trip.

National Park Service The National Park Service administers 84,375 sq miles in Alaska, including Denali, Glacier Bay and Katmai National Parks and Preserves. These three parks have maintained campgrounds and are accessible by either an Alaska Airlines flight or by road. The seven campgrounds in Denali National Park are scattered across the park. Morino Campground, at the entrance to the park, is a no-frills area for backpackers without vehicles.

Two other national parks, Kenai Fjords and Wrangell-St Elias, also have roads leading into them. Kenai Fjords' booming attendance is due to the growing number of marine cruises out of Seward and the ease of seeing Exit Glacier. Wrangell-St Elias is not nearly as developed for visitors as Denali, and many people consider that a plus. In Wrangell-St Elias, except in the McCarthy-Kennicott area, you can escape the mid-summer crush of tourists that the other parks suffer.

The National Park Service also oversees three other national parks (Gates of the Arctic, Kobuk Valley and Lake Clark), three national preserves (Bering Land Bridge, Noatak and Yukon-Charley Rivers), two national historical parks (Sitka and Klondike Gold Rush) and the Aniakchak and Cape Krusenstern National Monuments. With the exception of the popular historical parks, these areas are only accessible by bush plane or boat and offer no facilities. Most visitors reach them through guide companies that venture into the wilderness areas by raft, kayak or foot.

If you want to escape into the wilderness, the least visited national park in North America is Kobuk Valley, which receives less than 3000 visitors a year, compared to Yosemite's four million visitors. Even more remote is the Yukon-Charley Rivers National Preserve, northwest of Eagle. Just 1825 people visiting the area in 1997.

For addresses and more information on the individual parks, check the regional chapters. For general information on all parks, contact the main National Park Service offices: Alaska Public Lands Information Center (☎ 907-271-2737), 605 W 4th Ave, Suite 105, Anchorage, AK 99501-2231, or access the National Park Service website (www.nps.gov/parklists/ak.html) for Alaskan parks.

Bureau of Land Management The Bureau of Land Management (BLM) is the federal agency that maintains much of the wilderness around and north of Fairbanks. It has developed almost 30 camping areas and a dozen public-use cabins in the Interior, and two popular trails (Pinnell Mountain and White Mountain) off the highways north of Fairbanks. Most of the cabins are in the White Mountains National Recreation Area, whose trails are primarily winter routes that are often impassable during the summer. Camping, free in most BLM campgrounds, is handled on a first-come, first-served basis. Cabins are $20 a night, and most are within 100 miles of Fairbanks.

The BLM offices have good publications on paddling national wild rivers such as the Gulkana, Fortymile and Delta. For more information, contact the BLM Alaska State Office (☎ 907-271-5076), 222 W 7th Ave, Suite 13, Anchorage, AK 99513, or the BLM district office in Fairbanks (☎ 907-474-2200), 1150 University Ave, Fairbanks, AK 99709. You can also get information through the BLM website (www.ak.blm.gov).

US Fish & Wildlife Service This arm of the Department of the Interior administers 16 wildlife refuges in Alaska, more than 120,312 sq miles. The largest, Yukon Delta, which surrounds Bethel in Western Alaska, covers almost 31,250 sq miles.

Wildlife refuges protect habitats; visitor use and developed recreational activities are strictly an afterthought. Many of the refuges are in remote areas of the Bush with few, if any, developed facilities. Guide companies are the only means by which most travelers visit them. The one exception is Kenai National Wildlife Refuge, which can be reached by road from Anchorage. This preserve has 14 campgrounds, of which the Kenai-Russian River Campground is by far the most popular, and over 200 miles of hiking trails and water routes, including the popular Swanson River canoe route.

The Kodiak National Wildlife Refuge, although considerably more remote and more expensive to reach than Kenai, does offer eight wilderness cabins, similar to USFS cabins, for $20 per night. For more information on individual areas, see the regional chapters. For general information, contact the US Fish & Wildlife Service regional office (☎ 907-786-3487, www.r7.fws.gov), 1011 E Tudor Rd, Anchorage, AK 99503.

Alaska Division of Parks The Alaska Division of Parks and Outdoor Recreation controls more than 100 areas in the Alaskan state park system, ranging from the 2344-sq-mile Wood-Tikchik State Park, north of Dillingham on Bristol Bay, to small wayside parks along the highway. The areas also include state trails, campgrounds, wilderness parks and historic sites, all maintained by the state.

Among the more popular parks that offer a variety of recreational opportunities are Chugach, Denali State Park south of Mt McKinley, Nancy Lake Recreational Area just south of Willow, Captain Cook State Recreation Area on the Kenai Peninsula and Chilkat State Park south of Haines. Most campgrounds cost $8 a night, with the more popular ones charging $15. A growing number of parks, including Chugach and Independence Mine State Historical Park north of Palmer, now charge a $5 per vehicle entry fee.

If you plan to spend a summer camping in Alaska, it's possible to purchase a state park camping pass allowing unlimited camping for a year for $200. The state parks division also rents out recreational cabins in the Southeast, the Southcentral and the Interior regions for $30 to $50 a night, depending on the cabin. To obtain an annual Alaska Camping Pass in advance, send a check or money order to one of the following offices: Alaska Division of Parks (☎ 907-269-8400), 3601 C St, Suite 200, Anchorage, AK 99503-5929, or the Alaska Division of Parks (☎ 907-465-4563), 400 Willoughby Center, Juneau, AK 99801. The Division of Parks has an excellent website (www.dnr.state.ak.us/parks) that provides information on cabins and other recreational opportunities.

Backcountry Essentials

If you're planning to wander beyond roadside parks, don't take your adventure lightly. You must be totally independent in the wilderness – a new experience for most city dwellers. Camping, hiking and backpacking in Alaska are more dangerous than in most other places. The weather is more unpredictable, the climate harsher, and encounters with wildlife are a frequent occurrence. Unpredictable situations such as getting lost, snowstorms in the middle of the summer or being socked in by low clouds and fog for days while waiting for a bush plane happen to hundreds of backpackers annually in Alaska. You need the knowledge and equipment to sit out bad weather, endure an overturned boat or assist an injured member of your party. For that information, consult a survival manual such as *Walking Softly in the Wilderness* by John Hart. Campers in Alaskan wilderness *must* be prepared before entering the woods.

See the What to Bring section in the Facts for the Visitor chapter for what expedition equipment to bring, and stock up on food and supplies at the last major town you pass through before entering such wilderness areas as Glacier Bay, Denali or Katmai National Parks.

Backcountry Conduct Always check in with the nearest USFS office or National Park headquarters before entering the backcountry. By letting them know your intentions, you'll get peace of mind from knowing that someone knows you're out there. If there is no ranger office in the area, the best organization to advise of your travel plans is the air charter service responsible for picking up your party.

Do not harass wildlife while traveling in the backcountry. Avoid startling an animal, as it will most likely flee, leaving you with a short and forgettable encounter. If you flush a bird from its nest, leave the area quickly, as an unattended nest leaves the eggs vulnerable to predators. Never attempt to feed wildlife; it is not healthy for you or the animal.

Finally, be thoughtful when in the wilderness. It is a delicate environment. Carry in your supplies and carry out your trash. Never litter or leave garbage smoldering in a fire pit. Always put out your fire and cover it with natural materials or, better still, don't light a fire in heavily traveled areas. Use biodegradable soap and do all washing away from water sources. In short, leave no evidence of your stay. Only then can an area remain a true wilderness.

Map & Compass Backpackers should carry a compass into the wilderness and have some basic knowledge of how to use it correctly. You should also have the correct US Geological Survey (USGS) map for the area in which you are planning to travel.

USGS topographical maps come in a variety of scales, but most hikers prefer the smallest scale, 1:63,360, in which each inch equals a mile. Canoeists and other river runners can get away with the 1:250,000 map. The free maps of Tongass and Chugach National Forests produced by the US Forest Service will not do for any wilderness adventure. They cover too much area and lack the detail that backpackers rely on. See the Maps section of the Facts for the Visitor chapter for information on how to obtain maps in advance. Check the regional chapters for where to purchase maps once you've arrived.

Wilderness Camping Choosing a spot to pitch a tent in a campground is easy, but in the wilderness, the choice is more complicated and should be made carefully to avoid problems in the middle of the night. Throughout much of Alaska, especially the Interior, river bars are the best places to pitch a tent. Strips of sand or small gravel patches along rivers provide good drainage and a smoother surface than tussock grass on which to pitch a tent.

Take time to check out the area before unpacking your gear. Avoid animal trails (whether the tracks are moose or bear), areas with bear scat and berry patches with ripe fruit. In late summer, stay away from streams choked with salmon runs.

In the Southeast and other coastal areas of Alaska, search out beaches and ridges with southern exposures; they provide the driest conditions in these rainy zones. Old glacier and stream outwashes (sand or gravel deposits) make ideal campsites, as long as you stay well above the high-tide line. Look for the last ridge of seaweed and debris on the shore and then pitch your tent another 20 to 30 yards above that to avoid waking up with salt water flooding your tent. Tidal fluctuations along Alaska's coast are among the largest in the world – with tidal changes up to 30 feet in some places.

Hikers and backpackers should be equipped to purify water in the backcountry and plan to carry at least 1 quart of water per day per person. Alaska's water is affected by *Giardia lamblia*, or 'beaver fever' as it is known among trekkers. The parasite is found in surface water, particularly beaver ponds, and is transmitted between humans and animals. The simplest way to purify water is to boil it for 10 minutes. Filtering is acceptable if you use giardia-rated filters, which are designed to take out whatever you shouldn't be drinking, including *Giardia lamblia*. For more on drinking water and filters, see the Water Purification section in Facts for the Visitor chapter.

Guide Companies

Much of Alaska's wilderness is inaccessible to the first-time visitor; travelers either don't know about wilderness areas or don't know how to get to them, which makes guide companies very useful. Guides are not only for novice campers. Their clients can be experienced backpackers who want to explore the far reaches of Alaska's wilderness but don't have the time or money to put together an expedition on their own. Guides can arrange the many details of a large-scale trip into the backcountry – everything from food and equipment to air charter.

Guided expeditions cost money, and most budget travelers prefer unguided trips. However, many guide companies offer adventures to areas that are only visited by a few people each year, an inviting prospect. Trips can range from a day hike on a glacier to a 12-day raft trip or a three-week ascent of Mt McKinley, and costs range from $175 to more than $250 per day, depending upon the amount of air travel involved. Expeditions usually have five to 12 clients; guide companies are extremely hesitant to take larger groups because of the environmental impact. The tour season extends from late May to September, and a select group of companies specialize in winter Nordic (cross-country) skiing or dogsledding expeditions.

Although most companies begin taking reservations in April, don't hesitate to call one after you've arrived in Alaska. Often, you can score a discount of 30% to 50% in the middle of the summer, as guide companies are eager to fill any remaining places on a scheduled trip.

The following is a list of recreational guide companies in Alaska. Don't confuse them with hunting or fishing guides, whose main interest is to make sure that their client gets a trophy to hang on the wall of the family room. Also don't confuse expeditions with fishing camps or wilderness lodges. The camps and lodges are established rustic resorts in the wilderness where travelers have many of the comforts of home but see little beyond the immediate area.

Southeast Southeast Exposure (☎ 907-225-8829, burd@ptialaska.net) PO Box 9143, Ketchikan, AK 99901, rents kayaks and offers guided trips to Misty Fjords National Monument. A four-day paddle to the heart of Rudyerd Bay – the most scenic part of Misty Fjords – Manzanita Bay and Behm Canal is $700 per person and includes the boat trip from Ketchikan. A six-day trip that includes Walker Cove is $950.

Alaska Discovery (☎ 800-586-1911, akdisco@alaska.net, www.akdiscovery.com) 5449 Shaune Drive, Suite 4, Juneau, AK 99801, was organized in 1972 and is one of the oldest and largest guide companies in Alaska. It used to operate mainly in the Southeast but now has raft trips down the Kongakut River in the Arctic National Wildlife Refuge. Still, kayak trips in Glacier Bay and Russell Fjord, home of Hubbard Glacier, are the company's specialty. Among its expeditions are a five-day paddle in Glacier Bay for $1675 per person and a seven-day Hubbard Glacier adventure for $1775. It also offers 10- to 12-day raft trips down the spectacular Tatshenshini River for $2250.

Chilkat Guides company (☎ 907-766-2491, raftalaska@aol.com), PO Box 170, Haines, AK 99827, offers a handful of raft trips from its base in Haines and is best known for its expeditions down the Tatshenshini and Alsek Rivers. Both are spectacular trips past dozens of glaciers. The 'Tat' is a 10-day float that costs $1975, and the Alsek, with a helicopter flight to bypass Turnback Canyon, is a 13-day trip for $2400.

Spirit Walker Expeditions (☎ 907-697-2266, 800-529-2537, 72537.555@compuserve .com), PO Box 240, Gustavus, AK 99826, is based near Glacier Bay and offers sea-kayaking trips along the coastline of Chichagof Island, just south of the national park, and to Hubbard Glacier near Yakutat. The company prides itself on sighting whales and on providing memorable dinners

Alaska by Dogsled

Wilderness guides will you take into almost any region of Alaska or down any river, but the growth of the guiding industry in the past few years has been in dog mushing. More than two dozen outfitters, from Bettles to Homer, will set you up with a team and then lead you into a winter wilderness. Some outings are only three or four hours long; others may be as long as an eight-day journey into the Brooks Range with your own team. The best time for such an adventure is late February to early April, when the days are long and the temperatures are much more agreeable but the snow base is still deep. You do not need previous experience with dog teams or mushing, but you should be comfortable with winter camping and have cold-weather clothing and gear. Accommodations on such trips range from wall tents with small stoves and remote cabins to mountain lodges. Interested? Here is a sampling of outfitters now using dog mushing to attract travelers to Alaska in the winter:

Lucky Husky Kennels (☎ 907-495-6470, info@luckyhusky), HC 80, PO Box 256, Willow, AK 99688, is based in Willow and offers two-hour rides ($125), half-day rides ($150) and mushing tours in which you drive your own dog team. The kennel's three-day tour to a rustic cabin in the foothills of Mt McKinley is $1195 per person.

Earthsong Lodge (☎ 907-683-2863, earthsong@mail.denali.k12.ak.us), PO Box 89, Healy, AK 99743, is a lodge with a sled dog kennel on the edge of Denali National Park. Winter tours take place in the park, range from three to six days in length and utilize trapper's cabins for lodging on the trail.

Outback Kachemak Dogsled Tours (☎ 907-235-6333), PO Box 1797, Homer, AK 99603, explores the backcountry around Homer and often combines dog mushing with skijoring, in which a dog pulls a cross-country skier. An hour of mushing is $40, and two-day packages are $350 including lodging.

Denali West Lodge (☎ 907-674-3112), PO Box 40, Lake Minchumina, AK 99757, has a six-day package in which you stay at the lodge but mush each day in and around Denali National Park, for $2600.

Chena Dogsled Adventures (☎ 907-488-5845, sleddogs@ptialaska.net), PO Box 16037, Twin Rivers, AK 99716, has full-day and half-day trips and dog-handler trainee sessions. As a trainee, you learn to harness and run a team and how to feed and clean the dogs and prepare them for a tour. The cost to be a trainee is $150 per day (four days minimum) and includes accommodations, all meals and transportation from Fairbanks.

Sourdough Outfitters (☎ 907-692-5252, info@sourdoughoutfitters.com), PO Box 66, Bettles, AK 99726, is based in Bettles, the unofficial capital of dog-mushing outfitters. A handful of companies here offer long-term expeditions that range from six to 14 days and allow groups to travel extensively into the Brooks Range and Gates of the Arctic National Park. You mush your own team, travel 15 to 25 miles a day and usually sleep in large wall tents. Sourdough Outfitters provides several different trips, including a six-day excursion for $1915.

Bettles Lodge (☎ 907-692-5111, bttlodge@alaska.net), PO Box 27, Bettles, AK 99726, is also based in Bettles and offers both multiday adventures and winter packages in which guests stay at the lodge and mush each day. A four-day lodge-based adventure is $1700.

that range from halibut kebabs to fresh Dungeness crabs. Prices range from $685 for a two-night paddle to $1875 for a seven-day trip along Chichagof Island.

Anchorage & Southcentral Wilderness Alaska (☎ 907-345-3567, macgill@alaska .net, www.gorp.com/wildak), PO Box 113063, Anchorage, AK 99511, is an Anchorage-based company that runs trips throughout the state, from backpacking in the Arctic National Wildlife Refuge to kayaking in Prince William Sound. A seven-day float on the John River in the Gates of the Arctic National Park is $1995, and a six-day kayak trip to view the glaciers of Harriman Fjord in Prince William Sound is $1095.

Alaska Wilderness Journeys (☎ 907-349-2964, 800-349-0064, akwildj@alaska.net, www.alaska.net/~akwildj), PO Box 220204, Anchorage, AK 99522, is a highly respected company that also runs trips throughout the state. A six-day float down the Copper River in Wrangell-St Elias National Park is $1175, and a six-day rafting and base camp hiking adventure in the Talkeetna Mountains costs $1825. One of the more unusual trips is an eight-day volcano hike and paddle in Aniakchak National Monument for $2725.

Hugh Glass Backpacking Co (☎ 907-344-1340), PO Box 110796, Anchorage, AK 99511, is a small but long-established guide company that offers kayak trips in Kenai Fjords National Park and Arctic wilderness fishing expeditions. Among its outings is a seven-day trip on the Stuyuhok River for salmon, trout, char and grayling for $1995 and an eight-day trip on the Goodnews River for silver salmon and trout for $2395.

Sunny Cove Sea Kakaying (☎ 907-345-5339, 800-770-9119, kayakak@alaska.net), PO Box 111283, Anchorage, AK 99511, specializes in paddling trips in Resurrection Bay and Kenai Fjords National Park near Seward. Its five-day trip into the national park's Northwestern Fjord includes charter transportation to cut down on the long paddle out of Seward and costs $1195.

Anadyr Adventures (☎ 907-835-2814, 800-865-2925, anadyr@alaska.net, www.alaska .net/~anadyr), PO Box 1821, Valdez, AK 99686-1812, offers trips, paddling classes and kayak rentals for use in Prince William Sound. Guided trips range from one-day paddles and a three-day trip to the Columbia Glacier for $499 to an eight-day tour in the Sound that includes charter boat drop-off for $1499.

Alaska Wildtrek (☎ 907-235-6463, aktrek@ xyz.net), PO Box 1741, Homer, AK 99603, offers guided tours throughout the state, from the Brooks Range to the Alaska Peninsula. Directed by Chlaus Lotscher, a German transplant in Alaska, the company caters almost entirely to Europeans, especially Germans. Among the wilderness trips it offers is a 10-day rafting adventure down the Hulahula River in the Arctic National Wildlife Refuge for $2495 and a five-day float along the Chilikadrotna in Lake Clark National Park for $1495.

Alaskan Wilderness Sailing and Kayaking (☎ 907-835-5175, awss@alaska.net, www .alaskanwilderness.com), PO Box 1313, Valdez, AK 99686, offers kayaking and sailing trips from its Growler Island camp, a wilderness island south of Columbia Glacier. Accommodations and food at the camp are $100 a night; a full-day kayak rental is $89.

Mt McKinley & the Interior St Elias Alpine Guides company (☎ 888-933-5427, 907-277-6867, www.steliasguides.com), PO Box 111241, Anchorage, AK 99511-1241, specializes in mountaineering and glacier-skiing adventures at Wrangell-St Elias National Park. It also offers a 13-day trip down the Copper River to Cordova for $2275 and an 11-day backpacking trip around Chitistone Canyon of the Wrangell-St Elias National Park for $2175. Want to climb a mountain? The 17-day ascent of Mt Blackburn (elevation 16,390 feet) is only $2900.

Alaska Wilderness Journeys (☎ -349-0064, journeys@alaska.net), PO Box 743, Talkeetna, AK 99676, runs a variety of float trips, glacier treks and backpacking adventures around Denali National Park and Brooks Range above the Arctic Circle. A unique two-day raft trip begins on the flag-stop train of the Alaska Railroad and includes overnighting in a rustic cabin. The cost is $460. The company also has a three-day South Denali base camp trip featuring day hiking high in the Talkeetna Mountains for $650.

Denali Raft Adventures company (☎ 888-683-2234, 907-683-2234, denraft@mtaonline.net), Drawer 190, Denali Park, AK 99755, offers a variety of day-rafting trips down the Nenana River near Denali National Park. Some are in calm waters, but others involve two hours of white-water rafting. Prices are $50 to $70 per person for two- to four-hour trips. The company also has a full-day trip.

Nova (☎ 907-745-5753, 800-746-5753, nova@alaska.net, www.novalaska.com), PO Box 1129, Chickaloon, AK 99674-1129, specializes in river rafting. Its trips range from a day run down the Matanuska River for $60 per person to a three-day journey along the Talkeetna River that involves flying to the heart of the Talkeetna Mountains and grade IV white water for $950. The company handles trips to the Copper River in Wrangell-St Elias National Park (six days for $1450) as well as sea-kayaking adventures and glacier hikes.

Fairbanks & Brooks Range CanoeAlaska (☎ 907-479-5183, canoeak@mosquitonet.com), PO Box 81750, Fairbanks, AK 99708-1750, specializes in canoeing trips that teach boating skills and explore scenic rivers. Throughout the summer, the guide company runs trips on the Chena, Delta, Gulkana and Fortymile Rivers that last three to 10 days. The cost is $150 to $250 per person per day, depending on the river and the length of the trip.

Alaska Fish & Trails Unlimited (☎ 907-479-7630), 1177 Shypoke Dr, Fairbanks, AK 99709 runs backpacking, kayaking and canoeing trips in the Gates of the Arctic National Park that include a 14-day backpack and raft trip from Anaktuvuk Pass in the Brooks Range to Bettles for $1800. The company also offers an unguided raft-and-backpack trip from Summit Lake along the Koyukuk River for $1000.

Arctic Treks (☎ 907-455-6502), PO Box 73452, Fairbanks, AK 99707, is a family operation that specializes in treks and rafting in the Gates of the Arctic National Park and the Arctic National Wildlife Refuge. A 10-day backpacking trip to the high mountain valleys of the Brooks Range is $2050 per person, and a 10-day float down the Hulahula River through the Arctic North Slope costs $2875.

Sourdough Outfitters guides (☎ 907-692-5252, info@sourdoughoutfitters.com, www.sourdoughoutfitters.com), PO Box 66, Bettles, AK 99726, runs canoe, kayak and backpacking trips to the Gates of the Arctic National Park, Noatak and Kobuk Rivers and other areas.

The outfitters also provide unguided trips for individuals who have the experience to make an independent journey but want a guide company to handle the logistics (such as trip planning, transportation and canoe or raft rental) of a major expedition. Unguided trips throughout the Brooks Range are $420 to $960 per person, depending on the number of people in your party. Guided trips include an eight-day backpacking trek in the Gates of the Arctic National Park for $14250, a 10-day canoe trip along the Noatak River for $2000 and a five-day paddle of the Wild River in the Brooks Range for $1350.

ABEC's Alaska Adventures (☎ 907-457-8907, abec@polarnet.com), 1550 Alpine Vista Court, Fairbanks, AK 99712, is another outfitter that concentrates on trips in the Arctic National Wildlife Refuge and Gates of the Arctic National Park. Its 12-day Hulahula River raft trip is $2650, and a 12-day backpack trek to witness the caribou migration is $1800.

Arctic Wild (☎ 907-479-8203, arctic@willowbud.com), PO Box 80562, Fairbanks, AK 99708, offers a range of floats and treks in the Brooks Range and Arctic National Wildlife Refuge. The 11-day Hulahula float in the ANWR is $2600, and a six-day caribou migration backpack is $1875. Other rivers floated include the Noatak, the Aichlik on the border of the ANWR and the Alanta on the south side of the Brooks Range.

Backpacking

The following hikes are along routes that are popular and well developed. Backpackers still need the proper gear and knowledge but can undertake these adventures on their own without the services of a guide. Bring a tent on any wilderness trek. Always check with the offices or park headquarters listed for current trail conditions. A few of the trails have US Forest Service (USFS) cabins along the way, but these must be reserved well in advance. Trail sections and distances follow the Information section of each trail description. For more detailed descriptions of the hikes, see Lonely Planet's *Hiking in Alaska*.

CHILKOOT TRAIL

The Chilkoot is unquestionably the most famous trail in Alaska and often the most popular during the summer. It is the route used by the Klondike gold miners in the 1898 gold rush, and walking the trail is not so much a wilderness adventure as a history lesson. The well-developed and well-marked trail is still littered with artifacts of the era – from entire ghost towns and huge mining dredges to lone boots lying next to the trail. The trip is 33 to 35 miles long (depending on where you exit) and includes the Chilkoot

Pass – a steep climb up to 3525 feet, where most hikers scramble on all fours over the loose rocks and boulders. The trail can be attempted by anyone in good physical condition, with the right equipment and enough time. The hike normally takes three to four days, though it can be done in two days by experienced hikers.

The Chilkoot Trail is so popular that Parks Canada, which oversees the northern half, now charges a fee for hiking permits and limits backpackers to 50 per day in order to protect the natural and cultural resources. If you plan to walk the trail during the height of the summer season (July through mid-August), call Parks Canada (☎ 867-667-3910, 800-661-0486) to reserve your permit in advance.

The highlight of the hike for many is riding the historic White Pass & Yukon Route (WP&YR) railroad, which restored its service for hikers from Lake Bennett and to Skagway in 1998. There are cheaper ways to return, but don't pass up the train. Experiencing the Chilkoot and returning on the WP&YR is probably the ultimate Alaska trek, combining great scenery, a firsthand view of history and an incredible sense of adventure.

Getting Started

The Chilkoot Trail can be hiked from either direction (starting at Skagway or Lake Bennett), but it's actually easier and safer when you start from Skagway/Dyea in the south and climb up the loose scree of the Chilkoot Pass rather than down. Besides, following the footsteps of the Klondike miners makes this a special adventure. As gold miners did at the turn of the century, most hikers arrive at Skagway (the historic gold-rush town) by ferry and spend a day or so walking the wooden sidewalks and purchasing supplies from stores with false fronts. The hikers then continue north along the Chilkoot Trail.

From Skagway, make your way to Dyea 8 miles to the northwest, the site of the trailhead. Mile 0 of the Chilkoot is just before the Taiya River crossing. Near the trailhead is the Dyea Camping Area (22 sites, no fee) and a

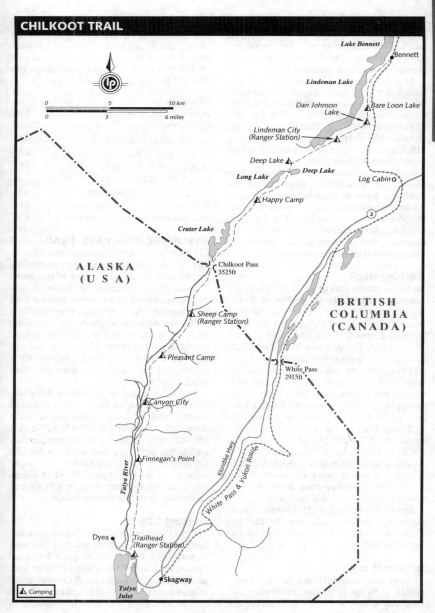

CHILKOOT TRAIL

Lake Bennett

Bennett

Lindeman Lake

Dan Johnson Lake

Bare Loon Lake

Lindeman City (Ranger Station)

Deep Lake

Deep Lake

Long Lake

Log Cabin

Happy Camp

Crater Lake

2

Chilkoot Pass 3525ft

ALASKA (USA)

BRITISH COLUMBIA (CANADA)

Sheep Camp (Ranger Station)

Pleasant Camp

White Pass 2915ft

Canyon City

Klondike Hwy

Finnegan's Point

Taiya River

White Pass & Yukon Route

Dyea

Trailhead (Ranger Station)

Skagway

Taiya Inlet

0   5   10 km
0   3   6 miles

Camping

ranger station managed by the National Park Service. Reaching Dyea by hitchhiking is tough, due to the steep and narrow road and its blind curves. After the first 2 miles, there are few places for motorists to pull over.

Many B&Bs and hotels in Skagway include a trip to the trailhead with the price of a room, or you can contact any of the taxi companies. Frontier Excursions (☎ 983-2517) and the Dyea Shuttle, run by the Skagway Home Hostel (☎ 983-2131), charge $10 for a ride out to the trailhead, which seems to be the going rate.

In Skagway, stop at the Chilkoot Trail Center (☎ 983-3655), across from the WP&YR depot on Broadway St, to obtain a backpacking permit. The US permit is free, but Parks Canada charges C$35 per adult and C$17.50 for children for its permit. You also need to sign the Canada Customs log here before departing up the trail.

Getting Back

At the northern end of the trail, hikers can catch the train on the White Pass & Yukon Route (☎ 800-343-7373) June through August. The train departs from the Lake Bennett Depot at 9 am and again at 1 pm daily, except Tuesday and Wednesday. The one-way fare to Skagway is $65.

There are two other ways to leave the trail at the northern end: you can hike 6 miles south from Bare Loon Lake Campground to the Log Cabin, on Klondike Hwy, or take the WP&YR train from Bennett just to Fraser ($25 one way). An Alaskon Express (☎ 983-2241) bus stops at the Log Cabin at 6:15 pm daily on its way south to Skagway, and a northbound bus reaches the warming hut at 9:15 am on its way to Whitehorse. The one-way fare from the Log Cabin to Skagway is $20 and from the Log Cabin to Whitehorse is $55. Frontier Excursions also makes daily runs to the Log Cabin and offers a drop-off and pickup ticket for $25.

Information

Stop at the National Park Service visitor center in Skagway, in the refurbished railroad depot on the corner of 2nd Ave and Broadway St, for current weather and trail conditions, exhibits and films on the area's history and hiking maps. For more information, contact the National Park Service (☎ 907-983-2921, www.nps.gov/klgo/), PO Box 517, Skagway, AK 99840.

section	miles
Dyea to Canyon City	7.7
Canyon City to Sheep Camp	5.3
Sheep Camp to Chilkoot Pass	3.5
Chilkoot Pass to Happy Camp	4.0
Happy Camp to Deep Lake	2.5
Deep Lake to Lindeman City	3.0
Lindeman City to Bare Loon Lake	3.0
Bare Loon Lake to the Log Cabin	6.0
Bare Loon Lake to Lake Bennett	4.0

RESURRECTION PASS TRAIL

Located in the Chugach National Forest, this 39-mile trail was carved by prospectors in the late 1800s and today is the most popular hiking route on the Kenai Peninsula. It is also an increasingly popular trail for mountain bikers, who can ride the entire route in one long Alaskan day. A strong hiker can be do the whole trip in three days, but most people prefer four to five days to make the most of the immense beauty of the region and the excellent fishing in Trout, Juneau and Swan Lakes.

Eight USFS cabins are along the route ($35 to $45 per night). They must be reserved in advance through the National Recreation Reservation Center (☎ 877-444-6777, 515-885-3639 for overseas, www.reserveusa.com) and, being quite popular, are fully booked for most of the summer. Last-minute reservations are almost impossible. Most hikers take a tent and a camp stove, as fallen wood can be scarce during the busy summer.

Getting Started

The northern trailhead is 20 miles from the Seward Hwy and 4 miles south of Hope on Resurrection Creek Rd. Hope, a historical mining community founded in 1896 by gold seekers, is a charming, out-of-the-way place to visit, but Hope Hwy is not an easy road to hitchhike. It does receive a fair amount of

RESURRECTION PASS TRAIL

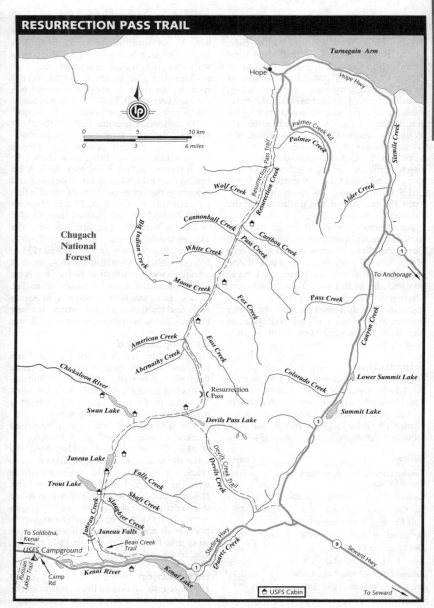

Turnagain Arm

Hope

Hope Hwy

Palmer Creek Rd

Sixmile Creek

Palmer Creek

0   5   10 km
0   3   6 miles

Resurrection Creek

Wolf Creek

Alder Creek

Resurrection Pass Trail

Cannonball Creek

Caribou Creek

Chugach National Forest

Big Indian Creek

White Creek

Pass Creek

Moose Creek

To Anchorage

1

Pass Creek

Fox Creek

Canyon Creek

American Creek

East Creek

Abernathy Creek

Colorado Creek

Lower Summit Lake

Chickaloon River

Resurrection Pass

Swan Lake

Devils Pass Lake

Summit Lake

1

Juneau Lake

Falls Creek

Devils Creek Trail

Devils Creek

Trout Lake

Shaft Creek

Slaughter Creek

Juneau Creek

Juneau Falls

Bean Creek Trail

9

Seward Hwy

To Soldotna, Kenai

USFS Campground

Russian Lakes Trail

Camp Rd

Sterling Hwy

Quartz Creek

Kenai River

Kenai Lake

1

☐ USFS Cabin

To Seward

traffic in the summer, but patience is the key; eventually someone will give you a lift.

From Hope Hwy, you turn south at the posted Resurrection Pass Trail signs onto Resurrection Creek Rd, passing the fork to Palmer Creek Rd. The southern trailhead is on the Sterling Hwy, near Cooper Landing, 53 miles east of Soldotna and 106 miles south of Anchorage. Hitchhiking is easy on the Sterling and Seward Hwys in either direction, or you can hop on a Kachemak Bay Transit bus out of Anchorage (see the Bus section in the Getting Around chapter). A quarter mile east of the southern trailhead along the Sterling Hwy is the Russian River USFS Campground (84 campsites, $6 per night for tents) and the trailhead for the Russian Lakes Trail.

An alternate route that avoids traveling to the remote northern trailhead is the Devils Pass Trail, which is posted at Mile 39 of the Seward Hwy, 88 miles south of Anchorage. The 10-mile path leaves the highway and climbs to Devils Pass at 2400 feet, where it joins the Resurrection Pass Trail. By using the Devils Pass Trail and the lower portion of Resurrection Pass Trail, you can hike from the Seward Hwy to the Sterling Hwy in two days.

Information

For more information on the trail contact the USFS Seward Ranger District (☎ 907-224-3374), 334 4th Ave, Seward, AK 99664, or the Alaska Public Lands Information Center (☎ 907-271-2737), 605 W 4th Ave, Suite 105, Anchorage, AK 99501-2231.

section	miles
Resurrection Creek Rd to Caribou Creek Cabin	6.9
Caribou Creek to Fox Creek Cabin	4.7
Fox Creek to East Creek Cabin	2.8
East Creek to Resurrection Pass	4.9
Resurrection Pass to Devils Pass Cabin	2.1
Devils Pass to Swan Lake Cabin	4.4
Swan Lake to Juneau Lake Cabin	3.3
Juneau Lake to Trout Lake Cabin	2.7
Trout Lake to Juneau Creek Falls	2.3
Juneau Creek Falls to Sterling Hwy	4.4

RUSSIAN LAKES TRAIL

This 21-mile, two-day hike is ideal for hikers who do not want to overextend themselves in the Chugach National Forest. The trail is well traveled, well maintained and well marked during the summer, and not too demanding on the legs. Most of the hike is a pleasant forest walk broken up by patches of wildflowers, ripe berries, lakes and streams.

Its highlights include the possibility of viewing moose or bears, the impressive glaciated mountains across from Upper Russian Lake or, for fishers, the chance to catch your own dinner. The trek offers good fishing for Dolly Varden, rainbow trout and salmon in the upper portions of the Russian River; rainbow trout in Lower Russian Lake, Aspen Flats and Upper Russian Lake; and Dolly Varden in Cooper Lake near the eastern trailhead.

Three USFS cabins are on the trail ($35 to $45 per night), but you must reserve them in advance (see Resurrection Trail). One is on Upper Russian Lake, 9 miles from the Cooper Lake trailhead. Another is at Aspen Flats, and another is 3 miles northwest along the trail, 12 miles from the western trailhead.

Getting Started

It is easier to start from the Cooper Lake trailhead, the higher end of the trail. To reach the trailhead, turn off at Mile 47.8 of Sterling Hwy onto Snug Harbor Rd. The road leads 12 miles to Cooper Lake and ends at a marked parking lot and the trailhead.

The western trailhead is on a side road marked 'Russian River USFS Campground' at Mile 52.7 of the Sterling Hwy. Hike 0.9 miles to the end of the campground road to reach a parking lot at the beginning of the trail. There is a $2 fee if you leave a car here. If you're planning to camp at Russian River the night before starting the hike, keep in mind that the campground is extremely popular during the salmon-running season, from mid-June to mid-July, and fills up with anglers by early afternoon.

Information

For more information on the trail, contact the US Forest Service Seward Ranger District

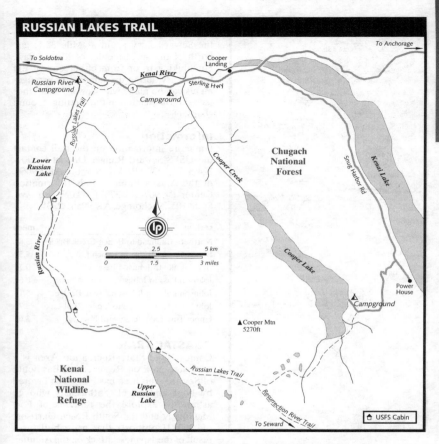

RUSSIAN LAKES TRAIL

To Anchorage

To Soldotna

Russian River Campground

Kenai River

Cooper Landing

Sterling Hwy

Campground

Russian Lakes Trail

Lower Russian Lake

Chugach National Forest

Cooper Creek

Snug Harbor Rd

Kenai Lake

Russian River

0   2.5   5 km
0   1.5   3 miles

Cooper Lake

Kenai National Wildlife Refuge

Upper Russian Lake

Russian Lakes Trail

▲ Cooper Mtn 5270ft

Power House

Campground

Resurrection River Trail

To Seward

🏠 USFS Cabin

(☎ 907-224-3374), 334 4th Ave, Seward, AK 99664, or the Alaska Public Lands Information Center (☎ 907-271-2737), 605 W 4th Ave, Suite 105, Anchorage, AK 99501-2231.

section	miles
Cooper Lake trailhead to junction of Resurrection River Trail	5.0
Trail junction to Upper Russian Lake	4.0
Upper Russian Lake to Aspen Flats Cabin	3.0
Aspen Flats to Lower Russian Lake	6.0
Lower Russian Lake to Russian River Campground	3.0

JOHNSON PASS TRAIL

In the same area as the Resurrection Pass and Russian Lakes trails, and nearly as popular, is the Johnson Pass Trail, a two-day and 23-mile hike over a 1550-foot alpine pass. The trail was originally part of the old Iditarod Trail blazed by prospectors from Seward to the golden beaches of Nome and later was used as part of the old Seward mail route.

Most of the trail is fairly level, which makes for easy hiking and explains the growing numbers of mountain bikers seen on it. Anglers will find arctic grayling in

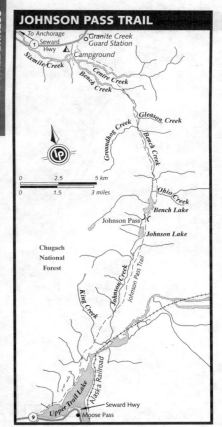

JOHNSON PASS TRAIL

south over Johnson Pass and then to the shore of Upper Trail Lake before reaching the Seward Hwy again at Mile 32.5, just north of the small hamlet of Moose Pass. Hitchhiking to or from either end of the trail is easy during the summer, or arrangements can be made with Seward Bus Lines (see the Bus section in the Getting Around chapter).

Information

For more information on the trail contact the USFS Seward Ranger District (☎ 907-224-3374), 334 4th Ave, Seward, AK 99664, or the Alaska Public Lands Information Center (☎ 907-271-2737), 605 W 4th Ave, Suite 105, Anchorage, AK 99501-2231.

section	miles
Northern trailhead to Bench Creek Bridge	3.8
Bench Creek Bridge to Bench Lake	5.5
Bench Lake to Johnson Pass	0.7
Johnson Pass to Johnson Lake	0.6
Johnson Lake to Johnson Creek Bridge	5.1
Johnson Creek Bridge to Upper Trail Lake	3.7
Upper Trail Lake to Seward Hwy	3.6

COASTAL TRAIL

Caines Head State Recreation Area is a 6000-acre park on Resurrection Bay south of Seward. This area has long been favored by boat and kayak enthusiasts who go ashore to explore the remains of Fort McGilvray and the South Beach Garrison, old WWII outposts that were built as a result of the Japanese attack on the Aleutian Islands. Along with the remains of an army pier, firing platforms and the garrison ghost town at South Beach, the park also has much natural beauty, including a massive headland that rises 650 feet above the water and provides sweeping views of Resurrection Bay.

Bench Lake and rainbow trout in Johnson Lake. Plan to camp at either Johnson Lake or Johnson Pass, but keep in mind that these places are above the tree line, making a small stove necessary. There are no cabins on this trail.

Getting Started

The trail can be hiked from either direction. The northern trailhead is at Mile 64 of the Seward Hwy, 96 miles south of Anchorage; a gravel road marked 'Forest Service Trail No 10' leads from there a short way to a parking lot and the trail. The trail goes

The Coastal Trail is a 4.5-mile one-way hike from Lowell Point to North Beach, where you can continue along old army roads to Fort McGilvray and South Beach. Along the way you pass a walk-in campground, vault toilets and a picnic shelter at Tonsina Point; two state park cabins ($50, reservations) just before reaching North Beach; and a campground, picnic shelter and ranger station at North Beach. This hiking trail makes an excellent overnight trip, combining history, great scenery and an opportunity to climb a spur trail into alpine areas; it's also affordable, as the trailhead is an easy walk from Seward.

Getting Started
The trailhead is at the end of Lowell Point Rd, 3 miles south of Seward's Alaska Sea-Life Center. Before leaving town, purchase a tide book; the 1.5-mile stretch between Tonsina Point and Derby Cove can only be hiked during low tide. Plan to leave Seward two hours before low tide, to avoid becoming stranded along the way. Due to steep cliffs along the shoreline, it's not possible to follow the beach from the trailhead to Tonsina Point. The trek to North Beach is a two- to three-hour walk. You must stay until the next low tide (12 hours after the last low tide) before returning.

Information
Contact Alaska Division of Parks and Outdoor Recreation (☎ 907-262-5581), PO Box 1247, Soldotna, AK 99669, for a brochure on the park.

section	miles
Northern trailhead to Tonsina Point	1.5
Tonsina Point to North Beach	3.0
North Beach to Fort McGilvray	2.0
North Beach to South Beach	2.5

CHENA DOME TRAIL
Fifty miles west of Fairbanks in the Chena River State Recreation Area, this 29.5-mile loop trail makes an ideal three- or four-day backpacking trip. The trail circles the entire Angel Creek drainage area and, for the first 3 miles, cuts through forest and climbs to the tree line. The vast majority of the hike follows tundra ridge tops where the route has been marked by rock cairns.

For those people who enjoy romping in the alpine area, this route is a treat. Four times the trail reaches summits that exceed

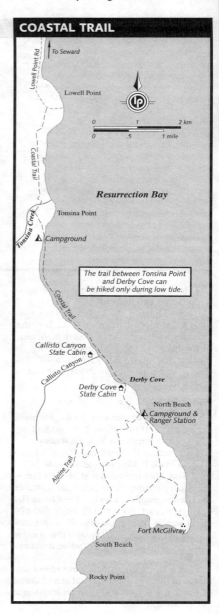

COASTAL TRAIL

To Seward

Lowell Point Rd

Lowell Point

0 — 1 — 2 km
0 — .5 — 1 mile

Resurrection Bay

Coastal Trail

Tonsina Point

Tonsina Creek

▲ Campground

The trail between Tonsina Point
and Derby Cove can
be hiked only during low tide.

Coastal Trail

Callisto Canyon
State Cabin ♠

Callisto Canyon

Derby Cove
Derby Cove ♠
State Cabin

North Beach
▲ Campground &
Ranger Station

Alpine Trail

Fort McGilvray

South Beach

Rocky Point

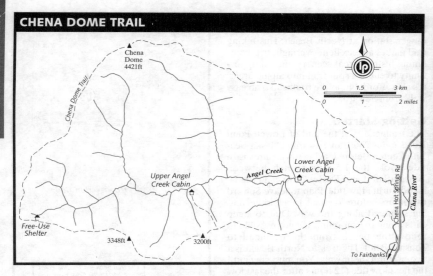

CHENA DOME TRAIL

3000 feet, and in between, it is made up of steep climbs and descents.

Chena Dome is the highest point on the trail, a flat-topped ridge at 4,421 feet that provides awesome views. Other highpoints of the hike are the wildflowers in July, the blueberries in August, wildlife, a free-use shelter and a public-use cabin that can be rented in advance.

Getting Started

It's easier to hike the loop by beginning at the northern trailhead at Mile 50.5 of the Chena Hot Springs Rd. When traveling west, you'll come to the trailhead 0.7 miles past Angel Creek Bridge on the left side of the road. The other trailhead is at Mile 49. Hitching is easy during the summer, as traffic on the road is generally good, or the Chena Hot Springs Resort van (☎ 452-7867, 800-478-4681) will provide roundtrip transportation for $30 per person. You can also rent a car in Fairbanks and pay $40 a day while it sits and you hike.

Pack a stove, since open fires are not permitted in the area. Also, carry at least 3 quarts of water per person and then replenish it at every opportunity along the trail. For the most part, water will be collected from small pools in the tundra and must be treated.

Mosquitoes and gnats can be a major nuisance from June to early August, so bring powerful insect repellent with Deet. And most importantly, obtain the USGS topos for Big Delta D5 and Circle A5 and A6, along with the trail map produced by Alaska Division of Parks and Recreation.

The free-use shelter is at Mile 17, and there are plans to add a second one at Mile 7.5. The Upper Angel Creek Cabin ($25, reservations) makes a welcome place for spending the third night, but it's a 1.5-mile, 1500-foot descent from the main trail. Another nice treat is to reserve a room or cabin at Chena Hot Springs Resort for after the trek (see Fairbanks chapter). There's nothing like a day or two to soak those tired muscles after rambling for 30 miles in an alpine area.

Information

For a trail information sheet or to reserve the Angel Creek Cabin, contact Alaska Division of Parks & Recreation (☎ 907-451-2695), 3700 Airport Way, Fairbanks, AK 99709.

section	miles
Mile 50.5 trailhead to timberline	3.0
Timberline to military plane wreck	5.5
Plane wreck to Chena Dome summit	2.0
Chena Dome to spur to free-use shelter	6.5
Free-use shelter to final descent off ridge	10.0
Final descent to Mile 49 trailhead	2.5

PINNELL MOUNTAIN TRAIL

The midnight sun is the outstanding sight on the Pinnell Mountain Trail, a 27.3-mile trek, 85 miles northeast of Fairbanks on the Steese Hwy. From June 18 to 25, the sun never sets on the trail, giving hikers 24 hours of light each day. You can view and photograph the sun sitting above the horizon at midnight at several high points on the trail, including the Eagle Summit trailhead.

The route is mostly tundra ridge tops that lie above 3500 feet and can be steep and rugged. Water is scarce in the alpine sections, so bring your own. The other highlight of the trip is the wildflowers (unmatched in much of the state) that carpet the Arctic-alpine tundra slopes, beginning in late May and peaking in mid-June. Hikers may spot small bands of caribou, grizzly bears, rock rabbits and an occasional wolf in the valleys below, but binoculars are necessary to really see any wildlife. The views from the ridge tops are spectacular, with the Alaska Range visible to the south and the Yukon Flats to the north.

Getting Started

The trail is a natural three-day adventure, with backpackers covering eight to 10 miles a day. Most hikers begin at the Eagle Summit trailhead on Mile 107.3 of the Steese Hwy, the higher end of the trail. The western end lies closer to Fairbanks at Twelvemile Summit, at Mile 85 of the Steese Hwy. Two small shelters built by the Youth Conservation Corps (YCC) are open to anyone, without

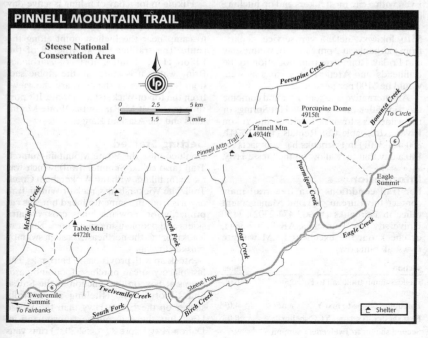

PINNELL MOUNTAIN TRAIL

Steese National Conservation Area

0   2.5   5 km
0   1.5   3 miles

Porcupine Creek

Porcupine Dome 4915ft

Bonanza Creek

To Circle

Pinnell Mtn 4934ft

Pinnell Mtn Trail

Ptarmigan Creek

6

Eagle Summit

McKinley Creek

North Fork

Bear Creek

Eagle Creek

Table Mtn 4472ft

6

Twelvemile Summit

To Fairbanks

Twelvemile Creek

Steese Hwy

South Fork

Birch Creek

⌂ Shelter

reservations or fees. They are great places for waiting out a storm or cooking a meal on a windy evening, but bring a tent with good bug netting to sleep in at night.

Snow cover can be expected in May (with patches remaining to June) and mid-September. These patches are good sources of water, which is scarce on this trail. Bring at least 2 quarts of water per person and then refill your supply at either snow patches, springs or tundra pools at every opportunity. Boil or filter all standing water from pools and slow-running springs.

The winds can be brutal in this barren region, as there are no trees to slow the gusts that can come howling over the ridges. Bring a windscreen for your camp stove; otherwise, cooking can become a long ordeal.

Traffic on the Steese Hwy is light this far out of Fairbanks, but there is still a steady trickle. Hitching is possible if you are willing to give up a day getting out there and back. Even with a car, most hikers end up hitching back to the trailhead where they began.

The Steese Highway Stage Line (☎ 520-5610, loki@xyz.net), a van service, departs from Fairbanks at 2 pm Monday, Wednesday and Friday. Roundtrip transportation to the trailheads, and Arctic Hot Springs as well, would be $100 per person.

An alternative is to rent a car and combine the trip with a drive to Circle Hot Springs or the wilderness town of Circle on the Yukon River. Affordable Car Rentals (☎ 452-7241, 800-471-3101) in Fairbanks has compacts for $40 a day that they allow on the Stesse Hwy.

Information

For trail conditions or a free trail map, contact the Bureau of Land Management office in Fairbanks (☎ 907-474-2302), 1150 University Ave, Fairbanks, AK 99709-3844, or check out the excellent BLM website (www.ak.blm.gov/).

section	miles
Eagle Summit trailhead to Porcupine Dome	6.0
Porcupine Dome to first YCC shelter	4.0
First shelter to second YCC shelter	8.0
Second shelter to Twelvemile Summit	9.5

WHITE MOUNTAINS SUMMIT TRAIL

The Bureau of Land Management (BLM), which maintains the Pinnell Mountain Trail, also administers the White Mountains National Recreation Area, which includes the Summit Trail. This 20-mile, one-way route was especially built for summer use and includes boardwalks over the wettest areas. The route winds through dense spruce forest, traverses scenic alpine ridge tops and Arctic tundra, and ends at Beaver Creek, in the foothills of the majestic White Mountains.

On the opposite bank of the creek from the trail is the Borealis-Le Fevre Cabin, which was rebuilt in 1996 and can be reserved for $20 a night. But you must bring tent! Beaver Creek is rarely low enough to ford safely. The grayling fishing is outstanding here, but most parties end the day camping above the tree line, as opposed to dealing with the low-lying swamp.

Hiking in for a day of fishing is a five-day adventure. Even if stopping short of Beaver Creek, hikers still require two or three days to camp near the highest point along the route. The trailhead is at Mile 28 of the Elliott Hwy, 31 miles north of Fairbanks. Bring water; it is scarce in the alpine sections. Highlights of the trek are the views from the top of Wickersham Dome. It's possible to see Mt McKinley, the White Mountains and the Alaskan Range.

Getting Started

Don't confuse the White Mountain Summit Trail (also called Summer Trail), which was made for hikers, with the Wickersham Creek Trail. The Wickersham Creek or Winter Trail departs from the same trailhead but was cut primarily for snow machines, cross-country skiers and people using snowshoes. This trail leads more to the northeast, through swampy muskeg lowlands.

Stock up with provisions in Fairbanks. The last place you can purchase food and gasoline is at Fox, on the junction of the Steese and Elliott Hwys. Hitching is generally slower on the Elliott Hwy than the Steese Hwy, but there is public transportation. Dalton Hwy Express (☎ 452-2031) runs vans

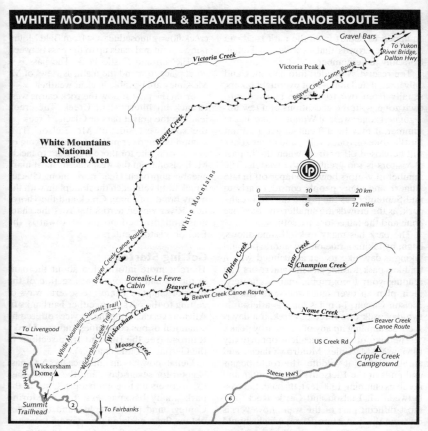

WHITE MOUNTAINS TRAIL & BEAVER CREEK CANOE ROUTE

to Prudhoe Bay twice a week and charges $70 roundtrip to the trailhead.

Information

For a trail map, contact the Bureau of Land Management office in Fairbanks (☎ 907-474-2302), 1150 University Ave, Fairbanks, AK 99709-3844, or check out the excellent BLM website (www.ak.blm.gov). The office will also have current information on trail conditions and the availability of water, and is the place to reserve the Borealis-Le Fevre Cabin. Call ☎ 800-437-7021 to reserve the cabin in advance.

section	miles
Summit trailhead to Wickersham Dome	6.0
Wickersham Dome to 3100-foot high point	4.0
3100 High Point to Wickersham Creek Trail junction	8.0
Trail junction to Borealis-Le Fevre Cabin	2.0

DENALI NATIONAL PARK – MT EIELSON CIRCUIT

Not the budget destination it once was, Denali National Park and Preserve is still a paradise for backpackers. The combination of terrain, scenery and wildlife that will make

THE WILDERNESS

your heart pound make this park a popular attraction with all visitors. Only backpackers equipped to depart from the park road can escape the crowds that descend on Denali from July to September.

The reserve is divided into 43 zones, and only a regulated number of overnight hikers, usually from two to 12, are allowed into each zone, with the exceptions of a few un-regulated zones west of Wonder Lake. In the summer, it may be difficult to get a permit for the zone of your choice, and other zones will be closed off entirely when the impact of visitors is too great for the wildlife. The number of visitors begins to taper off in late August, and many people consider early to mid-September as the prime time to see the park, as the crowds are smaller, the bugs are gone and the fall colors are setting in.

The park has many treks. If time allows, begin by taking a ride on the shuttle bus and taking a day hike to get acquainted with a trail-less park, fording streams and rivers, and reading your topographic map accurately; then, plan an overnight excursion. The Mt Eielson Circuit, 14 miles long, is a leisurely two-day walk or a three-day trek, if a day is spent scrambling up any of the nearby peaks.

The hike offers an excellent opportunity to view Mt McKinley, Muldrow Glacier and an abundance of wildlife. The route begins and ends at the Eielson Visitor Center and involves climbing 1300 feet, through the pass between Mt Eielson and Castle Rock. The most difficult part of the walk, however, is crossing the Thorofare River, which should be done wearing tennis shoes and with an ice axe or sturdy pole in hand.

From Eielson Visitor Center, Mile 66 of the park road, you begin the route (heading southeast) by dropping down the steep hill to Gorge Creek, crossing it and continuing south to the Thorofare River. Follow the tundra shelf along the east side of the river until you cross Sunrise Creek, which flows into the Thorofare River.

After fording Sunrise Creek, you must then ford Thorofare River. Search the braided river in this area for the best crossing place and then proceed with extreme caution. Once you're on the west bank of the river, continue

hiking south until you reach the confluence of Contact Creek and the Thorofare River. The creek flows almost due west from Bald Mountain Summit and leads up to the pass between Mt Eielson and Castle Peak. The pass is a good place to spend the night, as views of Mt McKinley are possible in clear weather.

From the pass, follow the rock cairns west to pick up Intermittent Creek. The creek leads to the gravel bars of Glacier Creek on the southwest side of Mt Eielson. This section of the river makes for easy hiking or a good campsite for those who want to tackle Mt Eielson from the west side, its most manageable approach. Head north along Glacier Creek until you reach the floodplain with the many braids of Camp Creek and the Thorofare River woven across it. Cross the channels and proceed northeast towards the Eielson Visitor Center.

Getting Started

There is more information about the park in the Denali National Park section of the Interior chapter. There are several ways of getting to the park from either Fairbanks or Anchorage, including the services offered by a handful of bus companies and the Alaska Railroad (see the Bus and Train sections in the Getting Around chapter).

Denali now has an entrance fee; a $5 pass is good for seven days, and the family pass ($10) covers up to eight people. Once in the park, many backpackers stay at Morino Campground ($12 a night), and then they obtain their backcountry permit from the visitor center at Riley Creek. Permits are free and handed out on a first-come, first-served basis one day before the trip. Keep in mind the zones around the Eielson Visitor Center are among the most popular in the park. If you arrive in July or early August, you might have a three- to four-day wait before obtaining a permit to one. Once you receive a permit, reserve a seat on the special camper bus ($15). Both visitor centers sell topographical maps: the circuit is contained on one section – Mt McKinley B-1. A small store within the park entrance area sells food and camp-stove fuel, but it is best to stock up in Anchorage or Fairbanks.

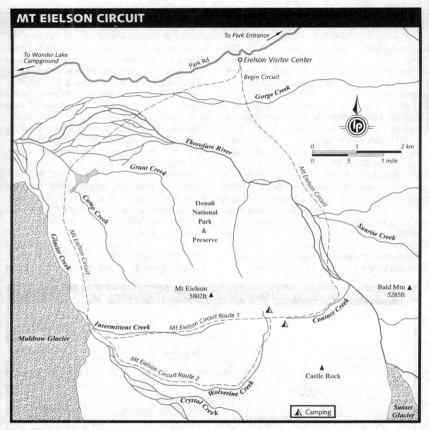

MT EIELSON CIRCUIT

Information

For more information on reserving campgrounds and shuttle bus seats in advance or additional tips for getting into the backcountry, check the Denali National Park section of the Interior chapter. You can also contact Denali National Park and Preserve (☎ 907-683-2294, 907-683-9640 for a recorded message, www.nps.gov/dena/), PO Box 9, Denali Park, AK 99755.

If you are in Anchorage, contact the Alaska Public Lands Information Center (☎ 271-2737), 605 W 4th Ave, Suite 105, Anchorage, AK 99501-2231 for information.

section	miles*
Eielson Visitor Center to Gorge Creek	1.0
Gorge Creek to Sunrise Creek-Thorofare River junction	2.0
Junction to Contact Creek	1.0
Contact Creek to Bald Mountain Summit pass	1.2
Pass to Glacier Creek	3.3
Glacier Creek to floodplains	2.5
Floodplains to Eielson Visitor Center	3.0

* This is a route not a trail, so all distances are rough estimates only.

DEER MOUNTAIN TRAIL

Located in Ketchikan, the Deer Mountain Trail is often a visitor's first hike in the North Country, and it rarely disappoints them. The trail is a steady but manageable climb to the sharp peak above the city, with incredible views of the Tongass Narrows and the surrounding area.

What many backpackers don't realize is that the Deer Mountain Trail is only part of a challenging, overnight alpine trail system. This 11-mile trip, which could include spending the night in a USFS cabin, begins with the 3-mile Deer Mountain Trail and leads into the Blue Lake Trail. This path is a natural route along an alpine ridge extending 4 miles north to John Mountain. Here, hikers can return to the Ketchikan road system by taking the John Mountain Trail for 2 miles to Upper Silvis Lake and then following an old access road from the hydroelectric plant on Lower Silvis Lake to the parking lot off the S Tongass Hwy.

Deer Mountain is well-maintained and is a heavily used trail during the summer. Even though it is a steady climb, the hike to the summit is not overly difficult. A quarter mile before the summit, you pass the junction to Blue Lake and the posted trail to the Deer Mountain USFS Cabin. The cabin, located above the tree line, sleeps eight people and used to be free. But it was improved, and now the USFS rents it out for $35 per night. The Blue Lake Trail crosses alpine country with natural but good footing, although in rainy weather it may be difficult to follow. The scenery from the trail is spectacular.

Within 2 miles of the junction of the Deer Mountain Trail, you arrive at the shore of Blue Lake. This lake, at 2700 feet, is above the tree line in a scenic alpine setting.

If you are going to trek along the John Mountain Trail, it is marked by a series of steel posts and has 20% grades on the first mile from Upper Silvis Lake. After this, it passes through alpine country. The John

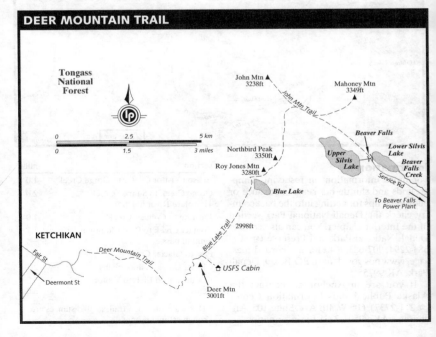

DEER MOUNTAIN TRAIL

Mountain Trail is a fairly difficult track to follow and presents hikers with a challenge in reading their topographic maps and choosing the right route.

Getting Started

The trailhead for the Deer Mountain Trail can be reached by following the gravel road from the corner of Fair and Deermount Sts in Ketchikan, past a subdivision (to the southeast). Just before reaching the former landfill (now closed), a trail sign points left to a side road that leads to the trailhead and small parking lot.

To get to the start of the John Mountain Trail, hitchhike 12.9 miles east of Ketchikan along the S Tongass Hwy (also known as the Beaver Falls Hwy) to its end at the power plant. There is a 2-mile hike along an old access road from the power plant at the tidewater to the hydroelectric plant on the south side of Lower Silvis Lake. From the road you pick up a trail that climbs steeply to the upper lake. The John Mountain Trail begins at the old outlet at the western end of the upper lake.

Information

Rent the cabin in advance through the National Recreation Reservation Center (☎ 877-444-6777, 515-885-3639 for overseas, www.reserveusa.com). The cabins and trails are maintained by the USFS, which staffs the Southeast Alaska Visitor Center (☎ 907-228-6214), 50 Main St, Ketchikan, AK 99901. Information can also be obtained through the USFS website (www.fs.fed.us/recreation/states/ak.html).

section	miles
Deer Mountain trailhead to Deer Mountain summit	3.1
Summit to Blue Lake	2.2
Blue Lake to John Mountain	2.0
John Mountain to Upper Silvis Lake	2.0
Upper Silvis Lake to S Tongass Hwy	2.0

PETERSBURG LAKE TRAIL

A short hop across the Wrangell Narrows from the fishing community of Petersburg is Petersburg Lake Trail and Portage Mountain Loop, which can be combined for a trek to two USFS cabins. The Petersburg Lake Trail is well planked and provides backpackers with a wilderness opportunity and access to a USFS cabin without expensive bushplane travel. Those planning to continue on to Portage Bay or Salt Chuck along Portage Mountain Loop should keep in mind that the trails on the loop are not planked or maintained and are, at best, only lightly marked. The 7-mile trek to Portage Cove is very challenging and involves crossing wet muskeg areas or stretches flooded out by beaver dams.

Bring a fishing pole, as there are good spots in the creek for Dolly Varden and rainbow trout. In August and early September, there are large coho and sockeye salmon runs throughout the area that attract anglers and bears.

The trek begins across Wrangell Narrows from Petersburg, at the Kupreanof Island public dock. From the dock, a partial boardwalk leads south 2 miles, past a handful of cabins, and then turns northwest up the tidewater arm of the creek, almost directly across Wrangell Narrows from the ferry terminal. A well-planked trail goes from the saltwater arm and continues along the northern side of the freshwater creek to Petersburg Lake USFS Cabin on the eastern end of the lake. From the cabin, Portage Mountain Loop continues north to Portage Bay.

Getting Started

The only hitch to this trip is getting across Wrangell Narrows to the public dock on Kupreanof Island. The USFS office above the post office in Petersburg provides a list of charter-boat operators, or contact Petersburg Creek Charters (☎ 772-2425), which charges $20 roundtrip per person.

The cheapest way to get across Wrangell Narrows is to hitch a ride with one of the boats that cross the narrows every day. Go to the skiff float in the North Harbor (Old Harbor) near the harbormaster's office on the waterfront and ask around for boats crossing. A small population lives on the

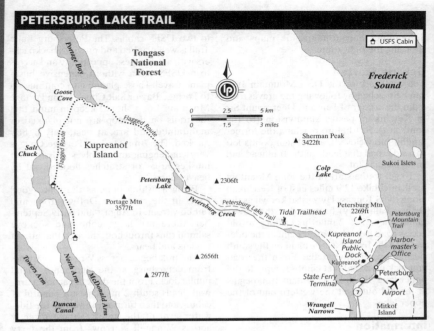

PETERSBURG LAKE TRAIL

other side of the narrows, so boats are constantly crossing, though at times you might have to wait a bit.

Travelers who arrive at Petersburg with their own kayak can paddle to the creek during high tide, to avoid much of the hike along the tidewater arm. This is one trip that you'll want good waterproof clothing and rubber boots for. Bring a tent or plan on reserving the cabins at least two months in advance, even earlier if you want to tackle the route in August during the salmon runs.

Information

The Petersburg District US Forest Service office is on the 2nd floor of the post office along Main St. You can also contact the Petersburg Ranger District (☎ 907-772-3871), PO Box 1328, Petersburg, AK 99833, in advance or check the USFS website (www.fs.fed.us/recreation/states/ak.html). Contact the National Recreation Reservation Center

(☎ 877-444-6777, 515-885-3639 for overseas, www.reserveusa.com) to rent the cabin in advance.

section	miles
Kupreanof Island dock to tidewater arm	2.0
Tidewater arm to Petersburg Creek	2.5
Trail by creek to USFS cabin	6.0
USFS cabin to Portage Bay	7.0
Portage Bay to Salt Chuck East Cabin	4.5

DAN MOLLER TRAIL

Across the Gastineau Channel from the center of Juneau is the Dan Moller Trail. It was originally built during the 1930s for downhill skiers and, at one time, had three warming huts along it. Today, the skiers continue along the N Douglas Hwy to the Eaglecrest Ski Area, and the Dan Moller Trail has become a popular access to the alpine meadows in the middle of Douglas Island.

The trail is 3.3 miles long and leads to a beautiful alpine bowl where the USFS has restored the remaining ski cabin. As with all USFS cabins, you have to reserve it in advance ($35), but from 10 am to 5 pm, it's shared by everybody as a warming hut.

Even if you can't secure the cabin, don't pass up this trail. Camping in the alpine bowl is superb, and an afternoon or an extra day can be spent scrambling up and along the ridge that surrounds the bowl and forms the backbone of Douglas Island. From the ridge, there are scenic views of Douglas Island, Admiralty Island and Stephens Passage. See the Around Juneau map in the Southeast Alaska chapter.

Getting Started

The trailhead is 1.5 miles from the Juneau International (AYH) Hostel. You can easily walk to it or catch the minibus to Douglas and get off at Cordova St, which leads to a growth of apartments and condominiums known as West Juneau. From Cordova St, turn left (southeast) onto Pioneer Ave and follow it to the end of the pavement.

Beyond the pavement is the posted trailhead and a small parking area. An old jeep track serves as the first part of the trail, before it emerges into open muskeg. Most of the trail is planked, but waterproof boots are a must. The hike is a steady climb to the alpine bowl but is not overly tiring; plan on six hours for the roundtrip.

Information

For additional information, contact the Forest Service Information Center (☎ 907-586-8751), Juneau Centennial Hall, 101 Egan Dr, Juneau, AK 99801) or the USFS website (www.fs.fed.us/recreation/states/ak.html).

Rent the cabin in advance through the National Recreation Reservation Center (☎ 877-444-6777, 515-885-3639 for overseas, www.reserveusa.com).

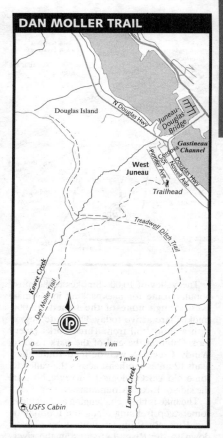

DAN MOLLER TRAIL

section	miles
Hostel to Dan Moller trailhead	1.5
Dan Moller trailhead to junction with Treadwell Ditch Trail	0.8
Trail junction to upper cabin	2.5

KATMAI NATIONAL PARK – VALLEY OF 10,000 SMOKES

Katmai National Park, an expensive side trip, is an intriguing place for a long-term wilderness adventure. A series of volcanic eruptions in 1912 left the area with unique land formations, including the eerie, barren landscape of the Valley of 10,000 Smokes. Wildlife is plentiful, with the brown bear the most prominent animal. Moose live in most parts of the park, and the fishing is often said to be among the best in Alaska, as Katmai is an important spawning area for salmon.

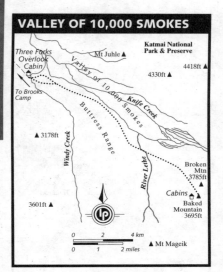

VALLEY OF 10,000 SMOKES

Katmai National Park & Preserve

Three Forks Overlook Cabin

To Brooks Camp

Mt Juhle ▲

Valley of 10,000 Smokes

Knife Creek

4418ft ▲

4330ft ▲

▲ 3178ft

Buttress Range

Windy Creek

River Lethe

Broken Mtn 3785ft ▲

Cabins ▲ ▲
Baked Mountain 3695ft

3601ft ▲

0   2   4 km
0   1   2 miles

▲ Mt Mageik

The Valley of 10,000 Smokes is the most popular route for backpacking in Katmai, even though none of the famed '10,000 smokes' are active today. The route begins with a short trail from Three Forks Overlook Cabin at the end of the park road to Windy Creek. A well-defined route then leads 12 miles southeast across the valley to some old US Geological Survey cabins on the side of Baked Mountain.

The hike is fairly challenging and includes some steep trekking along the foothills of the Buttress Range followed by a drop down to the River Lethe. From the river, you head for the divide between Broken Mountain and Baked Mountain. You then head southeast to climb the short, steep slope of Baked Mountain to the cabins.

Getting Started

Turn to the Katmai National Park section in the Bush chapter for travel information on getting to and from Katmai National Park, but be prepared to pay around $450 round-trip from Anchorage, 290 miles away. The only developed facilities in the park, apart from a couple of expensive wilderness lodges, are at Brooks Camp.

In recent years, Katmai has become extremely popular, forcing the National Park Service to institute quotas and fees. There is now a $10 per person per day fee for those at Brooks Camp, in addition to a $5 per person per night fee to stay at the campground. You must have reservations before arriving at Brooks Camp. You can begin making them in early January (the date varies from year to year) for the following summer through the National Park Reservation Service (☎ 800-365-2267, 301-722-1257 for overseas).

Like Denali National Park, Katmai has a shuttle bus that travels the park road daily. The fare is $72 roundtrip, and a spot should be reserved in advance. Hikers who have a week in the park can skip the bus fare by walking the 23 miles out to Three Forks Overlook from Brooks Camp or take the bus just one way and pay $40.

Brooks Camp has lodging, a restaurant and a park store that sells limited quantities of freeze-dried food, topographic maps and white gas for camp stoves. The park store also rents tents, canoes, camp stoves and fishing rods, among other things. It is best to stock up on food and fishing tackle in Anchorage to avoid emptying your entire money pouch here. The weather in the area can be consistently poor even by Alaskan standards; the skies are clear for only 20% of the summer, and from September onwards, strong winds are fairly frequent.

Information

In Anchorage, contact the Alaska Public Lands Information Center (☎ 271-2737), 605 W 4th Ave, Suite 105, Anchorage, AK 99501-2231, for information about Katmai National Park. In advance of your trip, contact Katmai National Park and Preserve (☎ 907-246-3305, www.nps.gov/katm), PO Box 7, King Salmon, AK 99613.

section	miles*
Brooks Camp to Three Forks via Park Rd	23.0
Three Forks to Windy Creek	1.0
Windy Creek to River Lethe via the Buttress Range	7.0
River Lethe to Baked Mountain Cabins	4.0
*Marked distances are rough estimates only.	

Bald eagle

Flowers in the tundra

Salmonberries

Brown bear

Backpackers on the Petersburg Lake Trail

Exploring Prince William Sound

Camping along the Noatak River in Arctic Alaska

WRANGELL-ST ELIAS NATIONAL PARK – DIXIE PASS

Even by Alaskan standards, Wrangell-St Elias National Park is a large tract of wilderness. At 20,625 sq miles, it's the largest US national park, contains the most peaks over 14,500 feet in North America and has the greatest concentration of glaciers in the continent.

The park is a mountainous wilderness with three mountain chains (Wrangell, St Elias and Chugach) converging here. Dall sheep, moose, three herds of caribou and, of course, lots of bears are found in the park. The rivers are full of grayling, and trout thrive in the lakes.

The most common trek is to spend a day hiking up to Bonanza Mine or Root Glacier (see the Wrangell-St Elias National Park section in the Southcentral chapter). Dixie Pass offers a longer, more rugged and more authentic wilderness adventure into the interior of this park. The trek up to Dixie Pass and back is 24 miles, but plan to camp there at least one or two extra days to take in the alpine beauty and explore the nearby ridges. This itinerary requires three or four days and is of moderate difficulty.

To get to the trailhead, hike 2.5 miles up the Nugget Creek/Kotsina Rd and then another 1.3 miles along Kotsina Rd after Nugget Creek Trail splits off to the northeast. The Dixie Pass trailhead is posted on the right-hand side of Kotsina Rd, usually as a pile of rocks with a stick in it. It's a definite trail but easy to miss. The route begins as a level path to Strelna Creek, reached in 3 miles, and then continues along the west side of the creek for another 3 miles to the first major confluence.

After fording the creek, you continue along animal trails, fording the creek when necessary to avoid rock bluffs. It's 5 to 6 miles to the pass, and along the way you cross two more confluences and hike through an interesting gorge. The ascent to the pass is a fairly obvious route. Dixie Pass offers superb scenery, good camping and opportunities to spend an extra day or two hiking the ridges. The vast majority of people then backtrack to Nugget Creek/Kotsina Rd.

Getting Started

Pick up supplies in Copper Center and stop at the park headquarters to fill out a backcountry trip itinerary and obtain your US Geological Survey quadrangle maps (Valdez C-1 and McCarthy C-8). Then make arrangements to be dropped off from Glennallen or Chitina and picked up at Nugget Creek/Kotsina Rd, 14.5 miles east of Chitina, through Backcountry Connection (☎ 822-5292 in Glennallen) on its daily run to McCarthy. One-way fare from Glennallen to McCarthy is $49. See the McCarthy section of the Southcentral chapter for details. It's possible to hitch to the trailheads and then on to McCarthy as well.

This trip is affordable and easy to arrange, but you still must be well prepared; it could take several days for help to reach you if you should have a mishap. Bears may be present anywhere, and stream fording must be attempted with extreme caution. Pack extra food, good waterproof clothing and woolens, as the weather can change quickly.

Information

In advance of your trip, contact the headquarters of the Wrangell-St Elias National

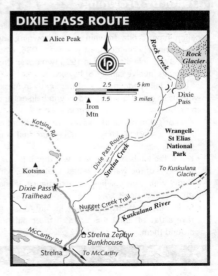

DIXIE PASS ROUTE

Park (☎ 907-822-5234, www.nps.gov/wrst/), PO Box 439, Copper Center, AK 99573. In Anchorage, contact the Alaska Public Lands Information Center (☎ 271-2737), 605 W 4th Ave, Suite 105, Anchorage, AK 99501-2231, for trail information.

section	miles
McCarthy Rd to trailhead	3.8
trailhead to Strelna Creek	3.0
Strelna Creek to Dixie Pass	8.5

Paddling

Blue-Water Paddling

'Blue water,' in Alaska, refers to the coastal areas of the state, which are characterized by extreme tidal fluctuations, cold water and the possibility of high winds and waves. Throughout Southeast and Southcentral Alaska, the open canoe gives way to the kayak, and blue-water paddling is the means of escape into the beauty of the coastal wilderness.

Don't confuse white-water kayaking with ocean touring. River running, wearing helmets and wet suits, in light, streamlined kayaks and executing Eskimo rolls has nothing to do with paddling coastal Alaska in ocean-touring kayaks. Every year, hundreds of backpackers with canoeing experience arrive in the North Country and undertake their first blue-water kayak trip in such protected areas as Muir Inlet in Glacier Bay National Park or Tracy Arm Fjord, south of Juneau.

Tidal fluctuations are the main concern in blue water areas. Paddlers should always pull their boats above the high-tide mark and secure them by tying a line to a rock or tree. A tide book for the area should be in the same pouch as the topographic map – paddlers schedule days around the changing tides, traveling with the tidal current or during slack tide for easy paddling. Check with local rangers for the narrow inlets or straits where riptides or whirlpools might form, and always plan to paddle these areas during slack tides.

Cold coastal water, rarely above 45°F in the summer, makes capsizing more than unpleasant. Even with a life jacket, survival

Death by Drowning

Planning to go canoeing, kayaking or rafting while in Alaska? Then be forewarned: Alaska leads the nation in per-capita drownings. The drowning rate for boaters in the 49th state is 10 times the national average. The deadliest year was 1986, when 53 people drowned in boating mishaps. But in 1992, 32 people died, and in 1998 two dozen drowned in the first half of the summer alone. Most drownings involve canoes or kayaks.

Don't take paddling adventures lightly in Alaska. If you flip, you can rarely swim to shore. Arctic water is so cold it quickly renders you helpless and then kills you with hypothermia. Here are some commonsense rules to boating in Alaska:

- Do not get into a canoe, kayak or raft without a good flotation life jacket. Moving, frigid water is always a shock. A life jacket will ensure that your head and mouth are high enough to be free of water.
- Know the limits of your boat, whether it is a white-water kayak, a lake canoe or a raft, and the demands of the water, whether a calm lake, white water or a tidal bay.
- Know your own abilities and experience. If the paddle is too hard, hire a qualified outfitter to guide you or don't go.
- In difficult situations, don't be reluctant to stay put or get out and walk. If the seas are too rough, take a day off until they calm. If the rapids are too nasty for your taste, portage your canoe around them.

time in the water is less than two hours; without one, the time is considerably less. Plan your trip to run parallel with the shoreline and arrange your schedule so you can sit out rough weather without missing your pickup date. If you do flip, stay with the boat and attempt to right it and crawl back in. Trying to swim to shore in Arctic water is risky at best.

Give a wide berth to marine mammals such as sea lions, seals and especially any whales. Glacial ice should also be treated with respect. Don't get closer than a half mile to a glacier face, as icebergs can calve suddenly and create a series of unmanageable waves and swells. Never try to climb onto floating icebergs. They are extremely unstable and can roll without warning.

Framed backpacks are almost useless in kayaks; gear is better stowed in duffel bags or small day packs. Carry a large supply of assorted plastic bags, including several garbage bags. All gear, especially sleeping bags and clothing, should be stowed in plastic bags, as water tends to seep in even when you seal yourself in with a cockpit skirt. For getting in and out of kayaks and pulling them across muddy tidal flats, over-the-calf rubber boots, so-called Southeast sneakers, are the best footwear to have. You might also want to invest in a pair of felt liners to help keep your toes warm. For any bluewater paddling include an extra paddle, a large sponge for bailing the boat, sunglasses and sunscreen, extra lines and a repair kit of duct tape and a tube of silicon sealant for fiberglass cracks.

White-Water Paddling

Throughout Alaska's history, rivers have been the traditional travel routes through the rugged terrain. Many rivers can be paddled in canoes; others, due to extensive white water, are better handled in rafts or kayaks. If access is available by road, hardshell canoes and kayaks can be used. If not, you might have to arrange for a folding boat, such as a Klepper kayak, or an inflatable canoe or raft. Or you can pay for an additional bush flight so a hard-shell canoe can be carried in on the floats.

Alaska's rivers vary from one end of the state to the other, but you will find they share characteristics not found on many rivers in the Lower 48. Water levels tend to change rapidly in Alaska. Due to temperature changes, rainfall and other factors, a river's depth and character can change noticeably even within a day. Many rivers are heavily braided and boulder-strewn and require a careful eye in picking out the right channel to avoid spending most of the day pulling your boat off gravel. And count on there being cold water, especially in any glacial-fed river, where the temperatures will be in the mid-30s (F). You can survive flipping your canoe in an Alaskan river, but you'll definitely want a plan of action in case you ever do.

North Slope rivers in the Arctic tend to be extremely braided, swift and free-flowing by mid-June. They remain high and silty for several weeks after that, but by mid-July even the sea ice is open enough to permit paddling in coastal lagoons.

Rivers flowing from the south slope of the Brooks Range are moving by early June and have good water levels through mid-August, and rivers in Fairbanks and Interior areas can usually be run from late May to mid-September. Farther south, around Anchorage and the Southcentral region, the paddling season lasts even longer – from May to September.

Much of the equipment for canoeists is the same as it is for blue water paddlers. You want all gear in dry storage bags, especially extra clothing, sleeping bag and tent. Tie everything into the canoe; you never know when a whirlpool or a series of standing waves will be encountered. Wear a life jacket at all times. Many paddlers stock their life jacket with insect repellent, waterproof matches and other survival gear in case they flip and get separated from their boat.

Always make a float plan before you depart and leave it with either the bush pilot who flies you in or the nearest BLM or USFS office. Research the river you want to run and make sure you can handle whatever class of water it's rated. Descriptions of paddling conditions follow:

Class I – easy

The river ranges from flat water to occasional series of mild rapids.

Class II – medium

The river has frequent stretches of rapids with waves up to 3 feet high and easy chutes, ledges and falls. The best route is easy to identify, and the entire river can be run in open canoes.

Class III – difficult

The river features numerous rapids with high, irregular waves and difficult chutes and falls that often require scouting. These river are for experienced paddlers who either use kayaks and rafts or have a spray cover for their canoe.

Class IV – very difficult

Rivers with long stretches of irregular waves, powerful eddies and even constricted canyons. Scouting is mandatory, and rescues can be difficult in many places. Suitable in rafts or whitewater kayaks with paddlers equipped with helmets.

Class V – extremely difficult

Rivers with continuous violent rapids, powerful rollers and high, unavoidable waves and haystacks. These rivers are only for white-water kayaks and paddlers who are proficient in the Eskimo roll.

Class VI – highest level of difficulty

These rivers are rarely run except by very experienced kayakers under ideal conditions.

MISTY FJORDS NATIONAL MONUMENT

The Misty Fjords National Monument, which encompasses 3594 sq miles of wilderness, lies between two impressive fjords – Behm Canal, 117 miles long, and Portland Canal, 72 miles long. The two natural canals give the preserve its extraordinarily deep and long fjords with sheer granite walls that rise thousands of feet out of the water. Misty Fjords is named after the rainy weather that seems to hover over it much of the year; the annual rainfall is 14 feet.

But don't let the rain put you off. Misty Fjords is an incredible place to spend a few days paddling. Lush forests, dramatic waterfalls plunging out of granite walls and diverse wildlife make the monument a kayaker's delight.

The destinations for many kayakers are the smaller but equally impressive fjords of Walker Cove and Punchbowl Cove in Rud-

yerd Bay, off Behm Canal. Dense spruce-hemlock rain forest is the most common vegetation throughout the monument, and sea lions, harbor seals, killer whales, brown and black bears, mountain goats, moose and bald eagles can all be seen there.

Ketchikan is the departure point for most trips into Misty Fjords. Several tour boats run day trips into the area, and there are the usual expensive sightseeing flights on small bush planes. Kayakers can either paddle out of the city (a seven- to 12-day trip, for experienced paddlers only) or have one of the tour boats drop you off deep in Behm Canal near Rudyerd Bay and protected water.

Those contemplating paddling all the way from Ketchikan should remember that the currents around Point Alava and Alava Bay are strong and tricky, often flowing in unusual patterns.

Rounding the point into Behm Canal should be done at slack tide, which means leaving the city at high tide. The 3- to 4-mile crossing of Behm Canal should also be done with caution, as northerly winds can create choppy conditions.

The Misty Fjords National Monument, which is administered by the US Forest Service, has 15 cabins ($25 to $45, reservations) and 15 miles of trails. Two of the cabins, at Alava Bay and Winstanley Island, are right on Behm Canal and allow kayakers to end a day of paddling at the doorstep of a cabin. Many of the others are a short hike inland.

Getting Started

Alaska Cruises, a Ketchikan tour company, offers a kayaker drop-off service to Misty Fjords, including a variety of boat and plane trips into the monument. During the summer, the company will drop you off and pick you up at the entrance of Rudyerd Bay, one of the most scenic areas, daily for $200 per person. This allows inexperienced paddlers to avoid much of the open water of Behm Canal and to experience only the protected and spectacular areas.

To rent a kayak, contact Southern Exposure Sea Kayaking. This guiding company will rent a double fiberglass kayak for $50

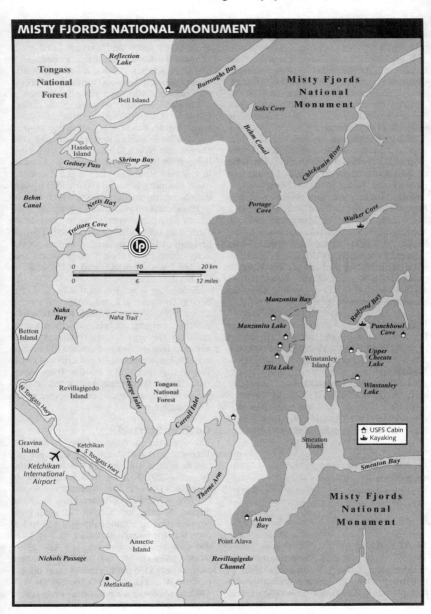

MISTY FJORDS NATIONAL MONUMENT

Tongass
National
Forest

Reflection
Lake

Burroughs Bay

Misty Fjords
National
Monument

Bell Island

Saks Cove

Behm Canal

Chickamin River

Hassler
Island

Shrimp Bay

Gedney Pass

Behm
Canal

Neets Bay

Portage
Cove

Walker Cove

Traitors Cove

0   10   20 km
0   6   12 miles

Naha
Bay

Naha Trail

Manzanita Bay

Rudyerd Bay

Punchbowl
Cove

Betton
Island

Manzanita Lake

Revillagigedo
Island

George Inlet

Tongass
National
Forest

Ella Lake

Winstanley
Island

Upper
Checats
Lake

Winstanley
Lake

N Tongass Hwy

Carroll Inlet

USFS Cabin
Kayaking

Gravina
Island

Ketchikan

S Tongass Hwy

Smeaton
Island

Ketchikan
International
Airport

Thorne Arm

Smeaton Bay

Annette
Island

Alava
Bay

Point Alava

Misty Fjords
National
Monument

Nichols Passage

Revillagigedo
Channel

Metlakatla

per day and a single for $40 per day, for one to five days. Rent it six or more days and the rate drops.

If possible, plan ahead and reserve your kayaks before the busy summer season. Contact Southeast Exposure (☎ 907-225-8829), PO Box 9143, Ketchikan, AK 99901, and Alaska Cruises (☎ 907-225-6044, 800-228-1905), PO Box 7815, Ketchikan, AK 99901, for reservations .

You cannot do this trip without good rain gear or a backpacker's stove, as wood in the monument is often too wet for campfires. Be prepared for extended periods of rain and have all gear sealed in plastic bags.

Either order your maps ahead of time or hope that the sections you want are in stock at the Tongass Trading Company, 203 Dock St in Ketchikan. Then, take the maps to the Southeast Alaska Visitor Center, at 50 Main St, and have somebody point out the camping spots in the area where you are going to paddle. Since much of the monument is comprised of steep fjords, good campsites are scarce in many areas.

Information

For information on the monument, contact the Southeast Alaska Visitor Center (☎ 907-228-6214), 50 Main St, Ketchikan, AK 99901. Information can also be obtained through the USFS website (www.fs.fed.us/recreation/states/ak.html). Rent cabins in advance through the National Recreation Reservation Center (☎ 877-444-6777, 515-885-3639 for overseas, www.reserveusa.com).

section	miles
Ketchikan to Thorne Arm	13.0
Thorne Arm to Point Alava	9.0
Point Alava to Winstanley Island	21.0
Winstanley Island to Rudyerd Bay	9.0
Rudyerd Bay to Walker Cove	10.0

TRACY ARM

Tracy Arm, like Glacier Bay, is a fjord in the Southeast that features tidewater glaciers and steep 2000-foot granite walls that rise straight out of the water. This 30-mile arm

was an ideal choice for novice kayakers, as calm water is the norm here due to the protection the steep and narrow fjord walls provide. However, the arm has become a major attraction for tour ships and other motorized boats, detracting from the wilderness experience. If you have more experience as a kayaker, consider exploring the other fjords that adjoin Tracy Arm at Holkham Bay. Just to the south, is Endicott Arm, another 30-mile fjord that was carved by the Dawes and North Dawes Glaciers. The icebergs from these glaciers, some as large as three-story buildings, often make it into the main shipping lanes of Stephens Passage, delighting travelers on the state ferries.

Endicott Arm also has considerably more places to pitch a tent at night than Tracy Arm. The only other camping spots in the first half of Tracy Arm are two valleys almost across from each other, 8 miles north along the fjord, and a small island at the head of the fjord.

Extending from Endicott Arm is Fords Terror. This narrow water chasm was named after a US sailor who, in 1889, found himself battling surging rapids, whirlpools and grinding icebergs for six terrifying hours when he tried to row out against the incoming tide. Endicott Arm, Tracy Arm and Fords Terror together make up the Tracy Arm-Fords Terror Wilderness Area, a 992-sq-mile preserve where you can easily spend seven days paddling.

Getting Started

The departure point for Tracy Arm-Fords Terror Wilderness Area is Juneau. Kayaks can be rented from Juneau Outdoor Center (☎ 586-8220), located in a warehouse in Douglas Harbor, or Adventure Sports (☎ 789-5696), 8757 Glacier Hwy, near the airport. Rentals are $40/50 a single/double per day, plus an additional fee of $10 to $20 each way for transportation of the kayaks to the tour boats downtown. Try Adventure Bound Alaska (☎ 800-228-3875), which charges only $135 per person for drop-off and pickup. Wilderness Swift Charters (☎ 463-4942, tongass@alaska.net) offers drop-offs at

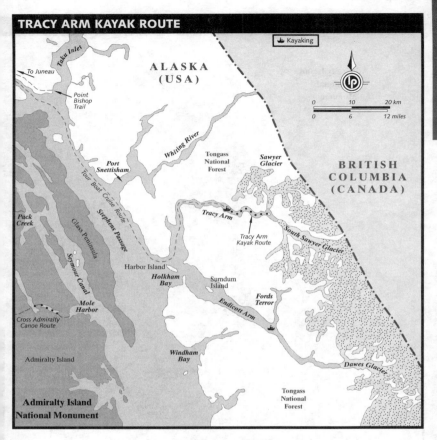

the entrance of Endicott Arm for $100. Add another $100 if you want to be picked up later. This makes the trip considerably easier, as it is a two- or three-day paddle in open water to either Endicott or Tracy Arm.

It is a pleasant two- to three-day paddle from one end of the arm to the other. Most kayakers camp on Harbor Island, near the entrance of Tracy and Endicott Arms, for at least one night, even though level ground for a tent is difficult to find.

Purchase topographic maps from Foggy Mountain Shop, 134 N Franklin St in Juneau,

and then head over to the USFS Information Center in Centennial Hall at 101 Egan Drive to locate campsites inside the arms. Also get a tide book, available in town, and plan your paddle with the tides for an easier trip.

Information

Tracy Arm Wilderness Area is managed by the USFS. For additional information contact Forest Service Information Center (☎ 907-586-8751), Juneau Centennial Hall, 101 Egan Dr, Juneau, AK 99801, or the USFS website (www.fs.fed.us/recreation/states.ak.html).

CROSS ADMIRALTY CANOE ROUTE

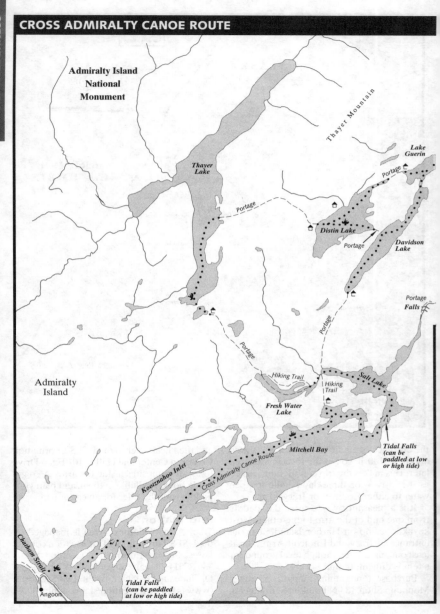

Admiralty Island
National
Monument

Thayer Mountain

Lake Guerin

Thayer Lake

Portage

Portage

Distin Lake

Davidson Lake

Portage

Portage
Falls

Portage

Portage

Admiralty Island

Hiking Trail

Hiking Trail

Salt Lake

Fresh Water Lake

Mitchell Bay

Kootznahoo Inlet

Cross Admiralty Canoe Route

Tidal Falls
(can be paddled
at low or high tide)

Chatham Strait

Angoon

Tidal Falls
(can be paddled
at low or high tide)

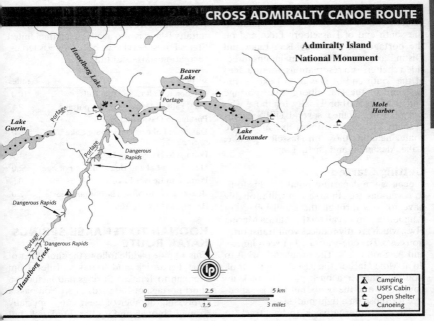

CROSS ADMIRALTY CANOE ROUTE

Admiralty Island
National Monument

Hasselborg Lake

Beaver Lake

Portage

Lake Guerin

Portage

Portage

Dangerous Rapids

Lake Alexander

Mole Harbor

Dangerous Rapids

Portage

Dangerous Rapids

Hasselborg Creek

	Camping
	USFS Cabin
	Open Shelter
	Canoeing

0   2.5   5 km
0   1.5   3 miles

CROSS ADMIRALTY ISLAND CANOE ROUTE

Admiralty Island National Monument, about 50 miles southwest of Juneau, is the site of one of the few canoe routes in the Southeast. This preserve is a fortress of dense coastal forest, ragged peaks, and brown bears that outnumber anything else on the island, including humans. The island also supports one of the largest bald-eagle nesting areas, and Sitka black-tailed deer can be seen throughout the monument.

The Cross Admiralty canoe route is a 32-mile paddle that spans the center of the island from the village of Angoon to Mole Harbor. Although the majority of the route consists of calm lakes connected by streams and portages, the 10-mile paddle from Angoon to Mitchell Bay is subject to strong tides that challenge even experienced paddlers.

Avoid Kootznahoo Inlet, as its tidal currents are extremely difficult to negotiate;

instead, paddle through the maze of islands south of it. Leave Angoon at low tide, just before slack tide, so the water will push you into Mitchell Bay. Keep a watchful eye out for tidal falls and whirlpools. When paddling to Angoon, leave Salt Lake four hours before the slack tide, after high tide.

From the west end of Salt Lake there is a 3.5-mile portage to Davidson Lake, which is connected to Lake Guerin by a navigable stream. Between Lake Guerin and Hasselborg Lake is a 1.7-mile portage followed by a half-mile portage on the east side of Hasselborg Lake to Beaver Lake.

Canoeists can paddle from Beaver Lake to the east end of Lake Alexander, where they can take a 2.5-mile trail to Mole Harbor. This is the route most commonly followed by canoeists, but there are numerous trails in the area, including portages leading to Thayer Lake and a route along Hasselborg Creek that connects Salt Lake with Hasselborg Lake.

Good campsites are at Tidal Falls on the eastern end of Salt Lake, on the islands at the south end of Hasselborg Lake and on the portage between Davidson Lake and Distin Lake. The USFS also maintains three-sided shelters (no reservations or rental fee) at the south end of Davidson Lake, at the east end of the Hasselborg Lake portage and at Mole Harbor. Finally, for those who can plan in advance, several USFS cabins ($25 to $45, reservations) are along the route, including those on Hasselborg Lake, Lake Alexander and Distin Lake.

Getting Started

Juneau is the departure point for this four- to seven-day trip, though you will probably have to pass through the small village of Angoon, a port of call on the Alaska Marine Hwy, which greatly reduces your transportation costs. The one-way fare between Juneau and Angoon is $24. The problem is what to do at Mole Harbor, the east end of the trail. You can charter a bush plane to pick up your party and the boats, but that is expensive for those on a tight budget.

The best alternative is to backtrack to Angoon and return to Juneau on the ferry, which charges only $9 for canoes or kayaks. This means setting up your trip around the ferry schedule, but the savings are enormous.

Renting a boat for this trip is an even bigger challenge. In Juneau, you can rent a kayak at Juneau Outdoor Center (☎ 586-8220) or Adventure Sports (☎ 789-5696), but it's a hassle to portage across the trails.

The preferred boat is a canoe. In Angoon, Favorite Bay Inn (☎ 788-3123) has canoes for rent for $50 a day, less if you rent for six days or more. But that means paddling a return trip to the small village. Purchase your topographic maps in Juneau and then take them to the USFS information center in Centennial Hall to have someone point out where strong tidal currents exist.

Information

This is a USFS-maintained preserve, and trip information or a Cross Admiralty Island Canoe map ($3) can be obtained from the US Forest Service Information Center (☎ 907-586-8751), Centennial Hall, 101 Egan Dr, Juneau, AK 99801). Information on Admiralty Island is also available on the United States Forest Service website (www.fs.fed.us/recreation/states.ak.html).

section	miles
Angoon to Salt Lake Tidal Falls	10.0
Tidal Falls to Davidson Lake portage	2.5
Portage to Davidson Lake	3.5
Davidson Lake to Hasselborg Lake portage	6.0
Portage to Hasselborg Lake	1.7
Hasselborg Lake to Beaver Lake portage	2.0
Portage to Beaver Lake	0.5
Beaver Lake to Mole Harbor portage	3.0
Portage to Mole Harbor	2.5

HOONAH TO TENAKEE SPRINGS KAYAK ROUTE

This 40-mile paddle follows the shorelines of Port Frederick and Tenakee Inlet from Hoonah to Tenakee Springs and includes a short portage of 100 yards or so. You pass a depressing number of clear cuts, especially around Hoonah and up Port Frederick, but there are few other signs of civilization along the route once you are beyond the two villages.

The area is part of the Tongass National Forest and consists of rugged and densely forested terrain populated by brown bears, which are often seen feeding along the shoreline.

It is important to carry a tide book and to reach the portage at high tide. Boot-sucking mud will be encountered along the portage, but take heart, it is just a short walk over a low ridge to the next inlet. Highlights of the trip include the scenic south shore of Tenakee Inlet, with its many bays and coves. The village of Tenakee Springs has a public bathhouse around its natural hot springs that will soothe any sore muscles resulting from the paddle.

Getting Started

This adventure is within the grasp of many backpackers on a budget, as ferry service connects both Hoonah and Tenakee Springs to Juneau. The one-way fare from Juneau to Hoonah is $20 (to Tenakee Springs $22), with a $9 charge for kayaks.

The best way to start the paddle is from Hoonah, in order to end the trip in Tenakee Springs, a charming village. However, this has to be planned carefully, as there is only one ferry every three to five days to Tenakee Springs. Kayaks ($40/50 a single/double per day) can be rented in Juneau from Adventure Sports (☎ 789-5696) or Juneau Outdoor Center (☎ 586-8220). For an additional fee, the staff at either shop will transport the boat to the Auke Bay Ferry Terminal.

Information
Contact the Forest Service Information Center (☎ 907-586-8751), Centennial Hall, 101 Egan Dr, Juneau, AK 99801, or the USFS office in the Hoonah (☎ 907-945-3631), PO Box 135, Hoonah, AK 99829-0135, for more information about the route or the surrounding area.

GLACIER BAY NATIONAL PARK – MUIR INLET
More than anything else, Glacier Bay is a kayaker's paradise. When you combine the stunning alpine scenery of the Fairweather Mountains with more than a dozen glaciers and the marine wildlife, you can understand the attraction for blue-water paddlers, despite the high costs of getting there. People with some extra change in their pocket and a few spare days can put together a paddle past three tidewater glaciers in Muir Inlet, including the one that John Muir 'discovered' in his famous trip to the area.

By utilizing the tour-boat service, you can be dropped off at Sebree Island, near the entrance of the inlet, and avoid the long paddle from Bartlett Cove, the park headquarters. Many kayakers then travel the length of the inlet to McBride, Riggs and Muir Glacier at the north end before returning to Sebree Island for a pickup. Such a trip would require five to six days of paddling. Those with more time but less money can book just a drop-off and then paddle back to Bartlett Cove, an eight- to 10-day trip. A roundtrip paddle out of Bartlett Cove to the

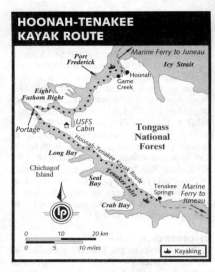

HOONAH-TENAKEE KAYAK ROUTE

Marine Ferry to Juneau

Port Frederick

Icy Strait

Hoonah
Game Creek

Eight Fathom Bight

USFS Cabin

Portage

Tongass National Forest

Hoonah-Tenakee Kayak Route

Long Bay

Chichagof Island

Seal Bay

Tenakee Inlet

Tenakee Springs

Marine Ferry to Juneau

Crab Bay

0   10   20 km
0   5   10 miles

Kayaking

glaciers of Muir Inlet is usually a two-week adventure for most people.

Getting Started
Turn to the Glacier Bay section in the Southeast chapter for general information about Glacier Bay National Park and Preserve. Once at Bartlett Cove, backpackers can stay in the free campground while preparing for their excursion up the bay. Call at the visitor center to obtain a backcountry permit and purchase the proper topographic maps.

It's best to arrange both kayak rental and tour boat passage in advance. Glacier Bay Sea Kayaks Kayaks (☎ 697-2257, kayakak@ seaknet.alaska.edu, www.he.net/~kayakak), PO Box 26, Gustavus, AK 99826, will rent two-person kayaks for $50 a day or $40 a day for a rental five days or longer. The company also has singles for $40 a day or $30 for more than five days. The price includes paddles, life vests, spray covers and loading the kayaks on the tour boat. The *Spirit of Adventure*, which departs daily at 7:30 am, will provide drop-off and pickup near Mt Wright at the mouth of Muir Inlet from mid-May to late September. One-way drop-offs are $90 per person, roundtrip $180. A multidrop pass, which allows you to explore more than one area, is an additional $24.

You must pack waterproof clothing (pants, parka) and a camp stove. Stock up on supplies in Juneau to avoid having to purchase anything in Gustavus. To reserve a kayak, and you almost have to in July and August, contact Glacier Bay Sea Kayaks (☎ 907-697-2257, kayakak@seaknet.alaska.edu), PO Box 26, Gustavus, AK 99826.

The alternative is to rent a kayak in Juneau (see Juneau in Southeast chapter) and then use either Auk Nu Tours (☎ 789-5701, 800-820-2628) or Kayak Express (☎ 780-4591) for transportation to Gustavus. Auk Nu is considerably cheaper, but it would still cost $135 roundtrip to get you and your boat over to the Gustavus Dock.

Information

In Juneau, contact the Forest Service Information Center (☎ 586-8751), Centennial Hall, 101 Egan Dr, Juneau, AK 99801. For information before you depart, contact Glacier Bay National Park (☎ 907-697-2230), PO Box 140, Gustavus, AK 99826-0140.

section	miles
Mt Wright to Wachusett Inlet	16.0
Wachusett Inlet to Riggs Glacier	9.0
Riggs Glacier to Muir Glacier	8.0
Muir Glacier to Mt Wright	33.0

SWANSON RIVER & SWAN LAKE

In the northern lowlands of the Kenai National Wildlife Refuge, there is a chain of rivers, lakes, streams and portages (of course) that make up the Swanson River and Swan Lake canoe routes. The trips are perfect for novice canoeists, as rough water is rarely a problem and portages do not exceed half a mile on the Swan Lake system or 1 mile in the Swanson River area.

Fishing is good for rainbow trout in many of the lakes, and wildlife is plentiful; a trip on either route could result in sightings of moose, bears, beavers or a variety of waterfowl. Both routes are well marked and maintained, with open shelters along the way and are popular among Anchorage canoeists.

The Swanson River system links more than 40 lakes and 46 miles of river, and a one-way trip is 80 miles, ending at Cook Inlet in Captain Cook State Park. It's a more challenging trip than the Swan Lake paddle, especially when the water is low, but also a more popular one. More than 1,500 paddlers float the river annually because of the numerous moose in the area, the silver salmon run in late summer and the lack of portages.

The easier Swan Lake route connects 30 lakes with forks of the Moose River; the one-way trip is 60 miles. A common four-day trip on Swan Lake begins at the west entrance of the canoe route and ends at Moose River Bridge on the Sterling Hwy.

Getting Started

To reach the Swan Lake or Swanson River canoe routes, travel to Mile 84 of the Sterling Hwy east of Soldotna and turn north on Robinson Lake Rd, just west of Moose River Bridge. Robinson Lake Rd turns into Swanson River Rd and leads to Swan Lake Rd 17 miles north from the Sterling Hwy. East on Swan Lake Rd are the entrances to both canoe systems, with the Swanson River route beginning at the very end of the road. The west entrance for Swan Lake is at Canoe Lake and the east is another 6 miles beyond at Portage Lake; both are well marked.

During the summer, the Great Alaska Fish Camp, a lodge at Mile 81.7 of the Sterling Hwy where it crosses the Moose River, rents out canoes and runs a shuttle bus service to the head of Swan Lake canoe route. You conveniently end up back at Moose River Bridge and the camp to eliminate any need for a pickup. To rent a canoe for three days costs $295, which includes shuttle transportation to the western entrance or the eastern entrance of the trail. The outfitter also has a four-day package that includes canoe, gear storage, vehicle parking, shuttle transportation and one night's accommodations at the lodge for $195 per person. Contact the Great Alaska Fish Camp (☎ 907-262-4515, 800-544-2261 in the winter, www.greatalaska.com), PO Box 218, Sterling, AK 99672-9702, for information.

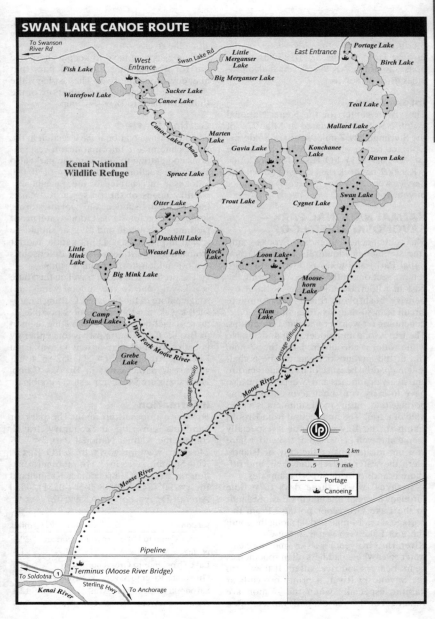

SWAN LAKE CANOE ROUTE

To Swanson River Rd

Swan Lake Rd

Little Merganser Lake

East Entrance

Portage Lake

Birch Lake

West Entrance

Fish Lake

Sucker Lake

Big Merganser Lake

Waterfowl Lake

Canoe Lake

Teal Lake

Marten Lake

Mallard Lake

Canoe Lakes Chain

Gavia Lake

Konchanee Lake

Kenai National Wildlife Refuge

Spruce Lake

Raven Lake

Swan Lake

Trout Lake

Cygnet Lake

Otter Lake

Duckbill Lake

Rock Lake

Loon Lake

Little Mink Lake

Weasel Lake

Moose-horn Lake

Big Mink Lake

Camp Island Lake

West Fork Moose River

Clam Lake

Grebe Lake

(passage difficult)

(passage difficult)

Moose River

Moose River

N

0   1   2 km
0   .5   1 mile

Pipeline

- - - - Portage
⚓ Canoeing

Terminus (Moose River Bridge)

To Soldotna 1

Sterling Hwy   To Anchorage

Kenai River

You can also rent canoes in Soldotna from the Sports Den (☎ 262-7491), 44176 Sterling Hwy, Soldotna, AK 99669, or the Fishing Hole (☎ 262-2290), 139 B Warehouse, Soldotna, AK 99669, which also provides drop-off service.

Information

The visitor center for the Kenai National Wildlife Refuge is situated at Mile 97.9 of the Sterling Hwy, 2 miles south of Soldotna. Contact Kenai National Wildlife Refuge (☎ 907-262-7021), PO Box 2139, Soldotna, AK 99669, or check the US Fish and Wildlife Service website (www.r7.fws.gov/) in advance of your trip.

KATMAI NATIONAL PARK – SAVONOSKI RIVER LOOP

This route begins and ends at Brooks Camp (the summer headquarters of Katmai National Park) and takes paddlers into more remote sections of the preserve, offering the best in wilderness adventures without expensive bush-plane travel. The complete circuit is an 80-mile, six- to eight-day paddle, depending on weather and wind conditions. The trip is long and moderately difficult. No white water is encountered, but the 12-mile run of the Savonoski River can be a challenging paddle because of its braided nature and many deadheads and sweepers. You also have to carry your boat across a mile-long portage that, during most summers, is a mud hole of a trail. The first section from Brooks Camp to the Bay of Islands is especially scenic and well protected at the end, where you dip in and out of the Bay of Islands. Here the water is deep and clear, and offshore islands provide superb campsites.

It takes two to three days to paddle through Naknek Lake and the Bay of Islands to the Lake Grosvenor portage. From this portage, it is a 14-mile paddle along the south shore of Lake Grosvenor to the Grosvenor River. The Grosvenor is a slow-moving clearwater river where you often spot moose, bears, beavers and river otters. It flows into the Savonoski River, a prime brown-bear habitat, especially when the salmon are running. For this reason, park rangers often recommend paddling the 12 miles of the Savonoski in a single day and not camping along the river.

Canoeists also have to keep a sharp eye out for obstructions and sand bars that may develop in the river. The last leg is the 20-mile paddle along the south shore of the Iliuk Arm back to Brooks Camp.

Getting Started

See the Katmai National Park section in the Bush chapter for information on reservations and getting to and from the park; also check the section on the Valley of 10,000 Smokes in this chapter for the special backcountry needs of the preserve. Katmai is famous for its sudden and violent storms, some lasting for days. Good waterproof clothing is essential, and all gear should be sealed in plastic bags. Don't paddle too far from shore, as it leaves you defenseless against sudden storms or high winds.

The preferred mode of travel on this route is a kayak, due to the sudden winds and rough nature of the big lakes. Getting a hardshell kayak into the park is now possible, as there is a jet-boat service from King Salmon to Brooks Camp, but most visitors either fly in with a folding kayak or rent a kayak from Lifetime Adventures (☎ 800-952-8624, adventures@matnet.com) in Brooks Camp. Hard shells are $40/45 for a single/double.

Information

For more information about the park or handouts covering backcountry travel, contact the Katmai National Park (☎ 907-246-3305, www.nps.gov/katm/), PO Box 7, King Salmon, AK 99613. For more information on Brooks Camp contact Katmailand Inc (☎ 907-243-5448, 800-544-0551), 4550 Aircraft Dr, Anchorage, AK 99502.

section	miles
Brooks Camp to Lake Grosvenor portage	30.0
portage	1.0
Lake Grosvenor to Grosvenor River	14.0
Grosvenor River to Savonoski River	3.0
Savonoski River to Iliuk Arm	12.0
Along Iliuk Arm to Brooks Camp	20.0

SAVONOSKI RIVER LOOP

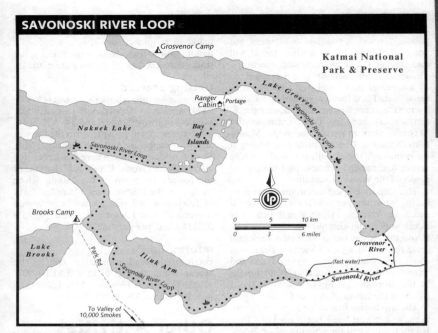

Katmai National
Park & Preserve

Grosvenor Camp

Lake Grosvenor

Ranger
Cabin   Portage

Savonoski River Loop

Naknek Lake

Bay
of
Islands

Savonoski River Loop

Brooks Camp

Lake
Brooks

Iliuk Arm

Savonoski River Loop

Grosvenor
River

(fast water)

Savonoski River

To Valley of
10,000 Smokes

0   5   10 km
0   3   6 miles

CHENA RIVER

The Chena River is one of the finest rivers for canoeing in the Fairbanks area, and a longtime favorite among local residents. It flows through a landscape of rolling forested hills with access to alpine tundra above 2800 feet. The river features no white water and paddlers only have to watch out for the occasional sweeper or logjam.

Wildlife in the area includes brown bears, moose, red foxes, beavers and river otters, and the fishing is excellent for grayling and northern pike. With the Interior's long, hot summer days, this trip can be an outstanding wilderness adventure.

Getting Started

Chena Hot Springs Rd provides access to the river at Mile 27.9 east of Fairbanks, Mile 28.6, Mile 29.4, Mile 33.9 at Four Mile Creek and Mile 39.6 at North Fork Chena River, where there is a state campground (20 sites, $6 fee). From Mile 39.6 of Chena Hot Springs Rd, the paddle along the river to Fairbanks is a 70-mile trip that can be done comfortably in four to five days.

You can rent canoes from 7 Bridges Boats & Bikes (☎ 479-0751). Boats cost $35 a day, but you will probably get a better deal for a weeklong rental. More importantly, transportation out along Chena Hot Springs Rd can be provided for a $1.50 a mile.

The other alternative is to rent a used car in Fairbanks (see the Getting Around section in the Fairbanks chapter), drop off the canoe, return the car to Fairbanks and hitchhike back to the trailhead. See the Chena Hot Springs Road map in the Fairbanks chapter.

Information

Much of the river lies in the Chena River State Recreation Area, which is administered by the Alaska Division of State Parks. Contact the Fairbanks Division of Parks office for more information (☎ 907-451-2695), 3700 Airport Way, Fairbanks, AK 99709.

BEAVER CREEK

Travelers with lots of time and a yearning to paddle through a roadless wilderness, but not a lot of funds for bush-plane travel, will find Beaver Creek the ultimate adventure. The moderately swift stream, characterized by long clear pools and frequent rapids, is rated Class I in difficulty and can be handled by novice canoeists with previous expedition experience. The BLM manages the 111-mile creek as part of the White Mountains National Recreation Area, where it flows through rolling hills forested in white spruce and paper birch and past the jagged peaks of the White Mountains.

The scenery is spectacular, the chances of seeing another party remote, and you'll catch so much grayling you'll probably never want to eat another one after the trip. If you take a day off at Victoria Creek and scale the 5000-foot high Victoria Peak, you should see wildlife such as moose, bears and mountain sheep. You can also spend a night in the Borealis-Le Fevre Cabin, a BLM cabin on the banks of Beaver Creek.

The trip begins from Mile 57 of the Steese Hwy, where you head north on US Creek Rd for 6 miles and then northwest on Nome Creek Road to the new Ophir Creek Campground (19 sites, $6). From the campground, you can put in at Nome Creek and easily paddle to its confluence with Beaver Creek. Most paddlers then plan on six to nine days to reach Victoria Creek, a 90-mile trip, where gravel bars nearby are used by bush planes to land and pick paddlers up.

From the confluence with Nome Creek to Victoria Creek, the paddle along Beaver Creek is through the White Mountains, where the stunning scenery includes limestone towers, buttes and spires. Large gravel bars provide plenty of places to pitch a tent along the river here, which generally poses few technical difficulties.

A day's paddle beyond Victoria Creek, Beaver Creek spills out of the White Mountains into Yukon Flats National Wildlife Refuge, where it slows down and meanders through a marshy area. Eventually it flows north into the Yukon River, where after two or three days, you'll pass under the Yukon River Bridge on the Dalton Hwy, avoiding another airfare if arrangements have been made to be picked up. This is a 395-mile paddle and a three-week expedition – the stuff great Alaskan adventures are made of.

Getting Started

Rent a canoe through Beaver Sports (☎ 479-2494, www.beaversports.net) in Fairbanks. Steese Highway Stage Line (☎ 520-5610, loki@xyz.net) will provide drop-off for you and your canoe, for $30 per person, at Mile 57 of the Steese Hwy, where US Creek Rd leads down to Nome Creek Rd. The end of the paddle for many is the Yukon River Bridge on the Dalton Hwy, 175 miles north of Fairbanks, and pickup can be arranged through Dalton Highway Express (☎ 452-2031) for $35 per person.

Information

For more detailed information contact the Steese-White District of the BLM (☎ 907-474-2200, www.ak.blm.gov), 1150 University Ave, Fairbanks, AK 99709-3899).

Other Activities

WILDERNESS FISHING

Many people have a 'fish-per-cast' vision of angling in Alaska. They expect every river, stream and lake, no matter how close to the road, to be bountiful, but often go home disappointed when their fishing efforts produce little to brag about. Serious anglers visiting Alaska carefully research the areas to be fished and are equipped with the right gear and tackle. They often pay for guides or book a room at remote camps or lodges where rivers are not 'fished out' by every passing motorist.

If, however, you plan to undertake a few wilderness trips, by all means pack a rod, reel and some tackle. You can purchase a backpacking rod that breaks down into five sections and has a light reel; it takes up less room than soap, shaving cream and a wash rag. In the Southeast and Southcentral regions, backpackers can catch cutthroat trout, rainbow trout and Dolly Varden (a fish similar to the other two). Farther north, especially around Fairbanks, you'll get grayling, with its sail-like dorsal fin, and arctic char; during August, salmon seem to be everywhere.

If angling is just a second thought, load an open-face spinning reel with light line, something in the four to six-pound range, and take along a small selection of spinners and spoons. After you arrive, you can always purchase the lures used locally, but in most wilderness streams, I've rarely had a problem catching fish on Mepps spinners, sizes No 1 to No 3. Other lures that work well are Pixies, Dardevles and Krocodiles.

For fly fishing, a No 5 or No 6 rod with a matching floating line or sinking tip is well suited for Dolly Vardens, rainbows and grayling. For species of salmon, a No 7 or No 8 rod and line are better choices. For ease of travel, rods should break down and be carried in a case.

A nonresident's fishing license costs $50 a year ($15 for residents), or you can purchase a three-day license for $20 or a 14-day one for $30; every bait shop in the state sells them.

The Alaska Department of Fish and Game puts out a variety of material for fishers, including the *Alaska Sport Fishing Guide*. You can obtain the brochure by contacting the Department of Fish & Game (☎ 907-465-4180), PO Box 25526, Juneau, AK 99802-5526. You can also request one through the state website (www.state.ak.us) by clicking on Alaska Fish and Game under Departments.

Perhaps the most comprehensive angler's guide to the state is *Alaska Fishing* by Gunnar Pedersen and Rene Limeres. The authors begin with a detailed look at the different species of Alaskan fish, including the best fishing techniques, and then follow with a review of each region and major river system throughout the state.

Equally good for fly fishing is *Flyfishing Alaska* by Anthony Route. Route writes a fly fishing column for the *Anchorage Daily News* and

does a particularly good job covering the species found in Alaska's rivers, streams and lakes and the tackle and equipment you need to catch them.

For those who want to combine a cabin rental with fishing there is *Fishing Alaska on Dollars a Day* by Christopher and Adela Batin. The guide describes Forest Service cabins that can be rented for $25 to $45 per day, fishing in the immediate area and gateway cities.

Here is a brief synopsis of the most common non-salmon species you find in lakes and streams all summer long.

Rainbow Trout

This is without a doubt the best fighting fish and the most sought after by most anglers. Fishing from shore in lakes is best in late spring and early summer, just after ice breakup, and again in the fall when water temperatures are cooler. During the height of the summer, rainbows move into deeper water in lakes, and you usually need a boat to fish them.

Fish them at dawn and dusk when, on calm days, they can be seen surfacing for insects. Use spinners, size No 1 to No 3, and flashy spoons, but avoid treble hooks (or clip one or two of the hooks on them), as they make releasing fish hard. The workhorse fly is the lake leech, in either purple or olive, fished with a slow retrieve on sinking-tip lines.

Cutthroat Trout

The cutthroat picks up its name from the reddish-orange slash along the inner edge of the fish's lower jaw. Outside Southeast Alaska, most traveling anglers end up casting for resident cutthroats that spend their entire lives in the streams and lakes as opposed to larger anadromous (those migrating upstream to breed) cutthroats that migrate to saltwater where food is more abundant. This trout likes to stay around submerged logs, aquatic vegetation or near other cover and is an aggressive feeder.

In most lakes, you can take them on small spinners, size No 0 up to No 2, but they also will

THE WILDERNESS

hit on larger spoons, especially red-and-white Dardevles. For fly fishing, a floating line with a nine-foot leader and a slowly twitching mosquito-larva fly can be very effective. The best time to fish is early morning and at dusk when light is low and cutthroats are often cruising the shallows for food.

Dolly Varden

One of the most widespread varieties of fish in Alaska, Dolly Varden's aggressive behavior makes them easy to catch. Dolly Varden are often caught near the entrances of streams or along weed beds near shore, making them accessible to backpacking anglers. With spinning gear, use spinners in sizes No 1 and No 2 or small spoons. Fly fishers often use a blue smolt fly on a sinking-tip line and a short leader and use an erratic strip retrieve. Other streamers work as well, and a pinhead muddler and a floating line are often used in shallow rivers or when Dolly Varden are holding in shallow water.

Arctic Char

A closely related cousin to the Dolly Varden, the arctic char is not quite as widespread in Alaska. Often anglers will confuse the two species. Arctic char will be encountered predominantly in the Alaska Peninsula and Bristol Bay areas, on Kodiak Island, in some lakes in the Kenai Peninsula and in the Brooks Range and to the north. Spawning male char turn brilliant red or gold with red or orange spots, while Dolly Varden are just as brightly colored but only on their lower body. For the most part, anglers use the same tackle and techniques for catching both species.

Grayling

There's no mistaking the grayling. Its long dorsal fin allows travelers to identify the fish even if they have never hooked one. Grayling in streams feed at the surface or in mid-water drift and almost exclusively on insects or larvae. In other words, they are a fly fisher's dream. They are extremely receptive to dry flies and rarely are so selective as to choose one pattern over another. Generally small flies (sizes No 16 to No 18) will

produce more rises than larger ones. Even if you have spinning gear, tie on a clear plastic bubble 4 to 6 feet above a dry fly and fish for grayling with that.

BICYCLING

The mountain bike's durable design, knobby tires and suspension are ideal for Alaska. With such a bike you can explore an almost endless number of dirt roads, miner's two-tracks and even some hiking trails that you would never consider with a road bike. By exploring rough 4WD roads, you can escape RVs and see more wildlife.

Always pick your route carefully before heading out. Make sure the length of the route and the ruggedness of the terrain are within your ability and the equipment you are carrying. Stay away from trails and areas that ban mountain bikes. If you choose a route already dedicated to vehicle use, such as an ATV trail, your trip is unlikely to contribute to erosion.

There is much mountain bike activity around Anchorage, with several places to rent bikes (see the Anchorage chapter). One of the more popular trails is the Powerline Pass Trail, an 11-mile roundtrip into the mountains of Chugach State Park. Within the Kenai Peninsula, the Resurrection Pass, Russian River and Johnson Pass Trails in the Chugach National Forest have become popular among off-road cyclists. There are also many two-tracks along Glenn Highway that can be explored on a mountain bike.

If you have the ability to carry equipment on your bike (sleeping bag, food and tent), you can enjoy a variety of overnight trips or longer bicycle tours. The 92-mile Denali Park Road is closed to vehicles, but you can explore it on a mountain bike. Another excellent dirt road for such an adventure is the 135-mile Denali Hwy from Passon to Cantwell. For popular bicycle touring routes, see the Bicycle section of the Getting Around chapter.

For additional information before your trip write to Arctic Bicycle Club (PO Box 140269, Anchorage, AK 99514) or check their website (arcticbike.alaska.net).

ROCK CLIMBING

Rock climbing has been growing in popularity in recent years in Alaska. On almost any summer weekend, you can watch climbers working bolt-protected sport routes just above Seward Hwy along Turnagain Arm. Canyons in nearby Portage are also capturing the attention of rock climbers. Off Byron Glacier, several routes grace a slab of black rock polished smooth by the glacier. Not far from Portage Lake, a short hike leads to the magnificent slate walls of Middle Canyon.

Fairbanks climbers head north of town to the limestone formations known as Grapefruit Rocks or else pack along a tent and sleeping bag for the Granite Tors Trail off the Chena Hot Springs Rd. A 7-mile hike from the trailhead brings them to the tors, a series of 100-foot granite spires in a wilderness setting.

For equipment and more information in Anchorage, contact REI (☎ 272-4565), 1200 Northern Lights Blvd, Anchorage, AK 99503. In Fairbanks, contact Beaver Sports (☎ 479-2494), 3480 College Rd, Fairbanks AK 99709, for equipment.

WILDLIFE WATCHING

The BLM says that, to see wildlife in Alaska, the first thing you have to do is not pack high expectations. Every year visitors arrive thinking they will see herds of wildlife, only to go home with a photo of a squirrel that was raiding their picnic table.

To see a variety of wildlife, you have to leave the roads, travel into the backcountry and learn how to 'watch wildlife.' Here's what the BLM recommends:

• Look for wildlife signs. There's added enjoyment in recognizing animals by their tracks, droppings or vocalizations. To do that, you might want to carry a field guide or two (see the Books section in the Facts for the Visitor chapter).

Wildlife tracks (not drawn to scale)

• Keep your distance. Don't try to get too close with camera in hand. Most wild animals react with alarm when approached by humans on foot or in vehicles. Repeated disturbances may cause animals or birds to leave the area for good. Also learn animal behavior patterns that will tip you off when you are too close. Mammals often raise their heads high with ears pointed in your direction if you are closing in too fast. They might also exhibit signs of skittishness or display aggressive behavior. You are too close to birds if they also seem skittish or raise their heads to watch you. They may preen excessively, give alarm calls, flush repeatedly or even feign a broken wing when threatened by your presence.

• Don't hurry. The more time you take in the backcountry, the greater the opportunity to observe wildlife. Instead of moving camp every day, set up a base camp and do nothing at dawn or dusk but scan areas for wildlife.

• Use proper equipment. You will see more by carrying high-quality binoculars or even a spotting scope. If you're set on photographing wildlife, make sure you have a telephoto lens, tripod and the right film for low-light conditions to deliver those close-up shots.

• Blend in. Wear muted colors, sit quietly and even avoid using scented soaps and perfumes.

Flora & Fauna of Alaska

The main attraction for many visitors to Alaska is the state's abundance of wildlife. From the road, most people see more wildlife in Alaska than they do in a lifetime elsewhere. From the trails, such encounters are often the highlight of an entire trip; you can spot an animal, watch it quietly and marvel at the experience when the creature moves on leisurely.

With a relatively small human population that's concentrated in a handful of cities, Alaska is one of the few places in the USA where entire ecosystems are still intact and ancient migratory routes uninterrupted. Some species that are threatened or endangered elsewhere – browns bears and bald eagles, to name but two – are thriving in the 49th state. More caribou live in Alaska (900,000) than people (606,000), and birds are in no short supply either. More than 400 species have been spotted in the state, with 20 million shorebirds and waterfowl migrating through the Copper River Delta near Cordova every spring. Pods of humpback whales spend summers in the Icy Straits of Southeast Alaska. Come August, streams and rivers are choking with millions of spawning salmon.

While the numbers are impressive, it's important to remember that Alaska's wildlife is spread over an area the size of a small continent. Some species, particularly large land mammals, need a vast territory to survive the harsh climactic conditions and short growing season of their food supply. Many species migrate as the seasons change, and others are concentrated in specific locations across the state.

If the main intent of your trip to Alaska is to see as much wildlife as possible, take the time to research particular species in advance of arriving. You'll increase your chances of encountering wild animals if you know the habitats they prefer, the best places to encounter them and the months when they are most active. An excellent resource guide is the Wildlife Notebook Series by the Alaska Department of Fish and Game, which covers the life history, habitat, foods and range for 88 species of mammals, birds and fish. The collection of loose-leaf notebook pages is $10 and can be purchased at any Alaska Public Lands Information Center or ordered in advance from the Alaska Natural History Association (☎ 907-274-8440).

FLORA

The flora of Alaska, like everything in the state, is diverse, changing dramatically from one region to the next. In the coastal regions of Southeast and Southcentral Alaska, mild temperatures in winter and summer and frequent rains produce lush coniferous forests of Sitka spruce (the state tree) and western hemlock. Any opening in the forest is often a bog or an area filled with alder or spiny devil's club, a mildly poisonous plant. The tree line is often between 2000 and 3000 feet, where thick alder takes over before giving way to alpine meadows.

In the Interior, the large area of plains and hills between the Alaska Range and the Brooks Range is dominated by boreal forests of white spruce, cottonwood and paper birch, while on north-facing slopes and in moist lowlands you'll find a stunted forest of scrawny black spruce. Continue traveling north and you'll enter a zone known as taiga, characterized by muskeg, willow thickets and more stunted spruce, before you reach the tundra of the Arctic coastal region.

The Arctic tundra is a bizarre world, a treeless area except for a few small stands on gravel flood plains of rivers. Plant life hugs the ground – even willow trees that only grow 6 inches in height still produce pussy willows. Other plants, including grasses, mosses and a variety of tiny flowers, provide a carpet of life for a short period in July and August despite little precipitation and a harsh climate.

Tundra can make for tough hiking for those who travel this far north in Alaska. Wet and moist tundra sits on top of permanently frozen ground known as permafrost. The tundra thaws in the summer but remains waterlogged because the permafrost prevents drainage. The caribou can navigate these soggy conditions because their dew claws and spreading cleft hooves help support their weight on the soft ground. Hikers are not so lucky.

Trees

There are 33 native species of trees, the fewest of any state in the USA, and only 12 of these are classified as large trees (more than 70 feet in height). Not surprisingly, nine of these species live in the coastal regions of Southeast and Southcentral Alaska.

Sitka Spruce Alaska's state tree, the Sitka spruce *(Picea sitchensis)*, thrives in the coastal regions of Southcentral and Southeast Alaska. The largest species of spruce in the USA, Sitka spruce grows quickly and can reach heights of 225 feet and diameters of 8 feet. The short, sharp needles are dark green on top, silvery blue underneath.

The tree's lumber is strong and lightweight, making it ideal for the construction of aircraft, gliders and boats. It is also a popular tonewood for guitar bodies. Native Alaskans used its roots for basket weaving. Commercially, the Sitka spruce is the most valuable species in Alaska.

Western Hemlock Occupying the same regions as the Sitka spruce is the western hemlock *(Tsuga heterophylla)*. In Southeast Alaska, the western hemlock makes up more than 70 percent of the trees in coastal spruce/hemlock forests. Hemlocks can grow to 190 feet in height and 5 feet in diameter and live to be 500 years old. Their needles are short, soft and rounded at the tip. Needles grow on only two sides of a twig, giving the branches a flat, feathery appearance.

Like the Sitka spruce, hemlock is commercially harvested, with much of the wood used for construction lumber. Poor quality hemlock goes into pulp to make paper; the bark was once used extensively for tanning leather.

White Spruce Found primarily in Interior Alaska, white spruce *(Picea glauca)* is considerably smaller than the Sitka spruce, rarely exceeding 50 feet in height and 1 to 2 feet in diameter. Needles are less than an inch long and yellow to blue-green in color. Moose and sheep occasionally feed on the white spruce twigs, and porcupines gnaw the inner bark.

Black Spruce This subarctic species of spruce can withstand severe winds and extreme cold. Pockets of dwarfed black spruce *(Picea mariana)* exist in the Brooks Range, and in bogs, wetlands and tundra areas farther south.

Paper Birch Widely found in the Interior and Southcentral regions, paper birch *(Betula papyrifera)* is easily identified by its dull white, peeling bark. The tree reaches heights of 70 feet and diameters of 1 to 3 feet. Its green, pointed leaves range from 1 to 4 inches long. Birch is an important food source for wildlife, as the twigs are cropped by moose and mountain goats, the seeds by songbirds and the inner bark by porcupines and beavers.

Alder Ranging from the size of a shrub to a small tree, alder is found in the southern half of the state and is the most common broadleaf tree in the Southeast. The dark green leaves are 1 to 3 inches wide with serrated edges, and the gray bark is smooth. The species produces a small, nutmeg-shaped nut.

Alder is a pioneer species, a rapid invader of bare soil that has been newly exposed by glaciers, avalanches or loggers clear-cutting a track of hemlock. There are three species of alder in Alaska: red alder *(Alnus rubra)*, the largest, lives predominantly in the Southeast; Sitka alder *(Alnus sinuata)* is more widespread; mountain alder *(Alnus tenuifolia)* exists at higher elevations in the Interior.

Willow Various species of willow can be found alongside alder in stream beds or in newly scarred areas. It's the tangle of willow and alder that makes cross-country trekking such a nightmare in many parts of Alaska. Willow has light, gray-green leaves that are 2 to 5 inches long, smooth and oblong. The telltale signs of willow are the caterpillar-shaped catkins that explode with white fluff in the spring. The three main species of willow are the Sitka willow *(Salix sitchensis)*, feltleaf willow *(Salix alaxensis)* and scouler willow *(Salix scoulerana)*.

Black Cottonwood Commonly found mixed with alder, the black cottonwood *(Populus trichocarpa)* lives throughout Southeast and Southcentral Alaska, often in river valleys. It's one of the tallest of Alaska's broadleaf trees, often reaching heights of 80 feet; one cottonwood found near Haines in 1965 measured 101 feet. Cottonwood leaves are dark green on top and silvery white beneath, with smooth edges (unlike the alder's toothed leaves).

Wild Berries

From a hiker's point of view, Alaska's wild berries may be the most interesting kinds of flora. Blueberries *(Vaccinium uliginosum)*, which grow throughout much of the state, can reach heights of 6 feet in the Southeast. Thickets of salmonberries *(Rubus spectablis)* thrive in moist woods and lower mountain slopes from the Alaskan Peninsula to Southcentral and Southeast Alaska. A cousin of the raspberry, the fruit looks similar but can range in color from red to yellow to orange.

You'll encounter raspberries *(Rubus idaeus)* in fields and thickets in the Interior, Southcentral and Southeast regions. Wild strawberries *(Fragaria chiloensis)* grow in scattered clumps throughout Southeast and Southcentral Alaska and the Aleutian Islands, particularly on beaches. Other edible species worth learning to identify include red huckleberries *(Vacciium parvifolium)*, lowbush and highbush cranberries *(Vaccinium vitis idaea* and *Vaccinium edule)* and red currants or gooseberries *(Ribes triste)*, which have an excellent flavor without the skunklike smell associated with many species of currants.

If you plan to feast on wild berries, take the time to learn which ones are inedible. The most common poisonous variety is the baneberry *(Actaea rubra)*, which often appears as a white berry in the Southeast and the Interior.

Wildflowers

Alaska's state flower is the forget-me-not *(Myosotis sylvatica)*, a delicate, sky-blue flower with a yellow eye. It grows 6 to 20 inches in height. Blue-violet wild lupine *(Lupinus perennis)* can reach heights of up to 4 feet; it thrives along coastal shores and in alpine areas. Even more impressive is fireweed *(Epilobium angustifolium)*, whose pink blossoms can be found throughout much of subarctic Alaska, in open areas such as meadows, riverbanks and clear-cuts. If conditions are right, fireweed can grow up to 7 feet tall.

In the bogs and wetlands of Southeast and Southcentral Alaska, you'll most likely see – and definitely smell – skunk cabbage *(Lysichitum americanum)*. The yellow-brown

Forget-me-not

flower often appears while snow is still on the ground, and the leaves soon follow. Prickly wild rose *(Rosa acicularis)* features five pink petals, which you may spot anywhere from Sitka north to the Alaska Range and as far west as Unalaska. Its fruits, rose hips, are often collected in the fall and are an excellent source of vitamin C.

Other common wildflowers in Alaska are pink and red primrose *(Oenothera)*, yellow mountain marigold *(Caltha leptosepala)*, blue mountain harebell *(Campanula lasiocarpa)*, white Arctic daisy *(Chrysanthemum arcticum)* and the dark blue monkshood *(Aconitum leptosepala)*, a member of the buttercup family.

A good identification guide to bring along is *A Field Guide to Alaskan Wildflowers* by Verna Pratt. It's available through the Alaska Natural History Association (☎ 907-274-8440), Mail Order Services, 605 W 4th Ave, Suite 85, Anchorage, AK 99501.

Fireweed

Lupine

FAUNA
Bears

Bears and visitors to Alaska have a love-hate relationship. Nothing makes you more afraid in the backcountry than the thought of encountering a bear, but you would hate leaving the state without having seen a bear in the wild. After a handful of bear encounters, most people develop a healthy respect for these magnificent animals. There are three species of bear in Alaska – brown, black and polar bears – and you're most likely to see the brown bears, since these have the greatest range.

Brown Bears At one time, brown and grizzly bears were listed as separate species, but now both are classified as *Ursus arctos*. The difference isn't so much genetics but size. Browns live along the coast where abundant salmon runs help them grow to a large size (often exceeding 800lb). The famed Kodiak brown bear has been known to stand 10 feet tall and tip the scales at 1500lb. Grizzlies are browns found inland, away from the rich salmon runs. Normally a male ranges from 500 to 700lb, and females weigh half to three-quarters as much.

The color of a brown bear can range from almost black to blond, with the darker individuals resembling black bears. One way biologists tell them apart is by measuring the upper rear molar. The length of the crown of this tooth in a brown is always more than an inch and a quarter. A less dangerous approach is to look for the prominent shoulder hump, easily seen behind the neck when a brown bear is on all fours.

In June and July, you can see brown bears fishing along rivers. In late summer and early fall, bears will often move to the tundra area and to open meadows to feed on berries. Browns occasionally act like predators but only in the spring, when the young are most vulnerable.

There are more than 40,000 brown bears in Alaska. They live everywhere in the state except for some islands in Frederick Sound in the Southeast, the islands west of Unimak in the Aleutian chain and some Bering Sea islands. One famous place to watch them is Brooks River in Katmai National Park, but brown bears are also common in Denali National Park, on Admiralty Island in the Southeast and in Wrangell-St Elias National Park.

Brown bear

Black Bears Though black bears *(Ursus americanus)* are the most widely distributed of the three bear species in the USA, their range is more limited in Alaska than that of their brown cousin. They usually live in most forested areas of the state, but not north of the Brooks Range, on the Seward Peninsula or on many large islands like Kodiak and Admiralty.

The average male weighs 180 to 250lb and can range in color from black to a rare creamy white color. A brown or cinnamon black bear often appears in Southcentral Alaska, leaving many backpackers confused about what the species is. Beyond measuring that upper rear molar, look for the straight facial profile to confirm it's a black bear.

Black bears, as well as brown, are creatures of opportunity when it comes to eating. Bears are omnivorous, and their common foods include berries, grass, sedge, salmon and any carrion they happen to find in their travels.

Bears don't hibernate but enter a stage of 'dormancy' – basically a deep sleep while denning up during the winter. Black bears usually enter their dens in November or December and reemerge in April or May. In the more northern areas of the state, some bears may be dormant for as long as seven or eight months a year.

Polar Bears Polar bears *(Ursus maritimus)* have always captured our interest because of their large size and white color, but they're not easy to encounter in person. Plan on stopping at the zoo in Anchorage if you want to see one in Alaska. Polar bears occur only in the Northern Hemisphere and almost always in association with Arctic Sea ice. Past studies have shown that few polar bears make their dens along the north Alaska coast.

A male usually weighs between 600 and 1200lb but occasionally tops 1400lb. The polar bear's adaptations to a life on the sea ice include its white, water-repellent coat, dense underfur, specialized teeth for a carnivorous diet (primarily seals), and hair that almost completely covers the bottom of its feet.

Moose

Moose *(Alces alces)* are improbable-looking mammals: long-legged to the extreme but short-bodied, with a huge rack of antlers and a drooping nose. Standing still, they look uncoordinated until you watch them run or, better still, swim – then their speed and grace are astounding. They're the largest members of the deer family in the world, and the Alaskan species is the largest of all moose. A newborn weighs in at 35lb and can grow to more than 300lb within five months. Cows range from 800 to 1200lb and bulls from 1000lb to more than 1500lb.

In the wild, moose may live to be more than 20 years old and often travel 20 to 40 miles to find their main forage of birch, willow, alder and aspen saplings. In the spring and summer, you often encounter them feeding in lakes, ponds and muskegs, with those huge noses below the water as they grab for aquatic plants and weeds.

The population ranges from an estimated 120,000 to 160,000 animals, and historically moose have always been the most important game animal in Alaska. Athabascan Indians survived by utilizing the moose as a source of food, clothing and implements, and professional hunters in the 19th century made a living by supplying moose meat to mining camps. Today, some 35,000 Alaskans and nonresidents harvest 9000 moose, or a total of five million pounds of meat, during the hunting season each year.

Moose are widespread throughout the state and range from the Stikine River in the Southeast to the Colville River on the North Slope. They're most abundant in second-growth birch forests, on timberline plateaus and along the major rivers of Southcentral Alaska and the Interior. Moose are frequently sighted along the Alcan, and Denali National Park is an excellent place to watch them. But the best place to see the biggest moose is the Kenai Peninsula, especially if you take time to paddle the Swanson River or Swan Lake canoe routes in the Kenai National Wildlife Refuge. The refuge even maintains a Moose Research Center 50 miles from Soldotna, and you can often see the animal there.

Caribou

Although an estimated 900,000 caribou *(Rangifer tarandus)* live in Alaska's 32 herds, these animals are relatively difficult to view as they travel from the Interior north to the Arctic Sea. Often called the 'nomads of the north,' caribou range in weight from 150lb to more than 400lb. They migrate hundreds of miles annually between their calving grounds, rutting areas and winter home. In the summer, they feed on grasses, grasslike sedges, berries and small shrubs of the tundra. In the winter, they eat a significant amount of lichen called 'reindeer moss.'

The principal predators of caribou are wolves, and some wolf packs on the North Slope have been known to follow caribou herds for years, picking off the young, old and victims of disabling falls caused by running in tightly massed herds. Bears, wolverines, foxes and eagles will also prey on calves, and every year several thousand nonresident hunters come to Alaska in search of a bull. The caribou, however, are most important to the Inuit and other Native Alaskans, who hunt more than 30,000 a year to support their subsistence lifestyle.

The best place for the average visitor to see caribou is Denali National Park. Occasionally, you can see them from the park road, but if the day is warm and still, you'll often encounter them above the tree line, where they head to seek relief from insects. In late spring, look for them around the remaining patches of snow.

Perhaps one of the greatest wildlife events left in the world today is the migration of the Western Arctic herd of caribou, the largest such herd in North America, with 450,000 animals. The herd uses the North Slope for its calving area, and in late August many of the animals begin to cross the Noatak River on their journey southward. During that time, the few visitors lucky enough to be on the river are often rewarded with the awesome experience of watching 20,000 or more caribou crossing the tundra toward the Brooks Range.

Caribou

Deer

The Sitka black-tailed deer *(Odocoileus hemionus sitkensis)* is native to the coastal rain forests of Southeast Alaska, but its range has expanded to Prince William Sound and Kodiak Island. The deer is a favorite target of hunters, but it's not the abundant source of meat that the moose is. The largest black-tailed deer weighs 212lb, but most weigh an average of 100lb, with bucks around 150lb.

The deer's coat is reddish-brown in summer and gray in winter. The antlers are small, usually with three points on each side, and the deer's tail is indeed black. Sitka black-tailed deer respond readily to calls. Most 'calls' consist of a thin strip of rubber or plastic stretched between two pieces of wood; they're held between the teeth and blown. The high-pitched note they produce simulates a fawn's cry and can stop a deer in its tracks and turn the animal around. Some old-time hunters can make the call by simply blowing on a leaf.

Mountain Goats

The mountain goat *(Oreamnos americanus)* is the single North American species in the widespread group of goat-antelopes. All are characterized by short horns and a fondness for the most rugged alpine terrain.

Although goats are often confused with Dall sheep, they are easily identified by their longer hair, black horns and deep chest. They're quite docile, making them easy to watch in the wild, and their gait, even when they're approached too closely, is a deliberate pace. In the summer, they normally frequent high alpine meadows, grazing on grasses and herbs, while in the winter they often drop down to the tree line.

In Alaska, the goats range through most of the Southeast, fanning out north and west into the coastal mountains of Cook Inlet as well as the Chugach and Wrangell Mountains. Good places to spot them include Glacier Bay National Park, Wrangell-St Elias National Park and many of the alpine trails in Juneau. But you have to climb to see some.

Dall Sheep

Dall sheep *(Ovis dalli dalli)* are more numerous and widespread than mountain goats. They number close to 80,000 in Alaska and live principally in the Alaska, Wrangell, Chugach and Kenai mountain ranges. Often sheep are spotted in Denali National Park when the park shuttle bus crosses Polychrome Pass on its way to Wonder Lake.

Rams are easy to spot thanks to their massive curling horns, which grow throughout the life of the sheep, unlike deer antlers, which are shed and regrown annually. The horns – like claws, hooves and your fingernails – grow from the skin, and as rams mature, the horns continue their ever-increasing curl, reaching a three-quarters curl in four to five years and a full curl in seven years.

It's spectacular to watch two rams in a horn-clashing battle, but contrary to popular belief, they are not fighting for a female, just for social dominance. Dall sheep do not clash as much as their big-horn cousins to the south, but you can spot the activity throughout the summer and into fall.

Dall sheep prefer rocky, open alpine tundra regions. In the spring and fall, however, they tend to move to lower slopes where the grazing is better. The best time to spot rams and see them clash is right before the rut (their mating period), which begins in November. At that time, they are moving among bands of ewes and often encountering other unfamiliar rams.

Wolves

While the wolf *(Canis lupus)* is struggling to survive throughout most of the USA, its natural distribution and population numbers still seem to be unaffected by human undertakings in Alaska. Throughout history no animal has been more misunderstood than the wolf. Unlike human hunters, who seek out the outstanding physical specimens, wolves can usually only catch and kill the weak, injured or young, thus strengthening the herd they are stalking. A pack of wolves is no match for a healthy 1200lb moose.

Eight thousand wolves live in packs scattered throughout Alaska, in almost every region except for some islands in the Southeast and Prince William Sound and in the Aleutian chain. Most adult males average 85 to 115lb, and their pelts

Gray wolf

can be gray, black, off-white, brown and yellow, with some tinges approaching red. Wolves travel, hunt, feed and operate in the social unit of a pack. In the Southeast, their principal food is deer; in the Interior, it's moose; in Arctic Alaska, it's caribou.

Even if you're planning to spend a great deal of time away from the road wandering in the wilderness, your chances of seeing wolves are rare. You might, however, find evidence of them in their doglike tracks, their howls at night and the remains of their wild kills.

Other Land Mammals

In the lowlands, hikers have a chance to view red fox *(Vulpes vulpes)*. A shy animal, the fox can occasionally be seen darting across roads or meadows into woody, bushy areas. Other lowland mammals you might see include pine marten *(Martes americana)*, snowshoe hare *(Lepus americanus)*, red squirrel *(Tamiasciurus hudsonicus)*, porcupine *(Erethizon dorsatum)* and, on very rare occasions, wolverines *(Gulo gulo)*.

Around lakes and rivers you stand a good chance of spotting river otters *(Lutra canadensis)* and beavers *(Castor canadensis)*. Both live throughout the state with the exception of the North Slope. Often larger than their relatives farther south, otters range from 15 to 35lb, and beavers weigh between 40 and 70lb, although 100lb beavers have been recorded in Alaska. In alpine areas, look for the ever-curious hoary marmot *(Marmota caligata)*, a large ground squirrel.

Marine Mammals

The most commonly spotted marine mammals are seals, often seen basking in the sun on an ice floe. Six species of seal exist in Alaska, but most visitors will encounter just the harbor seal *(Phoca vitulina)*, the only seal whose range includes the Southeast, Prince William Sound and the rest of the Gulf of Alaska. The average weight of a male is 200lb – achieved through a diet of herring, flounder, salmon, squid and small crabs.

Two other species, ringed seals *(Phoca hispida)* and bearded seals *(Erignathus barbatus)*, occur for the most part in the northern Bering, Chukchi and Beaufort Seas where sea ice forms during the winter. Although travel on land or ice is laborious and slow for seals, they're renowned divers. During a dive, their heartbeat may slow from a normal 55 to 120 beats per minute to 15. This allows them to stay underwater for more than five minutes, often reaching depths of 300 feet or more. Harbor seal dives of 20 minutes or longer have been recorded by biologists.

Many visitors also see dolphins and harbor porpoises *(Phocaena vomerina)*, even from the decks of the ferries. Occasionally, ferry travelers spot a rare treat: a pod of killer whales or orcas *(Orcinus orca)*, whose high black-and-white dorsal fins make them easy to identify from a distance. Orcas, which can exceed 20 feet in length, are actually the largest members of the dolphin family, which also includes the beluga *(Delphinapterus leucas)* or white whale. Belugas range in length from 11 to 16 feet and often weigh more than 3000lb. The 57,000 belugas that live in Alaskan waters travel in herds of more than 100. Their range includes the Arctic waters north of Bristol Bay and also Cook Inlet, where most visitors will spot them, especially in Kenai, which has a beluga observation area.

The three most common whales seen in coastal waters are the 50-foot-long humpback *(Magaptera novaeangliae)*, with its humplike dorsal fin and long flippers; the smaller bowhead whale *(Balaena mysticetus)*; and the gray whale *(Eschrichtius robustus)*. Other marine mammals include Steller's sea lions *(Eumetopias jubatus)*, sea otters *(Enhydra lutris)* and walruses *(Odobenus rosmarus divergens)*.

The best-known destination for sighting marine mammals, particularly whales, is Glacier Bay National Park in the Southeast. If you can spare a few days to kayak the glaciated sections of the bay, you'll increase your chances of seeing a whale. Kayak and boat tours in Prince William Sound, particularly around Kenai Fjords National Park near Seward, should result in encounters with marine mammals. Just a trip on the ferry from Seward to Kodiak offers an opportunity to see a colony of sea lions.

Salmon

The salmon runs (when thousands of fish swim upstream to spawn) rank among Alaska's most amazing sights and are common throughout much of the state. From late July to mid-September, many coastal streams are choked with salmon. You won't see just one fish here and there, but thousands – so many that they have to wait their turn to swim through narrow gaps of shallow water. The salmon are famous for their struggle against the current and their magnificent leaps over waterfalls, as well as for the density of salmon carcasses that cover stream banks after the spawning ends. Five kinds of salmon populate Alaskan waters: sockeye *(Oncorhynchus nerka)* (also referred to as red salmon), king or chinook *(Oncorhynchus tshawytscha)*, pink or humpie *(Oncorhynchus gorbuscha)*, coho or silver *(Oncorhynchus kisutch)* and chum *(Oncorhynchus keta)*.

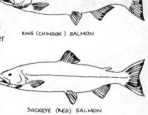

KING (CHINOOK) SALMON

SOCKEYE (RED) SALMON

Birds

More than anything, Alaska is a haven for winged wildlife. Biologists have identified 437 species of bird in the state, and only 65 of them are accidental visitors.

The most impressive bird in Alaska's wilderness is the bald eagle *(Haliaeetus leucocphalus)*, whose white tail and head – and wingspan that often reaches 8 feet – have become the symbols of a nation. While elsewhere the bird is on the endangered species list, in Alaska it thrives. The eagle can be sighted almost daily in most of the Southeast and is common in Prince William Sound. It also migrates once a year in a spectacle that exceeds even the salmon runs. As many as 3500 bald eagles gather along the Chilkat River north of Haines from late October to December. They come to feed on the late chum salmon run and create an amazing scene during the bleakness of early winter. Bare trees, without a leaf remaining, support 80 or more white-headed eagles, four or five to a branch.

The state bird of Alaska is the ptarmigan *(Lagopus)*, a cousin of the prairie grouse. Three species of the ptarmigan can be found throughout the state in high treeless country. The birds are easy to spot during the summer, as their wings remain white while their head and chest turn brown. In the winter, they sport pure white plumage.

Alaskan seabirds include the playful horned puffin *(Fratercula corniculata)*, six species of auklet *(Aethia)* and three species of albatross *(Diomedea)*, which boost a wingspan of up to 7 feet. The best way to see a variety of seabirds, including the rare black-footed albatross, is to board the Alaska Marine Hwy ferry for its special run along the Alaska Peninsula to Unalaska in the Aleutian Islands. Shorter and much more affordable is the tour of Gull Island in Kachemak Bay. It's offered daily in the summer, departing from Homer.

An amazing variety of waterfowl also migrate to Alaska, including the trumpeter swans *(Cygnus buccinator)*. The swan is the world's largest member of the waterfowl family and occasionally tips the scales at 30lb. Other waterfowl include Canada geese *(Branta canadensis)*, of which more than 130,000 nest in Alaska; all four species of eider *(Somateria)* in the world; the colorful Harlequin duck *(Histrionicus histrionicus)*; and five species of loons *(Gavia)*.

The Pribilof Islands in the Bering Sea attract birders from around the world. If you can't afford that trip, visit Potter Marsh south of Anchorage, a sanctuary that attracts more than 100 species annually. If you're serious about birding, then try to come to Alaska during the spring migration in May and attend either the Copper River Delta Shorebird Festival in Cordova or the Kackemak Bay Shorebird Festival in Homer.

Southeast Alaska

The North Country begins in Southeast Alaska, as do the summer adventures of many visitors to the state, and for good reasons. The Southeast is the closest part of Alaska to the Lower 48 – Ketchikan is only 90 minutes away from Seattle by air or two days away from Bellingham, Washington, on the Alaska Marine Hwy ferry – and travel to and around the Southeast is easy. The ferry connects this roadless area to the Lower 48 and provides transportation around the area, making the Alaskan Marine Hwy the longest (and many think the best) public ferry system in North America. Relaxing three-day cruises through the maze of islands and coastal mountains of the Southeast's Alexander Archipelago are a pleasant alternative to the long and often bumpy Alcan (Alaska Hwy). The ferry connects 14 ports and serves 64,000 residents, 75% of which live in Juneau, Ketchikan, Sitka, Petersburg and Wrangell.

The Southeast, affected greatly by warm ocean currents, has the mildest climate in Alaska and offers warm summer temperatures averaging 69°F, with an occasional heat wave that sends temperatures to 80°F. The winters are equally mild, and subzero days are rare. Residents who have learned to live with an annual rainfall of 60 to 200 inches call the frequent rain 'liquid sunshine.' The heavy precipitation creates the dense, lush forests and numerous waterfalls most travelers come to cherish.

The best reason to begin and end your trip in the Southeast is its scenery. Few places in the world have the spectacular views found in the Southeast. Rugged snow-capped mountains rise steeply from the water to form sheer-sided fjords decorated by cascading waterfalls. Ice-blue glaciers that begin among the highest peaks fan out into valleys of dark-green Sitka spruce trees and melt into wilderness waters that support whales, sea lions, harbor seals and huge salmon runs.

In recent years, the Southeast has experienced an incredible boom in summer tourism, but there is still room to breathe. At one time, the Southeast was the heart and soul of Alaska, and Juneau was not only the capital but the state's major city. However, WWII and the Alcan shifted the state's growth to Anchorage and Fairbanks. The population density in the Southeast is now about 2.5 people per sq mile and will probably stay that way. Much of the region now lies in the Tongass National Forest – at 26,563 sq miles the largest national forest in the USA – or in federal monuments and preserves such as the spectacular Glacier Bay National Park

Highlights

- Gaze at the totems and shoreline scenery of Sitka National Historical Park
- Soak in the hot springs of the Tenakee Springs bathhouse
- View Mendenhall Glacier from above by hiking the West Glacier Trail in Juneau
- Float past icebergs, glaciers and seals on a boat tour of Tracy Arm Fjord
- Watch brown bears feed on salmon at Pack Creek on Admiralty Island
- Experience stunning mountain scenery with a ride on the historic White Pass & Yukon Route railway

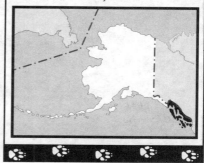

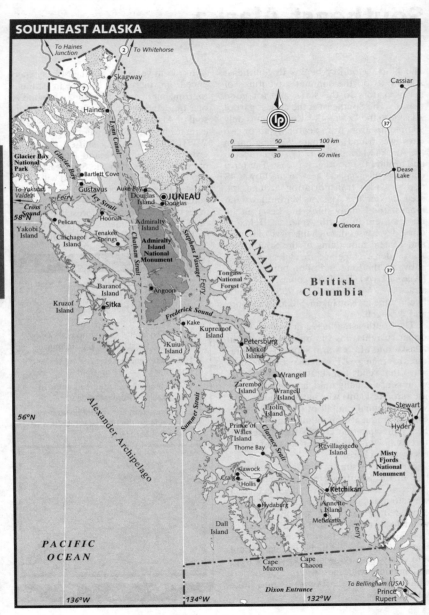

SOUTHEAST ALASKA

To Haines Junction
To Whitehorse
Cassiar
Skagway
Haines
Glacier Bay National Park
Bartlett Cove
Gustavus
Icy Strait
Auke Bay
Douglas Island
JUNEAU
Douglas
To Yakutat Valdez
Cross Sound
58°N
Pelican
Hoonan
Tenakee Springs
Admiralty Island
Yakobi Island
Chichagof Island
Chatham Strait
Admiralty Island National Monument
Stephens Passage
Tongass National Forest
CANADA
Dease Lake
Glenora
British Columbia
Baranof Island
Angoon
Kruzof Island
Sitka
Frederick Sound
Kake
Kupreanof Island
Kuiu Island
Petersburg
Mitkof Island
56°N
Alexander Archipelago
Summer Strait
Zarembo Island
Wrangell
Wrangell Island
Etolin Island
Stewart
Hyder
Clarence Strait
Prince of Wales Island
Thorne Bay
Revillagigedo Island
Misty Fjords National Monument
Klawock
Craig
Hollis
Ketchikan
Hydaburg
Annette Island
Metlakatla
Dall Island
PACIFIC OCEAN
Cape Muzon
Cape Chacon
Dixon Entrance
To Bellingham (USA)
Prince Rupert
136°W
134°W
132°W

Ferry

SOUTHEAST

0   50   100 km
0   30   60 miles

Kayaking on the Inside Passage

Wrecked fishing boat at Hubbard Glacier

Floatplane dock in Ketchikan

Totem Bight State Park, north of Ketchikan

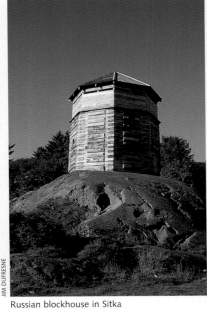

Russian blockhouse in Sitka

and Preserve, Admiralty Island and Misty Fjords National Monuments, Klondike Gold Rush National Historical Park and the Tracy Arm-Fords Terror Wilderness.

More than anywhere else in Alaska, each community in the Southeast clings tightly to its own character, color and past. There you'll find Norwegian-influenced Petersburg and Russian-tinted Sitka. You can feel the gold fever in Skagway, see lumberjacks and fishers in Ketchikan or venture to Juneau for a hefty dose of government, glaciers and un-controlled growth. The best way to visit the Southeast is to purchase a ferry ticket from Bellingham to Skagway ($252 one way) and make lengthy stops at a handful of towns. To rush from the Lower 48 to Juneau and then fly to Anchorage is to miss some of the best things that Alaska has to offer.

Ketchikan

Ketchikan (population 8320), otherwise known as the First City, is on the southwest side of Revillagigedo Island, only 90 miles north of Prince Rupert. It is the first stop the ferry makes in Alaska, so tourists pile off the boat for their first look at the North Country, and rarely does Ketchikan disappoint them.

History

The city's first residents were Tlingit families who camped on the banks of Ketchikan Creek during the great salmon runs. The runs also attracted huge numbers of bald eagles, and the name Ketchikan is a deriva-tive of a Tlingit word that means 'thundering wings of eagles.'

In 1885, Mike Martin, scouting for a cannery site for a Portland company, landed at the site of present-day Ketchikan and purchased it from local Natives. The town grew around salmon canneries and sawmills. A saltry for preserving fish was built at the mouth of Ketchikan Creek in the mid-1800s, and in 1883, the first cannery was built, leading the city to eventually crown itself the 'Canned Salmon Capital of the World.' The title first appeared in 1920s, when resi-dents erected an arch across Mission St, but

was changed to 'Salmon Capital of the World' when the arch was replaced in 1951, reflecting the fact that, by then, most of the canneries had left.

A sawmill was built in the center of Ketchikan in 1903, and in 1954 the huge Ketchikan Pulp Mill was constructed at Ward Cove. In the 1970s, strikes began to mar the logging industry. Just as Ketchikan began to recover from hard times, Louisiana-Pacific closed the sawmill in the city center after a strike in 1983. Two years later the his-torical downtown mill was razed for a parking lot. In 1997, the company perma-nently closed the Ketchikan Pulp Mill, and hundreds of workers lost their high-paying jobs. The pulp mill was the last in Southeast Alaska, and Ketchikan's largest employer.

The city and the people survived, a credit to their frontier spirit. Although the First City's industries include government serv-ices, a small shipyard and, increasingly, tourism, timber and fishing are still its trade-mark industries. Despite overfishing that nearly collapsed the salmon fisheries in the 1970s, fishing provides almost 20% of the city's economy and 230 commercial fishers are based in Ketchikan. The timber industry now consists of logging, a sawmill at Gravina Island and a veneer plant. These industries have given the city its rough-and-tumble character, and on a Saturday night, Ketchi-kan bars are full, loud and lively.

If you stay in Ketchikan longer than an hour, chances are good that it will rain at least once, if not several times. The average annual rainfall is 162 inches, but in some years it has been known to be more than 200 inches. Despite all the rain, the only people with umbrellas are tourists. First City residents never use umbrellas or let the rain interfere with daily activities, even outdoor ones. If they stopped everything every time it drizzled, Ketchikan would cease to exist.

Orientation

The town of Ketchikan is spread out. Several miles long and never more than 10 blocks wide, Ketchikan is centered on one road, Tongass Ave, which runs along the shores of – and sometimes over – Tongass

SOUTHEAST

KETCHIKAN

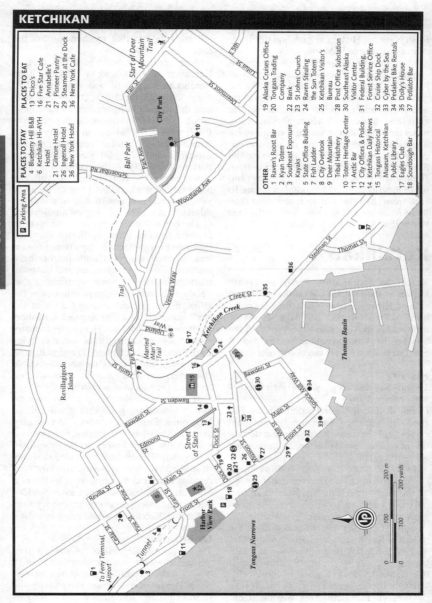

PLACES TO STAY
4 Blueberry Hill B&B
6 Ketchikan HI-AYH Hostel
21 Gilmore Hotel
26 Ingersoll Hotel
36 New York Hotel

PLACES TO EAT
13 Chico's
16 Five Star Cafe
21 Annabelle's
27 Pioneer Pantry
29 Steamers at the Dock
36 New York Cafe

OTHER
1 Raven's Roost Bar
2 Kyan Totem
3 Southeast Exposure Kayaks
5 State Office Building
7 Fish Ladder
8 City Overlook
9 Deer Mountain
10 Tribal Hatchery
11 Totem Heritage Center
12 Arctic Bar
14 City Offices & Police
15 Tongass Historical Museum, Ketchikan Public Library
17 Eagles Club
18 Sourdough Bar
19 Alaska Cruises Office
20 Tongass Trading Company
22 Bank
23 St Johns Church
24 Raven Stealing the Sun Totem
25 Ketchikan Visitor's Bureau
28 Post Office Substation
30 Southeast Alaska Visitor Center
31 Federal Building, Forest Service Office
32 Cruise Ship Dock
33 Cyber by the Sea
34 Pedalers Bike Rentals
35 Dolly's House
37 Potlatch Bar

🅿 Parking Area

Narrows. Crossroads appear mostly in the city center and the area surrounding the ferry terminal, known as West End. Ketchikan did not have traffic signals until 1984, and the first one was installed despite the objections of many residents. Many businesses and homes are suspended above the water or cling to the hillside and have winding staircases or wooden boardwalks leading to their front doors.

On a clear day – and there are a few during the summer – Ketchikan is a bustling community. It is backed by forested hills and surrounded by a waterway that hums with floatplanes, fishing boats, ferries and large cruise ships; to the south is the distinctively shaped Deer Mountain. Whether basking in sunshine or painted with a light drizzle, Ketchikan is an interesting place to start an Alaskan summer.

Information

Tourist Offices The Ketchikan Visitor's Bureau (☎ 225-6166, 800-770-3300,www .visit-ketchikan.com), on the city dock, can supply general information about Ketchikan and the city bus system. The bureau is open 8 am to 5 pm Monday to Friday and when the cruise ships are in on Saturday and Sunday.

For information about hiking trails, cabin reservations or other outdoor opportunities, head to the trip-planning room of the Southeast Alaska Visitor Center (☎ 228-6214), on the corner of Bawden and Mill Sts. Managed by the US Forest Service (USFS), the room contains reference guides, topo maps and a huge selection of videos to watch. Hours are 8:30 am to 4:30 pm daily in the summer.

Money National Bank of Alaska has an office downtown on Main St (☎ 225-2184) and a branch in the Plaza Mall (☎ 225-4141).

Post The main post office is near the ferry terminal on Tongass Ave, and there is a post office substation on Mission St between Main St and Bawden St.

Email & Internet Access You can retrieve email at Cyber by the Sea, a small book-and-coffee shop at 5 Salmon Landing near the city dock. You can also access the Internet at the Ketchikan Library, but you must first purchase a temporary library card.

Travel Agencies Ketchikan Travel (☎ 225-2100) has a location downtown in the National Bank of Alaska Building on Main St and an office in the airport (☎ 225-6600).

Bookstores The best place to purchase books on Alaska is at the Southeast Alaska Visitor Center. There is also a Waldenbooks (☎ 225-8120) in the Plaza Mall.

Libraries Near the corner of Park Ave and Dock St is the Centennial Building, which houses the Ketchikan Public Library (☎ 225-3331). It is open 10 am to 8 pm Monday to Wednesday, 10 am to 6 pm Thursday to Saturday and 1 to 6 pm Sunday. Often the library has used books for sale.

Laundry Highliner Laundromat (☎ 225-5308), which also has showers, is at 2703 Tongass Ave, and the Mat Laundry & Showers (☎ 225-0628) is at 989 Stedman St.

Medical Services Ketchikan General Hospital (☎ 225-5171) is at 3100 Tongass Ave, between the ferry terminal and the downtown area.

Things to See

The best way to explore Ketchikan is on foot, with a three-hour, 2-mile walk around the city center. Start at the visitor bureau, a brown building on the busy city dock, and pick up a free *Ketchikan Walking Tour Map*. Head up Mission St and swing (southwest) over to Mill St. Within three blocks, on the corner of Mill and Bawden Sts, is the **Southeast Alaska Visitor Center**. Three huge totems greet visitors in the lobby, and a school of silver salmon, suspended from the ceiling, lead into the exhibit hall and a slice of rain forest. Admission to the theater and exhibit hall is $3; the bookstore and the trip-planning room are free. Hours are 8:30 am to 4:30 pm daily during the summer months.

SOUTHEAST

By turning right (southwest) on Stedman St, you cross Ketchikan Creek and come to **Creek St**, a boardwalk built over the creek on pilings. This was the famed red-light district in Ketchikan for half a century, until prostitution became illegal in 1954. During Creek St's heyday, it supported up to 30 brothels. The first house, with its bright red doors and windows, is **Dolly's House**, the parlor of the city's most famous madam, Dolly Arthur. The house is now a museum dedicated to this infamous era and is open only when cruise ships are in port – almost daily during summer. For a $4 admission fee, you can see the brothel, including its bar, which was placed over a trapdoor to the creek for quick disposal of bootleg whiskey. There are another 20 buildings on Creek St, including small shops and a restaurant. Perhaps the best attraction on this unusual street is free – watching the salmon swim up Ketchikan Creek to spawn.

Across from Creek St (to the south) is **Thomas Basin**, one of three boat harbors in the city. It is nearly impossible to stay in Ketchikan and not spend time at the waterfront. The lifeblood of this narrow city is found in its collection of harbors, floatplanes and fishing boats that stretch along the lapping waters of the Tongass Narrows.

Thomas Basin, along with Thomas St (another boardwalk built on pilings) is the most picturesque harbor. An hour or so spent at the docks will acquaint you with Ketchikan's fishing fleet and the three kinds of fishing boats – gillnetters, power trollers and seiners. You may even end up at the colorful Potlatch Bar on Thomas St having a brew with someone from the fishing fleet.

Head east onto Deermont St to reach the **Totem Heritage Center**, where totem poles salvaged from deserted Tlingit communities are restored. The total collection, the largest in Alaska, numbers more than 30. Five of the poles are on display in the central gallery, along with indigenous art and a model of a Southeast Alaskan fish camp from the 1920s. Guided tours are scheduled around the times when the large cruise ships are in port. The center (☎ 225-5900) is open 8 am to 5 pm daily in the summer; admission is $4.

A bridge from the Totem Heritage Center crosses Ketchikan Creek to the **Deer Mountain Tribal Hatchery and Eagle Center** (☎ 225-5158, 800-252-5158), a fascinating place where biologists annually raise 150,000 king salmon and an equal number of coho salmon and then release them into the nearby stream. Observation platforms, outdoor displays and friendly workers provide an interesting lesson in the salmon's life cycle. In July or later, you'll see not only the salmon fry but returning adult fish swimming upstream to spawn. Hours are 8 am to 4:30 pm daily, and admission is $6, which includes a performance of Alaskan Native dancers and a sample of smoked salmon in the gift shop. A ticket to both the hatchery and Totem Heritage Center is $8. Next to the hatchery is **City Park**, a quiet spot with numerous small streams and wooden bridges. The park is a pleasant place to escape from the bustling crowds and tour groups that fill the city when a cruise ship is in town.

From the hatchery, head down Park Ave, cross Ketchikan Creek again and, on the other side of the road, you will soon see the Upland Way stairs. A climb up the stairs takes you to a viewing platform overlooking the city center, Thomas Basin and Creek St. Beyond Upland Way on Park Ave, another bridge crosses Ketchikan Creek. A **fish ladder** at the creek's falls enables salmon to reach upstream spawning gravel; it's a magnificent sight when these fish leap against the current during the late-summer migration. Next to the bridge is one end of **Married Man's Trail**, a delightful boardwalk that leads back to Creek St.

Park Ave merges into Bawden St, which heads south into the city center. Along the way, you pass the Centennial Building, home of the **Tongass Historical Museum** and the library. The museum features a small collection of local and indigenous artifacts, many tied in with Ketchikan's fishing industry. Hours are 8 am to 5 pm daily; admission is $3. Near the Centennial Building is the Raven Stealing the Sun totem, which was commissioned by the city in 1983.

Head west along Dock St. Edmond St, alongside the Ketchikan Daily News Building, is also called the **Street of Stairs**, as it leads to a system of long staircases. Back along Dock St, the next crossroad to the west is Main St, which leads north to the Ketchikan HI-AYH Hostel on the corner of Grant St and to the huge **Kyan Totem** another block beyond that.

Hiking

There are a variety of trails in the Ketchikan area, but the majority are either out of town or the trailhead must be reached by boat. The one exception is the Deer Mountain Trail, a 3.1-mile climb that begins near the city center and provides access to a USFS cabin ($35 a night, reserve in advance) and two other alpine trails (see the Backpacking section in the Wilderness chapter).

This trail is extremely well maintained and is a great way to escape the masses from the cruise ships that overtake the downtown area. An excellent lunch spot and view of Ketchikan is just 2 miles up the trail.

Ward Lake Nature Walk This is an easy trail around Ward Lake that begins near the shelters at the far end of the lake. The trail is 1.3 miles of flat terrain with information signs. To reach the lake, follow N Tongass Hwy 7 miles out of the city to the pulp mill on Ward Cove, turn right on Ward Lake Rd and follow it for a mile.

Perseverance Trail This trek is a 2.2-mile walk from Ward Lake Rd to Perseverance Lake, through mature coastal forest and muskeg. The view of the lake with its mountainous backdrop is spectacular, and the hiking is easy, as the trail consists mainly of boardwalks and steps. The trailhead is 1.5 miles from the start of Ward Lake Rd.

Talbot Lake Trail This trail starts from Connell Lake Rd, a gravel road that heads east 3 miles from the start of Ward Lake Rd. The 1.6-mile trail is a mixture of boardwalk and gravel and leads north from the Connell Lake Dam to Talbot Lake, where it ends at private property. The more adventurous, however, can cross a beaver dam at the south end of the lake and hike eastward

The Rise and Fall of Totems

Ironically, Europeans both stimulated and then almost ended the art of carving totems by Native Alaskans in the Southeast region. Totems first flourished in the late 18th century, after clans had acquired steel knives, axes and other cutting tools through the fur trade with white explorers.

Between 1880 and the 1950s, the art form was almost wiped out when a law forbidding potlatches took effect and banned the Native ceremony for which most totems were carved. When the law was repealed in 1951, a revival of the totem carving took place and still continues.

Generally, the oldest totems are 50 to 60 years old. After they reach this age, the heavy precipitation and acidic muskeg soil of Southeast Alaska takes its toll on the cedar pole, until the wood rots and the totem finally tumbles.

onto the north ridge of Brown Mountain to eventually reach its 2978-foot summit. Keep in mind that this is steep country with no established trail.

Bicycling

Ketchikan has two bicycle trails along Tongass Ave. The most scenic is the 2.5-mile trail that follows the water from the downtown area to Saxman Totem Park. The other trail follows North Tongass Hwy to Ward Lake Recreation Area, a one-way ride of 6.4 miles. You can rent mountain bikes or road bikes at the Pedalers (☎ 225-0440), 330 Spruce Mill Way. Rentals are $25/40 per half/full day.

You can also rent bikes at Southeast Exposure Kayaks (☎ 225-8829), 515 Water St, for $12/22 a half/full day.

Paddling

Many short and long-term kayak trips begin in Ketchikan and range from an easy paddle in well-protected waters to a weeklong trip to Misty Fjords National Monument and back (see the Paddling section in the Wilderness chapter). Kayaks can be rented from Southeast Exposure (☎ 225-8829), 515 Water St, and transported to some areas through Alaska Cruises (☎ 225-6044, 800-228-1905). Double kayaks rent for $50 a day or $45 for six days or more. Singles are also available. Southeast Sea Kayaks (☎ 225-1528, 800-287-1607) also rents boats in Ketchikan. Before any trip, purchase the topographic map of the area you'll be traveling in from Southeast Alaska Visitor Center, 50 Main St, or Tongass Trading Company, 201 Dock St.

If you just want to try kayaking without the rigors of an overnight paddle on your own, Southeast Exposure has two great paddling tours. The first is a three-hour waterfront day trip in which a guide leads you past the historic downtown area of the city. The cost is $50 per adult and includes all equipment. The second trip is an extended day trip to a number of areas, including Carroll Inlet, George Inlet or Naha Bay. The cost is $80 for six hours of paddling.

Naha River Trail From the end of the North Tongass Hwy, it's an 8-mile paddle to the trailhead for the Naha River Trail, a 6.5-mile path that follows the river and leads to two USFS cabins and two lakes. The trailhead is on Naha Bay, a body of water that leads through a narrow outlet from Roosevelt Lagoon. Kayakers trying to paddle into the lagoon must enter it at high slack tide, as the narrow pass becomes a frothy, roaring chute when the tide is moving in or out. The current actually changes directions depending on the tide.

The trail is a combination of boardwalk, suspension bridges and an uphill walk to the Jordan and Heckman Lake cabins. Both cabins ($35 per night) must be reserved in advance through the National Recreation Reservation Service (☎ 877-444-6777 or 518-885-3639 for overseas, www.reserveusa.com). This trail is an interesting side trip, as locals fish these waters for salmon and trout, and in August it's possible to see bears catching salmon at a small waterfall 2 miles up the trail from the Roosevelt Lagoon.

Wolf Creek Trail An even easier paddle is the 5-mile trip from the end of North Tongass Hwy to the trailhead for the Wolf Lake Trail at Moser Bay. The 2.5-mile trail passes through timber slopes and over muskeg to a three-sided shelter (no reservation or rental fee) at the outlet of Wolf Lake. A steep hill is encountered near the salt water, but this should not discourage the average hiker.

George & Carroll Inlets At the end of S Tongass Hwy, past Herring Bay, you are already in George Inlet, which makes this three- to four-day paddle an easy one, in water that is usually calm. North winds do occasionally whip down George Inlet, but both waterways are protected from southwesterlies, the prevailing winds in the Ketchikan area.

While not on the same dramatic scale as Misty Fjords, the two inlets are scenic, and paddling is an easy way to explore some of Ketchikan's backcountry. The return trip from Herring Bay to the end of George Inlet is a 25-mile paddle.

Organized Tours

Need a tour of the city? Ketchikan, being the cruise ship port that it is, has a bundle of different tours you can sign up for. Tour giant Gray Line has Ketchikan tours, but for something more personal, and cheaper, try the local companies. Little Red Riding Tours (☎ 225-0411) uses a small red bus for a two-hour tour that includes the Totem Heritage Center, Creek St and even a short walk through a rain forest, for $20 per person. City Tour (☎ 225-9465) has a nonstop, one-hour tour ($15) and a two-hour tour that includes Totem Bight State Park ($25). Rainbird Deluxe Tours (☎ 888-505-8810, 254-8810) uses 25-passenger buses to show you the sights downtown, Saxman Village and a rain forest walk in a two-hour tour ($20). You can book any of these tours at the visitor bureau on the city dock.

Special Events

Ketchikan has three major festivals during the summer. The 4th of July celebration, the biggest and the best, includes a parade, contests and softball games, an impressive display of fireworks over the channel and a logging show sponsored by the Alaska Loggers Association.

The Blueberry Festival, on a smaller scale, takes place in the lower floor and basement of the State Office Building and the Main Street Theater in mid-August. The festival consists of arts and crafts, singers and musicians and food stalls that serve blueberries in every possible way.

Places to Stay

When booking a bed in Ketchikan, be prepared for an additional 11.5% in city tax and bed tax, or $6 to $9 above the prices quoted here.

Camping Ketchikan has four public campgrounds, but none of them are close to town. *Settler's Cove*, 16 miles north of the ferry terminal, has 12 sites for $8 and is worth the hassle of getting there. The state recreation area where the campsite is located features a scenic beach and coastline, picnic shelters and a quarter-mile trail to a waterfall and observation deck. Because it is so far from town, this campground is not nearly as busy as the ones situated at Ward Lake.

The other three campgrounds are on Ward Lake Rd, in the Ward Lake Recreation Area. Take N Tongass Hwy 4 miles north of the ferry terminal and then turn right onto Ward Lake Rd just before the pulp mill on Ward Cove. The first campground is *Signal Creek* (19 sites, $10), a mile up the road. It is followed by *CCC Campground* (four sites, $10) a quarter mile farther and *Last Chance Campground* (25 sites, $10), another 1.8 miles along Ward Lake Rd. A night spent in one of these campgrounds is worth all the effort it takes to reach them. The area has four scenic lakes and three trails into the surrounding lush rain forest.

Cabins There are 30 US Forest Service cabins in the Ketchikan area; most cabins must be reserved in advance through the National Recreation Reservation Service

(☎ 877-444-6777 or 518-885-3639 for overseas, www.reserveusa.com) and cost $35 to $45 per day. With the exception of *Deer Mountain Cabin* (see the Hiking section earlier), which you can hike to, you must fly to the cabins. The following cabins are close to the city, which reduces air-charter time, the biggest cost factor in using them (see Getting There & Away for information on bush planes).

Alava Bay Cabin is on the southern end of Behm Canal. It provides ample opportunity for hiking and beachcombing along the coast, freshwater fishing and viewing of wildlife such as black bear and Sitka deer. The cabin is 20 air miles from Ketchikan.

Fish Creek Cabin is connected by a short trail to Thorne Bay. You can either paddle to it (a three- to four-day trip) or fly in, as it is only 18 air miles from Ketchikan. A trail leads to nearby Low Lake; fishing for cutthroat trout, rainbow trout and Dolly Varden is possible in the creek.

The *Patching Lake Cabins* (there are two cabins) are 20 air miles from Ketchikan. Patching Lake has good fishing for cutthroat trout and grayling.

Hostels In the center of town is the *Ketchikan HI-AYH Hostel* (☎ 225-3319), in the United Methodist Church, at Grant and Main Sts. It's open from Memorial Day to Labor Day and provides kitchen facilities, showers and a space on the floor with a mat to sleep on. The hostel is interesting because it always seems full of travelers heading north for a long trip. Since Ketchikan is their first Alaskan stop, they fill the recreation room with travel talk and excitement in the evenings. The fee is $8 for hostel members, $11 for nonmembers. If you're arriving at night, call the hostel to check whether space is available.

The *Rain Forest Inn* (☎ 225-7246, 2311 Hemlock St) has dormitory bunks but is very run-down and should be avoided at all costs.

B&Bs Ketchikan Reservation Service (☎ 247-5337, 800-987-5337) will book a room in a B&B in advance for you. B&Bs in the city have to charge the full 11.5% tax; those outside the city limits add only the 6% bed tax. You might consider the *Great Alaska Cedar Works* (☎ 247-8287), on N Tongass Hwy 11 miles north of the city, which was once the home of a foreman of a salmon cannery. This B&B has two cottages, including one on the beach, for $75 for two people.

B&Bs within easy walking distance of downtown include *Captain's Quarters* (☎ 225-4912, captbnb@ptialaska.net, 325 Lund St), which has singles or doubles for $80 and *Innside Passage* (☎ 247-3700, raaum@ktn.net, 114 Elliot St), a halfmile north of the city center, with rooms for $65/80 singles/doubles. Right downtown is Blueberry Hill B&B, (☎ 247-2584, bluberry@ ptialaska.net, 500 Front St) with two rooms for $80. Almost 4 miles south of downtown, *House of Stewart* (☎ 888-348-3725, 247-3343, hosbnb@ptialaska.net, 3725 S Tongass Hwy) has two rooms for $60 singles\doubles and $55 for two more nights.

Hotels Avoid the Union Rooms Hotel, a flophouse on Mill St. The *Gilmore Hotel* (☎ 225-9423, 326 Front St) was another run-down place, before undergoing major renovations that give it a historical flavor. Rooms begin at $68/73. Nearby, the *Ingersoll Hotel* (☎ 225-2124, 303 Mission St) has rooms for $79/89. Also downtown, the *New York Hotel* (☎ 225-0246, 207 Stedman St), near the Thomas Basin Boat Harbor, is a charming eight-room hotel furnished with antiques and with a view of the waterfront. Singles/doubles are $69/79.

Farther out, the *Super 8 Motel* (☎ 225-9088, 2151 Sea Level), a half mile south of the ferry terminal, has rooms for $90/100. The *Best Western Landing* (☎ 225-5166, 800-428-8304, 3434 Tongass Ave), across from the airport ferry, has singles/doubles for $115/125.

Places to Eat

Ketchikan has many places to eat, but the expensive Alaskan prices usually send the newly arrived visitor into a two-day fast. If this is your first Alaskan city, don't fret – it gets worse as you go north!

The downtown area has several good restaurants. For breakfast, there is the

Pioneer Pantry (124 Front St), which opens at 7 am. Three eggs, potatoes and toast cost $7. *Annabelle's*, in the Gilmore Mall on Front St, is a chowder house and saloon with 1920s decor. A stack of sourdough pancakes in the morning will only set you back $4. The chowder of the day is $5; chowder in a sourdough bowl is $8; and an excellent selection of salads cost $8 to $10. If you want to splurge, try the tequila prawns for dinner.

Equally charming is the *New York Cafe*, where you can get a window table overlooking Thomas Basin Harbor. For local seafood and waterfront dining, there's *Steamers at the Dock* (76 Front St); for Mexican, try *Chico's* (435 Dock St).

The best restaurant for vegetarian dishes and other 'healthy stuff' is the *Five Star Cafe*, in the Star Building on Creek St, a pleasant restaurant with a variety of art on display. The menu includes homemade soups and baked goods, a nice variety of sandwiches for around $6, salads and espresso drinks. Try the PNTHB (peanut butter, tahini with honey and sliced bananas sandwich).

Outside the downtown area, there is a *McDonald's* at Plaza Mall on Tongass Ave if you have a Big Mac attack. Nearby, *Godfather's Pizza*, in the Ketchikan Entertainment Center at 2050 Sea Level Drive, features medium pizzas with one item for $13 and an all-you-can eat salad bar and lunch buffet specials. Also in the complex is *Roller Bay Bar & Grill*.

Closer to downtown is *Waterfront Cafe* (1287 Tongass Ave), overlooking a floatplane dock. The cafe has an adjoining bar and outdoor deck and opens at 6 am for breakfast. Sandwiches and burgers are $7 to $8, seafood dinners $16 to $24.

Next door to the Plaza Mall is *Carrs Quality Center*, with an excellent salad bar for $4 a pound, espresso bar, deli and ready-to-eat items including stir-fry. It's open 24 hours and has a seating area inside that overlooks the Tongass Narrows.

Entertainment

After hiking all day, if you're still raring to go, try the *First City Saloon* (830 Water St), a sprawling bar with giant TV screens, pool tables, a cigar shop, live music, a small dance floor and an impressive selection of beers. Edgar Winter once played here (obviously at the end of his career). There is a cover charge. More live music is featured a couple nights a week at **KJ's Raven's Roost** *(522 Water St)*, at the north end of the tunnel.

The **Sourdough Bar** *(301 Front St)*, at the north end of the city dock, has walls covered with photos of fishing boats, and ship bells, ring floats and other fishing memorabilia hang from the ceiling. Just up Tongass Ave, before the tunnel, is the **Arctic Bar**, a quiet little place where you can go for an afternoon brew on a hot summer day. The bar is built on pillars above the water and has a sundeck that overlooks Tongass Narrows. Here you can enjoy the sea breeze while watching the floatplanes take off and land, as Taquan Air is next door and moors its planes right below the deck.

Ketchikan's longtime fisher's pub is the **Potlatch Bar** *(126 Thomas St)*, just above the Thomas Basin Boat Harbor. For cheap beer without all the fixings, try the **Eagles Club** on Creek St, where pints are under $4 and small pitchers $6.

Getting There & Away

Air Alaska Airlines (☎ 225-2145) flies to Ketchikan, with stops at other major Southeast communities, Anchorage and Seattle. There are several flights between Ketchikan and Juneau, including one that locals call the 'milk run,' as it stops at Petersburg, Wrangell and Sitka and is little more than a series of takeoffs and landings.

Ketchikan has many bush-plane operators; two of the more reliable ones are Taquan Air (☎ 225-8800, 800-770-8800, www .taquanair.com), 1007 Water St, Ketchikan, AK 99901, and Promech Air (☎ 225-3845, 800-860-3845, promech@visit.ktn.net), 1515 Tongass, Ketchikan, AK 99901.

Boat It's an exceptional day when there isn't a ferry departing from Ketchikan for other Southeast destinations or Bellingham. The one-way fares from Ketchikan to Wrangell are $24, Petersburg $38, Juneau $74, Sitka $54 and Haines $92. The M/V *Aurora* provides service to Metlakatla and Hollis on Prince of Wales Island. The trip runs almost daily during the summer, and the one-way fare is $20 to Hollis and $14 to Metlakatla. For exact sailing times call the ferry terminal (☎ 225-6181).

Getting Around

To/From the Airport The Ketchikan airport is on one side of Tongass Narrows, and the city is on the other. To go from one to the other, you can hop on the airport ferry, which travels from the airport to a ramp next to the ferry terminal at 15 and 45 minutes past the hour. The fare is $2.50 one way for walk-on passengers. The Airporter (☎ 225-5429) bus will take you to the downtown area for $12, ferry fare included.

Bus The city bus system consists of small buses that hold up to 30 passengers and follow a circular route from the ferry terminal to the area south of Thomas Basin, circling back by the Totem Heritage Center and within a half mile of the Deer Mountain trailhead. The route does not include Saxman Totem Park or anything north of the ferry terminal. Buses run from 5:30 am to 9:30 pm during the week and less on Saturday and Sunday. Fare is $1.

Car Alaska Car Rental (☎ 225-5123, 800-662-0007), with an office in the airport terminal and another at 2828 Tongass Ave, rents vehicles for $47 a day with unlimited mileage. For two to four people, this is a good way to spend a day seeing the sights out of town. Southeast Auto Rental (☎ 225-8778), 7480 N Tongass Hwy, has compacts for $40 a day.

AROUND KETCHIKAN
Saxman Totem Park

For a look at the world's largest standing collection of totem poles, head 2.3 miles south of Ketchikan on S Tongass Hwy, to Saxman Totem Park. The park's 24 poles were brought here from abandoned villages around the Southeast and were restored or recarved in the 1930s. At the entrance to the park is the impressive **Sun & Raven totem**,

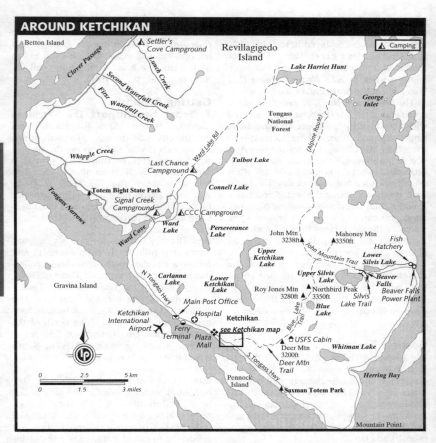

AROUND KETCHIKAN

Betton Island

Clover Passage

Settler's Cove Campground

Revillagigedo Island

Lunch Creek

Second Waterfall Creek

First Waterfall Creek

Lake Harriet Hunt

George Inlet

Whipple Creek

Ward Lake Rd

Tongass National Forest

(Alpine Route)

Last Chance Campground

Talbot Lake

Totem Bight State Park

Connell Lake

Signal Creek Campground

CCC Campground

Tongass Narrows

Ward Cove

Ward Lake

Perseverance Lake

John Mtn 3238ft

Mahoney Mtn 3350ft

Fish Hatchery

Upper Ketchikan Lake

John Mountain Trail

Lower Silvis Lake

Gravina Island

Carlanna Lake

N Tongass Hwy

Lower Ketchikan Lake

Upper Silvis Lake

Roy Jones Mtn 3280ft

Northbird Peak 3350ft

Beaver Falls

Silvis Lake Trail

Beaver Falls Power Plant

Main Post Office

Ketchikan International Airport

Hospital

Ketchikan see Ketchikan map

Blue Lake Trail

Blue Lake

Ferry Terminal

Plaza Mall

USFS Cabin

Deer Mtn 3200ft

Deer Mtn Trail

Whitman Lake

Pennock Island

S Tongass Hwy

Herring Bay

Saxman Totem Park

Mountain Point

Camping

0   2.5   5 km
0   1.5   3 miles

probably the most photographed totem pole in Alaska, and the rest of the park is uphill from there. Among the collection is a replica of the **Lincoln Pole**; the original is in the Alaska State Museum in Juneau. This pole was carved in 1883, using a picture of Abraham Lincoln, to commemorate the first sighting of white people.

Saxman Totem Park, an incorporated Native Alaskan village of more than 300 residents, also has a community hall, clan house and theater where you can see a slide and sound show about the park and Tlingit culture. This cultural center (☎ 225-4846) is

open daily in the summer, with the hours depending on when the cruise ships are in port. Most people see the village through an organized tour. You can book one at the visitors bureau in Ketchikan or call the center, but expect to pay $20 for a two-hour tour. If you can do without the slide show and cultural performances, just head down to the park and wander around.

From Saxman, S Tongass Hwy continues another 12 miles. Although there are no stores, restaurants or campgrounds here, this is a very scenic stretch, more scenic than driving N Tongass Hwy. You end up at

Beaver Falls Hatchery, where the trailhead for Silvis Lake Trail is located.

North Tongass Hwy
Ten miles north of Ketchikan, is **Totem Bight State Park** (no entry fee), which contains 14 restored or recarved totems and a colorful community house. Just as impressive as the totems are the park's wooded setting and the coastline. A viewing deck overlooks the Tongass Narrows. The N Tongass Hwy ends 18 miles north of Ketchikan at Settler's Cove State Campground, a scenic coastal area with a lush rain forest bordering a gravel beach and rocky coastline.

Misty Fjords National Monument
This spectacular, 3570-sq-mile national monument begins just 22 miles east of Ketchikan and is best noted for its sea cliffs, steep fjords and rock walls that jut 3000 feet straight out of the ocean. Walker Cove, Rudyerd Bay and Punchbowl Cove (the most picturesque areas of the preserve) are reached via Behm Canal, the long inlet that separates Revillagigedo Island from the Coast Mountains on the mainland.

Wildlife at Misty Fjords includes brown or black bears, mountain goats, Sitka deer, bald eagles and a multitude of marine mammals. As the name suggests, the monument can be a drizzly place, with an average annual rainfall of 150 inches, but many people think the real beauty of Misty Fjords lies in the granite walls and tumbling waterfalls wrapped in a veil of fog and mist.

The preserve is popular with kayakers (see the Paddling section of the Wilderness chapter), but less-adventurous visitors can view it on day cruises or sightseeing flights. Viewing Misty Fjords from a charter plane costs $150 per person for 1½ hours and most charter companies in town offer the trip (see Getting There & Away). The time actually spent viewing the monument is short, however, and the area's peaceful atmosphere is lost when the pilot has to yell at you over the roar of the bush plane. The best deal is probably through Island Wings (☎ 888-845-2444, 225-2444, islewing@ktn.net), a one-

plane, one-pilot company. Michelle Masden offers an hour flight with a stopover for $145 per person and a three-hour tour that includes a two-hour hike for $225.

Tour ships offer a more dramatic perspective of the preserve at a much more leisurely pace. Alaska Cruises (☎ 225-6044, 800-228-1905, akcruise@ptialaska.net), 220 Front St, offers an 11-hour cruise for $145. The boat leaves at 8 am every Tuesday, Thursday, Saturday and Sunday, and the cruise includes three meals. A shorter six-hour tour, in which return is via a bush plane, is $198. If you can plan ahead, the best way to experience Misty Fjords is to rent one of the 15 USFS cabins ($35 to $40 per night) in the area. Reserve a cabin in advance through the National Recreation Reservation Center (☎ 877-444-6777 or 515-885-3639 for overseas, www.reserveusa.com).

Metlakatla
Metlakatla, 12 miles southwest of Ketchikan on the west coast of Annette Island, is a well-planned community in the heart of the Annette Island Indian Reservation, the only reservation in Alaska. The village (population 1537) bustles during the summer as its boat harbor overflows with fishing vessels and its cold storage plant and cannery, which has been operating continuously since 1901, is busy handling the fleet's catch.

This small Native Alaskan community used to be a common day trip out of Ketchikan, until the ferry M/V *Chilkat* was taken out of service. Metlakatla is now served five times a week by the M/V *Aurora*; on Saturday the ferry visits the community twice, making it possible to do a day trip from Ketchikan. The rest of the week, the ferry stays in port only as long as it takes to unload, generally half an hour, which means viewing the town requires either staying overnight or flying back to Ketchikan.

Things to See From the ferry or from the shore near the terminal, you can see one of the community's fish traps, a large collection of logs and wire with a small hut off to one side. The fish traps, illegal everywhere else in Alaska, catch salmon by guiding the fish through a series of funnels, keeping them alive until they're ready to harvest.

The main attraction in town is **Father Duncan's Cottage**, now preserved as a museum. Metlakatla was founded when William Duncan, a Scottish-born minister, led several hundred Tsimshian Indians here from British Columbia in 1887, after a dispute with Anglican Church authorities. In 1891, Congress granted reservation status to the entire island, and under Duncan's supervision, the tribe prospered after building a salmon cannery and sawmill. Duncan lived in the cottage until his death in 1918, and it now features the minister's personal artifacts and many photographs of turn-of-the-century Metlakatla. The museum is open 10 am to noon Monday to Friday; there is a small admission charge.

A traditional **tribal longhouse**, down by the small boat harbor, has displays of log carvings and indigenous art and is the site of the community salmon bake whenever a cruise ship is in port.

Nearby you can stop at **Annette Island Packing Company**, a cannery owned and operated by the residents of Metlakatla. Inside, you can watch the bounty of the sea being unloaded and processed or sample the locally caught salmon.

Metlakatla Native Village Tours (☎ 247-8737, 886-8687) offers a 2½-hour bus tour of the island that includes the tribal longhouse and tribal dance performances at various times during the week, when cruise ships are in. Individuals can join the tours, if there is space, for $27. They also have a tour that includes a salmon bake for $55. You can book this at the visitors bureau in Ketchikan.

Hiking The hike to Yellow Hill provides good views of the western side of the island. Walk south along Airport Rd for 1.5 miles and look for the boardwalk on the right; it's an easy 30-minute walk to the top. Another hike in the area is the 3-mile Purple Lake Trail, 1.8 miles down Purple Mountain Rd. You can reach Purple Mountain Rd by traveling 2.7 miles south on Airport Rd. This trail involves a steep climb to the mountainous lake area.

Places to Stay & Eat At the *Metlakatla Hotel* (☎ 886-3456), a single/double is $78. A small cafe in back overlooks the cannery. Keep in mind the town is 'dry,' and camping on the island is discouraged. It's better and much cheaper to visit Metlakatla on Saturday, bring your own lunch and plan on spending the night back in Ketchikan.

Getting There & Away Five days a week the ferry M/V *Aurora* makes a single run to Metlakatla, but on Saturday it visits the community twice. The first run departs Ketchikan at 6:15 am, arriving in Metlakatla in about an hour. The second run leaves Metlakatla at 8:45 pm, giving tourists almost a full day on the island. Since the ferry terminal is only a mile east of town, there's enough time to walk to Metlakatla for an interesting and cheap trip. The one-way ferry ticket from Ketchikan to Metlakatla is $14.

You can also take a plane to Metlakatla. Taquan Air (☎ 225-8800, 800-770-8800, www.taquanair.com) provides daily, regularly scheduled flights for $49 roundtrip.

Hyder

Hyder is a ferry port at the head of Portland Canal, on the fringe of Misty Fjords National Monument. Nass Indians regularly visited the area to hunt birds, pick berries and, more often than not, hide from the aggressive Haida tribes. In 1896, Captain DD Gailland explored the Portland Canal for the US Army Corps of Engineers and built four stone storehouses, the first masonry buildings erected in Alaska, which still stand today.

But Hyder and its British Columbian neighbor Stewart didn't boom until Yukon gold-rush prospectors began settling in the area at the turn of the century. Major gold and silver mines were opened in 1919, and Hyder, enjoying its heyday, became the supply center for more than 10,000 residents. It's been going downhill ever since, and the population has now shrunk to around 100 year-round residents, the reason it's called 'the friendliest ghost town in Alaska.'

Because of Hyder's isolation from the rest of the state, and the country for that matter, residents are almost totally dependent on the much larger Stewart (population 2300), just across the Canadian border. They use Canadian money in Hyder, set their watches to Pacific time (not Alaska time), use a British Columbian area code and send their children to Canadian schools. All this can make a side trip here a little confusing.

Things to See & Do The most famous thing to do in Hyder is drink at one of its 'friendly saloons.' The historic **Glacier Inn** is the best known and features an interior papered in signed bills, creating the '$20,000 Walls' of Hyder. Next door is **First and Last Chance Saloon**, and both bars hop at night.

Near the Alaskan/Canadian border is the **Hyder Information Center and Museum** (☎ 250-636-9148). The **Stewart Museum** is at 6th and Columbia Sts and is open afternoons Monday to Friday. Displays concentrate mostly on the area's mining heritage and the Premier Mine, which before it closed in 1948, was Canada's largest gold mine.

From late July to September, you can head 4 miles north of town to **Fish Creek Bridge** and watch brown and black bears feed on chum salmon runs. Continue along the road and you cross back into British Columbia at Mile 11. At Mile 23, at 4300 feet, is a point from which to view the impressive **Bear River Glacier**, the fifth largest in Canada. Most visitors reach Fish Creek or the glaciers in their own vehicles, but contact Grand View Express (☎ 250-636-9148) or Seaport Limo Service (☎ 250-636-2622) if you don't have any wheels.

There are hiking trails in the area, and during the summer the US Forest Service (☎ 250-634-2367, summer only) sets up an office in the Hyder Community Building, which also contains a post office and the town's library.

Places to Stay & Eat In Stewart, you can pitch a tent at the **Bear River RV Park** (☎ 250-636-9205) for C$15 per night for two people. Or, secure a bed at the **King Edward Hotel** for C$58/68 for a single/double or the **King Edward Motel** (☎ 250-636-2244), at

The Border Patrol at Hyder

Hyder may be part of Alaska, but it uses Canadian currency, sends its children to a Canadian school across the border and sets its clocks to Canadian time (Pacific time). The only way to reach the village of 90 people from the US is by air or sea. If you want to drive to Hyder, you first must go through Canada.

Hyder and Stewart (population 2000), Hyder's larger neighbor to the east in British Columbia, are so intertwined that the Canadians removed their formal border crossing in 1985, but a new post went up in 1998, with custom officials staffing it 24 hours a day in the summer and 12 hours a day the rest of the year. The reason for the crackdown at the border? Drugs or gun running perhaps? No, something much more dear to the heart of the Canadian government: tax revenue. A carton of cigarettes in Hyder costs C$30, but in Stewart it costs C$55, thanks to federal taxes. Other heavily taxed items in Canada – particularly hard liquor, beer and wine – are also much more expensive in Stewart than just two miles down the road in Alaska. Custom officials said they were losing millions of dollars in tax revenues each year because Canadians were smuggling these goods back into British Columbia from Hyder.

5th and Columbia Sts, where the rooms include a kitchenette for C$68/78. In Hyder, you don't have to pay the 7% city tax that you do in Stewart, so at the **Grand View Inn** (☎ 250-636-9174), a mile from the ferry terminal, a single/double is C$50/55.

Both towns have a handful of cafes and coffee shops. In Stewart, the **Bitter Creek Cafe**, on 5th Ave, has local seafood, pizza or pasta, and nearby **Brother's Bakery** has sandwiches. In Hyder, you can head to the **Border Cafe**, conveniently located across the street from the saloons.

Getting There & Away Hyder is a possible side trip from Ketchikan because the ferry

M/V *Aurora* departs Ketchikan twice a month at 1:45 am on a Tuesday and reaches Hyder at 12:30 pm. It then departs Hyder at 3:45 pm and reaches Ketchikan at 12:30 am the next day, giving you three hours to explore the town (or drink in the bars). The one-way fare is $40, and the trip includes cruising scenic Portland Canal. If you want to stay overnight, you might have to charter a flight. Taquan Air (☎ 225-8800, 800-770-8800, www.taquanair.com) charges $200 roundtrip between Hyder and Ketchikan.

Prince of Wales Island

If time is no problem and out-of-the-way places or different lifestyles intrigue you, then this accessible island, with Native Alaskan villages and logging camps, can be an interesting jaunt. At 135 miles long and covering more than 2230 sq miles, Prince of Wales Island is the third largest island in the USA, after Kodiak and Hawaii. The island's landscape is characterized by steep forested mountains, deep U-shaped valleys, lakes, saltwater straits and bays that were carved out by glaciers long ago. The mountains rise to 3000 feet, and the spruce-hemlock forest is broken up by muskeg and, unfortunately, more clear-cuts than most visitors ever dreamed they would see. The 900-mile coastline has numerous bays, coves, inlets and protective islands, making it a kayaker's delight.

Getting There & Away

The ferry M/V *Aurora* makes a daily run, except on Tuesday, from Ketchikan to Hollis during the summer, including two trips on Saturday. The one-way fare is $20. Once you're at Hollis, where there are few visitor facilities and no stores or restaurants, getting around the island is a little more difficult.

Getting Around

The island has a 500-mile network of roads, more than the entire Southeast put together. Some stretches in the center of the island are now paved, but the vast majority of the roads are rough dirt. Logging roads connect Hollis with remote backcountry and the villages of Craig, Klawock, Thorne Bay and Hydaburg. Two of the 22 USFS cabins, Stanley Creek Cabin and Red Bay Lake Cabin, can be reached from the road; check with the USFS information center in Ketchikan for availability and then reserve them through National Recreation Reservation Service (see Cabins in Ketchikan section).

Taxi Jackson Cab (☎ 755-2557), in Klawock, will meet the ferry at Hollis. The fare for the trip back to Klawock is $23, and you can either arrange for pickup in advance or after you've arrived. Ask the ticket agent at the ferry terminal if anybody is offering van service around the island. It's generally cheaper than a cab.

Car If there are three or four of you, an ideal way to get around the island is to rent a vehicle at Ketchikan's Alaska Car Rental (☎ 225-5123, 800-662-0007) or Southeast Auto Rental (☎ 225-8778) and take it over on the ferry for an additional $26 one way. Or you can rent a car through Wilderness Rent-A-Car in Craig (☎ 826-2205). With a car, you can explore the far reaches of the island and fish the highly productive streams (accessible by road) for cutthroat trout, Dolly Varden and salmon.

Bicycle For someone carrying a mountain bike through Alaska, a week on Prince of Wales Island is worth all the trouble of carting the bike around. With a mountain bike you can explore the island and its network of logging roads. The main roads are gravel; the rest are logging roads and their condition depends on the weather and the amount of traffic. It's not unusual to find a culvert missing or a section washed out completely and passable only by four-wheel-drive vehicles – in other words, a mountain biker's dream come true. The fare to carry a bike over on the ferry is $8 one way, but invest another $3 for a copy of the *Prince of Wales Road Guide*, which can be purchased at USFS offices in Ketchikan or Craig.

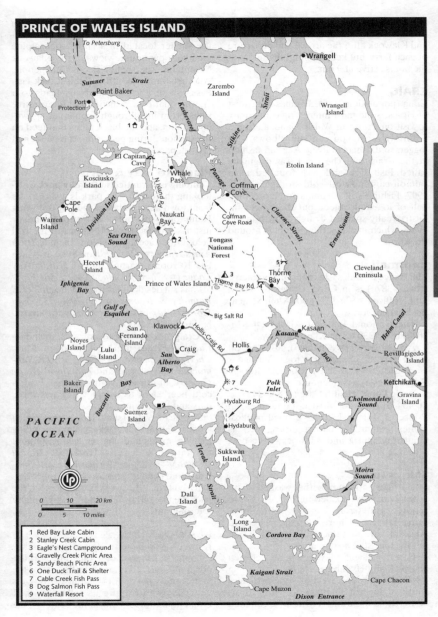

PRINCE OF WALES ISLAND

To Petersburg

Sumner Strait

Point Baker

Port Protection

Zarembo Island

Wrangell

Wrangell Island

Kashevarof

Stikine Strait

1

El Capitan Cave

Whale Pass

Kosciusko Island

N Island Rd

Passage

Coffman Cove

Etolin Island

Cape Pole

Davidson Inlet

Naukati Bay

Coffman Cove Road

Clarence Strait

Ernest Sound

Warren Island

Sea Otter Sound

2

Tongass National Forest

Heceta Island

Iphigenia Bay

Gulf of Esquibel

3

Prince of Wales Island

Thorne Bay Rd

4

5

Thorne Bay

Cleveland Peninsula

Big Salt Rd

Klawock

Hollis-Craig Rd

Kasaan

Kasaan Bay

Behm Canal

Noyes Island

San Fernando Island

Craig

Hollis

Revillagigedo Island

Lulu Island

San Alberto Bay

6

Baker Island

Bucareli Bay

7

Polk Inlet

8

Ketchikan

Gravina Island

9

Suemez Island

Hydaburg Rd

Cholmondeley Sound

PACIFIC OCEAN

Hydaburg

Tlevak Strait

Sukkwan Island

Moira Sound

0   10   20 km
0   5   10 miles

Dall Island

Long Island

Cordova Bay

Kaigani Strait

Cape Muzon

Dixon Entrance

Cape Chacon

1 Red Bay Lake Cabin
2 Stanley Creek Cabin
3 Eagle's Nest Campground
4 Gravelly Creek Picnic Area
5 Sandy Beach Picnic Area
6 One Duck Trail & Shelter
7 Cable Creek Fish Pass
8 Dog Salmon Fish Pass
9 Waterfall Resort

SOUTHEAST

Hitchhiking You can always hitchhike, as there is a small amount of traffic to Craig and Klawock after the arrival and departure of each ferry, but keep in mind that most of the boats arrive at 9 pm.

CRAIG

Craig (population 2136), 31 miles southwest of Hollis, is the most interesting community to visit on Prince of Wales Island, and on a Saturday night you can rub elbows with loggers and fishers in lively Alaskan fashion at the Craig Inn. The town was originally called Fish Egg and was founded as a salmon-canning and cold-storage site in 1907. Fishing still accounts for more than half of its employment, but the timber industry really sparked Craig's growth in the 1980s, which explains the clear-cuts around the town.

Information

The Prince of Wales Chamber of Commerce (☎ 826-3870) is in Craig. Craig also has a USFS office (☎ 826-3271), 900 Main St, near the boat harbor.

The National Bank of Alaska (☎ 826-3040) is at 1330 Craig-Klawock Hwy.

Air Sea Travel (☎ 826-3845), 401 Front St, is the only travel agency in town. Voyageur Book Store (☎ 826-2333), 330 Cold Storage Rd, doubles as a coffeehouse.

Craig Public Health Care (☎ 826-3433) is at 404 Spruce St. Most communities on Prince of Wales Island have small medical clinics, and major communities, such as Craig, Hydaburg and Klawock, have post offices.

Things to See

Other than a totem pole that washed up on a beach and was erected in front of the old school gym, Craig has no 'attractions.' Travelers come here to experience an Alaskan town that doesn't turn itself inside out for tourists every summer.

East of Craig, on Hydaburg Rd between Klawock and Hydaburg, are two interesting US Forest Service recreation sites. Two miles south of the road's junction with Hollis-Craig Rd is the trail for **One Duck Shelter**.

The trail is a steep hike, climbing 1400 feet in 1.2 miles, but it ends at a three-sided free-use shelter located in a large, open alpine area with panoramic views of the Klawock Mountains. The shelter sleeps four people. Another 6 miles south is **Cable Creek Fish Pass**, where a short boardwalk leads to a viewing platform, benches and interpretive signs. From July through September, spawning salmon, and the black bears that feed on the salmon during peak runs, can be seen at the fish pass.

Places to Stay & Eat

Camping is permitted in the *city park* overlooking the ocean. The park is a short hike from town and can be reached by following Hamilton Drive onto Graveyard Island, or just ask any local for directions to the ball field. Other accommodations include *Ruth Ann's Hotel* (☎ 826-3378), on Main St, which has 10 rooms starting at $90. *Haida Way Lodge* (☎ 826-3268, 800-347-4625, 501 Front St) has singles/doubles for $85/95, and *TLC Laundry & Rooms* (☎ 826-2966, 333 Cold Storage Rd) has bunkrooms with shared bathrooms for $35.

Craig has several restaurants, including *Lacey's Pizza*, in the Thibodeau Mall; *Cherlyn's Espresso (402 Front St)*; *TK Submarina*, on Water St; and *Thompson House Grocery*, at 4th and Water Sts. Just want a cold beer? Not to worry. Craig has three bars and three liquor stores.

Prince of Wales Island has several fishing lodges that provide package stays including lodging, meals and charter fishing. One of the largest lodges is *Waterfall Resort* (☎ 800-544-5125, www.waterfallresort.com), a restored cannery southwest of Craig originally built in 1912. At Waterfall Resort, the packages begin at $2860 for a three-night/four-day stay.

KLAWOCK

Klawock (population 673) is a Tlingit village 24 miles northwest of Hollis and 6 miles north of Craig. The town was the site of the first cannery in Alaska (built in 1878) but is better known today for its collection of 21 totem poles. **Totem Park**, in the center of the village, features 21 totems, including replicas and originals that were found in the abandoned Native Alaskan village of Tuxekan in the 1930s.

The best place to stay is at *Log Cabin Campgrounds* (☎ 755-2205, 800-544-2205), a half mile up Big Salt Rd, which offers tent space and showers for $7 per person and rustic cabins along the beach for $50 for two people. It also rents canoes that can be used in either Big Salt Lake or Klawock Lake, for $20 per day. Be forewarned that the campground and cabins are often fully booked during August, when the silver salmon are running. In town, *Fireweed Lodge* (☎ 755-2930), Mile 7 Hollis-Craig Hwy, has singles/doubles for $95. Head to *Dave's Diner* (779 Big Salt Lake Rd) for the cheapest meals or to nearby *Panhandle Grill & Spirits* to have a beer with your burger.

You can wash up at P&P Laundromat.

HYDABURG

Hydaburg (population 369) was founded in 1911, when three Haida villages were combined. Today, most of the residents are commercial fishers, but subsistence is still a necessary part of life. Located 36 miles southwest of Hollis, Hydaburg was not connected to the rest of the island by road until 1983.

This scenic village is known for an excellent collection of restored Haida totems in **Totem Park**, near the school, that was developed in the 1930s. On the way to Hydaburg, you can view **Dog Salmon Fish Pass**. At the junction of the paved road to Craig, head south almost 9 miles on the unpaved Hydaburg Rd and then east on Polk or No 21 Rd 16.7 miles. The fish pass was built in 1989 as an Alaskan steep-pass fish ladder. Between July and September, you can see salmon using the fish pass, and black bears, from an observation platform.

Lodging and meals are available at *Marlene Edenshaw Boarding House* (☎ 285-3254), which charges $100 for a bed and three meals or just $65 for the bed. There is also a grocery store and gasoline station in town.

THORNE BAY

Thorne Bay (population 582) was established in 1962, when Ketchikan Pulp Company moved its main logging camp here, 59 miles northeast from Hollis the original site in Hollis. Some people say the town still looks like a logging camp, but it lies in a picturesque setting.

On Thorne Bay Rd 18 miles west of Thorne Bay, *Eagles Nest Campground* overlooks a pair of lakes. The 11-site facility is also a canoe launching site for Balls Lake and features a half-mile boardwalk along the shore. The fee is $8 a night. Thirteen miles farther east is the **Gravelly Creek Picnic Area**. The facility has fireplaces, pit toilets and an open shelter. The Thorne River, less than a mile away, offers excellent fishing for cutthroat trout, Dolly Varden, rainbow trout and steelhead. Another scenic spot, just 6 miles north of Thorne Bay on Forest Rd 30, is **Sandy Beach Picnic Area**, which has tables, pit toilets and fireplaces. It's a great place to set up camp as there are spectacular views of Clarence Strait.

Northwest of Thorne Bay, a 94-mile drive from Hollis, are a pair of caves that have become increasingly popular with travelers in recent years. **El Capitan Cave**, 11 miles west of Whale Pass on Forest Rd 15, is so popular that the USFS erected a gate across the entrance to prevent further damage to the rock formations. You can descend into the cave during a free, two-hour tour that the USFS conducts Wednesday through Sunday in the summer. Tours are limited to six people and involve a 370-step stairway trail. Call the Thorne Bay USFS Office (☎ 828-3304) for tour times and reservations. **Cavern Lake Cave** is nearby and features an observation deck that allows visitors to peer into the cave's mouth at the stream gushing inside.

In Thorne Bay, supplies can be obtained at *Thorne Bay Market* (400 Shoreline Drive) and a meal at *Some Place to Go* (1219 Shoreline Drive). Nearby *McFarland's Floatel* (☎ 828-3335, 888-828-3335) has beachfront log cabins that sleep four for $200 a night. The USFS office, at 1312 Federal Way, provides recreational information for the area.

Wrangell

The next major town north from Ketchikan along the ferry route is Wrangell (population 2549). The community's claim to history is that it was the only Alaskan fort to have existed under three flags – Russian, British and American. Its strategic location near the mouth of the Stikine River has given it a long and colorful history.

History

The Russians founded the town when they arrived in 1834 and built a stockade they called Redoubt St Dionysius. The town's purpose then was to prevent encroachment by the Hudson's Bay Company traders working their way down the Stikine River. But in 1840, the Russians leased the entire Southeast coastline to the British for an annual payment of 2,000 otter skins. The British immediately took over the fort and renamed it Fort Stikine.

The Americans gained control of the fort when they purchased Alaska, and in 1868 changed the name to Fort Wrangell. Wrangell thrived as an important supply center for fur traders and later for gold miners, who used the Stikine River to reach gold rushes in British Columbia, at the Cassiar fields in the early 1870s, and then the Klondike fields in the Yukon. By the turn of the century, Wrangell was thriving on salmon canneries. Most of the workers were Native Alaskans or Chinese. Because the Asians believed that a dead man's spirit cannot rest in peace unless buried at the place of his birth, the Chinese who died at Wrangell were often placed in pickle barrels and stored at Simonof Island until a ship from their native land arrived to take them home. Eventually the spot became known locally as Dead Man's Island.

Wrangell's most famous visitor was John Muir, who visited in 1879 and again in 1880 and stayed with Presbyterian minister S Hall Young, using the town as a base for exploration. Muir later wrote that 'the Wrangell village was a rough place. It was a lawless draggle of wooden huts and houses, built in

crooked lines, wrangling around the boggy shore of the island for a mile or so.'

Today, the town is still considered colorful by Southeast residents, but for different reasons. Wrangell is a proud, traditional and sometimes stubborn community that clings to old Alaskan ideas of independence from excess government and freedom to use the land and natural resources to earn a living.

As the rest of the state is pushed into the 21st century, with heavy regulations on industries such as mining, logging and fishing, Wrangell often finds itself lagging behind economically and resisting the ideas of preserving the environment and setting aside wilderness. It's not that the town lynches environmentalists every Saturday night, but the issues surrounding timber sales in the Tongass National Forest hit Wrangell and its residents harder than most other towns in the Southeast.

When Alaska Pulp Corp closed its mill in 1994, the company eliminated 250 of the best-paying jobs in the area. The sawmill provided 20% of the jobs in the town and 30% of the payroll. Wrangell is still staggering from the closure, with a 20% unemployment rate that is triple the state average. Today Wrangell residents try to survive on a limited fishing fleet, government jobs and tourism in the summer.

Information

The Wrangell Visitor Center (☎ 874-3901, 800-367-9745) is an A-frame hut on Outer Drive, in front of City Hall. During the summer, the visitor center is open 8 am to 5 pm weekdays, Saturday mornings and Sunday afternoons. The city also has a website (www.wrangell.com). Nearby is the Wrangell Sentinel, on Lynch St, which publishes the free *Wrangell Visitors Guide*, the best source of information for the area.

The US Forest Service office (☎ 874-2323), 0.75 miles north of town at 525 Bennett St, is open 8 am to 5 pm Monday to Friday. It is the source of information for USFS cabins, trails and campgrounds in the area.

First Bank (☎ 874-3363) is across from Benjamin's Supermarket, at 224 Brueger St.

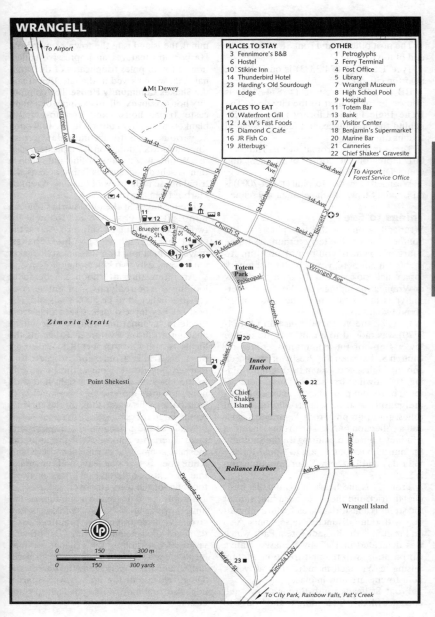

WRANGELL

PLACES TO STAY
3 Fennimore's B&B
6 Hostel
10 Stikine Inn
14 Thunderbird Hotel
23 Harding's Old Sourdough Lodge

PLACES TO EAT
10 Waterfront Grill
12 J & W's Fast Foods
15 Diamond C Cafe
16 JR Fish Co
19 Jitterbugs

OTHER
1 Petroglyphs
2 Ferry Terminal
4 Post Office
5 Library
7 Wrangell Museum
8 High School Pool
9 Hospital
11 Totem Bar
13 Bank
17 Visitor Center
18 Benjamin's Supermarket
20 Marine Bar
21 Canneries
22 Chief Shakes' Gravesite

To Airport

▲Mt Dewey

Evergreen Ave

3rd St

Cassiar St

2nd St

McKinnon St

Gillet St

Mission St

Park Ave

St Michael's St

2nd Ave

To Airport,
Forest Service Office

1st Ave

Bennett St

9

Church St

Reid St

6 7 8

11 12

10

Brueger St

Lynch St

Front St

13

14

15 16

17

19

18

St Michael's St

Wrangell Ave

Totem Park

Episcopal St

Church St

Case Ave

Zimovia Strait

20

21

Inner Harbor

Chief Shakes Island

22

Point Shekesti

Case Ave

Zimovia Ave

Reliance Harbor

Ash St

Wrangell Island

Peninsula St

Wrangell Hwy

0   150   300 m
0   150   300 yards

Berger St

23

To City Park, Rainbow Falls, Pat's Creek

SOUTHEAST

Also in town is National Bank of Alaska (☎ 874-3341), 115 Front St.

The post office is up Front St, at the north end of town.

Tyee Travel (☎ 874-3383) is on Front St, near the city dock.

BB Brock's Bookstore (☎ 874-3185) is also on Front St, next to the city dock. The Irene Ingle Public Library is on 2nd St, behind the post office, and features several totems out front.

There is a Laundromat in the Thunderbird Hotel, on the corner of Front St and Outer Drive.

Wrangell General Hospital (☎ 874-7000) is on Bennet St, next to the elementary school.

Things to See

Wrangell is one of the few places in the Southeast where the ferry terminal is in the heart of town. If you're not planning to spend a night here, you can still disembark for a quick look around. To get a good view of Wrangell, including a stroll out to see petroglyphs along the shoreline, you'll need about two hours.

In 1994, the **Wrangell Museum** (☎ 874-3770) was moved to an interim site on the lower floor of the community center on Church St, between the Presbyterian church and the high school, when its original building, the town's first schoolhouse, deteriorated beyond repair. The collection features indigenous artifacts, petroglyphs, local relics, photographs from Wrangell's past and a collection of Alaskan art that includes a Sidney Laurence painting. In the summer, the museum is open 10 am to 5 pm Monday to Friday and 1 to 5 pm Saturday; admission is $3.

Front St is the heart of Wrangell's business district, and the eastern (uphill) side of the street is a historical area featuring buildings with quite distinctive false fronts. Also on Front St is the **Kiksadi Totem Park**, which was dedicated in 1987 by Sealaska Native Corporation with the first traditional totem raising in Wrangell in more than 40 years. Four totems are now in place.

Front St heads south through town and becomes Shakes St, leading to the bridge to

Chief Shakes Island, Wrangell's most interesting attraction. A mile from the ferry terminal, the island is in the town's Inner Boat Harbor and features an impressive collection of totem poles (duplicates of the originals that were carved in the late 1930s) and the **Shakes Community House**. The community house is an excellent example of a high-caste tribal house and contains tools, blankets and other cultural items. It is open at various times to accommodate cruise ships, and a $3 donation is requested. Call the Wrangell Museum to find out when a tour is scheduled. Just as impressive as the tribal house is the view of bustling Wrangell Harbor from the island.

From Shakes St (heading north) you can turn right onto Case Ave and follow it for two blocks to Wrangell Shipyard. Across the street on the hillside is **Chief Shakes' gravesite**, enclosed by a Russian-style picket fence topped by two killer-whale totems.

An interesting afternoon can be spent looking for **petroglyphs** – primitive rock carvings believed to be 8000 years old. The best set lies three-quarters of a mile from the ferry terminal and can be reached by heading north on Evergreen Rd or, as the locals call it, Old Airport Rd. Walk past Stough's Trailer Court and proceed to a marked boardwalk. Follow the boardwalk to the beach and then turn right and walk north towards the end of the island. With your back to the water, look for the carvings on the large rocks.

Many of the petroglyphs are spirals and faces. There are almost 50 in the area, but most are submerged during high tide. Check a tide book before you leave and remember that the entire walk takes an hour or two – too long for the ferry stopover.

People used to make rubbings of the images with paper, but archaeologists now strongly discourage the practice, as it damages the ancient carvings. To prevent visitors from rubbing the original carvings, locals copied 10 of the glyphs onto six rocks in 1999 and lined them along the boardwalk. Tlingit elders cut the images with sharper edges so rubbings can be made faster and easier.

Anan Bear Observatory
The most interesting USFS cabin in the area (see the Places to Stay section for information on other cabins) is on the mainland at Anan Bay, 28 air miles from Wrangell. Near the Anan Bay Cabin is a mile-long trail that leads to a bear observation & photography platform. The observatory is on the creek from Anan Lake and can be used to safely watch black bears and a few browns feeding on the largest pink salmon run in Southeast Alaska. The cabin is a 50-minute flight from Wrangell or a 31-mile paddle.

Even if you don't have access to the cabin for a night, you can still visit the Anan Creek Bear Observatory and, in late July to early August, a fascinating day can be spent photographing the bears and eagles feeding on the salmon. A number of charter companies, including Breakaway Adventures (☎ 874-2488) and Stikine Wilderness Adventures (☎ 874-2085, 800-874-2085), will take you, via jet boat, to the trailhead. Trips range from five to eight hours and generally cost $155 per person with a minimum of three people chartering the boat.

Hiking
Mt Dewey Trail This half-mile trail winds its way up a hill to an observation point overlooking Wrangell and the surrounding waterways. From Mission St, walk a block and turn left at the first corner, 3rd St. Follow the street past a brown and red A-frame house with a white balcony. The trail, marked by a white sign, begins 50 yards past the house on the right. Once you arrive at the trailhead, the hike to the top takes 15 minutes or so, but the trail is often muddy. John Muir fanatics will appreciate the fact that the great naturalist himself climbed the mountain in 1879 and built a bonfire at the top, alarming the Tlingits living in the village below.

Rainbow Falls Trail The trailhead for the Rainbow Falls Trail is signposted 4.7 miles south of the ferry terminal on the Zimovia Hwy. The trail begins directly across from the Shoemaker Bay Recreation Area and just before the Wrangell Institute Complex.

From the trailhead it is a mile hike to the waterfalls and then another 2.5 miles to an observation point overlooking Shoemaker Bay on Institute Ridge, where the USFS has built a three-sided shelter. The lower section of the trail can be soggy at times, so rubber boots are useful. Upper sections of the trail are steep. The views are worth the hike, and a pleasant evening can be spent on the ridge. A roundtrip takes four to six hours.

Thoms Lake Trail At the end of the paved Zimovia Hwy is a dirt road, known officially as Forest Rd 6290, that extends 30 miles south along Wrangell Island. On this road, 23 miles south of Wrangell, is the Thoms Lake Trail, which leads 1.2 miles to a state park recreation cabin and a skiff on the lake. Since there is no state park office in Wrangell, you have to reserve the cabin through the Division of Parks office in Juneau (☎ 465-4563). Keep in mind that this trail cuts through muskeg and can get extremely muddy during wet weather. It is a 1½-hour hike to the cabin.

Long Lake Trail The trailhead for the Long Lake Trail is 27 miles southeast of Wrangell on Forest Rd 6270. This pleasant hike is only 0.6 miles long and is planked the entire way. It leads to a shelter, skiff and outhouses on the shores of the lake. Plan on an hour for the trek into the lake and back.

Highbush Lake Trail This very short (300-foot) path leads to the lake, where there's a skiff and oars. Fishing is fair and the surrounding views excellent. The parking lot for the trailhead is off Forest Rd 6265 and Forest Rd 50040, 29 miles southeast of Wrangell.

Paddling
A narrow, rugged shoreline and surrounding mountains and glaciers characterize the beautiful, wild Stikine River. It is the fastest navigable river in North America. The river's highlight is the Grand Canyon, a steep-walled enclosure of the waterway where churning white water makes river travel impossible.

SOUTHEAST

Trips from below the canyon are common among rafters and kayakers; they begin with a charter flight to Telegraph Creek in British Columbia and end with a 160-mile float back to Wrangell. Travelers who arrive at Wrangell with a kayak but not enough funds to charter a bush plane can undertake a trip from the town's harbor across the Stikine Flats, where there are several USFS cabins, and up one of the three arms of the Stikine River. By keeping close to shore and taking advantage of eddies and sloughs, experienced paddlers can make their way 30 miles up the Stikine River to the Canadian border, or even farther, passing 12 USFS cabins and the two bathing huts at Chief Shakes Hot Springs along the way. But you must know how to line a boat upstream and navigate a highly braided river and, while in the lower reaches, accept the fact there will be a considerable amount of jet-boat traffic.

The USFS office in Wrangell can provide information on the Stikine River, including a very helpful brochure and map entitled *Stikine River Canoe & Kayak Trips*. You can't rent a canoe or kayak in Wrangell, so if you are still intrigued by the Stikine River, plan to rent a boat in Juneau or Ketchikan.

Guide companies no longer offer boat trips down the Stikine, probably due to a lack of demand. Several charter captains will run up the river, but usually only for a day of fishing or sightseeing. Call Stikine Wilderness (☎ 800-874-2085) or Breakaway Adventures (☎ 874-2488) for such a trip and expect to pay $155 for a five- to seven-hour ride up the river.

Special Events

The only major event during the summer, other than the local salmon derby, is the 4th of July celebration. All of Wrangell, like most small Alaskan communities, gets involved in the festival, which features a parade, fireworks, a logging show, street games, food booths and a salmon bake in town.

In the third week of April, Wrangell stages its Garnet Festival (see the 'Garnet Sellers of Wrangell' boxed text). The weeklong event is timed with the large spring gathering of bald eagles in the area and includes wildlife tours and photography workshops, live music, a street fair and a craft show.

Garnet Sellers of Wrangell

Garnet Ledge, located 8 miles northeast of Wrangell on the mainland, has been mined for more than a century, including by the first all-woman corporation in the USA. The all-woman Alaska Garnet Mining and Manufacturing Co was based in Minneapolis and operated at the ledge from 1912 to 1922, using the garnets to make hatpin heads, watch fobs and other such jewelry of the day. In 1962, former mayor Fred Hanford deeded the ledge to the children of Wrangell and placed the ledge in the care of the local Boy Scout council. Now only children are allowed to sell garnets.

Garnets grow out of minerals that undergo crystallization brought about by heat and pressure, and Wrangell garnets have long been recognized for their faceted, luminous beauty. But the garnets' structure and color make them difficult to cut into attractive stones for jewelry. Still, they are popular souvenirs, and young garnet sellers meet most cruise ships that dock in Wrangell.

To collect garnets on your own, first obtain a $10 permit through the Wrangell Museum (☎ 874-3770) and contact a charter operator, through the visitor center, for a trip to the ledge. When you return from the ledge you must donate 10% of your garnet collection to the museum. The revenue from the sale of the garnets helps to support the local Boy and Girl Scout troops in town.

If you happen to be in Southeast Alaska around the third week of April, Wrangell stages its Garnet Festival then. The weeklong event celebrates the famous Garnet Ledge and the large spring gathering of bald eagles in the area with workshops and tours to collect the gems or spot eagles.

Places to Stay

Wrangell has a 7% city tax and a $3 bed tax for hotels, B&Bs and the hostel.

Camping The nearest campground to town is the *city park*, 1.8 miles south of the ferry terminal on Zimovia Hwy. This waterfront park is immediately south of the cemetery and city ball field and provides picnic tables, shelters and rest rooms. Camping is free, but for tents only, and there is a one-night limit.

Farther out of town, across from the trailhead to the Rainbow Falls Trail, is the *Shoemaker Bay Recreation Area*, 4.7 miles south of the ferry terminal on Zimovia Hwy. Camping is in a wooded area near a creek. There is a 10-day limit but no fees for tents. The fee for RVs is $6 to $10.

Still farther south is *Pat's Creek*, Mile 11 Zimovia Hwy, where it becomes a narrow forest service road. There are two dirt roads heading off to the left; the first is to the lake and the second is to the campground, which is basically just a clear spot to park vehicles. Near the campground there is a trail along the creek that leads back to Pat's Lake, where there are some excellent spots to fish for cutthroat trout and Dolly Varden.

Cabins The 20 USFS cabins in the Wrangell Ranger District are not as busy as those around Juneau or Ketchikan. Six of them (Binkley Slough, Koknuk, Little Dry Island, Sergief Island and two on Gut Island) lie on the Stikine River flats, 12 to 15 miles from Wrangell. The cabins can be reached by paddling or by a 30-minute bush-plane flight.

Hostels The *Wrangell Hostel* (☎ 874-3534, 220 Church St) was organized in Wrangell in 1994 in the First Presbyterian Church, the oldest continuously operating Protestant church in Alaska, dating back to 1877. The hostel provides affordable accommodations, kitchen facilities and showers for $10 a night.

B&Bs If staying in a private home interests you, the area has a handful of B&Bs, including several downtown. You can get a complete list from the visitor bureau or try *Grand View B&B* (☎ 874-3225), Mile 2 Zimovia Hwy, which has four rooms that range in price from $75 for a small double to $105 for the one-bedroom apartment. The *Anchor B&B* (☎ 874-2078, 325 Church St) is five minutes from town, and *Fennimore's by the Ferry* (☎ 874-3012), across from the ferry terminal, offers a private entrance and the use of bicycles. Both charge around $65/70 singles/doubles.

Hotels The cheapest hotel in town is the *Thunderbird Hotel* (☎ 874-3322, 223 Front St), with rooms at $65/75. The *Stikine Inn* (☎ 874-3388, 107 Front St), near the cruise ship dock, is a nicer place, with rooms for $75/80. A mile south of town is *Harding's Old Sourdough Lodge* (☎ 874-3613, 800-874-3613, 1104 Peninsula Ave), with 20 rooms, a sauna, a steam bath and free transportation from the ferry or airport. Rooms are $75/85 singles/doubles, and meals are available.

Places to Eat

The cheapest place for a meal is undoubtedly the *Diamond C Cafe*, in the Kadin Building on Front St and Outer Drive. It is open daily and has breakfasts for around $6, sandwiches and hamburgers for around $7 and local seafood. Nearer to the ferry terminal and open later at night is *J&W's Fast Foods*, at the city dock, which sells fish sandwiches and shrimp burgers. *JR Fish Co (120 Front St)* offers take-out fish sandwiches, soups and shrimp salads, and *Jitterbugs (309 Front St)* is an espresso stand that serves up lattes, cappuccinos and Italian sodas. You can join the guests at *Harding's Old Sourdough Lodge (1104 Peninsula Ave)* for homestyle meals. Breakfast and lunch are $10 per person and dinner $20. The top place to eat, featuring local shrimp and other seafood, is the *Waterfront Grill*, on the ground floor of the Stikine Inn, which has an excellent view of the harbor. Full dinners hover around $20, or a hand-thrown pizza that will feed two is $15.

Benjamin's Supermarket (223 Brueger St), off Outer Drive, has an in-store bakery and ready-to-eat items in its deli.

SOUTHEAST

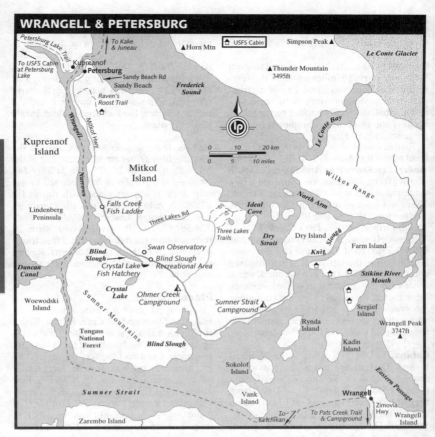

WRANGELL & PETERSBURG

Entertainment

Wrangell's bars are often where the town's true spirit shines through. Mingle with locals at the *Totem Bar* on Front St or with people from the fishing industry at the *Marine Bar*, on Shakes St near Chief Shakes Island. During a night run on the ferry, you have time to get off for a beer at the *Stikine Inn Lounge*, which has live music and the only dance floor in Wrangell.

Getting There & Away

Air Alaska Airlines (☎ 874-3308) provides year-round jet service to Wrangell, with a daily northbound and southbound flight. Many claim that the flight north to Petersburg is the 'world's shortest jet flight,' since the 11-minute trip is little more than a takeoff and landing.

Boat There is an almost daily northbound and southbound ferry service from Wrangell in the summer. The next stop north is Petersburg via the scenic, winding Wrangell Narrows. The ferry terminal in Wrangell is open 1½ hours before each ferry arrival and from 2 to 5 pm on weekdays. Call ☎ 874-3711 for 24-hour ferry information.

Getting Around
Practical Rent-A-Car (☎ 874-3975) is located at the airport. Compacts begin at $43 per day.

Petersburg

When the ferry heads north from Wrangell, it begins one of the most scenic and exciting sections of the Inside Passage. After crossing over from Wrangell Island to Mitkof Island, the ferry threads its way through the 46 turns of Wrangell Narrows, a 22-mile channel that is only 300 feet wide and 19 feet deep in places. At one point, the sides of the ship are so close to the shore that you can almost gather firewood for the evening.

At the other end of this breathtaking journey lies Petersburg (population 3415), one of the hidden gems of Southeast Alaska. This busy little town, an active fishing port during the summer, is decorated by weathered boathouses on the waterfront, freshly painted homes along Nordic Drive and the distinctive Devil's Thumb peak and other snowcapped mountains on the horizon.

History
Peter Buschmann arrived in the area in 1897 and found a fine harbor, abundant fish and a ready supply of ice from nearby Le Conte Glacier. He built a cannery and enticed his Norwegian friends to follow him there, and the resulting town was named after him. Today, a peek into the local phone book will reveal evidence of the strong Norwegian heritage that unifies Petersburg.

Petersburg is the youngest community in the Southeast but boasts of having the largest home-based halibut fleet in Alaska, some say the world. The economy has blossomed on fishing as the town processes more than $45 million worth of seafood annually through four canneries and two cold-storage plants that draw an army of summer workers from the Lower 48. Several of the canneries sit above the water on pilings, overlooking boat harbors bulging with vessels and a constant flow of barges, ferries

and seaplanes. Even at night, you can see small boats trolling the nearby waters for somebody's dinner.

Without a dependency on timber, Petersburg enjoys a healthier economy than Wrangell or Ketchikan. This partly explains why the town doesn't go out of its way for tourists. The other reason is that it lacks a deepwater port for large cruise ships to dock. For independent travelers this is good and bad: you won't be overrun by masses of tourists pouring out of the Love Boat, but the lack of a youth hostel and viable camping areas near town often leaves little choice but to book an $80 room for the night.

Information
Tourist Offices The Petersburg Visitor Center (☎ 772-3646, www.petersburg.org), at Fram and 1st Sts, has both community and USFS information. It's open until 5 pm daily during the summer.

For information about hiking trails, paddling, camping or reserving cabins, head over to the US Forest Service office (☎ 772-3871), upstairs in the federal building on Nordic Drive. The office is open 8 am to 5 pm weekdays.

Money National Bank of Alaska (☎ 772-3833) has an office at 201 Nordic Drive.

Post The post office is in the first level of the federal building on Nordic Drive.

Email & Internet Access Head to the Petersburg Public Library in the Municipal Building or Chips, a small computer shop behind Kito's Kave on Sing Lee Alley, for email and Internet access.

Travel Agencies Viking Travel (☎ 772-2571, 800-327-2571) is on the corner of Harbor Way and Chief John Lott St.

Bookstores Sing Lee Alley Books, on Sing Lee Alley of course, is a delightful little bookstore with an impressive selection of Alaska material. You can purchase topographic maps at Diamante (☎ 772-4858), a gift shop on Nordic Drive.

SOUTHEAST

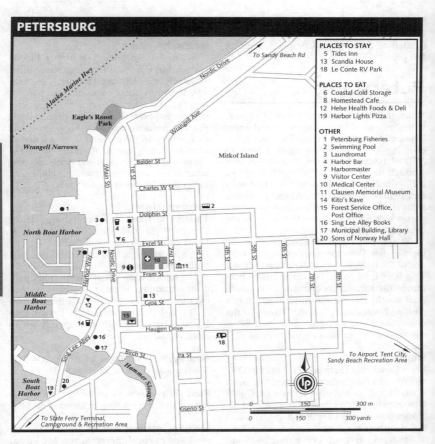

PETERSBURG

PLACES TO STAY
5 Tides Inn
13 Scandia House
18 Le Conte RV Park

PLACES TO EAT
6 Coastal Cold Storage
8 Homestead Cafe
12 Helse Health Foods & Deli
19 Harbor Lights Pizza

OTHER
1 Petersburg Fisheries
2 Swimming Pool
3 Laundromat
4 Harbor Bar
7 Harbormaster
9 Visitor Center
10 Medical Center
11 Clausen Memorial Museum
14 Kito's Kave
15 Forest Service Office,
   Post Office
16 Sing Lee Alley Books
17 Municipal Building, Library
20 Sons of Norway Hall

Libraries The Petersburg Public Library is on the second level of the Municipal Building at Nordic Drive and Haugen Drive. It's open daily, and until 9 pm Monday through Thursday, and often has used books for sale.

Laundry Glacier Laundry, on Nordic Drive, is open until 10 pm and has showers for $3.

Medical Services Petersburg Medical Center (☎ 772-4291), at 1st and Fram Sts, is the local hospital.

Things to See
On the waterfront near the corner of Dolphin St and Nordic Drive is **Petersburg Fisheries**, founded in 1900 by Peter Buschmann and today a subsidiary of Icicle Seafoods of Seattle. On Harbor Way, at the end of Gjoa St, is the long pier that leads out to **Ocean Beauty Seafoods**. The canneries, the backbone of the Petersburg economy, are not open to the public and do not offer tours.

Continuing south, Harbor Way passes Middle Boat Harbor and turns into **Sing Lee**

Alley. This was the center of old Petersburg, and much of the street is built on pilings over Hammer Slough. The **Sons of Norway Hall**, begun by Buschmann in 1897 and finished in 1912, is the large white building with the colorful rosemaling, a flowery Norwegian art form.

Hammer Slough provides photographers with the most colorful images of Petersburg. Both Sing Lee Alley and Birch St follow the tidal area and wind past clusters of weathered homes and boathouses suspended on pillars above a shoreline of old boats, nets and crab pots. Sing Lee Alley crosses Hammer Slough and then joins Nordic Drive. To the south, Nordic Drive turns into Mitkof Hwy and heads out past the ferry terminal; to the north Nordic Drive heads back into the center of Petersburg.

Turn east up Fram St from Nordic Drive to the **Clausen Memorial Museum** (☎ 772-3598) on the corner of 2nd St. Outside the museum is the *Fisk*, an 11-foot bronze sculpture commemorating the town's life by the sea. Inside the museum is an interesting collection of local artifacts and relics, most tied in with the history of fishing in Petersburg. The largest king salmon ever caught – 126lb – is in the back room. The giant lens from the old Cape Decision Lighthouse is also on display. The museum is open until 4:30 pm daily during the summer; admission costs $3.

From the downtown area, Nordic Drive heads north and then curves east at **Eagle's Roost Park**, a small hilltop park where you can often see eagles perched in the trees. A little farther is Hungry Point View Area, where the Wrangell Narrows merges into Frederick Sound, and finally **Sandy Beach Recreation Area**, 2 miles from downtown. The day-use area features three enclosed shelters and Tlingit petroglyphs that can be seen at low tide. Call the USFS office about interpretive walks at Sandy Beach to look at the petroglyphs.

Hiking

Raven's Roost Trail This 4-mile trail begins at the water tower on the southeast side of the airport, accessible from Haugen Drive. A boardwalk crosses muskeg areas at the start of the trail, and much of the route is a climb to beautiful open alpine areas at 2013 feet; some of it is steep and requires a little scrambling. A two-story US Forest Service cabin (reservations needed, $35 per night) is above the tree line in an area that provides good summer hiking and spectacular views of Petersburg, Frederick Sound and Wrangell Narrows.

Petersburg Mountain Trail On Kupreanof Island, this trail ascends 2.5 miles from Wrangell Narrows behind Sasby Island to the top of Petersburg Mountain. The best views in the area are here: of Petersburg, the Coast Mountains, glaciers and the Wrangell Narrows. Plan on three hours to the top of the mountain and two hours for the return. To get across the channel, go to the skiff float at the North Boat Harbor (Old Boat Harbor) and hitch a ride with somebody who lives on Kupreanof Island. From the Kupreanof Public Dock, head right on the overgrown road towards Sasby Island. You can also call Petersburg Creek Charters (☎ 772-2425), which runs hikers across the channel for $20 roundtrip per person.

Petersburg Lake Trail This 10.5-mile trail, part of a trail system in the Petersburg Creek-Duncan Salt Chuck Wilderness on Kupreanof Island, leads to a USFS cabin (reservations needed, $35 per night). See the Backpacking section in the Wilderness chapter for further details.

Three Lakes Trails These four short trails, connecting three lakes and Ideal Cove, are off Three Lakes Rd, a forest service road that heads east off Mitkof Hwy at Mile 13.6 and returns at Mile 23.8. Beginning at Mile 14.2 of Three Lakes Rd is a 3-mile loop with boardwalks leading to Sand, Crane and Hill lakes, which are known for their good trout fishing.

On each lake there is a skiff and a picnic platform. Tennis shoes are fine for the trail, but to explore around the lakes you need rubber boots. There is a free-use shelter on Sand Lake. From the Sand Lake Trail there is a 1.5-mile trail to Ideal Cove on Frederick Sound.

Blind River Rapids Boardwalk Starting at Mile 14.5 of the Mitkof Hwy, this easy mile-long boardwalk winds through muskeg before arriving at the rapids, a popular fishing spot during the summer.

Paddling

There are a variety of interesting trips in the Petersburg area, most of which are blue-water paddles requiring a week or more. Kayak rentals are difficult to come by in Petersburg. Try Tongass Kayak Adventures (☎ 772-4600, tonkayak@alaska.net), which offers a five-hour guided tour up Petersburg Creek for $55 and multiday trips to Le Conte Glacier. You might also try Sea Wind Charters (☎ 772-4389, Seawind@alaska.net), which offers trips that combine cruising on a sailboat with kayaking near the glacier.

For transportation, there's Alaskan Scenic Waterways (☎ 772-3777, 800-279-1176) and Kaleidoscope Cruises (☎ 800-868-4373, bbsea@alaska.net) which makes runs to both Le Conte Glacier and Thomas Bay. Contact the chamber of commerce office for a current list of all the charter operators.

Le Conte Glacier The most spectacular paddle in the region is to Le Conte Glacier, 25 miles east of Petersburg, the southernmost tidewater glacier in North America. From town, it takes three to four days to reach the frozen monument, including crossing Frederick Sound north of Coney Island. The crossing should be done at slack tide, as winds and tides can cause choppy conditions. If the tides are judged right, it is possible to paddle far enough into Le Conte Bay to camp within view of the glacier.

To skip the paddling but still see the glacier, check with Kupreanof Flying Service (☎ 772-3396) for a flightseeing trip, but expect to split $150 among three passengers

for the trip. More worthwhile is a cruise to the glacier with Alaskan Scenic Waterways (☎ 772-3777, 800-279-1176), which has a full-day cruise that includes the Stikine River for $155 per person.

Thomas Bay Almost as impressive as Le Conte Glacier is Thomas Bay, 20 miles from Petersburg and north of Le Conte Bay on the east side of Frederick Sound. The bay features a pair of glaciers, including Baird Glacier, where many paddlers spend a day hiking. The mountain scenery surrounding the bay is spectacular, and there are three USFS cabins (reservations needed, $35 per night): Swan Lake Cabin, Spurt Cove Cabin and Cascade Creek Cabin. Paddlers need four to seven days for the roundtrip out of Petersburg.

Kake to Petersburg Backpackers can take the ferry to the Native Alaskan village of Kake and paddle back to Petersburg. This 90-mile route follows the west side of Kupreanof Island through Keku Strait, Sumner Strait and up the Wrangell Narrows to Petersburg. The highlight of the trip is Rocky Pass, a remote and narrow winding waterway in Keku Strait that has almost no boat traffic other than the occasional kayaker. Caution has to be used in Sumner Strait, which lies only 40 miles away from open ocean and has its share of strong winds and waves. Plan on seven to 10 days for the trip.

Whale Watching

In recent years, whale watching has become a popular trip out of Petersburg. Humpback whales, which winter in Baja and Hawaii, migrate annually to summer feeding grounds in Southeast Alaska. One of the better areas to view whales is Frederick Sound just east of Petersburg. Biologists estimate as many as 450 whales enter the sound every summer from mid-May to mid-September, with the peak feeding period in July and August. Other wildlife that can be spotted during whale cruises include Steller's sea lions, orcas and seals.

Most charter boat operators in town offer whale watching as either half- or full-day tours. A full-day trip is eight hours long and runs $125 to $150 per person. Kaleidoscope Cruises (☎ 800-868-4373, bbsea@alaska.net) and Alaska Passages Adventure Cruises (☎ 888-434-3766, 772-3967, akpassag@alaska .net) offer such trips, or you can get a complete list of charter operators from the visitors bureau.

Special Events

Petersburg puts on its own 4th of July celebration with the usual small-town festivities and a couple of salmon derbies during the summer. The community's best event, and one that is famous around the Southeast, is the Little Norway Festival, held on the weekend closest to Norwegian Independence Day on May 17, usually before most tourists arrive. If you are even near the area, hop over to Petersburg for it. The locals dress in old costumes, Nordic Drive is filled with a string of booths and games, and several dances are held in local halls. The best part of the festival is the fish feed, when the town's residents put together a potluck feast.

Places to Stay

Petersburg adds 10% to the price of any bed in town.

Camping It is difficult to camp near town. Petersburg has *Tent City*, on Haugen Drive, half a mile or a 10-minute walk northwest of the airport. The city-operated campground provides 50 wooden pads, each holding three to five tents, to avoid the wet muskeg. However, the facility was designed primarily for young cannery workers who invariably arrive in the early summer months and occupy an entire pad by building plastic shelters around them. By the time most travelers arrive, there are few, if any, spaces available to pitch a tent. An on-site campground manager is there most evenings to collect the $5 fee.

Within town *Le Conte RV Park* (772-4680), at 4th St and Haugen Drive, charges $7 for a tent site. Out of town, the *Ohmer*

Creek Campground, Mile 22 Mitkof Hwy, is a free facility with 15 sites, an interpretive trail, fishing in the creek and a scenic setting.

Backpackers have a couple of ways to avoid the lack of budget accommodations in Petersburg. There is no camping within the city limits, and if you pitch a tent at the Sandy Beach Recreation Area, on the corner of Sandy Beach Rd and Haugen Drive 3 miles north of town, local police will most likely kick you out in the middle of the night. However, by hiking half a mile beyond Sandy Beach Recreation Area out on Frederick Point, you can camp on the scenic beach. Bring drinking water and pitch your tent above the high-tide line. You can also camp up along the Raven's Roost Trail, which begins near the airport, but you will have to walk more than a mile uphill before finding a site that isn't muskeg.

Hostels Petersburg doesn't have a hostel, but it does have *Bunk & Breakfast* (☎ 772-3632, ryn@alaska.net). Bunk & Breakfast is a 10-minute walk from the downtown area and has eight bunks for $25, including breakfast. You must call in advance for the location and availability of beds.

B&Bs Petersburg has a half dozen B&Bs, and practically all of them charge around $70/90 for singles/doubles. At *Nordic House* (☎ 772-3620), three blocks north of the ferry terminal, guests enjoy a spectacular view of the Narrows. The B&B has four rooms that range in price from $70 to $100. *Water's Edge B&B* (☎ 772-3736, 800-868-4373, 705 Sandy Beach Rd) has the same rates and is north of town overlooking Frederick Sound. *Harbor Day B&B* (☎ 772-3971, 404 Noseeum St) is a half mile from either the ferry terminal or downtown and has some of the best rates in town. Singles/doubles are $60/70. The visitor center has brochures for all of the B&Bs.

Hotels Hotel rooms in Petersburg are expensive. The *Tides Inn* (☎ 772-4288, 800-665-8433), at 1st and Dolphin Sts, has singles/doubles for $70/85, including a continental breakfast, and some rooms have kitchenettes. **Scandia House** (☎ 772-4281), on Nordic Drive, is in the center of town and has 33 rooms for $75 to $175.

Places to Eat

Locals eat at **Homestead Cafe** (106 Nordic Drive), which can be a little greasy at times but is open 24 hours and has breakfasts for $6 to $7. The hamburgers ($5 to $8) are served with a huge scoop of potato salad. **Harbor Lights Pizza**, opposite the Sons of Norway Hall on Sing Lee Alley, offers pasta dinners ($7), pizzas ($12 to $15), beer on tap, wine and a good view of the busy boat harbor. The best pizza is at **Pelleritos Pizza** (1105 S Nordic Drive), near the ferry terminal, and good Chinese can be enjoyed at **Joan Mei** (1103 S Nordic Drive). Dinners here cost $9 to $14.

Another interesting place in town is **Helse Health Foods & Deli** (17 Sing Lee Alley). The health-food store and restaurant is a pleasant place for tea during a rainy afternoon and features soups or seafood chowder with a thick slice of homemade bread for $5. The best seafood is at **Coastal Cold Storage**, downtown at 306 Nordic Drive. You can purchase shrimp sandwiches and salads, live crab, oysters and clams, or takeaways such as halibut beer bits with french fries ($7).

Petersburg's main supermarket is **Hammer & Wikan** (1300 Howkan), out by the airport, which features a bakery and a deli counter.

Entertainment

To listen to the fishers' woes or meet cannery workers, go to the **Harbor Bar** (310 Nordic Drive). For something livelier, try **Kito's Kave** (11 Sing Lee Alley). This bar and liquor store has live music and dancing most nights after 9 pm. When the boats are in it can be a rowdy place that hops until well after 1 am.

Getting There & Away

Air The Alaska Airlines (☎ 772-4255) milk run through the Southeast provides a daily northbound and southbound flight out of Petersburg. The airport is a mile east of the post office on Haugen Drive.

Boat The Alaska Marine Hwy terminal (☎ 772-3855) is about a mile south along Nordic Drive from the southern edge of town. One northbound ferry usually arrives daily. Travelers continuing on to Juneau should consider taking the M/V Le Conte on Tuesday if it fits into their schedule. This ship sails from Petersburg to Juneau but stops at Kake, Sitka, Angoon, Tenakee and Hoonah along the way; the one-way fare is $44.

Getting Around

Car The Tides Inn is also an Avis dealer and has midsize cars for $66 a day. During the summer you should call ahead to reserve a vehicle.

Bicycle Northern Bikes Sports (☎ 772-3978), 110 Nordic Drive, rents mountain bikes for $5 an hour or $25 a day.

AROUND PETERSBURG

There are a few sights around Petersburg, although it's debatable whether it's worth the hassle of getting out to see them. Travelers without transportation can either rent a vehicle or contact Tongass Traveler Tours (☎ 772-4837), which offers a three-hour van tour. For $25, Patti Norheim takes you to a shrimp cannery and fish hatchery, among other things, and then returns you to her home in town, where you sit on her deck enjoying wine and a shrimp cocktail.

One of the best fishing spots in the area is at Mile 14.5 of the Mitkof Hwy, south of Petersburg, where a 0.3-mile boardwalk leads through a muskeg meadow to the **Blind River Rapids Recreation Area**. There is a small trail shelter along the river where anglers come to catch Dolly Varden, cutthroat trout and steelhead from mid-April to mid-May, king salmon in June and July and coho salmon after mid-August.

Farther south, the **Crystal Lake Fish Hatchery**, at Mile 17.5 of the Mitkof Hwy, is a $2.2 million facility used to stock coho, king salmon and trout throughout the Southeast. No formal tours are offered, but hatchery personnel are pleasant and informative. It is open 8 am to 4 pm weekdays. Nearby, in Blind Slough Recreation Area is the **Trumpeter Swan Observatory**, designed to permit sheltered photography and viewing of this majestic bird.

On the way back to town, stop at the **Falls Creek Fish Ladder** at Mile 13.7 of the Mitkof Hwy, an impressive sight in August, when coho and pink salmon leap along its steps.

Sitka

In a region of Alaska already strong in color and history, Sitka (population 8733) is a gem in a beautiful setting. Facing the Pacific Ocean, the city is overshadowed to the west by Mt Edgecumbe, an extinct volcano with a cone similar to Japan's Mt Fuji. The waters offshore are broken up by a myriad of small, forested islands that are ragged silhouettes during the sunsets, and to the east, the town is flanked by snowcapped mountains and sharp granite peaks. On a clear day Sitka, the only city in Southeast Alaska that actually fronts the Pacific Ocean, rivals Juneau for the sheer beauty of its surroundings.

History
Along with its natural beauty, Sitka is steeped in history. The Russians may have landed in Sitka Sound as early as 1741, after two ships under explorer Vitus Bering became separated in a storm. While Bering was in Mt St Elias to confirm the presence of a continent, the other ship was much farther south, where it sent two longboats ashore in Sitka Sound in search of water. The boats never returned, and the Russians wisely departed.

What the sailors undoubtedly encountered were members of two powerful Tlingit tribes: the Kiksadi and the Kogwanton, who over time had developed the most advanced culture of any group of Native Americans in Alaska. The Tlingits were still there in 1799 when the Russians returned and established the first nonindigenous settlement in the Southeast. Aleksandr Baranov built a Russian fort near the present ferry terminal

to continue the rich sea-otter fur trade. He was in Kodiak three years later when Tlingits, armed with guns from British and American traders, overwhelmed the fort, burned it to the ground and killed most of its inhabitants.

Baranov returned in 1804, this time with an imperial Russian warship, and after destroying the Tlingit fort, established a settlement called New Archangel at the present site of Sitka, making it the headquarters of the Russian-American Company that controlled the fur trade. Sitka flourished both economically and culturally on the strength of the fur trade and was known as the 'Paris of the Pacific' in its golden era.

In 1867, Sitka picked up its present name, after the USA took control of the town following the purchase of Alaska. After the territorial capital was transferred to Juneau in 1900, Sitka fell upon some hard times, but it boomed again during WWII, when a military base was built on nearby Japonski Island. Today, the city is supported by a fishing fleet, cold-storage plants, several federal agencies that have offices in the area and, of course, tourism. A pulp mill that closed in 1993 hurt Sitka economically but didn't devastate the town, as was the case a year later in Wrangell.

The charm of Sitka is not only its natural beauty but the way the residents cling to the area's strong Russian heritage and pride themselves on being the cultural center of the Southeast, if not of all Alaska. It seemed only natural to those living in Sitka that when author James Michener decided to write his epic novel *Alaska* he chose their town as his home base to conduct research.

Orientation
When arriving in Sitka by ferry, you will sail through the Sergius Narrows, a tight waterway that ships must navigate at slack tide. At any other time, the passage is too hazardous for vessels to negotiate the fierce currents caused by the tides. This often forces the ferry to take a three-hour stop at Sitka while waiting for the tide and allows travelers a quick view of the city, even if they're not disembarking.

SITKA

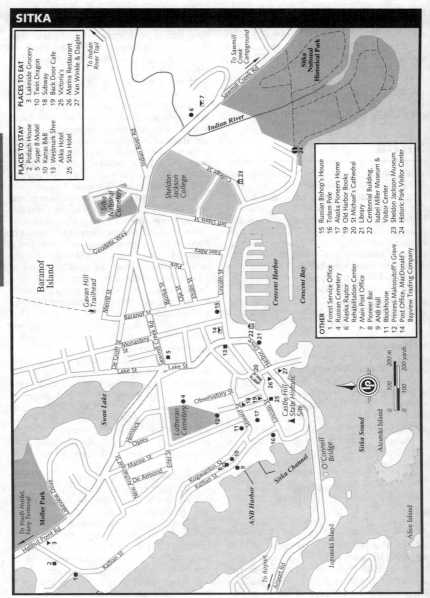

SOUTHEAST

PLACES TO STAY
2 Potlatch House
5 Super 8 Motel
10 Karras B&B
13 Westmark Shee Atika Hotel
25 Sitka Hotel

PLACES TO EAT
3 Lakeside Grocery
10 Twin Dragon
18 Subway
19 Back Door Cafe
25 Victoria's
26 Marina Restaurant
27 Van Winkle & Daigler

OTHER
1 Forest Service Office
4 Russian Cemetery
6 Alaska Raptor Rehabilitation Center
7 Main Post Office
8 Pioneer Bar
9 ANB Hall
11 Blockhouse
12 Princess Maksoutoff's Grave
14 Post Office, MacDonald's Bayview Trading Company
15 Russian Bishop's House
16 Totem Pole
17 Alaska Pioneers Home
19 Old Harbor Books
20 St Michael's Cathedral
21 Library
22 Centennial Building, Isabel Miller Museum & Visitor Center
23 Sheldon Jackson Museum
24 Historic Park Visitor Center

Baranof Island

Gavan Hill Trailhead

Sitka National Cemetery

Sitka National Historical Park

To Indian River Trail

To Sawmill Creek Campground

To Sawmill Creek Rd

Indian River

Sheldon Jackson College

Indian River Rd

College St

Jeff Davis St

Geodetic Way

Merrill St

De Groff St

Monastery St

Sawmill Creek Rd

Baranof St

Park St

Bjorka St

Ola St

Etolin St

Finn Alley

Lincoln St

Lake St

Lake St

Crescent Harbor

Crescent Bay

Swan Lake

Hemlock St

Osprey St

New Archangel St

Marine St

Erler St

Lutheran Cemetery

Observatory St

Seward St

Lincoln St

Harbor Drive

Castle Hill State Historic Site

Kogwanton St

Katlian St

Sitka Channel

ANB Harbor

O'Connell Bridge

Sitka Sound

Aleutski Island

Alice Island

Japonski Island

To Airport

Airport Rd

To Youth Hostel, Ferry Terminal

Moller Park

Lakeview Drive

Halibut Point Rd

Katlian St

0   100   200 m
0   100   200 yards

The ferry terminal is 7 miles north of town, too far to see anything on foot, but Sitka Tours (☎ 747-8443) does run a bus tour for those waiting for the ferry to depart (see Organized Tours).

Information

Tourist Offices The Sitka Visitor Bureau (☎ 747-5940, www.sitka.org) is part of the Isabel Miller Museum in the Centennial Building off Harbor Drive next to the Crescent Boat Harbor. The bureau is open 8 am to 6 pm daily in the summer. The US Forest Service office (☎ 747-6671), the place to go for trail information, cabin reservations and brochures about enjoying the wilderness, is in a three-story red building on the corner of Siginaka and Katlian Sts, across from the Thomas Boat Harbor. The office is open 8 am to 5 pm weekdays.

Money There are two banks downtown on Lincoln St, including National Bank of Alaska (☎ 747-3226).

Post The main post office is a mile out of town on Sawmill Creek Rd. In the downtown area, there is a substation in the MacDonald's Bayview Trading Company building, 407 Lincoln St.

Email & Internet Access The Highliner Coffee, in the Seward Mall on Kimsham St, is a cybercafe with Internet access and email.

Travel Agencies Totem Travel (☎ 747-3251, 800-478-3252) is at 903 Halibut Point Rd.

Bookstores & Libraries Books and topographic maps can be purchased downtown at Old Harbor Books (☎ 747-8808), 201 Lincoln St. Next door to the Centennial Building is the city's impressive Kettleson Memorial Library (☎ 747-8708), an excellent rainy-day spot that's open daily.

Laundry & Showers You can wash your clothes, or get a shower, at Homestead Laundromat, 713 Katlian St, behind Potlatch Motel, or Duds 'n' Suds at 906 Halibut Point Rd.

Medical Services The Sitka Community Hospital (☎ 747-3241), 209 Moller Drive at Halibut Point Rd and Brady St, is located just north of town.

Things to See

Within the Centennial Building is the **Isabel Miller Museum**, which has a collection of relics from the past and a model of the town as it appeared in 1867. Outside is a hand-carved Tlingit canoe made from a single log. The museum is open 8 am to 5 pm daily in the summer; $2 donation requested.

At the heart of the city center is **St Michael's Cathedral**, on Lincoln St two blocks west from the Centennial Building. Built between 1844 and 1848, the church stood for over 100 years as the finest Russian Orthodox cathedral in Alaska, until fire destroyed it in 1966. The priceless treasures and icons inside were saved by Sitka's residents, who built a replica of the original cathedral. The church is open 1:30 to 5:30 pm daily and longer if there is a cruise ship in town; $2 donation requested.

Continue west on Lincoln St for the walkway to **Castle Hill**. This was the site of an early stronghold of the indigenous Kiksadi clan and later the foundation of a succession of Russian buildings, including Baranov's Castle, which housed the governor of Russian America in 1837. It was here, on October 18, 1867, that the official transfer of Alaska from Russia to the USA took place.

More Russian cannons can be seen in **Totem Square**, near the end of Lincoln St. Next to the square is the prominent, yellow **Alaska Pioneers Home**. Built in 1934 on the old Russian Parade Ground, the home is for elderly Alaskans. Visitors are welcome to meet the 'old sourdoughs' and listen to their fascinating stories of gold-rush days or homesteading in the wilderness. A gift shop on the first floor sells handicrafts made by the residents. The 13-foot bronze prospector statue in front of the state home was dedicated on Alaska Day in 1949 and is modeled on longtime Alaskan resident William 'Skagway Bill' Fonda.

Another remnant of Sitka's Russian background can be seen on the hill west of

SOUTHEAST

the Alaska Pioneers Home. On the corner of Kogwanton and Marine Sts is the replica **blockhouse** of the type the Russians used to guard their stockade and separate it from the Indian village. Originally, three blockhouses on a wall kept the Tlingits restricted to an area along Katlian St. Adjacent to the wooden blockhouse, in the Lutheran Cemetery, is **Princess Maksoutoff's Grave**, marking the exact spot where the wife of Alaska's last Russian governor is buried. More old headstones and Russian Orthodox crosses are at the end of Observatory St, in the **Russian Cemetery**.

The **Russian Bishop's House**, the oldest intact Russian building in Sitka, is the first of many sights at the east end of town. The soft-yellow structure on Lincoln St, across from the west end of Crescent Harbor, was built in 1842 and is one of the few surviving examples of Russian colonial architecture in North America. Bishop Ivan Veniaminov, who eventually was canonized St Innocent, was the first resident of the home, which was later used as a school, chapel and office.

The National Park Service has renovated the building to its 1853 condition. A museum dedicated to its Russian occupants is on the 1st floor. The 2nd floor has been restored as the bishop's personal quarters and the Chapel of the Annunciation. Hours are 9 am to 1 pm and 2 to 5 pm daily in the summer; admission is $3.

Farther east along Lincoln St, past the boat harbor, is Sheldon Jackson College, where Michener stayed and worked for much of the three summers he spent in Alaska. Among the buildings on campus is the octagonal **Sheldon Jackson Museum**. Constructed in 1895, it's the oldest cement building in Alaska and today houses one of the best indigenous-culture collections in the state.

The artifacts were gathered by Dr Sheldon Jackson, the general agent for education, from 1880 to 1900, making the collection the oldest in the state. It features an impressive display of indigenous masks, hunting tools and baskets from such peoples as the Inuit, Tlingit, Haida and Aleut. Hanging from the ceiling, and equally im-

pressive, is the collection of boats and sleds used in Alaska – from reindeer sleds and dogsleds to kayaks and umiaks. The museum (☎ 747-8981) is open 9 am to 5 pm daily in the summer; admission is $3.

For a lot of visitors, Sitka's most colorful area is **Katlian St**, which begins off Lincoln St at the west end of town. The road is a classic mixture of weather-beaten houses, docks and canneries, where there always seem to be fishing boats unloading their catch. Katlian St portrays the sights and sounds of the busy Southeast fishing industry. Even the vacant yards along the street – with discarded fishing nets or stacks of crab pots – reflect dependence on the sea. In short, it is a colorful, bustling place and a photographer's delight. The **Alaskan Native Brotherhood Hall**, which was built by the ANB in 1914 and today is a registered national historic landmark, is also on Katlian St.

Sitka's most noted attraction is **Sitka National Historical Park**, which is at the east end of Lincoln St. This 107-acre park features a trail that winds past 15 totem poles, which were displayed in the Louisiana Purchase Exposition in St Louis in 1904, in a beautiful forest setting next to the sea. The site is at the mouth of the Indian River, where the Tlingit Indians were finally defeated by the Russians in 1804, after defending a wooden fort for a week. The Russians had arrived with a warship and three other ships to revenge a Tlingit Kiksadi clan raid on a nearby outpost two years earlier. Despite the Russian's cannons, they did little damage to the walls of the Tlingit fort and, when the Russian soldiers stormed the structure with the help of Aleuts, they were repulsed in a bloody battle. It was only when the Tlingits ran out of gunpowder and flint and slipped away at night that the Russians were able to enter the deserted fort.

Begin at the park's visitor center (☎ 747-6281), where there are displays of Russian and indigenous artifacts and carvers who demonstrate traditional arts. A mile-long self-guided loop leads past the totems to the site of the Tlingit fort near Indian River. The fort is long gone, but its outline can still be seen and is marked by posts. Admission is free and the visitor center is open 8 am to 5 pm daily in the summer.

Nearby on Sawmill Creek Rd, just beyond the Indian River Bridge, is the **Alaska Raptor Rehabilitation Center**. A raptor is a bird of prey, and at ARRC you'll see eagles, hawks and owls that are sick or injured and are undergoing treatment intended to enable them to survive in the wild. There are also more than a dozen bald eagles, and you can watch the exercise sessions that are staged several times a week in a nearby muskeg areas. The birds are secured by a loose line and are encouraged to fly from one stand to the next.

The center offers tours ($10) only when cruise ships are in, generally most mornings. Call the ARRC (☎ 747-8662) about tours, times and when the birds will be exercised.

Also at the east end of town is the **Sitka National Cemetery**, a place of interest mainly to history buffs. The plot is off Sawmill Creek Rd, just west of the Public Safety Academy, and can be reached from Sheldon Jackson College along Jeff Davis Rd. The area was designated a national cemetery by past president Calvin Coolidge and includes headstones of Civil War veterans, members of the Aleutian Campaign in WWII and many notable Alaskans.

Hiking

Sitka offers superb hiking in the beautiful but tangled forest that surrounds the city. Second only to Juneau for the variety and number of trails that can be reached on foot, Sitka has eight trails that start from its road system and total over 40 miles through the woods and mountain areas.

Indian River Trail This easy trail is a 5.5-mile walk along a clear salmon stream to the Indian River Falls, an 80-foot waterfall at the base of the Three Sisters Mountains. The hike takes you through a typical Southeast rain forest and offers the opportunity to

SOUTHEAST

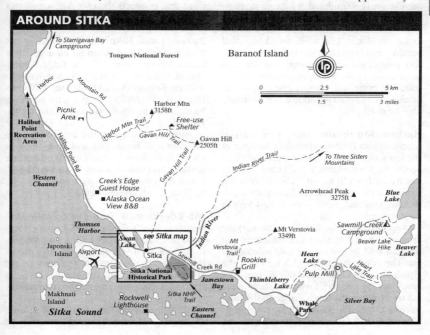

AROUND SITKA

view black bears, deer and bald eagles. The trailhead, a short walk from the center of town, is off Sawmill Creek Rd, just east of the Sitka National Cemetery. Pass the driveway leading to the Public Safety Academy parking lot and turn up the dirt road that has a gate across it. This leads back to the city water plant, where the trail begins left of the pump house. Plan on four to five hours for a roundtrip to the falls.

Gavan Hill Trail Also close to town is the Gavan Hill Trail, which ascends almost 2500 feet over 3 miles to the Gavan Hill peak. The trail provides excellent views of Sitka and the surrounding area. From the end of the trail, the adventurous hiker can continue on to the peaks of the Three Sisters Mountains.

Gavan Hill is also linked to Harbor Mountain Trail. Halfway across the alpine ridge is a free-use shelter. Built in 1991 by the USFS, the shelter is used on a first-come, first-gets-a-bunk basis and is 3.5 miles from the Gavan Hill trailhead, a hike of three to four hours.

From Lincoln St, head north up Baranof St for six blocks. The trailhead and a small parking area is reached just before the cemetery gate at the end of Baranof St. There is good camping in the alpine regions of the trail, but bring water and a camp stove, as drinking water and wood are not available above the tree line.

Harbor Mountain Trail This trail is reached from Harbor Mountain Rd, one of the few roads in the Southeast that provides access to a subalpine area. Head 4 miles northwest from Sitka on Halibut Point Rd to the junction with Harbor Mountain Rd. A parking area and picnic shelter are 4.5 miles up the rough dirt road.

Another half mile farther is the parking area at the end of the road, where an unmarked trail begins on the east side of the lot. The trail ascends for 1.5 miles to the alpine meadows, knobs and ridges where the views are spectacular. From here a recently cut trail follows the tundra ridge to the free-use shelter on the saddle between Harbor Mountain and Gavan Hill, where you can

pick up the Gavan Hill Trail. Plan on spending two to four hours if you are just scrambling through the alpine area above Harbor Mountain Rd.

Mt Verstovia Trail This 2.5-mile trail is a challenging climb of 2550 feet to the 'shoulder,' a small summit that is the most common end of the trail, although it is possible to climb to 3349 feet, the actual peak of Mt Verstovia. The view from the shoulder on clear days is spectacular, undoubtedly the best in the area.

The trailhead is 2 miles east of Sitka, along Sawmill Creek Rd. Once you reach Rookies Grill on the left, look for the trailhead marked 'Mount Verstovia Trail.' The Russian charcoal pits (signposted) are reached within a quarter mile and shortly after that the trail begins a series of switchbacks. Plan on a four-hour roundtrip to the shoulder. From the shoulder, the true peak of Mt Verstovia lies to the north along a ridge that connects the two. Allow an extra hour each way to hike to the peak.

Beaver Lake Hike This short trail starts from Sawmill Creek Campground, which is reached from Sawmill Creek Rd, 5.5 miles east of Sitka. Across from the former pulp mill on Sawmill Creek Rd, turn left onto Blue Lake Rd for the campground; the trailhead is on the southern side of the campground.

Although steep at the beginning, the 0.8-mile trail levels out and ends up as a scenic walk through open forest and along muskeg and marsh areas to Beaver Lake, which is surrounded by mountains. Plan on an hour for the roundtrip.

Mt Edgecumbe Trail The 6.7-mile trail begins at Fred's Creek USFS Cabin (reservations needed, $35 per night), and ascends to the crater of this extinct volcano. Needless to say, the views from the summit are spectacular on a clear day. About 3 miles up the trail is a free-use shelter (no reservations required).

Mt Edgecumbe lies on Kruzof Island, 10 miles west of Sitka, and can only be reached by boat because large swells from the ocean prevent floatplanes from landing. Stop at the Sitka Visitor Bureau or call Alaska Adventures Unlimited (☎ 747-5576, 800-770-5576) for a list of local operators who will drop off and pick up hikers for around $80 one way per party. Actual hiking time is five to six hours one way, but by securing Fred's Creek Cabin, you can turn the adventure into a pleasant three-day trip with nights spent in two shelters.

Paddling

Sitka also serves as the departure point for numerous blue-water trips along the protected shorelines of Baranof and Chichagof Islands. You can rent kayaks in town from Sitka Sound Ocean Adventures (☎ 747-6375, delongb@ptialaska.net) and Baidarka Boats (☎ 747-8996, email@kayaksite.com), 201 Lincoln St. Sitka Sound Ocean Adventures, which operates from a blue bus in the main harbor, charges $40/50 a day for singles/doubles. Baidarka Boats rents rigid kayaks (single/double $35/50 a day) and folding doubles ($60 a day) and both places offer guided day trips north of town.

Katlian Bay This 45-mile roundtrip, from Sitka Harbor to scenic Katlian Bay on the northern end of Kruzof Island and back, is one of the most popular paddles in the area. The route follows narrow straits and well-protected shorelines in marine traffic channels, making it an ideal trip for less-experienced blue-water paddlers who will never be far from help.

A scenic side trip is to hike the sandy beach from the Katlian Bay around Cape Georgiana to Sea Lion Cove on the Pacific Ocean. Catch the tides to paddle the Olga and Neva Straits on the way north and return along Sukot Inlet, spending a night at the USFS cabin on Brent's Beach, if you can reserve it. Plan on four to six days for the paddle.

Shelikof Bay You can combine a 10-mile paddle to Kruzof Island with a 6-mile hike across the island from Mud Bay to Shelikof Bay along an old logging road and trail.

Once on the Pacific Ocean side you'll find a beautiful sandy beach for beachcombing and the Shelikof USFS Cabin (reservations needed, $35 per night).

West Chichagof The western shoreline of Chichagof Island is one of the best blue-water trips in Southeast Alaska for experienced kayakers. Unfortunately, the trip often requires other transportation, because few paddlers have the experience necessary to paddle the open ocean around Khaz Peninsula, which forms a barrier between the north end of Kruzof Island and Slocum Arm, the south end of the West Chichagof-Yakobi Wilderness. Either rent a folding kayak and then book a floatplane or contact Southeast Alaska Ocean Adventures (☎ 747-5011), who will transport your kayak on their 50-foot sailboat.

The arm is the southern end of a series of straits, coves and protected waterways that shield paddlers from the ocean's swells and extend over 30 miles north to Lisianski Strait. With all its hidden coves and inlets, the trip is a good two-week paddle. Travelers with even more time and a sense of adventure could continue another 25 miles through Lisianski Strait to the fishing village of Pelican, where the ferry stops twice a month in the summer. Such an expedition would require at least two to three weeks.

Organized Tours

Sitka land tours include the ferry-stopover adventure by Sitka Tours (☎ 747-8443), for ferry passengers stuck in Sitka waiting for the tide to switch. The tour briefly covers the major sites: Sitka National Historical Park, St Michael's Cathedral and the Isabel Miller Museum. The cost is $10/5 adults/children. The same company also offers a historical tour ($25 for three hours) that includes Castle Hill, the Russian Blockhouse and a performance of Russian folk dances by the New Archangel Dancers.

Harbor Mountain Tours (☎ 747-8294, h.g.ulrich@worldnet.att.net) is slightly different. Its tour begins in downtown Sitka but includes driving to the breathtaking views above the tree line along Harbor

Mountain Rd. The sea level-to-2500-foot tour lasts three hours and costs $25 per person.

Whale Watching You can also book marine wildlife tours in Sitka. Allen Marine Tours (☎ 747-8100) offers a two-hour trip to view whales, sea otters and other wildlife for $49 per person. The tour departs Crescent Harbor at 2 pm Friday to Sunday and 10 am Tuesday throughout the summer. Other charters that offer half-day trips in the Sitka Sound to spot whales and seabirds include Tall Tale Ocean Tours (☎ 747-6965, dyoung@aol.com) and Bare Island Charters (☎ 747-4900). Expect to pay $65 to $80 for a four- to five-hour cruise.

If you don't have the funds for a whale-watching cruise, then try Whale Park, 6 miles south of town along Sawmill Creek Road. Dedicated in 1995, the park has a boardwalk and spotting scopes overlooking the ocean for whale watching. Fall is the best time to be at the park. As many as 80 whales have been known to gather in the waters off Sitka from mid-September through the end of the year.

Special Events

Extending its reputation as the cultural center of the Southeast, the city sponsors the Sitka Summer Music Festival, over three weeks in June, at Centennial Hall. The festival brings together professional musicians for chamber music concerts and workshops. The highly acclaimed event is popular, so it can be hard to obtain tickets to the twice-weekly evening concerts. Rehearsals, however, are open to the public, easier to attend and usually free.

A bit of Russian culture is offered during the summer months. Whenever a cruise ship is in port, the New Archangel Russian Dancers, more than 30 dancers in Russian costumes, take to the stage at Centennial Hall for a half-hour show. A schedule is posted at Centennial Hall; admission is $6.

On the weekend nearest October 18, the city holds its Alaska Day Festival by reenacting, in costumes (and even beard styles) of the 1860s, the transfer of the state from Russia to the USA. A parade highlights the three-day event.

In the first weekend of November, the city stages WhaleFest! to celebrate the large gathering of humpbacks in the fall.

Places to Stay

Sitka has a 5% city tax and a 4% bed tax, so travelers can add a hefty 9% to the price of accommodations.

Camping There are two campgrounds in the Sitka area but neither is close to town. *Starrigavan Campground* is a USFS campground about a mile north of the ferry terminal, at Mile 7.8 of Halibut Point Rd. The campground (28 sites, $10 per night) is in a scenic setting adjacent to a saltwater beach and hiking trails, but the gate is locked at 10 pm, making it unavailable to late-night ferry arrivals. On your way to the area you'll pass Old Sitka State Park, which features trails and interpretive displays dedicated to the site of the original Russian settlement.

Sawmill Creek Campground is 6 miles east of Sitka, on Blue Lake Rd off Sawmill Creek Rd, and has nine sites. It has mountain scenery and an interesting trail to Blue Lake, a good fishing spot.

Cabins A number of USFS cabins are close to Sitka and require less than 30 minutes of flying time to reach. The following cabins, which cost $35 per night, should be reserved in advance by calling the National Recreation Reservation Service (☎ 877-444-6777 or 518-885-3639 for overseas) or through its website (www.reserveusa.com).

For information on Fred's USFS Cabin, Brent's Beach USFS Cabin and Shelikof USFS Cabin on Kruzof Island (the site of Mt Edgecumbe) see the Sitka Hiking and Paddling sections. Local air-service operators that can handle chartering requests are Taquan Air (☎ 747-8636) and Harris Aircraft Service (☎ 966-3050).

Redoubt Lake Cabin is an A-frame cabin at the north end of Redoubt Lake, a narrow body of water south of Sitka on Baranof Island. The cabin is a 20-minute flight from Sitka. You can also reach it by paddling to the head of Silver Bay from town and then hiking along a 5-mile trail south to the cabin.

Baranof Lake Cabin is a favorite among locals, as it has a scenic, mountainous setting on the east side of Baranof Island and a mile trail to Warm Springs Bay. At the bay there is a bathhouse constructed around the natural hot springs, which can be used for $2.50. The cabin is a 20-minute flight from Sitka.

Lake Eva Cabin on Baranof Island has a skiff with oars, an outdoor fire pit and a woodstove inside. A trail from the lake outlet, which can be fished for Dolly Varden, cutthroat trout and salmon in the late summer, leads down to the ocean. The cabin is a 20-minute flight from Sitka.

White Sulphur Springs Cabin is just a 45-minute flight to the western shore of Chichagof Island and is popular with Southeasterners because of the hot springs bathhouse in front of it. The free hot springs are used by cabin renters and fishers and kayakers passing through.

Hostels The *Sitka HI-AYH Hostel* (☎ 747-8661, 303 Kimsham Rd) is in the basement of the Methodist church. Follow Halibut Point Rd northwest out of town and then turn right onto Peterson Rd, a quarter mile past the Lakeside Grocery Store. Once on Peterson Rd, immediately veer left onto Kimsham Rd. Facilities include a kitchen, lounge and eating area. Open only in the summer, the hostel charges $9/13 for members/nonmembers. Buses from the ferry will drop you right at the doorstep.

You might also check *Sheldon Jackson College* (☎ 747-2540, 801 Lincoln St). From mid-May to mid-August, the small college rents out its student rooms to travelers for $45/55 for a singles/doubles.

B&Bs The Sitka area has more than a dozen B&Bs that offer rooms with a good meal in the morning for around $55/60 singles/doubles. Stop at the Sitka Visitor Bureau for an updated list.

Creek's Edge Guest House (☎ 747-6484, 109 Cascade Creek Rd) overlooks Sitka Sound and Mt Edgecumbe and has rooms for $60 to $100. A little closer to downtown is *Karras B&B* (☎ 747-3978, 230 Kogwanton St), with four rooms for $55/85 singles/

doubles. *Alaska Ocean View B&B* (☎ 888-811-6870, 747-8310, aovbb@ptialaska.net, 1101 Edgecumbe Drive) is a three-story cedar home within walking distance of the city center and one block from the ocean. It has three rooms for $75 to $100 for a single and $85 to $120 for a double.

If you have some extra funds and want a unique experience, call the *Rockwell Lighthouse* (☎ 747-3056), the last lighthouse built in Alaska. The three-minute skiff ride from town is provided, and you'll get the whole lighthouse to yourself. From the hot tub on the deck, there is an excellent view of town and the rugged coastline around it. Staying here is not cheap though, at $150 a day per couple or $200 for four people. You almost need to book a year in advance if you're planning to stay in summer.

Hotels There are five hotels and motels in Sitka. Recently upgraded but still the most affordable is the *Sitka Hotel* (☎ 747-3288, 118 Lincoln St), with 60 rooms for $65/70 singles/doubles. The *Potlatch House* (☎ 747-8611, 713 Katlian St), near the intersection with Halibut Point Rd, has singles/doubles for $75/85.

Super 8 Motel (☎ 747-8804, 404 Sawmill Creek) has rooms starting at $78, and at the impressive *Westmark Shee Atika* (☎ 747-6241, 800-544-0970, 330 Seward St), downtown, you'll spend at least $120 a night.

Places to Eat

If you want coffee, the *Highliner Coffee* (215 Kimsham) opens at 5:30 am, has a variety of espresso drinks for under $4, serves bagels and croissants and even provides Internet and email service. The *Back Door Cafe*, accessed through Old Harbor Bookstore on Lincoln St, has sandwiches and the best espresso in town.

Victoria's (118 Lincoln St), next to the Sitka Hotel, used to be a 1950s diner but now has a decor that reflects 'the Victoria era.' It's where locals go for a breakfast ($6 to $10) that is served all day. The biscuits and gravy will stay with you almost to dinner. The *Bayview*, upstairs in the MacDonald Bayview Trading Company building, across

SOUTHEAST

from Crescent Harbor, has a variety of hamburgers and fresh seafood dinners for $12 to $16. The Bayview also serves beer and wine in a setting that offers every table a view of the boat harbor across the street. The best hamburgers and some of the largest portions are at *Rookies Grill (1617 Sawmill Creek Rd)*, at the Mount Verstovia trailhead. The ocean view is excellent and the burgers affordable at $7 to $9.

The best pasta and pizza is at *Marina Restaurant (205 Harbor Drive)*. For Chinese head to *Twin Dragon (210 Katlian St)*. Lunch specials begin at $6; dinners cost $10 to $15. The city's *McDonald's (913 Halibut Point Rd)* is a mile out of town, but closer fast food is at *Subway (327 Seward St)*, behind the Westmark Shee Atika Hotel, where subs cost $3 to $7.

Try the *Channel Club (2906 Halibut Point Rd)* and *Van Winkle & Daigler (228 Harbor Drive)* for good local seafood. The Channel Club also has the best steaks in town, a great salad bar and a view of Sitka Sound. The restaurant is 7 miles from town, but it offers a shuttle service. The more upscale Van Winkle & Daigler has an Alaska bouillabaisse of king crab, oysters, salmon and halibut. Expect to pay $12 to $25 at either place for dinner.

Sitka's largest supermarket, *Sea Mart (1867 Halibut Point Rd)*, features a bakery, deli, ready-to-eat items and a dining area overlooking Mount Edgecumbe. Closer to town is *Lakeside Grocery (705 Halibut Rd)*, which has sandwiches, soups and a salad bar.

Entertainment

Sitka's most interesting nightspot is the *Pioneer Bar (212 Katlian St)*, the classic fishers' pub down by the waterfront. The walls are covered with photos of fishing boats, and the scoreboard for the pool table often has 'help wanted' messages scrawled across it from fishers looking for black-cod crew or notes from fishers seeking work on trollers. Above the long wooden bar is a large brass bell, but put off the urge to ring it unless you want to buy a round of drinks for the house.

A more upscale bar is the lounge in the *Westmark Shee Atika*, and the only dance floor in Sitka is at *Rookies Grill* on Sawmill Creek Rd.

Getting There & Away

Air Sitka is served by Alaska Airlines (☎ 966-2422), with flights throughout the Southeast as part of the milk run. There are a handful of flights to Juneau during the summer; the one-way fare is $50. The airport is on Japonski Island, 1.8 miles west of the town center. On a nice day it can be a scenic 20-minute walk from the airport terminal over the O'Connell Bridge to the heart of Sitka. Otherwise, the white airport minibus meets all jet flights and charges $3 for a ride to the city hotels.

The only air-charter companies with floatplane service to small communities and forest service cabins is Taquan Air (☎ 747-8636) and Harris Aircraft Service (☎ 966-3050). During the summer, Taquan offers regular service to Pelican for $105 one way and Tenakee Springs for $84 one way.

Boat The Alaska Marine Hwy terminal (☎ 747-8737) is 7 miles north of town on Halibut Point Rd, and there are northbound or southbound departures almost daily.

Passage from Sitka to Juneau is $26, Sitka to Angoon $22, Sitka to Petersburg $26 and Sitka to Tenakee Springs $22. The Ferry Transit Bus (☎ 747-8443) meets all ferries for a trip into town. You can also catch the minibus out to the ferry terminal from the Westmark Shee Atika when it picks up hotel guests. The one-way fare to the ferry terminal is $3.

Getting Around

Bus Sitka doesn't have a public bus system, but during the summer it runs a visitor's transit shuttle (☎ 747-7290) 12:30 to 4:30 pm Monday through Friday. The shuttle stops every 25 minutes at Crescent Harbor shelter, Sitka National Park, Sheldon Jackson Museum, the Raptor Rehab Center and the downtown area. The fare is $5 per day for unlimited use.

Car & Bicycle Allstar Rental (☎ 966-2552, 800-722-6927) can provide a subcompact vehicle for $44 per day with unlimited mileage. The dealer is adjacent to the airport terminal. Yellow Jersey Cycle Shop (☎ 747-6317, 805 Halibut Point Rd) is less than a mile from downtown and has mountain bikes for $25 a day, less if you rent for longer.

Secondary Ports

On the ferry runs between Sitka and Juneau, you can stop at a handful of secondary ports to escape the cruise ships and tourists found at the larger towns. Some stops are scenic; others are not; all are a cultural experience of rural Alaska.

KAKE
Kake is an Indian beachfront community (population 745) on the northwest coast of Kupreanof Island, the traditional home of the Kake tribe of the Tlingit Indians. Today the community maintains subsistence rights and also runs commercial fishing, fish processing and logging enterprises to supplement its economy. Kake is known for having the tallest totem pole in Alaska (and some say the world), a 132-foot carving that was first raised at Alaska's pavilion in the 1970 world's fair in Osaka, Japan.

The ferry M/V *Le Conte* stops twice a week at Kake on its run between Petersburg and Sitka. The one-way fare from Petersburg is $22. Within town, 1.5 miles from the ferry terminal, are three general stores, a Laundromat, the *Nugget Inn* (☎ 785-6469, 2½ Keku Rd) for meals and the *Waterfront Lodge* (☎ 785-3472, 222 Keku Rd), where rooms are $70/85 for singles/doubles. Rough logging roads lead south from town and eventually reach scenic Hamilton Bay, which is 20 miles southeast of Kake.

Unless you want to spend three or four days in Kake, you can fly out on regularly scheduled flights with LAB Flying Service (☎ 785-6435, 800-426-0543) to Juneau. The one-way fare is $90.

Tebenkof Bay Wilderness
Kake serves as the departure point for bluewater trips into Tebenkof Bay Wilderness, a remote bay system composed of hundreds of islands, small inner bays and coves. The return paddle is a scenic 10-day adventure that can lead to sightings of bald eagles, black bears and a variety of marine mammals. Paddlers should have experience in ocean touring and be prepared to handle a number of portages. Kayaks can be rented in either Juneau or Sitka and then carried on the ferry to Kake.

The most common route is to paddle south from Kake through Keku Strait into Port Camden, where at its western end there is a 1.3-mile portage trail to the Bay of Pillars. From the Bay of Pillars, you encounter the only stretch of open water, a 3-mile paddle around Point Ellis into Tebenkof Bay. The return east follows Alecks Creek from Tebenkof Bay into Alecks Lake, where there is a 2.3-mile portage trail to No Name Bay. From here paddlers can reach Keku Strait and paddle north to Kake via the scenic Rocky Pass.

TENAKEE SPRINGS
What began in the late 1800s as a winter retreat for fishers and prospectors on the east side of Tenakee Inlet has today evolved into a rustic village known for its slow and relaxed pace of life. At the turn of the century, the springs were enlarged when the locals blasted out the surrounding rock. The forest service followed up by building a concrete container around the springs in 1915 to keep the hot water out and brushed back a path along the shoreline that for years served as the town's main street.

Tenakee Springs (population 93) is slowly changing. Logging has begun in the area, and the town now has a dirt road called Tenakee Ave and a handful of three-wheel motorized carts. But for the most part, the settlement is still a ferry dock, a row of houses on pilings and the hot springs, the town's main attraction, which comes bubbling out of the ground at 108°F. Tenakee's alternative lifestyle is centered around the public bathhouse at the end of the ferry dock. The building encloses the principal spring, which flows through the concrete bath at 7 gallons per minute. Bath hours, separate for men and

Love Boat Go Home

It's not that the residents of Tenakee Springs dislike tourists; they just like them a few at a time. If you spend an evening 'tubbing' at the bathhouse or an afternoon hiking to Indian River, the Tenakeeans you meet will be as polite and friendly as residents in any small Alaskan town.

But if you arrive with a hundred other camera-clicking tourists on a cruise ship, they'll be appalled or even angry, as the passengers on the *World Discoverer* discovered. The cruise ship first arrived in 1997, when it unloaded 120 tourists at the dock, more than doubling the town's population.

Having never experienced a gangplank stampede before, the locals were horrified as the passengers stomped flower beds, used private outhouses, picked berries from gardens, even snapped pictures of people inside their houses. One man entered a home uninvited, surprising a woman in her bathrobe. When the *World Discoverer* arrived the following summer, almost half of the town's 90 residents were at the dock to protest.

Tenakeeans complained to the ship's expedition leader, tempers grew short, some raw language – even for Alaskans – was used. 'We don't want you here,' said one resident. 'We're not built for this industrial-scale tourism.' Finally the Tenakeeans relented, but only after being promised the visitors wouldn't toss their Coke cans in the yards or photograph the inside of local houses.

Within an hour, the 120 passengers were aimlessly wandering the one dirt path that runs the length of this carless community. Most of the residents, on the other hand, hid out-of-sight. The Part-Time Bakery hung a 'Closed' sign on the door. The Blue Moon Cafe stayed dark. The town's only gift shop, the Shamrock Artists Coop, lowered its shades. The tourists looked at the shuttered town, snapped a few pictures of the community janitor burning garbage on the shore and finally returned to their ship.

The cruise company, embarrassed when the incident made the national news, promised not to return. Many small Alaska communities cheered the residents of Tenakee Springs. For months letters arrived addressed to simply 'City Council of Tenakee Springs.' 'It's encouraging to hear,' said one letter from Haines, 'that there is at least one town with the character to say "we are not for sale" to the tourist industry.'

women, are posted, and most locals take at least one good soak per day, if not two.

Tenakee Springs can be an interesting, relaxed and inexpensive side trip, especially if you use the ferry M/V *Le Conte*'s Friday night run from Juneau, thus saving accommodation expenses.

Hiking & Paddling

There is good fishing in the local streams for trout, salmon and Dolly Varden, and day hikes begin at each end of town. The dirt road extends 8 miles east of town, where the road ends at an old cannery on Coffee Cove, and more than 7 miles to the west of town, passing a few cabins in either direction.

Tenakee Springs is also one end of a common paddle from Hoonah (see the Paddling section in the Wilderness chapter); obtain supplies and a kayak from Juneau.

Whether paddling or hiking along the shore, always keep an eye out for marine mammals such as humpback whales, which are commonly sighted in Tenakee Inlet, killer whales and harbor porpoises. You may also see brown bears while paddling or hiking in the area, as Chichagof Island is second only to Admiralty Island in the Southeast for the density of its bear population.

Places to Stay & Eat

For a cheeseburger, there's **Rosie's Blue Moon Cafe**, or head to the **Part-Time Bakery**, which is closed on Tuesday, Wednesday, Saturday and Sunday. Opposite the bathhouse, at the foot of the ferry dock, is the **Snyder Mercantile Company** (☎ 736-2205). Founded by Ed Snyder, who arrived in a rowboat full of groceries in 1899, the store has been in business ever since. In

1976, Snyder Mercantile installed the town's first phone. It sells limited supplies and groceries, and also rents seven cabins, including several small ones at $45 a night for two people. To be sure of getting a cabin, you must reserve them in advance (PO Box 505, Tenakee Springs, AK 99841) and check in during store hours, 9 am to 5 pm Monday to Saturday and 9 am to 2 pm Sunday. You also need a sleeping bag.

Your ferry may arrive in the middle of the night, in which case plan on camping out for the first evening. Either pitch your tent near the boat harbor or plan on hiking out of town a fair way before finding an available spot to camp.

The best place to pitch a tent, if you plan to stay a few days, is at the rustic campground a mile east of town, at the mouth of the Indian River. It's quiet, picturesque and equipped with several tables and a covered picnic shelter. Keep the camp clean, however, to discourage brown bears from investigating your site, especially during the salmon runs in late August.

Getting There & Away

The ferry M/V *Le Conte* stops at Tenakee Springs three to four times a week, connecting it to Angoon, Hoonah, Sitka, Juneau and occasionally even Haines and Skagway. Study the ferry schedule carefully to make sure you don't have to stay in the town longer than you want. The one-way fare from Tenakee Springs to Juneau or Sitka is $22.

Wings of Alaska (☎ 789-0790 in Juneau, 736-2247 in Tenakee springs) has three flights from Juneau to Tenakee Springs from Monday to Saturday and two on Sunday. The one-way fare is $76. Alaska Seaplane Service (☎ 789-3331, 800-478-3360) also has scheduled service six days a week and charges $75 one-way.

HOONAH

As you head north on the ferry M/V *Le Conte*, the next stop after Tenakee Springs before reaching Juneau is Hoonah (population 877), the largest Tlingit village in Southeast Alaska. The Huna, a Tlingit tribe, have lived in the Icy Strait area for hundreds of

years, and legend tells of their being forced out of Glacier Bay by an advancing glacier. A store was built on the site of Hoonah in 1883, and an established community has existed there ever since.

Hoonah's population is roughly 80% indigenous people. The town lacks the charm and friendliness – as well as the public bathhouse – of Tenakee Springs, and in recent years even its coastal beauty has been stripped due to intense logging of Port Frederick. The logging controversy is a sticky one, because in this predominantly Native Alaskan village it's their own Native Alaskan corporation that is removing the timber and leaving behind barren mountainsides. As loggers cut the old growth trees, many local families wonder if their lifestyle is being diminished for quick cash. Except for a protected swath behind the town, Hoonah's Huna Totem Corporation has logged or sold to be logged all of its commercially viable trees.

Like the streams and valleys north of Fairbanks that have been reduced to rubble by gold miners and sluice boxes, the naked hillsides around Hoonah can be a depressing sight for many visitors traveling to Alaska to enjoy its natural beauty.

Things to See

The most photogenic area lies a mile northwest of Hoonah, where the faded red buildings of the old **Hoonah Packing Cannery** serenely guard Port Frederick. There is good fishing for Dolly Varden from this point.

In town, or actually on a hill overlooking Front St, is the **Cultural Center & Museum** (☎ 945-3545), which displays indigenous art and artifacts. The center, open 8 am to 4:30 pm Monday to Friday, has no admission charge.

Hiking & Paddling

The Spassky Trail, a 3.3-mile walk, begins 3.5 miles east of Hoonah and winds to Spassky Bay on Icy Strait.

The Pavlof Trail is a 3-mile walk along the Pavlof River, past two fish ladders between the lake and harbor of the same name. During mid- to late August, the salmon runs can be impressive here. Originally, the trail was accessible only by boat and plane, but now you reach the trailhead from Forest Development Road 8515. Pick up a copy of *Hoonah Area Road Guide* ($3) from the USFS office, if you want to go looking for this trail.

Hoonah lies southeast of Glacier Bay National Park across Icy Strait, but the paddle to the preserve is an extremely challenging trip, recommended for advanced kayakers only. An overnight kayak trip can be made to the Salt Lake Bay USFS Cabin (reservations needed, $35), 14 miles from Hoonah on Port Frederick.

Originally a trapper's cabin, the structure is small but can still sleep four, and it is not heavily used. There is a log-transfer facility across the bay and active logging in the area, so be ready for clear cuts.

Contact the USFS office (☎ 945-3631) at PO Box 135, Hoonah, AK 99829, for more information about hiking or paddling in the area.

Places to Stay & Eat

Harbor Lights Mini-Mart (286 Front St) has limited groceries. You can occasionally purchase fresh seafood directly from the *cold storage plant*. You'll find showers and a Laundromat at the marina, and accommodations and meals at the *Huna Totem Lodge* (☎ 945-3636), on Garteeni Hwy, 1.4 miles from the ferry terminal. In town, there is *Hubbard's B&B* (☎ 945-3414, 709 Huna Ct) and *Mary's Inn Restaurant*.

Getting There & Away

The M/V *Le Conte* docks in Hoonah three days a week on its route between Tenakee Springs and Juneau. The ferry terminal (☎ 945-3292), half a mile from town, is open two hours before the ferry arrives. Wings of Alaska (☎ 945-3275) and LAB Flying Service (☎ 945-3661) also maintain offices in Hoonah and provide daily services to Juneau. One-way fare is $50.

PELICAN

If you time it right, you can catch a ferry to Pelican, a lively little fishing town on Lisian-

ski Inlet on the northwest coast of Chichagof Island. The M/V *Le Conte* makes a special run to Pelican (population 137) twice a month, providing a unique day trip from Juneau for only $64.

The cruise through Icy Straits is scenic, with a good possibility of seeing humpback whales, and the hour and a half in port is more than enough time to walk the length of town, and even have a beer, in one of the last true boardwalk communities in Southeast Alaska.

The town was established in 1938 by a fish packer and named after his boat. Fishing is Pelican's reason for being. The town is the closest harbor to the rich Fairweather salmon grounds, and its population doubles from June to mid-September when commercial fishers and cold-storage workers arrive for the trolling season. Although the town's lifeblood, Pelican Seafoods, closed briefly in 1996, the Kake Native corporation since purchased the company, and Pelican again seems economically stable.

Pelican is a photographer's delight. Most of it is built on pilings over tidelands, and its main street, dubbed Salmon Way, is a mile-long wooden boardwalk. Only 2 miles of rough gravel road run beyond that. The main attraction is *Rosie's Bar & Grill* (☎ 735-2265), where you can get a burger, a beer or even a bed – there are four basic rooms for rent for $65 for singles/doubles. This is a classic Alaskan fisherman's bar, though when legendary Rose Miller gave up the place in 1996 due to poor health, it lost some of its charm. Still, you can mingle with trollers, longliners and Pelican Seafood workers or marvel at the half-king-salmon-half-blacktailed-deer mounted on the wall.

If you plan to stay over, there are a handful of places to secure a bed, including *Otter Cove B&B* (☎ 735-2259), a short walk from town. Located on a small cove, the house is built on stilts over a stream has a front-deck view of Lisianski Inlet. Singles/doubles costs $75/90, and a kayak is available for rent. Two miles northwest of Pelican is *Lisianski Inlet Lodge* (☎ 735-2266), a remote homestead accessible only by boat or floatplane. The rate is $180/260 for singles/doubles but includes three full meals a day and transportation from Pelican.

Pelican also has a small library, another bar, the *Lisianski Inlet Cafe*, a Laundromat, general store, a liquor store with adjoining steam baths and showers and kayak rentals at Loken Air, which has an office on the boardwalk. Alaska Seaplane Service (☎ 789-3331, 800-478-3360) – also known as Loken Air – has scheduled flights six days a week to Juneau for $97 one way.

Juneau

First appearances are often misleading, and Juneau (population 30,852) is a case in point. Almost half the northbound ferries arrive in the capital city between midnight and 6 am at the Auke Bay Ferry Terminal, 14 miles from the Juneau city center, leaving disgruntled backpackers and tired travelers to sleepily hunt for transportation and lodging. At that point, you might be unappreciative of Juneau, but give it a second chance. Few cities in the USA, and none in Alaska, are as beautiful as Juneau. Residents claim it is the most scenic capital in the country, and others describe it as a 'little San Francisco.'

The city center, which hugs the side of Mt Juneau and Mt Roberts, has many narrow streets running past a mixture of new structures, old storefronts and slanted houses, all held together by a network of staircases. The waterfront is bustling with cruise ships, tankers, fishing boats, a few kayakers and floatplanes buzzing in and out like flies. The snowcapped peaks of Mt Juneau and Mt Roberts provide just a small part of the superb hiking found in the area.

History

Although the Gastineau Channel was a favorite fishing ground for local Tlingit Indians, the town was founded on gold nuggets. In 1880, Sitka mining engineer George Pilz offered a reward to any local chief who could lead him to gold-bearing ore. Chief Kowee of the Auk Tlingit tribe arrived with such ore and Pilz sent Joe Juneau and Dick Harris, two vagabond

prospectors, to investigate. The first time the prospectors arrived, they found little that interested them in Gold Creek, but at Kowee's insistence, Pilz sent the two men back to the Gastineau Channel. The second time they hacked their way through the thick rain forest to Snow Slide Gulch, the head of Gold Creek, and found, in the words of Harris, 'little lumps as large as peas and beans.' On October 18, 1880, the two men staked out a 160-acre townsite, and almost overnight a mining camp appeared. It was the state's first major gold strike, and within a year the camp became a small town, the first to be founded after Alaska's purchase from the Russians.

Initially, the town was called Harrisburg and then Rockwell, then in 1881 the miners met and officially named it after Juneau. The post office was established shortly later, and the name has stuck. After the declining whaling and fur trade reduced the importance of Sitka, the capital of Alaska was moved to Juneau in 1906.

Almost 75 years later, in 1974, Alaskans voted to move the state's capital again, this time to a small highway junction called Willow that lay in Anchorage's strong sphere of influence. The so-called 'capital move' issue hung over Juneau like a dark cloud, restricting its growth and threatening to turn the place into a ghost town, as 50% of the residents work for the federal, state or local government.

The issue became a political tug-of-war between Anchorage and the Southeast, until the voters, faced with a billion-dollar price tag to construct a capital at Willow, defeated the funding in 1982. Although the conflict will probably never go away, the statewide vote gave Juneau new life, and the town burst at its seams, booming in typical Alaskan fashion.

McDonald's and Taco Bell fast-food chains appeared, new office buildings sprang up and apartments and condominiums mushroomed. The sudden growth was too much too soon for many of the residents, who were disgusted at the sight of wooded hillsides being bulldozed for yet another apartment complex.

SOUTHEAST

JUNEAU

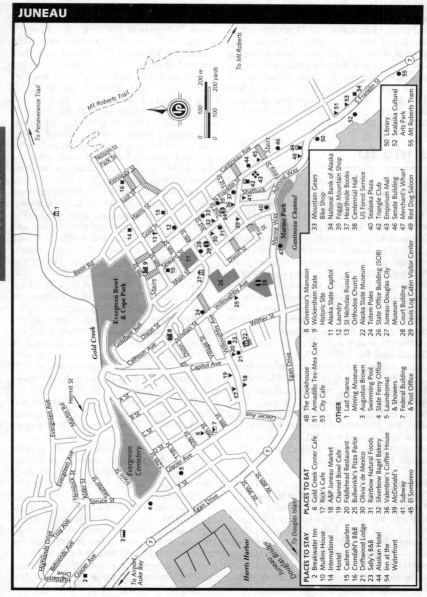

PLACES TO STAY
2 Breakwater Inn
10 Mullins House
14 International
     Hostel
15 Cashen Quarters
16 Crondall's B&B
21 Driftwood Lodge
23 Sally's B&B
44 Alaskan Hotel
54 Inn at the
     Waterfront

PLACES TO EAT
6 Gold Creek Corner Cafe
17 Rick's Cafe
18 A&P Juneau Market
19 Channel Bowl Cafe
20 Fiddlehead Restaurant
25 Bullwinkle's Pizza Parlor
30 Olivia's de Mexico
31 Rainbow Natural Foods
32 Silverbow Bagel Bakery
36 Valentine's Coffee House
39 McDonald's
41 Subway
45 El Sombrero

48 The Cookhouse
51 Armadillo Tex-Mex Cafe
53 City Cafe

OTHER
1 Last Chance
    Mining Museum
3 Augustus Brown
    Swimming Pool
4 State Ferry Office
5 Laundromat
    & Showers
7 Federal Building
    & Post Office

8 Governor's Mansion
9 Wickersham State
    Historic Site
11 Alaska State Capitol
12 Laundry
13 St Nicholas Russian
     Orthodox Church
24 Alaska State Museum
27 Totem Poles
27 Juneau-Douglas City
     Museum
28 State Office Building (SOB)
28 Court Building
29 Davis Log Cabin Visitor Center

33 Mountain Gears
     Bike Shop
34 National Bank of Alaska
35 Foggy Mountain Shop
37 Hearthside Books
38 US Forest Service
40 Sealaska Plaza
42 Triangle Club
43 Emporium Mall
46 Senate Building
47 Merchant's Wharf
49 Red Dog Saloon

50 Library
52 Sealaska Cultural
     Arts Park
55 Mt Roberts Tram

The city entered the 1990s with new concerns over growth and development, this time surrounding a growing interest in opening historical mines. By 1989, the Green Creek Mine, the largest silver mine in North America, was opened on Admiralty Island and had a workforce of 260 people who were living in Juneau and traveling daily to the mine via a catamaran. There was also interest in reopening the Kensington Mine, 40 miles north of the city near Berners Bay, where engineers believed there was an estimated $855 million worth of gold still lying below the surface.

But the heart of the mining controversy surrounded an effort by a Canadian company to reopen the Alaska-Juneau Mine for gold production. The A-J Mine operated from 1893 until WWII forced its closure, due primarily to a shortage of labor. During that time, it produced 3.5 million ounces of refined gold, or about a fourth of all the lode gold ever produced in Alaska. As Echo Bay Exploration began to plot the reopening of the A-J, environmental concerns swept through Juneau. Other people pushed for the project to proceed, seeing the new interest in mining as a way for Juneau to lessen its dependency on government. The heated issue ended quietly in 1997, when the company decided not to reopen the mine after new drilling revealed there was less recoverable gold than originally estimated.

Regardless of the issues facing this city, travelers will find Juneau to be a fine place offering a variety of accommodations, good

SOUTHEAST

A Road to Somewhere Else

Juneau is not only one of the most nerve-racking airline approaches in the USA (jumbo jets must search for a runway planted between two tree-topped ridges) but it's the only capital in North America you can't reach by road. Alaska's state capital has more than 100 miles of pavement around it, but none of it goes anywhere.

Meanwhile, every year 200 scheduled flights never make it into the city because of bad weather. That's fuel for the long-running debate on whether Alaska should move its seat of government closer to its largest population center – Anchorage.

In 1997, an environmental impact study was released that concluded that a 65-mile highway could be punched through to Skagway. From there – via the Alaska Hwy – it's only 832 miles to Anchorage and 710 miles to Fairbanks. The state Department of Transportation estimated it would cost $232 million to carve a two-lane road that would skirt the east side of Lynn Canal and traverse 58 known avalanche areas. Federal highway funds would pay for much of the construction, but inevitably motorists would pay a toll; $25 a car is what some officials predict.

The thought of a road reaching Juneau has the city in an uproar. Almost immediately, a pro-road group, Alaskans for Better Access, formed, arguing that land transportation would cool the capital-move debate and bring economic prosperity to a city that now has to barge in most heavy freight from Seattle.

But many residents aren't so sure. A road into Juneau renews the old conflict about what Alaska is and what people were looking for when they moved there. Build a road and a little more of that unique remoteness will be lost.

Build a road, say critics, and you're guaranteeing that an endless stream of Winnebagos will invade every summer, trying to negotiate downtown Juneau's narrow, winding one-way streets. Some residents imagine with horror the scene when the hoard of recreational vehicles meets the wave of tourists off the cruise ships.

'This is the only place where we'd be having this discussion: Should we build a road to our town,' said the city manager. 'But if it's built, Juneau is going to be the end of it. The question is, what are we going to do with all those buses and trailers and Winnebagos once they get here?'

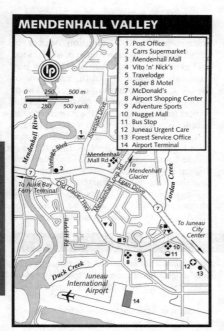

MENDENHALL VALLEY

1 Post Office
2 Carrs Supermarket
3 Mendenhall Mall
4 Vito 'n' Nick's
5 Travelodge
6 Super 8 Motel
7 McDonald's
8 Airport Shopping Center
9 Adventure Sports
10 Nugget Mall
11 Bus Stop
12 Juneau Urgent Care
13 Forest Service Office
14 Airport Terminal

SOUTHEAST

restaurants and transportation services. It also serves as the departure point for several wilderness attractions, including Glacier Bay National Park and Admiralty Island National Monument.

Orientation

While the downtown area clings to a mountainside, the rest of the city 'officially' sprawls over 3100 sq miles to the Canadian border, making it one of the largest cities, in area, in the USA. There are five sections to Juneau, with the city center being the busiest and most popular area among visitors during the summer. From there, Egan Drive, the only four-lane highway in the Southeast, heads northwest to Mendenhall Valley.

Known to locals as simply 'the Valley,' this area contains a growing residential section, much of Juneau's business district and the world-famous Mendenhall Glacier. In the Valley, Egan Drive turns into Glacier Hwy, a two-lane road that leads to Auke Bay, the

site of the Alaska Marine Hwy terminal, more boat harbors and the last spot for purchasing food or gas until the end of the road at Echo Cove.

Across the Gastineau Channel is Douglas, a small town southeast of Juneau that at one time was the area's major city. The road north out of this sleepy little town, Douglas Hwy, runs around Douglas Island to the fifth area of Juneau, known to locals as North Douglas. Around there, you'll find the Eagle Crest Ski Area, many scenic turnoffs, and a lot of half-hidden cabins and homes owned by people who work in Juneau but don't want to live in its hustle-bustle.

Information

Tourist Offices The main visitor center is the Davis Log Cabin (☎ 888-581-2201, 586-2201), at 134 3rd St, open 8:30 am to 5 pm daily during the summer. The city of Juneau also maintains a website (www.juneau.com) with travel information. Smaller visitor information booths are in the Juneau airport terminal out in the Valley and at Marine Park on the city waterfront.

For information about cabin rentals, hiking trails, Glacier Bay, Admiralty Island or any outdoor activity in the Tongass National Forest, stop at the information center (☎ 586-8751), in the Centennial Hall at 101 Egan Drive. The center is staffed by both US Forest Service and national park personnel and is open 8 am to 5 pm daily in the summer.

For state park information the Alaska Division of Parks and Outdoor Recreation office (☎ 465-4563), 400 Willoughby Ave, is open 8 am to 4:30 pm Monday to Friday.

Money Juneau has almost a dozen banks. National Bank of Alaska (☎ 586-3324) has a branch downtown at the corner of Seward and 2nd streets and another towards the Valley at 9150 Glacier Hwy. American Express (☎ 789-0999) is in the Nugget Mall in the Valley.

Post The main post office in Juneau is on the first floor of the federal building, at 9th St and Glacier Ave.

Email & Internet Access Juneau's main library has computers available for email and Internet access.

Travel Agencies US Travel (☎ 463-5446, 800-478-2423), 111 S Seward, is in the downtown area.

Bookstores Juneau's best bookstore, Hearthside Books, has two locations: downtown (☎ 586-1726), 254 Front St, and in the Mendenhall Valley (☎ 789-2750), 8745 Glacier Hwy.

Libraries If for no other reason, you should stop at Juneau's main public library (☎ 586-5249), 292 Marine Way, for the view. From the top of a parking structure, the windows of the library provide a panorama of downtown Juneau leading up to Mount Juneau. Open daily and until 9 pm Monday through Thursday, this excellent facility often has used books for sale.

Laundry Harbor Washboard (☎ 586-1133), 1114 Glacier Ave across Egan Drive from the small boat harbor, also has showers. The Dungeon, in the basement of an apartment building at 4th St and N Franklin St, is a small Laundromat with no attendant or showers. It's not well posted outside, but the entrance is a stairway on N Franklin St.

Medical Services Bartlett Memorial Hospital (☎ 586-2611) is off Glacier Hwy, between the downtown area and Lemon Creek, and is a stop along the city bus route. Near Nugget Mall in the Valley is Juneau Urgent Care (☎ 790-4111), 8505 Old Dairy Rd, a medical clinic with walk-in service.

City Center

Much of your sightseeing time will be spent in the city center, where nothing more than a good pair of walking shoes is needed. Start at the **Marine Park**, a delightful waterfront park across from the Sealaska Building at the southern end of Egan Drive, where there is an information kiosk, open daily. Among the handouts they offer is a walking-tour map.

The tour leads from the park along Admiralty Way to **S Franklin St**, a historical district that underwent major renovation in 1985. The buildings along this stretch, many dating back to the early 1900s, have since been turned into bars, gift shops and restaurants and are stormed by mobs of visitors every time a cruise ship docks.

At Hearthside Bookstore, the tour veers left onto Front St and then continues onto Seward St, where it passes the **Davis Log Cabin**, a replica of the first public school in Juneau. The cabin is another information center and houses a small collection of local historical relics and objects.

Swing left (southwest) onto 3rd St and head uphill on Main St, where first you'll pass an impressive life-size bronze sculpture of a bear before reaching the **state capitol**, though you might not recognize it as such. Built in 1929–31 as the territorial federal building, to many the capitol looks more like a high school than the Alaskan seat of government. Inside are the legislative chambers, the governor's office and offices for the hundreds of staff members who arrive in Juneau for the winter legislative session. Within the lobby is a visitor desk where free 30-minute tours of the building are offered every half hour from 9 am to 4:30 pm daily during the summer.

The walking tour returns to Seward St, climbs one block up and then turns right (northeast) on 5th St to the **St Nicholas Russian Orthodox Church**, probably the most photographed structure in Juneau. The octagonally shaped building was built in 1894, making it the oldest church in the Southeast, and has exhibits of Russian icons, original vestments and religious relics. Informal tours are conducted 9 am to 5 pm Monday to Saturday during the summer; donation requested.

Backtrack to the corner of 4th and Main Streets to reach the **Juneau-Douglas City Museum** (☎ 586-3572). Housed in the old Memorial Library Building, the museum has local artwork, a large custom relief map of the area and audiovisual presentations. Its best exhibits are interpretive displays covering the gold-mining history of Juneau and

Douglas. The museum is open during the summer 9 am to 6 pm Monday through Friday and 10 am to 6 pm Saturday and Sunday; admission is $3.

Across from the museum is the **State Office Building**, or the **SOB** as it is known locally. Inside the SOB on the 8th floor is the grand court, which features a century-old totem pole and a restored 1928 Kimball organ played for office workers and visitors each Friday at noon. The **Alaska State Library** is also off the grand court. The panoramic view of Juneau's waterfront and Douglas Island from the adjoining outdoor balcony is most impressive – an excellent place to have lunch on a sunny day.

Heading west from the SOB, 4th St curves north and becomes Calhoun Ave; in a block it reaches the six-pillared **Governor's Mansion**. Built and furnished in 1912 at a cost of $44,000, the structure has a New England appearance but is accented by a totem pole carved in 1940 by Tlingit Indians and presented to the governor as a gift.

Behind the Governor's Mansion is Indian St, which curves sharply into 9th St. Follow 9th St southwest to the **federal building**, where there is a 1994 time capsule with a collection that can be viewed through a pair of windows next to the main post office on the 1st floor. The federal building is at the junction of 9th St and Glacier Ave, a major bus stop for buses to the Valley or Douglas.

Glacier Ave curves east and becomes Willoughby Ave, and in a few blocks you reach Whittier St. Turn right (south) on Whittier St to the **Alaska State Museum**, an impressive white building. This outstanding museum provides Alaskans with a showcase of their past, including artifacts from all four indigenous groups: Athabascan, Aleut, Inuit and northwest coast people. There are also displays relating to the Russian period, major gold strikes in the state, and the Trans-Alaska Pipeline.

By far the most impressive sight is the full-size eagle's nest that sits on top of a tree that is as high as the 2nd floor of the museum. A circular staircase allows you to view the nest from all angles. The museum is open 9 am to 6 pm Monday to Friday and from 10 am to 6 pm Saturday and Sunday; admission is $4.

From Whittier St, you can turn left (east) onto Egan Drive to the **Centennial Hall**, where there is a USFS information center and exhibits. During the summer, films and slide presentations are shown in the adjoining theater.

A made-for-the-cruise-ship attraction is the **Mt Roberts Tram** (☎ 463-3412), just down S Franklin St. The tram commenced operation in 1996 and takes passengers from the cruise ship dock to the tree line of Mount Roberts for $20. On top there is a restaurant, gift shops and a small theater, or you just spend the day hiking in the alpine.

On 7th St, at the top (northern end) of Main St, is the **Wickersham State Historical Site** (☎ 586-9001), the historical home of Judge James Wickersham, a pioneer judge and statesman of Alaska. The house was built in 1898 and was occupied by the judge, who served as Alaska's first delegate to Congress from 1928 to 1939. Inside are photographs, books and other memorabilia from the judge's colorful career. The house is supposed to be open 9 am to 4 pm Monday through Friday and noon to 4 pm Sunday, but the hours seem sporadic; call first. Admission is $3.

Gold Mines

Gold fever and gold mines built Juneau, and today mining companies are staging a resurgence in and around the city. There are several interesting and free places that will help you gain an idea of what must have been an incredible era in Alaska's history. First, head to the Juneau-Douglas City Museum for its exhibit and pick up the *Perseverance Trail* booklet and *Treadwell Mine Historic Trail* brochure for a small fee.

A hike up Basin Rd to the start of Perseverance Trail, a 2-mile walk from the city center, will take you to the remains of the compressor house for the Alaska-Juneau Mine on the Gastineau Channel. Today, the building is the **Last Chance Mining Museum** (☎ 586-5338), where you can view the impressive complex of railroad lines, ore cars and repair sheds. Hours are 9:30 am to

6:30 pm daily; admission is $3. To reach the area, follow N Franklin St up the hill to its end and turn right (southeast) onto 6th St. Turn immediately left (northwest) on Gold St, which turns into Basin Rd. The ruins are half a mile down this scenic road.

At the end of nearby Perseverance Trail (see the Juneau Hiking section) is the **Glory Hole**, a caved-in mine shaft that was connected to the Alaska-Juneau Mine, along with the remains of the **Silver Bowl Basin Mine**.

Perhaps the most interesting areas to explore are the **Treadwell Mine** ruins, across the Gastineau Channel near Douglas. From the Capital Transit bus turnaround in Douglas, continue south towards the Sandy Beach Recreation Area, past the softball fields and Douglas Boat Harbor. The beach was made from the tailings of the Treadwell Mine, and the old pilings from its shipping dock still stand.

Take one of the staircases from the beach to St Ann's St, right above Sandy Beach, and follow the street farther south to Old Treadwell Rd. The dirt road leads to the old foundations, the shells of boarding houses and the mine shaft, another glory hole, of the Treadwell Mining Community. The operation closed down in 1922, after a 1917 cave-in caused the financial collapse of the company. During its heyday at the turn of the century, the mine made Douglas the major city on the channel, with a population of 15,000.

Across the channel from Treadwell is the **Alaska-Juneau Mine**, on the side of Mt Roberts. The mine closed down in 1944 after producing more than $80 million in gold, then valued at $20 to $35 an ounce.

Many visitors passing through the Southeast are fascinated with gold-rush history and want to try gold panning themselves. Any hardware store in Juneau will sell you a gold pan (black plastic ones are the cheapest and easiest to see those flecks of gold in), and the best public creeks to pan are Bullion Creek in the Treadwell Mine area, Gold Creek up by the Last Chance Basin, Sheep Creek on Thane Rd and Salmon, Nugget and Eagle Creeks off Egan Drive and Glacier Hwy north of the city center.

Glaciers

Juneau is also known as the 'Gateway to the Glaciers.' Several glaciers are in the area, including the Mendenhall Glacier, Alaska's famous drive-in glacier. The ice floe is 13 miles from the city center, at the end of Glacier Spur Rd. Head out along Egan Drive and at Mile 9 turn right onto Mendenhall Loop Rd, staying on Glacier Spur Rd when the loop curves north to head back to Auke Bay.

The Mendenhall Glacier flows 12 miles from its source, the Juneau Ice Field, and has a 1.5-mile face. On a sunny day it's beautiful, with blue skies and snowcapped mountains in the background. On a cloudy and drizzly afternoon, it can be even more impressive, as the ice turns shades of deep blue.

Near the face of the glacier is a US Forest Service visitor center (☎ 789-0097) that was rebuilt and enlarged in 1999. Inside are a variety of exhibits, a large relief map of the ice field and glaciers, a theater with slide presentations and films and an information desk with trail information. It's open from 8 am to 5 pm daily during the summer, and admission is $3. The area has several hiking trails, including a half-mile nature trail, the East Glacier Trail and the Nugget Creek Trail (see the Juneau Hiking section).

The cheapest way to see the glacier is to hop on a Capital Transit bus in the city center and get off at the corner of Mendenhall Loop and Glacier Spur Rds. The fare is $1.25, and buses depart from the state capitol and the federal building every half hour or so. From the Loop Rd, it is another mile to the visitor center. Or try Mendenhall Glacier Transport (☎ 789-5460), whose two-and-a-half-hour city tour includes 40 minutes at the glacier. The cost is $17.50 per person.

On your way out to Mendenhall Valley, when you pass Lemon Creek, look high in the mountains to your right to see the remains of the Lemon Creek Glacier. By hiking, you can get a close and uncrowded look at Herbert Glacier on Mile 27.5 of Glacier Hwy or Eagle Glacier at Mile 28.4 (see the Juneau Hiking section) north of Juneau.

SOUTHEAST

One way to see all the glaciers and the ice field is to splurge on a sightseeing flight. They're not cheap, at around $125 per person for a 45-minute flight, but on a clear day you will get a spectacular overview of the ice field. All the air-charter companies run flights. Wings of Alaska (☎ 789-0790) offers scenic flights during the summer from the airport, and from Marine Park at the city waterfront when there is a cruise ship in port.

You can also marvel at the ice field and glaciers from a helicopter, landing on the sea of ice and spending about 20 minutes walking around. Temsco Helicopters (☎ 789-9501) and Era Aviation (☎ 800-843-1947) offer such tours lasting almost an hour. The price to stand on ice? How about $160 per person.

Hiking

Few cities in Alaska have such a diversity of hiking trails as Juneau; it's the area's top attraction. Many of these hiking routes are shown on the Around Juneau map later in this chapter.

For those who don't feel up to walking the trails on their own, Juneau Parks & Recreation (☎ 586-2635) holds adult hikes every Wednesday, and family hikes along easier trails every Saturday. The hikes begin at the trailhead at 10 am; on Wednesday there is often carpooling to the trail, with hikers meeting at Cope Park, a short walk from the hostel. Call Juneau Parks & Recreation for a schedule.

If you need to rent overnight equipment: a tent, sleeping bag or a stove, call Gearing Up (☎ 586-2549) or Adventure Sports (☎ 789-5696).

Perseverance Trail This trail system off Basin Rd is the most popular one in Juneau and includes the Perseverance, Mt Juneau and Granite Creek Trails. Together, the trails can be combined into a rugged 10-hour walk for hardy hikers or an overnight excursion into the mountains that surround Alaska's capital city.

A violent storm and landslide in 1996 washed out large sections of the Perseverance Trail, including several bridges. Work to repair it began the following summer, but, as of 1999, wasn't completed due to a budget dispute in the state legislature. You can still hike the trail, but for a few years at least, it won't be the easy walk it once was.

To reach the trailhead from the international hostel, take 6th St one block southwest to Gold St, which turns into Basin Rd, a dirt road that curves away from the city into the mountains as it follows Gold Creek. After crossing the bridge over the creek look for the posted trailhead on the left.

From the Perseverance Trail, it is possible to pick up the Granite Creek Trail and follow the path to the creek's basin, a beautiful spot to spend the night. From there, you can reach Mt Juneau by climbing the ridge and staying left of Mt Olds, the huge rocky mountain. Once on the summit of Mt Juneau, you can complete the loop by descending along the Mt Juneau Trail, which joins Perseverance Trail a mile from its beginning.

The hike to the 3576-foot peak of Mt Juneau along the ridge from Granite Creek is an easier but longer trek than the ascent from the Mt Juneau Trail. The alpine sections of the ridge are serene, and on a clear day in the summer, there are outstanding views. From the trailhead for the Perseverance Trail to the upper basin of Granite Creek is a 3.3-mile one-way hike. From there, it is another 3 miles along the ridge to reach Mt Juneau.

Mt Roberts Trail This is the other hike that starts close to the international hostel. The trail is a 4-mile ascent to the mountain above the city. The trail begins at a marked wooden staircase at the northeastern end of 6th St and consists of a series of switchbacks with good resting spots. When you break out of the trees at Gastineau Peak, you will come to a wooden cross and the new tram station and nature center. From the peak there are good views of Juneau, Douglas and the entire Gastineau Channel. The Mt Roberts summit is a steep climb from Gastineau Peak through the alpine brush to the north of the city.

If you hike up, a ride down on the Mt Roberts Tram to S Franklin St is only $5.

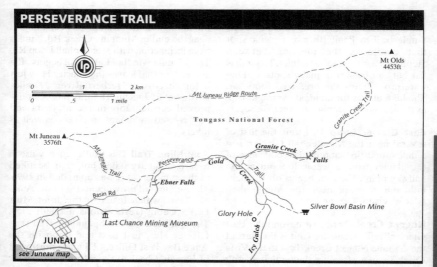

PERSEVERANCE TRAIL

Mt Olds
4453ft

Mt Juneau Ridge Route

Tongass National Forest

Granite Creek Trail

Mt Juneau ▲
3576ft

Granite Creek

Falls

Mt Juneau Trail

Perseverance   Gold

Creek

Ebner Falls

Basin Rd

Silver Bowl Basin Mine

Last Chance Mining Museum

Glory Hole

Icy Gulch

JUNEAU
see Juneau map

0   1   2 km
0   .5   1 mile

Purchase $5 worth of food or drink at the visitor center at the top, and the ride down is free.

Dan Moller Trail This 3.3-mile trail leads to an alpine bowl at the crest of Douglas Island, where there is a USFS cabin (reservations needed, $35 per night). See the Backpacking section in the Wilderness chapter for further details.

Treadwell Ditch Trail Also on Douglas Island, this trail can be picked up either a mile up the Dan Moller Trail or just above D St in Douglas. The trail stretches 12 miles north from Douglas to Eagle Crest, although most people only hike to the Dan Moller Trail and then return to the road, a 5-mile trip. The path is rated as easy and provides views of the Gastineau Channel and winds through scenic muskeg meadows.

Mt Bradley Trail This 2.6-mile trail begins in Douglas, through a vacant lot behind section 300 of 5th St, and is a much harder climb than the hikes up Mt Roberts or Mt Juneau. Both rubber boots and sturdy hiking boots are needed, as the trail can be muddy in the lower sections before you reach the

beautiful alpine areas above the tree line. The climb to the 3337-foot peak should only be attempted by experienced hikers.

Cropley Lake Trail Another trail on Douglas Island is the 1.5-mile route to Cropley Lake. The trail was built primarily for cross-country skiing, but in the summer it can be hiked to the alpine lake, which provides good scenery and camping. The start is up Fish Creek Rd, a short way past the Eagle Crest Ski Lodge in a creek gully to the right.

Sheep Creek Trail Southeast of Juneau along Thane Rd is the very scenic Sheep Creek Trail, a 3-mile walk into the valley south of Mt Roberts, where there are many historic mining relics. The trailhead is 4 miles from Juneau, at a staircase on the gravel spur to a Snettisham Power Plant substation. The trail is fairly flat in the valley, from where you scramble up forested hillsides to the alpine zone. Many hikers follow the power line once they are above the tree line to reach the ridge to Sheep Mountain. You can continue from Sheep Mountain over Mt Roberts, returning to Juneau along the Mt Roberts Trail. This is a 10- to 12-hour day hike.

Point Bishop Trail At the end of Thane Rd, 7.5 miles southeast of Juneau, is this 8-mile trail to Point Bishop, a scenic spot that overlooks the junction between Stephens Passage and Taku Inlet. The trail is flat but can be wet in many spots, making waterproof boots the preferred footwear. The hike makes for an ideal overnight trip, as there is good camping at Point Bishop.

East Glacier Loop This trail, the first of several near the Mendenhall Glacier, is a 3-mile roundtrip that provides good views of the glacier from a scenic lookout at the halfway point. The trail begins off the half-mile nature walk near the Mendenhall Glacier Visitor Center.

Nugget Creek Trail Just beyond the East Glacier Trail's scenic lookout is the start of the 2.5-mile Nugget Creek Trail to the Vista Creek Shelter, a free-use shelter that doesn't require reservations. The total roundtrip to the shelter from the Mendenhall Glacier Visitor Center is 8 miles. Hikers who plan to spend the night at the shelter can continue along the creek towards Nugget Glacier, though the route is brushy and hard to follow at times.

West Glacier Trail This is one of the most spectacular trails in the Juneau area. The 3.4-mile trail begins off Montana Creek Rd past Mendenhall Lake Campground and hugs the mountainside along the glacier, providing exceptional views of the icefalls and other glacial features. It ends at a rocky outcropping, but a rough route continues from there to the summit of Mt McGinnis, another 2 miles away. Plan on four to five hours for the West Glacier Trail, or plan on a long day if you want to tackle the difficult Mt McGinnis route.

Montana Creek & Windfall Lake Trails These two trails connect at Windfall Lake and can be combined for an interesting 11.5-mile overnight hiking trip. It is easier to begin at the trailhead at Montana Creek and follow the Windfall Lake Trail out to the Glacier Hwy.

The 8-mile Montana Creek Trail, known for its high concentration of bears, begins near the end of Montana Creek Rd, 2 miles from its junction with Mendenhall Loop Rd. The 3.5-mile Windfall Lake Trail begins off a gravel spur that leaves the Glacier Hwy just before it crosses Herbert River, 27 miles northwest of Juneau. The trail has been improved considerably in recent years and now is used by mountain bikers as well as hikers.

Spaulding Trail This trail's primary use is for cross-country skiing, but it can be hiked in the summer, as it was upgraded in 1996. The 3-mile trail provides access to the Auke Nu Trail, which leads to the John Muir USFS Cabin (reservations needed, $35). The trailhead for the Spaulding Trail is at Glacier Hwy just past and opposite the Auke Bay Post Office, 12.3 miles northwest of Juneau. Check at the information center in the Centennial Building about the availability of the cabin.

Peterson Lake Trail This 4-mile trail provides access to good Dolly Varden fishing in both Peterson Creek and Peterson Lake. The trailhead has been moved to avoid private property and is now 20 feet before the Mile 24 marker on Glacier Hwy, north of the Shrine of St Terese. Wear rubber boots, as it can be muddy during the summer. A USFS cabin (reservations needed, $35) is at Peterson Lake.

Herbert Glacier Trail This level trail extends 4.6 miles along the Herbert River to Herbert Glacier. The trail is easy, though wet in some places, and the roundtrip takes four to five hours. The trail begins just past the bridge over Herbert River at Mile 28 of Glacier Hwy in a small parking lot to the left.

Amalga Trail Also known as the Eagle Glacier Trail, this level route winds 7.5 miles one way to the lake formed by Eagle Glacier, where there is now a USFS cabin (reservations needed, $35) 0.8 miles from its face. The view from the Eagle Glacier Cabin is well worth the effort of reserving it in advance. The trailhead is beyond the Glacier Hwy bridge, across Eagle River, 0.4 miles past the trailhead for the Herbert Glacier Trail. Plan on a roundtrip of seven to eight hours to reach the impressive Eagle Glacier and return to the trailhead.

Paddling

Both day trips and extended three- to five-day paddles are possible out of the Juneau area in sea kayaks. Boats can now be rented from several places in the area, with the best being Juneau Outdoor Center (☎ 586-8220) near the Douglas Boat Harbor. Adventure Sports (☎ 789-5696), at 8757 Glacier Hwy, also rents kayaks near the airport. Doubles are $50 a day, singles $40, and either outfitter can arrange transportation to any location on the Juneau road system. Topographic maps can be obtained in Juneau at the Foggy Mountain Shop (☎ 586-6780), across from the Baranof Hotel on N Franklin St.

Guided Tours If you are unsure about kayaking, Alaska Discovery (☎ 800-586-1911) offers a guided day trip daily in Juneau, where you get a chance to paddle the coastal islands of Lynn Canal. Tours are limited to 10 people, and everything is provided, including boats, lifejackets, rubber boots and transportation from the downtown area. The cost is $95 per person.

Auke Bay The easiest trip is to paddle out and around the islands of Auke Bay. You can even camp on the islands to turn the adventure into an overnight trip.

Taku Inlet This waterway is an excellent four- to five-day trip with close views of Taku Glacier. Total paddling distance is 30 to 40 miles, depending on how far you travel up the inlet. It does not require any major crossing, though rounding Point Bishop can be rough at times. It is possible to camp at Point Bishop and along the grassy area southwest of the glacier, where brown bears are occasionally spotted.

Berners Bay At the western end of Glacier Hwy, 40 miles from Juneau, is Echo Cove, where kayakers put in for paddles in the protected waters of Berners Bay. The bay, which extends 12 miles north to the outlets of the Antler, Lace and Berners Rivers, is ideal for an overnight trip or longer excursions up Berners River.

Oliver Inlet On the northeast coast of Admiralty Island is Oliver Inlet State Marine Park. A 0.8-mile portage tramway connects the inlet to scenic Seymour Canal, known for one of the greatest concentrations of nesting bald eagles in the world and its large population of brown bears. Seals, sea lions and whales also spend the summer feeding in the canal. The paddle to Oliver Inlet is 18 miles and involves crossing Stephens Passage, a challenging open-water crossing, for experienced kayakers only. At the south end of the portage tram from Oliver Inlet is the Seymour Canal Cabin, a state park cabin that rents for $25 a night and can be reserved through the Juneau state park office (☎ 465-4563).

Organized Tours

City Tours A number of companies offer city tours through Juneau and the surrounding area for those travelers with limited time. Gray Line (☎ 586-3773) departs from the Baranof Hotel, 127 N Franklin St, and offers a 2½-hour Mendenhall Glacier tour with a few historic sights in town for $35. Mendenhall Glacier Transport's (☎ 789-5460) tour, which has basically the same thing for only $17.50, is much better.

Tracy Arm This steep-sided fjord, 50 miles southeast of Juneau, has a pair of tidewater glaciers and a gallery of icebergs that float down the length of it. Tracy Arm makes an interesting day trip, especially if you don't have the time or funds for Glacier Bay. You're almost guaranteed to see seals inside the arm, and there's a possibility of spotting whales on the way there.

A handful of tour boats make the run to the head of the fjord, and they all take off from Marine Park and maintain a ticket office in the area. The trip is usually a full-day cruise that includes a light lunch, cash bar and costs $100. But Adventure Bound Alaska (☎ 463-2509, 800-228-3875) sells the trip to hostel members for $80. Also offering the cruise for $100 is Auk Nu Tours (☎ 586-8687).

For something different, call Wilderness Swift Charters (☎ 463-4942, tongass@ alaska.net). Lynn Schooler offers three- and four-day outings for six passengers in which you camp on shore each night and bring your own food. The cost is $499 per person and includes Admiralty Island's Pack Creek and Tracy Arm.

If you don't have camping equipment, you can rent it for an additional $65.

Special Events

Juneau's main festival during the summer is on the 4th of July, when the celebrations include a parade, a carnival, fireworks over the channel and a lot of outdoor meals from Sandy Beach in Douglas to Juneau's city center. In mid-April there is the weeklong Alaska Folk Festival (☎ 364-2658), when the city stages the largest gathering of musicians from around the state for a week of performances, workshops and dances at Centennial Hall. The similar Juneau Jazz and Classics festival (☎ 463-3378) is the third week in May and Gold Rush Days, a festival of logging and mining events, is in late June.

Places to Stay

Juneau tacks on 12% to the price of most lodging. Downtown hotels and B&Bs tend to be heavily booked during the summer tourist season.

Camping There are some fine campgrounds beyond Mendenhall Valley. **Mendenhall Lake Campground**, 13 miles from downtown Juneau and 5 miles northeast of the Auke Bay Ferry Terminal, is one of the most beautiful USFS campgrounds in Alaska. The recently expanded campground (80 sites) has a separate seven-site backpacking unit on Montana Creek Rd, a dirt road that runs off Mendenhall Loop Rd. The tent sites are alongside a lake, and many have spectacular views of the nearby glacier. The nightly fee is

$8 per site. The only drawback of this campground is that the campsites can be reserved in advance through the National Recreation Reservation Service (☎ 877-444-6777, www .reserveusa.com), so the campground is going to be filled through much of the summer.

The other USFS campground is **Auke Village**, 2 miles from the ferry terminal on Glacier Hwy. The area (12 sites) provides shelters, tables, wood and an interesting beach to walk along. The fee is also $8, but no advance reservations are accepted. **Eagle Beach campsites**, on Glacier Hwy 15 miles from the ferry terminal, is operated by Alaska State Parks and is a 5-acre gravel site a quarter mile from Eagle Beach Picnic Area. You're 28 miles from downtown Juneau, but the area is very scenic. The fee is $3 per night.

The rest of the campground facilities are for recreational vehicles. The city of Juneau allows RV parking at **Savikko Park** in Douglas for $5 a night; nearby there is a trailer dump station and water. **Auke Bay RV Park** (☎ 789-9467), 1.5 miles east of the ferry terminal, is a full-service campground that charges $20 per night. Closer to town is **Juneau RV Park** (☎ 790-6444, 2850 Engineers Cutoff Rd), which also charges $20. Many RVers just park for free in the Valley at Carrs (3033 Vintage Blvd), K-Mart (6525 Glacier Hwy) and Fred Meyer (8181 Glacier Hwy).

Glacier Hwy ends 41 miles north of Juneau at a pleasant spot called Echo Cove. There are no developed facilities here, but it's a nice spot to camp for a while and a favorite among locals. There is usually good offshore salmon fishing in August. Other scenic but undeveloped areas are Eagle Beach on Glacier Hwy, and Fish Creek on N Douglas Hwy.

Cabins Numerous USFS cabins are accessible from Juneau, but all are heavily used, requiring reservations in advance (☎ 877-444-6777, www.reserveusa.com). If you're just passing through, check with the USFS information center in the Centennial Building for a complete list of cabins in the area.

The John Muir, Peterson Lake and Dan Moller Cabins and the new Eagle Glacier Cabin, accessible by foot from the Juneau road system, have already been mentioned in the Juneau Hiking section.

The following cabins are within 30 minutes' flying time from Juneau; the air charter costs range from $200 to $250 per person for return transport. Alaska Seaplane Service (☎ 789-3331, 800-478-3360) and Wings of Alaska (☎ 789-0790) can provide air services on short notice.

The *West Turner Cabin* is one of the most scenic and by far the most popular cabin in the Juneau area. This unit is a 30-minute flight from Juneau on the western end of Turner Lake, where there is good fishing for trout, Dolly Varden and salmon. A skiff is provided.

The *Admiralty Cove Cabin* is on a scenic bay and has access to Young Lake along a very rough 4.5-mile trail. The unit is a 30-minute flight from Juneau in a tidal area where floatplanes can land only during high tide. Brown bears frequent the area.

Young Lake has a USFS cabin at each end, and both cabins are provided with a skiff. The lake offers good fishing for cutthroat trout and landlocked salmon. An overgrown trail connects North Young Lake Cabin with Admiralty Cove. There is no trail between South and North Young Lake Cabins.

Hostels The *Juneau International Hostel* (☎ 586-9559), at Harris and 6th Sts, is one of the best hostels in Alaska. The large yellow house has an ideal location – five blocks from the state capitol, four blocks from the Mt Roberts Trail and two blocks from Basin Rd and the beginning of the scenic Gold Creek area.

The hostel has cooking and laundry facilities, showers, and a common room with a fireplace. Check-in time is from 5 to 11 pm, checkout is 9 am, and reservations are accepted if accompanied by the first night's fee and sent with a self-addressed, stamped envelope. Fees are $10 a night. For reservations contact the Juneau International (AYH) Hostel, 614 Harris St, Juneau, AK 99801.

B&Bs Juneau has more than 50 B&Bs with rates that range from $70 to $90 per couple per night. The only problem is securing a room after stepping off the ferry late at night. For that reason, it's wise to book ahead, even a day or two while traveling through the region. An easy way to do this is to contact the Alaska Bed & Breakfast Association Reservation Service (☎ 586-2959, alaskabednbreakfast@cheerful.com), which covers most of the Southeast, including Juneau, of course.

Downtown B&Bs include *Sally's B&B* (☎ 780-4708, 465 Whittier St), which has six rooms with private baths and kitchenette for $80 for a double. Just a block up from the state capitol is the *Mullins House* (☎ 586-3384, 526 Seward St), with rooms for $70/80 singles/doubles. In the historic Starr Hill neighborhood is *Crondahls' B&B* (☎ 586-1464, jcrondah@ptialaska.net, 626 5th St), with great views of the channel and two rooms for $60/70.

In Douglas, there is *Windsock Inn* (☎ 364-2431, 410 D St), with two rooms for $50/55. In North Douglas, try *Blueberry Lodge* (☎ 463-5886, jayjudy@alaska.net, 9436 N Douglas Hwy), which has five rooms near the Eaglecrest Ski Facility and a great view of the Gastineau Channel. Rooms are $75/85.

Hotels The cheapest hotel is the *Alaskan Hotel* (☎ 586-1000, 800-327-9347, akhotel@ptialaska.net, 167 S Franklin St), which has historical decor in its lobby and rooms dating back to 1913. Rooms without baths cost $60/75. Just to the south is the *Inn at the Waterfront* (☎ 586-2050, 455 S Franklin), a small hotel where a single with a shared bath is $60 but includes a light breakfast. Another small hotel is *Cashen Quarters* (☎ 586-9863, jsclc3@ptialaska.net, 303 Gold St), with five rooms with baths and kitchens for $80/88 singles/doubles.

One of the best places to stay downtown is *Driftwood Lodge* (☎ 586-2280, 800-544-2239, driftwood@gci.net, 435 Willoughby Hwy), near the Alaska State Museum. Rooms without kitchens cost $68/78, and the motel has a courtesy van that runs out to both the airport and the ferry terminal.

Near the airport are several motels. **Super 8 Motel** (☎ 789-4858, 2295 Trout St), next door to McDonald's, has a van that meets flight and ferry arrivals, and rooms that begin at $92/102 singles/doubles. Even closer to the airport is **Travelodge** (☎ 789-9700, 9200 Glacier Hwy), with rooms for $100/120.

Places to Eat

Juneau's size allows it to have an excellent range of restaurants that no other Southeast town could possibly support. There are more than 50 in the area, principally downtown, with a couple in Douglas and the rest in the Mendenhall Valley.

Restaurants Juneau has several salmon bakes. The best is **Thane Ore House** (☎ 586-3442), 4 miles south of town on Thane Rd. The all-you-can-eat dinner of grilled salmon, halibut and ribs costs $18.50 and includes a salad bar, corn, baked beans, the usual. At 7 pm the Gold Nugget Revue starts, and the show and dinner set you back $27. Call if you need bus transportation from the downtown area. There is also **Gold Creek Salmon Bake** (☎ 586-1424), which charges $24. To combine flightseeing, glacier viewing and a salmon bake, you should try **Taku Glacier Lodge** (☎ 586-8258), which is reached via a 15-minute floatplane flight up Taku Inlet. The tour last three hours but is a little pricey at $178 per person.

Cheap dinners of pizza or sandwiches can be obtained at **Bullwinkle's Pizza Parlor** (318 Willoughby Ave), across from the State Office Building. Good-sized sandwiches cost $5 to $7, and medium pizzas begin at $11. They also have wine, a large selection of imported beer, and silent movies shown on the back wall at night. The best pizza downtown is at **Pizzeria Roma**, in Merchant's Wharf on Marine Way. The small restaurant has a full bar, beer on tap and medium thin-crust pizzas for $15 to $20. For hot subs and large salads, try **Rick's Cafe** (730 Willoughby Ave), across from A&P Juneau Market.

Next door to the Red Dog Saloon is the **Cookhouse** (200 S Franklin St), which claims to serve the largest hamburger in Alaska, so big it feeds two. For $16, you can judge for

yourself. The gold-rush theme restaurant is a bit touristy for me, but others find it fun. Full dinners of steak and prime rib are about $24.

Of the handful of Mexican restaurants in the city center, the best is the **Armadillo Tex-Mex Cafe** (431 S Franklin St), where you can fill up on enchiladas, *pollo loco* (crazy chicken) or a vegetarian taco – among other delights. Two tacos with pinto beans and rice cost $10, a fajita dinner $13. If the place is full, and often it is, then head north to **El Sombrero** (157 S Franklin St) or **Olivia's de Mexico** (222 Seward St), the most affordable of the three.

A longtime favorite, **Fiddlehead Restaurant** (☎ 586-3150, 429 W Willoughby Ave) serves the best vegetarian cuisine in Juneau, as well as seafood. The food is excellent, but dinners cost $10 to $18, and just the bean burger is $8. The place is a good spot for afternoon tea and freshly baked foods, and upstairs is the Fireweed Room for cocktails, fine dining and live music at night. **Hangar on the Wharf** (☎ 586-5018), Merchant's Wharf, is a waterfront restaurant with Southeast Alaska's largest selection of microbrews, more than 100. Dinners cost $8 to $22.

In the same price range but much more quaint is **Summit Restaurant** (☎ 586-2050, 455 S Franklin St), at the Inn on the Waterfront. Call ahead and make a reservation; the restaurant is charming but small.

Just north of the airport is **Vito 'n' Nick's** (9342 Glacier Hwy), a small Italian restaurant. Deep-dish pizzas begin at $12 for a medium; pasta dinners are under $10; and on Tuesday, all the spaghetti you can consume costs $9. Next door is **Valley Restaurant**, which serves the usual cafe food and stays open to 4 am on Friday and Saturday for late ferry arrivals.

Cafes The cheapest place for breakfast or lunch is the **Federal Building Cafeteria**, 2nd floor of the federal building, which also provides a nice view of the Gastineau Channel for its diners. Open 7 am to 3:30 pm, the restaurant offers eggs, potatoes, toast and bacon for around $6, and hamburgers and sandwiches for under $5.

Across from the federal building is **Gold Creek Corner Cafe** (740 W 9th St), a quaint restaurant with Persian fare. The daily special is $7; a half order is $4.50 and is a meal in itself. Also nearby is **Channel Bowl Cafe** (608 Willoughby Ave), across from the A&P Juneau Market, a local hangout known for large portions and reasonable prices for breakfast. Try the Mt Jumbo, a heaped plate of eggs, potatoes and peppers, onions and cheese for $7. It will keep you full until dinner.

Another interesting restaurant is **City Cafe** (439 S Franklin St), near the Mt Roberts Tram. Breakfasts are $7 to $10 and include a recommended garden omelette. The cafe also has an interesting selection of Filipino and Indonesian dishes and cheap beer on tap; small pitchers are only $5.

The **Silverbow Bagel Bakery** (120 2nd St) bakes the best bagels in the Capital City. For breakfast, you can enjoy an egg-cheese and salmon sausage bagel ($4) or just a bagel with cream cheese and a cup of coffee ($2.50). The restaurant is open for lunch and dinner as well featuring salads, deli sandwiches for under $7 and homemade pasta.

On the 1st floor of the Emporium Mall is the **Heritage Coffee Co & Cafe**, Juneau's most popular coffee shop. Large, double-shot lattes are $4, huge bagels and cream cheese $3 and breakfast sandwiches $4. Not far away is **Valentine's Coffee House** (111 Seward St), with espresso drinks and fresh baked goods.

In Douglas, of the two restaurants on this side of the channel, I prefer the **Douglas Cafe** (913 3rd St), next door to the Perseverance Theater. Breakfast begins at $5; almost 20 types of gourmet hamburgers are $7 to $8; and dinners are $13 to $16.

Fast Food Juneau has two **McDonald's**, at 130 Front St and in the Valley across from the Nugget Mall. Also, a **Subway** (205 Front St) is downtown, and in the Valley, there is a **Taco Bell** in Mendenhall Mall.

Markets In the city center, **A&P Juneau Market**, on Willoughby Ave across from the federal building, has a good selection of local seafood, an espresso counter, a salad bar for $3.50 a pound, ready-to-eat items and a small seating area. It's open 24 hours.

Also located downtown is **Rainbow Natural Foods**, corner of 2nd and Seward Sts, a health food store.

An excellent **Carrs**, on the corner of Egan Hwy and Vintage Blvd, has a salad bar, stir-fry counter, bakery and eating area. It's open 24 hours.

Entertainment

Bars With a population that is larger, younger and a little more cultured than in most other Southeast towns, Juneau is able to support a great deal more nightlife. The most famous nightspot is the **Red Dog Saloon**, which is mentioned in every travel brochure and is the first destination of every cruise ship passenger. The bar is interesting, with its sawdust floor and relics covering the walls, but the Red Dog is not a place to spend an entire evening drinking unless you can put up with point-and-shoot cameras flashing at the stuffed bear.

S Franklin St as a whole is Juneau's drinking section. Many places are local hangouts that will undoubtedly turn you off, which is fine with those leaning against the bar inside. The **Triangle Club**, at Front and S Franklin Sts, however, is a pleasant little spot. Although there is limited seating inside, the bar offers wide-screen television and good hot dogs to go along with a mug of beer. Hidden in the back of the **Alaskan Hotel** (167 S Franklin St) is a unique bar with an interior and cash register that matches the rest of the hotel's historical decor. Often there is folk or jazz music.

To sip a beer and watch the floatplanes take off and land on the Gastineau Channel, go to the **Hangar on the Wharf**, on Merchant's Wharf, which also features a wide-screen TV. For a view of the harbor, head to the **Breakwater Inn** (1711 Glacier Ave), past the high school in the west end of the downtown area. The bar is on the 2nd floor and overlooks the Aurora Basin Boat Harbor, an active place in the summer.

Out in the Valley is **Hoochie's Sports Pub** (9121 Glacier Hwy), in the Airport Shopping

Center, Juneau's liveliest dance bar. There is live music almost nightly in the summer, and until the band starts playing, large pitchers are only $9.

Theater Juneau is blessed with the *Perseverance Theater* (☎ 364-2421, 914 3rd St), which produces classic and original plays. The theater, founded in 1979, is Alaska's only genuine full-time professional company. In the past, it has struggled financially, but it somehow has survived and has become the state's leader in fostering work by Alaskan writers. That includes *The Mineola Twins*, which premiered at the Perseverance Theater in 1996 and then went on to achieve national notice in New York and win playwright Paula Vogel a Pulitzer Prize in 1998.

Juneau's melodrama is the *Gold Nugget Revue*, a show of cancan dancers, music and local history. It's staged at the Thane Ore House (☎ 586-1462); tickets, without the salmon bake, are $8.50.

Getting There & Away

Air Alaska Airlines (☎ 789-5538) has scheduled service to Seattle, all major Southeast communities, Glacier Bay, Anchorage, and Cordova daily during the summer. Recent airfare wars have pushed the one-way fare from Juneau to Anchorage to as low as $110. The one-way fare from Juneau to Cordova, which allows continued travel on the state ferries to Valdez, Seward, Homer and Kodiak, is $127 if purchased 21 days in advance. To Ketchikan the one-way fare is usually about $100. Air North (☎ 800-764-0407) flies three times a week to Whitehorse.

The smaller air-service companies have a number of scheduled flights to small communities in the area that are considerably cheaper than chartering a plane there. LAB Flying Service (☎ 789-9160, 800-426-0543) flies to Hoonah for $50 one way and Haines for $75. Wings of Alaska (☎ 789-0790) offers a $76 flight to Tenakee Springs, and an $80 flight to Angoon. Alaska Seaplane Service (☎ 789-3331, 800-478-3360) has scheduled floatplane service to Pelican for $97 one-way, as well as service to Angoon, Elfin Cove and Tenakee Springs.

Boat The ferry arrives and departs from the Auke Bay Ferry Terminal, 14 miles from the downtown area. There are daily ferry departures during the summer for Sitka ($26), Petersburg ($44), Ketchikan ($74), Haines ($24) and Skagway ($32). A smaller ferry, the *Le Conte*, connects Juneau to Hoonah, Angoon and Tenakee Springs.

During the summer the M/V *Malaspina* makes a North Lynn Canal trip daily, departing Juneau at 7 am and arriving at Skagway at 1:30 pm. It stays in port for two hours, then begins a return trip to the Capital City, stopping at Haines along the way. Once a month, the M/V *Kennicott* departs Juneau for a trip across the Gulf of Alaska to Valdez and then Seward. One-way fare from Juneau to Seward is $148, and space should be reserved in advance. The main ticket office for the ferry (☎ 465-3941, 800-642-0062) is at 1591 Glacier Ave.

There are no state ferries to Gustavus, the gateway to Glacier Bay, but Auk Nu Tours (☎ 789-5701, 800-820-2628) runs a 78-foot catamaran daily, departing from near the Auke Bay post office at 9:30 pm. The round-trip fare is $85; transporting kayaks costs an additional $25.

Getting Around

To/From the Airport & Ferry Late-night arrivals at the ferry terminal should catch the Mendenhall Glacier Transport bus (☎ 789-5460) that meets all ferries. It will take you to the airport or downtown for $5. An airporter bus (☎ 780-4977) makes hourly runs from major hotels to the airport for $8 a person. There are always taxis, of course, but expect to pay around $22 from the ferry terminal and $16 from the airport.

The city bus system also runs out to the airport, but only from 7:30 am to 5:30 pm on weekdays. On the weekends and in the evening, it's possible to walk to the nearest public bus stop for a $1.25 ride into town. From the ferry terminal, walk south along the Glacier Hwy for a little over a mile, to Dehart's Grocery Store, near the Auke Bay terminal.

From the airport terminal, stroll to the backside of Nugget Mall, across the street from Mendenhall Auto, where there is a bus stop with a posted schedule.

Bus Capital Transit (☎ 789-6901), Juneau's public bus system, runs hourly during the week, with alternating local and express services from 7 am to 6 pm, and 9 am to 6 pm on Sunday. The main route circles the downtown area, stopping at the city dock ferry terminal, the capitol building, the federal building, and then heading out to the Valley and Auke Bay Boat Harbor via Mendenhall Loop Rd, where it travels close to Mendenhall Lake Campground. A bus also runs every hour from city stops to Douglas. Fares are $1.25 each way. Grab a map and schedule the first time you board a bus.

Car There are almost a dozen car rental places in Juneau, for those needing a vehicle – a great way for two or three people to see the sights out of the city or to reach a trailhead. Few companies have a mileage charge, because all the roads in Juneau don't total much more than 100 miles. For a $35 special, call Rent-A-Wreck (☎ 789-4111) at 9099 Glacier Hwy, which provides pickup and drop-off service. Allstar Rent-A-Car (☎ 790-2414) also provides these services, as does Evergreen Motors (☎ 789-9386), which has compacts for around $40 a day.

Bicycle Juneau has several bike paths, including a 9-mile route from Auke Bay downtown to the Mendenhall Glacier, from the Juneau-Douglas Bridge to Douglas and a new 2.5-mile path along Mendenhall River. Because most of Juneau's trails are steep, mountain biking is limited, but Windfall Lake and Peterson Lake trails are popular areas for off-road cyclists. You can rent mountain bikes at Mountain Gears (☎ 586-4327), 126 N Franklin St, which charges $6 an hour or $25 a day. The bike shop also has organized cycling tours.

AROUND JUNEAU
Gastineau Salmon Hatchery Visitor Center, just 3 miles north of downtown at 2697 Channel Drive, is part of the new $7 million, state-of-the-art Douglas Island

Pink & Chum Hatchery (☎ 463-4810). The entire facility is a major producer of salmon for the northern region of Southeast Alaska and is geared for visitors, with underwater viewing windows that allow you to see fish spawning, fish ladders and interpretive displays explaining the lifecycle of salmon and the different hatchery operations. The hatchery is close to a bus stop, and tours are offered 10 am to 6 pm Monday to Friday and 10 am to 5 pm Saturday and Sunday; admission is $3.

Other sights outside the city include the **Alaska Brewing Company** (☎ 780-5866) on Shaune Drive in the Lemon Creek area. Juneau's only brewery offers free tours every half hour from 11 am to 4:30 pm Tuesday to Saturday, with a glass of suds at the end. **Glacier Gardens** (☎ 790-3377) is nearby at 76000 Glacier Hwy. The 50 acres of gardens opened up in 1998 and include ponds, waterfalls and pathways that climb to the 500-foot elevation of Thunder Mountain. Plans call for extending the paths to the 900-foot level, where you would be rewarded with a view of Mendenhall Glacier. Better like your rhododendrons if you stop by; admission is $18. Hours are 9 am to 8 pm daily, 9 am to 6 pm Sunday.

The **Auke Bay Marine Lab** is 12.5 miles northwest of Juneau and a mile south of the Alaska Marine Hwy terminal. The research facility has a self-guided tour of displays and saltwater tanks and is open 8 am to 4:30 pm weekdays. South of the lab on the shores of Auke Lake is the **University of Alaska campus**, a small college in a beautiful setting. Among the many buildings are a student union and a bookstore, and Egan Library features a Northwest Coast Native art collection of masks, baskets, hats and wooden panels.

At Mile 23.3 of Glacier Hwy is the **Shrine of St Terese**, a natural stone chapel on an island that is connected to the shore by a stone causeway. As well as being the site of numerous weddings, the island is situated along the Breadline, a well-known salmon-fishing area in Juneau. The island is perhaps the best place to fish for salmon from the shore.

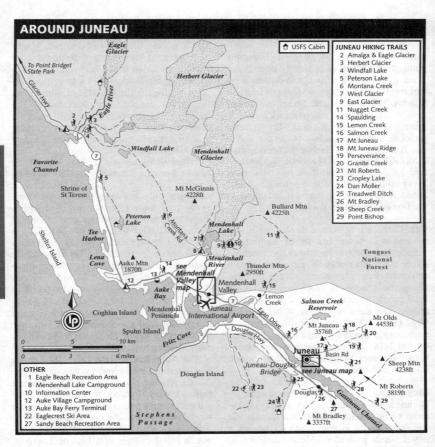

AROUND JUNEAU

⌂ USFS Cabin

JUNEAU HIKING TRAILS
2 Amalga & Eagle Glacier
3 Herbert Glacier
4 Windfall Lake
5 Peterson Lake
6 Montana Creek
7 West Glacier
9 East Glacier
11 Nugget Creek
14 Spaulding
15 Lemon Creek
16 Salmon Creek
17 Mt Juneau
18 Mt Juneau Ridge
19 Perseverance
20 Granite Creek
21 Mt Roberts
23 Cropley Lake
24 Dan Moller
25 Treadwell Ditch
26 Mt Bradley
28 Sheep Creek
29 Point Bishop

OTHER
1 Eagle Beach Recreation Area
8 Mendenhall Lake Campground
10 Information Center
12 Auke Village Campground
13 Auke Bay Ferry Terminal
22 Eaglecrest Ski Area
27 Sandy Beach Recreation Area

Juneau's only state park is **Point Bridget State Park**, a 2800-acre park at Mile 39 of Glacier Hwy. Point Bridget overlooks Berners Bay and Lynn Canal and is known for its excellent salmon fishing off the Berners Bay beaches and in Cowee Creek. Three hiking trails wander through rain forest, along the park's rugged shoreline and past two rental cabins (reservations needed, $35) that can be reserved by calling the Alaska State Division of Parks and Outdoor Recreation (☎ 465-4563). Cowee Meadow Cabin is a 2.5-mile hike in. Blue Mussel Cabin is a 3.4-mile walk.

Scenic viewing points include N Douglas Hwy, for a look at Fritz Cove and Mendenhall Glacier from afar, and **Eagle Beach Recreation Area**, at Mile 28.6 of Glacier Hwy, for stunning views of the Chilkat Mountains and Lynn Canal. Bird enthusiasts should stop at the scenic view at Mile 6 of Egan Drive, which overlooks the **Mendenhall Wetlands and Refuge**. There's a viewing platform with signboards that explain the natural history of the refuge. If the temperatures top 80°F, head over to **Sandy Beach** and watch the pale locals cram in as much tanning as they can under the midnight sun.

Admiralty Island

Only 15 miles southeast of Juneau is Admiralty Island National Monument, a 1493-sq-mile preserve, of which 90% has been designated as wilderness. The Tlingit Indians, who know Admiralty Island as Kootznoo-woo, 'the Fortress of Bears' (the name was well chosen), have resided on the 96-mile-long island for more than 1000 years.

Admiralty Island has a wide variety of wildlife. Bays like Mitchell, Hood, Whitewater and Chaik contain harbor seals, porpoises and sea lions. Seymour Canal, the island's largest inlet, has one of the highest densities of nesting eagles in the world, and humpback whales often feed in the waterway. Sitka black-tailed deer are plentiful, and the streams choke with spawning salmon during August. But more than anything else Admiralty Island is known for its bears.

The island has one of the highest populations of bears in Alaska. It is estimated that 1500 to 1700 bears live there – or about one bruin for every 1600 sq miles. Bears enjoy a good life on the island, roaming the drainage areas for sedges, roots and berries much of the year but feasting on salmon in August before settling into dens on the upper slopes to sleep away most of the winter.

Admiralty is a rugged island, with forested mountains that rise to 4650 feet. Numerous lakes, rivers and open areas of muskeg break up the coastal rain forest of Sitka spruce and western hemlock. Around 2500 feet, the tree line is reached, and beyond that you'll find alpine tundra and even permanent ice fields.

Although you can fly in for a stay at a USFS cabin or an expensive lodge, most visitors to the monument are people looking for a wilderness experience who take the Cross Admiralty Island canoe route (see the Paddling section in the Wilderness chapter) or spend time paddling Seymour Inlet and Mitchell Bay or one of many other bays.

Most visitors arrive from Juneau. Before arriving, secure supplies in Juneau and obtain information from the USFS office at Centennial Hall on Egan Drive or the Admiralty Island National Monument office (☎ 586-8790), 8461 Old Dairy Rd, out in Mendenhall Valley.

ANGOON

The lone settlement on Admiralty Island is Angoon, a predominantly Tlingit community of 650 residents. Tlingit tribes occupied the site for centuries, but the original village was wiped out in 1882, when the US Navy, sailing out of Sitka, bombarded the indigenous people after they staged an uprising against a local whaling company.

Today, the economy is a mixture of commercial fishing and subsistence, and in town the strong indigenous heritage is evident in the painted fronts of the 16 tribal community houses. The old lifestyle is still apparent in this remote community, and time in Angoon can be spent observing and gaining some understanding of the Tlingit culture. Tourism seems to be tolerated only because the village is a port-of-call for the ferry.

Angoon only has 3 miles of road. The village itself is at one end, perched on a strip of land between Chatham Strait on the west coast of Admiralty Island and turbulent Kootznahoo Inlet, which leads into the interior of the national monument. The community serves as the departure point for many kayak and canoe trips into the heart of the monument, including the 32-mile Cross Admiralty canoe route to Mole Harbor (see the Paddling section of the Wilderness chapter).

Many people are content to just spend a few days paddling and fishing Mitchell Bay and Salt Lake. To rent a canoe or kayak in Angoon, call Favorite Bay Inn (☎ 788-3123, 800-423-3123), which charges $60 a day, less for a rental of six days or longer. The tides here are among the strongest in the world; the walk between the airport and the town allows you to view the turbulent waters at midtide. Before undertaking such an adventure, stop at the USFS office (☎ 788-3166), in the Old City Office Building on Flagstaff Rd in Angoon, for information on the tides in Kootznahoo Inlet and Mitchell Bay. The office is open 8 am to 5 pm Monday to Friday.

SOUTHEAST

Places to Stay & Eat

By far the best place to stay in Angoon is the *Favorite Bay Inn* (☎ 788-3123, 800-432-3123, favoritebayinn@juno.com), a large, rambling log home 2 miles from the ferry terminal. A bed and a hearty breakfast is $89/129 for singles/doubles. *Kootznahoo Inlet Lodge* (☎ 788-3501), on Kootznahoo Rd, has 10 rooms for $85 singles/doubles.

Angoon is a dry community, and the only cafe in town is *Ramona's Coffee Shop* (350 Anaya Rd), a hangout for teenagers at night. Groceries and limited supplies can be picked up at the *Angoon Trading Company* (☎ 788-3111, 145 Kootznahoo Rd), but it's best to arrive with a full supply of your own food.

Getting There & Away

Approximately three southbound and two northbound ferries a week stop at Angoon on the run from Sitka to Juneau during the summer. The one-way fare to Angoon is $24 from Juneau and $22 from Sitka. The ferry terminal is 3 miles from town.

Wings of Alaska (☎ 788-3530 in Angoon) and Alaska Seaplane Service (☎ 789-3331 in Juneau) have scheduled flights between Juneau and Angoon for $75 one-way.

PACK CREEK

On the eastern side of Admiralty Island, spilling into Seymour Canal, is Pack Creek. Swan Cove is to the north, and to the south is Windfall Harbor. All three areas have extensive tide flats that draw a large number of bears to feed, making these spots favorites for observing and photographing the animals.

Within this area is the **Stan Price State Wildlife Sanctuary**, named for the pioneering researcher who spent a good part of his life living at Pack Creek. The sanctuary includes an area that has been closed to hunting since the mid-1930s, and thanks to Price, the bears have become used to the presence of humans. The bears are most abundant in July and August, when the salmon are running, and most visitors are boaters who go ashore to view the animals and then camp somewhere else. At Pack Creek, you watch the bears from the viewing sand spit

or an observation tower along the creek reached by a mile-long trail. The only place to camp in the area is on the east side of Windfall Island, a half mile away, making a boat necessary for those who plan to spend more than a day in the area. To the south, there is a free, three-sided shelter in Windfall Harbor.

A food cache is provided near the south sand spit, as you should never enter the area with food in your pack. Do not leave the viewing sand spit to get closer to the bears. Stay on the spit, wait for the bears to move into range and use a telephoto lens for close-up shots.

In recent years, Pack Creek has become so popular that the area buzzes with planes and boats every morning from early July to late August. Anticipating this daily rush hour, most resident bears escape into the forest, but a few adult females and cubs hang around to feed on salmon, having long since been habituated to the human visitors. Seeing five or six bears at one time would be a good viewing day at Pack Creek.

Permits

In the 1980s, the number of visitors to Pack Creek grew from 100 per year to more than 1000, forcing the USFS and Alaska Department of Fish and Game to institute a permit system to limit visitors. Only 24 people are allowed per day from July through August. One- to three-day permits are reserved in advance and are $50 per adult per day. Four guiding and tour companies receive 16 of the permits, leaving only eight for individuals who want to visit Pack Creek on their own.

Permits are available from March 1 and are usually gone within two or three weeks. A handful are kept as spares, however, and handed out three days in advance at the monument office. Call the USFS Information Center (☎ 586-8751) in Juneau about obtaining one.

Getting There & Away

Experienced kayakers can rent a boat from Juneau Outdoor Center (☎ 586-8220) in Douglas or Adventure Sports (☎ 789-5696) in Juneau and paddle to the refuge. The run down Gastineau Channel and around Douglas Island isn't bad, but the Stephens Passage crossing to reach Oliver Inlet has to be done with extreme care and a close eye on the weather. From the inlet, the Alaska Division of Parks and Outdoor Recreation operates the Oliver Inlet tramway, which can be used to cross the mile-long portage into Seymour Canal. At the south end of the portage is the Seymour Canal Cabin that can be rented for $25 per night by calling the State Division of Parks office (☎ 465-4563) in Juneau.

You can also arrange to be dropped off and picked up by Alaska Seaplane Service (☎ 789-3331, 800-478-3360), which departs at 8:30 am daily for Pack Creek and returns at 4 pm ($130 roundtrip). Alaska Discovery (☎ 800-586-1911) offers guided trips into the area. The one-day tour ($450 per person), a flight to Admiralty Island and then kayaking to Pack Creek for a day of watching bears before returning to Juneau. There is also a three-day trip for $895.

Glacier Bay National Park

Sixteen tidewater glaciers that spill out of the mountains and fill the sea with icebergs of all shapes, sizes and shades of blue have made Glacier Bay National Park and Preserve an icy wilderness renowned throughout the world.

When Captain George Vancouver sailed through the ice-choked waters of Icy Strait in 1774, Glacier Bay was little more than a dent in a mountain of ice. In 1879, John Muir made his legendary discovery of Glacier Bay and found that the end of the bay had retreated 20 miles from Icy Strait. Today, the glacier that bears his name is 60 miles from Icy Strait, and its rapid retreat has revealed plants and animals that have fascinated naturalists since 1916.

Apart from having the world's largest concentration of tidewater glaciers, Glacier Bay is the habitat for a variety of marine life, including whales. The humpbacks are by far the most impressive and acrobatic, as they

heave their massive bodies in spectacular leaps (called 'breaching') from the water. Adult humpbacks often grow to 50 feet and weigh up to 37 tons. Other marine life seen at Glacier Bay includes harbor seals, porpoises, killer whales and sea otters, and other wildlife includes brown and black bears, wolves, moose, mountain goats and over 200 species of birds.

Glacier Bay is a park of contrasts. It is an area of lush spruce and hemlock forests, bare shores recently exposed by glaciers, steep fjords, the flat terrain around Gustavus and an inlet full of icebergs. It's also the site of a controversy that's brewing between the cruise-ship lines and environmentalists. To the operators of the huge 10-story cruise ships, Glacier Bay is the jewel that attracts customers to these high-priced trips. To environmentalists, these floating resorts are trouble, causing humpback whales to leave the park and bringing smog to the middle of the wilderness.

After the number of whales dropped dramatically in 1978, the National Park Service reduced ship visits from 103 to 79 during the three-month season. But the industry lobbied the US Congress (the US way of getting what you want) to increase the number to 200 a year, or two a day, during the season. When Alaska's Republican senators pushed through a 30% increase in ships allowed in the bay, environmentalists filed suit in 1997.

Among the more bizarre problems the ships bring is smog, which is created when the ships park for an hour or so in front of a glacier. An air inversion leaves a haze hovering over the ice. To kayakers and backcountry users, such a ship is a hotel on water, with 1000 passengers waving from the railing and a public-address system announcing happy hour. In an effort to separate the groups, the National Park Service has designated Muir Inlet, or the East Arm, as wilderness water, prohibiting the large boats from sailing there.

The park is many things to many people, but it's never a cheap side trip. Of the more than 300,000 annual visitors, over 90% arrive aboard a cruise ship and never leave the boat. The rest are a mixture of tour-group

GLACIER BAY NATIONAL PARK

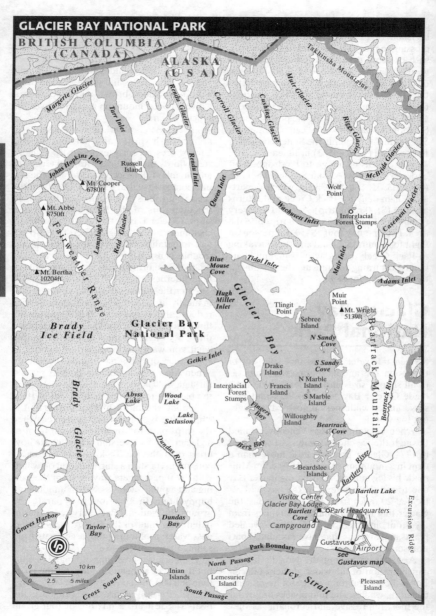

members who head straight for the lodge and backpackers who wander toward the free campground. Plan on spending at least $400 for a trip from Juneau to Glacier Bay, but remember that the cost per day drops quickly after you've arrived.

GUSTAVUS

The park is serviced by a small settlement called Gustavus, an interesting backcountry community of 400 residents. The citizens of Gustavus include a mixture of professional people – doctors, lawyers, former government workers and artists – who have decided to drop out of the rat race and live on their own in the middle of the woods. Electricity only arrived in the early 1980s, and in some homes, you still must pump the water at the sink or build a fire before you can have a hot shower.

There is no town center in Gustavus. The town is merely an airstrip left over from WWII and a road to Bartlett Cove, officially called Main Road and then Park Road but known to most locals as 'the Road.' They refer to every other road and dirt path in the area as 'the Other Road,' regardless of which road. Along the Road there is little to see, as most cabins and homes are tucked away behind a shield of trees. The heart of Gustavus is the bridge over the Salmon River; near it are Salmon River Park, the Gustavus Inn and the only grocery store in the area.

Places to Stay & Eat

Thanks to the growing popularity of Glacier Bay, there has been a boom in fine inns and lodges in Gustavus, most charging $100 or more a night.

The original is the **Gustavus Inn** (☎ 697-2254, 800-649-5220), a charming family homestead lodge that has 16 rooms and space for 26 people. The inn is mentioned in every travel book and brochure on Alaska, and rooms are hard to obtain at the last minute. Nightly rates are $135 per person, including meals. The inn is really known for its gourmet dinners, which include home-grown vegetables and main courses of local seafood such as salmon, crab, halibut and

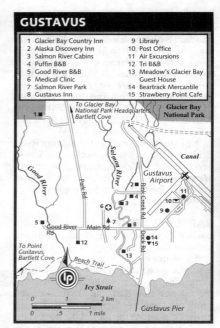

GUSTAVUS

1 Glacier Bay Country Inn
2 Alaska Discovery Inn
3 Salmon River Cabins
4 Puffin B&B
5 Good River B&B
6 Medical Clinic
7 Salmon River Park
8 Gustavus Inn
9 Library
10 Post Office
11 Air Excursions
12 Tri B&B
13 Meadow's Glacier Bay
   Guest House
14 Beartrack Mercantile
15 Strawberry Point Cafe

SOUTHEAST

trout served family style. Dinners cost $25 per person, and you have to call ahead for a space at the table.

Another fine place is the **Glacier Bay Country Inn** (☎ 697-2288, 800-628-0912, gbci@thor.he.net), which offers a room, three meals a day and your transfers for $324 for two people. The **Alaska Discovery Inn** (☎ 800-586-1911) is a quaint lodge with singles/doubles for $95/105. The **Meadow's Glacier Bay Guest House** (☎ 697-2348, meadowguest@iname.com) has three rooms that range from $99 to $179 for a double that includes breakfast, use of bicycles and transfers.

A cheaper alternative for lodging in Gustavus is the **Salmon River Cabins** (☎ 697-2245), on a road that heads northeast just before you cross the Salmon River Bridge from the airport. Cabins are $70 per night for two people and can accommodate up to four. Each has a woodstove and a gas camp stove, and bicycles can be rented.

Puffin B&B *(☎ 800-478-2258 in Alaska or 697-2260)* has five cabins, with and without attached bathrooms, near the Salmon River that range from $90 to $130 for two people, along with a Laundromat and bicycles for guests. Other homes with lodging include ***Good River B&B*** *(☎ 697-2241, gva@ goodrive.com)*, a spacious log home with free bicycles. Singles/doubles are $70/80. The ***Tri B&B*** *(☎ 697-2425, tribay@pluto.he.net)* offers individual cabins for $70/90.

A quarter mile south of the Salmon River Bridge on the way to the dock is the ***Strawberry Point Cafe***. Next door, ***Beartrack Mercantile*** sells groceries at outrageous prices. It's best to purchase supplies before leaving Juneau.

BARTLETT COVE

Bartlett Cove is the park headquarters and includes the Glacier Bay Lodge, a restaurant, a visitor center, a campground and the main dock where the tour boats depart for excursions up the bay. The cove lies within the Glacier Bay Park but is still 40 miles south (and another high-priced trip) of the nearest glacier. At the foot of the dock is the park's visitor center, where you can obtain backcountry permits, seek out information or purchase a variety of books or topographic maps that cover the park.

Hiking

Glacier Bay has few trails, and in the backcountry, foot travel is done along riverbanks, on ridges or across ice remnants of glaciers. The only developed trails are in Bartlett Cove.

Forest Trail This mile-long nature walk begins and ends near the Bartlett Cove Dock and winds through the pond-studded spruce and hemlock forest near the campground. There are daily ranger-led walks along this trail; inquire at the lodge.

Bartlett River Trail This 1.5-mile trail begins just up the road to Gustavus, where there is a posted trailhead, and ends at the Bartlett River estuary. Along the way, it meanders along a tidal lagoon and passes

through a few wet spots. Plan on two to four hours for the 3-mile roundtrip.

Point Gustavus Beach Walk This walk, along the shoreline south of Bartlett Cove to Point Gustavus and Gustavus, provides the only overnight trek from the park headquarters. The total distance is 12 miles, and the walk to Point Gustavus, an excellent spot to camp, is 6 miles. Plan on hiking the stretch from Point Gustavus to Gustavus at low tide, which will allow you to ford the Salmon River as opposed to swimming across it. Point Gustavus is an excellent place to sight killer whales in Icy Strait.

Paddling

Glacier Bay offers an excellent opportunity for people who have experience on the water but not a lot as kayakers. By utilizing the tour boat, you can skip the long and open paddle up the bay and enjoy only the well-protected arms and inlets where the glaciers are located. Transportation is on the *Spirit of Adventure,* which departs daily at 7:30 am and will put you ashore at Mt Wright, near where the East and West Arms divide, Geikie Inlet near Hugh Miller Inlet, or Gilbert Peninsula in the West Arm. The most dramatic glaciers are in the West Arm, but occasionally the upper areas of the arm have been off limits to campers and kayakers due to aggressive brown bears. Many paddlers, however, prefer Muir Inlet, because cruise ships and tour boats are prohibited there. Plan on a week to paddle from Mt Wright up the arm and return to the pickup point, from eight to 10 days for a drop-off in the West Arm with a return paddle to Bartlett Cove. For more detailed information on kayaking this route, see the Glacier Bay section of the Wilderness chapter.

Paddlers who want to avoid the tour-boat fares but still long for a kayak adventure should try the Beardslee Islands. While there are no glaciers to view, the islands (a day's paddle from Bartlett Cove) offer calm water, protected channels and pleasant beach camping. Wildlife includes black bears, seals and bald eagles, and the tidal pools burst with activity at low tide. The islands make for an easy three-day paddle.

Alaska Discovery also offers single-day guided trips that begin and end at Bartlett Cove. Kayaks, life vests, rubber boots, paddles and rain gear are supplied. You supply $119. The paddles are only to Beardslee Islands, and not the glaciers, and it's best to reserve a spot on the trip at the Juneau office (☎ 800-586-1911). Spirit Walker Expeditions (☎ 697-2266, 800-529-2937) has a single-day paddle to Pleasant Island, outside of the park, for $115, and an overnight trip for $370 per person.

Places to Stay

The *campground* is free and always seems to have space. It is a quarter mile south of the Glacier Bay Lodge in a lush forest just off the shoreline. It provides a bear cache, eating shelter and pleasant surroundings in which to pitch a tent. Coin-operated showers are available in the park, but there aren't any places that sell groceries or camping supplies.

Glacier Bay Lodge (☎ 800-622-2042) has 55 rooms that cost $165 per night for a double. It also offers dormitory bunks at $28 a night, but the campground is still a better place to spend the night. In the evening, there is a crackling fire in the lodge's huge stone fireplace, and the adjoining bar usually hums with an interesting mixture of park employees, backpackers and locals from Gustavus. Nightly slide presentations, ranger talks and movies held upstairs cover the natural history of the park.

Getting There & Away

You can now fly to or take a boat to Gustavus. There is no ferry service to Gustavus, but Auk Nu Tours (☎ 789-5701, 800-820-2628) leaves Juneau's Auke Bay at 11 am daily and then departs Gustavus at 5:45 pm the same day for the return trip. Roundtrip fare is $86.

Alaska Airlines departs Juneau daily at around 4:30 pm for the 15-minute trip to Gustavus; the roundtrip fare is $80. The cheapest flight is through Air Excursions (☎ 697-2375), which has three flights daily

between the two towns and charges only $100 roundtrip.

Once at Gustavus airport, you are still 10 miles from Bartlett Cove, the park headquarters. The Glacier Bay Lodge bus meets all airline flights but charges $10 for the ride. You can also hitchhike, as there is always a stream of traffic shuffling between Gustavus and the park headquarters.

The other way to reach Glacier Bay is to book a total package tour out of Juneau, which usually includes return airfares and boat passage up the bay to view the glaciers. Such packages are offered by Glacier Bay Tours and Cruises (☎ 800-451-5952). The company offers a six-day cruise of the park that begins with a flight to Gustavus and returns to Juneau via the ship *Wilderness Explorer*. The cost is around $1,500 per person and includes berth, meals and kayaks for paddling in the park. There is also a two-day tour of the park ($481) in which you fly to Gustavus, tour the bay and spend a night at the Glacier Bay Lodge. The company also offers one-day tours out of Juneau ($346), Haines ($440) and Skagway ($462), but that is a lot to pay for a quick trip into the park.

Tour Boats The *Spirit of Adventure*, a 220-passenger catamaran, departs Bartlett Cove at 7:30 am daily, for a nine-hour trip up the West Arm. It returns at 4 pm, when a waiting bus will whisk you away in time to catch the Alaska Airlines flight back to Juneau. The tour of the West Arm glaciers, the reason you've spent so much money to get here, is another $158, but that does include lunch – what a deal!

Haines

Haines (population 1775), in the northern reaches of the Inside Passage, is an important access point to the Yukon Territory (Canada) and Interior Alaska. While the town itself may lack the charm of Sitka or Petersburg, the surrounding scenery is stunning. Travelers who arrive on the ferry will travel up Lynn Canal, the longest and deepest fjord in

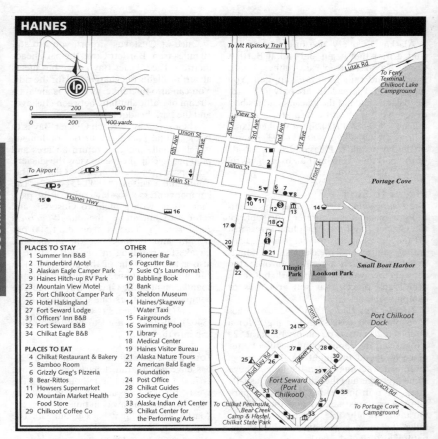

HAINES

To Mt Ripinsky Trail

Lutak Rd

To Ferry
Terminal,
Chilkoot Lake
Campground

0   200   400 m
0   200   400 yards

To Airport

To Chilkat Peninsula,
Bear-Creek
Camp & Hostel,
Chilkat State Park

View St

Union St

4th Ave

3rd Ave

2nd Ave

1st Ave

Front St

Dalton St

Main St

Haines Hwy

6th Ave

5th Ave

Portage Cove

Tlingit
Park

Lookout Park

Small Boat Harbor

Port Chilkoot
Dock

Fort Seward
(Port
Chilkoot)

Totem St

Mud Bay Rd

FAA Rd

Portage St

Beach Rd

To Portage Cove
Campground

PLACES TO STAY
1 Summer Inn B&B
2 Thunderbird Motel
3 Alaskan Eagle Camper Park
9 Haines Hitch-up RV Park
23 Mountain View Motel
25 Port Chilkoot Camper Park
26 Hotel Halsingland
27 Fort Seward Lodge
31 Officers' Inn B&B
32 Fort Seward B&B
34 Chilkat Eagle B&B

PLACES TO EAT
4 Chilkat Restaurant & Bakery
5 Bamboo Room
7 Grizzly Greg's Pizzeria
8 Bear-Rittos
11 Howsers Supermarket
20 Mountain Market Health
    Food Store
29 Chilkoot Coffee Co

OTHER
5 Pioneer Bar
6 Fogcutter Bar
7 Susie Q's Laundromat
10 Babbling Book
12 Bank
13 Sheldon Museum
14 Haines/Skagway
    Water Taxi
15 Fairgrounds
16 Swimming Pool
17 Library
18 Medical Center
19 Haines Visitor Bureau
21 Alaska Nature Tours
22 American Bald Eagle
    Foundation
24 Post Office
28 Chilkat Guides
30 Sockeye Cycle
33 Alaska Indian Art Center
35 Chilkat Center for
    the Performing Arts

North America. Passengers scramble to the left side of the boat when the US Forest Service guide announces the approach of Davidson and Rainbow Glaciers to the west.

Mountains seem to surround Haines on all sides. To the west, looming over Fort Seward, are the jagged Cathedral Peaks of the Chilkat Mountains; to the east is the Chilkoot Range; and standing guard behind Haines is Mt Ripinsky.

History

Haines is 75 miles north of Juneau on a wooded peninsula between the Chilkat and Chilkoot Inlets. Originally, it was a stronghold of the wealthy Chilkat Tlingit Indians, who called the settlement Dtehshuh, meaning 'end of the trail.' The first white person to settle was George Dickinson of the Northwest Trading Company, who arrived in 1878 and was followed by missionaries and a trickle of other settlers. Eventually, of course, the gold prospectors stampeded through the town.

In 1897, Jack Dalton, a gun-toting entrepreneur, turned an old Indian trade route into a toll road for miners seeking an easier way to reach the Klondike. He charged $2 per head of cattle. The Dalton Trail quickly became a heavily used pack route to mining districts north of Whitehorse, and Dalton himself reaped the profits until the White Pass & Yukon Railroad in Skagway put him out of business in 1900.

The army established Alaska's first permanent post at Haines in 1903 and named it Fort William H Seward, after the secretary of state who negotiated the purchase of the state. It was renamed Chilkoot Barracks in 1922, to avoid confusing it with the town of Seward, and for the next 20 years was the only army post in Alaska.

The fort was used as a rest camp during WWII, and from there soldiers moved on to various points in the state, where they formed the nuclei of new army installations. By 1946, the fort was deactivated and declared surplus.

WWII also led to the construction of the Haines Hwy, the 159-mile link between the Southeast and the Alcan (Alaska Hwy). By 1942, the Japanese had captured two Aleutian islands and were headed, many believed, toward a land war in Alaska. Military planners, seeking a second link to the sea and another possible evacuation route, chose to connect Haines to the Alcan. Construction began two months after the Alcan was completed and engineers merely followed Jack Dalton's trail. The route through the mountains is so rugged it would be 20 years before US and Canadian crews even attempted to keep the 'Haines Cut-off Road' open during the winter and, up until the early 1970s, a radio check system was used to make sure cars made it through. By the 1980s, the Haines Hwy was paved, and now more than 50,000 travelers in cars, RVs and buses follow in annually.

Logging and fishing have been the traditional industries of Haines, but in the 1970s the town became economically depressed as the lumber industry fell on hard times. Haines' residents have since swung their economy towards tourism, and the town is surviving as a major Southeast tourist destination. And why not? Haines has spectacular scenery, comparatively dry weather (only 53 inches of rain annually) and is accessible by road. What other Southeast Alaska town can boast that?

Information

Tourist Offices The Haines Visitors Bureau (☎ 766-2234, 800-458-3579, hainesak@wwa.com, www.haines.ak.us), at 2nd Ave and Willard St, is open 8 am to 8 pm daily during the summer. The center has racks of free information for tourists, rest rooms, a small message board and a used-book exchange.

For information on the town's three state parks, head to the Alaska Division of State Parks office (☎ 766-2292) on Main St above Helen's Shop. The office is open 8 am to 4:30 pm Monday to Friday.

Money First National Bank of Anchorage (☎ 766-2321) is on the corner of 2nd Ave and Main St.

Post The post office is on the corner of the Haines Hwy and Mud Bay Rd, near Fort Seward.

Email & Internet Access The Haines Library provides free email and Internet access, and the Haines Visitors Bureau has a modem line for those packing a computer. Chilkat Eagle B&B (☎ 766-2763) is also wired, so you can pick up your email or surf the Web.

Travel Agencies The Travel Connection Agency (☎ 766-2681) is on 2nd Ave, across from the visitor bureau.

Bookstores & Libraries On Main St is the Babbling Book (☎ 766-3356). South of Main St is the Haines Public Library (☎ 766-2545), 103 3rd Ave, which is open daily and until 9 pm Monday to Thursday.

Laundry Susie Q's Laundromat, near the eastern end of Main St by the boat harbor, also has showers.

Medical Services For medical needs, there is the Haines Medical Center (☎ 766-3121), 131 1st Ave.

Things to See

The **Sheldon Museum** (☎ 766-2366) is near the waterfront at the eastern end of Main St, just off Front St. It features a collection of indigenous artifacts and relics from Haines' pioneer and gold-rush days, including the sawed-off shotgun Jack Dalton used to convince travelers to pay his toll. Twice a day the museum also shows *Last Stronghold of the Eagles,* an excellent movie by Juneau filmmaker Joel Bennett about the annual gathering of bald eagles. The museum is open 1 to 5 pm daily and 9 am to noon Tuesday to Friday; admission is $3.

Across Front St from the museum, the **small boat harbor** bustles during the summer with fishing and pleasure boats. A walk up Main St will take you through the heart of the Haines' business district, and south on Front St is **Lookout Park**, a vantage point where you can get good views of the boat harbor to the left (north), Port Chilkoot Dock to the right and the Coast Mountains all around. A display points out the various peaks that rise above Haines.

Continue south on Front St as it curves around Portage Cove to merge into the Haines Hwy. If you head north on the highway, you'll pass the post office and come to Haines' newest attraction, **American Bald Eagle Foundation** (☎ 766-3094). The nonprofit center opened in 1994 and features an impressive wildlife diorama with more than 100 species on display. A tree full of eagles occupies the middle of the hall, and a small video room shows the annual winter eagle congregation on the Chilkat River. Hours are 10 am to 5 pm daily; donation requested.

If you turn uphill (east) at the Front St-Haines Hwy junction, you reach **Fort Seward**. The old army fort was designated a national historical site in 1972 and is slowly being renovated. In the center of the fort are the parade grounds, and to the north is Building No 53, formerly the commanding officers' quarters and now the Hotel Halsingland. A walking-tour map of the fort is available in the lobby of the hotel.

Within the parade ground is **Totem Village**. Although not part of the original fort, it provides an interesting view of two tribal houses, totem poles and **Sea Wolf Art Studio** (☎ 766-2558), which features the work of Tresham Gregg, one of Haines' best-known indigenous artists.

More art can be seen in Fort Seward at the **Alaska Indian Arts Center** (☎ 766-2160), in the former post hospital, and in the **Chilkat Center for the Performing Arts** – a refurbished cannery building and the site of nightly productions from the Chilkat Dancers and Lynn Canal Community Players. The arts center features indigenous artists carving totems, masks and war clubs or weaving Chilkat blankets; many of these items are available for purchase. The center is open 9 am to noon and 1 to 5 pm Monday to Saturday during the summer.

Hiking

There are two major trail systems near Haines: south of town are the Chilkat Peninsula trails that include the climb to Mt Riley; north of Haines is the path to the summit of Mt Ripinsky. Stop at the visitor bureau in town before hiking and pick up the brochure *Haines is for Hikers,* which describes the trails in more detail.

Mt Ripinsky Trail The trip to the 3563-foot summit of Mt Ripinsky (also known as the South Summit) is an all-day hike with a sweeping view of the land from Juneau to Skagway. The route, which includes Peak 3920 and a descent from 7 Mile Saddle to Haines Hwy, is either a strenuous 10-hour journey for experienced hikers or an overnight trip.

To reach the trailhead, follow 2nd Ave north to Lutak Rd (the road to the ferry terminal) and past the fire station. Leave Lutak Rd when it curves right and head up the hill on Young St. Turn right along an old, buried pipeline and follow it for a mile to the start of the trail, just as the pipeline heads downhill to the tank farm.

The trail crosses a pair of streams, passes by an old reservoir and then ascends steadily through spruce and hemlock, reaching open muskeg at 1300 feet. After a second climb, you come to Johnson's Creek at 2500 feet, where there is drinking water and views of the Southeast's snowcapped mountains all the way to Admiralty Island. From here, the route goes from dwarfed hemlock to open slope that has snow until late summer.

The North Summit has a benchmark and a high wooden surveyor's platform. You can camp in the alpine area between the two peaks and then continue the next day by descending the North Summit and hiking west along the ridge to Peak 3920. From here you can descend to 7 Mile Saddle and then to the Haines Hwy, putting you 7 miles northwest of town. This is a 10-mile loop and a challenging overnight hike; the trail is steep in places and easily lost. The views, however, are spectacular.

Battery Point Trail This 2-mile trail is a flat walk along the shore to Kelgaya Point, where you can cut across to a pebble beach and follow it to Battery Point for excellent views of Lynn Canal. The trail begins a mile beyond Portage Cove Campground at the end of Beach Rd. Plan on about two hours roundtrip.

Mt Riley Trails This climb to a 1760-foot summit is considerably easier than the one to Mt Ripinsky, but it still provides good views in all directions, including Rainbow and Davidson Glaciers. One trail up the mountain begins at a junction 2.2 miles up the Battery Point Trail out of Portage Cove Campground. From here, you hike 3 miles over Half Dome and up Mt Riley.

Another route, closer to town, begins at the end of FAA Rd, which runs behind the Officers' Row in Fort Seward. From the road's end, follow the water-supply access route for 2 miles to a short spur that branches off to the right and connects with the trail from Mud Bay Rd. The hike is 3.9 miles one way and eliminates having to find a ride out to the third trailhead to Mt Riley, three miles out on Mud Bay Rd. The trailhead off Mud Bay Rd is posted. This 2.8-mile route is the steepest but most direct to the summit. Plan on five to six hours roundtrip.

Seduction Point Trail This trail begins at Chilkat State Park Campground and is a 6.5-

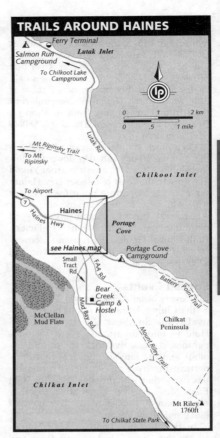

TRAILS AROUND HAINES

Ferry Terminal
Salmon Run Campground
Lutak Inlet
To Chilkoot Lake Campground
Lutak Rd
Mt Ripinsky Trail
To Mt Ripinsky
Chilkoot Inlet
To Airport
7
Haines
Haines Hwy
Portage Cove
see Haines map
Portage Cove Campground
Small Tract Rd
FAA Rd
Battery Point Trail
Bear Creek Camp & Hostel
McClellan Mud Flats
Mud Bay Rd
Chilkat Peninsula
Mount Riley Trail
Chilkat Inlet
Mt Riley 1760ft
To Chilkat State Park

0   1   2 km
0   .5   1 mile

SOUTHEAST

mile, one-way hike to the point that separates Chilkoot and Chilkat Inlets. The trail swings between inland forest and beaches and provides excellent views of Davidson Glacier.

If you have the equipment, this trail can be turned into an excellent overnight hike by setting up camp at the cove east of Seduction Point. Carry in water and check the tides before departing, as the final stretch along the beach after David's Cove should be walked at low or midtide. The entire roundtrip takes most hikers from nine to 10 hours.

River Running

Haines is also the departure point for numerous raft trips in the area. Chilkat Guides (☎ 766-2491, raftalaska@aol.com) offers a four-hour float down the Chilkat River that provides plenty of opportunity to view bald eagles and possibly brown bears; there is little white water. The guide company runs the trip daily, beginning from its shop on Beach Rd in Fort Seward. The cost is $80/40 adults/children.

On a much grander scale of adventure is the exciting 10-day raft trip down the Tatshenshinin/Alsek River system, from Yukon Territory to the coast of Glacier Bay. Haines serves as the departure point for this river trip, which is unmatched by any other Alaskan raft trip for its scenic mix of rugged mountain ranges and dozens of glaciers. Both Chilkat Guides and Alaska Discovery (☎ 586-1911) run the trip, which costs around $2000 per person.

Special Events

Like every other Alaskan town, Haines has a 4th of July celebration, but its biggest festival is the Southeast Alaska State Fair. Held in mid-August, the event includes parades, dances, livestock shows and exhibits and the famous pig races that draw participants from all Southeast communities. Coinciding with the state fair is the Bald Eagle Music Festival, which brings together more than 50 musicians for five days of blues and bluegrass music.

In the third weekend of May, Haines stages the Great Alaska Craft Beer and Home Brew Festival, when most of the state's microbrews compete for the honors of being named top suds. In mid-November, Haines stages the Alaska Bald Eagle Festival, a three-day event at what is usually the peak time of the winter gathering of eagles.

Places to Stay

Haines tacks on a 5.5% tax to the price of lodging.

Camping Haines has several state campgrounds. The closest to town is *Portage Cove*, half a mile southeast of Fort Seward. This scenic beach campground for backpackers and cyclists is only 2 miles from the center of town and has water, pit toilets and nine sites for $6 a night. Follow Front St south (which becomes Beach Rd as it curves around the cove near Fort Seward), and the campground is at the end of the gravel road. Five miles north of the ferry terminal is *Chilkoot Lake State Park*, on Lutak Rd. The campground has 32 sites for $10 a night and picnic shelters. There is good fishing for Dolly Varden on Chilkoot Lake, a turquoise-blue lake surrounded by mountain peaks.

If you have some spare time in Haines, spend a night at *Chilkat State Park*, 7 miles southeast of Haines on Mud Bay Rd. The park, situated towards the end of the Chilkat Peninsula, has good views of Lynn Canal and of the Davidson and Rainbow Glaciers, which spill out of the mountains into the canal. There are 15 sites ($6).

Within town is *Port Chilkoot Camper Park* (☎ 766-2000, 800-542-6363), behind the Hotel Halsingland, where a full hookup for RVers is $18.50 and a tent site is $8 a night. The private campground has wooded sites, a Laundromat and showers for $1.50. Other RV campgrounds include *Alaskan Eagle Camper Park* (☎ 888-306-7521, 766-2335, 755 Union St) and *Haines Hitch-up RV Park* (☎ 766-2882), on the corner of the Haines Hwy and Main St. Outside of town is *Salmon Run RV Campground* (☎ 766-4229, salmonrun@juno.com), on Lutak Rd 1.8 miles north of the ferry terminal. Overlooking a mountainous stretch of Lutak Inlet, this campground features wooded sites, showers and a day lodge selling coffee and giant cinnamon rolls in the morning. A tent site is $12.50 a night.

Hostels *Bear Creek Camp & Hostel* (☎ 766-2259, hostel@kcd.com) is on Small Tract Rd 2.5 miles south of town. Follow 3rd Ave south onto Mud Bay Rd near Fort Seward. After a half mile, veer left onto Small Tract Rd and follow it for 1.5 miles to the hostel. There is room for 20 people in the hostel's dorms; the cost is $14 per night.

There are also tent sites for $12 per night for two people (shower included) and two-person cabins for $38 per night. New owners have improved the rustic camp considerably by cleaning it up and adding a coin-operated laundry, free ferry pickup, bike rentals and a hot tub.

B&Bs The *Summer Inn B&B* (☎ 766-2970, 247 2nd Ave), 4 miles from the ferry terminal, has five bedrooms with shared bath for $70/80 singles/doubles, most with a good view of Lynn Canal. There are several B&Bs in the buildings at the fort. *Fort Seward B&B* (☎ 766-2856, 800-615-6676, fortseward@ yahoo.com) is in the former home of the army's surgeon, where rooms with shared baths are $74/84. *Officers' Inn B&B* (☎ 766-2000, 800-542-6363, halsinglan@aol.com) has some economy rooms for $50/55.

Finally *Chilkat Eagle B&B* (☎ 766-2763, eaglebb@kcd.com) is also in the fort and has four rooms for $65/75. The B&B provides a full breakfast and a courtesy kitchen.

Hotels In Haines there are eight hotels and lodges. The *Fort Seward Lodge* (☎ 766-2009, 800-478-7772, ftsewardlodge@wytbear.com), the former post exchange in the fort, is the cheapest hotel, with single/doubles beginning at $50/55. Also in the former fort is *Hotel Halsingland* (☎ 766-2000, 800-542-6363 halsinglan@aol.com), where rooms cost $89/98. Near the entrance to the fort, on Mud Rd, *Mountain View Motel* (☎ 766-2900, 800-478-2902 budget@mtviewmotel.com) has rooms with kitchenettes at $69/74. In town, *Thunderbird Motel* (☎ 766-2131, 800-327-2556, t-bird@kcd.com) has singles/doubles for $69/79.

Places to Eat

The popular place for breakfast among locals is the *Chilkat Restaurant and Bakery*, on the corner of Main St and 5th Ave, which opens at 7 am. A plate of eggs, potatoes and toast is $6, and you can get coffee and a warm muffin for around $2.50. On Friday night, they have an all-you-can-eat Mexican dinner for $13.

The *Commander's Room*, in the Hotel Halsingland in Fort Seward, provides a historical setting (with a nice view of the surrounding mountains) in which to eat. The cost of breakfast is similar to the Chilkat Restaurant and Bakery and the portions are filling. At night, the restaurant serves a variety of seafood, including prawns, scallops and salmon, with dinners ranging from $14 to $22. The best breakfast value in town is at the *Bamboo Room*, on the corner of 2nd Ave and Main St, where a plate of blueberry pancakes and a coffee costs under $6.

For sandwiches or sourdough pizza by the slice, try *Grizzly Greg's Pizzeria*, across from the Bamboo Room on 2nd Ave. Vegetarian sandwiches and an espresso bar are found at *Mountain Market Health Food Store*, 3rd Ave and Haines Hwy. If staying near Fort Seward, you'll find your morning latte at *Chilkoot Coffee Company*, on Portage St. Locally caught seafood ends up on a variety of menus in Haines. For Mexican food with a seafood twist, try halibut tacos ($4), shrimp burrito ($7) or Alaskan shrimp nachos ($11) at *Bear-Rittos*, next door to Susie Q Laundromat on Main St.

The town's salmon bake, *Port Chilkoot Potlatch*, takes place nightly from 5 to 8 pm at Totem Village in the center of Fort Seward. For $22 per person, you can enjoy all the grilled salmon, salad and baked beans you can handle in one sitting. To take some salmon or crab back to your campsite, go to *Howsers Supermarket* (335 Main St), which has a distinctive storefront with large moose antlers.

Entertainment

To get beer on tap and rub elbows with the locals, stop at the *Fogcutter Bar* (122 Main St) or the *Pioneer Bar* (13 2nd Ave), next to the Bamboo Room. Both spots can get lively and full at night, as Haines is a hard-drinking town. At Fort Seward, the nights can get lively at the *Hotel Halsingland Pub*.

Other activities at night include performances by the Chilkat Dancers in full traditional Tlingit costume at the *Chilkat Center for the Performing Arts* (☎ 766-2160), at Fort Seward. The performances start at 7:30 pm Sunday, Monday, Tuesday and Thursday and 8:30 pm on Wednesday; admission is $10.

Getting There & Around

Air There is no jet service to Haines, but several charter companies run regularly scheduled north- and southbound flights. Wings of Alaska (☎ 766-2030), Haines Airways (☎ 766-2646) or LAB Flying Service (☎ 766-2222) all offer daily flights to Juneau. One-way is around $65, roundtrip $130. Any of them will arrange a sightseeing flight over Glacier Bay National Park; the park is only a 10-minute flight from Haines. For a 60- to 70-minute flight, which is enough air time to reach the park's famous glaciers, expect to pay $100 per person, with a two-person minimum. On a clear day, it's money well spent.

Bus From Haines, you can catch buses north to Whitehorse, Anchorage or Fairbanks. Alaskon Express has a bus departing from the Hotel Halsingland at 8:45 am Sunday, Tuesday and Thursday that overnights at Beaver Creek and then continues on to Anchorage, reaching the city at 7:30 pm the following day. The fare from Haines to Anchorage is $195 and does not include lodging.

On the same runs, you can also make connections at either Haines Junction or Beaver Creek for Fairbanks, Whitehorse or Skagway, though why anybody would want to ride a bus instead of a ferry to Skagway is beyond me. The one-way fare to Fairbanks is $182 and Whitehorse $86.

Boat State ferries arrive and depart daily from the terminal (☎ 766-2111) in Lutak Inlet north of town. The one-way fare north to Skagway is $17 and south to Juneau is $24.

Haines Taxi (☎ 766-3138) runs a ferry shuttle bus, meets all arrivals, and for $5 will take you the 4 miles into town. The bus also departs town 30 minutes before each ferry arrival and stops at the Hotel Halsingland and near the visitor bureau in town, before heading out to the ferry terminal.

For a day trip to Skagway, contact Haines-Skagway Water Taxi (☎ 888-766-3395, 766-3395, h2otaxi@kcd.com). The 80-passenger boat departs twice daily, first at 9:30 am and then again at 3:45 pm, from the boat harbor in the heart of Haines; roundtrip fare is $32, one-way $20. Tickets can be purchased in advance from the water taxi office at the Haines small boat harbor.

Chilkat Cruises (☎ 888-766-2103, 766-2100) also runs a ferry between Haines and Skagway, with departures at 11:15 am and 5 pm daily from near Port Chilkoot dock. Roundtrip is $30.

Car To enjoy the sites out on the road, especially to visit the Chilkat Bald Eagle Preserve on your own, there are five car rental agencies in Haines. The best rates are with Affordable Cars at Captain's Choice Motel (☎ 766-3111), which has compacts for $49 a day with unlimited mileage, but you have to stay in the USA. It's $69 with unlimited mileage if you're going into Canada. You can also try Thunderbird Motel Car Rental (☎ 766-2131).

Bicycle Sockeye Cycle (☎ 766-2869, cycleak@ibm.net) rents mountain bikes and road bikes by the hour, day or even weekly, as well as selling parts. Rates are $6 an hour and $30 a day, with discounts on two- and three-day rentals. The shop also offers bike tours that range from one-hour to one-day journeys or will arrange van transport to those who want to cycle on their own.

A three-hour bicycle tour to Chilkoot Lake is $80.

AROUND HAINES
Alaska Chilkat Bald Eagle Preserve

In 1982, the state reserved 48,000 acres along the Chilkat River to protect the largest known gathering of bald eagles in the world. Each year from October to January, more than 4000 eagles congregate here to feed on chum salmon. They come because an upwelling of warm water prevents the river from freezing and encourages the late run of salmon. It's a remarkable sight, hundreds of birds along the banks of the river sitting in the bare trees that line the river, with often six or more birds to a branch.

The eagles can be seen from the Haines Hwy, where lookouts allow motorists to park and view the birds. The best view is between Mile 18 and Mile 22, where telescopes, interpretive displays and paved walkways along the river were added in 1997. You really have to be here after November to enjoy the birds in their greatest numbers, but unfortunately, most travelers have long departed Alaska by then. Still there are more than 200 resident eagles that can be spotted throughout the summer.

The state park office in Haines can provide a list of state-authorized guides who conduct tours into the preserve. Among them is Alaska Nature Tours (☎ 766-2876; aknature@kcd.com), which conducts three-hour tours ($50) daily during the summer. The tours cover much of the scenery around the Haines area but often concentrate on the river flats and river mouths where you usually see 40 to 50 eagles in the summer, many nesting.

Kluane National Park

Kluane National Park, 120 miles north of Haines, is one of Canada's most spectacular parks. The preserve encompasses 8649 sq miles of rugged coastal mountains in the southwestern corner of the Yukon Territory. There are no roads in this wilderness park but the Haines Hwy runs along its eastern edge, providing easy access to the area. The 159-mile Haines Hwy, which follows Jack Dalton's gold-rush toll road, is paved and makes an extremely scenic and smooth drive ending at the Alcan in Haines Junction.

Amid the lofty mountains of Kluane National Park lies Mt Logan, Canada's highest peak at 19,636 feet and the most extensive nonpolar ice field in the world, from which glaciers spill out onto the valley floors. Wildlife is plentiful and includes Dall sheep, brown bears, moose, mountain goats and caribou.

The park's visitor center (☎ 867-634-7207), in Haines Junction on the Alcan, is open 9 am to 7 pm (Yukon time) daily in the summer. Along with displays and a free slide show covering the area's natural history, the center can provide you with information, backcountry permits and topographic maps for overnight hikes into the park.

The main activity in Kluane is hiking, and trails consist primarily of old mining roads, animal trails or natural routes along riverbeds or ridges. The trailheads for eight hiking routes are located along the Haines and Alaska Hwys.

Alsek Pass Trail This 15-mile trail is a flat walk, most of the way, along an old abandoned mining road. It begins 6 miles west of Haines Junction at Mackintosh Lodge and ends at Sugden Creek.

Sheep Creek Trail This 3-mile trail is reached by turning left on the first gravel drive just north of the Sheep Mountain Visitors Center on Haines Hwy. Follow the old mining road to the Warden's Cabin and park there. Continue another half mile on the mining road to the posted trailhead. The trail involves some climbing but will lead you to panoramic views of Kluane Lake and Kaskawulsh Glacier. Plan on four to five hours for the roundtrip hike of 6 miles.

Cottonwood Trail This 53-mile loop begins at the Kathleen Lake Campground, 12 miles south of Haines Junction. It ends at Dezadeash Lodge off the Haines Hwy. The route runs along old mining roads that require some climbing and fording of streams. Wildlife sightings, especially brown bears, are plentiful on this four-day hike.

Slims River Trail This 16-mile trail is one of the most scenic in Kluane National Park, passing old mining relics and ending at Observation Mountain, which you can scramble up for a view of the spectacular Kaskawulsh Glacier. The trailhead is about 40 miles west of Haines Junction near a park information center.

Skagway

Skagway (population 825), a place of many names, much history and little rain, is the northern terminus of the Alaska Marine Hwy. The town lies at the head of the Lynn Canal and, at one time or another, has been called Skaguay, Shkagway and Gateway to the Golden Interior. It is also known as the Home of the North Wind, and residents tell visitors that it blows so much here you'll never breathe the same air twice.

Skagway is also one of the driest places in what is often the soggy Southeast. While Petersburg averages over 100 inches of rain a year and Ketchikan a drenching 154 inches, Skagway only gets 26 inches of rain annually.

Much of Skagway is within the Klondike Gold Rush National Historical Park, which extends from Seattle to Dawson in the Yukon Territory. The National Park Service is constantly restoring the old shop fronts and buildings so the town looks similar to the boomtown it was in the 1890s, when the gold rush gave birth to Skagway.

History

The town and the nearby ghost town of Dyea were the start for over 40,000 gold-rush stampeders who headed to the Yukon by way of either the Chilkoot Trail or the White Pass Trail. The Chilkoot Trail, which started from Dyea, was the most popular, as it was several miles shorter. The White Pass Trail, which began in Skagway and was advertised as a 'horse trail,' was brutal. In the winter of 1897–98, some 3000 pack animals were driven to death by overly anxious owners; the White Pass was called the 'Dead Horse Trail.'

In 1887, the population of Skagway was two; 10 years later, 20,000 people lived there and the gold-rush town was Alaska's largest city. A center for saloons, hotels and dance halls – Skagway became infamous for its lawlessness. For a time, the town was held under the tight control of Jefferson Randolph 'Soapy' Smith and his gang, who conned and swindled naive newcomers out of their money and stampeders out of their gold dust. Soapy Smith was finally removed from power by a mob of angry citizens. In a gunfight between him and city engineer Frank Reid, both men died, and Smith's reign as the 'uncrowned prince of Skagway' ended, having lasted only nine months.

At the height of the gold rush, Michael J Heney, an Irish contractor, convinced a group of English investors that he could build a railroad over the White Pass Trail to Whitehorse. Construction began in 1898 with little more than picks, shovels and blasting powder, and the narrow-gauge railroad reached Whitehorse, the Yukon capital, in July 1900. The construction of the White Pass & Yukon Railroad was nothing short of a superhuman feat, and the railroad became the focal point of the town's economy after the gold rush and during the military buildup of WWII.

The line was shut down in 1982 but was revived in 1988, to the delight of backpackers walking the Chilkoot Trail and cruise-ship

Soapy Smith's gang

SKAGWAY

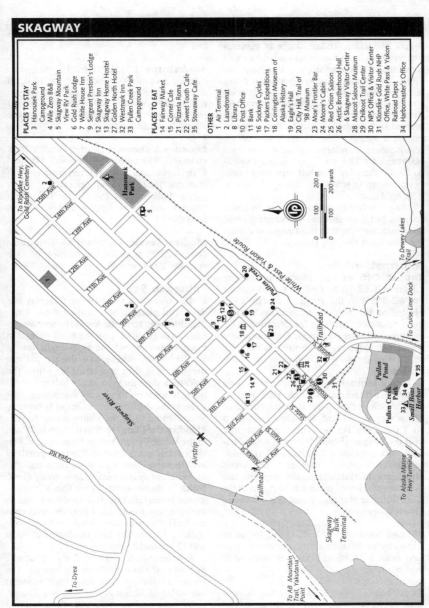

PLACES TO STAY
3 Hanousek Park Campground
4 Mile Zero B&B
5 Skagway Mountain View RV Park
6 Gold Rush Lodge
7 White House Inn
9 Sergeant Preston's Lodge
12 Skagway Inn
13 Skagway Home Hostel
27 Golden North Hotel
32 Westmark Inn
33 Pullen Creek Park Campground

PLACES TO EAT
14 Fairway Market
15 Corner Cafe
21 Pizzeria Roma
22 Sweet Tooth Cafe
35 Stowaway Cafe

OTHER
1 Air Terminal
2 Laundromat
8 Library
10 Post Office
11 Bank
16 Sockeye Cycles
17 Packers Expeditions
18 Corrington Museum of Alaska History
19 Eagle's Hall
20 City Hall, Trail of '98 Museum
23 Moe's Frontier Bar
24 Moore's Cabin
25 Red Onion Saloon
26 Arctic Brotherhood Hall & Skagway Visitor Center
28 Mascot Saloon Museum
29 Chilkoot Trail Center
30 NPS Office & Visitor Center
31 Klondike Gold Rush NHP Office, White Pass & Yukon Railroad Depot
34 Harbormaster's Office

SOUTHEAST

tourists. Although the train hauls no freight, its rebirth was important to Skagway as a tourist attraction. Today, Skagway survives almost entirely on tourism, as bus tours and more than 200 cruise ships visit to turn this village into a modern-day boomtown every summer. When two or three ships arrive on the same day, this is where Alaska can really get crowded. On July 1997, seven cruise ships arrived and dumped almost 7,000 passengers on the town for 12 hours. With ship crews, independent travelers and the town's own 800 residents, Skagway's population swelled to 10,000 that day. The last time that many people were in town was during the Klondike gold rush.

Skagway has to make a living in three months, but if the throngs of tourists are still too much for you, skip this town and depart the Southeast through Haines.

Information

Tourist Offices For information on the Chilkoot Trail, go to Chilkoot Trail Center (☎ 983-3655) in the restored Martin Itjen House at the foot of Broadway St. The center is a clearinghouse for information on permits and transportation. There is also a 13-minute video on hiking the Chilkoot for those who are not sure if they're up to the adventure.

For information on local trails and camping, contact the National Park Service Visitor Center (☎ 983-2921) on the corner of Broadway St and 2nd Ave. Hours are 8 am to 7 pm daily. For any other information, visit the Skagway Visitor Center (☎ 888-762-1898, 983-2854, inforskag@ptialaska), which in 2000 is scheduled to return to the Arctic Brotherhood Hall, diagonally opposite the NPS office. Hours are 8 am to 5 pm daily. The visitor center also maintains a website (www.skagway.org).

Money National Bank of Alaska began in Skagway in 1916 and still maintains that first branch (☎ 983-2265) at Broadway St and 6th Ave.

Post The post office is on Broadway St, next door to the National Bank of Alaska.

Travel Agencies Skagway Travel Service (☎ 983-2500) is at the Westmark Inn on 3rd Ave.

Bookstores & Libraries The Skagway Library is at 8th Ave and State St. It's open daily except Sunday. Skagway News Depot is a small bookstore on Broadway Ave that has an excellent selection on Alaska and the Klondike Gold Rush.

Laundry & Showers Garden City RV Park (☎ 983-2378) is on State St between 15th and 17th Aves and has a Laundromat with showers. There are coin-operated showers ($1) at Pullen Creek Park in the RV campground and at the harbormaster's office, next door.

Medical Services Skagway Medical Clinic (☎ 983-2255) is at the intersection of 11th Ave and Broadway St.

Things to See

Unlike most Southeast towns, Skagway is a delightful place to arrive aboard the ferry. The dock and terminal are at the southwestern end of Broadway St, the main avenue in town. You step off the ferry right into a bustling town, where half the people are dressed as if they are trying to relive the gold-rush days and the other half are obviously tourists off the luxury liners.

Near the dock, on the corner of Broadway St and 2nd Ave, is the visitor center for the **Klondike Gold Rush National Historical Park**, in the White Pass & Yukon Route depot. The visitor center is open from 8 am to 8 pm daily and features displays, ranger talks and the movie *Days of Adventure, Dreams of Gold,* which is shown every hour. The 30-minute movie is narrated by Hal Holbrook and is the best way to slip back into the gold-rush days. The center also leads a 45-minute walking tour of the historic district at 9, 10 and 11 am and 2 pm daily.

A seven-block corridor along Broadway St, part of the historic district, is home to the restored buildings, false fronts and wooden sidewalks of Skagway's golden era. Diagonally opposite the National Park Service office is the **Arctic Brotherhood Hall**, which serves as the Skagway Visitor Center. The hall is hard to miss, as there are 20,000 pieces of driftwood tacked to the front of it, making it one of the most distinctive buildings in Alaska and probably the most photographed.

Near the corner of 3rd Ave and Broadway St is the **Mascot Saloon**, the latest renovation project completed by the National Park Service. Built in 1898, the Mascot was one of 70 saloons during Skagway's heyday as 'the roughest place in the world.' On the 1st floor are exhibits depicting the old saloon at the height of the gold rush, including beer bottles and gambling tokens; admission is free.

Just up Broadway St at 5th Ave is the **Corrington Museum of Alaska History** (☎ 983-2580). This private museum in the back of a gift shop covers the state's history, beginning with the Bering Land Bridge, on 40 pieces of scrimshaw, hand-carved ivory from walrus tusks. Admission is free.

A block southeast of the museum on 5th Ave is **Moore's Cabin**, the oldest building in Skagway. Captain William Moore and his son built the cabin in 1887, when they staked out their homestead as the founders of the town. Moore had to move his home to its present location, however, when gold-rush stampeders overran his homestead. The National Park Service has since renovated the building and, in doing so, discovered that the famous Dead Horse Trail that was used by so many stampeders actually began in the large lawn next to the cabin. Nearby, at 5th Ave and Spring St, is **Bernard Moore House**, which was restored in 1997 and now features exhibits and furnishings depicting family life during the gold rush.

At the southeastern end of 7th Ave is the **city hall**, a granite building built in 1900 as McCabe College. The building later served as a US court, until the city obtained it in 1956. Outside city hall is a restored train and engine and historic displays about the Pullen House, Alaskan Natives and why Skagway is known as the 'Garden City of Alaska.' The **Trail of '98 Museum**, inside city hall, is open 9 am to 5 pm daily in the summer. The museum is jammed with gold-rush relics, including many items devoted to the town's two leading characters, 'Soapy' Smith and Frank Reid. You can purchase a copy of the July 15, 1898 *Skagway News* that described all the details surrounding the colorful shoot-out between the two men; admission to the museum is $3.

For visitors who become as infatuated with Smith and Reid as the locals are, there is the walk out to the **Gold Rush Cemetery**. From the ferry terminal, it is a 2.5-mile stroll northeast along State St, which runs parallel to Broadway St, to the graveyard. Follow State St until it curves into 23rd Ave and look for the sign to Soapy's grave across the railroad tracks. A wooden bridge along the tracks leads to the main part of the cemetery, the site of many stampeders' graves and the plots of Reid and Smith. From Reid's gravestone, it is a short hike uphill to the lovely **Reid Falls**, which cascade 300 feet from the mountainside.

In 1898, Skagway's rival city, **Dyea**, at the foot of the Chilkoot Trail, was on the shortest route to Lake Bennett, where stampeders began their float to Dawson City. After the White Pass & Yukon Railroad was completed in 1900, Dyea quickly died. Today, the town is little more than a few old crumbling cabins, the pilings of Dyea Wharf and Slide Cemetery, where 47 men and women were buried after perishing in an avalanche on the Chilkoot Trail in April 1898. During the summer, the National Park Service leads interpretive walks through the area. Check the NPS Visitor Center for times.

Dyea Rd, a scenic drive, winds 9 miles from Skagway to the ghost town. The hairpin turns are a headache for drivers of camper vans. **Skagway Overlook**, a scenic turnoff with a viewing platform, is 2.5 miles out of town along the Dyea Rd. The overlook offers an excellent view of Skagway, its waterfront and the peaks above the town. Just before crossing the bridge over the Taiya River, you pass the Dyea Camping Area (22 sites), a free campground where an NPS ranger is stationed in the summer to assist hikers on the Chilkoot Trail, which starts near the campground.

A Bridge to Dyea

When Skagway was hitting its peak during the Klondike gold rush at the turn of the century, so was Dyea, 9 miles away. Located on the tidal flats of the Taiya River, Dyea had long been a camp for Chilkoot Tlingits, who developed the Chilkoot Trail as a trading route into the Interior.

When the stampeders arrived in 1897, Dyea appeared almost overnight. By 1899, it rivaled Skagway, with a population of 8000 and more than 150 businesses, including hotels, saloons, bathhouses and even its own newspaper. Dyea's darkest hour occurred on Palm Sunday in 1898, when an avalanche above Sheep Camp on the Chilkoot Trail claimed 60 victims. But it was the White Pass & Yukon Railroad, which began operations in 1900 and made the Chilkoot Trail obsolete, that sealed Dyea's fate. The town died almost as quickly as it was born. Many buildings were torn down and their lumber shipped for use elsewhere. The only ruins that remain today are a few foundations of buildings, the rotting stubs of the town's Long Wharf and Slide Cemetery.

In the past, visiting this bit of Klondike history meant fording an arm of the Nelson Slough, which was sometimes a bit of a problem. The Dyea Flats have one of the largest tidal ranges in the world, as much as 24 feet in six hours. At high tide, the Nelson Slough rises from its normal 18 inches to about 4 feet. The problem of access to the ghost town was solved in 1998, when the city of Skagway received a grant and built a bridge over the slough. The US Forest Service provided both the money and the timber, highly prized Alaskan yellow cedar logged from Chichagof Island. The new footbridge is simple, strong, attractive and, being cedar, also aromatic. 'It's probably the best-smelling bridge in Alaska,' said the Juneau engineer who designed it.

Even if you have no intentions of hiking the Chilkoot Trail, Dyea makes an interesting and cheap side trip from Skagway. A number of tour companies will run out to the area for $10 person, and camping at Dyea Campground is free. You can then hike over the historic townsite on your own or join a free walking tour that the National Park Service stages daily during the summer.

Hiking

The Chilkoot Trail (see the Backpacking section in the Wilderness chapter) is probably the most popular hike in the Southeast, but there are other good hikes around Skagway. There is no USFS office in Skagway, but the NPS Visitor Center has a brochure entitled *Skagway Trail Map*.

Dewey Lakes Trail System This series of trails leads east of Skagway to a handful of alpine and subalpine lakes, waterfalls and historic sites. From Broadway St, follow 3rd Ave southeast to the railroad tracks. On the east side of the tracks are the trailheads to Lower Dewey Lake (0.7 miles), Icy Lake (2.5 miles), Upper Reid Falls (3.5 miles) and Sturgill's Landing (4.5 miles).

Plan on taking an hour roundtrip for the hike to Lower Dewey Lake, where there are picnic tables, camping spots and a trail that circles the lake. At the northern end of the lake is an alpine trail that ascends steeply to Upper Dewey Lake, 3.5 miles from town, and Devil's Punchbowl, another 0.7 miles south of the upper lake.

The hike to Devil's Punchbowl is an all-day trip or an ideal overnight excursion, as the views are excellent and there is a free-use USFS shelter on Upper Dewey Lake that is in rough condition but does not require reservations. There are also campsites at Sturgill's Landing.

AB Mountain Trail Also known as the Skyline Trail, this route ascends 5.5 miles to the 5100-foot summit of AB Mountain, named for the 'AB' that appears on its south side when the snow melts every spring. The trailhead is on Dyea Rd, about a mile from Skagway via the Skagway River footbridge off the northwest end of 1st Ave. The trail is very steep and requires a full day to complete.

Denver Glacier Trail This trail begins at Mile 6 of the White Pass & Yukon Route, where the USFS has renovated a WP&YR caboose into a rental cabin (reservations needed, $35 per night). Hikers need to make arrangements with the White Pass & Yukon Route to be dropped off at the caboose. The trail heads up the East fork of the Skagway River for 2 miles, then swings south and continues another 1.5 miles up the glacial outwash to Denver Glacier. Most of the trail is overgrown with brush, but the second half is particularly tough hiking.

Laughton Glacier Trail At Mile 14 of the White Pass & Yukon Route is a 1.5-mile hike to a USFS cabin (reservations needed, $35 per night). The cabin overlooks the river from Warm Pass but is only a mile from Laughton Glacier, an impressive hanging glacier between the 3000-foot walls of the Sawtooth Range. The alpine scenery and ridge walks in this area are worth the $52 ticket WP&YR charges to drop off and pick up hikers. There are two excursion trains from Skagway, so this could be a possible day hike. But it's far better to carry in a tent and spend a night in the area.

Organized Tours
Without a doubt the most spectacular tour from Skagway is the Lake Bennett Adventure on the White Pass & Yukon Route. The day-long journey begins at the railroad depot, where you board parlor cars for the trip to White Pass on the narrowgauge line built during the 1898 Klondike gold rush.

This segment is only a small portion of the 110-mile route to Whitehorse, but it contains the most spectacular scenery, including crossing Glacier Gorge and Dead Horse Gulch, viewing Bridal Veil Falls and then making the steep 2885-foot climb to White Pass, only 20 miles from Skagway. At the end of the trip, you end up at the historic Lake Bennett Railroad Depot, where there is a two-hour layover for lunch and time to explore this beautiful area.

The Lake Bennett trip departs from Skagway at 8 am daily during the summertime,

except on Wednesday and Tuesday. The fare is $128 per adult. Fares for children are half price.

The three-hour Summit Excursion is a shorter tour on the historic railroad, a roundtrip ride to White Pass Summit. The tour is offered at 8:30 am and 1 pm daily and at 4:30 pm on Tuesday and Wednesday. Tickets are $78 and can be purchased at the White Pass & Yukon Route railroad depot (☎ 983-2217, 800-363-7373).

There are numerous tour companies in town, but the most interesting is the Skagway Streetcar Company (☎ 983-2908), which uses eight-door White Motor Company vehicles from 1937. The two-hour tours ($36) are presold by the cruise ships, so you need to book a seat a week in advance. Most other tour companies use vans or minibuses, take you to Gold Rush Cemetery, White Pass Summit, Skagway Overlook and a handful of other sights in two to three hours and charge around $30. For such a tour, call Frontier Excursions (☎ 983-2512), Gold Rush Tours (☎ 983-4444, grt@ptialaska.net) or Gray Line (☎ 983-2241).

Sockeye Cycles (☎ 983-2851), on 5th Ave off Broadway St, offers several bike tours out of Skagway. It's Klondike Tour begins with van transportation to Klondike Pass, elevation 3295 feet, on the Klondike Hwy. From there it's a 15-mile, downhill ride back to town, with plenty of stops to view waterfalls and the White Pass & Yukon Route. The price is $69 and includes use of a bicycle.

Skagway Float Trips (☎ 983-3508) offers a two-hour raft trip through the mild white water of the Skagway River ($40). For kayak trips, call Klondike Water Adventures (☎ 983-3769).

Special Events
Skagway's most unusual celebration is Soapy Smith's Wake, on July 8. Locals and the cast of the *Days of '98 Show* celebrate with a hike out to the grave and a champagne toast, with champagne often sent up by Smith's great-grandson from California. The 4th of July celebrations feature a footrace, parade and fish feed.

Places to Stay

Skagway has an 8% bed tax that is applied to all lodging.

Camping The city manages two campgrounds that serve RVers and backpackers. *Hanousek Park* (☎ 983-2378), at Broadway St and 14th Ave, provides tables, pit toilets and water in a wooded setting for $8 per tent site. Near the ferry terminal is *Pullen Creek Park Campground* (☎ 983-2768, 800-936-3731). There are 30 sites with electricity and water that cost $20 per night and tent sites for $10. *Skagway Mountain View RV Park* (☎ 983-3333), at 12th Ave and Broadway St, has 62 tent sites for $12 a night.

Near the Chilkoot trailhead in Dyea, about 9 miles north of Skagway, the free *Dyea Camping Area* (☎ 983-2921) is operated by the NPS on a first-come, first-served basis. There are 22 sites, vault toilets, tables and fire pits but no water.

Hostels The *Skagway Home Hostel* (☎ 983-2131), on 3rd Ave near Main St, is a very pleasant place to stay, a half mile from the ferry terminal. Reservations are advised – call the hostel or write to the Home Hostel, PO Box 231, Skagway, AK 99840. Along with a kitchen and baggage storage area, there are laundry facilities and bikes. A bunk is $15; a room for couples is $40.

B&Bs The *Skagway Inn* (☎ 983-2289, 800-478-2290 in Alaska, sgyinn@ptialaska.net), at Broadway St and 7th Ave, is in an 1897 Victorian home. The B&B provides breakfast in the morning and free transport to the Chilkoot trailhead. Rooms are $85/100. Equally elegant is the *White House Inn* (☎ 983-9000, whitehse@ptialaska.net), at 8th Ave and Main St, with 10 rooms that begin at $100 per couple. *Mile Zero B&B* (☎ 983-3045), at 9th Ave and Main St, has rooms for $80/$105.

Hotels The recently renovated *Golden North Hotel* (☎ 888-222-1898, 983-2294), at Broadway St and 3rd Ave, is Alaska's oldest hotel and has rooms with shared baths for $60. *Sergeant Preston's Lodge* (☎ 983-2521), at 6th Ave and State St, has rooms with shared baths for $75/95. The *Westmark Inn* (☎ 983-6000), on 3rd Ave between Broadway and Spring Sts, charges $89 for doubles, as does the *Gold Rush Lodge* (☎ 983-2831), at 6th Ave and Alaska St.

Places to Eat

In the past few years, the number of restaurants in Skagway has almost doubled. If you stumble off the ferry early, head up Broadway Ave for breakfast at the *Sweet Tooth Cafe*, which opens at 6 am. The coffee is weak, but the breakfasts are agreeable at $6 to $8. *Corner Cafe*, nearby at 4th Ave and State St, has a wide range of seafood and broiled, stuffed, poached or barbecued salmon or halibut dinners for around $15. When the weather is nice, there are a few tables outside.

The best place for pizza is *Pizzeria Roma II*, on 3rd Ave between State and Broadway Sts, where a 15-inch thin crust is $14 to $23 and daily pasta specials with focaccia bread are $9. *Northern Lights Pizzeria*, up Broadway, has pasta, Greek or Mexican dinners ($10 to $13) and huge portions.

There are also an assortment of espresso shops, lunch wagons and small delis in town, and a couple of fine restaurants. The best is the *Stowaway Cafe* (☎ 983-3463), just past the harbormaster's office. The small cafe has a handful of tables, a view of the boat harbor and excellent fish, seafood gumbo and Cajun-style steak dinners for $16 to $20.

Fairway Market, at 4th Ave and State St, has groceries for those camping or staying at the hostel, and the *Packers Expeditions*, on 5th Ave off Broadway St, features a limited supply of freeze-dried food, white gas for hiking trips and topographic maps.

Entertainment

Bars For a town with only 800 permanent residents, there's a lot to do in Skagway at night. The town's most distinctive and lively bar is the *Red Onion Saloon*, at Broadway St and 2nd Ave, which frequently features live music, or at least a ragtime piano player. This former brothel, built in 1898, is now a gold-rush saloon, complete with mannequins leering down at you from the 2nd story to depict turn-of-the-century working girls.

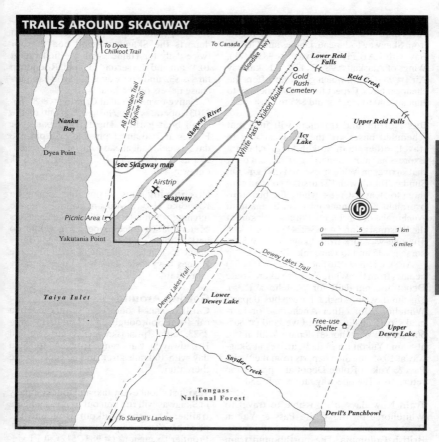

TRAILS AROUND SKAGWAY

The most historic brewery in Alaska is **Skagway Brewing Co**, in the Golden North Hotel. Brewmaster Dennis Corrington discovered the town was home to three breweries during its gold-rush days, so he snatched up the expired Skagway Brewing Co trademark and started brewing. If you like dark beer, try the Blue Top porter. Just up the street is **Moe's Frontier Bar**, a local hangout that can get lively late at night.

Theater Skagway has the best melodrama in the Southeast. Gambling for prizes and drinking begins in the back room of the **Eagle's Hall**, Broadway St and 6th Ave, every night at 7:30 pm. This is followed at 8:30 pm by the entertaining and lively production of the *Days of '98 Show,* which covers the town's gold-rush days and the full story of Soapy Smith and his gang; admission is $14 for both the play and preshow entertainment.

Equally entertaining is 'Buckwheat' Donahue's performance of Robert Service ballads and other tall tales of the North at the NPS Visitor Center every Monday at 7:30 pm. The performance is free and includes howling lessons.

Getting There & Away

Air There are regularly scheduled flights from Skagway to Juneau, Haines and Glacier Bay with LAB Flying Service (☎ 983-2471), Wings of Alaska (☎ 983-2442), and Skagway Air (☎ 983-2218), which generally offers the cheapest fares. Expect to pay $80 one way to Juneau, $40 to Haines and $85 to Gustavus.

Bus Northbound travelers will find that scheduled buses are the cheapest way to travel, other than hitchhiking. Alaskon Express has a bus departing at 7:30 am daily that arrives in Whitehorse at 11:30 am. On Sunday, Tuesday, and Thursday, you can continue to Beaver Creek, where the bus stops overnight and connections can be made to Anchorage or Fairbanks. Purchase tickets at the Westmark Inn (☎ 983-2241) on 3rd Ave. The one-way fare from Skagway to Whitehorse is $45 and to Fairbanks $206.

Alaska Direct Busline (☎ 800-770-6652) departs from the White Pass & Yukon Route Depot at 3 pm daily for Whitehorse ($35). On Sunday, an Alaska Direct bus departs Whitehorse for either Anchorage or Fairbanks. And finally, Alaska Overland (☎ 867-667-7896 in Whitehorse) departs Whitehorse at 8 am (Yukon time) daily, arrives at Skagway at 10:45 am, then departs from the White Pass & Yukon Route Depot at 3 pm for the return trip. The one-way fare is only $30.

Train Nowadays, it's possible to travel to Whitehorse on the White Pass & Yukon Route, with a bus connection at Fraser, British Columbia. The northbound train departs the Skagway depot (☎ 983-2217) at 12:40 pm daily during the summer and passengers arrive in Whitehorse by bus at 6 pm. The one-way fare is $95, quite a bit more than the bus, but the ride on the historic, narrow-gauge railroad is worth it.

Boat The Alaska Marine Hwy ferry (☎ 983-2941) departs daily, during the summer, from the terminal and dock at the southwest end of Broadway St. There are lockers in the terminal, but the building is only open three hours prior to the arrival of a ferry and then while the boat is in port.

Haines-Skagway Water Taxi (☎ 888-766-3395) operates an 80-passenger boat that departs the Skagway small boat harbor twice daily for Haines, with the first run at 10:45 am and the second at 5 pm. Roundtrip fare is $32 and one-way is $20; you can purchase tickets on the boat.

Native-owned Chilkat Cruises (☎ 888-766-2103) operates the *Fairweather* out of the small boat harbor. The ferry departs for Haines at 7:30 am, 1 pm and 6:15 pm five days a week. Call ahead for its weekly schedule, as the days change. Roundtrip is $30, one-way $19.

Hitchhiking This is possible along the Klondike Hwy if you are patient and are hitching when a ferry pulls in. Backpackers contemplating hitchhiking north would do better, however, if they bought a $17 ferry ticket to Haines and hitchhiked along the Haines Hwy instead, as it has considerably more traffic.

Getting Around

Car If you need some wheels, you can rent a car from Sourdough Car Rentals (☎ 983-2523, rental@ptialaska.net), at 6th Ave and Broadway St. Cars range from $40 to $50 a day, with 100 miles free and 30 cents a mile thereafter.

Taxi Just about every taxi and tour company in Skagway will run you out to Dyea and the trailhead for the Chilkoot Trail, and the price hasn't gone up in years – $10 a head. Frontier Excursions (☎ 983-2512), at Broadway St and 7th Ave, has trips at 7 and 9 am, and 2 and 7 pm.

Bicycle Several places in town rent bikes, including Sockeye Cycle (☎ 983-2851), at 5th Ave and Broadway St. Rates are $6/30 an hour/day for mountain bikes.

AROUND SKAGWAY
Golden Circle Route

If you're not heading into the heart of Alaska but still want a taste of the Interior, take the Golden Circle Route, a 372-mile drive that forms a loop between Skagway,

Whitehorse and Haines. It can be covered in as little as two days of hard driving, or you could spend a week or more enjoying the spectacular alpine scenery, especially Kluane National Park, the numerous campgrounds and the eagles of the Chilkat River north of Haines.

The 100-mile Klondike Hwy, from Skagway to Whitehorse, is particularly scenic as it parallels the White Pass Trail and then passes Emerald and Kookatsoon Lakes near Carcross, where there are a handful of campgrounds.

From Whitehorse, you drive a 105-mile portion of the Alaska Hwy and then head south back into Alaska at Haines Junction on the Haines Hwy. The Alaska Marine Hwy would then complete the loop with transportation back to Skagway or a return to Juneau.

Head to the Skagway Visitor Center for maps and information before starting out. In Whitehorse, stop at the Whitehorse Information Center (☎ 867-668-8687, dodds@city.whitehorse.yk.ca), 2121 2nd Ave, or check its website (www.city.whitehorse.yk.ca) for material on the Yukon capital.

Also pick up a copy of *Skaguay Alaskan,* the visitor guide published by the *Skagway News,* for a good mile-by-mile description of the Klondike Hwy.

Yakutat

Yakutat (population 800), the most northern Southeast community, was once isolated but is now linked to the rest of the state by both jet and ferry service. The town became an Alaska Marine Hwy port in 1998, when the M/V *Kennicott* began its once-a-month trips from Juneau to Seward. Thanks to the occasional ferry and Alaska Airlines jet that stops on its way to Cordova, travelers will slowly begin discovering Yakutat, a Tlingit village in a stunning setting. Visitor facilities are still limited and expensive, but the side trip is worth it if you have the funds and the time.

The town is surrounded by lofty peaks, including Mt Elias (18,114 feet) to the west

and Mt Fairweather (15,388 feet) to the east. Northwest of Yakutat lies **Malaspina Glacier**, the largest glacier in North America and the main attraction in the area. During the Klondike gold rush, a few foolish stampeders tried to reach the goldfields by crossing the glacier, and it's unknown if any of them survived the ordeal.

The glacier can be seen from town, but for a closer view you can book a sightseeing flight through Gulf Air Taxi (☎ 784-3240), the local air-charter operator based at the airport. A one-hour flight in a Cessna 185 would be enough to see both the Malaspina and Hubbard Glaciers; it costs $230 for three people. For $460, three passengers can enjoy two hours in the air – enough time to include Mt Elias.

Other visitors come to beach-comb the miles of sandy beach that surround Yakutat, searching for Japanese glass balls (used as floats for fishing nets) blown ashore by the violent Pacific storms.

Information

The best place to go for information on the area is the USFS Yakutat Ranger Station (☎ 784-3359), 712 Ocean Cape Rd, 4 miles from the Yakutat Airport on the way to town. It's open 8 am to 5 pm Monday through Friday.

Places to Stay & Eat

The USFS maintains 10 cabins ($35) in the area, but none of them are in the Russell Fjord Wilderness to the northeast. Five of the cabins in the area can be reached from Forest Hwy 10, which extends east from Yakutat. It's best to reserve the cabins in advance through the National Recreation Reservation Service (☎ 877-444-6777, 518-885-3639 from overseas, www.reserveusa.com). If you're passing through Juneau, you can check on the cabins' availability at the USFS office in Juneau Centennial Hall (☎ 586-8751).

Camping in Yakutat is possible at ***Cannon Beach***, a picnic area near town that's run by the USFS. Yakutat also has lodges and a couple of B&Bs. ***Glacier Bear Lodge*** *(☎ 784-3202)* has singles/doubles for $90/120 and a restaurant. *The Mooring Lodge* (☎ *888-551-2836, 784-3300*) rents rooms with kitchens for $125/175. The *Blue Heron Inn* (☎ *784-3287*), near the boat harbor, is a B&B with five rooms for $120. In town, you'll find a restaurant and two grocery stores.

Getting There & Away

Air Alaskan Airlines (☎ 800-426-0333) stops at Yakutat daily on both its northbound and southbound flight between Juneau and Cordova. Roundtrip fare to Yakutat from either city is $165. You can also purchase a one-way ticket between the two cities with a stopover in Yakutat for $167.

Boat The M/V *Kennicott* will make a whistle stop at Yakutat during the summer on its once-a-month Juneau-to-Valdez run, if there are vehicle reservations. One-way fare between Juneau and Yakutat is $54 for an adult.

AROUND YAKUTAT

Yakutat was an obscure Alaskan town until 1986, when Hubbard Glacier captured national attention by galloping across Russell Fjord at an amazing speed, turning the long inlet into a lake. For much of the year, scientists and geologists set up camp to monitor the unusual event while environmental groups debated whether man should interfere with Mother Nature by trapping and airlifting to safety the doomed seals caught inside Russell Fjord.

Eventually Hubbard receded to reopen the fjord, but to this day the 8-mile-wide glacier remains one of the most active in Alaska. The rip tides and currents that flow

between Gilberts Point and the face of the glacier, a mere 1000 feet away, are so strong that they cause Hubbard to calve almost continuously at peak tides. The entire area is part of the 545-sq-mile Russell Fjord Wilderness and is one of the most interesting places in Alaska to kayak.

Kayakers often begin their journeys in the southern end of the fjord, a short and cheap flight from Yakutat, and then paddle up to Hubbard Glacier and back again. The trip takes a week or more and requires a folding kayak. You can't rent such a boat in Yakutat, but they're available in Sitka at Baidarka Boats (see Paddling in the Sitka section of the Southeast Alaska chapter). Gulf Air or Totem Air (☎ 784-3563) will drop off and pick up two kayakers and their equipment for $150 each way.

The other option is to rent a hard-shell kayak in Yakutat from Chris Widdows (☎ 784-3261), who charges $45/65 per day for single/double boats. You can then transport your kayak into Russell Fjord by taking a charter boat that will drop you off at the north end, or by carrying the kayak along the Russell Fjord Trail from FH 10, the road that crosses the Situk River. Contact the USFS Yakutat Ranger Station (☎ 784-3359) for details on the trail or for a list of charter boats.

Finally, Alaska Discovery (☎ 800-586-1911) offers a seven-day trip into the area that includes a night's lodging at Yakutat, charter flights and a kayaking trip up Russell Fjord to the face of Hubbard Glacier. You can begin or end the trip from Yakutat, Anchorage or Juneau. The cost is $1775 per person.

Anchorage

Anchorage, the hub of Alaska's road system and home for almost half of the state's residents, is a city of prosperity and controversy. Those who live in the Anchorage area (population 259,391) claim there is no other city like it. In Alaska's Big Apple, everything you could possibly want is only a short hop away: glaciers, mountains, hiking trails or whitewater rivers are just a 30-minute drive from the city. Within a couple hours' drive, there's the recreation paradise of the Kenai Peninsula and a handful of state and national preserves that offer unlimited camping, hiking and fishing. Anchorage is so close to the wilderness that in 1996 a wolf killed and ate a yearling moose in a city park, as locals driving on a highway watched.

Yet, in Anchorage, you can enjoy all the comforts and attractions offered by any large US city, including a modern performing arts center, enclosed shopping malls and major retailers such as Kmart, Wal-Mart and Computer City, which bring the lowest cost of living in Alaska to Anchorage. At night, brewpubs, bars and nightclubs buzz into the late hours.

But many of the state's residents shake their head and say, 'Anchorage is great; it's only 20 minutes from Alaska.' To some, everything that Alaska is, Anchorage isn't. The city is a mass of urban sprawl – in down-to-earth terms, 'a beer can in the wilderness.' It has billboards, traffic jams, dozens of fast-food restaurants and, occasionally, smog and crime.

With the exception of New York, no other city provokes such a love-hate relationship. No other city, in any other state, has such pull or gobbles up so much of the public funds as Anchorage. But if you're a traveler in Alaska, you'll probably pass through Anchorage at least once, if not several times.

Anchorage has the advantage of being north of the Kenai Mountains, which shield the city from the excess moisture experienced by Southcentral Alaska. The Anchorage Bowl – the city and surrounding area –

receives only 14 inches of rain annually. Nor does the area have the extreme temperatures of the Interior. The average temperature in January is 13°F, and at the height of the summer it's only 58°F. The area does, however, have more than its fair share of overcast days, especially in early and late summer.

History
Although Captain James Cook sailed up Cook Inlet in 1778 looking for the elusive

Highlights

- Gaze at Sydney Laurence's 10-foot painting of Mt McKinley at the Anchorage Museum of History and Art

- Rent a bicycle and enjoy the views of Cook Inlet and the Alaska Range from the Tony Knowles Coastal Trail

- Watch videos of brown bears and other wildlife at the Alaska Public Lands Information Center

- Laugh at Alaskans making fun of Spam and themselves at Mr Whitekeys' Fly by Night Club

- Touch an iceberg at Portage Glacier's Begich-Boggs Visitor Center

- Visit a historic gold mine in a beautiful alpine setting at Hatcher Pass

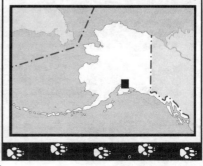

ANCHORAGE

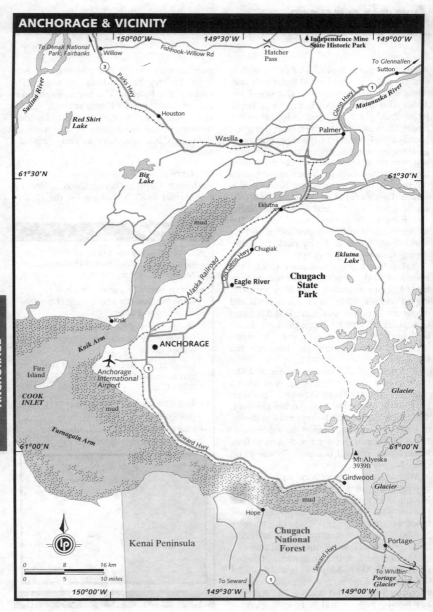

ANCHORAGE & VICINITY

150°00'W   149°30'W   149°00'W

To Denali National Park, Fairbanks

Willow

Fishhook-Willow Rd

Hatcher Pass

Independence Mine State Historic Park

To Glennallen

Sutton

Glenn Hwy

Parks Hwy

Susitna River

Red Shirt Lake

Houston

Wasilla

Matanuska River

Palmer

61°30'N   61°30'N

Big Lake

Eklutna

mud

Eklutna Lake

Chugiak

Alaska Railroad

Old Glenn Hwy

Eagle River

Chugach State Park

Knik

Knik Arm

ANCHORAGE

Fire Island

COOK INLET

Anchorage International Airport

mud

Glacier

Turnagain Arm

61°00'N   61°00'N

Mt Alyeska 3939ft

Girdwood

Glacier

mud

Hope

Seward Hwy

Chugach National Forest

Portage

Kenai Peninsula

0   8   16 km
0   5   10 miles

To Whittier
Portage Glacier

To Seward

150°00'W   149°30'W   149°00'W

ANCHORAGE

Northwest Passage, Anchorage wasn't founded until 1914, when surveyors chose the site as the work camp and headquarters for the Alaska Railroad. In 1915, the 'Great Anchorage Lot Sale' was held. Some 655 lots were sold for $225, and soon there was a tent city of 2000 people. From then on, the area's growth occurred in spurts caused by increased farming in the Matanuska Valley in the 1930s, the construction of military bases during WWII and the discovery of oil in Cook Inlet in 1957.

Two events literally reshaped Anchorage and created the city we know today. The first was the Good Friday Earthquake of 1964, the largest earthquake ever recorded in the Western Hemisphere. Originally measured at 8.4 on the Richter scale, the quake was later upped to 9.2. It lasted an unprecedented five minutes, and when it was finished the north side of 4th Ave was 10 feet lower than the south side. In one neighborhood, more than 100 homes slid off a bluff into the Knik Arm, some as far as 1200 feet. Nine people were killed, and a city lay in shambles. Four years later, Atlantic Richfield discovered a $10 billion oil reserve at a place called Prudhoe Bay.

Though the Trans-Alaska Pipeline doesn't come within 300 miles of Anchorage, as the headquarters for the petroleum and service companies, the city gushes with oil money.

During the late 1970s, when a barrel of crude cost more than $20 and Alaska couldn't spend its tax revenue fast enough, Anchorage received the lion's share. The downtown area was revitalized with such projects as the Sullivan Sports Arena, the Egan Civic Center and the stunning Alaska Center for the Performing Arts. A 122-mile network of bicycle trails was paved as well, and the Anchorage Museum of History and Art was expanded.

The city that has stage plays and snowy peaks also has pork-barrel power, with 42% of the state's population. Translated into political muscle, nine of the 20 state senators and 17 of the 40 state representatives represent the municipality of Anchorage. This causes problems if you don't happen to live in Anchorage. The biggest rivalry exists between Anchorage and Fairbanks, with

83,773 residents the second largest municipality. Fairbanks has long accused its sister to the south of trying to have major departments at the Fairbanks campus of the University of Alaska (the main one) moved to UA Anchorage. Juneau, the third largest city (population 30,852), has no love for Anchorage either, seeing it as the power broker in an effort to move the state capital north.

What can't be debated is that Anchorage is truly the heart of Alaska and the center of the state's commercial and financial communities. Though the wide Anchorage Bowl is boxed in by the Chugach Mountains to the east and Cook Inlet to the west, the city continues to sprawl and seems to be in a constant state of rebuilding. Although the decline of oil prices in the late 1980s and 1990s has slowed its economy, Anchorage is still the fastest-growing city in Alaska. Love Anchorage or hate it, one thing is certain – as long as oil gushes in Alaska, this city will prosper.

Orientation

If you fly into Anchorage, you'll arrive at the airport in the southwest corner of the city. If you drive in from the south on Seward Hwy or from the north on Glenn Hwy, the roads lead to the downtown area, where they end less than a mile from each other.

Downtown Anchorage is a somewhat undefined area boxed in by 3rd Ave to the north, 10th Ave to the south, Minnesota Drive and L St to the west and A St to the east. What is commonly referred to as Midtown Anchorage is an area that extends east and west from Minnesota Drive to Seward Hwy and north and south from Fireweed Lane to International Airport Rd. The heart of Midtown is the heavily commercialized area around Northern Lights and Benson Blvds. Finally, South Anchorage is generally considered to be the area south of Dowling Rd, including the Hillside Park residential areas on the doorstep of Chugach State Park.

You will not find a charming historic downtown area in Anchorage, as you do in Juneau or Sitka, but you will discover that Alaska's largest city is tied together by a

ANCHORAGE

ANCHORAGE

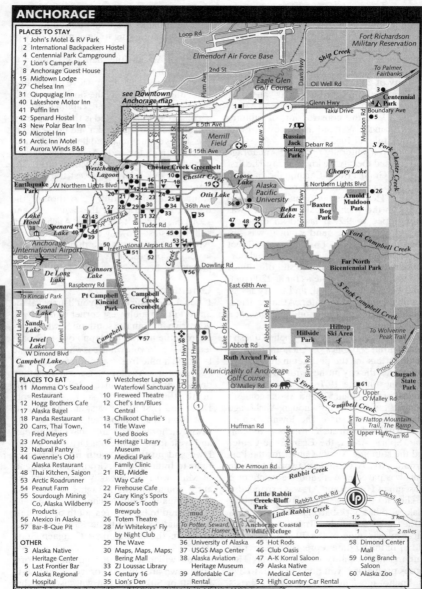

PLACES TO STAY
1   John's Motel & RV Park
2   International Backpackers Hostel
4   Centennial Park Campground
7   Lion's Camper Park
8   Anchorage Guest House
15 Midtown Lodge
27 Chelsea Inn
31 Qupqugiag Inn
40 Lakeshore Motor Inn
41 Puffin Inn
42 Spenard Hostel
43 New Polar Bear Inn
50 Microtel Inn
51 Arctic Inn Motel
61 Aurora Winds B&B

PLACES TO EAT
11 Momma O's Seafood Restaurant
12 Hogg Brothers Cafe
17 Alaska Bagel
18 Panda Restaurant
20 Carrs, Thai Town, Fred Meyers
23 McDonald's
32 Natural Pantry
44 Gwennie's Old Alaska Restaurant
48 Thai Kitchen, Saigon
53 Arctic Roadrunner
54 Peanut Farm
55 Sourdough Mining Co, Alaska Wildberry Products
56 Mexico in Alaska
57 Bar-B-Que Pit

9   Westchester Lagoon Waterfowl Sanctuary
10 Fireweed Theatre
12 Chef's Inn/Blues Central
13 Chilkoot Charlie's
14 Title Wave Used Books
16 Heritage Library Museum
19 Medical Park Family Clinic
21 REI, Middle Way Cafe
22 Firehouse Cafe
24 Gary King's Sports
25 Moose's Tooth Brewpub
26 Totem Theatre
28 Mr Whitekeys' Fly by Night Club
29 The Wave
30 Maps, Maps, Maps; Bering Mall
33 ZJ Loussac Library
34 Century 16
35 Lion's Den

OTHER
3   Alaska Native Heritage Center
5   Last Frontier Bar
6   Alaska Regional Hospital

36 University of Alaska
37 USGS Map Center
38 Alaska Aviation Heritage Museum
39 Affordable Car Rental

45 Hot Rods
46 Club Oasis
47 A-K Korral Saloon
49 Alaska Native Medical Center
52 High Country Car Rental

58 Dimond Center Mall
59 Long Branch Saloon
60 Alaska Zoo

magnificent system of trails and parks and that the locals who use them are vibrant and active.

Information

Tourist Offices Anchorage has several visitor centers. The main one is the Log Cabin Visitor Center (☎ 274-3531), on the corner of W 4th Ave and F St, open 7:30 am to 7 pm daily June to August, 8:30 am to 6 pm May and September and 9 am to 4 pm the rest of the year. Along with many services and handouts, this center operates an emergency language bank that has speakers of 27 languages to help foreign travelers in distress. It also has a 24-hour recording (☎ 276-3200) listing events taking place in the city that day.

There is another visitor center (☎ 266-2437), open 9 am to 4 pm, at the Anchorage International Airport in the baggage claim level of the south (domestic) terminal. Self-service information areas are in the north (international) terminal and the Alaska Railroad Depot downtown. The Anchorage Convention and Visitors Bureau (☎ 276-4118, info@anchorage.net) also maintains a website (www.anchorage.net).

Backpackers and hikers should contact the Alaska Public Lands Information Center (☎ 271-2737), in the Old Federal Building at W 4th Ave and F St (diagonally opposite the Log Cabin Visitors Center), for information and handouts on any national park, federal refuge or state park in Alaska. Head here when planning wilderness adventures and to purchase topographic maps and books. They'll answer 99% of your questions. It is open 9 am to 5:30 pm daily in the summer.

If the public lands office can't help you, you can contact several other centers. Information on state parks can also be obtained from the Alaska Department of Natural Resources Public Information Center (☎ 269-8400), 3601 C St. The Chugach National Forest office (☎ 271-2500), Suite 300, 3301 C St, has details on any USFS national forest, trail or cabin. The US Fish & Wildlife Service (for the Kenai National Wildlife Refuge; ☎ 786-3487) maintains an office at 1011 E Tudor Rd.

Money Banks and ATMs abound in Anchorage. Key Bank of Alaska has several locations, including one downtown (☎ 257-5500) at 601 W 5th Ave and another in Midtown (☎ 562-6100) at 101 W Benson Blvd. Thomas Cook Currency Service (☎ 278-2822) has an office in the Anchorage Hilton, at 311 F St.

Post The main post office downtown is at the Post Office Mall, at W 4th Ave and D St, with an entrance off W 3rd Ave.

Email & Internet Access ZJ Loussac Public Library (☎ 261-2845), Denali St at W 36th Ave, has five computers on the 2nd floor for Internet access. The best cybercafe is Surf City, at W 4th Ave and L St, which has 10 superfast PCs and Macs. Many B&Bs and hostels in Anchorage also offer Internet access.

Travel Agencies US Travel (☎ 561-2434, 800-478-2434), at 1415 E Tudor Rd, can assist in booking tours and rooms. World Express Travel (☎ 786-3200), 206 W 34th Ave, will arrange airline tickets to anywhere outside Alaska.

Bookstores For the best selection of books on Alaska, head to either the Alaska Public Lands Information Center (see the Tourist Offices section of this chapter) or Cook Inlet Book Co (☎ 258-4544), 415 W 5th Ave, which always has autographed copies of titles by local authors. Title Wave Used Books (☎ 278-9283), 1068 W Fireweed Lane, carries a great selection of used but still readable paperbacks, most priced at half of what they cost new. For almost any Alaska newspaper and many out-of-state and foreign papers, go to Sourdough News & Tobacco (☎ 274-6397), 735 W 4th Ave.

Libraries Anchorage's main library is ZJ Loussac Public Library (☎ 261-2845), in the Midtown area at Denali St and 36th Ave. This impressive 140,000-sq-foot facility is open daily, has several lounges, an excellent section called the Alaska Collection and a complete set of topographic maps for the state.

ANCHORAGE

Laundry Dirty clothes can be taken care of at Don Dee's Laundromat (☎ 279-0251), at Northern Lights Blvd and Minnesota Ave.

Outdoor Equipment & Supplies Whatever you need, a bicycle spoke or a tent stake, you'll find it somewhere along Northern Lights Blvd, between Minnesota Drive and New Seward Hwy. For backpacking, kayaking or camping gear, there's an impressive REI (☎ 272-4565), 1200 W Northern Lights Blvd in the Northern Lights Shopping Center, or Gary King's Sports (☎ 272-5401), nearby on E Northern Lights Blvd. Across the street from REI is R&R Bicycle (☎ 276-8536). The Sears Mall, near New Seward Hwy, has a Carrs Supermarket on one side of it and a Fred Meyers on the other to replenish your food bag.

Medical Services The Alaska Regional Hospital (☎ 276-1131) is at the corner of DeBarr Rd and Airport Heights, near Merrill Field, and has 24-hour emergency service. Medical Park Family Clinic (☎ 279-8486), 2211 E Northern Lights Blvd, has walk-in service and is open on Saturday.

Walking Tour

Begin any visit to the city at the **Log Cabin Visitors Center** at W 4th Ave and F St. Among the handouts and maps provided is the *Anchorage Visitors Guide,* which describes a three- to four-hour walking tour of the downtown area.

The beautiful thing about getting around Anchorage is the simplicity of the street layout, especially in the city center. Numbered avenues run east and west and lettered streets north and south.

The city walking tour begins by heading over to the **Alaska Public Lands Information Center**, in the Old Federal Building. Even if you're not into backpacking or camping, you will find the exhibits excellent. Among the wildlife displays, a series of monitors show videos on topics ranging from glaciers and salmon in the Kenai River to Inuit whaling.

By backtracking to E St and heading north, you pass the **Cadastral Survey Monument** on the corner of W 2nd Ave and then swing around near the **Alaska Railroad Depot**. The monument notes the original 1915 Anchorage townsite survey and has four etchings that trace the development of Anchorage from the first auction of public land to a current city map. The railroad depot, at the base of the hill, features historical photos and a railroading gift shop in its lobby, totem poles outside and Engine No 1 on a platform.

The tour, however, misses the depot, turning west at 2nd Ave and passing the **Alaska Statehood Monument** and the start of the **Tony Knowles Coastal Trail** (see the Cycling section of this chapter).

Back on 4th Ave, head west of the Log Cabin Visitor Center to K St and turn right. Half a block north on K St is the eye-catching statue entitled **The Last Blue Whale**.

Nearby, at the west end of 3rd Ave, are **Resolution Park** and the **Captain Cook Monument**, which honor the 200th anniversary of the English captain's sailing into Cook Inlet (with officers George Vancouver and William Bligh at his side). If not overrun by tour-bus passengers, this observation deck has an excellent view of the surrounding mountains, including the Talkeetnas to the northeast and the snow-covered Alaska Range to the west. On a clear day you can see Mt McKinley and Mt Foraker to the north. To the west is Mt Susitna, known as 'the Sleeping Lady,' which marks the southwest end of the Alaska Range.

The tour continues south to **Oscar Anderson House** (☎ 274-2336), in the delightful Elderberry Park on M St just north of W 5th Ave. Anderson was the 18th person to set foot in Anchorage, and his home was the first wood-frame house built in the city. Now, it's the only home museum in Anchorage. It's open 11 am to 4 pm Tuesday to Saturday; admission is $3.

At W 6th Ave and H St is the **Oomingmak Musk Ox Producers Co-op** (☎ 272-9225). The cooperative handles a variety of garments made of arctic musk-ox wool, hand-knitted in isolated Inuit villages. Outside, a mural depicts a herd of musk oxen, and inside the results of this cottage industry are sold.

The Art of Sydney Laurence

Of all the artists who have been inspired by Alaska – and the grandeur of this land has inspired a lot of them – none is more widely recognized than Sydney Laurence, the 'Painter of the North.' Born in Brooklyn, New York, in 1865, Laurence was exhibiting paintings by the time he was 22 and was involved in the founding of the American Fine Arts Society in 1889. But the lure of gold was a strong fever, and in 1904, the painter left his wife and two children and made his way to Alaska.

For the next nine years, Laurence did little painting and a lot of panning for gold in Southcentral Alaska but never found any great quantities of the precious metal. In 1913, he was commissioned by a group of Valdez businessmen to produce a painting of Mt McKinley for the Panama Pacific Exposition in San Francisco. The grand painting never made it to the expo but was added to the Smithsonian Institution collection in 1915, the same year Laurence set up a photography studio in a bustling little tent city called Anchorage.

The painter lived in Anchorage until his death in 1940 and during those years was enormously prolific. While the rest of the country may not have always recognized his name, in Alaska, Laurence has become an almost mythical figure, and his paintings still mesmerize thousands of people each summer. As one art critic put it in an issue of *Southwest Art* magazine:

> The message of his work is clear: the Alaskan landscape was immeasurably greater than the deeds of the men and the women who inhabited it. Not so much hostile as indifferent, the northern landscape had the same mystique of unspoiled, seemingly limitless horizon that the American west had a half century earlier.

Laurence's most impressive work, a 6-by-10-foot painting of Mt McKinley, is the centerpiece of the historical art collection of the Anchorage Museum of History and Art, which has a room devoted to oils by Laurence. You can also enjoy a half dozen more of his works, including several smaller paintings of Mt McKinley (his favorite subject), at the fine Heritage Library Museum in the National Bank of Alaska building on Northern Lights Blvd.

The **Imaginarium** (☎ 276-3179), 725 W 5th Ave, is a hands-on science museum and a place to go if you have children tagging along. The award-winning center features more than 20 exhibits that explain the northern lights, earthquakes, oil exploration, bears and other Alaskan topics. You can even enter a polar bear's den or dabble your fingers in a marine-life touch tank. The museum is open 10 am to 6 pm daily; admission costs $5/4 adults/children.

Across from the transit center, on the north side of W 6th Ave, is the **Alaska Center for the Performing Arts**. Alaskan artists designed the lobby and contributed a number of art pieces, including 23 Native American masks. During the summer, tours are given at 1 pm on Wednesday and Friday for a donation, or you can just buy your lunch from a street vendor on W 4th Ave and eat on a hillside seat in **Town Square Park**, which overlooks the arts center and surrounding flower beds.

Eventually, the walking tour leads to the **Anchorage Museum of History and Art** (☎ 343-4326), near the corner of W 7th Ave and A St. In 1984, the museum was expanded to triple its original size and is now an impressive center for displays on Alaskan history and indigenous culture and an art gallery featuring work by regional, national and international artists. The Alaska Gallery, upstairs, traces the history and people of this land in three-dimensional exhibits. The museum is open 9 am to 6 pm daily during the summer, and the admission of $5 is well worth it.

Heritage Library Museum

The Heritage Library Museum (☎ 265-2834), on the 1st floor in the National Bank of

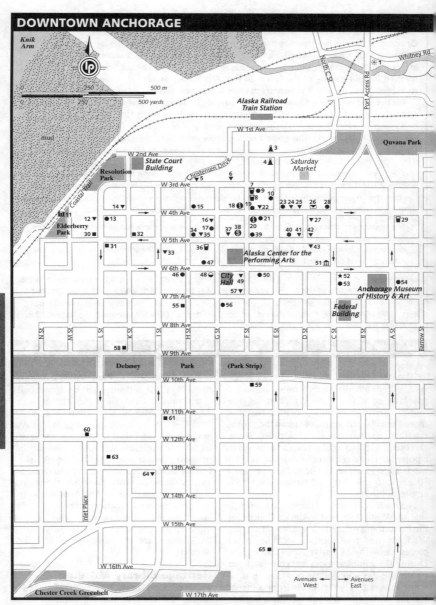

DOWNTOWN ANCHORAGE

Knik Arm

500 m
500 yards

mud

Alaska Railroad Train Station

W 1st Ave

Quvana Park

W 2nd Ave

State Court Building

Resolution Park

Christensen Drive

Saturday Market

W 3rd Ave

Elderberry Park

W 4th Ave

W 5th Ave

Alaska Center for the Performing Arts

W 6th Ave

City Hall

Anchorage Museum of History & Art

W 7th Ave

Federal Building

W 8th Ave

N St
M St
L St
K St
I St
H St
G St
F St
E St
D St
C St
B St
A St
Barrow St

W 9th Ave

Delaney   Park   (Park Strip)

W 10th Ave

W 11th Ave

W 12th Ave

Inlet Place

W 13th Ave

W 14th Ave

W 15th Ave

W 16th Ave

Avenues ← West   → Avenues East

Chester Creek Greenbelt

W 17th Ave

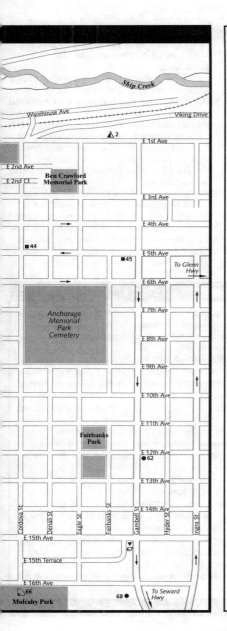

PLACES TO STAY
2 Ship Creek Landings Campground
30 Copper Whale Inn
31 Caribou Inn
32 Hotel Captain Cook
44 Days Inn
45 Econo Lodge
55 Hostelling International Anchorage
58 Snowshoe Inn
59 B&B on the Park
60 12th & L B&B
61 I Street B&B
63 Inlet Tower
65 Walkabout Town B&B

PLACES TO EAT
5 Snow Goose Restaurant
6 Marx Bros Cafe
12 Simon & Seafort's Saloon & Grill
14 Cafe Del Mundos
16 Side Street Espresso
22 Downtown Deli
24 Tito's Gyros
25 Blondie's Cafe
27 Cyrano's Books & Cafe
33 Wings N Things, Muffin Man
35 Glacier Brewhouse
37 Sack's Cafe
41 Phyllis's Cafe
42 China Express
43 Sullivan's Steakhouse, Burger King
49 Humpy's Great Alaskan Alehouse
57 Bear Paw Coffee
64 New Sagaya's City Market
67 Twin Dragon Restaurant

OTHER
1 Ship Creek Salmon Viewing Platform
3 Alaska Statehood Monument
4 Cadastral Survey Monument
7 Sports Edition Bar
8 F Street Station
9 Alaska Airlines
10 Rumrunner's Old Towne Bar
11 Oscar Anderson House
13 Surf City
15 Sourdough News & Tobacco
16 Darwin's Theory
17 All Alaska Tours
18 Alaska Public Lands Information Center
19 Gray Line
20 Log Cabin Visitor Center
21 Old City Hall
23 Post Office Mall
26 Post Office
28 Downtown Bicycle Rental, One-Hour Photo Shop
29 The Hub
32 Crow's Nest
34 Imaginarium
36 Penthouse Lounge
38 Bank
39 Convention Center
40 Cook Inlet Book Co
46 Oomingmak Musk Ox Producers Co-op
47 Alaska Experience Center
48 Transit Center
50 Library
51 Wolf Song of Alaska
52 Police
53 Fire
54 Nenana Creative Arts
56 Arco Building
62 Denali Car Rental
66 Mulchay Ball Park
68 Sports Arena

ANCHORAGE

Alaska Building at Northern Lights Blvd and C St, is the place to see fine Native Alaskan artwork. The center features an impressive collection of Native American tools, costumes and weapons; original paintings, including several by Sydney Laurence; and lots of Native scrimshaw. Much of the carved ivory is from the gold-rush days in Nome and was purchased by miners as proof that they had been in Alaska, despite not bringing any gold home. The museum is open noon to 5 pm weekdays, and admission is free.

Parks

Earthquake Park Among other things, the 1964 earthquake caused 130 acres of land on the west side of the city to slip 2000 feet towards the sea. The east end of that strip was Turnagain Heights, a neighborhood where 75 homes were destroyed and three

people died. The other end was undeveloped and today is Earthquake Park, at the west end of Northern Lights Blvd on the Knik Arm.

An interpretive walkway that includes a series of displays describing the effects of the quake and the tsunamis that followed was added to the park in 1997. It ends with a series of benches offering panoramic views of Anchorage's skyline set against the Chugach Mountains. On a clear day, you can also see Mt McKinley and Mt Foraker, from the Tony Knowles Coastal Trail at the lower area of the park.

Back in the 1970s, the park was a moonscape of barren land, but Mother Nature's healing hand has since covered the jagged crease in the middle with brush. You now have to poke around the saplings and trees to get a sense of the power that hit Anchorage that day.

Native Alaskan Culture in Anchorage

The Anchorage area served as a summer fish camp for the Dena'ina Indians, and archaeological digs indicate that there was frequent contact between the Dena'ina Athabascan Indians, Chugach Aleuts and the Inuit here. Despite the past, Native Alaskans did not have a cultural center of their own in the state's largest city until almost the new millennium.

Twelve years after first being conceived, the first phase of the $15 million Alaska Native Heritage Center opened in 1999 on 26 acres near Muldoon Rd and the Glenn Hwy. The complex features a 26,000-sq-foot Welcome House with a theater and exhibition space devoted to the history, lifestyle and arts of Native Alaskans. Open studios in the Welcome Center feature artists carving baleen or sewing skin boats, and a half-mile trail outside leads past a smokehouse, covered carving shed and other traditional village structures.

Later phases call for a small lake surrounded by five replicate villages – Athabascan, Yupik, Inupiat, Aleut and Tlingit/Haida – where people will be involved in such traditional activities as splitting and drying salmon, tanning hides or building kayaks. Hours for the center (☎ 343-4326) are 9 am to 9 pm daily. Admission is $20.

Another excellent place to experience Native culture is the Alaska Native Medical Center (ANMC) at Turdor Rd and Boniface Pkwy. The ANMC opened in 1997 and from the start was committed to funding Native arts. Glass display cases are now found throughout the building showcasing everything from 4-foot-high grass baskets, baleen carvings and raincoats of seal intestine to spirit masks and soapstone carvings. There are even display cases in the stairwells.

Equally interesting is the ANMC gift shop, which is open 10 am to 2 pm Monday through Friday. Volunteers run the shop, and the pieces are sold on consignment. The prices are excellent, and most of the money goes back to the person who carved the ivory earrings, wove the baleen basket or sewed the sealskin slippers. Viewing the hospital's art collection or window-shopping at the gift shop is free.

Delaney Park Within the city center is Delaney Park, known locally as the 'Park Strip,' because it stretches from A to K Sts between W 9th and W 10th Aves. The greenbelt, the site of the 50-ton bonfire celebrating statehood in 1959 and later where Pope John Paul II gave an outdoor mass in 1981, is a good place to lie down on a hot afternoon.

Russian Jack Springs Park Named after the original homesteader of the site, this 300-acre park is south of Glenn Hwy on Boniface Pkwy and can be reached by bus No 12. The city park has tennis courts, 4 miles of hiking and biking trails and a picnic area. Near the entrance are the **Mann Leiser Memorial Greenhouses** (☎ 333-8610), which have tropical plants, exotic birds and fish. They are open 9 am to 3 pm daily.

Far North Bicentennial Park This park is comprised of 4000 acres of forest and muskeg in east central Anchorage. The park features 20 miles of trails for hiking and mountain biking and **Hilltop Ski Area**, whose chalet (☎ 346-1446) can provide you with a trail guide. In the center of the park is **BLM's Campbell Tract**, a 700-acre wildlife oasis where it's possible to see moose and bears in the spring and brilliant fall colors in mid-September. To reach the Hilltop Ski Area, take O'Malley Rd east to Hillside Drive and follow the road to the parking area.

Westchester Lagoon Sanctuary More wildlife, mostly ducks and geese, can be seen closer to the downtown area at this sanctuary. On the corner of Spenard Rd and W 19th Ave, the small preserve is a year-round home for a variety of birds and features displays and a half-mile nature trail around the small lake. Call the city's department of parks & recreation (☎ 343-4474), for information on park activities.

Lakes

If the weather is hot enough, several lakes in the area offer swimming or simply a place to sit and watch the water. The closest one to downtown is **Goose Lake**, on Northern Lights Blvd, near the UA Anchorage campus (take bus No 3 or 45). It is connected to Goose Lake Park by footpaths. You can also swim at **Spenard Lake**, 3 miles south of the downtown area on Spenard Rd and west on Lakeshore Drive (take bus No 7 or 36), and at **Jewel Lake**, 6.5 miles southwest of the city center on Dimond Blvd (take bus No 7).

Wildlife Centers

Maybe it's me, but there is something weird about coming all the way to Alaska and then going to a zoo to view caged animals. Others, however, think the $7 admission is worth paying at the **Alaska Zoo** (☎ 346-2133), 4731 O'Malley Rd, where you can see such resident species as brown bears, musk oxen and otters and a few that are definitely not native to Alaska, like an elephant. The animal most visitors want to see is a polar bear, and in 1999 the zoo added a $1.7 million exhibit that allows you to watch Ahpun the polar bear swimming and diving. Hours are 9 am to 6 pm daily. Here are a few other wildlife centers that are cheaper and more appealing:

Elmendorf AFB Wildlife Museum This museum (☎ 552-2282) has more than 200 Alaskan mammals, fish, birds and a 10½-foot-high brown bear that misses the world record by an eighth of an inch, as well as hands-on exhibits. The museum is open 3 to 5 pm Monday to Thursday and noon to 5 pm on Friday; admission is free. The museum can be reached by bus No 75 from the transit center.

Fort Richardson Wildlife Center The center (☎ 384-0431) features 250 specimens. It is open 9 am to 4:30 pm weekdays, except Thursday, when it is closed in the morning; admission is free. The center can be reached by bus No 75 from the transit center.

Wolf Song of Alaska This nonprofit center (☎ 274-9653) is at W 6th Ave and C St and features exhibits and dioramas that focus on the natural history of the wolf. The center is open from 10 am to 7 pm weekdays and until 6 pm Saturday and 5 pm Sunday. Admission is $3.

University of Alaska Anchorage

This is the largest college campus in the state, but there is far less to do here than at its sister school UA Fairbanks. Still the school is impressive and connected with bike paths to Goose Lake, Chester Creek Greenbelt and Earthquake Park. Stop in at the Campus Center, where you'll find an Olympic-size pool with open swims, a small art gallery, and the bookstore, where you can buy clothing with Alaska on it. On the ground floor is the University Pub, where there are affordable sandwiches and occasionally live music. Bus Nos 3, 11, and 45 swing past the campus.

Lake Hood Air Harbor

Those enchanted by Alaska's bush planes and small air-taxi operators will be overwhelmed by Lake Hood, the world's busiest floatplane base (and ski-plane base in the winter). Almost every type of small plane imaginable can be seen flying onto and off of the lake's surface. The floatplane base makes an interesting afternoon trip when combined with a swim in adjoining Lake Spenard (take bus No 7 or 36).

Alaska Aviation Heritage Museum

On the south shore of Lake Hood, at 4721 Aircraft Drive, is the Alaska Aviation Heritage Museum (☎ 248-5325). In an effort to preserve Alaska's unique approach to aviation, the museum has films, displays on such pioneer pilots as Ben Eielson, Noel Wein and Russell Merrill, vintage aircraft and an observation deck. Summer hours are 9 am to 6 pm; admission is $5.75.

Ship Creek Viewing Platform

From mid- to late summer, king, coho and pink salmon spawn up Ship Creek, the historical site of Tanaina Indian fish camps. The overlook, a half mile east from the Alaska Railroad Depot, is where you can watch the return of the salmon. Follow C St north as it crosses Ship Creek Bridge and then turn right on Whitney Rd.

Bicycling

Anchorage has 122 miles of paved bicycle paths that parallel major roads or wind through many of its parks and greenbelt areas. You can rent bicycles at Downtown Bicycle Rental (☎ 279-5293), at W 4th Ave and C St, which has mountain bikes and road bikes for $29 a day and $15 for three hours. The rental includes a helmet, lock and gloves. You can also rent bicycles in the Midtown area at the Bicycle Shop (☎ 272-5219), 1035 W Northern Lights Blvd, or CycleSights (☎ 344-1771), at W 5th Ave and M St in Elderberry Park.

For information on organized tours for both road trips and mountain biking, call the Arctic Bicycle Club hot line (☎ 566-0177). Alaskan Bicycle Adventures (☎ 243-2329, 800-770-7242) offers a couple of vehicle-supported rides out of Anchorage, including a seven-day ride on the George Parks, Denali and Richardson Hwys. The cost is $2345 and includes a bicycle.

The following are some of the better bike trails:

Chester Creek Trail One of the more popular routes is the 4-mile path through the Chester Creek Greenbelt from UA Anchorage and Goose Lake Park to Westchester Lagoon overlooking Knik Arm.

Tony Knowles Coastal Trail The most scenic route is the 11-mile Tony Knowles Coastal Trail, which begins at the west end of 2nd Ave downtown and reaches Elderberry Park within a mile. From there, it winds 10 miles west of Anchorage through Earthquake Park, around Point Woronzof and finally to Point Campbell in Kincaid Park. Along the way you are treated to good views of Knik Arm and the Alaska Range.

Turnagain Arm Bike Path This 14-mile paved bicycle path begins at Potter Marsh Refuge and then hugs the shoreline for sweeping views of Turnagain Arm until it ends at Bird Creek. Plans call for someday connecting the Tony Knowles Coastal Trail with this path.

Glenn Hwy Trail Head north on this paved path out of the city. It begins at the corner of Muldoon Rd and Glenn Hwy and then parallels the highway for 14 miles to Chugiak Elementary School.

Chugach State Park Excellent mountain biking begins at the Hillside area trailheads (see Hiking section) for Chugach State Park, and an easy way to get there is via People Mover buses. In 1997, the public system added racks to the outside of its buses that carry two bicycles each. Rent a mountain bike for the day and then pick up a free *Bike Hanger* card from the transit center at W 6th Ave and G St to learn how to use the racks (the driver can't leave the bus to help you).

With your *Bike Hanger* card in hand, jump on bus No 2 for the corner of Lake Otis Pkwy and Abbott Rd and then continue east along Abbott Rd. Head south on Hillside Rd and then climb Upper Huffman Rd, following the signs for 2.7 miles to the Glen Alps park entrance, where you can access several trails. The most popular trail among mountain bikers is Powerline Pass Trail, an old roadbed that extends 11 miles through the heart of the state park and gains 1300 feet along the way.

Far North Bicentennial Park Within this 4000-acre park are more than 20 miles of trails, many of them open to mountain bikes. Hilltop Ski Area (☎ 346-1446) rents mountain bikes here daily during the summer for $17/26 half/full day.

Rock Climbing

You can free climb and rappel a short drive from downtown Anchorage at several rock faces along the Seward Hwy. The most prominent, known as Boy Scout Rock, is a few miles before the Alyeska Hwy at Girdwood. You can also climb indoors at the Alaska Rock Gym (☎ 562-7265), 4840 Fairbanks St. The gym features a 30-foot-high, 5500-sq-foot climbing wall. For information on more serious climbing, contact the Mountaineering Club of Alaska (☎ 272-1811).

Hiking

With the Chugach Mountains at its doorstep, Anchorage has excellent day hikes that

begin on the outskirts of the city and quickly lead into the beautiful alpine area to the east. Most of the hikes begin in the Hillside area of the city, which borders Chugach State Park, the second largest state preserve in Alaska, at 773 sq miles.

At $1 a ride, the People Mover bus was the cheapest way to get to the trails. Unfortunately, in the fall of 1999, the bus system dropped routes 90, 91 and 92, which took hikers to within a short walk of the Glen Alps and Prospect Heights parking areas of Chugach State Park. If you don't have a vehicle, you now have to walk or hitch several miles from bus No 2 or take a taxi, which from downtown would be around a $17 fare.

You can rent tents, stoves, sleeping bags and other equipment at REI (☎ 272-4565) on Northern Lights Blvd. Cheaper rentals are possible at the Campus Center Information Desk at UA Anchorage (☎ 786-1204) or Moseley Sports Center at Alaska Pacific University (☎ 564-8314), but sometimes they can be hard to deal with if you are not a student or faculty member.

The USGS Earth Science Information Center (☎ 786-7011) sells topos for the entire state. The center is in Grace Hall at Alaska Pacific University at the east end of

Providence Drive and is open from 8:30 am to 4:30 pm weekdays. It can be reached on bus No 11 or 45. You can also purchase maps at the Alaska Public Lands Information Center (see Information) or Maps, Maps, Maps (☎ 563-6277), an excellent store in the Bering Mall, 601 W 36th Ave, that sells USGS topos and a variety of other recreational maps to the state.

For descriptions of the trails along Seward Hwy towards Portage, see the South of Anchorage section of this chapter. Also, for information on guide companies that run hiking trips see the Organized Tours section in this chapter.

Flattop Mountain Trail Because of its easy access, this trail is the most popular hike near the city. The path to the 3550-foot peak is not difficult to walk, and from the summit, there are good views of the Alaska Range (to the north) and most of Cook Inlet. The trail begins at the Glen Alps entrance to the Chugach State Park.

From Hillside Rd, head east 0.7 miles along Upper Huffman Rd and then turn right on Toilsome Hill Drive and follow it for 2 miles. This switchback road ascends steeply to the Glen Alps park entrance, a parking lot where trailhead signs point the way to Flattop Mountain. The roundtrip is 3.5 miles, with some scrambling over loose rock on steep sections near the top of the mountain. Plan on three to five hours for the entire hike.

Wolverine Peak Trail This path ascends to a 4455-foot triangular peak, which can be seen to the east of Anchorage. It is a strenuous but rewarding full-day trip, resulting in good views of the city, Cook Inlet and the Alaska Range.

From Hillside Drive and O'Malley Rd, head east up Upper O'Malley Rd for a half mile, until you reach a T intersection, and turn left (north) onto Prospect Drive. After 1.1 miles, this ends at the Prospect Heights entrance and parking area of the Chugach State Park. The marked trail begins as an old homesteader road that crosses the south fork of Campbell Creek and passes junctions with two other old roads in the first 2.3 miles.

Keep heading east, and the road will become a footpath that ascends above the tree line and eventually fades out. Make sure to mark its whereabouts in order to find it on the way back. From there, it is 3 miles to Wolverine Peak.

The roundtrip from the corner of O'Malley Rd and Hillside Drive is 13.8 miles, a nine-hour hike. Many people just trek to the good views above the tree line, shortening the trip to 7.8 miles.

The Ramp This is another of the many alpine summit hikes from the east side of the city that wander through tranquil tundra valleys, providing a good chance of seeing Dall sheep during the summer. Begin at the Glen Alps entrance to the state park (see the Flattop Trail for directions to the entrance).

Instead of following the upper trail to Flattop Mountain at the parking lot, hike the lower one a half mile to Powerline Pass Trail. Turn right and follow the power line for 2 miles, past 13 power poles, to where an old jeep trail crosses over from the left and heads downhill to the south fork of Campbell Creek.

The trail then crosses the creek and continues up the hill beyond it to a valley on the other side. Hike up the alpine valley to Ship Lake Pass, which lies between the Ramp to the north, at 5240 feet, and the Wedge to the south, at 4660 feet. Either peak can be climbed. The roundtrip from the Glen Alps entrance is 14 miles, or an eight- to 10-hour hike.

Williwaw Lakes Trail This hike leads to the handful of alpine lakes found at the base of Mt Williwaw. The trail makes a pleasant overnight hike and many hikers consider it the most scenic outing in the Hillside area of Chugach State Park. The hike begins on the same lower trail as the Ramp, from the Glen Alps entrance parking lot (see the Flattop Mountain Trail for directions to the entrance).

Walk half a mile to the Powerline Pass Trail and then turn right. This time, walk only about 300 yards and then turn left on a trail marked 'Middle Fork Loop Trail.' This trail leads down and across the south fork of Campbell Creek and then heads north for 1.5 miles to the middle fork of the creek. Here you reach a junction; continue on the right-hand trail, which is posted 'Williwaw Lakes.' This trail follows the middle fork of Campbell Creek until it reaches the alpine lakes at its end. The roundtrip from Glen Alps is 13 miles, or seven to nine hours of easy hiking.

McHugh Lake Trail This trail was built to replace Rabbit Lake Trail, which was closed due to an access dispute between the state and a private landowner. The McHugh Lake trailhead is at McHugh Creek Picnic Area, 15 miles south of Anchorage at Mile 111.8 of the Seward Hwy. The route follows the McHugh Creek valley, and in 7 miles reaches Rabbit and McHugh Lakes, two beautiful alpine lakes nestled in the shadow of the 5000-foot Suicide Peaks.

The first 3 miles feature some good climbs, and the roundtrip trek makes for a long day. It's better to haul in a tent and then spend the afternoon exploring the open tundra country and nearby ridges. For more on other trails along the Seward Hwy, see the South of Anchorage section.

Rendezvous Peak Route The trek to this 4050-foot peak is an easy five-hour roundtrip, less from the trailhead, and rewards hikers with incredible views of Mt McKinley, Cook Inlet, Turnagain and Knik Arms and the city far below. Take bus No 75 for 6.5 miles northeast on Glenn Hwy, to Arctic Valley Rd. Turn right (east) on Arctic Valley Rd (this section is also known as Ski Bowl Rd), and continue 7 miles to the Arctic Valley Ski Area. From the parking lot, a short trail leads along the right-hand side of the stream up the valley to the northwest. It ends at a pass where a short ascent to Rendezvous Peak is easily seen and climbed.

The roundtrip from the ski area parking lot is only 3.5 miles, but it is a much longer day if you are unable to thumb a ride up Arctic Valley Rd.

Organized Tours

City Tours The Anchorage Historical Properties conducts an hour-long walking tour of the downtown area beginning in the lobby of the renovated Old City Hall at 1 pm Monday through Friday during the summer; admission is $5. It's even cheaper to hop on the People Mover's Downtown Anchorage Short Hop bus, which is free.

A number of companies offer a bus tour of Anchorage. Almost all of these tours are three to four hours long and include Resolution Park, Lake Hood and usually an hour or so at the Anchorage Museum of History and Art. Just about all the tours – Gray Line (☎ 277-5581, 800-478-6388), Alaska Sightseeing (☎ 276-1305, 800-666-7375) and Princess Tours (☎ 550-7711, 800-835-8907) – charge around $27.

For something quicker and cheaper, Anchorage Trolley (☎ 276-5603) has a $10, one-hour tour on its bright red trolley. Stops include Alaska Railroad Depot, Earthquake Park, Lake Hood and the Anchorage Museum of History and Art. The ticket office is at 612 W 4th Ave, and tours depart hourly from 9 am to 6 pm.

Flightseeing Tours Flightseeing – touring in a small plane – is popular all over Alaska and huge in Anchorage. The tours are short and expensive, but aerial views offer a sense of Alaska's grandeur that is hard to achieve when your feet are still on the ground. Mt McKinley, an impressive mountain when you're looking at it from Denali Park Rd, becomes a colossal white pyramid that fills every window in an airplane during a flightseeing tour.

More than a dozen charter companies in Anchorage specialize in flightseeing, and all of them have brochures at the Log Cabin Visitors Center. VernAir (☎ 258-7822, 800-478-8376) flies out of Merrill Field and offers a 40-minute flight to nearby Eagle River and Eagle Glacier for $60 per person. A two-hour wildlife tour on the west side of Cook Inlet costs $170 per person. Rust's Flying Service (☎ 243-1595, 800-544-2299) offers a three-hour Mt McKinley flight for $199 and for $249 will land on a glacier on the side of

ANCHORAGE

the mountain. For $399, you can join an all-day tour that includes landing at Redoubt Bay to watch brown bears feeding.

For the nostalgic, there is Era Aviation's classic DC-3, which departs daily for a two-hour tour of Mt McKinley, Prince William Sound or the Harding Ice Field, depending on which area has the best viewing weather. The plane's interior has been retrofitted to a 1940s theme, with big band music and vintage magazines. Passengers are served champagne while gazing out of specially installed large windows. Tickets cost $150 per person, and reservations (☎ 800-866-8394) are highly recommended.

Area Tours Gray Line offers a daily seven-hour Portage Glacier-Turnagain Arm tour for $60. It departs at 9 am and noon. The trip includes the USFS visitor center and a trip on Gray Line's *Ptarmigan,* which cruises past the face of Portage Glacier. For a more personal tour, check out Killer Whale Tours (☎ 258-7999). Longtime marine biologist Tony Carter leads small groups along Turnagain Arm in a tour that includes birding at Potter Marsh, sighting beluga whales and bore tides in the inlet and viewing Portage Glacier. The cost is $65.

You can also tour Seward and Kenai Fjords National Park in a day from Anchorage. The Alaska Railroad (☎ 265-2494, 800-544-0552) has a day in Seward that includes the train ride down and a half-day cruise to Bear Glacier on the edge of the national park. The fare is $139, and the train pulls out daily at 7 am.

A better and much cheaper way to spend an afternoon is to hop on People Mover bus No 74, 76 or 102 for the scenic trip north of Anchorage along Eagle River, through Chugiak and to Peter's Creek. The 48-mile roundtrip takes about two hours and costs a mere $2. Those who take the first bus out in the morning have been known to occasionally spot moose between Fort Richardson and Eagle River.

Package Tours Travelers on a tight schedule will find a variety of package tours to other areas of the state available in Anchorage. They include accommodations, transportation and meals and are a way to cover a lot in a day or two, if you are willing to pay the price.

The most popular trip out of the city is the cruise past Columbia Glacier to Valdez that returns to Anchorage along the scenic Richardson and Glenn Hwys. Gray Line (☎ 277-5581, 800-478-6388) offers a two-day/one-night package with an overnight stay at a Valdez hotel for $325 per person, based on double occupancy.

Gray Line and Alaska Sightseeing (☎ 276-1305, 800-666-7375), along with a few other large tour companies, have package tours everywhere, shuffling tour groups to such unlikely places as Barrow and Kotzebue. This is a quick way to see an interesting slice of Alaska, but not cheap. The Gray Line two-day/one-night tour of Kotzebue and Nome costs $520 per person, based on double occupancy.

Also offering a variety of package tours is Alaska Railroad (☎ 265-2494). Three of these tours are worth considering for those short on time. The Denali Overnight tour includes a roundtrip train trip to Denali National Park and a night's lodging in the park for $269 per person, based on double occupancy. It does not include, however, a bus ride through the park to Wonder Lake. Gray Line has a similar tour for $385.

If you don't book a package tour in advance and find yourself in Anchorage near the end of your stay with too much money in your pocket, try to cut a deal on 4th Ave. A number of booking and reservation centers along this downtown avenue might have better deals for you. Try All Alaska Tours (☎ 272-8687) on G St, next door to Darwin's Theory Bar.

Guide Companies Anchorage is home to a large number of guide companies that run hiking, kayaking and rafting trips to every corner of the state. Check the Wilderness chapter for the complete list and descriptions of their expeditions, and don't be shy about calling at the last minute. Often, you can get a place in a group and a hefty discount for filling up a leftover spot.

The Eagle River Nature Center (☎ 694-2108, www.alaska.net/~ernc) offers a guided three-day, 26-mile trek along the Historic Iditarod Trail, from the Cross Pass trailhead near Girdwood to Eagle River, throughout the summer. The cost is $165 and includes transportation from Anchorage or Eagle River. You need your own backpack, sleeping bags, tents and food.

The best white water in the Anchorage area is Eagle River, a 15-mile run of mostly Class I water, but with short stretches of Class II and even Class III. Midnight Sun River Runners (☎ 338-7238. 800-825-7238) runs the river daily in the summer, with four-hour trips departing at 8:30 am and 3 pm from downtown hotels. The cost is $69 per person.

Special Events

In the summer months, festivals include a large 4th of July celebration; a Renaissance Faire at the Hilltop Ski Area, with Shakespearean costumes and plays for two weekends in early June; and the Spenard Solstice Street Party on the weekend closest to June 21, with a parade on Saturday and food booths, bands and dancing the rest of the time. Also in early June is the Taste, a food fest held over the course of a weekend at Delaney Park Strip. Call the All About Anchorage recorded message (☎ 276-3200) to see if anything is happening while you're passing through town.

For a small-town festival, head to Girdwood on the 4th of July weekend for its Girdwood Forest Faire, or to Eagle River in mid-July (☎ 694-4702 for exact dates) for the Bear Paw Festival.

Places to Stay

Camping The Anchorage Parks and Recreation Department (☎ 343-4474) maintains two parks with overnight camping. *Centennial Park* (☎ 333-9711) has 89 sites, showers and rest rooms, but is 4.6 miles from the downtown area on Glenn Hwy. In recent years, theft has also been a problem at the campground. The cost is $15 per night, and there is a limit of seven days. Take the Muldoon Rd exit south of the highway and turn east onto Boundary Ave for half a block. Bus No 75, 3 or 4 runs past the corner of Muldoon Rd and Boundary Ave. The city also manages *Lion's Camper Park* (☎ 333-9711), in Russian Jack Springs Park, a wooded area close to town that is ideal for tent campers. The fee is $15 per night, and bus No 8 takes you within a quarter mile of the park on Boniface Pkwy. *Ship Creek Landings* (☎ 277-0877) offers 180 RV sites just off E 1st Ave. The tent rate is $17 per night; a full hookup costs $27.

Chugach State Park, which practically surrounds Anchorage, also has public campgrounds, but none are close to town, and they always fill up fast. The nearest facilities are at Bird Creek on the Seward Hwy (see the South of Anchorage section in this chapter) and at Eagle River off the Glenn Hwy (see the North of Anchorage section). RVers often simply park overnight in the parking lot of stores such as Fred Meyer or Wal-Mart.

Hostels The *Hostelling International Anchorage hostel* (☎ 276-3635, hipat@servcom.com, 700 H St) is downtown, one block south of the transit center. The cost is $16/19 members/nonmembers, and there are a few private rooms available for $40. There is a four-night maximum stay, unless special arrangements are made. Along with sleeping facilities, the hostel has a common room, kitchen, showers and even double rooms. Laundry facilities are available, and you can store extra bags here for $1 per day. This hostel is busy during the summer, so many travelers reserve a bunk ahead of time by calling in advance and using either a Visa card or MasterCard to secure the reservation. You can also mail a money order for the first night's stay, along with details of the number and gender of people arriving, to Hostelling International Anchorage, 700 H St, Anchorage, AK 99501.

A smaller but more personal hostel is *Spenard Hostel* (☎ 248-5036, spnrdhstl@alaskalife.net, 2845 W 42nd Place), off Turnagain Pkwy, near Gwennie's Old Alaska Restaurant. You can reach it on bus No 7. The fourplex apartment has couple and family rooms, a kitchen, laundry facilities and bike rentals. Rooms cost $15 a night.

Finally there's *International Backpackers Hostel* (☎ 274-3870, 3601 Peterkin Ave), on the east side of the city. The hostel is actually five homes in the same neighborhood that can accommodate up to 45 people a night, with two to four people per room. Facilities include a coin-operated laundry, a fully equipped kitchen and a TV and common room. Rates are $15 a night or $80 a week. To reach the hostel from the transit center, take bus No 45 to Bragaw St and Peterkin Ave and head west on Peterkin Ave for three blocks.

B&Bs B&Bs have blossomed in Anchorage. More than 400 residents have opened up their spare bedrooms to summer travelers. Most places are on the fringes of the city or in the suburbs and provide a clean bed, a good breakfast and local insight into both the city and the Alaskan way of life. The going rate is a bit steeper in Anchorage than in the rest of the state, as you generally pay $85 to $110 per couple a night. Stop at the Log Cabin Visitors Center for an entire rack of B&B brochures, or call Alaska Private Lodging (☎ 258-1717, apl@alaska.net) to arrange such accommodations.

In or near the downtown area, *12th & L B&B* (☎ 276-1225, 1134 L St) is located, you guessed it, on the corner of 12th Ave and L St. The three rooms cost $98 to $115 for a double, and there are laundry facilities. Not far away is *I St B&B* (☎ 277-4233, 1125 I St), with four rooms and rates that begin at $85/95 singles/doubles. Next door to Simon & Seafort's Saloon & Grill is *Copper Whale Inn* (☎ 258-7999, 440 L St), with a great view of Cook Inlet. Rooms cost $100 to $155 in the summer, and the B&B puts you within easy walking distance of most downtown restaurants, bars and delightful Elderberry Park.

Walkabout Town B&B (☎ 279-2918, 1610 E St), a three-bedroom apartment, is across from the Chester Creek Greenbelt, near a public bus stop. Doubles cost $85, and guests share a living room and kitchen. *B&B on the Park* (☎ 277-0878, 800-353-0878, 602 W 10th

Ave) is right on Delaney Park and has five rooms that run $100 a night single or double.

New in 1999, *Anchorage Guest House* (☎ 274-0408, house@alaska.net, 2001 Hillcrest Drive), off Spenard Rd, has rooms with king, double and single beds for $30 to $40 a night, and some bunks for $22. This excellent guesthouse also has Internet access, laundry facilities and rents mountain bikes ($20 a day), because it lies close to the Coastal Trail. Take People Mover bus No 3, 4 or 6 to West Anchorage High School or the bus from the airport to Spenard and Hillcrest.

In Anchorage's Hillside area is *Aurora Winds B&B* (☎ 346-2533, 800-642-9640, 7501 Upper O'Malley Rd). This place is unbelievable, with a mirrored gym, billiards, sauna and huge hot tub. There's even a white grand piano in the living room. A double room costs $125 to $175 a night.

Hotels A surge in the late 1990s has given Anchorage more than 70 hotels and motels and 6000 rooms for rent. It's easier to find a bed now in the middle of the summer, but you still must plan on spending what most travelers would consider a bundle for it. The average rate for a room hovers around $90 a night, and trying to find something for under $75 is very challenging. Passing through the city before June or after August saves you a bundle; rates often drop as much as 30% to 40% a night in the off-season. Remember that Anchorage has an 8% bed tax.

New hotels have popped up primarily around the Anchorage International Airport. Late night arrivals now have a choice of motels that offer courtesy transportation and are nearby on International Airport Rd or just north of it on Spenard Rd. But be prepared for Alaska-size rates of around $100 a night. Brand new *Microtel Inn* (☎ 245-5002, 5205 Northwood Drive) has a free airport shuttle and doubles that begin at $120. *Puffin Inn* (☎ 243-4044, 800-478-3346, 4400 Spenard Rd) is not as new but clean, has an airport shuttle and complimentary muffins, coffee and newspapers in the morning. Singles/doubles cost $99/119. Nearby is *Lakeshore Motor Inn* (☎ 248-3485, 800-770-3000, 3009 Lakeshore Drive), where rooms cost $114/129. The alternative is **Arctic Inn Motel** (☎ 561-1328, 842 W International Airport Rd). It's a $10 taxi ride from the airport and has rooms for $75/85. Each room has a small stove and refrigerator, and the motel has a laundry room.

The downtown area also has several motels. Avoid the shabby Inlet Inn across from the transit center. A cleaner and safer choice downtown is **Caribou Inn** (☎ 272-0444, 800-272-5878, 501 L St). It features 14 rooms that begin at $75/84 with shared bath but includes a full breakfast and courtesy pickup from the airport or train station. The Caribou fills fast, so try to book a room in advance. There's also the **Snowshoe Inn** (☎ 258-7669), at K St and W 9th Ave. Rooms with shared baths, including a light breakfast and laundry facilities, cost $95.

Entering the city from the Glenn Hwy, you end up on 5th Ave, where there is a cluster of motels. The best of the bunch is the newly remodeled **Econo Lodge** (274-1515, 642 E 5th Ave). Singles/doubles cost $114/124, and the motel offers free pickup from the airport and trail station. Nearby **Days Inn** (☎ 276-7226), at E 5th Ave and Cordova St, has singles or doubles for $155 and a coffee shop and car rental agency on site.

At the other end of the scale, if you want to spend your final night or two in Alaska in glorious comfort, there is the **Hotel Captain Cook** (☎ 276-6000), at W 5th Ave and K St, with an ideal location downtown. Rooms start at $230, but guests are pampered here. The **Inlet Tower** (☎ 276-0110, 800-544-0786, 1200 L St) also has 1st-class service, and spectacular views from its 180 suites. Rates in the summer are $130 to $190.

In the Midtown area, just off Spenard Rd, is **Midtown Lodge** (☎ 258-7778, 800-235-6546, 604 W 26th Ave). The spartan rooms are small, and you share the bath, but there is a group kitchen. Rates are only $55/65, which includes a light breakfast, soup and sandwiches later in the day and pickup at the airport. Across from Gwennie's Old Alaska Restaurant is **New Polar Bear Inn** (☎ 888-243-0533, 243-0533, 4332 Spenard Rd), with doubles for $109. Even farther south is **Qupqugiaq Inn** (☎ 562-5681, 640 W 36th

Ave), between Arctic Blvd and C St. This inn is actually a group of houses. Doubles with shared bath and a common kitchen begin at $39. The rate is cheap, but the rooms are small. Check the house before handing over your money, to make sure you feel comfortable in the situation. At the other end of the scale is **Chelsea Inn** (☎ 276-5002, 800-770-5002, 3836 Spenard Rd). Singles/doubles with shared bathroom cost $85/95, but the rooms are very clean and comfortable. A continental breakfast is provided, and there are kitchen facilities available. The inn also provides 24-hour pickup service for travelers, to and from the airport.

If you have a car, book a room on the outskirts of the city for better rates. If you're heading up from the Kenai Peninsula, the **Brown Bear Motel** (☎ 653-7000)), Mile 103 Seward Hwy, in Indian 20 minutes south of Anchorage, has clean rooms with private baths and TV for $40 a night. They don't come any cheaper than this, folks. Also on site is the Brown Bear Saloon. Just off the Glenn Hwy before it becomes 5th Ave is **John's Motel & RV Park** (☎ 277-4332, 800-478-4332, 3543 Mountain View Drive), where small rooms begin at $60 and full hookups on a gravel parking area cost $25.

Places to Eat

Anchorage offers just about any kind of food you might desire, at prices that range from budget to expensive. Because the restaurants are spread across the city they are divided here into areas.

Downtown For those on a strict budget, there's a choice of fast-food places, including **McDonald's**, at W 4th Ave and E St, and **Burger King** (520 W 5th Ave). Just as easy on the money pouch is the **Federal Building Cafeteria**, in the Federal Building just across from the Anchorage Museum of History and Art. It opens at 7 am weekdays and serves breakfast for around $5 and lunch in pleasant surroundings where you won't feel like gulping down your food. If the weather is nice, there is seating outdoors. On Saturday morning, from 10 am to 6 pm, there is the **Saturday Market**, at W 3rd Ave and E St, where fresh produce and seafood are sold along with arts and crafts.

For food and surroundings that are a little more distinct, the downtown area of Anchorage has a wonderful selection of cafes, eateries and espresso shops. *Blondie's Cafe*, at W 4th Ave and D St, is open 24 hours. Located adjacent to the start of the Iditarod race, the bright and cheery cafe is loaded with sled-dog paraphernalia, including an entire sled hanging on the wall. An egg breakfast costs $5, a huge Blondie burger $6. Farther west, in a bright yellow building, is *Tito's Gyros (411 W 4th Ave)*, where you can get a medium one-item pizza for under $12 and gyro sandwiches stuffed with lamb for $6. Still farther west on 4th Ave is the *Downtown Deli (525 W 4th Ave)*, unquestionably the city's best-known delicatessen. Breakfasts are great – eggs, potatoes and a lightly toasted bagel for $6. Deli sandwiches cost $6 to $9, and a bowl of reindeer stew with biscuits is $10. Highly recommended is *Sack's Cafe (625 W 5th Ave)*, especially the fresh shellfish. Dinners cost $19 to $22.

Other fine spots to enjoy lunch or dinner outdoors include *Phyllis's Cafe*, at W 5th Ave and D St. Art decorates the interior, and out back is a sawdust-covered courtyard. The salmon dinner costs $19, and the hamburgers ($6 to $9) are excellent. Try the Bristol Bay buffalo burger (yes, it is buffalo meat), the Rampart reindeer burger or the Moose Pass mushroom burger.

Cheap eats near the Anchorage International Hostel include *Wings N Things*, I St and W 6th Ave, which is open till 10 pm on the weekends. Chicken wings, vegetables and sauce (try their Nuke sauce if you want to burn your mouth) run $7; whole subs start at $7; and beer is available. Next door is *Muffin Man*, which opens for breakfast at 6 am. Muffins are 75¢; a full breakfast $6; and, of course, there's espresso.

Anchorage's most interesting grocery store, and another place to get cheap food, is *New Sagaya's City Market*, I St and W 13th Ave. It has an espresso bar, bakery, seafood counter, specialty food shop and several areas that sell ready-to-eat items like salad, wraps, pizza, pasta and Chinese and Thai entrees. A complete Asian meal with an egg roll and rice is under $6. The store also has seating inside and an outdoor court. *China Express (425 W 5th Ave)*, on the west side of the downtown area, has a $7 all-you-can-eat lunch buffet and family dinners with two or more entrees that begin at $10.

For an evening out, Anchorage has a long list of places for dinner. One of the best is *Simon & Seafort's Saloon & Grill* (☎ 274-3502, 420 L St), between W 4th and W 5th Aves. The restaurant has the decor of a turn-of-the-century grand saloon and a nice view of Cook Inlet, from which you can watch the sun set behind Mt Susitna. Locals rave about *Marx Bros Cafe* (☎ 278-2133, 627 W 3rd Ave), which woos you with views of Cook Inlet, great seafood and a 10,000-bottle wine cellar. Dinners at either restaurant are expensive – plan on spending $17 to $28, not counting your liquor – and reservations are a must. Another popular restaurant is *Glacier Brew-House* (☎ 274-2739, 737 5th Ave), where the wait can be a long one on the weekends for such entrees as spit-roasted prime rib ($20) or apple-grilled rockfish with mango salsa ($15).

The liveliest pub with the best food is *Humpy's Great Alaskan Alehouse*, at W 6th Ave and F St. Pass up the burgers to try halibut tacos or smoked salmon on pasta for under $10. Wash your meal down with one of 50 microbrews on tap. The place gets crowded, so be prepared to wait for a table.

One other eatery that has to be mentioned is *Peggy's Place (1675 E 5th Ave)*, across from Merrill Airfield. While not exactly downtown, this restaurant is well worth the extra effort required to reach it. This longtime favorite is famous for Peggy's homemade pies, 20 different types that range from Nutdelight and boysenberry to a strawberry cream pie that is 6 inches high. Breakfast costs $4 to $9 for Peggy's Special – ham, bacon, three eggs, toast and pancakes all smothered with country gravy. If that doesn't give you a stroke, nothing will.

There's no shortage of cappuccino in this city. You can't walk more than a block or two downtown without passing a coffee shop. Drive-through espresso shacks seem to be on every corner. There's even an espresso bar in some Kinko's Print Shops. Have a cafe latte while waiting for your copies.

Relax at **Side Street Espresso** (428 G St) just off 4th Ave. It has an interesting selection of prints on the walls, a used-book shelf in the corner and, by the afternoon, a couple of copies of the *Daily News* spread across the tables. Also downtown is one of the **Cafe Del Mundos**, W 4th Ave and K St, in the city, and nearby is **Surf City**, W 4th Ave and L St. The latter cafe has huge cinnamon buns and 20oz lattes that will set you back only $3.40 and doubles as a cybercafe. Sip and surf.

Farther east is **Bear Paw Coffee Co**, at F St and W 7th Ave, where you can get blasted awake in the morning with its 20oz latte with five shots of espresso ($5). The food here is very good – huge bagels with cream cheese ($2), giant Belgian waffles with strawberries, quiche and oatmeal-apple-pecan pancakes.

Another interesting place is **Cyrano's Books & Cafe** (413 4th Ave). Established in 1987, the shop is an offbeat bookstore with an excellent Alaska section and an espresso shop with a variety of baked goods, sandwiches and lunches. Idle away the afternoon with a latte, an order of quesadillas and a new book.

Midtown Head down Northern Lights Blvd or Benson Blvd, between New Seward Hwy and Minnesota Drive, for any fast-food restaurant you're craving. Even better is **Momma O's Seafood Restaurant** (2636 Spenard Rd), just near Northern Lights Blvd. Grilled halibut with a trip to a small but good salad bar costs $8. There are also clam, oyster, calamari and scallop dinners and fish sandwiches. The most affordable food, however, is at the **Carrs** Aurora Village store, at L St and Northern Lights Blvd, the largest of the Carrs chain. The salad bar is great at $3.50 a pound, and there are also a deli, an Orient express for stir-fry, a bakery, an espresso shop and seating.

There are also two very distinct places in this center slice of the city. **Hogg Brothers Cafe** (1049 W Northern Lights Blvd), at Spenard Rd, is a bizarre restaurant with 'piggy' decor, including a stuffed hog mounted on the wall. Breakfast is served all

day and the selection is creative. You could order two eggs, home fries and toast for $4, but why when there are more than 20 omelettes, like Mat-Zu-Mama (Canadian bacon, cheese and tomatoes). The place isn't as classic as the original that was next door to Chilkoot Charlie's, but the food is still good and plentiful.

Also serving breakfast all day is **Gwennie's Old Alaska Restaurant** (4333 Spenard Rd), west of Minnesota Drive. The portions are big, the prices reasonable and the artifacts are so numerous that the place mat doubles as a guide to what's on the walls. Order an omelette ($7 to $9) and then study the baleen sleds that Native Alaskans once used to haul freight, photos of the 1964 earthquake, pieces of the Trans-Alaska Pipeline or the 45,000-year-old bison head found in the Lucky Seven Mine.

To the south, in the Plaza Mall at 36th Ave and C St, is **Natural Pantry** (☎ 563-2727), a health-food store and a restaurant with a $6 lunch special that includes soup, a sandwich and a drink. The **Crazy Croissants French Bakery** (☎ 278-8787, 1406 W 31st Ave) is a hard-to-find eatery between Spenard Rd and Minnesota Drive, but the search is well worth the effort as the baked goods are excellent, salads and quiches wonderful and prices very reasonable.

A great selection of bagels (60¢ each) and bagel sandwiches ($6 to $7), breakfast bagels with eggs ($4 to $5) and cafe latte are at **Alaska Bagel Restaurant** (113 W Northern Lights Blvd) in the Great Alaska Mall. Next to the REI is the **Middle Way Cafe** (1200 W Northern Lights), which has tortilla-wrap sandwiches, good salads, fruit smoothies and other healthy dishes, along with espresso drinks.

Good Greek and Italian food and outdoor seating are at the **Greek Corner** (302 W Fireweed Lane). The moussaka plate ($13) will fill you up, and Italian dishes range from garlic-feta spaghetti ($11) to rigatoni al forno ($10.50). Beer and wine are also served here. Just west is one of the best steakhouses in Anchorage, **Black Angus Meat Market** (1101 Fireweed Lane). The restaurant has the dark wood panel interior

ANCHORAGE

you expect in a steakhouse, along with a butcher case to preview the cuts of meat. Steaks are excellent here and affordable, $11 to $17 for the 24oz porterhouse.

An interesting evening can also be enjoyed at *Flying Machine* (☎ 243-2300, 4800 Spenard Rd), the restaurant inside the Regal Alaskan Hotel. The dinners are excellent ($16 to $24), and from your table you can watch the floatplanes take off from Lake Hood. On the other side of town is the *Moose's Tooth* (☎ 258-2537, 3300 Old Seward Hwy), a brewpub with 15 homemade beers on tap, outdoor seating and possibly the best pizza ($11 to $17 for medium) in town.

Asian restaurants, from Thai and Mongolian barbecue to Chinese restaurants, are found in this part of the city. One of the best for traditional Chinese is *Panda* (605 E Northern Lights Blvd). The Cantonese and Szechuan dinners at the small restaurant are excellent and affordable, for $8 to $12. Nearby, across from the Sears Mall, is *Peking Palace* (605 E Benson Ave), for spicy northern Chinese cuisine. Full dinners, including soup, egg rolls and three main courses begin at around $11.

Excellent Mongolian barbecue, where you fill your bowl with raw vegetables, fish, chicken and beef and then hand it to the chef to cook on a round grill, can be found at *Twin Dragon* (612 E 15 Ave) near Gambell St. If that's too far away, you can get the same thing at *Golden China*, in a mall at 3020 Minnesota Drive. At both restaurants, an all-you-can eat dinner costs $11 or lunch, $7.

For Thai cuisine, a good choice is *Thai Town*, in the same mall as Carrs on Minnesota Drive and Northern Lights Blvd. Dinners cost $7 to $10. The restaurant has an extensive selection of vegetarian main courses and seafood. Try the sir-fry shrimp curry in a coconut-milk sauce. Also highly recommended is *Thai Kitchen* (3405 E Tudor Rd) in Tudor Square Mall. There are 103 items on the menu, dozens of which are vegetarian, with most entrees from $7 to $8 with all the steamed rice you can eat. In the same strip of stores is the best Vietnamese restaurant in Anchorage, *Saigon* (3561 E Tudor Rd).

South Anchorage The best place for a burger south of Tudor Rd is the original *Arctic Roadrunner*, at International Airport Rd and Old Seward Hwy. The 'Local Burgerman' has been serving big hamburgers for more than 35 years, and you can enjoy your food while looking at the restaurant's customer gallery. Among those enshrined are Norma Jean Saunders, the first woman to climb Mt McKinley; Mark Scherath, one of the first Alaskan-born players in the National Football League; and Bob Henderson, who once landed a 26lb northern pike with a muskrat in its stomach. Burgers range from under $3 to $4.35, for the Kenai Whopper. Across the street is the *Peanut Farm* (5227 Old Seward Hwy), a bar with good food, cheap beer and an outdoor deck. At this place you can drink until the staff start serving breakfast.

Nearby, the tourists are bused to the *Sourdough Mining Co* (☎ 563-2272), a half block of Old Seward Hwy at International Airport Rd and Juneau St. For $24, you can enjoy the sourdough seafood sampler (snow crab, salmon, halibut, prawns) and other dishes in the re-created miner's hall, or head outside for an all-you-can eat buffet in a dinner tent. There is also a nightly Alaskan show. Next door is the huge *Alaska Wildberry Products* store for dessert.

The best Mexican dishes are found in South Anchorage at *Mexico in Alaska* (7305 Old Seward Hwy), just south of Dowling Rd. Dinners of traditional Mexican cuisine cost $10 to $13. The beer list from Mexico is impressive, and there is an outdoor seating area if the weather is nice. It's a long way from downtown, but bus No 60 goes right past the restaurant. The best ribs are also on the south side of the city, at the *Bar-B-Que Pit* (1160 W Dimond Blvd), which has been slow cooking baby back ribs since 1960. A barbecue beef sandwich costs $5.25 and includes beans and coleslaw, and the polar bear delight – barbecue beef, ham *and* ribs, with a ton of side dishes – costs $15.

Entertainment

With its young and lively population, Anchorage has a lot to do after the midnight sun finally sets. The best way to check out what's happening is to pick up a copy of *Anchorage Press,* an alternative newspaper that features bar and dance club listings and movie reviews. It's free and distributed at most tourist places in the downtown area. In the Friday edition of the *Anchorage Daily News* is the equally good weekend entertainment section called '8.'

Cinemas The city has numerous movie theaters, including the *Fireweed Theatre* (☎ 275-3139), at Fireweed and Gambell Rd, and *Totem Theatre* (☎ 275-3188, 3131 Muldoon Rd). The largest, with 16 screens each, are *Dimond Center* (☎ 275-3102), in the Dimond Center Mall at Dimond Rd and Old Seward Hwy, and *Century 16* (☎ 929-3456, 301 E 36th Ave). Just about all the movie theaters open early for daily discount matinees.

At the *Sydney Laurence Theatre* (800-478-7328), *Sky Song* is shown on the hour 9 am to 9 pm daily. The 38-minute presentation includes over 300 slides of the northern lights set to classical music. Tickets cost $7. For something more touristy, head to the *Alaska Experience Center* (☎ 276-3730), at G St and W 6th Ave. The theater presents a 40-minute, 70mm film that is projected on a huge domed screen and is entitled *Alaska the Great Land;* admission is $7. For $10 you can also watch a second film, about the 1964 Good Friday Earthquake.

Performing Arts Anchorage has a civic opera (☎ 279-2557), a symphony orchestra (☎ 254-8668), several theater groups and a concert association (☎ 272-1471) that brings a number of dance companies and art groups to the city every year. Big-name performers and Broadway productions arrive more frequently now that the *Alaska Center for the Performing Arts* (☎ 263-2900) has been completed. Call the center for a schedule of who's in town and call its box office (☎ 263-2787) for the price and availability of tickets.

You'll also find live theater at the *Mainstage Theater* (☎ 263-2787), at the UA Anchorage Arts Building, and at the *Off Center Playhouse* at Cyrano's Books &

Cafe (☎ 274-2599, 413 D St). The unique coffee shop-bookstore also maintains a small stage for its 'Eccentric Theatre Company,' which formed in 1995 and puts on several productions throughout the year. Tickets are $12.50 and worth it.

Dance Clubs In Anchorage, you can hike all day in the mountains and dance all night in the bars. One of the more colorful places is *Chilkoot Charlie's* (2435 Spenard Rd), or 'Koots,' as the locals call it. The bar has been around for almost 30 years and has expanded to 10,000 sq feet, with three bands, dancing, horseshoes outside and a long bar with sawdust on the floor and rusty artifacts all over the walls. There is a cover charge, and liquor prices are Alaskan, but reasonable if you arrive before the bands start at 9 pm.

Other places with loud music and large dance floors are *Hot Rods* (4848 Spenard Rd), a '50s nightclub with a DJ; *Blondie's* (333 W 4th Ave); and *Club Oasis* (4801 Old Seward Hwy). The *Wave* (3103 Spenard Rd), Anchorage's gay dance club, prides itself on being 'totally straight-friendly.' This outrageous club has shows and special events Wednesday to Saturday, including gay and lesbian line dancing and drag queen bingo.

Jazz & Blues *Chef's Inn/Blues Central* (825 W Northern Lights Blvd) is the small but delightful jazz club featuring Blues Jam Night every Sunday, when there is great jamming and no cover. *Rumrunner's Old Towne Bar* (330 E St), in the Anchorage Hotel, also features rhythm & blues, as does *Sullivan's Steakhouse* (320 W 5th Ave) four nights a week and *Firehouse Cafe* (2911 Spenard Rd), a renovated fire station.

Country There's plenty of honky-tonk in Anchorage. Dance halls for country music and line dancing include *Last Frontier Bar* (369 Muldoon Rd), *Long Branch Saloon* (1737 E Diamond Blvd) and *A-K Korral Saloon* (2421 E Tudor Rd).

Other Music There's lighter acoustic music at *Humpy's* (610 6th Ave), and *Kaladi*

ANCHORAGE

Brothers Coffee Co, in the Brayton Mall at 68th Ave and Frontage St, often has folk music on the weekends. *Mr Whitekeys' Fly by Night Club* (☎ 279-7726, *3300 Spenard Rd*) has jazz, blues and early rock but is best known for its *Whale-Fat Follies*, a fun and raunchy look at Alaska that teaches you all you'll ever want to know about duct tape, spawning salmon and Alaska's official state fossil, the woolly mammoth. This place has a Spam fixation that will make you howl all night. The two-hour show starts at 8 pm Tuesday to Saturday; tickets cost $12 to $18, and reservations are a must.

Bars Downtown, there are a variety of low-key pubs and lively bars where you can go to cap off the evening. Locals head for *Darwin's Theory* (*426 G St*), where the popcorn is free. The *Sports Edition Bar* (*500 W 3rd Ave*), in the Anchorage Hilton, has 20 TVs of every size imaginable, for viewing whatever game is being played that night. You could also try the *Lion's Den* (*1000 E 36th St*), in the Western Golden Lion Hotel, where there are often free munchies, or the *Hub*, at W 4th Ave and A St, a favorite with locals and bush dwellers. Yuppie Anchoragites drink at *F Street Station* (*325 F St*), across from the Old Federal Building.

Great views of the area can be obtained for the (steep) price of a drink in the *Crow's Nest*, top of the Hotel Captain Cook at 5th Ave and K St, or at the *Penthouse Lounge*, top of the Westmark Hotel at 720 W 5th Ave, where floor-to-ceiling windows let you marvel at Mt McKinley on a clear day.

Shopping
The downtown area between 4th and 6th Aves is overrun with gift shops, many hawking the same tacky souvenirs: moose-nugget

---

Brewing Beer in Anchorage

When gold fever hit its peak in Alaska in the late 19th and early 20th century, more than 40 breweries helped stampeders to spend their fortunes or drown their sorrows. Prohibition destroyed Alaska's rich brewing history, as the beers of the gold rush era vanished forever. But a microbrew industry that began in Juneau in 1985 with the start-up of the Alaska Brewing Company took off in the mid-1990s. In 1996 alone, four brewpubs set up shop in Anchorage, three of them downtown. Alaska now has 15 microbreweries and brewpubs, and annual beer festivals in Haines and Chena Hot Springs. Anchorage has the lion's share of microbrew industry, with five brewery restaurants and three microbreweries.

The best brewpub in the city is *Cusack's* (*598 W Northern Lights Blvd*), in the Northern Lights Hotel. This is where serious beer drinkers come, as there are more than 20 varieties on tap, including the five house brews (try MacGrouder's Scottish Ale). Can't make up your mind? Then try several at once via the sampler glass. Before you leave, check out the record moose on display in the hotel lobby.

Other brewpubs include *Moose's Tooth Pub* (*3300 Old Seward Hwy*), *Snow Goose Restaurant* (*717 W 3rd Ave*) and *Glacier BrewHouse* (*737 West 5th Ave*). Glacier BrewHouse was the first downtown brewpub and now is one of the most popular restaurants in Anchorage. Snow Goose is the home of the Sleeping Lady Brewing Co, and an outdoor deck where you can sit for hours enjoying the midnight sun and glasses of Fish On Pale Ale. Another outdoor setting, more craft beer and excellent pizza are available at Moose's Tooth Pub. On the first Thursday of every month, the pub hosts First Tap Thursday, when suds connoisseurs gather to celebrate the release of a new beer.

Anchorage also has breweries to visit. *Midnight Sun Brewing Co* (*7329 Arctic Blvd*) holds an event at 6 pm every Friday to release their new beers. *Borealis Brewery* (*349 E Ship Creek Ave*) stages tours at 6 pm on Thursday, and to the north in Wasilla, *Great Bear Brewing Company* (*238 N Boundary St*) has regularly scheduled tours at 4 pm every Tuesday.

earrings, I-Kissed-a-Moose T-shirts, beer coasters in the shape of igloos. Among the better shops are Arctic Art, at 5th Ave and D St, for scrimshaw and soapstone carvings; TJ Shirts, at 6th Ave near E St, which carries LA Gear clothing with quality embroidery; and the shops in the Hotel Captain Cook. For the cheapest stuff, the place to go for that souvenir you promised your six-year-old cousin (who is just going to lose it within a day anyhow) is Polar Bear Gifts, at W 5th Ave and E St.

Be careful when purchasing Native Alaskan art (see Shopping in the Facts for the Visitor chapter). An excellent place to check out is the gift shop at the Alaska Native Medical Center (see 'Native Culture in Anchorage' boxed text). Across A St from the historical museum is Nenana Creative Arts (☎ 278-6748), a Native American arts cooperative, where you can watch artists work on ivory, soapstone and other materials.

Getting There & Away

Air Anchorage International Airport, 6.5 miles west of the city center, is the largest airport in the state, handling 130 flights daily from more than a dozen major airlines. You can catch a flight to anywhere in Alaska. Alaska Airlines (☎ 800-426-0333) provides the most intrastate routes to travelers, often through its contract carrier, ERA, which services Valdez, Homer, Cordova, Kenai, Iliamna and Kodiak.

Reeve Aleutian Airways (☎ 243-4700, 800-544-2248) offers flights throughout Southwest Alaska, including Pribilof Islands, King Salmon, Bethel and Unalaska. Yute Air Alaska (☎ 888-359-9883, 243-7090) flies to Bethel, Nome and 50 villages in western Alaska.

Bus A variety of bus and van companies operate out of Anchorage and provide service to almost everywhere in the state. You can count on the biggies, like Alaskon Express, but double-check the smaller companies by making a phone call.

For travelers heading toward Haines or Whitehorse, there are a couple possibilities.

Alaskon Express (☎ 227-5581, 800-478-6388) departs from its office on 745 W 4th Ave, and from a handful of major hotels, at 7:30 am on Sunday, Tuesday and Friday for Palmer, Glennallen, Tok and Beaver Creek in the Yukon Territory, where the bus stops overnight. From Beaver Creek, you can make connections to Whitehorse, Haines or Skagway. The one-way fare to Haines is $195 and to Glennallen $61. Alaska Direct (☎ 277-6652, 800-770-6652) has a bus that departs Anchorage at 6 am Sunday, Wednesday and Friday and arrives in Whitehorse at midnight. One-way fare is $145.

Taking a van service to Denali National Park and Fairbanks is the cheapest way to travel the George Parks Hwy, other than hitchhiking. Alaska Backpackers Shuttle (☎ 344-8775, 800-266-8625, abst@juno.com) departs Voyager Hotel at 5th Ave and K St at 8 am, reaches Denali at 1 pm and the Fairbanks Visitor Center at 5 pm. One-way to Denali is $40 and Fairbanks $60. Bicycles cost $5 extra. Several other companies offer the same service, including Parks Highway Express (☎ 888-600-6001, info@alaskashuttle.com). Most of the van companies that run to Denali don't depart the Parks Hwy for the 14-mile side trip to Talkeetna. You can reach this interesting little town through Alaska Tourquest (☎ 344-6667, 800-660-2688, ron@alaskaquest.com) or Talkeetna Shuttle Service (☎ 733-1725, 888-288-6008, tshuttle@alaska.net). The one-way fare is around $25.

To get to the Kenai Peninsula, take Seward Bus Line (☎ 224-3608), which departs from 3339 Fairbanks St at 2:30 pm daily for Seward, reaching the town at 5:30 pm. The one-way fare is $30. Also running between Anchorage and Seward is Kachemak Bay Transit (☎ 299-0994, 877-235-9191) and Alaska Backpacker Shuttle (☎ 344-8775). Kachemak Bay Transit departs Anchorage at 8 am from a variety of locations, including the Spenard Hostel, and arrives at Homer between 2:30 and 4:30 pm. One-way fare is $45. Homer Stage Line (☎ 235-7009) also runs the same route, leaving Anchorage at 3:30 pm and arriving at Homer at 8:30 pm, for the same fare.

Parks Highway Express (☎ 888-600-6001, info@alaskashuttle.com) began as van service to Denali National Park, but in 1999, expanded to offer service on the other two major highways, Glenn and Richardson. A bus leaves the Anchorage Hostel at 7th Ave and H St at 9 am Wednesday, Friday and Sunday and arrives at Valdez at 4:50 pm. You can also use this service to reach Palmer, Glennallen or other points in between. One-way from Anchorage to Valdez is $59. The company also has a bus pass ($145) for unlimited travel on any of the routes. The bus pass is good for the entire travel season, from late May through early September. Alaskon Express also has a bus for Valdez, departing from Anchorage at 8 am daily. The one-way fare is $68.

Train The Alaska Railroad (☎ 265-2494, 800-544-0552, akrr@Alaska.net) maintains its office in the depot at 421 W 1st Ave and provides services both north and south of Anchorage. The most popular run is the *Denali Express,* which departs Anchorage at 8:15 am daily for Denali Park and Fairbanks. The one-way fare to Denali is $104 and to Fairbanks $154. From mid-September to mid-May the schedule changes to one train per week, which departs Anchorage at 8:30 am on Saturday.

The local 'flag stop' train no longer departs from Anchorage from May to October, but rather from Talkeetna. The rest of the year the flag-stop service is from Anchorage to Hurricane Gulch, only on the first Thursday of the month. The train departs Anchorage at 8:30 am, and a roundtrip ticket costs $88.

Alaska Railroad's newest service is an Anchorage to Whittier run with a stop in Girdwood. The train departs Anchorage at 9 am daily, reaches Whittier at 11:30 am and then departs at 5:45 pm for the return trip. The roundtrip fare is $52, one-way $26, making it a slightly better deal than purchasing van shuttle service to Portage and a Portage-to-Whittier ticket on the railroad. You can also take the train to Seward. From Anchorage, the train departs at 6:45 am daily from mid-May to early September,

reaching Seward at 11:05 am. The roundtrip fare is $86.

Hitchhiking Hitching out of Anchorage can be made a lot easier by first spending $1 and hopping on a People Mover bus. Travelers heading north should take bus No 76 or 102 to Peter's Creek Trading Post on Glenn Hwy. If you're heading to Portage, Seward or the rest of the Kenai Peninsula, take bus No 60 and get off at Huffman Park Drive and Seward Hwy.

Boat The Alaska Marine Hwy (☎ 272-4482) doesn't service Anchorage but does have an office in the city, in the Old Federal Courthouse at 605 W 4th Ave. Here you can obtain information, make reservations or purchase advance tickets.

Getting Around

To/From the Airport The good news is the People Mover bus system has restored its service to the airport. The bad news is they operate the route only on the weekdays and only during the summer months. If you arrive between 7 am and 6:30 pm Monday through Friday, you can pick up bus No 6 at the domestic terminal and reach downtown Anchorage for only $1. Otherwise, call Borealis Shuttle (☎ 888-436-3600, 276-3600). A ride to the downtown hostel will cost $12.

Many hotels and B&Bs, mostly listed in the baggage claim area, also have courtesy van service. Finally, an endless line of taxis is eager to take your bags and your money. Plan on a $13 to $16 fare to the downtown area.

Bus Anchorage has an excellent public bus system in the People Mover, with clean buses and friendly drivers. All buses begin at the People Mover's downtown terminal, in the transit center at the corner of 6th Ave and G St. Most buses pass by every half hour, and the schedule is posted at every stop. The fare is $1 a ride or $2.50 for an all-day, unlimited ticket. If the trip requires more than one bus, ask the driver for a transfer, which allows you to ride on the connecting bus for an additional 10¢.

A full service of 17 routes operates 6 am to 10 pm Monday to Friday, with reduced service 8 am to 8 pm Saturday and 9:30 am to 6:30 pm Sunday. People Mover also operates a free bus called DASH, an acronym for Downtown Anchorage Short Hop, that travels between 5th and 8th Aves in the downtown area. For information on any route, call the Rideline at ☎ 343-6543.

In 1999, People Mover formed a working partnership with Mat-Su Community Transit (☎ 376-5000) to coordinate bus service from Anchorage to the Matanuska Valley. The service is offered Monday to Friday, and you switch lines at the Eagle River Transit Center on Business Park Blvd. The one-way fare from Anchorage to Palmer or Wasilla is $3.50, a bargain.

Car For two or more people, renting a used car is the most affordable way to see Anchorage, the surrounding area or the Kenai Peninsula. The cheapest deal is available from Denali Car Rental (☎ 276-1230), 1209 Gambell St, which has subcompacts for $32 a day or $210 a week from June through August and $25 a day before or after that. Affordable Car Rental (☎ 243-3370, 800-248-3765), 4707 Spenard Rd, across from the Regal Alaskan Hotel, advertises subcompacts for as low as $33 per day but never seem to have any vehicles available when you call. Its compacts cost $42 a day.

High Country Car Rental (☎ 562-8078, 888-685-1155), 512 W International Airport Rd, has subcompacts for $40 a day during the summer, but before June and after August prices are lower, sometimes as low as $30 a day. Both Ace Rent-A-Car and Affordable will provide transportation from your motel or to the airport before or after you rent the car. Other discounted car rental places include Airport Car Rentals (☎ 277-7662), U-Save Auto Rental (☎ 272-8728, 800-254-8728) and Denali Car Rental (☎ 276-1230).

All the national concerns (Avis, Budget, Hertz, Payless, National, etc) maintain counters in the ground transportation lobby of the south terminal at the airport. Reserve a car if you can; all car rentals in Anchorage are heavily booked in the summer.

South of Anchorage

Travelers who arrive in Anchorage and head south to the Kenai Peninsula will immediately be struck by Alaska's splendor; they no sooner leave the city limits than they find themselves following the edge of the spectacular Turnagain Arm. An extension of Cook Inlet, the arm is known for having some of the highest tides in the world and for the views of the Kenai Mountains to the south.

SEWARD HIGHWAY
The Seward Hwy, which runs along Turnagain Arm south of Anchorage, hugs the water and, at times, is carved out of the mountainside; it runs side by side with the Alaska Railroad. A bike path shoulders much of the road and, when completed, will connect the bike trails in Anchorage with those in Girdwood.

The Seward Hwy begins as New Seward Hwy in Anchorage, on the corner of 5th Ave and Gambell St at a junction with the Glenn Hwy. It heads south and reaches the coast near Rabbit Creek Rd. From there, the mileposts on the road measure the distance to Seward. People who live in Anchorage often play on the Kenai Peninsula. Add the usual RVers in summer, and on Friday afternoon, you have a major traffic tie-up heading south on Seward Hwy.

At Mile 118, 9 miles south of the Anchorage city center, the highway passes the first of many gravel Turnagain Arm lookouts. A mile farther, the highway reaches two lookouts and a massive boardwalk out onto the **Anchorage Coastal Wildlife Refuge**, a state game refuge. At the lookouts, you can often marvel at arctic terns and Canada geese nesting nearby. Some 130 species of birds and waterfowl have been spotted in this refuge at Anchorage's back door.

Two miles to the south, you enter Chugach State Park and pass the **Potter Section House**. A home for railroad workers who maintained the tracks when locomotives were powered by coal, the house is now a state historic site and museum with displays and railroad exhibits, including a vintage snowblower and working model train. It's open 8 am to 4:30 pm daily. Stop there or call (☎ 345-5014) for information on outdoor activities in Chugach State Park.

Across the street is the posted northern trailhead for the **Turnagain Arm Trail**, an 11-mile footpath. Originally, Native Alaskans used the route, and later, Russians, trappers and gold miners. It's an easy hike with a mountain goat's view of Turnagain Arm, alpine meadows and beluga whales feeding

in the waters below. From Potter, the trail heads southeast and reaches McHugh Picnic Area in 3.5 miles; Rainbow (with access to Seward Hwy) in 7.5 miles; and Windy Corner, at the trail's southern end, in 9.5 miles. Plan on five to seven hours for the entire walk.

In the next 10 miles, the highway passes numerous lookouts, many with scenic views of Turnagain Arm. Just beyond Mile 112 of Seward Hwy is McHugh Creek Picnic Area (30 picnic tables) and the second access to

Canaries of the Sea

Of all the whales that inhabit Alaskan waters, the beluga is one of the most intriguing and certainly the easiest to spot, due to its unusual white color. The word 'beluga' is actually Russian for 'sturgeon,' and Belukha was what the early Russians named the white whale they encountered in Alaskan waters. The animals have also been referred to as 'canaries of the sea,' because of their noisy chatter.

Belugas are small, toothed whales, adults averaging 12 to 16 feet in length, 3000lb in weight and reaching sexual maturity in five to six years. The beluga has no dorsal fin, which allows it to move easily under free ice. It's not unusual in the winter to see belugas sleeping under clear, newly formed ice.

The whale prefers the cold waters of the Bering Sea but is also found as far south as Cook Inlet and Yakutat Bay in Alaska and the Gulf of St Lawrence on the east coast of Canada. Belugas have been spotted swimming 1240 miles up the Amur River in Asia, 600 miles inland in the Yukon River and in Lake Iliamna on the Alaska Peninsula.

There are an estimated 70,000 belugas worldwide, with 25,000 in the Bering Sea. In recent years the Cook Inlet population has declined from more than 1000 to less than 800, due to hunting pressure (Alaskan Natives harvest 200 to 300 a year), development along rivers and coastal areas and pollution.

Still, the white heads of belugas are a common sight during the summer. Three good spots to see the belugas are in and around Anchorage. The best is at Beluga Point, 17 miles southeast of Anchorage along the Seward Hwy. The point overlooks Turnagain Arm and has picnic tables, benches, telescopes and an interpretive display. You can also look for belugas from the boat launch at Ship Creek, as the whales often will feed on salmon in the mouth of the creek, or from the Coastal Trail between Westchester Lagoon and Point Woronzof.

The city of Kenai has Beluga Whale Lookout, near the corner of Main and Mission Sts. Located on the edge of the bluff, the overlook provides a view of the mouth of the Kenai River, where belugas are occasionally seen following salmon runs during incoming tides. Another place to observe them on the Kenai Peninsula is Captain Cook State Recreation Area, 36 miles north of the city of Kenai.

When searching for the white whales, scan Cook Inlet or Turnagain Arm with binoculars during high tide. Look for white bumps in the gray water. Belugas don't leap but roll slowly as they swim, often breathing in unison. You can see beluga from May through September, or possibly even earlier in Turnagain Arm if the silver salmon are running.

the Turnagain Arm Trail and then **Beluga Point**. The point has a commanding view of the Turnagain Arm and features telescopes and interpretive displays to assist travelers in spotting the white whales in May and August. At Mile 103.6 is **Indian**, a town consisting mainly of a couple of bars and a restaurant. The ***Brown Bear Saloon*** (☎ 653-7000) is a rustic but fun watering hole that often has live music on the weekends. Nearby is the **Indian Valley Mine** (☎ 337-7749), one of only two underground mines in the area. For a small fee, you can now pan for gold or check out a museum at the mine.

Just west of Turnagain House and Indian Creek is a gravel road that leads 1.3 miles past a pump station and ends near Indian Creek, where there is parking space and the posted trailhead for the **Indian Valley Trail**, a 6-mile path to Indian Pass. The trail is easy, with only an occasional ford of Indian Creek, and leads to the alpine areas of the pass. In these areas, more experienced hikers can continue north to eventually reach the Ship Creek Trail, which ends at Ski Bowl Rd north of Anchorage. Plan on five to seven hours for the 12-mile roundtrip on the Indian Valley Trail.

The **Bird Ridge Trail** starts near Mile 10 of Seward Hwy – look for a large marked parking area to the north. From there, the trail to the ridge begins with an uphill climb to a power-line access road, follows it for 0.3 miles and then turns left and climbs Bird Ridge, which runs along the valley of Bird Creek. The hike is steep in many places but quickly leaves the bush behind for the alpine beauty above. You can hike more than 4 miles on the ridge itself, reaching views of the headwaters of Ship Creek below. Viewing points of Turnagain Arm are plentiful and make the trail a good mountain hike.

The ***Bird Creek State Campground***, just beyond Mile 101, has 27 sites for $10. The campground is scenic and known for its fine sunbathing, but is often full by early afternoon during the summer, especially on weekends.

The next 10 miles after Bird Creek Campground contain 16 turnoffs, all good spots to watch the **tidal bores**. Bores (barreling walls of water that often exceed 10 feet in height as they rush at 15mph back across the mud flats) are created twice a day by the powerful tides in Turnagain Arm.

There are more than 60 places around the world where tidal bores occur (the highest are the 25-foot bores on the Amazon basin) but the Turnagain and Knik Arms are the only places in the USA where they take place on a regular basis. To avoid missing the turbulent incoming waves, get the time of low tide from the *Anchorage Daily News* and add two hours and 15 minutes. At that time, the bore will be passing this particular point along the highway. Arrive early and then continue down the road after the bore passes your lookout, to view it again and again.

GIRDWOOD

At Mile 90 of Seward Hwy is the junction with Alyeska Hwy, the access road that goes to Girdwood, a small hamlet of 300 residents, 2 miles up the side road. The junction itself now has a strip mall housing a 7-Eleven, a taco shop and a video-rental store. For something less urban, pass this up for Girdwood. The town has a post office, grocery store and Kinder Park. Nearby is the Girdwood Fairgrounds, the site of the town's annual Forest Faire, usually held in the first week of July.

Head 3.5 miles up Crow Creek Rd to see the handful of historical buildings at **Crow Creek Mine** (☎ 278-8060). Built in 1898, the camp includes a mess hall, a blacksmith's shop, a bunkhouse and several other restored buildings. Admission is $3, but for $5 you can also get a gold-panning demonstration and then strike out on your own at a nearby creek. You can also camp here for $6 a night. An excellent way to reach the mine and continue up Crow Pass Rd is to rent a mountain bike from Girdwood Ski & Cyclery (☎ 783-2453). Bikes cost $25 a day or $15 for two hours.

Another mile east of Girdwood is the **Alyeska Ski Area**. The ski resort hums during the winter and is also a busy place during the summer, when tour groups leave the buses to wander through the gift shops and expensive restaurants or participate in hot-air

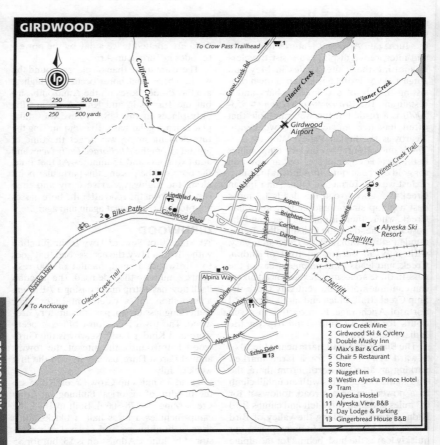

GIRDWOOD

1	Crow Creek Mine
2	Girdwood Ski & Cyclery
3	Double Musky Inn
4	Max's Bar & Grill
5	Chair 5 Restaurant
6	Store
7	Nugget Inn
8	Westin Alyeska Prince Hotel
9	Tram
10	Alyeska Hostel
11	Alyeska View B&B
12	Day Lodge & Parking
13	Gingerbread House B&B

balloon flights and horse-drawn carriage rides. The best thing about the resort is the scenic ride up Mt Alyeska. In 1993, the ski resort replaced the open chairlift with a pair of 60-passenger trams. The trip up is now a five-minute ride that ends at the 2300-foot level of Mt Alyeska, where you enjoy a view of Turnagain Arm and seven area glaciers. At the top are two restaurants: fine dining at Seven Glaciers or something cheaper and quicker at Glacier Express. The tram ride costs $16 per adult, but for an additional $3, Glacier Express will give you a ride-and-lunch combo.

During the summer, you can also use the resort's health center for $5. The center includes a swimming pool, weight room, sauna and a hot tub with a gorgeous view of the mountains.

Hiking
Just up the Alyeska Hwy from Seward Hwy is a Chugach National Forest ranger office (☎ 783-3242). The center is open daily during the summer and is a place to go for information on hiking trails not only in the Girdwood area but throughout the Kenai Peninsula.

Alyeska Glacier View Trail Begin the Alyeska Glacier View Trail by taking the tram to the top and then scrambling up the knob behind the sundeck. From there, follow the ridge into an alpine area with views of the tiny Alyeska Glacier. The roundtrip is less than a mile. You can continue up the ridge to climb the so-called summit of Mt Alyeska, a high point of 3939 feet. The true summit lies farther to the south but is not a climb for casual hikers.

Winner Creek Gorge This is an easy and pleasant hike that winds 3.5 miles through a tall spruce and hemlock forest and ends in the gorge itself, where Winner Creek flows through a small cleft in the rocks and becomes a series of small falls and cascades on its way to emptying into Glacier Creek. Pick up the trail at Alyeska Ski Resort by parking on Arlberg Rd and walking along the bike path past the Alyeska Prince Hotel, toward the bottom of the tram. Follow the edge of a ski trail above the tram and look for the footpath heading into the forest.

Crow Pass Trail Two miles up the Alyeska Access Rd and just before Girdwood is the junction with Crow Creek Rd, a bumpy gravel road. It extends 5.8 miles to a parking lot and the marked trailhead to the Crow Pass Trail, a short but beautiful alpine hike. It is 4 miles to Raven Glacier, the traditional turnaround point of the trail, and with a ride up and back on Crow Creek Rd, hikers can easily do the 8-mile roundtrip in four to six hours.

The trail is highly recommended, as it features gold-mining relics, an alpine lake and usually Dall sheep on the slopes above. There are also many possibilities for longer trips and a USFS cabin 3 miles up the trail (reservations needed, $35 per night). You can also camp around Crow Pass, turning the walk into a pleasant overnight trip. Or, you can continue and complete the three-day, 25-mile route along the Historic Iditarod Trail to the Chugach State Park's Eagle River Nature Center (see the North of Anchorage section in this chapter).

Places to Stay
During the summer the ski resort's **Nugget Inn** has rooms (call the Alyeska Prince Hotel), but they tend to be overrun by tour bus groups and rates reflect that. The **Westin Alyeska Prince Hotel** (☎ 754-2111, 800-880-3880), also at the Alyeska Ski Area, is the only hotel in Alaska to receive a four-star rating from the American Automobile Association. The eight-story hotel with over 300 rooms opened in 1994 and features four

Death in the Mud Flats

As you drive the Seward Hwy along the Turnagain Arm, the sand may look inviting when the tide is out but never venture out on it! Cook Inlet has the second highest tides in North America, with a range of nearly 40 feet, and the mud flats they expose are a deadly quicksand. In the past 30 years, three people have drowned after sinking into the ooze, and many duck hunters and clammers have been pulled out in dramatic fashion as the water rushed in.

The saddest incident occurred in 1989, when a husband and wife driving an all-terrain vehicle (ATV) across the flats became stuck. As the couple tried to push out the ATV, the wife, Adeana Dickison, also became mired in the mud. With the tide coming in, her husband rushed to the nearby Tidewater Cafe to call for help. The troopers arrived quickly, but the 38°F water was already at the woman's chest, and she was begging them to save her. Rescuers fought against the mud and onrushing water but to no avail. As the tide covered her head, Dickison was given a tube to breathe through, but she was already suffering from hypothermia and could not hold out for very long.

Six hours later, when rescuers went out to retrieve the body, one of the legs was still firmly trapped in the mud. All of Anchorage was shocked at such a horrible death, but nobody as much as the Girdwood rescuers, who later met with psychiatrists in an effort to come to terms with the ordeal.

restaurants, a 16-person whirlpool and an indoor pool that overlooks Mt Alyeska – as well as some steep rates. But if you want to be pampered, rooms begin at $175 per night and climb from there.

A small but charming hostel in the area can be reached by turning right into Timberline Drive before the ski lodge and then turning right again into Alpina Rd. The *Alyeska Hostel (☎ 783-2099)* is in a cabin with wood heating, gas lighting and a kitchen area, and includes the use of a wood-burning sauna. Unfortunately, the hostel only has 10 beds, so you might want to call ahead to try to secure space. There is a three-night maximum stay, and the nightly fees are $10/13 members/nonmembers. You can reserve a bed in advance but must send a money order in with your request (PO Box 953, Girdwood, AK 99587).

There are a growing number of B&Bs in Girdwood. *Gingerbread House (☎ 783-1952, DAchermann@aol.com)* has two rooms for $75 and $115 per couple, and *Alyeska View (☎ 783-2747)* has three rooms for $70 to $75 per couple. The hosts of Alyeska View, Heinrich and Emmy Gruber, speak German.

Places to Eat

There are two good restaurants in Girdwood. *Chair 5 Restaurant (5 Lindbald Ave)* is right in town and features gourmet burgers ($7), vegetarian sandwiches, salads, beer on tap and a friendly crew sitting at the bar. *Double Musky Inn (☎ 783-2822)*, on Crow Creek Rd, is one of the outstanding restaurants in the Anchorage area, specializing in Cajun dishes and blackened steaks and fish. It's open only for dinner and no reservations are taken, so be prepared for a long wait. Dinners cost $17 to $26, but the food is well worth the wait and expense.

At the strip mall along Seward Hwy, there is *Taco's*, where the menu is handwritten in neon chalk on two large blackboards, and the chunky salsa is made fresh daily. Burritos, tamales and nachos are all $4 to $6, or for $5, you can fill up on a chicken taco and a healthy portion of rice or beans. At night, head to *Max's Bar & Grill*, on Crow Creek Rd, a rustic bar with live music on the weekends and jam sessions on Sundays.

PORTAGE

From the Alyeska Access Rd, Seward Hwy continues southeast and, at Mile 81, reaches the **Wetland Observation Platform**, which was constructed by the BLM. The platform features interpretive plaques on the ducks, arctic terns, bald eagles and other wildlife that can often be seen from it.

Portage, the departure point for passengers and cars going to Whittier on the Alaska Railroad, is passed at Mile 80 of Seward Hwy. There is not much left of Portage, which was destroyed by the Good Friday Earthquake, other than a few structures sinking into the nearby mud flats. During the summer, the shuttle train departs the loading ramp several times daily, with one trip connecting with the M/V *Bartlett*, the ferry that cruises from Whittier to Valdez (see the Getting Around chapter).

This lack of development will most likely change after 2000, when the road to Whittier is scheduled to open. The controversial project (see 'A Road to Whittier' boxed text in the Southcentral chapter) is a 2.5-mile toll road that will depart from near Begich-Boggs Visitor Center at Portage Glacier and connect to the Alaska Railroad Tunnel. The tunnel will then be extensively revamped to accommodate trains and vehicles, allowing locals and tourists to drive to the small port on Prince William Sound.

PORTAGE GLACIER

A mile south of the loading ramp in Portage is the junction with Portage Glacier Access Rd. The road leads 5.4 miles past two campgrounds to a visitor center overlooking Portage Glacier, which has surpassed Denali National Park as Alaska's most visited attraction. The magnificent ice floe is 5 miles long and a mile wide at its face and is the Southcentral's version of the drive-in glacier. It's impressive, but in 1880 it filled what is now Portage Lake. Native Alaskans and miners used the ice as a route or 'portage' between Turnagain Arm and Passage Canal.

By 1890, the glacier had begun to retreat, and today more than 2.5 miles of the lake have been exposed. Retreating at more than 300 feet per year, the glacier is now expected to reach the end of the lake by the year 2020. What it will do at that point is anybody's guess.

More than 700,000 people view the glacier annually, with the number increasing sharply each year. This is evident during the summer, as a stream of tour buses and cars is constantly passing through. But even if you're trying to avoid crowds, Portage Glacier is not to be missed, as it is classic Alaskan imagery. The **Begich-Boggs Visitor Center** (☎ 783-2326) is also well worth viewing. The center houses, among other things, a simulated ice cave you can walk through to reach the Glacier Exhibit room, which has displays demonstrating the formation of crevasses, glacial motion and the range of glaciers today. Elsewhere, you can touch an iceberg, brought in fresh daily, take a close look at ice worms or take in the excellent movie *Voices from the Ice,* which is shown every hour in a 200-seat theater. Observation decks and telescopes from which to view the main attraction are scattered around the visitor center. During the summer the center is open 9 am to 6 pm daily.

For those who want to get even closer to the glacier, Gray Line offers hour-long cruises ($25) on board its tour boat, *Ptarmigan.* Don't get this cruise confused with a glacier cruise along Tracy Arm in the Southeast or College Fjord in Prince William Sound; you simply motor around the lake.

Check with the rangers about a planned trail to the face of Portage Glacier. Otherwise, hiking in the area consists of the **Byron Glacier Trail**, an easy 1-mile path to the base of Byron Glacier that begins on the road to the tour-boat dock. Once you reach the permanent snow in front of the glacier, look for ice worms in it. The worms, immortalized in a Robert Service poem, are black, threadlike and less than an inch long. They survive by consuming algae and escape the heat of the sun by sliding between ice crystals of glaciers and snowfields.

Places to Stay
There are only two campgrounds in the area: *Black Bear Campground* (12 sites, $9 fee) and *Williwaw Campground* (60 sites, $10 to $15 fee). Williwaw is particularly pleasant, as there is a salmon-spawning observation deck near it and a mile-long nature walk through beaver and moose habitat. Sites are unavailable late in the day at these campgrounds. With more than 700,000 people coming to see Portage Glacier annually, the facilities always seem to be full.

From Portage, Seward Hwy turns south and heads toward the scenic town of Seward on Resurrection Bay, 128 miles from Anchorage (see the Southcentral chapter).

North of Anchorage

GLENN HIGHWAY
The 189-mile Glenn Hwy begins on the corner of Medfra St and 5th Ave (Mile 0), just west of Merrill Field Airport in Anchorage, and extends to Glennallen and the Richardson Hwy. The first 42 miles head northeast to Palmer, the trade center of the Matanuska Valley, and have been converted into a true highway, featuring four lanes that enable motorists to pass road hogs in their RVs. Just west of Palmer, the Glenn Hwy forms a major junction with the George Parks Hwy. The George Parks Hwy heads to Fairbanks. Glenn Hwy curves east to Glennallen (see the Interior chapter). Mileposts on the highway show distances measured from Anchorage.

On the first 8 miles northeast from Anchorage, you pass the exits to Elmendorf Air Force Base, Centennial Campground and Arctic Valley Rd to Fort Richardson (see the Anchorage section). At Mile 11.5 of Glenn Hwy is the turnoff to *Eagle River State Campground*, on Hiland Rd, with 58 sites for $15 per night. The scenic campground is in a wooded area on the south bank of the Eagle River. The spot is popular and has a four-day limit. Don't drink the glacier-fed water of the Eagle River. Also, don't depend on getting a tent space if you happen to arrive late. This is one of the busiest campgrounds in the state.

Eagle River

At Mile 13.4 of Glenn Hwy is the exit to Old Glenn Hwy, which takes you through the bedroom communities of Eagle River and Chugiak. Eagle River (population 14,000) has a couple of plazas and just about every business you need. Chugiak is almost devoid of any commercial service, and at times it's even hard to know when you have passed through the town.

The **North Anchorage Visitor Center** is an unstaffed center with maps and brochures in the Parkgate Building across from the McDonald's on Old Glenn Hwy. Hours are 10 am to 6 pm. Next door is the **Alaska Museum of Natural History** (☎ 694-0819). Exhibits include Alaskan dinosaurs, the rare Alaskan lion from the Ice Age, minerals, fossils and wildlife displays of black and brown bears. Admission is $3, and hours are 10 am to 5 pm Monday through Saturday in summer.

The main reason to exit at Eagle River is to drive Eagle River Rd. This 12.7-mile road is paved and a beautiful side trip into the Chugach Mountains. It ends at the **Eagle River Nature Center** of the Chugach State Forest. The log cabin center (☎ 694-2108) is open 10 am to 5 pm Tuesday through Saturday and features wildlife displays, handouts for hikers, naturalist programs and telescopes with which to view Dall sheep in the surrounding mountains. There is also an outdoor picnic area with more telescopes and a stunning view of the Chugach Mountains. Admission is a $5 vehicle entry permit.

Hiking Two trails depart from the Eagle River Nature Center. One is the easy **Rodak Nature Trail**, a loop of less than a mile that passes a series of interpretive panels and an impressive observation deck straddling a salmon stream. **Albert Loop Trail** is a 3-mile hike through a boreal forest and along Eagle River.

The nature center also serves as the northern trailhead for the **Historic Iditarod Trail**, a

26-mile trek. Gold miners and dogsled teams used the route until 1918, when the Alaska Railroad was completed from Seward to Fairbanks. It is a three-day hike through excellent mountain scenery and up to Crow Pass, where you can view nearby Raven Glacier and Crystal Lake. From there you hike down the Crow Creek Trail and emerge on Crow Creek Rd, 7 miles away from the Seward Hwy (see the South of Anchorage section in this chapter).

Although this route involves fording several streams, including Eagle River itself, and some climbing to Crow Pass, it is one of the best hikes in the Southcentral and Anchorage regions. Backpackers in Anchorage can reach the junction of Eagle River Rd on People Mover bus No 74 or 76 and, from there, hitch to the visitor center. Or Alaska Backpacker Shuttle (☎ 344-8775) will transport groups of up to six to the center for $90 and then pick them up at the Crow Pass trailhead three days later for $120. Bring a stove, as campfires are not allowed in state park.

Northbound on Glenn Hwy, the Thunderbird Falls exit is reached at Mile 25.2 and leads 0.3 miles to a parking area and the trailhead for the **Thunderbird Falls Trail**. The mile-long trail is a quick uphill climb to the scenic falls formed by a small, rocky gorge. At the end is a deck with benches overlooking the cascade, a great place to enjoy lunch.

Places to Stay & Eat If the public campgrounds are filled and you're too tired to hassle with Anchorage, try the *Eagle River Motel* (☎ 694-5000, 11111 Old Eagle River Rd), which includes a Laundromat. Singles/doubles cost $76/85. There are also a dozen B&Bs in Eagle River. *Randy's Valley B&B* (☎ 694-8266, 10131 Chandalar St) is in the center of town and has three rooms for $65 to $75, and the host speaks German.

In town, there is a *Safeway* (12001 Business Blvd) with a salad bar and ready-to-eat items, and the *Sleepy Dog Coffee Co* (11525 Old Glenn Hwy) for a latte ($1.75 to $3.25) and an opportunity to surf the Internet. At night, the coffee club hops with live music and an open mike on Thursdays. Another

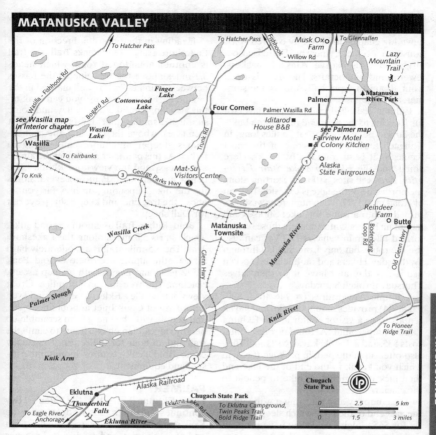

MATANUSKA VALLEY

excellent coffeehouse with music is **Jitters** *(11401 Old Glenn Hwy)*, in Eagle River Shopping Center, decorated in antiques and 1930s coffee memorabilia.

There are also the usual fast-food chains: McDonald's, Taco Bell, Subway and Pizza Hut. The best eatery is **Bombay Restaurant** *(11401 Old Glenn Hwy)*, in the Eagle River Shopping Center. The Indian cuisine is good enough for locals to justify the drive from Anchorage. **North Slope Restaurant** *(11501 Old Glenn Hwy)* includes a microbrewery (try the Copper River Amber) and live music on the weekends in a tavern

adorned with stuffed animals. There's dancing on the weekends at **Tips Bar** *(12349 Old Glenn Hwy)*.

Eklutna

The Native Alaskan village of Eklutna (population 434) is reached by taking the Eklutna Lake Rd exit at Mile 26.5 of Glenn Hwy and heading west. Dating back to 1650, Eklutna is the oldest continually inhabited Athabascan site in the region. Much of that history can be seen at the **Eklutna Village Historical Park** (☎ 696-2828). The park contains the Heritage House with displays on the indigenous lifestyle and art; the St Nicholas Russian Orthodox Church, a hand-hewn log chapel; and brightly colored spirit houses in a cemetery nearby. There is also a gift shop with Native Alaskan baskets, jewelry and handicrafts. The park is open from 10 am to 6 pm daily during the summer; admission is $3.50.

Eklutna Lake Rd bumps and winds east for 10 miles, to the west end of Eklutna Lake, the largest body of water (at 7 miles long) in Chugach State Park and one of the most scenic, as it is surrounded by peaks. Here you'll find the *Eklutna Lake State Recreation Area* (50 sites, $10 fee). Skirting along the north side of the lake is **Lakeside Trail**, an old road until 1977, when numerous washouts turned it into a route for hikers, horses and mountain bikers. Unfortunately, those on motorized all-terrain vehicles (ATVs) can also use the route, but only from Sunday through Wednesday. Hikers and mountain bikers can use it any day and have it to themselves Thursday through Saturday.

Lifetime Adventures (☎ 746-4644, 800-952-8624) provides mountain bike and kayak rentals from a visitor center at the Eklutna Lake Campground. A full-day bike rental costs $35, and a double kayak costs $45. They also offer a paddle/peddle package ($65), in which you kayak to the end of the lake and then pick up a mountain bike to peddle to the glacier.

The company also rents out a wall tent at the east end of the lake, which sleeps four to six for $45 a night. And they have drop-off and pickup service via a 21-foot pontoon boat. A trip down the lake costs $10 per person.

Hiking There is a separate parking lot for the trailhead with a $5-per-vehicle fee, a trail information kiosk and telescopes for viewing Dall sheep. Lakeshore Trail begins on the other side of Twin Peaks Creek and is an easy one-way walk of 13 miles. There are even mile markers and free campsites at Eklutna Alex Campground at Mile 9 and Kanchee Campground at Mile 11. If you are staying overnight, plan on hiking **Eklutna Glacier Trail** just past Mile 12. The 0.75-mile

trail ends at interpretive panels and a view of the glacier.

Heading in the opposite direction of the Lakeshore Trail is **Twin Peaks Trail**. The trail is another abandoned road, which heads 3.2 miles above the tree line to the passes between Twin Peaks. It is well marked in the beginning, and halfway up, you can soak up the views of the lake and valley and some sun, if it's shining that day (chances are it won't be). Above the tree line, the trail becomes steeper and more challenging to follow. At this point, scrambling in the alpine area is easy and the views of Eklutna Lake below are excellent. Plan on several hours for the hike, depending on how far you go above the tree line, and keep a sharp eye out for Dall sheep.

Bold Ridge Trail is another good hike, which starts 5.5 miles along the Lakeshore Trail. The 3.5-mile trail is a moderately hard hike to the alpine area below Bold Peak (7522 feet) and begins with a steep ascent, reaching the tree line in 1.5 miles. Great views of the valley, Eklutna Glacier and even Knik Arm of Cook Inlet are obtained here, and people with the energy can scramble up nearby ridges. Plan on two hours to climb the trail and an hour for the return. To actually climb Bold Peak requires mountaineering skill and equipment.

PALMER

From Eklutna Lake Rd, the Glenn Hwy continues north, crosses bridges over the Knik and Matanuska Rivers at the northern end of Cook Inlet, and at Mile 35.3 reaches a major junction with the George Parks Hwy. At this point, Glenn Hwy curves sharply to the east and heads into Palmer (population 4385), 7 miles away. If you are driving, a much more scenic way to reach Palmer is to leave Glenn Hwy just before it crosses Knik River and follow Old Glenn Hwy into town.

History

Although a train station was built here in 1916, Palmer was really born in 1935, when it was selected for an unusual social experiment during President Franklin Roosevelt's

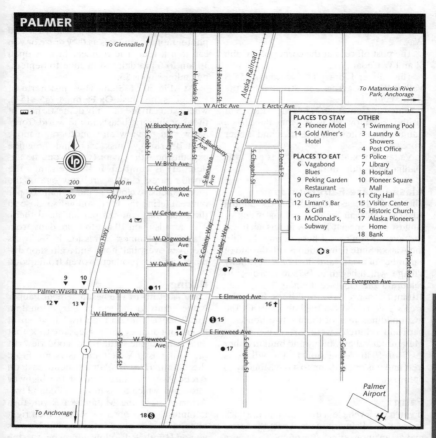

PALMER

To Glennallen

To Matanuska River
Park, Anchorage →

W Arctic Ave   E Arctic Ave

2 ■

W Blueberry Ave   ● 3

W Birch Ave

W Cottonwood Ave

E Cottonwood Ave

★ 5

W Cedar Ave

W Dogwood Ave

6 ▼

W Dahlia Ave   E Dahlia Ave

● 7

9   10
▼   ▼

Palmer-Wasilla Rd   W Evergreen Ave   ● 11   E Evergreen Ave

12 ▼   13 ▼

W Elmwood Ave   E Elmwood Ave

16 †

14 ■   ℹ 15

W Fireweed Ave   E Fireweed Ave

● 17

To Anchorage   18 ⑤

Palmer Airport

0   200   400 m
0   200   400 yards

Glenn Hwy

N Alaska St   N Bonanza St   Alaska Railroad
S Cobb St   S Bailey St   S Alaska Ave   E Blueberry Ave   S Bonanza Ave   S Colony Way   S Valley Way   S Denali St   S Chugach St   S Gulkana St   S Dimond St   Airport Rd

PLACES TO STAY	OTHER
2 Pioneer Motel	1 Swimming Pool
14 Gold Miner's Hotel	3 Laundry & Showers
	4 Post Office
PLACES TO EAT	5 Police
6 Vagabond Blues	7 Library
9 Peking Garden Restaurant	8 Hospital
10 Carrs	10 Pioneer Square Mall
12 Limani's Bar & Grill	11 City Hall
13 McDonald's, Subway	15 Visitor Center
	16 Historic Church
	17 Alaska Pioneers Home
	18 Bank

ANCHORAGE

New Deal relief programs. Some 200 farming families, hit hard by the Great Depression in the US Midwest, were moved north to raise crops and livestock in the Matanuska and Susitna Valleys.

The failure rate was high within this transplanted agricultural colony, but somehow Palmer survived, and today it is the only community in Alaska whose economy is based primarily on farming. The farms of the Matanuska Valley grow 60lb cabbages and 7lb turnips as a result of the midnight sun that shines up to 20 hours a day during the summer.

Information

Stop at the Palmer Visitor Center (☎ 745-2880), a rustic log cabin near the corner of Fireweed Ave and S Valley Way in the center of town. Open 8 am to 6 pm daily, the center has a small museum in the basement with relics from its 'colony' era. Outside are a picnic area and the **Matanuska Valley Agricultural Showcase**, a garden of flowers and the area's famous oversized vegetables. To see cabbages the size of basketballs or radishes that look like red softballs, you have to come from late July to late August. It is open 8 am to 7 pm daily in the summer.

Palmer has four banks, including Key Bank of Alaska (☎ 745-6100), 1150 S Colony Way.

The post office is at the corner of S Cobb St and W Cedar Ave.

The Palmer Library (☎ 745-4690), 655 S Valley Way, is across the street from the visitor center.

Gateway Center (☎ 745-6161), Mile 6.5 of Fishhook-Willow Rd to Hatcher Pass, has a Laundromat, showers, groceries and a beer store.

Valley Hospital (☎ 746-8600) is at 515 E Dahlia, east of the library.

Alaska State Fairgrounds

The town's biggest attraction is the annual Alaska State Fair, held in the last week of August (see Special Events in this section). But even if you're not here during the fair, the Alaska State Fairground is still the site of a number of events and the home of **Colony Village**, which began in 1975 as a project to celebrate the US bicentennial. The village attempts to preserve buildings from the area's 'colony' days of the late 1930s. Of the five buildings, four of them – two houses, a barn and a church – were part of the original Matanuska Valley Colony and built in either 1935 or 1936. Admission to the village is free, and it is open 10 am to 4 pm Monday to Saturday.

Farms

If you have a vehicle, a drive around the back roads of the Palmer area and past the farms makes an interesting afternoon. To view a few of the colony farms that survived, along with the original barns, head northeast 9 miles on Glenn Hwy and exit onto Farm Loop Rd. Keep an eye out for vegetable stands if you're passing through the area from mid- to late summer. The **Matanuska Farm Market** is at Mile 38 of the Glenn Hwy, and **Pyrah's Pioneer Peak Farm** is a pick-your-own-vegetables farm just before Mile 3 of Bodenberg Loop Rd south of Palmer.

At Mile 11.5 of Old Glenn Hwy, you pass near a farm of a different sort – one that raises reindeer. Turn onto Bodenberg Loop Rd, and within a mile, you'll reach the **Reindeer Farm** (☎ 745-4000). You can view and photograph the animals as they graze or you can join a tour. The reindeer farm is open 10 am to 6 pm daily from June to September; admission is $5.

At Mile 50 of Glenn Hwy, just north of Palmer, is the **Musk Ox Farm** (☎ 745-4151), where you can see the only domestic herd of these prehistoric beasts in the world. Tours allow you to view and photograph more than 100 shaggy musk oxen, and the guide explains how the qiviut (wool from the undercoat) is combed and woven into the world's rarest cloth – probably one of the most expensive cloths, at more than $60 per ounce. During the tour, you get so close to the oxen that you can pet and feed them. The farm is open 10 am to 6 pm daily from May to September; admission is $8. Tours are given every half hour, and a gift shop displays and sells products woven from qiviut.

Hiking

Lazy Mountain The best hike near Palmer is the climb to the top of Lazy Mountain (3720 feet). The 2.5-mile trail is steep at times, but makes for a pleasant trek that ends in an alpine setting with good views of the Matanuska Valley and its farms. From the Glenn Hwy in Palmer, head east on Arctic Ave, the third exit off the highway into town, which turns into Old Glenn Hwy. After crossing the Matanuska River, turn left into Clark-Wolverine Rd and then right after half a mile at a T intersection. This puts you on Huntly Rd; follow it for a mile, to the Equestrian Center parking lot at its end. The trailhead, marked 'Foot Trail,' is on the north side of the parking lot. Plan on three to five hours for the roundtrip.

McRoberts Creek Trail This is a backcountry hike up the McRoberts Creek valley and provides an easy approach to climbing Matanuska Peak (6119 feet). The trail reaches the tree line in 2.5 miles and 3880-foot Summit Ridge in 9 miles. The trek to Matanuska Peak would be an 18-mile hike. To reach the trailhead, take Old Glenn

Hwy from Palmer toward Butte and turn left onto Smith Rd at Mile 15.5. Follow Smith Rd for 1.4 miles, until it curves into Harmony Ave. There is no parking at the South Fork trailhead, so leave the car at the bend in the road.

Pioneer Ridge Trail This is a 5.7-mile route from Knik River Rd to the main ridge that extends southeast from Pioneer Peaks (6400 feet). The first half of the climb is through birch, cottonwood and alder, until you reach the alpine tundra at 3200 feet. Once you are on the ridge, South Pioneer Peak is a mile to the northwest and North Pioneer Peak is 2 miles away. To scale, either one requires rock-climbing experience and equipment. To the southeast, the ridge leads toward Bold Peak, the Hunter Creek drainage and eventually Eklutna Lake. To reach the trailhead, turn into Knik River Rd, just before crossing the river on Old Glenn Hwy, and follow it for almost 4 miles.

Organized Tours
Want to see a glacier? Knik Glacier Adventures (☎ 746-5133) offers a four-hour airboat tour of the 3-mile-long Knik Glacier at 10 am and 3:30 pm daily. It's $65 per person but includes a barbecue meal at the face of the glacier.

Special Events
The best reason to stop in Palmer is the Alaska State Fair, an 11-day event that ends on Labor Day. The fair features produce and livestock from the surrounding area, horse shows, a rodeo, a carnival and the largest cabbages you'll ever see.

There is more to eat at the fair than just corn dogs and cotton candy. You can feast on fresh salads, homemade desserts, seafood and barbecue ribs and chicken.

Within the state fairgrounds is the outdoor Borealis Theater, and during the 4th of July weekend, it is the site of a bluegrass festival worth attending if you are passing through. Admission to the fair is $8. For information on events and entertainment, call the fair office (☎ 745-4827).

Places to Stay
Like many Alaskan communities, Palmer has an 8% bed tax.

Camping You can pitch a tent or park a trailer at *Matanuska River Park*, less than a half mile east of town on Old Glenn Hwy. One half of the campground features wooded sites for $10 per night, showers and a series of trails that wind around ponds and along the Matanuska River. The other half is an open day-use area that includes a large softball complex.

B&Bs Outside the Palmer Visitor Center is a rack for the local B&Bs; you'll find more than a dozen in the area. You can also call the Mat-Su chapter of the B&B Association of Alaska (☎ 376-4461, 800-401-7444) in advance for a room in a B&B.

About a mile west of Palmer is *Iditarod House* (☎ 745-4348, iditabed@matnet.com, 12100 Woodstock Drive), on 7 secluded acres with a view of the mountains. There are two double rooms for $55 a night.

Hotels The cheapest hotel in town is the *Pioneer Motel* (☎ 745-3425), at N Alaska St and W Arctic Ave, where a double costs $53 per night in rooms that are small but clean, with some featuring kitchenettes. Also in Palmer is the *Gold Miner's Hotel* (☎ 745-6160, 800-725-2752, frontdesk@goldminers .com), W Elmwood Ave and S Colony Way, with doubles or singles from $70 to $90. The *Fairview Motel* (☎ 745-1505), across from the state fairgrounds, has singles/doubles for $54/65 and rooms with kitchenettes for $5 more.

Places to Eat
Palmer has a *McDonald's* and a *Subway* at the intersection of the Glenn and Palmer-Wasilla Hwys, and other fast-food chains will begin appearing soon. For something a little more personal, try *Colony Kitchen (1890 Glenn Hwy)*, next door to the Fairview Motel. A skillet of eggs and potatoes or homemade biscuits and gravy costs $6 and can be enjoyed in an interesting interior with

stuffed birds suspended from the ceiling (thus the restaurant's nickname, 'the Noisy Goose Cafe').

Vagabond Blues (642 S Alaska St), in the heart of Palmer, is a bakery, restaurant and coffeehouse with live music at night. The strawberry pie and homemade soups are excellent, or lunch on bagel sandwiches and pasta salads. *Limani's Bar & Grill* (800 W Evergreen) also has good food, a kickback atmosphere and blues and jazz musicians most weekends.

Carrs, in Pioneer Square Mall on Glenn Hwy, has cheap eats, and *Peking Garden* (775 W Evergreen), next to the mall, has an all-you-can-eat lunch buffet Sunday through Friday for $7. Dinners cost $8 to $15.

HATCHER PASS

Just northeast of Palmer, via the Fishhook-Willow Rd off Glenn Hwy, is the Hatcher Pass area (see the Interior map in the Interior chapter), an alpine paradise filled with panoramas of the Talkeetna Mountains, foot trails, gold-mine artifacts and even some unusual lodging possibilities. The area is probably the most photographed in the Mat-Su Valley and can be entered from either Wasilla, Willow or Palmer, but the drive from Palmer is the shortest and most scenic, as it follows the Little Susitna River through a steep-walled gorge. It also has the most traffic, making hitching a lot easier for those without a set of wheels.

The pass itself is 22 miles out of Palmer and, at 3886 feet, is an alpine area of meadows, ridges, steep drops and a beautiful body of water known as Summit Lake. It's also a popular destination for parasailing and, on most calm evenings, you can sit on a ridge and watch the daredevils strap themselves to the colorful sails and glide with the wind.

Independence Mine State Historical Park

This fascinating 272-acre state historical park, 18 miles north of Palmer, is entirely above the tree line. Within the beautiful bowl-shaped valley of the park are the remains of 16 buildings that were built in the 1930s by the Alaska-Pacific Mining Com-

pany (APC), which for 10 years was second only to Juneau's A-J Mine as the leading hardrock gold mine in Alaska.

Gold was first discovered in the area by a pair of Japanese prospectors shortly after 1900, and the rough nature of the gold was an indication to many miners that there was a mother lode waiting to be found higher in the Talkeetna Mountains. Robert Lee Hatcher discovered and staked the first lode claim in Willow Creek Valley in 1906, and within a few years, mining took off. From 1906 until 1950, more than 50 gold mines were worked in the Hatcher Pass area. The two most productive mines were the Alaska Free Gold Mine on Skyscraper Mountain and Independence Mine on Granite Mountain.

In 1938, the two mines were consolidated by APC, which controls a block of 83 mining permits, 1350 acres and 27 structures. At its peak, in 1941, APC employed 204 workers, blasted almost 12 miles of tunnels and recovered 34,416oz of gold worth $1.2 million. Today that gold would be worth almost $18 million.

WWII shut down the Independence Mine in 1943. The mine reopened in 1948 and briefly in 1950 before being finally abandoned in 1955. Now a state park, the Independence Mine and the company town that was built around it make for a fascinating afternoon. Admission is $5 per vehicle, but the state division of parks is considering turning the operation of the park over to a private company, so the admission price may change. Without an adequate budget for massive rehabilitation, state officials fear many of the buildings will soon collapse.

Begin at the Manager's House, which has been converted into a visitor center. There are video interviews of the old miners, displays on the different ways to mine gold (panning, placer mining and hardrock) and even a simulated mining tunnel.

The visitor center (☎ 745-2827) is open 11 am to 7 pm daily and can provide a walking-tour map of the park and a list of area hikes. Guided tours are conducted at 1:30 and 3:30 pm daily for an additional small fee.

Independence Mine State Historical Park

Little Susitna River, north of Palmer

Downtown Anchorage

Hikers along the Historic Iditarod Trail

Eklutna Lake from the Lakeside Trail

Potter Marsh, birding near Anchorage

From the center, follow Hardrock Trail past the buildings, which include bunkhouses and a mill complex that is built into the side of the mountain and looks like an avalanche of falling timber. Make an effort to climb up the trail to the water tunnel portal, where there is a great overview of the entire complex and a blast of cold air pouring out of the mountain.

Hiking

Gold Mint Trail This is one of the easiest hikes in the Hatcher Pass area. It begins at a parking lot across from Motherlode Lodge at Mile 14 of the Fishhook-Willow Rd. The trail follows the Little Susitna River into a gently sloping mountain valley. Within 3 miles you can spot the ruins of Lonesome Mine. Keep hiking, and you will eventually reach the head of the river at Mint Glacier.

Reed Lakes Trail A mile past Motherlode Lodge, a road to Archangel Valley splits off from Fishhook-Willow Rd and leads to the trailhead of Reed Lakes. The trail begins as a wide road and soon climbs to the crest of the valley. Lower Reed Lake is reached within a quarter mile after reaching the crest; Upper Reed Lake follows after a bit more climbing.

Craigie Creek Trail This trail, posted along the Fishhook-Willow Rd west of Hatcher Pass, actually starts out as a road that is occasionally used by 4WD vehicles. The trail follows a valley up to the head of the creek, where it's possible to cross a pass into the Independence Mine Bowl. The road climbs gently for 4 miles past several abandoned mining operations and then becomes a very steep trail for 3 miles to Dogsled Pass.

Places to Stay & Eat

At Mile 14 of Fishhook-Willow Rd is *Motherlode Lodge* (☎ 746-1464), which was originally built in the 1930s as part of the local mining operation. Today, it's been totally renovated and has double rooms for $68 a night, including breakfast. There is also a dining room here, with superb views of the mountains from every table, and a bar where you can sit out on the deck and take in more panoramas.

Closer to the pass itself, within Independence Mine State Park, is *Hatcher Pass Lodge* (☎ 745-5897), Mile 17.5 Fishhook-Willow Rd. Small cabins cost $115 a night per couple, and rooms cost $70. Both prices include breakfast. This lodge also has a restaurant, a bar where you can enjoy your favorite brew at 3000 feet above sea level, and a sauna built over a rushing mountain stream.

Getting Around

There is no place to rent a car in Palmer. Instead, head to Wasilla and pick up a vehicle at Denali Motors (☎ 376-1230).

ANCHORAGE

Southcentral Alaska

Known by many as the Gulf Coast region, Southcentral Alaska is really a continuation of Alaska's rugged coastal playground that begins in Ketchikan. Both Southeast and Southcentral Alaska boast spectacular scenery with glaciers, fjords and mountain ranges half buried by ice fields and covered at the base by lush forest; both areas are also affected by the Japanese Current, which produces a wet but mild climate. Fishing is an important industry in these regions, and the Alaska Marine Hwy ferry is one of the main modes of transportation.

Highlights

- Marvel at Columbia Glacier on a boat tour from Valdez

- Enjoy breakfast on the porch of the Kennicott Glacier Lodge and then visit the abandoned town of Kennicott

- See seals and humpback whales on a wildlife cruise in Kenai Fjords National Park

- Touch a sea anemone, pick up a starfish and watch puffins swim at Seward's Alaska SeaLife Center

- Dig for razor clams at Clam Gulch State Recreation Area

- Camp in front of Grewingk Glacier at Kachemak Bay State Park

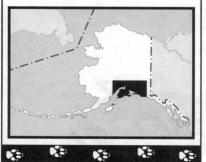

But Southcentral Alaska (the region around Prince William Sound and the Gulf of Alaska) has one important feature that the Panhandle (Southeast) doesn't have – a road system linking many of the towns. This alone makes Southcentral Alaska one of the cheapest, most accessible and most popular areas in the state to visit.

Southcentral can be divided into two main areas: Prince William Sound and the Kenai Peninsula. The first includes the communities of Cordova, Valdez and Whittier and features towering mountains, glaciers and abundant marine wildlife.

To the west of Prince William Sound, the Kenai Peninsula includes the towns of Seward, Kenai, Soldotna and Homer. This great forested plateau, bounded by the Kenai Mountains and the Harding Ice Field to the east, is broken up by hundreds of lakes, rivers and streams, making it an outdoor paradise for hikers, canoeists and anglers – as well as RVers, tour groups and almost half of Alaska's population, which lives just to the north in Anchorage. Because of this easy accessibility, facilities and lodging in the Kenai can get surprisingly crowded during the short tourist season.

Prince William Sound

Prince William Sound, the northern extent of the Gulf of Alaska, rivals the Southeast for the steepest fjords and the most spectacular coastlines and glaciers. The Sound is a marvelous wilderness area of islands, inlets, fjords, lush rain forests and towering mountains. Flanked to the west by the Kenai Mountains and to the north and east by the Chugach Mountains, Prince William Sound covers 15,000 sq miles and boasts abundant wildlife, including whales, sea lions, harbor seals, otters, eagles, Dall sheep, mountain goats and, of course, bears.

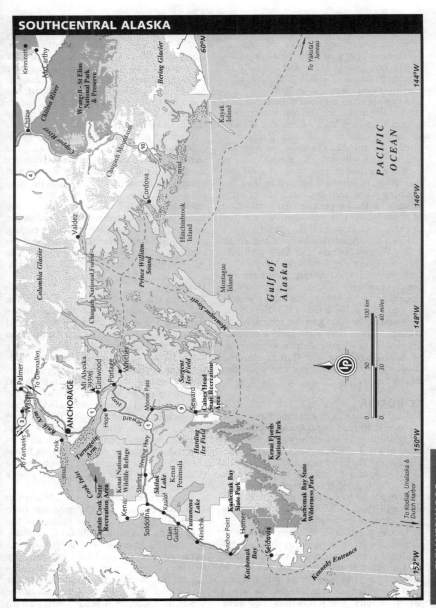

SOUTHCENTRAL ALASKA

Kennicott
McCarthy
Chitina
Chitina River
Copper River
Wrangell - St Elias National Park & Preserve
Bering Glacier
60°N
To Yakutat, Juneau
144°W

Columbia Glacier
Chugach Mountains
10
Cordova
mud
Kayak Island
PACIFIC OCEAN
146°W

Valdez
Chugach National Forest
Hinchinbrook Island
Prince William Sound
Montague Island
Gulf of Alaska
148°W

To Ottennallen,
Palmer
Wasilla
ANCHORAGE
Mt Alyeska 3939ft
Girdwood
Portage
Whittier
Moose Pass
Surgent Ice Field
Seward
Caines Head State Recreation Area

Hope
Seward Hwy
Sterling Hwy
Sterling
Kenai National Wildlife Refuge
Turnagain Arm
Kenai
Soldotna
Skilak Lake
Kasilof Lake
Kenai Peninsula
Tustamena Lake
Clam Gulch
Ninilchik
Anchor Point
Homer
Kachemak Bay State Park
Kachemak Bay State Wilderness Park
Kenai Fjords National Park
Harding Ice Field
Captain Cook State Recreation Area
Cook Inlet
Knik Arm
Knik
mud
3
To Fairbanks

Kachemak Bay
Seldovia
To Kodiak, Unalaska & Dutch Harbor
Kennedy Entrance
152°W
150°W

0   50   100 km
0   30   60 miles

Another trait the Sound shares with the Southeast is rain – lots of rain. The area receives an average of well over 100 inches of precipitation per year, with the fishing town of Cordova getting 167 inches annually, including 80 inches of snowfall. Summer temperatures range from 54° to 70°F.

At center stage in Prince William Sound is the Columbia Glacier. The bluish wall of ice, named after New York's Columbia University, is one of the most spectacular tidewater glaciers on the Alaskan coast, as it covers 440 sq miles with ice. The glacier's face is 3 miles wide, and in some places it is 262 feet high. If you're passing the glacier by boat, the stunning scene includes hundreds of seals sunning on the ice pack against a backdrop of mountains. You can usually hear the thunder of ice calving off the glacier's face.

From Southeast Alaska, you can reach Prince William Sound via an Alaska Airlines flight to Cordova or the Alaska Marine Hwy ferry to Valdez. At Valdez, you have the option of returning to the road if you're continuing on to Anchorage, but most travelers elect to stay on the ferry to Whittier on the west side of the sound, as this section of the Alaska Marine Hwy passes the Columbia Glacier. From Whittier, there is a rail service to Anchorage (see the Getting Around chapter). From Valdez, you can reach the city by bus.

CORDOVA

Nestled between Orca Inlet and Lake Eyak and overshadowed by Mt Eccles, Cordova is a beautiful little fishing town on the east coast of Prince William Sound. An isolated place worth the extra time and expense of a visit, Cordova is inaccessible by road (you'll notice the lack of RVs) and for years had been bypassed by the large cruise-ship lines that spill thousands of tourists into every major town in the Southeast.

This changed in 1998, when Norwegian Cruise Line began stopping at Cordova, unloading 800 passengers into the downtown area a dozen times during the summer. It remains to be seen whether other cruise lines will follow and whether this traffic will affect the city. Many travelers who have

been to Cordova fear this invasion of cruise ships and their tennis-shoe crowds. In the past, if you were an independent traveler, Cordova is where you went to get a feel for the real Alaska without the inflated prices or packaged approach that large tour companies have forced on Juneau or Seward. But some say it was just a matter of time before the cruise lines discovered the area's unique charm and moved in to profit from it.

Cordova has about 2400 permanent residents, but its population doubles during the summer, with an influx of fishers and cannery workers; the town's economy is centered around its fishing fleet and fish-processing plants. The area around Cordova is an outdoor paradise, and the town offers easy access to 14 USFS cabins, some good alpine hiking and the Copper River Delta, a nesting area for millions of birds. Childs Glacier is perhaps the most active and spectacular Alaskan glacier that can be reached by road.

History

The area was first settled by nomadic Eyak Indians who were drawn down the Copper River by the enormous salmon runs and abundance of shellfish. The first European in the area was Vitus Bering, a Danish navigator sailing for the tsar of Russia. He anchored his ship near Kayak Island, east of Copper River, in 1741, and 50 years later the Russians had established an outpost at Nuchek, a Chugach Inuit village on Hinchinbrook Island. But the Chugach Inuit, Eyaks and the Tlingits from the Yakutat area refused to hunt sea otters for the Russians, forcing the fur traders to bring Aleuts from the Aleutian Islands. Eventually the Aleuts intermarried, and today the Aleut language is the most common Native language in the area.

Early US fishers built a cannery here in 1889, but modern-day Cordova was born when Michael J Heney, the builder of the White Pass & Yukon Railroad from Skagway to Whitehorse, arrived in 1906. At that point, he had decided to transform the summer cannery site into the railroad terminus for his line from the Kennecott copper mines near McCarthy. Construction of the $23 million Copper River & Northwestern

CORDOVA

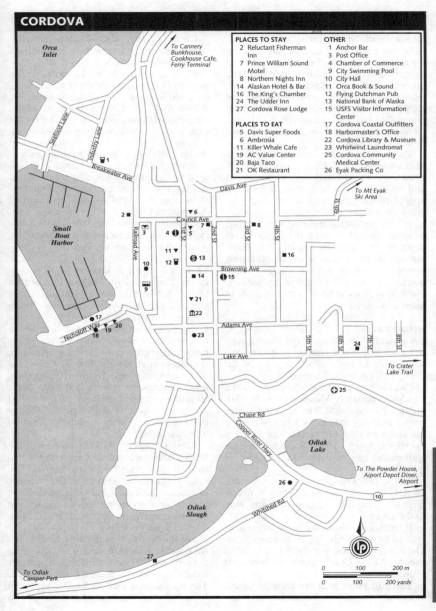

Orca Inlet

To Cannery
Bunkhouse,
Cookhouse Cafe,
Ferry Terminal

Seafood Lane

Industry Lane

Breakwater Ave

Small
Boat
Harbor

Railroad Ave

1st St

2nd St

3rd St

6th St

Davis Ave

Council Ave

Browning Ave

Adams Ave

Lake Ave

4th St

5th St

6th St

7th St

8th St

Nicholoff Way

To Mt Eyak
Ski Area

To Crater
Lake Trail

Chase Rd

Copper River Hwy

Odiak
Lake

Odiak
Slough

Whitshed Rd

To The Powder House,
Aiport Depot Diner,
Airport

To Odiak
Camper Park

PLACES TO STAY
2 Reluctant Fisherman Inn
7 Prince William Sound Motel
8 Northern Nights Inn
14 Alaskan Hotel & Bar
16 The King's Chamber
24 The Udder Inn
27 Cordova Rose Lodge

PLACES TO EAT
5 Davis Super Foods
6 Ambrosia
11 Killer Whale Cafe
19 AC Value Center
20 Baja Taco
21 OK Restaurant

OTHER
1 Anchor Bar
3 Post Office
4 Chamber of Commerce
9 City Swimming Pool
10 City Hall
11 Orca Book & Sound
12 Flying Dutchman Pub
13 National Bank of Alaska
15 USFS Visitor Information Center
17 Cordova Coastal Outfitters
18 Harbormaster's Office
22 Cordova Library & Museum
23 Whirlwind Laundromat
25 Cordova Community Medical Center
26 Eyak Packing Co

0   100   200 m
0   100   200 yards

SOUTHCENTRAL

Railroad began that year and was completed in 1911 – another amazing engineering feat by the 'Irish Prince.'

Within five years, Cordova was a boomtown, with more than $32 million worth of copper ore passing through its docks. The railroad and town prospered until 1938, when labor strikes and the declining price of copper permanently closed the Kennecott mines. The railroad ceased operations, and Cordova turned to fishing, its main economic base today.

The town's dependence on fishing explains why the 1989 Exxon oil spill devastated Cordova. Although most of the halibut and salmon swimming beneath the oil appear to have survived, the mishap canceled or postponed the fishing seasons in 1989. Commercial fishing boats were left idle, while stories of lifelong fishers breaking down in tears as they steered their boats through the slick were common. The only saving grace for the industry was that Exxon was forced into leasing many of the commercial fishing boats at $3400 a day or more to assist with the cleanup.

Information

For general information about Cordova, go to the Chamber of Commerce (☎ 424-7260, www.ptialaska.net/~cchamber), on 1st St. It's open 8 am to 4 pm weekdays.

But the best place for information is the Cordova Library & Museum (☎ 424-6665), Adams Ave at 1st St. The museum visitor center not only maintains a brochure rack but also a very helpful traveler's information notebook. As an added bonus, the museum staff will let you store a bag in the lobby for a few hours.

The USFS Visitor Information Center (☎ 424-7661), 612 2nd St, can help with any question about hiking, camping or kayaking in the area.

If you need cash, try the National Bank of Alaska (☎ 424-3258), 510 1st St across from Davis Super Foods, and there's an ATM in the AC Value Center store on Nicholoff Way.

The post office is at the corner of Railroad and Council Aves. You can access email

or surf the Internet at the Cordova Library & Museum, in the Centennial Building.

Cordova Travel (☎ 424-7102) is in the Reluctant Fisherman Inn on the corner of Railroad and Council Aves.

If you're looking for books about Alaska, head to Orca Book & Sound (☎ 424-7733), on 1st St in the same building as the Killer Whale Cafe, next door to the Cordova Chamber of Commerce. You can also try the Cordova Library & Museum (☎ 424-6667), Adams Ave at 1st St in the Centennial Building. It's open Tuesday to Saturday.

Wash clothes or take a shower at Whirlwind Laundromat (☎ 424-5110) at 1st St and Adams Ave. You can also shower at the City Swimming Pool (☎ 424-7200), on Railroad Ave next to City Hall.

Cordova Community Medical Center (☎ 424-8000), on Chase Rd, is a 22-bed hospital with emergency services.

Things to See & Do

In the Centennial Building is the **Cordova Library & Museum**, a small but interesting museum with displays on marine life, relics from the town's early history and the nearby Kennecott mine, Russian artifacts and a three-seater *bidarka* (kayak-style boat) made with spruce and 12 sealskins. At 3 pm, the museum shows the film *The Cordova Story*, covering local history. It also rents tapes and cassette players ($9) that offer a 60-minute, self-guided tour of town. The museum is open 10 am to 6 pm Monday through Saturday in the summer. Admission is by donation.

More natural exhibits can be seen at the **USFS Visitor Information Center**, in the historic former courthouse on 2nd St. The office features a whale skull; wildlife mounts, including a bald eagle, sea otter and beaver; and information on the area's amazing bird migration and hiking opportunities. It's open 8 am to 5 pm weekdays.

For the best view of the area, head to the **Mt Eyak Ski Area**, at the end of 6th St. During the summer, the Sheridan Ski Club operates its vintage chair lift if there is enough interest. The lift was first used in Sun Valley, Idaho from 1936 to 1969 before being shipped to

Alaska in 1974. At Sun Valley, it carried a number of famous people, including Clark Gable and Marilyn Monroe, John Wayne, Groucho Marx and Ernest Hemingway.

The ride up is a slow, relaxing trip that's perfect for taking in the stunning scenery. From the top, you can view Hawkins Island and Orca Inlet to the northwest; you may glimpse pods of killer whales there. To the south is the entrance to the Gulf of Alaska and southeast is the Copper River Delta. The club (☎ 424-7766) operates the chair Monday, Friday and Saturday, with a minimum of six people. Rides cost $7 per person.

Heading north on Railroad Ave from the city swimming pool, you'll reach the **small boat harbor**. In 1984, the harbor doubled in size to 845 slips, and it is now one of the five largest harbors in the state. More than in any other Alaskan town, with the exception of Petersburg, the harbor is the heart of this community. Between seasons and on weekends, it hums with the activity of boats and fishers. Surrounding the row of commercial fishing boats are marine supply businesses and processing plants. Cordova's fleet is composed primarily of salmon seiners and gillnetters, and the season runs from mid-May into September. Dungeness and tanner crabs are harvested for a few months during the summer and later in the winter.

To see where the catch is processed, ask at the Chamber of Commerce office about canneries offering tours or call **Eyak Packing Company** (☎ 424-5300). This small company, at the corner of the Copper River Hwy and Whitshed Rd, is a smokery and cannery that specializes in mail-order canned salmon. The owners give tours that include salmon-tasting opportunities. To purchase fresh seafood, head over to **Silver Lining/Norquest** (☎ 424-5390), on Railroad Ave across from City Hall, or **North Pacific Processors** (☎ 424-7111), on Seafood Lane.

Hiking

More than 35 miles of trails are accessible from Cordova roads. Several of these paths lead to USFS cabins (see Places to Stay, below). As in much of the Southeast, the hiking in this area is excellent, combining a lush forest with alpine terrain, great views and glaciers. For transportation to the trailheads, call Copper River/Northwest Tours (☎ 424-5356), which offers a drop-off and pickup service for $1 a mile.

Before venturing into the surrounding area, hikers should first stop at the USFS Visitor Information Center (☎ 424-7661), on the corner of Browning Ave and 2nd St, to pick up an assortment of free trail maps. It's open 8 am to 5 pm weekdays.

Mt Eyak Ski Hill After a quick scramble up the ski hill at the end of 6th Ave, hardy hikers can spend a day climbing from here to the top of Mt Eyak and down the other side to Crater Lake.

Crater Lake & Power Creek Trails The 2.4-mile Crater Lake Trail begins on Eyak Lake, about half a mile beyond the Municipal Airfield on Eyak Lake Rd across from Skaters Cabin. The trail ascends steeply but is easy to follow as it winds through lush forest. At the top, it offers panoramic views of both the Copper River Delta and Prince William Sound. Plan on two to four hours for the roundtrip from the road to the open country around Crater Lake.

Once at the lake, you can continue with a 5.5-mile ridge route to Alice Smith Cutoff, which descends to Power Creek Trail. The entire loop would be a 12-mile trek or an ideal overnight backpacking trip. Halfway along the ridge is a free-use shelter, while at the east end of Power Creek Trail is a USFS cabin (see Places to Stay, below). Arrange to be dropped off at the Power Creek trailhead by Copper River/Northwest Tours (☎ 424-5356) and then hike all the way back into town via the Mt Eyak Trail.

McKinley Lake & Pipeline Lakes Trails The 2.5-mile McKinley Lake Trail begins at Mile 21.6 of the Copper River Hwy and leads to the head of the lake and the remains of the Lucky Strike gold mine. Two USFS cabins, McKinley Lake Cabin and McKinley Trail Cabin, are on this path, making them accessible by foot from the highway.

SOUTHCENTRAL

Departing from the McKinley Lake Trail is the Pipeline Lakes Trail, which loops back to the Copper River Hwy at Mile 21.4. This 2-mile trail provides access to several small lakes that can be fished for grayling and trout and turns the trek to McKinley Lake into a 6-mile loop. The Pipeline Lakes Trail also provides excellent views of the surrounding Chugach Mountains, but the muskeg areas can be very wet in places and rubber boots are recommended.

Sheridan Mountain Trail This trail starts at the end of Sheridan Glacier Rd, southeast of town at Mile 13 of the Copper River Hwy. The road leads 4.3 miles to the north, ending at a picnic table with a partial view of the ice floe. Near the end is the trailhead for the Sheridan Mountain Trail. Most of the 2.9-mile, one-way trail is a moderate climb that passes through mature forests before breaking out into an alpine basin. From the basin, the view of mountains and the Sheridan and Sherman Glaciers is a stunning sight, and it only gets better when you start climbing the surrounding rim. During a dry spell, hiking boots are fine for the walk; otherwise, you might want to tackle this one in rubber boots.

Saddlebag Glacier Trail You reach this trail via a firewood-cutting road, at Mile 25 of the Copper River Hwy. It's an easy walk of 3 miles through cottonwoods and spruce until you emerge at the outlet of Saddlebag Lake. The view is outstanding, for the namesake glacier is at the far end of the lake and has littered it with icebergs. The lake and glacier are surrounded by peaks and cliffs, where you can often spot mountain goats. If you're mountain biking the highway, this is one of the few trails dry enough to ride.

Special Events

Because of the economic importance of the fishing season, few events take place during the summer in Cordova, other than a small July 4th celebration and a couple of salmon derbies. The town's biggest event is its Iceworm Festival in mid-February, when there is little else to do. On the first weekend of May, you can attend the Copper Delta

Shorebird Festival, which celebrates the largest migration in North America.

Places to Stay

Cordova has a 6% city sales tax that's added to the price of all rooms.

Camping The closest campground is the **Odiak Camper Park** (☎ 424-6200), a half mile from town on Whitshed Rd. This city campground is little more than a gravel parking lot with a rest room and some play equipment in the middle. It has an excellent view of Cordova with Mt Eyak looming overhead, but the smell of fish is often so strong you have to think twice about pitching a tent here. The tent rate is $3 per night and includes water, showers and rest rooms. RVers pay $12 for an electric hookup. An unofficial spot for pitching a tent is up 6th St at Mt Eyak Ski Hill.

Cabins Cordova is the gateway to 10 USFS cabins that have the lowest occupancy rate of all Southcentral cabins. Several area trails lead to USFS cabins, all of which require reservations and cost $35 per night. You'll find a cabin at the end of Power Creek Trail and two cabins on the McKinley Lake Trail (see Hiking, above). One of the best in the area is **Hook Point Cabin**, an A-Frame with three bunks and loft. Overlooking a wide beach on the south side of Hinchinbrook Island, it's a mile from a salmon stream. The 15-minute flight to the cabin from Cordova is $220 roundtrip for two to three people.

For more information on area cabins, contact the USFS Visitor Information Center (☎ 424-7661) in Cordova. Reserve them through the National Recreation Reservation Service (☎ 877-444-6777, 518-885-3639 from overseas, www.reserveusa.com).

B&Bs While there is no hostel in Cordova, there are now a dozen B&Bs operating in and around town. Check with the visitor center for a current list of B&Bs, as they often change.

The **Northern Nights Inn** (☎ 424-5356), 3rd St at Council Ave, has four rooms with rates beginning at $65. Just up the hill toward

Mt Eyak Ski Hill is **The King's Chamber** (☎ 424-3373), 4th St, with five rooms in two houses for $65/75 singles/doubles. Five minutes from downtown is **The Udder Inn** (☎ 424-3895, 601 Lake Ave), with four rooms and kitchen facilities for the same rates.

Then there is **Cordova Rose Lodge** (☎ 424-7673, cdvrose@ptialaska.net, 1315 Whitshed Rd), a barge that was converted into a floating B&B. Docked – sort of – in Odiak Slough, the lodge has six rooms and a cedar-lined sauna. Rooms with shared bathrooms cost $60/75, including a full breakfast.

Hotels Of the four hotels in town, the **Alaskan Hotel & Bar** (☎ 424-3299), 1st St, is the cheapest. A room with a shared bathroom costs $40; rooms with private bathrooms cost $60. The Alaskan, like all hotels in Cordova, is booked solid through most of the summer. Avoid the seedy Cordova Hotel on 1st St and instead book a room at the **Cannery Bunkhouse** (☎ 424-5920), above the Cookhouse Cafe on a dock on Orca Inlet. Singles/doubles cost $45/50. The **Prince William Sound Motel** (☎ 424-3201), 2nd St at Council Ave, is in the heart of downtown, with rooms for $75/85. At the **Reluctant Fisherman Inn** (☎ 424-3272, 800-770-3272), Railroad Ave at Council Ave, rooms start at $80/90 singles/doubles.

Places to Eat
True to its name, the **OK Restaurant**, near the museum on 1st St, has okay Chinese food, with an $8 lunch special and dinners that range from $11 to $14. If the weather is nice, head to **Baja Taco**, a converted school bus on Nicholoff Way near the small boat harbor. Meals are still cooked in the old red bus, and the menu is posted on a surfboard. You can sit outdoors with a view of the harbor or the mountains while feasting on a taco plate ($7.50) or an order of nachos ($5). This is as un-Cordova as it gets.

The **Ambrosia** (413 1st St) specializes in pizza and Italian food, with pasta dinners from $11 to $14, medium pizzas for $16 and soup and subs for $9. The **Killer Whale Cafe**, in the Orca Book & Sound store on 1st St, opens at 7 am to serve omelets for $8 and

French toast for $4, as well as the best coffee and espresso drinks in town. Excellent salads range from $6 to $8.

The **Cookhouse Cafe**, on 1st St next to the ferry dock, is the centerpiece of an old working cannery. At one time a worker's mess hall, the cafe serves reindeer omelets ($9), sourdough pancakes ($7) or grilled salmon, country fries and toast ($7), beginning at 6 am. The grilled halibut sandwich with fries is a filling lunch for $8.

Outside of town, at Mile 1.5 of the Copper River Hwy, is **The Powder House**, a bar that serves sandwiches, chili and barbecue dinners and has a deck overlooking Eyak Lake. Farther out still, the **Airport Depot Diner**, Mile 13 of the Copper River Hwy near the airport, offers good burgers ($7 to $9) and beer.

Places to pick up your own supplies include **Davis Super Foods**, 1st St, and **AC Value Center**, Nicholoff Way, which has an espresso bar, bakery and deli as well as a grocery store.

Entertainment
The Powder House Bar, which earns its name because it lies on the site of the original Copper River & Northwestern Railroad powder house, is a fun place that features folk, bluegrass and country music at night. If you happen to be there on a rare evening when it isn't raining, sit on the deck that overlooks Eyak Lake.

In town, the **Flying Dutchman Pub**, 1st St, offers music nightly, and the **Anchor Bar**, on Breakwater Ave across from the small boat harbor, attracts those who want to mingle with the fishers. The **Alaskan Hotel Bar**, 1st St, has live music.

Getting There & Away
Air Alaska Airlines (☎ 424-7151) makes a daily stop at Cordova on its run to Seattle, and its contract carrier, ERA, flies twice daily from Anchorage. An advance-purchase ticket is generally around $80 one-way and $160 roundtrip.

All jets arrive at and depart from Cordova's airport, 12 miles from town on the Copper River Hwy. Within the small terminal you'll find a used-book counter and a courtesy phone you can use to contact many area businesses. The Airport Shuttle (☎ 424-3272) greets all arrivals and charges $10 for the trip into town. For the return trip to the airport, you can catch the shuttle at the major hotels in town.

Boat During the summer, the M/V *Bartlett* stops at Cordova on Monday, Wednesday and Friday en route from either Valdez or Whittier. The fare from Cordova to Valdez is $30; it's $58 to Whittier. The ferry terminal (☎ 424-7333) is 1.5 miles north of town on Railroad Ave.

AROUND CORDOVA

More than 50 miles of road extend out from Cordova, with much of the road system centered around the Copper River Hwy. Built on the old railroad bed to the Kennecott mines, the road was originally going to connect Cordova with the Richardson Hwy and the rest of Alaska. Construction was halted in 1964, after the Good Friday Earthquake damaged the existing roadbeds and bridges, knocking out the fourth span of the famous Million Dollar Bridge in front of Childs Glacier.

The reason to come to Cordova is to drive this road to see Childs Glacier. At least a full day should be spent exploring the Copper River Hwy, but it's best to take two days, spending the night at the end of the road and stopping during the day to fish or hike. Before departing, pick up a copy of the brochure *Copper River Delta* at the USFS Visitor Information Center in Cordova. It includes a map and milepost listings of trailheads, undeveloped campsites, wildlife-viewing areas, and streams where you can cast a lure.

Copper River Delta

The highway provides access to the delta, a 60-mile arc formed by six glacial-fed river systems. Stretching for more than 700,000 acres, the delta is the largest continuous wetland on the Pacific coast of North America. Its myriad tidal marshes, shallow ponds and outwashes are used by millions of birds and waterfowl as staging areas during the spring and fall migrations, as well as nesting areas in the summer.

May is the prime month for birders, a period when as many as 20 million shorebirds rest and feed in the tidal flats, including seven million western sandpipers and the entire population of West Coast dunlins. Other common species include arctic terns, dusty Canada geese, trumpeter swans, great blue herons and bald eagles. A drive along the highway at dawn or dusk can also provide you with views of moose, brown bears, beavers and porcupines.

The wildlife is so abundant in this area that in 1962 the USFS, the US Fish & Wildlife Service and the state agreed to manage 33,000 acres of the delta as a game and fish habitat. The refuge has since been enlarged to 2.3 million acres, and in 1972 the delta on the east side of the Copper River Hwy was closed to off-road vehicles.

The delta region offers opportunities for hiking (see Hiking under Cordova), wildlife viewing, birding, rafting on swift glacial rivers and angling. The streams and rivers along the highway are renowned for their fishing and can provide the ultimate angling experience – fishing an isolated stretch of river with mountains around you and wildlife just beyond the next bend. Sockeye-salmon fishing begins in mid-June and peaks around July 4. Coho-salmon runs occur from August to September, and cutthroat trout and Dolly Varden trout can be caught throughout the summer and fall.

Childs Glacier

The Copper River Hwy also provides access to a handful of glaciers that flow out of the Chugach Mountains. The first you'll reach is the **Sheridan Glacier**, which you can view from the bridge over the Sheridan River 15 miles from Cordova or 3 miles beyond Cordova's airport. One mile before the bridge, the Sheridan Glacier access road leads 4.3 miles to the north, ending at a picnic table with a partial view of the ice floe. From here, a 1-mile trail leads to a dirt-covered glacial moraine, which you can climb for a dazzling view of ice and crevasses.

Several other glaciers can be seen spilling out of the mountains. The most impressive by far is **Childs Glacier** at the end of the road, 48 miles from Cordova. The 3-mile wide glacier is west of the Million Dollar Bridge and sits right above the Copper River. It moves forward 500 feet a year and constantly dislodges icebergs into the river. The glacier is especially active in late spring and summer, when the Copper River rises above the glacier's rocky bed, undercutting its icy blue face to halt any further advance. The discharging ice makes for a noisy show, since the 300-foot face of the glacier lies only 1200 feet from the observation platform.

Just before the Copper River Hwy crosses the Million Dollar Bridge, a short side road leads to the Childs Glacier Recreation Area, which has picnic tables and rest rooms. It's common for people to camp overnight here. From the parking area, short trails run through the woods to the river, passing a 15-foot high viewing platform with interpretive displays. You can go right down to the river's edge for even closer views of the glacier, but remember that the calving can cause large swells to rush onshore.

Nearby is one end of the Childs Glacier Trail. Beginning near the viewing platform, this 1.2-mile trail follows an old road along the Copper River, passing superb views of the glacier. It ends at another observation platform overlooking the **Million Dollar Bridge**, built in 1910. Though severely damaged by the 1964 earthquake, the bridge has been jerry-rigged to allow an occasional brave soul – mostly rafters looking to put in upstream – to drive across. By all means, walk to the middle of it, which you'll reach before the damaged span, for the million-dollar view. Less than a mile downstream is Childs Glacier, while 5 miles upstream is **Miles Glacier**. More amazing than the view is the fact that the original builders constructed the bridge when the north arm of Childs Glacier was only 1500 feet away.

Paddling The Copper River flows 287 miles, beginning at Copper Glacier near Slana in Alaska's Interior and ending at the Gulf of Alaska, east of Cordova. Most of the river is for experienced rafters, as rapids, glaciers and narrow cannons give it a white-water rating of Class II-III much of the way. Some rafters rate Wood Canyon, just below Chitina, as Class IV. The 20-mile stretch between the Million Dollar Bridge and Flag Point, at Mile 27 of the Copper River Hwy, is considerably wider and slower. Here you'll be more concerned with tidal fluctuations than rapids.

Experienced sea kayakers can run the river all the way through the Copper River Delta into the Gulf of Alaska. Below Flag Point, though, the river becomes heavily braided, which inevitably means dragging your boat through shallow channels.

Deadly Glaciers

With its 300-foot-high face only 1200 feet from the observation platform (or less if you stand on the banks of the Copper River), Childs Glacier is one of the closest tidewater glaciers you can view. It's so close that every year icebergs calving into the river cause swells to reach the opposite bank.

It is estimated that 20 to 50 times a year a berg creates a 10-foot wave that's high enough to cross the river and sweep through the day-use area. Every two years, a glacial calving produces a 20-foot wave, and in 1993, when a piece of ice half the size of a football field broke off, a monstrous 40-foot wave resulted.

The wave was so powerful that it hurled picnic tables more than 50 feet and swamped the people standing on the 15-foot-high observation deck. Slabs of ice the size of cars littered the day-use area after the water retreated, and two women who were standing on the beach admiring the glacier were seriously injured.

If that wasn't enough of a reminder of how dangerous glaciers can be, in the same month a 36-year-old Anchorage man was killed when a chunk of ice fell on him while he was kayaking around Blackstone Glacier near Whittier.

SOUTHCENTRAL

Copper River/Northwest Tours (☎ 424-5356) provides shuttle service for those who want to float the river from either Flag Point or the Million Dollar Bridge. The cost is $20 per person or $80 a trip for Flag Point and $30 per person or $120 a trip for the bridge. To rent kayaks, contact Cordova Coastal Outfitters (☎ 424-7424, 800-357-5145), in the small boat harbor. Singles/doubles are $35/55 per day; weeklong rentals are available at a discount.

Getting Around The major problem for travelers exploring the Copper River area is finding transportation. Hitchhiking along the Copper River Hwy is possible, though you might not encounter many passing motorists, even in the summer months. The number of rental cars available in Cordova is limited. At the airport, Cordova Car Rentals (☎ 424-5982) has vehicles for $65 per day with unlimited mileage. You can also try the Reluctant Fisherman Inn (☎ 424-3272, 800-770-3272), which rents cars for $75 per day.

Copper River/Northwest Tours (☎ 424-5356) offers a six-hour tour out to the Million Dollar Bridge for $35 per person, with a minimum of four people per trip, and is by far the most reasonable way to see this road. The company uses a 25-passenger bus and serves a box lunch at the Childs Glacier Recreation Area.

If you have a few days, an excellent way to explore the Copper River Hwy is by mountain bike. Plan on at least three days if you ride out to the end of the road and back, or two days if you arrange for a drop-off service at the end of the road and then ride the 48 miles back to town. Cordova Coastal Adventures (☎ 424-3842, 800-357-5145) rents mountain bikes for $15 a day, including a helmet, water bottles and a rack for gear. The company also offers rides to the end of the highway for $75 per trip for up to three people with gear. Each additional passenger is $5. The van holds seven.

VALDEZ

In the heart of Prince William Sound and less than 25 miles east of the Columbia Glacier is Valdez, which is the southern terminus of the Trans-Alaska Pipeline and the most northerly ice-free port in the Western Hemisphere.

History

The town and port of Valdez were named after a Spanish naval officer by Spanish explorer Don Salvador Fidalgo in 1790. Valdez boomed in 1897–98, when 4000 gold-seekers came looking for what had been billed as the 'All American Route' to Alaska's Interior and the Klondike goldfields. Talk about truth in advertising – what they found were a few tents set up above the tide line and one of the most dangerous routes to the Klondike.

Also known as the Valdez Trail, the route across the Chugach Mountains included a trek over two glaciers, beginning with the Valdez Glacier. It was a suicidal trip at best, and hundreds of lives were lost due to falls in crevasses, snow blindness and hypothermia. In the spring of 1899, Capt William Abercrombie arrived to find a devastated group of men, most of whom had scurvy. They also were short of supplies, never having anticipated a lack of them in Valdez. The army captain soon set up a hospital, made arrangements for supplies and began surveying a better route to the Interior. It was Abercrombie who found Keystone Canyon and Thompson Pass – a much more suitable place to cross the Chugach Mountains. Eventually the gold miners' trail evolved into a wagon trail and then a paved road in the 1920s, ultimately becoming the Richardson Hwy.

Valdez prospered briefly, with a few mines of its own and an army outpost. But by the early 1900s, the town began a long decline when, in a bitter fight, it lost the Copper River & Northwestern Railroad to Cordova despite blasting tunnels in Keystone Canyon in anticipation of a line.

In 1964, Valdez lost even more than its role as the main cargo route to the Interior. In four short minutes, the Good Friday Earthquake demolished the city. Valdez was one of the hardest hit settlements in Alaska, with the epicenter only 45 miles west of town. The earthquake caused the land to ripple like water and a 4000-foot slice of

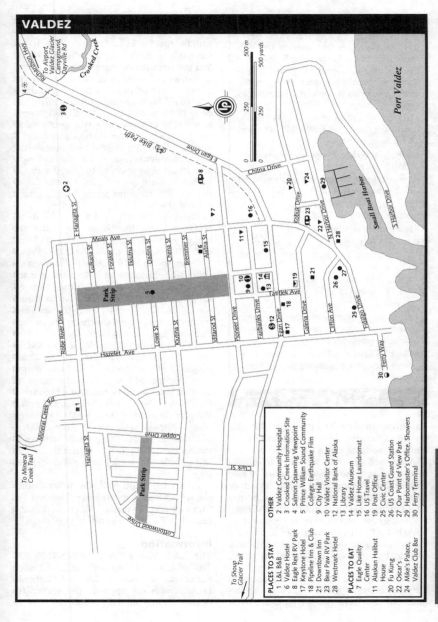

VALDEZ

To Airport,
Valdez Glacier
Campground,
Dayville Rd

Richardson Hwy

Crooked Creek

Richardson Hwy

4

To Mineral
Creek Trail

Mineral Creek Rd

E Egan Drive

Bike Path

3

8

2

E Hanagita St

Meals Ave

Gulkana St

Foraker St

Eklutna St

Dadina St

Chena St

Bremner St

Alatna St

7

11

6

16

Chitna Drive

Kobuk Drive

N Harbor Drive

20

24

29

23

28

22

Port Valdez

Small Boat Harbor

S Harbor Drive

Park Strip

5

10

9

17

13

14

18

15

19

21

26

27

Tatitlek Ave

Fidalgo Drive

Clifton Ave

25

Galena Drive

Egan Drive

12

Fairbanks Drive

Pioneer Drive

Idatarod St

Kluttna St

Lowe St

Rose River Drive

Hazelet Ave

Hanagita St

Copper Drive

Clark St

1

Park Strip

Cottonwood Drive

30

Ferry Way

To Mineral
Creek Trail

To Shoup
Glacier Trail

500 m

500 yards

250

250

0

PLACES TO STAY
1 L&L B&B
6 Valdez Hostel
8 Eagle Rest RV Park
17 Keystone Hotel
18 Pipeline Inn & Club
21 Downtown Inn
23 Bear Paw RV Park
28 Westmark Hotel

PLACES TO EAT
7 Eagle Quality
   Center
11 Alaskan Halibut
   House
20 Fu Kung
22 Oscar's
24 Mike's Palace,
   Valdez Club Bar

OTHER
2 Valdez Community Hospital
3 Crooked Creek Information Site
4 Salmon Spawning Viewpoint
5 Prince William Sound Community
   College, Earthquake Film
9 City Hall
10 Valdez Visitor Center
12 National Bank of Alaska
13 Library
14 Valdez Museum
15 Like Home Laundromat
16 US Travel
19 Post Office
25 Civic Center
26 US Coast Guard Station
27 Our Point of View Park
29 Harbormaster's Office, Showers
30 Ferry Terminal

Ten Years after the Spill

In 1999, Alaska residents marked the 10th anniversary of the Exxon oil spill, when the *Exxon Valdez* ran aground in Prince William Sound on March 24, 1989. Here are the sobering numbers 10 years later, according to *Newsweek* magazine:

- Number of gallons of oil lost: 11 million, making it the largest spill in US history and 53rd worst worldwide
- Miles of shoreline the spill covered with oil: 1300
- Percentage of the spill that was recovered by cleanup crews: 14
- Number of birds that died as a result of the oil: 250,000
- Number of sea otters that died: 2800
- Amount that Exxon spent in cleanup costs during the first two years after the disaster: $2.1 billion
- Amount of damages Exxon is paying to Alaska and the US in civil and criminal fines: $1 billion
- Amount that Exxon was ordered to pay in punitive damages to local fishermen, native hunters and others: $5 billion
- Punitive damages Exxon has paid as of 1999 because it is appealing the court decisions: $0

began in 1974, and the $9 billion project was completed in 1977; the first tanker was filled with the black gold on August 1, 1977. Today, the city's economy depends heavily on oil and the taxes the oil company pays.

Fishing and tourism also contribute to the economy, but oil has clearly made Valdez a rich city. Major projects completed in the early 1980s included a $50-million container terminal to enhance the city's reputation as the 'Gateway to the North' and the $7-million Civic Center. With oil money, the Chugach Mountains as a beautiful backdrop, and an ideal location in the middle of the Prince William Sound playground, Valdez and its 4100 residents seemed to have all a city could want.

However, the city paid a price for its involvement with the oil industry when the tanker *Exxon Valdez* rammed a reef and spilled 11 million gallons of oil into Prince William Sound in 1989. It was the worst oil spill in US history, and Valdez became the center of an environmental storm. Exxon officials directed the oil cleanup from Valdez during the first summer after the spill and created a money rush that hadn't been seen since the pipeline was built.

Thousands of people flocked to Valdez from all over the country in search of cleanup jobs that paid up to $20 an hour. Within a month, the oil company had created an army of 9000 workers, many of whom spent their days at the oil-soaked beaches of Prince William Sound but their nights in Valdez, whose population jumped from 3000 to 12,000, with people living out of tents or in the back of pickup trucks. Currently, 30% of the population works in pipeline-related jobs.

Apart from the spill, the town's other claim to fame is its weather. Dubbed the 'snow capital of Alaska,' Valdez received a record 46.7 feet of the stuff in 1989.

Information

The Valdez Visitor Center (☎ 835-4636, 800-770-5954, www.alaska.net/~valdezak) is on the corner of Chenega Ave and Fairbanks Drive, diagonally opposite the library. It's open 8 am to 8 pm daily in summer.

waterfront to slide into the harbor. It also produced massive tidal waves that left few buildings undamaged in the town.

Afterward, the residents voted to rebuild their city at a new site on more stable ground. It took more than two years before people could move into their new homes after paying $400 for their lots. The old town lies 4 miles east of Valdez on the Richardson Hwy, but all that remains today is a vacant field and a plaque dedicated to the 33 people who lost their lives during the frightful event.

Valdez regained its role as the gateway to the Interior when it was chosen as the terminus of the Trans-Alaska Pipeline. Work

There are two banks in Valdez, including the National Bank of Alaska (☎ 835-4745), 337 Egan Drive, which has a 24-hour ATM.

The post office is at the corner of Galena St and Tatitlek Ave. To check your email, visit the Valdez library, on Fairbanks St, which offers free Internet access.

The travel agency US Travel (☎ 877-835-8374, 835-8373) is in the Guesthouse Inn – Valdez lobby, 100 Meals Ave.

Diagonally opposite the Valdez Museum is the Valdez library, which runs a book and magazine swap for travelers on its lower floor. The library is open 10 am to 6 pm Monday and Friday, 10 am to 8 pm Tuesday to Thursday and noon to 6 pm Saturday.

Like Home Laundromat (☎ 835-2913), in the Valdez Mall on Egan Drive, has showers as well as coin-operated laundry machines. There are also showers at the harbormaster's office at the small boat harbor.

Valdez Community Hospital (☎ 835-2249), 511 Meals Ave, has an emergency room, while walk-in care is available next door at the Valdez Medical Clinic (☎ 835-4811), 912 Meals Ave.

Things to See & Do

Valdez's bustling **small boat harbor**, south of North Harbor Drive, features a long boardwalk with benches and ramps down to the various docks. With an impressive set of peaks in the background, the harbor is an excellent place to hang out in the evening, especially during July, when you can watch lucky anglers weighing in 100 or 200lb halibut right on the docks. At the west end of the harbor, near the corner of Clifton Ave and Fidalgo Drive, you'll find both the US Coast Guard Station and **Our Point of View Park**. The observation platform on the knoll is a good spot to view the old town site to the east, the pipeline terminal to the south and Valdez Narrows to the west. Nearby, on Fidalgo Drive near Hazelet Ave, is the **Civic Center**, with more picnic tables and panoramas of the area.

From the Civic Center, head two blocks north on Hazelet Ave and turn right (east) on Egan Drive to the **Valdez Museum** (☎ 835-2764), inside the Centennial Building. The museum is packed with displays, that include a model of the Trans-Alaska Pipeline, a 19th-century saloon bar, an exhibit on glaciers that usually includes a cooler full of ice from the Columbia Glacier and a photo display on Valdez. Opposite each other are two exhibits connected with the town's most important events (the 1964 earthquake and the 1989 Exxon oil spill). The museum is open 9 am to 6 pm Monday to Saturday, 8 am to 5 pm Sunday in summer; admission is $3.

To reach **Prince William Sound Community College**, follow Hazelet Ave north and turn right (east) on Lowe St. The small campus, a division of the University of Alaska, has three huge wooden carvings that are part of Peter Toth's collection of 50 sculptures dedicated to Native Americans. Also on the small campus is the PWSCC Bookstore, which has a nice selection of Alaskan titles, an espresso shop and a gold-rush-era photo exhibit. Throughout the summer, the store also shows a 1964 earthquake film ($3).

A half mile north of Pioneer Drive along the Richardson Hwy is the **Crooked Creek Information Site**. The wooden platform, the site of the old hatchery, is a good spot to watch salmon spawn in July and August. USFS naturalists operate programs here throughout the summer.

Hiking

In an area surrounded by mountains and glaciers, you would expect good hiking around Valdez, but this is not the case. Though many trails have been proposed and a new route has been cut to offer views of Shoup Glacier, the town is nowhere near the hiking meccas of Juneau or Anchorage. There's also no USFS office in Valdez and no nearby cabins.

Mineral Creek Trail The best walk away from town is the old road along Mineral Creek and the 1-mile trail from its end to the old Smith Stamping Mill. The road can be in poor condition at times, but most cars can usually manage it without bottoming out too much.

To reach the trailhead, follow Hazelet Ave north 10 blocks from Egan Drive to Hanagita St and turn left (west); then turn right (north) onto Mineral Creek Rd. The road bumps along for 5.5 miles and then turns into a mile-long trail to the old mill. Built by WL Smith in 1913, the mill required only two men to operate it and used mercury to remove the gold from the ore.

Following the trail beyond the mill at Brevier Creek requires considerable bush hacking. If you are hiking the entire road, the trip up the lush green canyon can be a pleasant 13-mile adventure that requires five to six hours. It's also a popular place for mountain biking.

Shoup Glacier Trail Built in 1999, Valdez's newest trail begins at the west end of town and skirts Port Valdez for 12 miles. It crosses Gold Creek along the way and ends in Shoup Bay, where there are views of Shoup Glacier. To reach the trailhead, follow Egan Drive west across Mineral Creek and into the Cottonwood subdivision. The trail begins from a parking lot at the end of the street.

Solomon Gulch Trail Another relatively new trail is located across from the Solomon Gulch Fish Hatchery on Dayville Rd, off the Richardson Hwy. This 1.3-mile trail is a steep, uphill hike that quickly leads to splendid views of Port Valdez and the city below. It ends at Solomon Lake, which is the source of 80% of Valdez's power.

Goat Trail The oldest trail in the area is Goat Trail, which originally was a Native American route that was discovered by Capt Abercrombie in his search of safe passage to the Interior. Today, you can pick up the posted trailhead at Mile 13.5 of the Richardson Hwy, just past Horsetail Falls in Keystone Canyon. The trail twists and turns for 2.5 miles as it follows the Lowe River until it stops at the original bridge over Bear Creek.

Paddling
Lowe River This glacial river cuts through the impressive Keystone Canyon and is only about 12 miles outside Valdez. Lowe River has become a popular float trip during the summer. It features Class III rapids, sheer canyon walls and waterfalls cascading from the sides. The highlight of the trip is passing Bridal Veil Falls, which drops 900 feet from the canyon walls.

Keystone Adventures (☎ 835-2606, 800-328-8460) offers day trips on the river, carrying passengers 6 miles through white water and past the cascading waterfalls that have made the canyon famous. The guide company runs the 1½-hour trip five times daily (beginning at 10 am and ending with a run at 6 pm) and charges $35 per person, or $60 including transportation from town.

For something a little wilder, sign up for the company's three-hour float on the Tsaina River, which has Class IV rapids. It costs $70 per person.

Shoup Bay Protected as a state marine park, this bay off Valdez Arm is the home of a retreating tidewater glacier of the same name and is the destination of a popular overnight kayaking trip. The glacier features two tidal basins and an underwater moraine, which makes it a protected area for harbor seals and other sea life. It's about 10 miles to the bay and another 4 miles up to the glacier. If you're planning a kayaking trip, take a tide book. You must enter the bay two hours before the incoming tide to avoid swift tidal currents.

Anadyr Adventures (☎ 835-2814, 800-865-2925) rents kayaks off N Harbor Drive across from the small boat harbor, where you can launch. Singles cost $45 per day, with doubles for $65, but there's a discount if you rent for more than two days. A guided day trip to the glacier costs $140 per person. You can also rent boats from Pangaea Adventures (☎ 835-8442, 800-660-9637, pangaea@pangaeaadventures.com) for $45/65.

Columbia Glacier This is the largest tidewater glacier in Prince William Sound and a spectacular spot to spend a few days kayaking among the crackling ice while watching seals and other wildlife. Only experienced paddlers should attempt to paddle the open water from Valdez Arm to the glacier, a three- to four-day trip. Others should arrange a drop-off and pickup service, which is tough to do if you're on a budget.

The best way to set up an unguided paddle to Columbia Glacier is to purchase a Growler Island tour through Prince William Sound Cruises (formerly Stan Stephens Cruises; ☎ 835-4731, 800-992-1297). The company maintains a number of heated wall tents at Elder Bay, putting you within easy paddling of the glacier. The cruise and one night's accommodation at the island is $100 per person.

On Growler Island, Alaska Kayaking & Sailing Adventures (☎ 835-5175, awss@alaska.net) rents single/double kayaks for $45/65 per day, with 20% off for each subsequent day. Many kayakers then paddle Heather Bay to view the ice and camp on Heather Island. Alaska Kayaking & Sailing Adventures also offers kayaking and camping adventures from the island for $175 per person per day. The cost includes kayaks and a guide, but you must bring your own food and camping gear. Anadyr Adventures (☎ 835-2814, 800-865-2925, anadyr@alaska.net) offers day trips to the glacier for $170 per person or four-day paddle trips for $550.

Special Events

Valdez has both a July 4th celebration and an end-of-summer festival called Gold Rush Days. The five-day festival takes place in mid-August and includes a parade, bed races, dances, a free fish feed and a portable jailhouse that's pulled throughout town by locals who arrest people without beards and other innocent bystanders.

Places to Stay

Valdez adds a 6% bed tax to the room rates B&Bs and motels quote you.

Camping Six miles out of town, past the airport, is the *Valdez Glacier Campground* (101 sites, $10) on Airport Rd. This campground features private wooded sites but lacks the charm of the state campgrounds you've been passing along the highway all day.

The private campgrounds in town offer a better deal. Downtown Valdez is full of RV campgrounds, and you'll be amazed how they pack them in around the harbor. Two of the commercial campgrounds, however, also cater to those who arrive with a tent. *Bear Paw RV Campground (☎ 835-2530, 101 N Harbor Drive)*, right near the small boat harbor, has sites for $17 a night in a special wooded area just for tents. It's on a small knob above the City Dock and includes its own shower and laundry building. The rate for RVers here is about $22. *Eagle Rest RV Park (☎ 835-2373, 800-553-7275)*, Pioneer Drive at the Richardson Hwy, also has tent sites for $15 a night, plus showers, a laundry room and a few old-model bikes.

In recent years, Valdez has begun to restrict unauthorized camping within the city, especially on the hill overlooking the waterfront across Chitna St. 'Hotel Hill,' a gravel camping area on the south side of the small boat harbor once used by seasonal cannery workers, was closed by the city in 1996. The best place to find an unauthorized campsite is to hike a mile or so up Mineral Creek Rd.

Cabins There aren't any USFS cabins near Valdez, but there are a pair of state cabins at Shoup Bay. Both McAllister Creek and Kittiwake Cabins sleep eight, can be reached by boat and rent for $50 per night. But Kittiwake is also at the end of the Shoup Glacier Trail, a 12-mile overland route from Valdez (see Hiking, above). Contact the Department of Natural Resources Public Information Center (☎ 269-8400), 3601 C St, Suite 200, Anchorage, AK 99503-5929, to rent the cabins in advance.

Hostels In 1999, the *Valdez Hostel (☎ 835-2155, vhostel@pobox.alaska.net, 139 Alatna St)* opened, providing travelers on a budget a great place to stay. Located less than a block from the Eagle Quality Center, the hostel is a dormitory-style apartment with a kitchen and washer and dryer on-site. Beds cost $20, but you need your own bedding.

B&Bs More than 30 B&Bs around town charge around $60/70 for singles/doubles.

The Valdez Visitor Center has a speed-dial phone outside and a bulletin board listing all the current B&Bs and their rates. Just pick a home and push a button. Or you can try **L&L B&B** (☎ 835-4447, mrlou@alaska.net, 533 W Hanagita St), which has five rooms ($65 with a shared bathroom, $75 with a private bathroom) and bikes for use.

Hotels Rates in the city's six motel/hotels range from $95 a night at the **Pipeline Inn** (☎ 835-4444, 112 Egan Drive) to $130 at the top-end **Westmark Hotel** (☎ 835-4391, 100 Fidalgo Drive). Newly remodeled **Keystone Hotel** (☎ 888-835-0665, 835-3851), Egan Drive at Hazelet Ave, has 106 rooms that cost $85/95 in the summer.

The best deal is **Downtown Inn** (☎ 835-2791, 800-478-2791 in Alaska only, 113 Galena Drive), which calls itself a B&B but in reality is more of a hotel, with 25 rooms. Near the post office, the inn has some rooms with shared bathrooms that begin at $80. You also get a filling breakfast in the morning, and the coin-operated washer and dryer cost half as much as those at the local Laundromat. Call for a room in advance.

Places to Eat

What used to be a Tastee Freez is now **Oscar's** (143 N Harbor Drive), across from the small boat harbor. Definitely a step up from the Tastee Freez, the restaurant serves eggs-toast-potatoes breakfasts for $6 to $8, hamburgers for $6 and, perhaps its best deal, homemade chowder served in a sourdough bread bowl for $7. More local seafood can be enjoyed at **The Alaskan Halibut House**, Meals Ave at Fairbanks Drive across from Village Inn. The closest thing Valdez has to a fast-food place, this spot has a salad bar and serves a fish-and-chips basket of halibut for $7 or catch-of-the-day (take your chances) for $5.

A little classier than the local hamburger joint is **Mike's Palace** (201 N Harbor Drive), which enjoys a view of the harbor. The place specializes in pasta and local seafood, especially halibut, and serves beer and wine. Dinners cost $11 to $16, but you can pick up a small pizza that will easily feed two or three people for under $13. A short walk from the small boat harbor is **Fu Kung** (207 Kobuk Drive). The Chinese restaurant is in an old military hut, but you wouldn't know it from the inside and the food is excellent. Dinners cost $10 to $14, but arrive before 2:30 pm and get a better deal with the lunch special: main dish, soup, fried rice and egg roll for $7.

Eagle Quality Center, Pioneer Drive at Meals Ave, has the cheapest supermarket prices in town along with a bar serving salad, hot soup and tacos, where $6 buys you a taco salad that will keep you filled until morning. Breakfast, served in take-away trays from 6 to 10 am, costs less than $5 for eggs, toast and hash browns – a deal almost unheard of anywhere else in Alaska.

Entertainment

Local nightspots include the **Valdez Club Bar**, next door to Mike's Palace, where you can hang out with local fishers.

The lounge at the **Pipeline Club** (112 Egan Drive) offers live music. It's the watering hole where Capt Hazelwood had his famous scotch-on-the-rocks before running the **Exxon Valdez** aground and causing the worst oil spill in the history of the country.

There are usually numerous activities, including performances by traveling theater groups and movies shown on a large screen, at the Civic Center (☎ 835-4400) during the summer. The Prince William Sound Community College also operates a live theater that taps into the tourism season. Call the Valdez Visitor Center (☎ 835-2984) to purchase tickets.

Getting There & Away

Air Alaska Airlines, through its contract carrier ERA Aviation (☎ 835-2636), provides five flights weekdays and three on Saturday and Sunday between Valdez and Anchorage for $75 to $85 one-way. The Valdez airport is 5 miles from town on Airport Rd, off the Richardson Hwy.

Bus Alaskon Express (☎ 835-4391), operating out of the Westmark Hotel, departs Valdez at 8 am daily and reaches Anchorage at 6 pm. The one-way fare is $68. You can also get off at Glennallen and pick up a connecting bus to just about anywhere in the state, including Fairbanks ($150). In 1999, Parks Highway Express (☎ 888-600-6001) also extended its service to Valdez, with a bus departing at 9 am on Monday, Thursday and Saturday, reaching Glennallen at noon and Anchorage at 4:30 pm. The one-way fare to Glennallen is $20, to Anchorage $59.

If you want to visit McCarthy and Wrangell-St Elias National Park, you have to take a bus to either Copper Center or Glennallen and then backtrack south via Backcountry Connection (☎ 822-5292, 800-478-5292 in Alaska only) to the historic town.

Boat The Alaska Marine Hwy ferry used to be the cheapest way to view the Columbia Glacier, but in 1999 politicians bowed to the pressure of the tourist industry and changed the route of the M/V *Bartlett*. Now the ferry swings farther away from the ice floe, forcing you to book a cruise with a private vessel if you want a close view.

The one-way Valdez-to-Whittier fare is $58. The ferry also connects Valdez to Cordova ($30), Seward ($58), Homer ($138) and Kodiak ($98), since both the M/V *Bartlett* and M/V *Tustumena* call at Valdez. Between the two ships, there are runs to Whittier five times a week, two weekly sailings to Cordova and a weekly run to Seward, Homer and Kodiak. Reservations for these popular runs are strongly recommended. If you don't have a confirmed space for you and your car, you can try your luck on standby. For the 7:15 am run to Whittier, the ferry terminal opens at 4:30 am, and it's best to get there as early as you can to be at the front of the line of standby vehicles. Normally there's enough extra space for two or three cars. The Valdez ferry terminal (☎ 835-4436) is at the southern end of Hazelet Ave.

AROUND VALDEZ

At the airport is Valdez's newest attraction, **Historic Alaska Heritage Center** (☎ 834-1625), opened by Prince William Sound

Community College in 1999. The center is devoted to Native Alaskan culture and features ivory, baleen and other artwork, historical photographs and displays on the state's natural history, including wildlife mounts. It's open 8 am to 8 pm daily.

Eight miles from town (and a few miles beyond the airport), Dayville Rd branches off from the Richardson Hwy, hugging the mountainside and passing the scenic **Solomon Gulch**. The **Copper Valley Hydro Project**, which supplies power for both Valdez and Glennallen, has been completed at Solomon Gulch. Across the road is the **Solomon Gulch Hatchery**, which has a self-guided interpretive walk open to visitors from 8 am to 5 pm daily. Admission is $1.

Dayville Rd ends at the **oil pipeline terminal**, the heart and soul of Valdez. Outside the terminal's visitor center, a bronze monument commemorates the construction workers who built the pipeline.

The terminal is nothing short of remarkable, as it contains more than 15 miles of pipeline, 18 oil-storage tanks and four tanker berths. Oil is pumped out of Prudhoe Bay on the Beaufort Sea in northern Alaska and travels 800 miles south through the pipeline to the terminal, where it is either stored or loaded into tankers. It is estimated that there are 9.6 billion barrels of oil under the North Slope and 1.7 million barrels flow out of the pipeline into tankers every day at the terminal.

Displays at the visitor center explain the history, and for many it's enough to stare at the facility from the entrance gate and then head back. If you want a closer look, Valdez Tours (☎ 835-2686) runs a two-hour tour ($15) that departs from the airport's visitor center several times daily. During the tour, you pass through a security check that's tougher than those you experience at most airports, and you only step off the bus twice. Despite being total PR for big oil companies, the tour is interesting, and unless you're a founding member of Greenpeace, you can't help but be a little impressed with all the security measures and safeguards here, especially in the wake of the *Exxon Valdez* oil spill.

COLUMBIA GLACIER

Columbia Glacier is the second-largest tidewater glacier in North America, spilling 40 miles out of the Chugach Mountains and ending with a 3-mile-wide face.

Most travelers can glimpse this magnificent tidewater glacier while crossing Prince William Sound to or from Valdez on the Alaska Marine Hwy ferry. But to get a closer view and to spend more time at the ice pack observing wildlife, you need to take a private tour boat. Keep in mind that the glacier has been rapidly retreating for almost 10 years, and it's now difficult for any boat to get close to the face. The bay is just too clogged with ice.

Privately run cruise ships do spend considerably more time threading their way through the icebergs, where you can often observe seals basking under the sun. Whether you're close to the 300-foot-high face or not, this sea of ice is still an awesome sight and a photographer's delight.

Prince William Sound Cruises (formerly Stan Stephens Cruises; ☎ 835-4731, 800-922-1297) is the largest tour operator, running five boats during the summer. A six-hour tour departs at 11 am daily and costs $69 per person. A nine-hour lunch cruise ($119) departs at 9 am and includes a buffet on Growler Island.

You can also ride from Valdez to Whittier on a glacier cruise. The six-hour crossing departs Valdez at 7:15 am, arrives at Whittier at 1:45 pm and costs $11 per person. Stop at Bear Paw RV Campground (see Camping) to purchase tickets or make reservations.

Glacier Wildlife Cruises (☎ 835-5141, 800-411-0090) runs the M/V *Lu-Lu Belle* and maintains an office on Kobuk Drive behind Totem Inn. The boat, which features a bar, departs at 1 pm daily for a five-hour cruise. During the height of the tourist season, there's an 8 am cruise as well. It's $70 per person for the 1 pm departure and $60 for the 8 am trip.

Smaller operators come and go, so shop around by walking the docks of the small boat harbor or carefully checking brochures at the visitor center.

RICHARDSON HIGHWAY TO MILE 115

The section of the Richardson Hwy from Valdez to Glennallen is an incredibly scenic route that includes canyons, mountain passes, glaciers and access to the massive Wrangell-St Elias National Park. Hitchhiking is fairly easy during the summer, making it convenient to stop often and enjoy the sights and campgrounds along the way.

The highway begins in the center of Valdez, but Mile 0 is near the site of old Valdez, as the mileposts were erected before the Good Friday Earthquake and were never changed. The junction with Dayville Rd, which leads to the pipeline terminal, is 6.9 miles from town, and at this point the Richardson Hwy swings north.

At Mile 13, you reach **Keystone Canyon**, with its many waterfalls and unusual rock formations high above the road. In the next mile, two magnificent waterfalls appear: Horsetail Falls and Bridal Veil Falls, half a mile farther. The canyon wall is so sheer that the waterfalls appear to be cascading straight down. They actually spray the road with mist.

At Mile 14.8 of the Richardson Hwy, in the northern end of the canyon, there is an abandoned hand-drilled tunnel that residents of Valdez began but never finished when they were competing with Cordova for the railroad to the Kennecott copper mines. A historical marker briefly describes how nine companies fought to develop the short route from the coast to the mines, leading to the 'shootout in Keystone Canyon.'

The **Trans-Alaska Pipeline** can be seen at Mile 20.4. At Mile 24, a short loop road leads to the first camping area, ***Blueberry Lake State Recreation Site***. The recreational area offers 10 sites ($10) and four covered picnic shelters in a beautiful alpine setting surrounded by lofty peaks. Often during the summer all the sites will be taken by RVers, but it's easy for backpackers to find a spot to pitch their tents near the trails. There's good fishing for rainbow trout in the nearby lakes. In Summit Lake, these fish can reach up to 18 inches long and are usually caught with flies, small spinners or salmon eggs.

Above the tree line, the weather can be windy and foul as the highway ascends toward **Thompson Pass** at Mile 26. There are several scenic turnoffs near the pass (elevation 2771 feet), which is covered in wildflowers in early summer. This spot also holds most of Alaska's snowfall records, including 62 inches of snow in a 24-hour period in December 1955. That's the reason for the L-shaped poles along the highway. The snow is so deep here in the winter that snowplows need the poles to guide them over the pass.

At Mile 28.6 is the turnoff to the **Worthington Glacier State Recreation Area**, where you can drive to the glacier's face on a short access road. The recreation area includes outhouses, picnic tables and a large covered viewing area. The mile-long **Worthington Glacier View Trail** begins at the parking lot and follows the crest of the moraine. It's a scenic hike that follows the edge of the glacier, but you must exercise caution. Never hike on the glacier itself. Thompson Pass and the surrounding area above the tree line are ideal for tramping, as hikers will have few problems climbing through the heather.

The pipeline continues to pop into view as you travel north on the Richardson Hwy, and at one point it passes beneath the road. At Mile 65, you'll reach *Little Tonsina River State Recreation Site*, a campground with 10 sites ($6). None of the sites is on the Little Tonsina River, but a path leads down to the water, where anglers can fish for Dolly Varden trout most of the summer. The *Squirrel Creek State Campground*, Mile 79.4 of the Richardson Hwy, offers a scenic little camping area with 14 sites ($10) on the banks of the creek. You can fish for grayling and rainbow trout in Squirrel Creek – the reason, no doubt, why the campground is often filled. Nearby is a roadhouse that serves meals, while across the street there's a small gas station with supplies.

The Edgerton Hwy junction, which leads to the heart of Wrangell-St Elias National Park, is 3 miles past the campground. You'll reach a lookout over **Willow Lake** at Mile 87.6. The lake can be stunning on a clear day, with the water reflecting the Wrangell

Mountains, a 100-mile chain that includes 11 peaks over 10,000 feet. The two most prominent peaks visible from the lookout are Mt Drum, 28 miles to the northeast, and Mt Wrangell, Alaska's largest active volcano, to the east. Mt Wrangell is 14,163 feet, and on some days you can see a plume of steam rising from its crater.

The Richardson Hwy now bypasses **Copper Center** (population 553), which used to be at Mile 101. You now have to make a special effort to see the small village, but you shouldn't hesitate. This town is a classic, especially compared with that dusty trailer park known as Glennallen to the north.

At the turn of the century, Copper Center was an important mining camp for the thousands of prospectors eyeing the goldfields in the Yukon and later in Fairbanks. Near the bridge over the Klutina River is the *Copper Center Lodge* (☎ 822-3245), which began in 1897 as the Blix Roadhouse and was the first lodge built north of Valdez. The lodge still serves as a roadhouse today. You can get a delicious plate of sourdough pancakes, reputedly made from century-old starter. The dining room is open 7 am to 9 pm; double rooms range from $84 (shared bathroom) to $94 (private bathroom).

Next door is the **George Ashby Museum**, open 1 to 5 pm Monday to Saturday (no admission fee). Inside the log cabin are mining artifacts from the Kennecott mines, as well as the record moose rack for Alaska. It's hanging over the door and, with a spread of almost 70 inches poised over your head, you pray it doesn't fall when you leave. Also check out the outhouse known as Copper Center City Hall; it's good for a laugh.

Copper Center has a gas station, a store for supplies, a post office and the *Silver Fox Drive Inn*, which is an old bus that serves everything from hamburgers to tacos for under $7. Before you return to the Richardson Hwy, you'll pass the **Wrangell-St Elias National Park Visitor Center**. During the summer, the center is open until 6 pm daily and is the place to go for topographical maps and trip suggestions. You can also leave your backpacking itinerary here. Even if you don't plan to enter the park's backcountry, the center has a few displays and videos on the area.

Just north of town on the Richardson Hwy is the **Chapel on the Hill**, built in 1942. During the summer, the log chapel features a short slide presentation on the history of the Copper River Basin area; admission is free.

At Mile 115 is the major junction between the Glenn and Richardson Hwys. The Richardson Hwy (see the Interior chapter) continues north to Delta Junction and eventually Fairbanks. The Glenn Hwy (see the Interior chapter) heads west to Glennallen, a short distance away, and on to Anchorage.

WRANGELL-ST ELIAS NATIONAL PARK

This national park, created in 1980, stretches north 170 miles from the Gulf of Alaska. It encompasses 13.2 million acres of mountains, foothills and river valleys bounded by the Copper River on the west and Canada's Kluane National Park to the east. Together, Kluane and Wrangell-St Elias National Parks make up almost 20 million acres and encompass the greatest expanse of valleys, canyons and towering mountains in North America, including the continent's second- and third-highest peaks.

This area is a crossroads of mountain ranges. To the north are the Wrangell Mountains; to the south, the Chugaches. Thrusting from the Gulf of Alaska and clashing with the Wrangells are the St Elias Mountains. There are so many mountains and so many summits in this rugged land that, as the park brochure says, 'you quickly abandon the urge to learn their names.'

Spilling out from the peaks are extensive ice fields and more than 100 major glaciers – some of the largest and most active in the world. The Bagley Ice Field near the coast is the largest subpolar mass of ice in North America. The Malaspina Glacier, which spills out of the St Elias Mountains between Ice Bay and Yakutat Bay, is larger than the state of Rhode Island.

Wildlife in Wrangell-St Elias National Park is more diverse and plentiful than in any other Alaskan park. Species in the preserve include moose, black and brown bears, Dall sheep, mountain goats, wolves, wolverines, beavers and three of Alaska's 11 caribou herds.

The Richardson Hwy borders the northwest corner of the park, and two rough dirt roads lead into its interior. The most popular access road by far is McCarthy Rd, with the historic mining towns of McCarthy and Kennicott serving as something of a visitor's area for the park. Whereas in the early 1980s a few hundred people would venture across the Kennicott River into McCarthy, today that many will show up on a good weekend, and annually both towns now attract more than 20,000 visitors.

Despite the rebirth of McCarthy, Wrangell-St Elias is still a true wilderness park, with few visitor facilities or services beyond the highway. An adventure into this preserve requires time and patience rather than money, but it can lead to a once-in-a-lifetime experience.

Information

The park's main office (☎ 822-5234, www .nps.gov/wrst) is at Mile 105 of the Richardson Hwy, 10 miles before the junction with the Glenn Hwy. It's open 8 am to 6 pm daily during the summer, and rangers can answer questions about the park as well as supply various handouts and rough maps of the area.

During the summer, rangers are also stationed in a log-cabin visitor center in Chitina (☎ 823-2205), at the end of the Edgerton Hwy. It's open 10 am to 6 pm daily. There's also a new Slana ranger station at the start of the road to Nebesna.

McCarthy Road

The Edgerton Hwy and McCarthy Rd combine to provide a 92-mile route into the heart of Wrangell-St Elias National Park, ending at the footbridge across the Kennicott River to McCarthy.

The 32-mile Edgerton Hwy, fully paved, begins at Mile 82.6 of the Richardson Hwy and ends at **Chitina**. The town, which has 90 or so permanent residents, is the last place to purchase gas and to get a reasonably priced

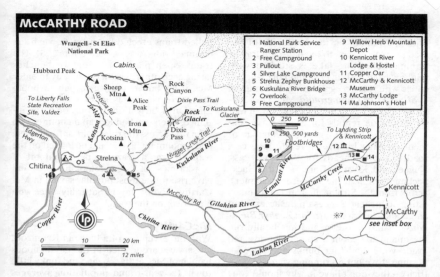

McCARTHY ROAD

Wrangell - St Elias
National Park

Hubbard Peak

Cabins

Rock Canyon

Sheep Mtn

Alice Peak

To Liberty Falls
State Recreation
Site, Valdez

Dixie Pass Trail

Rock Glacier

To Kuskulana Glacier

Iron Mtn

Kotsina

Dixie Pass

Kuskulana River

Nugget Creek Trail

Edgerton Hwy

Strelna

Chitina

McCarthy Rd

Gilahina River

Copper River

Chitina River

Laking River

1 National Park Service Ranger Station
2 Free Campground
3 Pullout
4 Silver Lake Campground
5 Strelna Zephyr Bunkhouse
6 Kuskulana River Bridge
7 Overlook
8 Free Campground
9 Willow Herb Mountain Depot
10 Kennicott River Lodge & Hostel
11 Copper Oar
12 McCarthy & Kennicott Museum
13 Kennicott Lodge
14 Ma Johnson's Hotel

To Landing Strip & Kennicott

Footbridges

Kennicott River

McCarthy Creek

McCarthy

Kennicott

McCarthy
see inset box

meal (at least, reasonably priced by Alaskan standards). Backpackers can camp along the 3-mile road south to O'Brien Creek or beside Town Lake within Chitina. The best spot to stop, however, is 10 miles before you reach Chitina, at **Liberty Falls State Recreation Site**. The campground has only three or four sites for RVs, but there are another six spots for tents, including four tent platforms right along rushing Liberty Creek. Although there's no piped-in water here, the campground does contain thundering Liberty Falls. Sites cost $10.

There is also a small free **campground** with eight sites next to the Copper River Bridge. It's maintained by the Alaska Department of Transportation and used primarily by dipnetters who descend on Chitina in July and August to scoop up red and king salmon.

Within Chitina, the National Park Service ranger station is open 10 am to 6 pm daily during the summer. Also in town, the delightful gallery Spirit Mountain Artworks plugs and patches flat tires. Owner Art Koeninger loves his art, but he undoubtedly makes a living repairing the tires that McCarthy Rd chews up.

Chitina also contains a grocery store, post office and two restaurants. Try **Chitina Cafe**, a good place to stop before the long drive out to McCarthy. The interior has – what else? – miners' decor. Prices range from $5 to $10 for breakfast; a hamburger costs $7. Try the homemade biscuits and gravy ($5), guaranteed to keep you fueled until you've reached McCarthy.

From Chitina, McCarthy Rd – a rough dirt road that is not regularly maintained – follows the abandoned Copper River & Northwest Railroad bed that was used to transport copper from the mines to Cordova. It leads 60 miles or so farther east to the Kennicott River. Your $40-a-day rental car can usually travel this stretch during the summer, but plan on three to four hours for the trip, and if it's been raining hard, don't plan it at all.

The road starts 2 miles west of Chitina, and the first few miles offer spectacular views of the Chugach Mountains, the east-west range that separates the Chitina Valley lowlands from the Gulf of Alaska. Peaks average 7000 to 8000 feet. You'll also cross the mighty Copper River, where it's possible to see a dozen fish wheels or, if your timing is right, hordes of dipnetters. Just before Mile 9, a pullout on the north side of the road provides access to the half-mile trail to Strelna Lake. The lake is stocked with rainbow trout and silver salmon that anglers entice with salmon eggs during the summer.

Silver Lake Campground, Mile 11 of McCarthy Rd, is a commercial facility with tent spaces, canoe rentals for Silver Lake and other limited services, gas not being one of them. At Mile 14.5, you'll reach the access road to the trailheads for the Dixie Pass, Nugget and Kotsina Trails (see the Backpacking section in the Wilderness chapter), across from the Strelna airstrip. For an interesting night, head 2 miles up the access road and book a bed at the *Strelna Zephyr Bunkhouse*. Sandy Kasteler and her family run the quaint log cabin accommodations, and inside you'll find four bunks and a woodburning stove but no running water or electricity – they don't have it, why should you? Nearby is a log sauna.

At Mile 17 of McCarthy Rd is the **Kuskulana River Bridge**. Built in 1910, this historic railroad bridge spans 525 feet across an impressive gorge that rises 238 feet above the river. From the time the road was opened to cars in the 1960s until the 1980s, this narrow, three-span railroad bridge was known as 'the biggest thrill on the road to McCarthy.' In 1988, however, the structure was completely upgraded by the state, which added guard rails and replanked it. Although it is no longer quite as thrilling, the view of the steep-sided canyon and rushing river from the middle of the bridge is mind-boggling, well worth the time to park at one end and walk back across it.

You cross two more bridges at Mile 28.5 and Mile 44; at the first one, you can still admire an impressive railroad trestle that was abandoned in the 1930s and left standing. At Mile 57.3, an overlook on the south side of the road offers a view of the town of McCarthy and a glimpse of Kennicott Glacier through the forest of spruce and poplar.

To continue the final mile to McCarthy, you have to leave the car behind and use the new footbridge to cross the Kennicott River. Built in 1996, the bridge replaced the handpulled trams erected by the state when the original bridge was washed out in 1981. The trams, open platforms with two benches facing each other, were a classic way to enter McCarthy, but as tourism began to boom they were viewed as neither efficient nor safe. On a busy Friday afternoon, for instance, when you had to wait an hour or two for a ride across the river, four or five people and a mountain bike would be loaded on the tram. It was a crazy scene – that bit of Alaska most of us came looking for – and gave rise to the most popular saying in McCarthy: 'Every day is Saturday once you cross over on the tram.'

McCarthy

With the exception of a lodge in Kennicott, all services are located in the mountainous hamlet of McCarthy, a scenic and funky little town. Its year-round population averages around 35 but fluctuates depending on who is sticking out the winter; during the summer, it swells to around 100. Once you've crossed the Kennicott River on the footbridge, follow the road to the McCarthy River, which you also cross on a footbridge. On the other side, the road leads half a mile to the **McCarthy & Kennicott Museum**, an old railroad depot that features old photographs and a few mining artifacts dating back to the mining days, along with a small coffee shop that serves giant muffins in the morning. From the museum, take the right fork into the town of McCarthy (the left fork is the main road to Kennicott).

Kennicott was a company town, selfcontained and serious. McCarthy, on the other hand, was created in the early 1900s for the miners as a place of 'wine, women and song.' In other words, it had several saloons, restaurants and a red light district. In its heyday, the town had several hundred residents, its own newspaper and school. Today both O'Neill's Hardware Store and the MotherLode Power House (the home of St Elias Alpine Guides) have been listed on the National Register of Historic Places.

Kennicott

In 1900, a pair of miners named Jack Smith and Clarence Warner stumbled up the east side of the Kennicott Glacier until they arrived at a creek and found traces of copper. They named the creek Bonanza, and was it ever – the entire mountainside turned out to hold some of the richest copper deposits ever uncovered. In the Lower 48, mines were digging up ore that contained only 2% copper. Here, the veins would average almost 13%, while some contained as much as 70%.

Eventually, a group of investors bought the existing stakes and formed the Kennecott Copper Corporation, named when a clerical worker misspelled 'Kennicott.' First the syndicate built its railroad, 196 miles of rails through the wilderness, including the leg that is now McCarthy Rd, and Cordova's famous Million Dollar Bridge. The line cost $23 million before it even reached the mines in 1911.

Then, the syndicate built the company town of Kennicott, a sprawling red complex that included offices, the crushing mills, bunkhouses for the workers, company stores, a theater, wooden tennis courts and a school, all perched on a mountainside above the Kennicott Glacier. From 1911 until 1938, the mines operated 24 hours a day, produced 591,000 tons of copper and reported a net profit of more than $100 million.

Then in November 1938, faced with falling world prices for copper, an uncertainty about the mine's future productivity and, most of all, a possible labor strike, the company managers decided to close the operation. They made the decision one night, and then the next morning they told the workers that the mine was shut down and that the last train out of Kennicott was leaving in two hours. The disgruntled miners left in what has to be one of the greatest exoduses from a town in the USA.

With the exception of two large diesel engines, everything was left behind and Kennicott became a perfectly preserved slice of US mining history. Unfortunately, when the railroad bed was converted to a road in the 1960s, Kennicott also became the biggest help-yourself hardware store in the country.

Locals were taking windows, doors and wiring while tourists were picking the town clean of tools, spikes and anything they could haul away as a souvenir. Despite the pillage, Kennicott is still an amazing sight for most travelers. The mill, where the ore was crushed and the copper concentrated, towers above the surrounding buildings and still has tram cables leading up to the mountain mines. The rest of the buildings, including bunkhouses, train depot, worker's cottages and power plant, sit above the Kennicott Glacier.

In 1998, the NPS purchased the mill, power plant and many of the buildings from private owners as the first step to restoring them. The project of saving this unique piece of Alaska history will undoubtedly take years. Until then, you have to be content with strolling through the center of town and admiring the mining history by peeping through the windows. Also keep in mind that many of the buildings are still privately owned, and it is illegal to enter them.

You can reach Kennicott from McCarthy by either walking the railroad grade, now the main road, or hiking or mountain biking up Old Wagon Rd, more of a trail than a road. It starts on the main road, at a junction marked with a 'To Glacier' sign. Either way it's a 5-mile trek. There is also a van service in McCarthy, and it's always possible to hitch a ride in summer, when there's a trickle of traffic between the two towns.

Hiking

St Elias Alpine Guides (☎ 888-933-5427, 554-4445), in the MotherLode Power House, offer a number of guided day hikes in the McCarthy area. A full-day's hike along the alpine ridges to the mining ruins at the base of Castle Mountain is $95 per person. A four- to six-hour hike on Root Glacier is $55, including crampons and other equipment. For $125, the outfitters will fly you in for a stunning four- to six-hour hike higher on the glacier.

If you'd rather set out on your own, you can purchase USGS topographic maps at the Willow Herb Mountain Depot, on McCarthy Rd just before you cross the Kennicott River.

SOUTHCENTRAL

Root Glacier Trail From Kennicott Glacier Lodge, Root Glacier Trail is a 2.5-mile roundtrip past the mine ruins to the sparkling white-and-blue floe of ice. Hike west of town and continue past an unmarked junction to Bonanza Mine, less than a quarter of a mile away. Along the way you cross Jumbo Creek; a plank upstream makes fording this creek easy in normal water conditions. In another half mile are campsites overlooking the end of Root Glacier, with a storage bin to keep the bears out of your food and an outhouse nearby.

You can climb the glacier, but use extreme caution if you're inexperienced or you lack the proper equipment for walking on ice (crampons, ice axe, etc). A safer alternative is to follow the rough trail that skirts the moraine along the glacier. The path continues another 1.5 miles, providing excellent views of the ice. For this trek, you'll need these topographic maps: USGS quads *McCarthy B-6* and *C-6*.

Bonanza Mine Trail One of the best hikes from Kennicott is the alpine trek along the trail to Bonanza Mine. It's a roundtrip of almost 7 miles to the mine and a steep uphill walk all the way. Plan on three to four hours to hike up if the weather is good, and half that time to get back down. The trail is actually a rough dirt road to the tree line and starts just west of town at a junction that makes a sharp 180° turn up the mountain. Once above the tree line (a three-hour climb for most people), the view is stunning, and you can clearly see the mountain where the mine still sits. To reach the mine, you have to scramble up a rocky slope to the remaining bunkhouse, shafts and tram platform.

There is water once you reach the top, but carry at least a quart if the day is hot. For those who want to skip the long haul up but still enjoy the alpine portion of the hike, Kennicott-McCarthy Wilderness Guides (☎ 554-4444, 800-664-4537) uses a 4x4 vehicle to take hikers above the tree line for $25, with a minimum of four passengers. From there, it's still a good 90-minute trek to the mine.

River Running

Kennicott River Beginning near the glacier itself, rafting companies float the Kennicott River on half-day trips that feature Class III white water. Copper Oar (☎ 800-523-4453, 554-4453 in the summer) maintains a small office on the west side of

the river near the tram platform. The company offers a two-hour run down the Kennicott for $50 per person.

Nizina River For a full-day float, rafting companies combine the Kennicott with the Nizina and a portion of the Chitina River and then return you to McCarthy via a bush plane for a view of the mountains from above. The high point of the day is the run through the vertical-walled Nizina River Canyon. Both St Elias Alpine Guides (☎ 888-933-5427, 554-4445), in the MotherLode Power House, and Copper Oar offer a full-day three-rivers trip for $195.

Organized Tours

For a guided walk through Kennicott, seek out Chris Richards, the town's only registered voter. The colorful, year-round resident lives across the street from the Kennicott Glacier Lodge and offers historic tours through Kennicott-McCarthy Wilderness Guides (☎ 554-4444, 800-664-4537). He provides a colorful two-hour tour ($25) and gives you an idea of what it's like to live in a one-person town in the winter (he reads a lot). Richards also offers half-day glacier treks.

St Elias Alpine Guides (☎ 554-4445), in the MotherLode Power House, offers a variety of day trips out of McCarthy, including a two-hour historical tour of the area for $25 per person. If you just want to wander through Kennicott on your own, stop at the McCarthy Museum and pick up a copy of its *Walking Tour of Kennicott* for $1.

If the day is clear, splurge on a flightseeing tour of the surrounding mountains and glaciers. Both McCarthy Air (☎ 554-4440) and Wrangell Mountain Air (☎ 554-4400, 800-478-1160) offer a wide range of scenic flights, with a 30-minute flight beginning at around $50. But if you do fly, invest in an hour-long flight at $100 per person, so you'll have enough time to fly around 16,930-foot Mt Blackburn and volcanic Mt Wrangell.

Places to Stay & Eat

It's hard to camp around either McCarthy or Kennicott due to private ownership of most of the land. But those determined to pitch a tent can find campsites along the west side of the Kennicott River. A mile before the end of the road, the National Park Service maintains a free camping area. At the end of the road, you have to pay $5 to camp on private land. There are vault toilets but no piped-in water.

When it gets crowded and dusty on the weekends, a better alternative is the ***Kennicott River Lodge & Hostel*** (☎ 554-4441), Mile 58 of McCarthy Rd. The two-story log lodge includes a common kitchen and large porches overlooking the Kennicott Glacier. Accommodations are bunkrooms in the lodge, cabins or wall tents. The rate is $25 per night.

In McCarthy, the accommodation options change almost seasonally, so it pays to walk around to see if anybody is renting out a cabin or has started up a B&B. A half mile from the Kennicott River, ***McCarthy B&B*** (☎ 554-4433), McCarthy Rd, has four cabins that cost $85 for a double without a bathroom. You enjoy an all-the-pancakes-you-can-eat breakfast in the home of the host, John Adams.

In the heart of McCarthy is the ***McCarthy Lodge*** (☎ 554-4402), a virtual museum full of mining relics and photographs of the era, and the place to get a bed, meal, shower or a cold beer in a frosty mug. The main lodge has a dining room where full dinners cost $17 to $22 and a lively bar with $4 beers. A lot for a beer maybe, but, hey, they're cold! Showers cost $5, so skip the shower and have a beer. Across the street, the lodge runs ***Ma Johnson's Hotel***, built in 1916 as a boarding house and today totally renovated, with rooms beginning at $95/110 (more if you want your meals included).

Next door to Ma Johnson's Hotel is ***Tailor Made Pizza***, where a pizza sets you back $15 and can be enjoyed with beer and wine. There's also ***McCarthy Gift Shop and Groceries***, with limited liquor, camping and food supplies.

In Kennicott, the ***Kennicott Glacier Lodge*** (☎ 800-582-5128 *outside Alaska*, 800-478-2350 *within the state*) offers beds, running water and electricity, but not a private bathroom, for $149/169. It also has a dining room, and for $255 per couple you get a bed, six meals and a guided walk of the mines. Even if you don't stay here, hike up in the morning and have breakfast on the long front porch. The meal is $12 but includes eggs, sourdough pancakes and sausage along with pitchers of juice and coffee, all enjoyed with a spectacular view of peaks and glaciers.

Getting There & Away

Air Several small air companies fly daily service between McCarthy and Glennallen. Ellis Air (☎ 800-478-3368 in Alaska, 822-3363) departs the Gulkana airstrip at 10 am on Wednesday and Friday, arrives in McCarthy at 11 am and then turns around and heads back. The one-way fare is $62. Wrangell Mountain Air (☎ 554-4440, 800-478-1160) also has service between McCarthy and Glennallen and even Chitina. A roundtrip flight between Chitina and McCarthy is $130 and doubles as a flightseeing trip that includes five glaciers and the mountaintop mines on Bonanza Peak.

Bus Hitchhiking McCarthy Rd is not nearly as challenging as it was 10 years ago, but it still can be a wait at times. The alternative is Backcountry Connections (☎ 800-478-5292 in Alaska, 822-5292). The small tour company departs Caribou Motel on Glenn Hwy in Glennallen at 7 am Monday to Saturday, reaching Chitina at 8:30 am and the McCarthy footbridge at noon. After a five-hour layover, enough time to see McCarthy and the ruins at Kennicott, the van returns to Glennallen, reaching the crossroads town at 8:30 pm. The roundtrip fare for the same day is $99, though this is a lot of time to spend in a van. The roundtrip fare for different days is $105; one-way, it's $70.

Getting Around

Once you're in McCarthy, you can pick up a ride to Kennicott from either McCarthy Air or Wrangell Mountain Air, which maintain log cabin offices in town. Both run vans up to the company town for $5 per person.

Mountain bikes clearly outnumber cars here, as most locals and travelers use them as a means of getting around the area. In fact, those old mining roads and trails, which are tough on vehicles, are ideal for fat-tire bikes, making McCarthy something of a biker's paradise. If you have your own bike, you can walk it across the footbridge. If not, then St Elias Alpine Guides (☎ 554-4445) rents Diamond Back mountain bikes for $35 a day.

WHITTIER

On the day the military was cutting the ribbon that marked the completion of the Alcan, the army was also having a tunnel 'holing through' ceremony outside Whittier. WWII and the Japanese invasion of the Aleutian Islands brought the US military searching for a second warm-water port in Southcentral Alaska, one that would serve as a secret port. Whittier was chosen because it was well hidden between the high walls of the Passage Canal Fjord and because consistently bad weather hangs over it.

In the Chugach Mountains, work began immediately on two tunnels that would connect the port to the main line of the Alaska Railroad. The tunnels, though overshadowed by the Alcan, were another amazing feat of engineering. The first was drilled through almost a mile of solid rock, while the second, begun simultaneously from the other side of the mountain, required carving a route 2.5 miles long. When General Simon Buckner blasted open the second tunnel during the 'holing through' ceremony in 1942, the two tunnels missed perfect alignment by an eighth of an inch.

Whittier owes both its existence and its skyscraper appearance to the military. After WWII, the port remained a permanent base during the Cold War, and tall concrete buildings were constructed to house and serve the personnel. One building, Begich Towers, is 14 stories tall. Nearby, the massive Buckner Building once housed 1000 people and had a bowling alley, theater, hospital, pool, jail and cafes. These skyscrapers look strange, but their upward-pointing design greatly reduces the need for the removal of snow, which exceeds 14 feet during some winters.

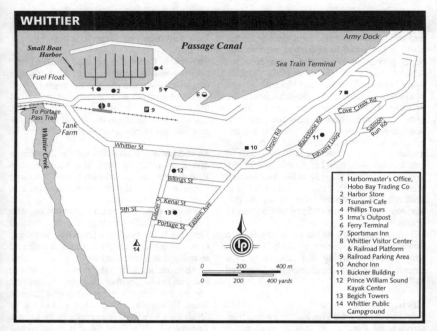

WHITTIER

Passage Canal

Army Dock

Small Boat Harbor

Fuel Float

Sea Train Terminal

Cove Creek Rd

To Portage Pass Trail

Tank Farm

Whittier Creek

Whittier St

Depot Rd

Blackstone Rd

Eshamy Loop

Salmon Run Rd

Billings St

Glacier St

Kenai St

Eastern Ave

5th St

Portage St

0   200   400 m
0   200   400 yards

1 Harbormaster's Office,
   Hobo Bay Trading Co
2 Harbor Store
3 Tsunami Cafe
4 Phillips Tours
5 Irma's Outpost
6 Ferry Terminal
7 Sportsman Inn
8 Whittier Visitor Center
   & Railroad Platform
9 Railroad Parking Area
10 Anchor Inn
11 Buckner Building
12 Prince William Sound
   Kayak Center
13 Begich Towers
14 Whittier Public
   Campground

The army declared the Whittier post unnecessary in 1960 but maintained it until 1968, in part because of the extensive damage the town suffered from the Good Friday Earthquake. The quake caused more than $5 million in damage, with 13 people killed and the harbor destroyed by a tidal wave. Whittier was incorporated in 1969, and in 1973 the city bought seven military buildings and 97 acres for $200,000. Begich Towers was quickly converted into 198 condominiums, with city offices located on the 1st floor and community businesses on the 2nd floor.

Today, over half of Whittier's 280 residents live in Begich Towers. On the first two floors, you'll find a laundromat, convenience store, beauty salon, post office, even a church. Since the military left, Whittier has survived thanks to some fishing and tourism. It's a port of call for both the Alaska Marine Hwy ferry and the Alaska Railroad.

All this could change by the year 2000, when the road to Whittier is scheduled to open. Work on the road, which starts at the Begich-Boggs Visitor Center at Portage Glacier, began in 1997 but has slowed due to litigation by opponents, many of them town residents (see the boxed text 'A Road To Whittier'). Once the road is completed, it remains to be seen how much of an economic stimulus it will be or how it will affect the character of what used to be a remote and isolated community.

Things to See & Do

The vast majority of travelers stay in Whittier only long enough to board the train to Anchorage or the ferry to Valdez. Although the town itself is nothing to brag about – many consider it to be dismal – the surrounding area is a scenic blend of mountains and glaciers; on a rare clear day, it's an interesting spot to spend an afternoon.

As soon as you disembark from the train, you'll spot the new **Whittier Visitor Center** (☎ 472-2379), housed in a rail car donated by the Alaska Railroad. It's part visitor center and part gift shop, but the staff are friendly and will point you in the right direction. Due north is the **small boat harbor**, with fishing boats, private craft and the numerous tour vessels that work the Columbia Glacier route between Whittier and Valdez.

On the 1st floor of the Begich Towers, the **Whittier Historical Museum** looks like a garage sale more than a museum and contains mostly historic photos and maritime specimens. Its most interesting display is a mounted wolffish that a six-year-old girl caught while fishing in Prince William Sound. The mouth of this rare fish is filled with sharp teeth and molars that the animal used to eat shellfish and, on occasion, to attack people. The museum is open 1 to 5 pm Wednesday to Friday.

From the southwest corner of the Begich Towers, a track leads west to Whittier Creek, while above it, falling from the ridge of a glacial cirque, is the picturesque **Horsetail Falls**.

Hiking

Portage Pass Trail This makes a superb afternoon hike, as it provides good views of Portage Glacier, Passage Canal and the surrounding mountains and glaciers. Even better, hike up in the late afternoon and spend the evening camping at Divide Lake.

The Portage Pass Trail is an old roadbed and is easy to follow. To reach the trailhead, walk west along the gravel road from the train platform as it parallels the tracks. Follow it 1.3 miles to the tank farm and the tunnel at Maynard Mountain, and turn left onto a road that crosses the tracks. Proceed along the right fork as it begins to climb steeply along the flank of the mountain. It's a steady ascent of a mile to a promontory (elevation 750 feet) that offers views of Portage Glacier or Passage Canal to the east.

The trail then descends to Divide Lake and the Portage Pass, reached in another half mile. At this point the trail ends, and a route through alder continues to descend to a beach on Portage Lake. It's a one-way, 2-mile hike from the trailhead to the lake and well

worth bashing some brush at the end. There are great views from the shores of Portage Lake and plenty of places to set up camp.

Smitty's Cove From the front of the Sportsman Inn, Smitty's Cove lies a quarter of a mile down the road to the right (northeast). At low tide you can beach-comb all of the cove to the point east of it. A favorite haunt of Alaska scuba divers, the area is occasionally referred to as Diver's Cove.

First Salmon Run A 0.8-mile walk along a dirt road leads to the First Salmon Run Picnic Area, so named because of the large king and silver salmon runs in the creek in June and late August.

From the northeast corner of the Buckner Building behind the Sportsman Inn, follow the road that leads up the mountain, staying to the right at the first fork and to the left at the second fork.

The road leads into the picnic area, where you can cross a bridge over the stream and continue another 3 miles to Second Salmon Run. This walk, along what is known as Shotgun Cove Rd, is exceptionally scenic, with views of Billings Glacier most of the way.

Paddling

Whittier is a prime location for sea kayakers, as it's practically surrounded by glaciated fjords and inlets. Prince William Sound Kayak Center (☎ 472-2452) can outfit you with a rental kayak and gear. Not a shop, the center is in a fenced-in storage area just off Glacier St a block from Begich Towers. It's best to reserve a boat in advance during the summer. A single kayak is $45 a day; a double is $70. The company also shuttles people out to Smitty's Cove or First Salmon Run for $5 per person.

Alaska Trail & Sail Adventures (☎ 346-1234), in the Whittier Harbor, rents kayaks for the same price and also offers a six-hour guided paddle trip for $99.

The most common overnight trip from Whittier is Blackstone Bay, which features a pair of tidewater glaciers: Blackstone and

Beloit. Many kayakers utilize charter boats to carry their kayaks and reach the more dramatic fjords to the north, including Harriman, College and Unakwik Inlet. Contact Lazy Otter Charters (☎ 345-3775, 800-587-6887, lazyottr@alaska.net) or Sound Eco Adventures (☎ 888-471-2312, 333-8209) about drop-off and pickup service.

Organized Tours

College and Harriman Fjords, north of Whittier, contain not one but 26 glaciers with such academic names as Harvard, Dartmouth, Yale and Vassar, after the colleges that supported the expedition leading to their discovery. On the way to Harriman Fjord, cruise ships pass so close to a kittiwake rookery

A Road to Whittier

Babe Reynolds arrived in Whittier in 1979, 'running from a husband.' She stayed in the small seaport and opened up the Hobo Bay Trading Company because she liked the isolation and the fact that people could only come by train or boat. But in the past few years, Reynolds has not only been flipping buffalo burgers but fighting what has become known around this community of 300 as 'The Road.'

Reynolds, along with a coalition of environmental groups and local municipalities, has lost. Sometime in 2000, the toll road to Whittier is scheduled to be open. It will depart from near the Begich Boggs Visitor Center at Portage Glacier, wind 2 miles along the shores of Portage Lake and then enter a 2.7-mile train tunnel that has been revamped to handle both trains and cars at different times. The total project exceeds $60 million, leading critics to call it 'Whittier's $24 million-a-mile road.'

Questions about the project remain. Once the road is open, what are people in Whittier going to do with all the cars? Or tourists? Or cruise ships? Some studies estimate that more than 2000 tour buses and cars will arrive in the town daily during the summer. Whittier, the closest community to Prince William Sound's spectacular glaciers, presently draws 100,000 tourists a year. Experts say that number could rise to 1.4 million by 2015, thanks to The Road. 'Where are they going to park?' Reynolds said to a magazine writer. 'Parking places are hard enough to find now. We'll be the world's biggest cul-de-sac.'

In the works for more than 20 years, the project finally leaped off the drawing board in 1993, when Gov Wally Hickel convinced the Alaska legislature to appropriate $15 million toward the construction. Ironically, the money came from the settlement that Exxon paid the state for its 1989 oil spill. The devastating spill that washed the eastern half of the Sound in oil is now, say road opponents, contributing to the over-commercialization of the western half.

Proponents argue that the road is needed. Whittier is surrounded by mountains – the reason the US Army built its self-contained base here in 1943 – that literally hold storms over the town. Whittier averages 15 feet of rain and more than 20 feet of snow annually. In the summer the train runs six times daily, but in the winter residents can be trapped for days at a time.

Most of all, a road will be a pipeline for large tour companies to funnel tourists from Anchorage to the wonders of Prince William Sound. Giants like Holland American Line pushed for The Road early on. With The Road, tourists can see the glaciers in College Fjord during the day and then spend the night in Anchorage.

But many others are saddened by the inevitable change that is about to occur in Whittier in the next few years. Already there is talk about adding a 400-room resort, doubling the size of the harbor and welcoming the return of the large cruise ships that abandoned Whittier in the early 1990s in favor of Seward. 'It isn't being done for us; it is being done to us,' said Reynolds.

that you can see the eggs of the black-legged birds in their nests.

Various tour boats that sail out of the small boat harbor in Whittier offer day cruises to this icy world, including the *Klondike Express*, a new high-speed catamaran operated by Phillips Tours (☎ 800-544-0529, 276-8023 in Anchorage). The boat departs Whittier at 11:45 am daily, so if you're coming from Anchorage, you need to catch the 10:20 am train. The 110-mile cruise lasts almost six hours and costs $122 per person.

Major Marine Tours (☎ 800-764-7300, 274-7300 in Anchorage) offers a six-hour tour to the glaciers at the head of Blackstone Bay onboard the 100-foot *Emerald Sea*. This boat, which includes a full bar, departs daily during the summer at 11:45 am. The difference between the two tours is that Blackstone Bay is cheaper – only $99 per person – but visits fewer glaciers.

Places to Stay & Eat

Whittier Public Campground is primarily a gravel surface for RVers behind Begich Towers, but you can also set up a tent for $5 per night. Or you can pitch a tent just about anywhere near town by walking into the bush and away from the road.

In town, you can book a bed through *June's Whittier B&B* (☎ 472-2396), in Begich Towers, which maintains three condos on the 5th, 8th and 15th floors. Rates begin at $75 single/double but jump to $90 if your room overlooks the bay and mountains. There are also two hotels in Whittier: the *Anchor Inn* (☎ 472-2354) and the *Sportsman Inn* (☎ 472-2352). Both sell groceries and have a dining room, public laundry, bar and rates of $70/75 for a single/double. The Anchor Inn is the less run-down of the two.

At the *Hobo Bay Trading Company*, in the harbormaster's office, Babs Reynolds has been flipping burgers for 20 years and will serve you a Buffalo Babs Burger topped with a hot pepper and served with good fries and a dose of local politics ($6 to $8). Her pies are a great way to end any meal.

The east end of the small boat harbor has been developed into something of a strip mall, Whittier style. Among the gift shops

here you'll find an information booth, a reindeer pen and *Irma's Outpost*, a spot serving hamburgers and corned beef sandwiches. Even better is *Tsunami Cafe* next door. The hamburgers are served on freshly baked buns ($7 to $9), or you can order a large shrimp-and-garlic pizza ($20) and enjoy it with a cold beer. If it's one of those rare sunny days in Whittier, you can even dine on the cafe's outdoor deck overlooking the harbor.

The *Harbor Store*, also overlooking the small boat harbor, carries groceries and other supplies.

Getting There & Away

There are two ways of getting out of Whittier, and neither one is by road – or not yet, anyhow. To go west, you take the Alaska Railroad; to head east, you take a boat.

Train Four trains depart Whittier on Wednesday and Thursday, with six trains the rest of the week. The one-way fare from Whittier to Portage is $12. Once in Portage, you can take a shuttle bus to Anchorage. Alaska Backpackers Shuttle (☎ 344-8775, 800-266-8625) meets all trains and charges a one-way fare of $20. The Alaska Railroad's newest service is a Whittier-to-Anchorage run. This train departs Whittier at 5:45 pm daily, and the one-way fare is $26, making it cheaper than the train to Portage and van service to Anchorage.

Boat The ferry M/V *Bartlett* goes east six times a week, departing at 2:45 pm from the ferry dock. On Monday, the boat sails to Cordova; all other departures go to Valdez. The one-way fare from Whittier to either Valdez or Cordova is $58.

Kenai Peninsula

Because of its diverse terrain, easy accessibility and close proximity to Anchorage, the Kenai Peninsula has become the state's top recreational area. It is well serviced, well developed and, unfortunately, well used during the summer. Although some trails are very

The Homer Spit extending out into Kachemak Bay

Cordova small boat harbor

Blackstone Bay at dawn, Prince William Sound

The Million Dollar Bridge, outside of Cordova

popular all summer and many campgrounds are always filled to near capacity, if you hike a little farther or climb a little higher you can find a tent space with only nature around you.

Two major highways and one minor one pass through the area. From Anchorage, the Seward Hwy follows the Turnagain Arm where the road has been carved out of mountains and then turns south at Portage, heading to the picturesque community of Seward on Resurrection Bay.

At Tern Lake Junction, 90 miles south of Anchorage, the Sterling Hwy heads west from the Seward Hwy. When it reaches the crossroads town of Soldotna, near Cook Inlet, it turns south, following the coast past some great clam-digging beaches and ending at Homer, the most delightful town on the peninsula. The third road is the Hope Hwy, which heads north from the Seward Hwy, 70 miles south of Anchorage, and leads to the small historical mining community of Hope, about 16 miles from the junction with the Seward Hwy.

Traffic is heavy on the main highways, making hitchhiking an easy form of travel during the summer. The area is connected to the rest of Prince William Sound by the ferry M/V *Tustumena*, which runs from Cordova and Valdez across the sound to Seward, over to Homer and then south to Kodiak. Alaska Airlines, through its contract carrier, also provides regularly scheduled services between Anchorage and Kenai, Homer and Kodiak. For more information, see the Getting Around chapter of this book.

SEWARD HIGHWAY

From Portage, it's easy traveling down the Seward Hwy into the heart of the Kenai Peninsula. The highway stretches for 127 miles and is another scenic gem in the state's fledgling road system.

The first section of the Seward Hwy – from Anchorage (Mile 127) to Portage Glacier (Mile 79) – is covered in the Anchorage chapter. When heading south, keep in mind that the mileposts along the Seward Hwy show distances from Seward, (Mile 0) to Anchorage (Mile 127).

Near Mile 68 the highway begins climbing into the alpine region of **Turnagain Pass**, where there's a roadside stop with garbage cans and toilets. In early summer, this area is a kaleidoscope of wildflowers.

Just past Mile 65 is the USFS *Bertha Creek Campground* (12 sites, $9) on the banks of the creek. You can spend a day climbing the alpine slopes of the pass here, or you can head down the road to the northern trailhead of **Johnson Pass Trail** (see the Hiking section in the Wilderness chapter), a 23-mile route over another alpine pass.

The USFS *Granite Creek Campground* (18 sites, $9 fee) is at *Mile 63* of the Seward Hwy and provides tables, water and a place to camp for hikers coming off the Johnson Pass Trail at its northern end. This campground, about halfway between Anchorage and Seward, is a convenient place to spend the evening, but recent logging has marred the beauty of the surrounding area.

The junction with Hope Hwy (see the Hope Hwy section in this chapter) is at Mile 56.7. From here, the paved Hope Hwy heads 18 miles north, ending a mile past the small hamlet of Hope. The Seward Hwy continues south of this junction, and at Mile 46 you cross the Colorado Creek Bridge and the short side road to the USFS *Tenderfoot Creek Campground* (28 sites, $9), a scenic campground on the shores of Upper Summit Lake.

The **Devil's Pass Trail** (see the Resurrection Pass Trail in the Hiking section of the Wilderness chapter), a 10-mile hike over a 2400-foot gap to Resurrection Pass Trail, is at Mile 39.4 of the Seward Hwy. Tern Lake Junction, the beginning of the Sterling Hwy at Mile 37, makes for an ideal place to stop and stretch the legs. Located at the junction is a USFS wildlife viewing area, and from the platform that extends into the marshy north end of the lake you can usually spot common loons, bald eagles or arctic terns. Look for beavers and river otters in the lake, while Dall sheep and mountain goats often feed on the slopes of the surrounding mountains. For more wildlife, head half a mile west from the junction to the US Forest Service *Tern Lake Campground* (33 sites, $9), where there's a

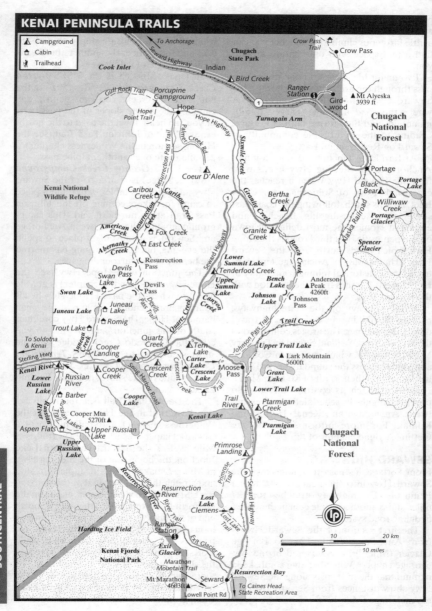

KENAI PENINSULA TRAILS

- △ Campground
- ⌂ Cabin
- 🎿 Trailhead

salmon-viewing platform on Dave's Creek. Occasionally brown and black bears come to the creek to feed on spawning salmon.

At Mile 33 of the Seward Hwy, the **Carter Lake Trail** provides quick (but steep) access to subalpine terrain. The 2.3-mile path, an old jeep trail, starts from a parking area on the west side of the highway and ascends almost 1000 feet to Carter Lake. From the lake, a trail continues another mile around the west side of the lake, headed toward Crescent Lake. You'll find good camping at the end of Carter Lake.

At Mile 29.4, the Seward Hwy passes through the village of **Moose Pass** (population 118) on the banks of Upper Trail Lake. This small town began in the Hope-Sunrise gold rush of the late 1800s but really came into its own when the original Iditarod Trail was cut around the lake in 1910–11. The abundance of moose in the area caused an early mail carrier to call the valley Moose Pass, and the name stuck when the first post office opened in 1928.

Moose Pass has a general store and bar, post office, a handful of B&Bs and ***Trail Lake Lodge*** (☎ 288-3103). The recently remodeled lodge features a restaurant, 35 rooms that begin at $89 for single or double with a shared bathroom, showers, a Laundromat and a salmon bake on the shores of the lake during the summer. Just down the road is ***Moose Pass RV Park***, with sites that overlook the lake for $12 a night.

The best time to visit the area is during the Moose Pass Summer Festival on the weekend nearest the summer solstice (usually June 21). This delightful two-day festival includes a halibut barbecue, games for the kids, arts and crafts booths and a beer tent.

Back on the Seward Hwy, at Mile 24 you'll meet an obscure dirt road that leads west to the USFS ***Trail River Campground*** (63 sites, $9). This campground features many campsites among the tall spruce along Kenai Lake and the Lower Trail River. Right before the Ptarmigan Creek Bridge, at Mile 23 of the Seward Hwy, is the entrance to the USFS ***Ptarmigan Creek Campground*** (26 sites, $9).

The 3.5-mile **Ptarmigan Creek Trail** begins in the campground and ends at Ptarmigan Lake, a beautiful body of water that reflects the surrounding mountains. A 4-mile trail continues around the north side of the lake, where there's good fishing for Dolly Varden trout at the lake's outlet to the creek. Plan on five hours for a roundtrip hike to the lake, as some parts of the trail are steep. The **Victor Creek Trail**, at Mile 19.7 on the east side of the highway, is a fairly difficult path that ascends 3 miles to good views of the surrounding mountains.

After crossing the bridge over South Fork Snow River at Mile 17.2, look west for the road that leads a mile to the USFS ***Primrose Landing Campground*** (10 sites, $9). This scenic campground is on the east end of the beautiful Kenai Lake and contains the trailhead for the Primrose Trail (see the Lost Lake Trail in the Seward Hiking section).

The **Grayling Lake Trail** leads 2 miles to Grayling Lake, a beautiful spot with views of Snow River. Side trails connect Grayling Lake with Meridian and Leech Lakes. At all three lakes, anglers stand a good chance of catching grayling. The trailhead is in a paved parking lot at Mile 13.2 on the west side of the Seward Hwy.

SEWARD

Seward (population 3000) is a scenic town flanked by rugged mountains on one side and the salmon-filled Resurrection Bay on the other. It's the only town on the eastern side of the Kenai Peninsula – and probably the only city of its size in Alaska – without a McDonald's. For that reason alone, you've got to love Seward.

History

The town was founded in 1903, when Alaska Railroad surveyors needed an ice-free port to serve as the ocean terminal for the rail line. The first spike was driven in during 1904, and the line was completed in 1923. During that time, Seward prospered, for it served as the beginning of the Iditarod Trail to Nome and thousands of prospectors stampeded their way through town. Dog teams hauled supplies and mail along this 1200-mile route

SEWARD

PLACES TO STAY
2 Breeze Inn
6 Murphy's Motel
7 Harborview Inn
9 Falcon's Way B&B
12 Moby Dick Hostel
14 Waterfront Campground
19 Van Guilder Hotel
25 Taroka Inn
28 Hotel Seward
34 Seward Waterfront Lodging

PLACES TO EAT
1 Ray's Waterfront
17 Peking Chinese Restaurant
21 Mt Marathon Cafe
26 Apollo
29 Harbor Dinner Club
33 Legends of the Mountain
35 Don's Kitchen

OTHER
3 Kenai Fjords Tours
4 Kenai Fjords National Park Visitor Center
5 National Bank of Alaska
8 Laundromat
10 Seward General Hospital
11 Railroad Car, Chamber of Commerce
13 Post Office
15 Resurrection Bay Historical Museum
16 USFS Ranger Station
18 Resurrect Art Gallery
20 Liberty Theater
22 City Hall
23 Rest Rooms
24 St Peter's Episcopal Church
27 Seward Saloon & Oyster Bar
30 Library
31 Northland Books & Charts
32 Yukon Bar
36 Marine Science Education Center
37 Alaska SeaLife Center
38 Chugach Heritage Center, Start of Iditarod Trail

To Seward Hwy, Ferry Terminal, Resurrection River Trail, Anchorage

Small Boat Harbor

Lagoon

2nd Lake

1st Lake

Two Lakes Trail

Van Buren St
D St
C St
B St
A St
Monroe St
Madison St
Jefferson St
Adams St
Washington St

Park

To Mt Marathon

Race Point Trail

Lowell Canyon Rd

0 100 200 m
0 100 200 yards

1st Ave
2nd Ave
3rd Ave
4th Ave
5th Ave
6th Ave

Ballaine Boulevard

Iditarod National Historic Trail

Church St

Bromwell St

Railway Ave

To Lowell Point, Caines Head State Recreation Area

Resurrection Bay

SOUTHCENTRAL

and returned with the gold. In 1910, one of the largest shipments of Nome gold arrived with miner Bob Griffis, who mushed his dogs into Seward accompanied by armed guards. Griffis's gold bags would have been worth more than $6 million today.

Like most towns in Southcentral Alaska, Seward began a new era of history in 1964 after the Good Friday Earthquake (or Black Friday, as Alaskans call it) caused fires and tidal waves that destroyed 90% of the town. At one point, a 3500-foot stretch of waterfront slid into the bay, and Seward was completely cut off from the rest of the state.

The only reminder of that natural disaster is at the public library, 5th Ave at Adams St across from City Hall, where the slide show *Seward is Burning* is shown at 2 pm Monday to Saturday. Admission is $3.

The town has completely rebuilt its fine small boat harbor and waterfront facilities, with a $10-million dock designed to be earthquake-proof. Most of the area's residents either work at Seward Fisheries (the largest halibut-receiving station on the US West Coast) or fish themselves, or they're otherwise connected with the town's growing maritime industry.

Information

Tourist Offices If downtown, head over to the Seward Railroad Car on the corner of 3rd Ave and Jefferson St. Built as a dining car by the Pullman Company in 1916, today it houses the Chamber of Commerce Information Cache, where you can pick up maps, information or a guide to a walking tour. Inside the car, you'll still find the original lunch counter and stools, where you can enjoy a 25¢ cup of coffee. The center is open 11 am to 5 pm daily in the summer.

If driving into town, stop at the year-round visitor center in the Chamber office (☎ 224-8051, www.seward.net/chamber) at Mile 2 of the Seward Hwy. The center has racks of information, brochures on most of the B&Bs in the area and courtesy phones to book rooms or tours. During the summer, the office is open 8 am to 6 pm daily. The rest of the year, the office is open 8 am to 5 pm weekdays.

The Kenai Fjords National Park Visitor Center (☎ 224-3175), in the small boat harbor, has information on the nearby park and is open 8 am to 7 pm daily during the summer. For information on Chugach National Forest trails, cabins and campgrounds, go to the USFS Ranger Station (☎ 224-3374) on the corner of 4th Ave and Jefferson St. It's open 8 am to 5 pm Monday to Friday.

Money There are two banks in Seward, including the National Bank of Alaska (☎ 224-5283), 3rd Ave at D St.

Post The post office is open on the corner of 5th Ave and Madison St.

Email & Internet Access Email and Internet access is available at the Seward library, on the corner of 5th Ave and Adams St.

Travel Agencies One of the largest in Seward is World Express Travel (☎ 224-5554), 300 4th Ave.

Bookstores Northland Books & Charts (☎ 224-3102) is in the Orca Building, 201 3rd Ave, and sells Alaskan titles as well as USGS topographical maps.

Libraries The Seward library (☎ 224-3646), 5th Ave at Adams St, often sponsors a used-book sale during the summer. It's open noon to 8 pm weekdays, noon to 6 pm Saturday.

Laundry Seward Laundry (☎ 224-5727), near the small boat harbor at 4th Ave and B St, also offers showers for $3.50.

Medical Services The Seward General Hospital (☎ 224-5205) is on 1st Ave at the west end of Madison St. The Family Medical Clinic of Seward (☎ 224-8911) is in the Seaview Plaza, 302 Railway Ave.

Walking Tour

Beginning at the Seward Railroad Car on 3rd Ave, look to the left, where you'll see a group of houses known as **Millionaires Row**. They were built around 1905 by railroad officials and bankers who had just

SOUTHCENTRAL

arrived in the newly created town. Nearby, on the corner of Jefferson St and 3rd Ave, is the **Resurrection Bay Historical Museum**, open 10 am to 5 pm daily. The museum features artifacts and photographs of the 1964 earthquake, including a clock that stopped the instant the disaster struck. There are also exhibits about the area's Russian era, when a shipyard was established in 1793, and about Seward's role in the Iditarod Trail. Admission is $1.

Head west on Jefferson St to Lowell Canyon Rd to see the start of the trail to Mt Marathon (see Race Point Trail in the Hiking section below). After you turn back toward town on Jefferson St, turn south (right) onto 1st St. At Adams St, turn east (left). On the corner of 2nd Ave is **St Peter's Episcopal Church**. Built in 1906, the church contains the famous mural of the Resurrection by Dutch artist Jan van Emple, who used Alaskan models and the nearby bay as his backdrop.

To the southeast, on the corner of 3rd and Railway Aves, is the **Marine Science Education Center**, operated by the University of Alaska-Fairbanks. The center has aquariums featuring live Alaskan marine specimens, as well as interesting displays and films on the state's important sea life. If you haven't seen a whale yet, you'll get a good idea of how large they are from the minke whale skull that fills the middle of the room. The center is open 10 am to 4 pm Tuesday through Sunday in summer. Admission is $3.

East on Railway Ave, next door to the Alaska Sealife Center, is the **Chugach Heritage Center**. Located in Seward's restored 1917 railroad depot, the center houses workshops for native artists and craftsmen, as well as a gift shop and interpretive displays. Native dance performances take place six times daily in a 40-seat theater. The center is open 10 am to 6 pm daily. Dance performances cost $8.

Alaska SeaLife Center

The most impressive attraction in Seward is the new Alaska SeaLife Center, which opened in 1998. Housed in what used to be the ferry terminal at the foot of 4th Ave, the $56-million marine center was funded in part by money from the *Exxon Valdez* oil spill settlement. It's the only cold-water marine science facility in the Western Hemisphere.

The facility is both a research station for the rehabilitation of fish, marine mammals and sea birds and an interpretive area for visitors. A tour begins with a ride up the only escalator in the Kenai Peninsula to view an ongoing movie on the rich marine life in Prince William Sound. Exhibit rooms follow and include displays on the oil spill; the Alaska Waters Gallery, which features fish in a kelp forest; and a tide pool touch tank where you can pick up and hold a sea anemone or star fish.

The most impressive area is a wing that houses a series of tanks 21 feet deep. The huge tanks are home to a variety of marine wildlife – chattering seabirds, playful puffins, diving harbor seals and sea lions sunning themselves – that you can view from above or from an underwater vantage point on a lower floor. The outdoor observation deck offers a picture-postcard view of the mountains ringing Resurrection Bay and a chance to watch salmon thrash their way up a fish ladder. At the foot of the deck is the beachfront, where veterinarians and volunteers worked tirelessly trying to save oiled sea otters in 1989.

This is truly one of Alaska's finest attractions. Plan to spend the better part of an afternoon here. The center (☎ 224-3080, 800-224-2525) is open 9 am to 9:30 pm daily. Admission is $12.50 per person.

Small Boat Harbor

The interesting small boat harbor, at the northern end of 4th Ave, hums during the summer with fishing boats, charter vessels and a large number of sailboats. It has also developed into a separate business district for Seward, especially as far as restaurants are concerned. The heart of the district is the **harbormaster's office**; look for the pair of huge sea anchors and impressive pile of chain displayed outside. Nearby is the **Kenai Fjords National Park Visitor Center**. The center has a bookshop, a few displays on the park and a fascinating oil-spill video, shown in a small theater. At the back, there are picnic tables and a free sighting scope overlooking the harbor and the bay – it's a nice place to enjoy lunch.

Hiking

Mount Marathon Trail The most popular trail near the town center heads toward the top of Mt Marathon, the mountain that sits behind the city. The route (also called Race Point Trail) is well known throughout Alaska. In 1909, two sourdough miners wagered how long it would take to run to the top and back and then dashed off for the peak. After that, it became an official event at the Seward July Fourth celebrations and today attracts hundreds of runners and an equal number of spectators who line the streets. The fastest time is 43 minutes and 23 seconds, set in 1981. Most runners come down the mountain in less than 10 minutes, usually by sliding halfway on their behinds.

Hikers, on the other hand, can take their time and enjoy the spectacular views of Seward and Resurrection Bay. The trail begins at the west end of Jefferson St (also known as Lowell Canyon Rd), up the Lowell Canyon. The marked trailhead is in a small gravel pit just past a pair of water tanks.

Scramble up the ridge to the right of the gully, and for fun return through the gully's scree. You never really reach Mt Marathon's summit, though you do reach a high point (known as Race Point) at 3022 feet on the broad east shoulder. Plan on three to four hours for the 3-mile roundtrip.

Iditarod National Historic Trail Although most of the world knows the Iditarod as a sled-dog race from Anchorage to Nome, the legendary trail actually begins in Seward. A historical marker in Hoben Park at the foot of 4th Ave marks Mile 0, and from there a paved bike path heads north along the beach.

A far more interesting segment of the trail for hikers, however, can be reached by heading east on Nash Rd just after the Seward Hwy crosses the Resurrection River. Within 2 miles you'll cross Sawmill Creek and arrive at a gravel parking lot on the north side of the road. From here you can follow the Iditarod Trail through the woods for a 4-mile hike to Bear Lake.

Two Lakes Trail This easy 1-mile loop goes through a wooded area, crosses a salmon-spawning creek and passes two small lakes at the base of Mt Marathon. Begin the hike near the first lake, behind the Alaska Vocational & Training Center on the corner of 2nd Ave and B St, and loop back on Hemlock St after you reach the second lake. Near the start of the trail you'll see a scenic waterfall.

Resurrection River Trail This 16-mile trail, built in 1984, is the last link in a 70-mile system across the Kenai Peninsula from Seward to Hope. This continuous trail is broken only by the Sterling Hwy and provides a long-term wilderness adventure on the peninsula, leading hikers through a diversity of streams, rivers, lakes, wooded lowlands and alpine areas.

The southern trailhead for the Resurrection River Trail is 8 miles up Exit Glacier Rd, which leaves the Seward Hwy at Mile 3.7. The northern trailhead joins the Russian Lakes Trail (see the Hiking section in the Wilderness chapter) 5 miles from Cooper Lake or 16 miles from the Russian River Campground off the Sterling Hwy. The hike from the Seward Hwy to the Sterling Hwy is a 40-mile trip, including walking up Exit Glacier Rd.

In 1995, floods severely damaged the trail, making the northern half a much more challenging hike. The route from Exit Glacier Rd to the USFS Resurrection River Cabin (see Places to Stay below), which is 6.5 miles from the southern trailhead, has been repaired, but the second half, from the cabin to the Russian Lakes Trail, has not been restored as of press time. Damage includes downed trees and two washed-out bridges. Due to budget cuts, the Forest Service is unsure when or if this portion of the trail will be repaired.

Lost Lake Trail This 7-mile trail to the alpine lake is one of the most scenic hikes the Kenai Peninsula has to offer in midsummer. The trailhead is in Lost Lake subdivision, a quarter mile from Mile 5.3 of the Seward Hwy. After 3 miles, you come to the summer trail that winds 1.5 miles south to the USFS Clemens Memorial Cabin (See Places to Stay, below). The final 2 miles of Lost Lake Trail are above the tree line, making the lake itself a glorious place to spend a night.

If you'd rather not return the same way, continue around the east side of Lost Lake to the Primrose Trail, another USFS-maintained route. This 8-mile trail leads through alpine country and ends at ***Primrose Campground*** (Mile 17.2 of the Seward Hwy). Plan on seven to 10 hours for the roundtrip to Lost Lake and bring a camp stove because there is no wood near the lake.

Caines Head State Recreation Area This 6000-acre preserve, 5.5 miles south of Seward on Resurrection Bay, contains military ruins, a 650-foot headlands and the Coastal Trail (see the Hiking section of the Wilderness Chapter). Even if you're not up for an overnight backpacking trip, the hike to Tonsina Point is an easy roundtrip hike of only 3 miles. At the point, you can view the salmon spawning up Tonsina Creek if it's July or early August.

Paddling

Kayaks can be rented from Kayak & Custom Adventures (☎ 224-3960, 800-288-3134, kayak@arctic.net) at Miller's Landing Campground for $30/55 a day for singles/doubles. The company also offers guided day trips, which include morning kayaking instructions; trips depart and return from Lowell Point, 3 miles south of town, and cost $95 per person. An overnight tour from Seward is $395, and a three-day tour is $575.

Special Events

Each summer, Seward holds two events that have become popular throughout Southcentral Alaska. The July 4th celebration is a big event in Seward, highlighted by the annual Mt Marathon Race, which draws runners from around the state. The city's most famous event, however, is the Silver Salmon Derby on the second Saturday of August.

Places to Stay

At the height of the summer season, a last-minute room is hard to secure in Seward, which adds 9% tax to all room rates. But many of the accommodations mentioned below lie just outside the city limits, in which case the tax is only 2%.

Camping Seward is one of the few towns in Alaska with an excellent and affordable campground right in the heart of its downtown area.

The ***Waterfront Campground***, along Ballaine Blvd, is managed by the city's Parks and Recreation Department (☎ 224-3331) and overlooks the bay. Most of it is open gravel parking for RVers, but you'll also find a grassy tent area that even has a few trees and shrubs. A day-use area contains grills, picnic tables and small shelters, while a paved bike path runs through the campground. In 1996, the city even began adding full hookups for RVers. Best of all is the price: $6 a night for tents, $10 for RVers to park and $15 for full hookup.

Forest Acres Campground, 2 miles north of town on the west side of the Seward Hwy, is in a wooded area that tends to be a little buggy at times. It's $6 to pitch a tent, and there's a 14-day limit. Farther out of town still, but free, is the 12-site ***Exit Glacier Campground***, 9 miles from Seward at the end of Exit Glacier Rd. This National Park Service facility is for tents only.

Cabins Around Seward there are a handful of remote cabins, administered and maintained by a handful of agencies: the state Parks and Outdoor Recreation Division, the USFS and the National Park Service. Three of these cabins can be reached on foot, saving the budget-minded trekker an expensive air-charter trip, but are not nearly as secluded as the others.

The ***Clemens Memorial Cabin*** ($35, reservations required) is a six-bunk Forest

Service cabin that can be reached on foot with a 4.5-mile trek up the Lost Lake Trail (see the previous Hiking section). The cabin is located at the tree line, providing spectacular views of Resurrection Peak, Mt Ascension and Resurrection Bay. The USFS **Resurrection River Cabin** ($35, reservations required) is 6.5 miles from the southern trailhead of the Resurrection River Trail (see the earlier Hiking section). Reserve these cabins through the National Recreation Reservation Service (☎ 877-444-6777, 518-885-3639 from overseas, www.reserveusa.com).

Derby Cove is a state cabin located just off the tidal trail between Tonsina Point and North Beach in Caines Head State Recreation Area. From the trailhead at Lowell Point to the cabin, it's a 4-mile trek that must be done during low tide. You could also rent kayaks (see Paddling, earlier) and paddle out to it. Situated on the backside of a marsh on Derby Cove, the cabin offers a bit of privacy for $50 a night.

Callisto Canyon is also located just off the tidal trail a half mile before you reach Derby Cove. Built in 1998, the state park cabin sleeps eight, also rents for $50 a night and can be reached by kayak. Check the availability of both cabins by calling the DNR Public Information Center (☎ 269-8400) in Anchorage or the Kenai Area Parks Office (☎ 262-5581) at Morgan's Landing. There is no longer a state park office in Seward.

In 1992, Kenai Fjords National Park built a series of wilderness cabins, which you can reach either by air charter or kayak. The closest to Seward is **Aialik Bay**, which is near one of the few beaches that you can hike in this portion of the bay. At low tide, you can beach-comb for more than a mile, exploring tidal pools as you go or looking out for whales that feed in the area. The cabin costs $30 a night and must be rented through the Kenai Fjords National Park Visitor Center (☎ 224-3175) in Seward.

Located across the bay is **Holgate Arm Cabin**, which features a spectacular view of Holgate Glacier. This unit is also $30 and must be reserved through the Kenai Fjords National Park Visitor Center (☎ 224-3175).

Hostels The always popular Snow River Hostel, 16 miles north of town on the Seward Hwy, closed in 1998. Seward has three other hostel-type accommodations to serve budget-minded travelers, all closer to town but none as pleasant as Snow River.

Kate's Roadhouse (☎ 224-5888), Mile 5.5 of the Seward Hwy, includes seven beds in a rustic bunkhouse ($17), private rooms ($59 for a double) and four cabins ($29 to $49).

Moby Dick Hostel (☎ 224-7072, 430 3rd Ave), between Madison and Jefferson Sts in town, has 18 bunks for $15 a night and a few small and dingy rooms for $65. **Meg & Pete's Hostel** (☎ 224-7137, megandpete@hotmail .net, 307 3rd Ave) has room for six people at only $12 a night.

B&Bs The number of B&Bs in and around Seward has exploded in recent years. They are often your best bet for obtaining a room at the last minute.

Downtown there's **Seward Waterfront Lodging** (☎ 224-5563, 550 Railway Ave) and **Falcon's Way B&B** (☎ 224-5757, 611 4th Ave). Waterfront Lodging is just down the street from the Alaska SeaLife Center and has doubles for $75 to $95. Falcon's Way has four rooms with shared bathroom for $50/65 single/double.

Many of the B&Bs are north of town off the Seward Hwy. Three miles north of town is **The Farm B&B** (☎ 224-5691, thefarm@ ptialaska.net), Salmon Creek Rd, which has a wide variety of accommodations. Rooms in the remodeled farmhouse range from $85 to $95 for two people. But there are also sleeping cottages complete with decks for $80, and small bungalows that sleep two for $65. At the beginning of Exit Glacier Rd are several inns and B&Bs, including **Creekside Cabins** (☎ 224-3834), which has four cabins that overlook Clear Creek and range from $55 to $80. The resort also features a sauna, bathhouse and two secluded tent sites ($15 for two people).

Farther out still is **Alaska's Treehouse** (☎ 224-3867), Mile 7 of the Seward Hwy via Timber St and Forest Rd, located in a wooded area. This B&B features a sauna, hot tub, espressos and lattes in the morning,

SOUTHCENTRAL

and great views of Hearth Mountain and Mt Alice. Rates are $85 to $105 for two people.

Hotels None of the hotels in town are cheap. Downtown, the *Taroka Inn* (☎ 224-8687, taroka@arctic net), 3rd Ave at Adams St, was a former officer's quarters during WWII. Nine rooms that include kitchenettes begin at $85 for a double. *Harborview Inn* (☎ 224-3217), 3rd Ave at C St, added 13 more rooms in 1998 and now charges $119 for a double in the new section and $109 for one of the eight original rooms. The inn serves free pastries and coffee in the morning.

The *Van Guilder Hotel* (☎ 224-3525, 800-204-6835, 307 Adams St) was built in 1916 and placed on the National Register of Historic Places in 1980. Restored to its original Edwardian charm, the hotel has a few 'pension rooms' for $75 a night, while double rooms with private baths start at $95.

The best place to stay downtown is *Hotel Seward* (☎ 224-2378, 221 5th Ave), with rooms ranging from $125 for a single to $215 for a room with a bay window overlooking Resurrection Bay.

In the small boat harbor area is *Breeze Inn* (☎ 224-5237), with singles/doubles at $109/119. Nearby, *Murphy's Motel* (☎ 224-8090, 911 4th Ave) has singles/doubles for $77/86, and the *Marina Motel* (☎ 224-5518, 603 3rd Ave), just up the highway, offers doubles for $105 to $120, but neither is as nice as Breeze Inn.

Places to Eat

In the downtown area, *Don's Kitchen (405 Washington St)* is open 24 hours and probably has the cheapest fare; breakfasts begin at $5, and the Yukon Scrambler for $6 will keep you going until late in the afternoon. A half-pound halibut dinner costs $11. *Mt Marathon Cafe*, 4th Ave near Adams St, has good deli sandwiches for $6 to $7 and fishing-charter lunches to go.

For something nicer, try *Legends of the Mountain*, 5th Ave at Washington St, where you can enjoy a view of the bay from any table. Dinners begin at $13, but head over for a late lunch of seafood sauté – halibut,

scallops and shrimp sautéed in white wine and herbs – for $10. The *Harbor Dinner Club (220 5th Ave)* is another upscale restaurant across from the Hotel Seward. The menu is made up almost entirely of seafood and usually includes an 'inflation-fighter' special for under $11. If fresh halibut cheeks are one of the appetizers, skip dinner and just order these with a few beers.

Want Chinese? The *Peking Chinese Restaurant*, 4th Ave at Jefferson St, is open until 10 pm daily and has dinners for two, which include egg rolls, two to four main dishes and fried rice, for $10 to $18 per person. Lunch specials cost $7. If it's Greek or Italian you're craving, *Apollo (229 4th Ave)* has both, with pasta dinners beginning at $8 and a gyro plate priced at around $10. Apollo also serves Alaskan seafood and pizza.

As you'd expect, the small boat harbor area features a number of seafood spots. *Smoke'N Alaska Seafood* serves fish and chips, smoked salmon and seafood chowder. The *Depot Grill*, near the small shelter where the train drops you off, has sandwiches and hamburgers that begin at $5 and a pleasant solarium area overlooking the harbor. Also look around the small boat harbor for *Red's*, a school bus converted to a grill where a good hamburger and fries are only $5.

Ray's Waterfront, overlooking the harbor, serves excellent seafood, including local salmon, halibut or pan-seared scallops. Try its Halibut Andaman ($22), a fresh fillet served in a roasted macadamia-nut crust and a sweet lime-chile sauce, or pan-seared Thai scallops ($20). This is Seward's nicest restaurant, with dinner prices ranging from $17 to $24.

For something a little healthier than milk-shakes and fried food, try *Le Barn Appetit*, Resurrection Rd just off Exit Glacier Rd. Seward's only health-food store is also a restaurant and bakery offering deli sandwiches, crepes, fresh-baked bread and quiche. The vegetarian cuisine is about $7 for dinner.

Entertainment

Feel like pinning a few dollars to the ceiling? Head over to the *Yukon Bar*, 4th Ave at

Washington St – Seward's most lively bar. You can order from a list of 20 imported beers or try a Yukon ice tea. From Wednesday to Saturday, the bar somehow packs a band in and offers live music. Just down the street is the competition, ***Tony's Bar***, which has live music on Friday and Saturday but not as much character.

If you don't like either one of these places, there are several other bars on 4th Ave, as well as the more upscale ***Seward Saloon & Oyster Bar*** *(209 5th Ave)*. For local color, head out to ***The Pit Bar***, Seward Hwy just past Exit Glacier Rd. This place can get lively on the weekends, with pool, darts and shuffleboard inside and Ping-Pong and horseshoes outside. If you have a cast-iron stomach, have the bartender snare one of Chet's smoked pickled eggs from the big jar behind the bar.

At the opposite end of the spectrum from The Pit Bar is ***Resurrect Art Gallery and Coffee House***, 320 3rd Ave. Located in an old church downtown, the coffee house includes an interesting gallery of Native Alaskan art, block prints and pottery. The menu features espresso drinks, Italian sodas, teas and light snacks. At night, local musicians or storytellers often entertain, or you can simply take your latte to the loft, where there are stacks of books and board games.

Liberty Theater *(☎ 224-5418)*, Adams St, is a great little movie theater next door to the Van Gilder Hotel. For budget travelers, the Kenai Fjords National Park Visitor Center in the small boat harbor offers free evening programs on wildlife or glaciers from 5 to 6 pm.

Getting There & Away
Bus Several bus companies now offer a run between Seward and Anchorage. Seward Bus Lines (☎ 224-3608) provides daily service to Anchorage during the summer, with a bus departing from the small depot at 1915 Seward Hwy at 9 am. The bus leaves Anchorage at 2:30 pm for the return trip to Seward; the one-way fare is $30.

Also offering bus service are Kachemak Bay Transit (☎ 235-3795), Alaska Backpacker

Shuttle (☎ 344-8775) and Alaskon Express (☎ 800-478-6388).

Train From May to September, the Alaska Railroad offers a daily run to Anchorage. Departing Seward at 6 pm, the train travels a spectacular route that includes glaciers, steep gorges and rugged mountain scenery. Even when leaving that late, you can still view the scenery, thanks to those long Alaskan days. The one-way fare is $50. There's no depot in Seward, so call the Anchorage terminal (☎ 800-544-0552) for more information.

Boat In 1995, the ferry terminal (☎ 224-5485) relocated from the downtown waterfront to the Alaska Railroad dock, north of the small boat harbor. From the Seward Hwy, head east on Port Ave and follow the signs to the office. Ferries from Kodiak or Valdez arrive in Seward twice a week, on Thursday and Friday, and depart for the same communities before continuing on to other Southcentral ports. The fare to Valdez is $58, to Kodiak $54 and to Homer $96. The trip to Valdez passes the Columbia Glacier. The boat to Kodiak Island goes by the Steller sea lions on the Chiswell Islands near the mouth of Resurrection Bay.

Getting Around
The Seward Trolley travels from the ferry terminal south to the downtown area, stopping at the library, museum, harbormaster's office and campgrounds. It runs from 10 am to 7 pm daily. The fare is $1.50 per ride, or $3 for a day pass.

KENAI FJORDS NATIONAL PARK
Seward serves as the departure point for most trips into Kenai Fjords National Park, which was created in 1980 and thrust into the news during the Exxon oil spill. The park covers 587,000 acres and consists mainly of the Harding Ice Field, the rugged coastline where tidewater glaciers calve into the sea and the offshore islands.

With its abundance of marine wildlife and glaciers, Kenai Fjords is a major tourist attraction but unfortunately not an inexpensive one. That's why easy-to-reach Exit Glacier is its main attraction, drawing more than 100,000 tourists each summer. The vast majority of visitors either take a quick trip to this glacier or splurge on a tour-boat cruise to the coastal glaciers (around $130).

For the adventurous, there is Harding Ice Field. One of the largest ice fields in North America, it remained undiscovered until the early 1900s, when a map-making team realized several coastal glaciers belonged to the same massive system. The Harding Ice Field is 50 miles long and 30 miles wide and in some places 200 inches deep. Eight glaciers extend from the field to the sea, including Exit Glacier, a remnant of a larger one that once extended into Resurrection Bay.

Hikers can reach the ice field's edge via the Harding Ice Field Trail, but only experienced mountaineers equipped with skis, ice axes and crampons can explore the 300 sq miles of ice. The many deep fjords and rich marine life also make the park a blue-water kayaker's dream; to reach the ice field, though, you either have to paddle the sections exposed to the Gulf of Alaska or pay for a drop-off service.

For more information, visit the Kenai Fjords National Park Visitor Center (☎ 224-3175), on 4th Ave overlooking Seward's small boat harbor. It's open 8 am to 7 pm daily. The ranger station at Exit Glacier is open 10 am to 5 pm daily in summer.

Exit Glacier

The 3-mile-long Exit Glacier is fast becoming a frozen tourist attraction, ranking right up there with Portage Glacier and Juneau's Mendenhall. It picked up its name when explorers, crossing the Harding Ice Field, found the glacier a suitable way to 'exit' the ice and mountains. It's believed that at one time the glacier extended all the way to Seward, and today it is still active, but now it's only retreating into the mountains.

You reach the ice on Exit Glacier Rd, which leaves the Seward Hwy at Mile 3.7 at a posted junction. The road first parallels the heavily braided Resurrection River, providing access to some unofficial but great camping spots on the surrounding gravel bars.

Within 7 miles, you pass the trailhead to the Resurrection River Trail (see the Seward Hiking section) and then cross over the river on a bridge that was built in 1985. At this point, the view of the glacier fills your windshield and dominates the scenery for the remaining 2 miles.

If you don't have a car, hitchhiking to Exit Glacier is fairly easy, or you can reach it through Glacier Quest Eco-Tours (☎ 877-444-5770, 224-5770), which charges $20 per person roundtrip and will pick you up anywhere in town.

At the end of Exit Glacier Rd, there's a ranger station with a few informational displays and books for sale, as well as the answers to any questions you might have. A short, ranger-led nature walk departs from the station daily around 10 am and 2 pm. Beginning at 8 am every Saturday, a ranger-led trek up to the Harding Ice Field lasts a good part of the day.

A paved, wheelchair-accessible trail leads a quarter mile to the overlook and information shelter. To continue farther, you have to take to the trails. The vast majority of people hike the Lower Loop Trail so that they can have their picture taken in front of the bluish ice.

Hiking

Nature Trail A half-mile nature trail departs from the ranger station and winds through cottonwood forest, alder thickets and old glacial moraines before emerging at the information shelter. It's a great way to return from the glacier if you're not up to facing the mass of humanity on the paved trail.

Exit Glacier Trails From the information center, a network of loops provides close access to the ice itself. The Lower Loop Trail is an easy half-mile walk to the outwash plain in front of the ice. A multitude of warning signs tell you to stay away from the face due to the danger of falling ice. But despite the signs, people are so determined to touch the ice or have their picture taken next to it that the park often posts a ranger out there to keep them away.

The Upper Loop Trail departs the first loop and climbs steeply to an overlook at the side of the glacier before returning. Both trails make for a short hike, not much more than a mile in length, and sections may be closed at times due to falling ice. Don't skip the short spur to Falls Overlook, a scenic cascade off the upper trail.

Harding Ice Field Trail Besides the nature trail from the ranger station to Exit Glacier, the only other developed hike in the glacier area is the trek to Harding Ice Field. This hike is a difficult ascent that follows a steep, roughly cut and sometimes slippery route on the north side of Exit Glacier, beginning at its base. It's a 5-mile, one-way hike to the ice field at 3500 feet; for reasonably fit trekkers, that's a good four-hour trip.

The all-day trek is well worth it for those with the stamina, as it provides spectacular views of not only the ice field but of Exit Glacier and the valley below. The upper section of the route is snow-covered for much of the year. You'll find the trailhead at the beginning of the Lower Loop Trail.

Paddling

Blue-water paddles out of Resurrection Bay along the coastline of the park are challenges for experienced kayakers or involve a costly drop-off/pickup fee, but reward you with almost daily wildlife encounters and close-up views of the glaciers from a unique perspective. The popularity of such trips is evident in the proliferation of kayaks for rent in Seward.

Sunny Cove Sea Kayaking Company (☎ 345-5339, 800-770-9119, kayakak@alaska .net), at the Alaska Saltwater Lodge on Lowell Point, charges $90/165 for singles/doubles for three days (the minimum time). Each additional day is $25/45. Kayak & Custom Adventures (☎ 224-3960, 800-288-3134, kayak@arctic.net) also rents rigid doubles and singles from Miller's Landing.

Either company will arrange drop-off service for those who want to skip the open water of the Gulf of Alaska. Best to plan on $200 to $230 for the roundtrip to Aialik Bay, depending how far up the bay you are dropped off, and $250 for the more remote Northwestern Lagoon.

These companies also offer guided kayak trips. Sunny Cove Sea Kayaking Company charges $95 for a daylong (10 am to 5 pm) paddle trip along the shoreline of Caines Head State Park, including all equipment and a shoreline lunch. The company's Fox Island trip includes a wildlife boat cruise, a three-hour kayaking tour around the island and a salmon bake lunch for $139.

Aialik Bay This is the more popular arm for kayakers to paddle. Many people hire tour boats to drop them near Aialik Glacier, then take three or four days to paddle south past Pedersen Glacier and into Holgate Arm, where they're picked up. The high point of the trip is Holgate Glacier, an active tidewater glacier that's the main feature of all the boat tours.

Northwestern Lagoon This fjord is more expensive to reach but much more remote, with not nearly as many tour boats. The wildlife is excellent, especially the seabirds and sea otters, and more than a half dozen glaciers can be seen, including three tidewater ones. Plan on three to four days if you're being dropped inside the lagoon.

Organized Tours

For most visitors, the best way to see the rugged fjords, glaciers and wildlife is on a tour boat. In the past few years, Kenai Fjords cruises have become Seward's main attraction, and all the operators maintain a booth or office in the small boat harbor, right next to the harbormaster's office. It always pays to shop around before booking, but keep in mind that there are Kenai Fjords tours and wildlife tours. The wildlife tours are just cruises inside Resurrection Bay that never get close to the glaciers and only offer glimpses of seabirds. If you want to view the national park, you're going to have to pay around $100.

Kenai Fjords Tours (☎ 800-478-3346, 224-8068) runs a six-hour tour of the park, with boats departing at 8 and 11:30 am and 3 pm daily, and an eight-hour trip along the same

SOUTHCENTRAL

route at 10 am. The fare is $99. Purchase tickets at the company's office on the board-walk in Seward's small boat harbor.

Likewise, Allen Marine Tours (☎ 888-305-2515) and Major Marine Tours (☎ 224-8030, 800-764-7300) offer the same cruise. Major Marine, which departs at 11:30 am, is the cheapest of the three at $89 per person. All three cruises head south into Aialik Bay, travel past several glaciers (including Hol-gate) and, if the sea gods are smiling on you that day, pass a variety of marine life, includ-ing sea otters, a sea lion colony and even humpback or minke whales.

Kenai Fjords Tours and Major Marine Tours, along with Renown Charters (☎ 224-3806, 800-655-3806), offer a shorter wildlife tour inside Resurrection Bay, including a swing past Bear Glacier, for $54 to $64. Renown Charters does the run in 2½ hours, with departures at 9 am, noon, 3 and 6 pm.

Finally, Kenai Fjords Tours offers a 10-hour tour into impressive Northwestern Lagoon. The boat departs at 9 am, and it's $139 per person but includes a deli lunch and beverages.

HOPE HIGHWAY

This paved road leads almost 18 miles north to the historical community of Hope and the northern trailhead for the Resurrection Pass Trail. Hope experienced a minor stampede in 1896, when news of a gold strike brought more than 3000 prospectors to the cluster of cabins and to nearby Sunrise, a tent city. Within a few years, the majority had left to look for gold elsewhere, and today Hope is a small village with a summer population of 225. Nothing remains of Sunrise.

Even if you are not planning to hike the Resurrection Pass Trail, Hope is a great side trip; tucked away in a very scenic area, the town takes you back in time. Hitchhiking is not hard, but plan on at least two days for this trip rather than a rushed overnight stop.

Near Mile 1 of the Hope Hwy is Nova River Runners (☎ 800-746-5753), which offer rafting trips on nearby Sixmile and Granite Creeks. Sixmile is renowned among white-water enthusiasts and is considered one of the most challenging rivers in Alaska. It runs

through three sheer-walled canyons where rafters battle Class IV and Class V rapids. A two-canyon float trip ($75) departs daily at 9 am. A three-canyon float trip ($135), which includes Class V rapids, departs at noon.

At Mile 16 is the junction of the Hope Hwy and Resurrection Creek Rd. Turn left (south) onto Resurrection Creek Rd; in 0.7 miles, Palmer Creek Rd branches to the left. Near the junction is the unattended Hope airstrip. Four miles down Resurrection Creek Rd is the northern trailhead of the Resurrection Pass Trail.

Palmer Creek Rd is a scenic drive that leads 7 miles to the *Coeur d'Alene Camp-ground*, a USFS campground that has five free rustic sites. Beyond the campground, the road is not maintained but leads another 5 miles to alpine country above 1500 feet and ends at the ruins of the abandoned Swet-mann mining camp. From the old mining buildings, it's easy to scramble through the tundra to several small alpine lakes.

Hope

To reach the town of Hope, turn right on Hope Rd at Mile 16.5 of the Hope Hwy. Hope Rd first leads past the post office. Across the street is the **Hope-Sunrise Mining Museum**, which was built out of logs in 1993. The displays here recall the Turn-again Arm gold rush of 1894–1899; historical photos show Hope and Sunrise during their boom times. The museum is open noon to 4 pm Monday, Friday and Saturday; noon to 2 pm Sunday. Admission is free.

Beyond the museum, Hope Rd winds past the many log cabins and some aban-doned log structures that have become fa-vorites among photographers. You end up near the waterfront at what is best described as 'downtown Hope.' Here you'll find a gift and mining shop, the Hope Social Hall, which has been hosting meetings and wed-dings since the turn of the century, and the Seaview Cafe – all quaint buildings in a scenic setting.

Gold Panning There are about 125 mining claims throughout the Chugach National Forest in Southcentral Alaska, but most of today's prospectors are recreational miners out there for the fun, searching their pans or sluice box for a little color. Some of the more serious ones actually make money from their time spent along the creeks, but most are happy to take home a bottle with a few flakes of gold in it.

The Hope area provides numerous opportunities for the amateur panner, including a 20-acre claim that the USFS has set aside near the Resurrection Pass trailhead for recreational mining. Some regulars are usually out there who don't mind showing newcomers how to swirl the pan. Other panning areas include Sixmile Creek, between Mile 1.5 and Mile 5.5 of the Hope Hwy, and many of the creeks along the Resurrection Pass Trail.

Hiking From Porcupine Campground (see Places to Stay & Eat, below), two fine trails lead to scenic points overlooking the Turnagain Arm. The first, Gull Rock Trail, is an easy 5.1-mile walk to Gull Rock, a rocky point 140 feet above the Turnagain shoreline. The trail follows an old wagon road built at the turn of the century, and along the way you can explore the remains of a cabin and a sawmill. You may also glimpse Turnagain Arm and even Mt McKinley on a clear day. The roundtrip takes four to six hours.

The second route, to Hope Point, follows an alpine ridge for incredible views of Turnagain Arm. Begin at the entrance sign to Porcupine Campground and follow an unmarked trail along the right-hand side of the small Porcupine Creek. After 0.3 miles, the trail leaves the side of the creek and begins to ascend a bluff to the right, reaching an outcrop with good views of Turnagain Arm in 45 minutes or so. From here, you can follow the ridge above the tree line to Hope Point, elevation 3708 feet. Except for an early-summer snowfield, you'll find no water after Porcupine Creek.

Bicycling Located near the north end of the Resurrection Pass Trail, a popular route for off-road riding, is Mountain Bike Alaska (☎ 248-7301). This shop rents a bike and

helmet for $15 for four hours or $25 for the whole day. A bridge 200 yards south of the trailhead connects the shop to the trail.

Experienced bikers in good shape can cover the trail in one long Alaskan day, but most people need to camp overnight. You also can set up camp on the Resurrection River near the trailhead and then spend an enjoyable day simply riding out and back.

Places to Stay & Eat Campsites abound all around Hope, but the USFS maintains the ***Porcupine Campground***, 1.3 miles beyond Hope at the end of the Hope Hwy; its 24 sites cost $9 per night. The campground features the usual spread-out sites, a scenic overlook to watch the tide and two trailheads to Hope Point and Gull Rock (see Hiking, above). Beware, the place is often filled on weekends and sometimes even in the middle of the week. Near the campground is ***Davidson Enterprises***, a general store that sells groceries, gasoline and liquor.

Hope has a general store, laundromat and a couple of lodges and cafes. For the most affordable accommodations, head to ***Raven Hill B&B*** (☎ 786-3411), off Resurrection Rd, which has a bunkhouse that sleeps six people for $16.50 per person. The place is hard to find, so call ahead for directions.

Near the junction of Resurrection Creek Rd and the Hope Hwy, ***Henry's One Stop*** (☎ 782-3222) offers meals, beers, showers and rooms with private bathrooms for $60 a night. Next door is ***Bear Creek Lodge*** (☎ 782-3141), a scenic resort in the woods with a small restaurant, a scattering of cabins and even a replica of an old log cache. The five restored, hand-hewn log cabins along the creek cost $75 a night.

Hope's favorite restaurant was the ***Discovery Cafe*** – 'where the goldminers meet and eat' – but it burned to the ground in January 1999. The locals immediately began to rebuild and planned to reopen by 2000. ***Bear Creek Lodge*** also has a restaurant serving soups, homemade bread and wonderful desserts. At the ***Seaview Cafe***, in the heart of Hope, you can get a plate of ribs or chicken for $11 and wash it down with a beer.

STERLING HIGHWAY TO KENAI NATIONAL WILDLIFE REFUGE

It is only 58 miles from Tern Lake Junction to Soldotna along the Sterling Hwy, not much more than an hour's drive. Yet the stretch contains so many hiking, camping and canoeing opportunities that it would take you a month to enjoy them all. Surrounded by the Chugach National Forest and Kenai National Wildlife Refuge, the Sterling Hwy and its side roads pass a dozen trails, 20 campgrounds and an almost endless number of lakes, rivers and streams.

More than anywhere else, this is Alaska's favorite playground. Despite all the campgrounds and facilities, the summer crowds that descend onto the area in July and August (both Alaskans and tourists) are crushing at times. Be prepared, if you're traveling by car at this time of year, to stop at a handful of campgrounds before finding an available site.

Mileposts along the highway show distances from Seward, making Tern Lake Junction, at Mile 37, the starting point of the Sterling Hwy. The first accommodation along the highway, 8 miles west of Tern Lake, is the **Sunrise Inn** (☎ 595-1222), Mile 45. The log lodge features a cafe and bar, while the 10-room motel has single or double rooms for $89. The first campgrounds are just past the Sunrise Inn, down Quartz Creek Rd. Follow the road south 0.3 miles to the USFS **Quartz Creek Campground** (31 sites, $10), on the shores of Kenai Lake, or 3 miles to the USFS **Crescent Creek Campground** (9 sites, $10).

The **Crescent Creek Trail**, about half a mile beyond the Crescent Creek Campground, has a marked trailhead and leads 6.5 miles to the outlet of Crescent Lake and a **USFS cabin** ($35, reservations required). The trail is an easy walk and is beautiful in September, thanks to autumn colors; the cabin offers access to the high country. Anglers can fish for arctic grayling in the lake during the summer. At the east end of the lake is the **Carter Lake Trail** to the Seward Hwy, with a rough path along the south side of the lake connecting the two trails.

Another half mile west on the Sterling Hwy is a large lookout where you can observe Dall sheep in the Kenai Mountains and mountain goats in the Cecil Rhode Mountains directly across Kenai Lake. Displays explain the life cycle of the animals. The Kenai River Bridge is at Mile 47.8. Immediately after it, Snug Harbor Rd leads south 12 miles to Cooper Lake and the eastern trailhead for the Russian Lakes Trail (see the Hiking section in the Wilderness chapter).

Cooper Landing

After skirting the north end of Kenai Lake, you enter scenic Cooper Landing (population 285) at Mile 48.4. This service center was named after Joseph Cooper, a miner who worked the area in the 1880s. A school was built here in 1929, and the first post office was established in 1937, a year before the town was connected by road to Seward.

The five-building national historic district includes the post office and a handful of homesteader's cabins. Situated right on the banks of the river, it makes for a very photogenic stop, with the towering mountains overhead.

Cooper Landing is best known, however, as an outpost for red-salmon fishing in the Russian River and as the starting point for raft trips down the Kenai River. A number of companies run the trip, including Alaska Wildland Adventures (☎ 800-478-4100) and the Alaska River Co (☎ 595-1226). Expect to pay around $50 for a three-hour, half-day trip, or about $100 for a full-day outing, which includes some Class III white water in the Kenai Canyon.

Guided fishing trips for either spin or fly fishers can be easily arranged at several places in Cooper Landing, including Gwin's Lodge (☎ 595-1266), on Mile 52 of the Sterling Hwy, and Alaska River Adventures (☎ 595-2000, 800-836-9027), next door to Hamilton's Place on the Sterling Hwy. Most guides charge $100 to $125 for a half-day trip on the river but will provide the drift boat, gear and lunch.

Even if you have no intention of baiting a hook, you can still enjoy the salmon runs on the Russian River. Head to the Russian River Campground at Mile 52 of the Sterling Hwy and park at the Pink Salmon or Grayling day-use parking areas. From here, steep stairs lead down to the river, where you can see sockeye spawn either in early June or during a second run in mid-July.

Just west of the campground, at Mile 52.6, is the **K'Beg Interpretive Site**. Built in 1997 by the USFS, the site includes a visitor cabin and a boardwalk that winds past a house pit, cache pit and other archaeological relics from the Kenaitize tribe, a branch of the Athabascan Indians. From May through August, there are guided tours of the site daily.

Places to Stay At Mile 50.7 of the Sterling Hwy is the USFS *Cooper Creek Campground* (27 sites, $9), where there are campsites on both sides of the highway, with several on the north side scenically located on the Kenai River.

The final USFS campground before you enter the Kenai National Wildlife Refuge is the *Russian River Campground*, a half mile past Gwin's Lodge at Mile 52.6, with 84 sites for $11 a night. A beautiful campground located where the Russian and Kenai Rivers merge, this is the area's most popular one by far. Both the Cooper Creek and Russian River Campgrounds lie in prime red-salmon spawning areas, and the campsites tend to fill up by noon in late summer. The Russian River Campground is so popular that it charges $5 just to park and fish.

A mile down Russian River Campground Rd is the trailhead and parking area for the Russian Lakes Trail, while a quarter mile west of the campground on the Sterling Hwy is the well-marked entrance to the Resurrection Pass Trail (see the Hiking section in the Wilderness chapter).

If you're looking for a bed, *The Hutch B&B* (☎ 595-1270), Mile 48.5 of the Sterling Hwy in Cooper Landing, is a 12-room inn with doubles ranging from $60 to $75. Just north of Cooper Landing is *Kenai River B&B* (☎ 595-1712), Mile 49 of the Sterling Hwy, which has two large suites with kitchenettes for $125. Since the B&B is right on

the Kenai River, you can practically fish from the deck of your room.

Gwin's Lodge (☎ 595-1266), Mile 52 of the Sterling Hwy, is the classic Alaskan roadhouse. The log lodge was built in 1952 and features a cafe, bar and liquor store next door to the old Russian River ferry, which serves as a monument to the red-salmon run that draws hundreds of anglers to the Russian River from June through July. The lodge also has log cabins at $99/104 for a single/double at peak season and rustic fishers' cabins that sleep four for $40 a night. At the restaurant, the helpings are huge and the prices are reasonable. Breakfast ranges from $6 to $8, and dinners cost $8 to $16.

Other accommodations include the lavish *Kenai Princess Lodge* (☎ 800-426-0500), Mile 47.7 of the Sterling Hwy. This Princess Cruises hotel charges $229 for a double.

KENAI NATIONAL WILDLIFE REFUGE
Once west of the Resurrection Pass Trailhead, you leave Chugach National Forest, administered by the USFS, and enter the Kenai National Wildlife Refuge, managed by the US Fish & Wildlife Service. The impressive populations of Dall sheep, moose, caribou and bear here have attracted hunters from around the world since the early 1900s. In 1941, President Roosevelt set aside 1.73 million acres as the Kenai National Moose Range, and the 1980 Alaska Lands Act increased it to almost 2 million acres.

Along with an abundance of wildlife, good fishing and great mountain scenery, the refuge offers an opportunity to hike some of the least-used trails on the Kenai Peninsula. Hikers who want to spend a few days trekking here should first go to the Kenai National Wildlife Refuge Visitor Station at Mile 58 of the Sterling Hwy or the visitor center in Kenai for information on all the trails or an update on their condition.

The first campground in the refuge is the *Kenai-Russian River Recreational Area*, Mile 55 of the Sterling Hwy, with 180 sites for $6 a night. West of the confluence of these two salmon-rich rivers, this campground attracts many anglers from mid- to late summer, and the fee applies whether you want to camp or just park.

A privately owned, 28-passenger ferry carries anglers to the opposite bank of the Kenai River for $6 roundtrip, with cables and the current propelling it across the river in both directions. The ferry transports more than 30,000 anglers during the salmon season, and at the peak hundreds line up by 5 am to catch the first trip across the river.

The 3-mile **Fuller Lakes Trail** begins at Mile 57 of the Sterling Hwy and ends at Fuller Lake just above the tree line. The trail, an old road blocked by logs, is well marked along the highway and begins as a rapid climb. Halfway up the trail, you reach Lower Fuller Lake, where you cross a stream over a beaver dam and continue over a low pass to Upper Fuller Lake. At the lake, the trail follows the east shore and then branches; the fork to the left leads up a ridge and becomes the **Skyline Trail**. This trail is not maintained and is unmarked above the bush line. It follows a ridge for 6.5 miles and descends to Mile 61 of the Sterling Hwy. Those who want to hike both trails should plan to stay overnight at Upper Fuller Lake, where there are several good campsites.

Just past the Fuller Lakes Trailhead on the Sterling Hwy is the **Skilak Lake Loop Rd** junction (at Mile 58) and the **Kenai National Wildlife Refuge Visitor Station**. The log cabin is open from 10 am to 7 pm daily and contains maps and brochures on the refuge. The 19-mile loop road, a scenic side trip on an already scenic highway, is a popular and often crowded recreational avenue. There are five USFS campgrounds along the road. Some, like Hidden Lake and Upper Skilak, cost $10 a night for a vehicle and $6 for a walk-in site, while others are free. All these campgrounds are well marked and, from east to west, are as follows:

campground	sites	location
Hidden Lake	44	Mile 3.6
Upper Skilak Lake	25	Mile 8.4
Lower Ohmer Lake	3	Mile 8.6
Engineer Lake	4	Mile 9.7
Lower Skilak Lake	14	Mile 14.0

The **Kenai River Trail**, 0.6 miles past the visitor station on the Skilak Lake Loop Rd, winds 5.1 miles to Skilak Lake and then turns into the **Hidden Creek Loop**. The 1.4-mile loop trail curves back to its beginning at Mile 4.6 of Skilak Lake Loop Rd. Both trails are easy walks along level terrain.

The **Skilak Lookout Trail** begins at Mile 5.5 of Skilak Lake Rd and ascends 2.6 miles to a knob (elevation 1450 feet) that offers a panoramic view of the surrounding mountains and lakes. Plan on four to five hours for the roundtrip and bring water, as there is none on the trail.

The **Seven Lakes Trail**, a 4.4-mile hike to the Sterling Hwy, begins at Mile 9.7 of Skilak Lake Loop Rd, at the spur to Engineer Lake. The trail is easy walking over level terrain and passes Hidden and Hikers Lakes before ending at Kelly Lake Campground on a side road off the Sterling Hwy. You'll find fair to good fishing in Kelly and Engineer Lakes.

If you choose to stay on the Sterling Hwy past the Skilak Lake Rd junction, you pass the small *Jean Lake Campground*, Mile 60, with three free sites. A side road at Mile 69 leads south to the *Peterson Lake Campground* (three sites, free) and *Kelly Lake Campground* (three sites, free), near one end of the Seven Lakes Trail. *Watson Lake Campground*, Mile 71.3 of the Sterling Hwy, also has three free sites. Four miles farther down the highway is the west junction with Skilak Lake Rd.

At Mile 81, the Sterling Hwy divides into a four-lane road, and you soon arrive in the small town of **Sterling** (population 1800), where the Moose River empties into the Kenai. Sterling meets the usual travelers' needs, with restaurants, lodges, gas stations and grocery stores.

Beyond the town is the *Izaak Walton Recreation Site* (Mile 82, at the confluence of the Kenai and Moose Rivers), with 25 sites for $10. A display explains the nearby archaeological site, where excavations suggest that the area was used by Inuit people 2000 years ago. The state recreational area is heavily used all summer, as anglers swarm here for the salmon runs, while paddlers end their Swan Lake canoe trip at the Moose

River Bridge. There, canoe rentals and transportation are available for those planning to paddle the Swan Lake and Swanson River canoe trails (see the Paddling section in the Wilderness chapter).

At Mile 85 of the Sterling Hwy, Swanson River Rd turns north for 18 miles, with Swan Lake Rd heading east for 3 miles at the end of Swanson River Rd. The roads offer access to the Swanson River and Swan Lake canoe routes and three campgrounds: *Dolly Varden Lake Campground* (12 sites, free), 14 miles up Swanson River Rd; the *Rainbow Lake Campground* (three sites, free), another 2 miles beyond; and the *Swanson River Campground* (four sites, free), at the very end of the road. Even without a canoe, you can spend a day or two here, as trails lead to many of the lakes that offer superb fishing.

Across the Sterling Hwy from Swanson River Rd is the entrance to Scout Lake Loop Rd, where you'll find the *Scout Lake Campground* (14 sites, $8) and *Morgans Landing State Recreation Area* (42 sites, $10). Morgans Landing, a 3.5-mile drive from the Sterling Hwy, is a particularly scenic area, as it sits on a bluff overlooking the Kenai River with the Kenai Mountains on the horizon. The Alaska Division of Parks and Outdoor Recreation office (☎ 262-5581) for the Kenai Peninsula is located here and offers information on both Kachemak Bay State Park to the south and Caines Head State Recreation Area in Seward. It's open 8 am to 5 pm weekdays.

KENAI
To reach Kenai (population 7000), you have to leave the Sterling Hwy at Mile 94.2 and head north on the Kenai Spur Hwy. For that reason, many people bypass it and instead stop in Soldotna, little more than a commercial crossroads without the scenic appeal or history of Kenai.

While Kenai does not have the charm of Seward or Homer, it offers good views of the active volcanoes across the inlet, along with a little Russian history. The town itself is at the mouth of the Kenai River on Cook Inlet, where you can view Mt Redoubt (the volcano that erupted steam and ash in December 1989) to the southwest, Mt Iliamna at the head of the Aleutian Range and the Alaska Range to the northwest.

History
Kenai is the second-oldest permanent settlement in Alaska and the largest city on the peninsula. It was established by Russian fur traders, who arrived in 1791 with 300 settlers and set up camp near the Dena'ina Indian village of Skitok. The next most important year in Kenai's history is probably 1957, when Alaska's first oil discovery was made at Swanson River. Today, the North Kenai industrial district around Mile 19 of the Kenai Spur Hwy boasts the largest concentration of oil industry infrastructure outside of Prudhoe Bay, while across the inlet 15 oil platforms pump out 42,000 barrels a day.

Information
The impressive Kenai Visitors & Cultural Center (☎ 283-1991, www.visitkenai.com) was built in 1991 to mark the city's 200th anniversary. The center, on the corner of Main St and the Kenai Spur Hwy, has racks of brochures on most of the B&Bs in the area and is open daily during the summer.

Bank of America (☎ 283-3369) is inside Carrs Supermarket on the Kenai Spur Hwy.

The post office is on Caviar St just north of the Kenai Spur Hwy.

The Kenai Community Library is on Main St Loop Rd, near Willow St, and is open Monday through Saturday.

Beluga Lookout RV Park, Mission St, has showers and laundry facilities.

For medical services, see Information under Soldotna.

Things to See & Do
The **Kenai Visitors & Cultural Center** features historical exhibits on the city's Russian heritage, wildlife displays and an audio-visual room with daily showings of videos on the state. Don't miss the wildlife room, as it includes dozens of mounts, with 13 eagles, wolverines, brown bears and a beluga whale. The cultural center is open 9 am to 8 pm weekdays and 11 am to 7 pm weekends. Admission is free.

SOUTHCENTRAL

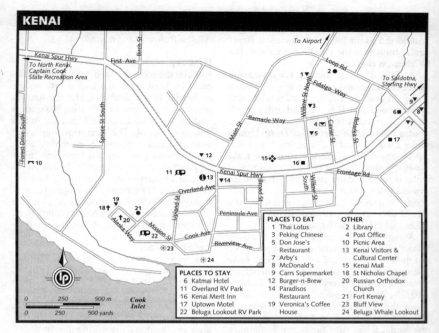

KENAI

To Airport
Kenai Spur Hwy
To North Kenai,
Captain Cook
State Recreation Area
First Ave
Birch St
Loop Rd
2
1
Fidalgo Way
To Soldotna,
Sterling Hwy
9
Willow St North
3
Barnacle Way
6
8
7
Main St
4
Caviar St
5
Blazka St
17
Spruce St South
12
15
16
Forest Drive South
10
Kenai Spur Hwy
Frontage Rd
11
13
14
Broad St
Willow St South
Overland Ave
19
20
18
21
Peninsula Ave
Upland St
Alaska Way
22
Mission St
Cook Ave
23
Riverview Ave
24

Cook
Inlet

PLACES TO EAT	OTHER
1 Thai Lotus	2 Library
3 Peking Chinese	4 Post Office
5 Don Jose's	10 Picnic Area
Restaurant	13 Kenai Visitors &
7 Arby's	Cultural Center
8 McDonald's	15 Kenai Mall
9 Carrs Supermarket	18 St Nicholas Chapel
12 Burger-n-Brew	20 Russian Orthodox
14 Paradisos	Church
Restaurant	21 Fort Kenay
19 Veronica's Coffee	23 Bluff View
House	24 Beluga Whale Lookout

PLACES TO STAY
6 Katmai Hotel
11 Overland RV Park
16 Kenai Merit Inn
17 Uptown Motel
22 Beluga Lookout RV Park

0   250   500 m
0   250   500 yards

From the visitor center, follow Overland Ave west to what locals refer to as 'Old Town.' Near Cook Inlet, the US military established **Fort Kenay** in 1867 and stationed more than 100 men here at one time. What stands today is a replica constructed as part of the Alaska Centennial in 1967.

Across Mission St from the fort is the **Russian Orthodox Church**, built in 1895 and today the oldest Orthodox church on mainland Alaska. West of the church is the blue-domed **St Nicholas Chapel**, built in 1906 on the burial site of Father Igumen Nicolai, Kenai's first resident priest. There are no regularly scheduled tours of either building, but both are a photographer's delight.

Head southeast on Mission St, and you'll be traveling along **The Bluff**, a good vantage point to view the mouth of the Kenai River or the mountainous terrain on the west side of Cook Inlet. On the corner of Main and Mission Sts is the **Beluga Whale Lookout**. From here, you can sometimes see groups of white whales in the late spring and early summer as they ride the incoming tides into the Kenai River to feed on salmon.

Places to Stay

Sadly, there is no public campground in or near Kenai. Within town, several commercial campgrounds are geared for RVers. Both **Beluga Lookout RV Park** (☎ 283-5999, 929 Mission St) and **Overland RV Park** (☎ 283-4512), Overland Ave, are within a five-minute walk of the visitor center and have laundry facilities, full hookups and showers. Expect to pay $15 a night.

Hotels in Kenai are expensive and tend to be filled during the king-salmon runs in June and July. If you're on a tight budget, either plan on camping in this area or head north along the Kenai Spur Hwy, where several motels cater to the oil workers and offer lower rates. Within town, the most affordable is the **Katmai Hotel** (☎ 283-6101), Kenai Spur Hwy at Main St Loop Rd. Rooms during the peak season start at $79/89 for a single/double. At **Kenai Merit Inn** (☎ 283-6131, 800-227-6131, 260 Willow St), a double costs $90. At most other places in town, such as **Uptown Motel** (☎ 283-3660, 800-777-3650, 47 Spur View Drive), double rooms cost more than $125.

Places to Eat

For cheap food in town, there's the salad-and-soup bar at **Carrs Supermarket**, Kenai Spur Hwy next door to Kmart. There's also an **Arby's** (10733 Kenai Spur Hwy) and a **McDonald's** (10447 Kenai Spur Hwy), but pass them up for **Burger-N-Brew**, on Kenai Spur Hwy across from the visitor center. This small restaurant has a sunroom and a menu that features 40 types of hamburgers ($5 to $7), as well as sandwiches, seafood, salad and soup. Everything can be washed down with a pitcher of beer.

On Willow St, just off the Kenai Spur Hwy, are three restaurants within walking distance of each other. The small **Thai Lotus** and the larger **New Peking Chinese** both have lunch buffets for under $8 and dinners that start around $11. Nearby is **Don Jose's Mexican Restaurant** (205 Willow St). Across from the visitor center is **Paradisos Restaurant**, Main St, a longtime favorite for Italian, Greek and Mexican dishes.

Also in the Old Town area is **Veronica's Coffee House** (604 Peterson Way), with good espresso, a pleasant atmosphere and live music by local musicians on Friday and Saturday evenings.

Getting There & Away

Air Kenai has the main airport on the peninsula and is served by ERA (☎ 283-3168). ERA offers more than a dozen daily flights between Anchorage and Kenai. The round-trip fare costs $90 for the 30-minute flight.

Bus Bus service has resumed to the west side of the Kenai Peninsula. Kachemak Bay Transit (☎ 877-235-9101, 235-3795) provides service between Homer and Anchorage, with stops at Soldotna or the junction of the Sterling and Kenai Spur Hwys. The one-way fare from Anchorage is $40.

CAPTAIN COOK STATE RECREATION AREA

By following the Kenai Spur Hwy north for 36 miles, you'll first pass the trailer parks and chemical plants of the North Kenai industrial district and then eventually reach this uncrowded state recreation area that encompasses 4000 acres of forests, lakes, rivers and beaches along Cook Inlet. The area offers swimming, camping and the beauty of Cook Inlet in a setting that is unaffected by the stampede for salmon to the south.

The Kenai Spur Hwy ends in the park after first passing Stormy Lake, where you'll find a bathhouse and a swimming area along the water's edge. Also within the park is the **Bishop Creek Campground** (12 sites, $8) and the **Discovery Campground** (57 sites, $10). Both camping areas are on the bluff overlooking the Cook Inlet, where some of the world's greatest tides ebb and flow.

The best hiking in the park is along the saltwater beach, but don't let the high tides catch you off guard. Those paddling the Swanson River canoe route (see the Paddling section in the Wilderness chapter) will find the park an appropriate place to end the trip.

SOLDOTNA

Soldotna (population 4140) is strictly a service center at the junction of the Sterling and Kenai Spur Hwys. The town was born when both roads were completed in the 1940s and WWII veterans were given a 90-day head start to homestead the area. But what used to be little more than a hub for anglers hoping to catch an 80lb-plus king salmon from the Kenai River is now one of the fastest growing commercial areas on the peninsula. The main reason for the boom in business is tourism. The Alaska Department of Fish and Game reports the Kenai River to be the most heavily fished stream in the state, as hundreds of thousands of anglers flood the area annually and congest the waterway with powerboats.

Just about everyone headed for the river (anglers, RVers and hitchhiking backpackers) have to pass through Soldotna – the reason, no doubt, there's a McDonald's in town.

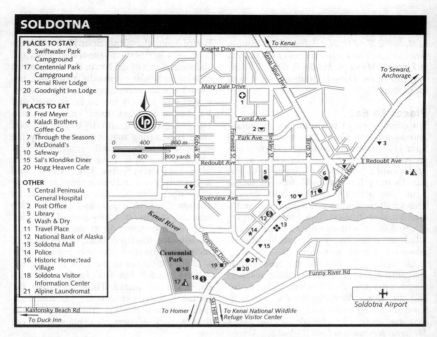

SOLDOTNA

PLACES TO STAY
8 Swiftwater Park
   Campground
17 Centennial Park
   Campground
19 Kenai River Lodge
20 Goodnight Inn Lodge

PLACES TO EAT
3 Fred Meyer
4 Kaladi Brothers
   Coffee Co
7 Through the Seasons
9 McDonald's
10 Safeway
15 Sal's Klondike Diner
20 Hogg Heaven Cafe

OTHER
1 Central Peninsula
   General Hospital
2 Post Office
5 Library
6 Wash & Dry
11 Travel Place
12 National Bank of Alaska
13 Soldotna Mall
14 Police
16 Historic Homestead
   Village
18 Soldotna Visitor
   Information Center
21 Alpine Laundromat

Information

The Soldotna Visitor Information Center
(☎ 262-9814) is in the center of town on the
Sterling Hwy, just south of the Kenai River
Bridge. The impressive center, open to 7 pm
daily during the summer, sits in a wooded
setting along the banks of the river. Outside,
a series of steps and landings leads down to
the water.

Soldotna's three banks are all on the Sterling Hwy, including National Bank of Alaska
(☎ 262-4435), 44552 Sterling Hwy.

The post office is on Corral Ave, just west
of the Kenai Spur Hwy and north of the Soldotna 'Y.'

If you need a travel agency, the Travel
Place (☎ 262-3992) is at 44096 Sterling Hwy.

The Joyce Carver Memorial Library
(☎ 262-4227), 235 Binkley St near the post
office, is open Monday through Saturday.
You can retrieve your email for free at the
library's two Internet stations. At 2 pm on
Saturday, the library shows Alaskan videos.

If you need to do laundry, try the Wash &
Dry, near the intersection of the Kenai Spur
and Sterling Hwys at the Soldotna 'Y,' or the
Alpine Laundromat, next to Dairy Queen
on the Sterling Hwy. Both have showers.

Central Peninsula General Hospital
(☎ 262-4404) is on Mary Dale Drive, just
west of the Kenai Spur Hwy, and serves both
Soldotna and Kenai.

Things to See & Do

The most interesting thing to do in Soldotna
is to drive on to Kalifonsky Beach Rd, just
after passing the bridge over the Kenai
River. The road heads west at first and
passes Centennial Park, where the Soldotna
Historical Society opened **Historic Homestead Village** in 1990. Spread out on 6 acres
within the park, the village consists of six
log buildings from early Soldotna, including
a log schoolhouse, the former tourist information building and Damon Hall. Many of
them now have historical displays or, in the

case of Damon Hall, wildlife exhibits. It's open 10 am to 4 pm Tuesday to Sunday in summer.

Opposite Kalifonsky Beach Rd near the Kenai River is the junction with Funny River Rd. Turn left (east) here and turn right (south) immediately onto Ski Hill Rd, following it for a mile to reach the **Kenai National Wildlife Refuge Visitor Center** (☎ 262-7021). The center features a series of wildlife displays, daily slide shows and wildlife films in its theater, with naturalist-led outdoor programs on the weekends. Three short trails begin at the visitor center and wind into the nearby woods or to a viewing platform on Headquarters Lake. Ask for a map. The center is open 8 am to 4:30 pm weekdays and 10 am to 6 pm weekends. Admission is free.

Places to Stay

Camping Soldotna operates two public campgrounds. *Centennial Park Campground*, Sterling Hwy at Kalifonsky Beach Rd near the Soldotna visitor center, has 108 sites for $6 per night. *Swiftwater Park Campground*, on E Redoubt Ave at Mile 94 of the Sterling Hwy, has 20 sites for the same rate. Both are on the Kenai River, so from June through July you'd better be there before noon to stake out a site.

B&Bs At the 30-plus B&Bs in the area, rates range from $60 to $90 for a single. Stop at the Soldotna visitor center for brochures and locations or call *Accommodations on the Kenai* (☎ 262-2139), a referral service for B&Bs, lodges and fish camps in the central Kenai Peninsula.

Near Soldotna, the *Denise Lake Lodge* (☎ 262-1789, 800-478-1789 in Alaska, 41680 Denise Lake Rd) features six rooms and a cabin, along with a large fireplace and a kitchen available to guests at night. Except in July (king-salmon season), singles/doubles begin at $79/98. *Spruce Avenue B&B* (☎ 262-9833, 44810 Spruce Ave), off the Kenai Spur Hwy, has four rooms ($55/65 for singles/ doubles with shared bathrooms). *Aksala Bunk & Breakfast* (☎ 283-9233), Kalifonsky

The Largest King of Them All

Thanks to its close proximity to Anchorage, ease of access and size of its king salmon, the Kenai River is Alaska's best-known fishery. Biologists believe that genetics and the fact that Kenai River salmon often spend an extra year at sea make them the largest salmon in Alaska. A trophy salmon elsewhere in Alaska is a 50lb fish. On the Kenai River, anglers don't get too excited until a king tops 75lb.

The possibility of such a wall hanger combined with the river's easy accessibility has led to what is called 'combat fishing' – anglers lining up shoulder-to-shoulder for a chance of to fill their coolers with fillets. The ticket to landing a lunker involves three key strategies: using heavy spoons, spinners or wobbling plugs, not getting your line tangled with the angler next to you and arriving with plenty of patience. There's also a lot of luck involved.

Such was the case with Les Anderson and his brother-in-law in May 1985. Fishing out of a boat at Pillars Drift, Anderson hooked into a king that immediately went airborne in what must have been a stunning sight. Anderson battled the large fish for more than an hour and then discovered his net was too small to land it. The pair ended up beaching the boat and wrestling the fish to shore. Later that day, it weighed in at 97.2lb, easily topping the previous world record of 93lb for a king salmon. Most experts agree that it's only a matter of time before the first 100lb king is hauled out of the Kenai.

Today you can marvel at Anderson's giant salmon at the Soldotna Visitor Information Center. Or, you can pick up a list of fishing guides and try to break the record yourself. There are more than 300 fishing guides registered to work the Kenai River, with half-day trips ranging from $125 to $160 per person.

Beach Rd 3.3 miles south of Bridge Access Rd, has bunks for $40, which includes a full breakfast.

Hotels Most of the hotels are geared toward RVers and anglers and are lined up along the Sterling and Kenai Spur Hwys – take your pick. Within town, the most affordable is the ***Goodnight Inn Lodge*** (☎ 262-4584, 800-478-4584 in Alaska, 44751 Sterling Hwy), across from the visitor center. Summer rates are $89 for a single or double. An even better deal – though it's farther away – is the ***Duck Inn*** (☎ 262-1849), 3.5 miles out on Kalifonsky Beach Rd, with singles or doubles for $70. More upscale is the ***Kenai River Lodge*** (☎ 262-4292, 393 Riverside Drive), where rooms overlook the river and cost $110.

Places to Eat

Chain restaurants on the Sterling Hwy include ***McDonald's***, ***Taco Bell*** and ***Burger King***, while ***Fred Meyer***, just before the Soldotna 'Y,' has a deli, bakery and ready-to-eat food items. ***Safeway*** (44428 Sterling Hwy) is open 24 hours and has a salad bar.

Sal's Klondike Diner, near the bridge on the Sterling Hwy, is open 24 hours. Breakfast begins at $4. You can amuse yourself with the menu before the eggs and toast arrive. A wider selection of breakfasts, especially omelets, can be found at ***Hog Heaven Cafe***, next door to the Goodnight Inn. More than 20 types of omelets start at around $7.

In the Soldotna Mall on the Sterling Hwy, you'll find a Chinese restaurant with a lunch buffet and ***Le Croissant Shoppe***, with espresso, salads and a variety of croissant sandwiches for about $7. There are also two Mexican restaurants, practically across from each other. ***Grand Burrito*** (44096 Sterling Hwy) serves quick Mexican food, with enchilada and taco platters at $7 and a small lunch buffet. For something more authentic that can be enjoyed with a frozen margarita, try ***Don Jose's*** across the street.

The best restaurant in Soldotna is ***Through the Seasons*** (☎ 262-5006), north of the 'Y' on the Sterling Hwy, tucked away in the woods and reached via a short boardwalk through the trees. The homemade soups and bread

make a great lunch, and at dinnertime you can splurge on such entrees as halibut baked in a Dijon sauce or peanut pesto fettuccine. In the evening, it's hard for two people to walk out of here for under $40.

Kaladi Brothers Coffee Co (315 S Kobuk St), which operates several popular coffee houses in Anchorage, has a shop in Soldotna. Next door is the ***Kenai Farmers Market***, where you can purchase locally grown produce and handmade crafts from 9 am to 2 pm on Saturday.

Getting There & Away

Kachemak Bay Transit (☎ 877-235-9101, 235-3795) provides service between Homer and Anchorage and stops at Soldotna. The one-way fare from Anchorage is $40.

STERLING HIGHWAY TO HOMER

At Soldotna, the Sterling Hwy rambles south, hugging the coastline and opening up to grand views of Cook Inlet every so often. This stretch is 78 miles long and passes through a handful of small villages near some great clamming areas, ending at the charming village of Homer. Take your time in this area; the coastline and Homer are worth every day you decide to spend there.

Kasilof

Kasilof (population 550), a fishing village, is at Mile 108.8 of the Sterling Hwy. Turn west on Kalifonsky Beach Rd and then travel 3.6 miles to reach the small boat harbor on the Kasilof River. The Sterling Hwy crosses a bridge over the Kasilof River a mile south of the Kalifonsky Beach Rd turnoff. On the other side of the bridge is the ***Kasilof River State Wayside Campground*** (11 sites, $8) on the riverbank. At Mile 111.5 of the Sterling Hwy, the Cohoe Loop Rd heads northwest towards the ocean, passing ***Crooked Creek State Recreation Area*** along the way. The rustic campsites here cost $8. Also along the road is ***Kasilof River Kabins*** (☎ 262-4946), with four cabins that sleep three or possibly four and rent for $100 a night. This fish camp also has a shared shower cabin and a great view; it's only a short walk to the river itself.

Southeast of the Cohoe Loop Rd intersection on the Sterling Hwy is Johnson Lake Access Rd, which quickly passes the *Johnson Lake Recreation Area* (43 sites, $10). Not open to motorized boats, Johnson Lake offers the chance to catch rainbow trout. At the end of the 7-mile access road is the *Tustumena Lake Campground* (10 sites, $8), which really lies on the Kasilof River, a mile from the large Tustumena Lake.

Clam Gulch

At Mile 117.4 of the Sterling Hwy, before reaching the hamlet of Clam Gulch (population 120), you pass the turnoff to a 2-mile gravel road. Just west on the road is *Clam Gulch State Recreation Area*, which has covered picnic tables, outhouses and a campground (116 sites, $8) on a steep bluff overlooking Cook Inlet. More importantly, the road provides access to the beaches below – the starting points for the area's great clam digging. Of all the beaches, the Clam Gulch beach is generally thought to be the best by clammers due to its easy access, the nearby campground and gradual gradient that makes for wide beds. If you don't camp but just stop to clam, you'll have to pay the $5 vehicle fee.

The village of Clam Gulch is less than a mile south of the gravel road on the Sterling Hwy and has a post office and gas station. More importantly, there's *Clam Shell Lodge* (☎ 262-4211), where you can rent a clam shovel for $5 and then, after a morning on the beach, take a shower and do some washing. If that sounds too much like work, the lodge restaurant serves clam chowder, razor clams and steamers (also a type of clam). Rooms are $70 for a single or double.

Ninilchik

Halfway between Soldotna and Homer is Ninilchik, a scenic area with a Russian accent, some great clamming beaches and four state campgrounds; three have views of those impressive volcanoes across Cook Inlet. For many travelers, Ninilchik is merely a stop for gas and a quick look at its Russian church. But this interesting little village is

well worth spending a night, if for no other reason than it has some of the most affordable accommodations on the west side of the Kenai Peninsula.

The community is actually the oldest on the Kenai Peninsula, having been settled in the 1820s by employees of the Russian-American Company. Many stayed even after imperial Russia sold Alaska to the USA, and their descendants form the core of the present community, which has about 680 residents.

Like so many other Kenai Peninsula towns, Ninilchik suffered heavily during the 1964 earthquake, when the village sank 3 feet and huge sections of land, including its landing strip, disappeared into the Cook Inlet. Subsequently, 'New Ninilchik' was built on the bluffs at Mile 135.5 of the Sterling Hwy between the Ninilchik River and Deep Creek.

Information There is no longer a bank in Ninilchik, but National Bank of Alaska maintains an ATM at Ninilchik General Store, Mile 135.7 of the Sterling Hwy.
The post office is on Kingsley Rd.

The Ninilchik public library (☎ 567-3333), on Sterling Hwy just north of Oilwell Rd, doubles as a visitor information center.

For a shower or laundry facilities, try *Hylen's Camper Park*, Kingsley Rd, or *Ninilchik Corners*, at the intersection of Kingsley and Oilwell Rds.

Things to See & Do Head west on Beach Access Rd, just south of the bridge over the Ninilchik River, and stop at the Village Cache Gift Shop to pick up a free *Tour of Ninilchik Village* brochure. **Old Ninilchik Village**, the site of the original community, is a postcard scene of faded log cabins in tall grass and beached fishing boats against the spectacular backdrop of Mt Redoubt. The walking tour of the old village points out a dozen buildings, including the town's first Russian school house and the **Sorensen/ Tupper Home**, built in 1895 with fir logs salvaged from fish traps.

The most spectacular building, however, is the **old Russian church**, which you reach from

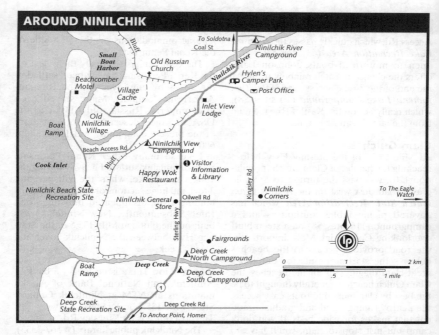

AROUND NINILCHIK

a posted footpath in the village. Built in 1901, the historic church, topped with the unique spires and crosses of the Russian Orthodox faith, is on a wide bluff and commands an unbelievable view of Cook Inlet and the volcanoes on the other side. A Russian Orthodox cemetery adjoins the church, and together they make for a photographer's delight on a clear day.

Also spend some time at **Village Cache**, a log cabin that was built in the late 1800s and then completely dismantled and restored, log by log, in 1984. Inside is a gift shop featuring unusual Native Alaskan and Russian artwork and jewelry, not moose-nugget earrings.

One of the most popular activities in Ninilchik is clamming. At low tide, head to either Ninilchik Beach State Recreation Site, across the river from the old village, or Deep Creek State Recreation Site, Mile 137.2 of the Sterling Hwy. (It costs $5 to park at the state recreation areas.) You can either

purchase a shovel at the Ninilchik General Store on the Sterling Hwy or rent one from the Village Cache in the old village.

The main event in Ninilchik is the Kenai Peninsula State Fair, the 'biggest little fair in Alaska,' which is held annually in town near the end of August.

Camping Sandwiched around the town are a handful of state campgrounds, with more just down the highway. Across the river from the old village is *Ninilchik Beach State Recreation Site* (50 sites, $8), an open area along the shoreline. It can get windy here at times, but the clamming is great. Just south of Beach Access Rd on the Sterling Hwy is *Ninilchik View Campground* (12 sites, $10), where the campsites sit on a wooded bluff just above the beach. Most are in the trees, but some have a great view of the village or Cook Inlet. A stairway leads down the bluff to the beach, the river and the village of Ninilchik.

Digging for Clams

Almost all of the beaches on the west side of the Kenai Peninsula (Clam Gulch, Deep Creek, Ninilchik and Whiskey Gulch) have a good supply of razor clams, considered by mollusk connoisseurs to be a true delicacy. Not only do razors have the best flavor, but they're also among the largest of the mollusks. The average razor clam is 3½ inches long, but most clammers have their heart set on gathering clams that reach 5, 6 or even 7 inches in length.

To go clamming, you first have to purchase a sportfishing license (a three-day visitor's license is $20, and a 14-day license is $30). The daily bag limit is 60 clams, but remember – that's an awful lot of clams to clean and eat. Two dozen per person are more than enough for a meal. While the clamming's good from April to August, the best time is July, right before spawning. Wait for the tide to drop at least a foot from the high-water mark or, better still, bide your time until it falls 4 or 5 feet.

For equipment, you'll need a narrow-bladed clam shovel that can either be purchased or, if you don't feel like hauling it around all summer, rented at many lodges and stores near the clamming areas. You also will want rubber boots, rubber gloves, a bucket and a pair of pants you're not terribly attached to.

Once you're on the beach, you have to play detective. Look for the clam's 'footprint,' a dimple mark left behind when it withdraws its neck. That's your clue to the clam's whereabouts, but don't dig directly below the imprint or you'll break its shell. Shovel a scoop or two next to the mark and then reach into the sand for the clam. You have to be quick, since a razor clam can bury itself and be gone in seconds.

Once you're successful, leave the clams in a bucket of seawater or, better yet, beer for several hours to allow them to 'clean themselves.' Many locals say a handful of cornmeal helps this process. The best way to cook clams is right on the beach over an open fire while you're taking in the mountain scenery across Cook Inlet. Use a large covered pot and steam the clams in saltwater or, better still, in white wine with a clove of garlic.

Here's where to go:

Clam Gulch This is the most popular and, many say, most productive spot by far. The Clam Gulch State Recreation Area is a half mile from Mile 118 of the Sterling Highway, where there's a short access road to the beach from the campground.

Ninilchik The best bet is to camp at Ninilchik View Campground, located above the old village of Ninilchik. From there, you can walk to beaches for clamming.

Deep Creek Just south of Ninilchik is the Deep Creek State Recreation Site, where there's camping and plenty of parking along the beach.0

Whiskey Gulch Look for the turnoff at about Mile 154 of the Sterling Hwy. Unless you have a 4WD vehicle, park at the elbow-turn above the beach.

Mud Bay On the east side of the Homer Spit is Mud Bay, a stretch abundant with Eastern soft-shells, nuttals, cockles and blue mussels. Some surf clams (rednecks) and razor clams can also be found on the Cook Inlet side of the Spit.

Some other highly edible mollusks on the western side of the Kenai Peninsula include:

Eastern Soft-Shell Clam An introduced species from the Atlantic Ocean, the Eastern soft-shell clam is most likely to be found in muddy, sandy or gravelly bottoms where the salinity has been reduced by a freshwater influx. Mud Bay is one good source for these clams.

Horse Clams The 'granddaddies' of the local mollusks, weighing in at 4½lb in some cases, these are available on the south side of Kachemak Bay along rocky beaches in the more protected bays.

Nuttals & Cockles These shellfish make a good chowder base. They're prevalent in Mud Bay.

Blue Mussels Often overlooked, blue mussels are abundant throughout Kachemak Bay and Cook Inlet, where they attach themselves to rocks and pilings. These mollusks can be delicious when prepared with care.

SOUTHCENTRAL

Across the Sterling Hwy from Coat Rd in northern Ninilchik is **Ninilchik River Campground** (43 sites, $8), in a wooded area away from the river. To the south, at Mile 137.2 of the Sterling Hwy, you'll reach the **Deep Creek State Recreation Site** (100 sites, $8), on the beach near the mouth of the creek. The facility features a boat launch, information board about clamming, parking for 300 cars and boat trailers and a pay phone. It's heavily used by campers, clammers and anglers who launch their boats in the creek. You can also camp on both sides of the Sterling Hwy Bridge across Deep Creek; sites cost $8.

If these are all full, continue south to **Stariski Creek State Recreation Site**, Mile 152 of the Sterling Hwy, with 13 campsites on a bluff overlooking Cook Inlet for $10.

Cabins You can rent cabins north of town at **Ninilchik Cabins & Fish Camp** (☎ 567-3635), Mile 128.3 of the Sterling Hwy, or **Ninilchik Point Overnighter** (☎ 567-3423), Mile 130.5 of the Sterling Hwy. The Overnighter, 5 miles from town, has a spectacular view of the volcanoes across the inlet. Smaller cabins are $60 for two people, and there are also tent sites for $7.

In Ninilchik, the **Inlet View Lodge** (☎ 567-3330), at Mile 135.4 of the Sterling Hwy, has 11 cabins for rent. All the cabins are very rustic and small, with a shared shower area, but cost only $30/35 for a single/double. The lodge also contains a restaurant and liquor store.

Hostels Ninilchik has a hostel that is a little out-of-the-way but well worth the effort to reach it. **The Eagle Watch** (☎ 567-3905), east of town at Mile 3 of Oilwell Rd, features eight bunks, a kitchen, showers and laundry facilities. The rural setting is spectacular, as the log home was built on a high bluff overlooking the Ninilchik River valley. The rate is $10 for members, $15 for non-members and $2 for bedsheet rental, as the owners don't allow sleeping bags.

Hotels Right on the beach in the old village is the **Beachcomber Motel** (☎ 567-3417),

Beach Rd, with a half dozen small rooms that rent for $60/70 for singles/doubles.

Places to Eat Ninilchik General Store, at Mile 135.7 of the Sterling Hwy, sells groceries, supplies, sandwiches and coffee at its espresso bar. But the best place for a bite to eat is the nearby **Happy Wok Restaurant**. A plate of fried rice begins at $7, while full dinners, which include soup, egg roll, two main dishes and fried rice, are $10 to $13.

Anchor Point

Twenty miles south of Ninilchik is Anchor Point (population 1200) and, as a monument here notes, 'the most westerly point on the North American continent accessible by a continuous road system.' Anchor Point was named in 1778 by Capt James Cook after the *Resolution* lost a kedge anchor to the tidal currents. Today, the town is a fishing hot spot during the summer, with Anchor River renowned for its population of salmon, steelhead and Dolly Varden trout. If you're bringing your rod and reel, make sure you pick up an Anchor River State Recreation Area brochure, which lists the seasons and even shows the favorite fishing holes along the river. But be prepared for massive crowds here in July and much of August.

Information At the junction of the Sterling and Old Sterling Hwys is the Anchor Point Visitor Center, housed in a log cabin and staffed by volunteers. If you stop by, you'll receive a certificate stating you've been to 'North America's Most Westerly Highway Point.' The center is open 10 am to 4 pm weekdays.

Places to Stay & Eat Old Sterling Hwy, or Anchor River Rd, leads to the Anchor River State Recreation Area. A beach access road on the south side of the Anchor River enters the recreation area and leads past five campgrounds. The last one, **Halibut Campground**, has 30 sites and overlooks Cook Inlet Beach, while the rest are on the river. Sites are $8 or $10.

Among the campgrounds are some RV parks and tackle shops – testimony to the king-salmon fever that runs through this place in July. (Good luck getting a site then.) The road ends at a beautiful stretch of beach with good views of Mt Redoubt and Mt Iliamna across the inlet. An observation deck has sighting scopes and an information display about 'the Ring of Fire' volcanoes.

Accommodations in town include the ***Anchor River Inn*** (☎ *235-8531, 800-435-8531*), Sterling Hwy at Old Sterling Hwy. The motel has small economy rooms called 'Fisherman's special' for $45/50 single/double and larger motel rooms for $90/95. Three miles north of Anchor Point is ***Eagle Crest RV Park*** (☎ *235-6651*), Mile 152.7 of the Sterling Hwy, with cabins that overlook Cook Inlet, along with a laundry facility and convenience store. Cabins cost $100 for two people; full hookups are $20.

For a cheeseburger ($7 includes fries) and a beer served on an outdoor deck, try ***Teri Ann's***, Mile 156.3 of the Sterling Hwy. For an espresso or deli sandwich while you wait for your wash to finish, stop in at the delightful ***Anchorage Point Roadhouse*** (*34115 Sterling Hwy*), just down the road.

HOMER
Arriving in Homer (population 4100) is like opening one of those pop-up greeting cards – it's an unexpected thrill. From Anchor Point, the Sterling Hwy ascends the bluffs overlooking Kachemak Bay. Three miles before Homer, the road provides a few teasers that whet your appetite but never fully prepare you for the charming, colorful fishing village that lies ahead. As the road makes a final turn east along the bluffs, Homer unfolds completely. It's a truly incredible panorama of mountains, white peaks, glaciers and Homer Spit, a long strip of land that stretches into beautiful Kachemak Bay.

History
In the beginning, the Spit was Homer, and it has always played a prominent role in the

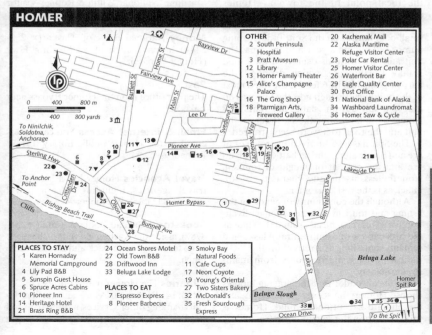

SOUTHCENTRAL

development of the city. The town was founded, and picked up its name, when Homer Pennock, an adventurer from Michigan, landed on the Spit with a crew of gold seekers in 1896, convinced that Kachemak Bay was the key to their riches. It wasn't, and in 1898 Pennock was lured away by the spell of the Klondike fields, though he also failed to find gold there.

Coal first supported the fledging town, and in 1899 the first dock on the Spit was built by the Cook Inlet Coal Field Company (CCC). It was later destroyed by ice. The second dock didn't come until 1938, when a combination of the CCC and local fundraising (including the efforts of the Homer Women's Club, which raised enough to build a warehouse) reconnected the city to the sea. When the first steamship arrived that fall, the residents celebrated the end of an era of dismal isolation.

Despite the arrival of the first gravel road to Homer in 1951, the Spit continued to be the focal point of the town as Homer switched from a coal-based economy to a fishing industry, which is centered in the small boat harbor on the Spit. Today, fishing pumps $30 million a year into the area. The Spit and the town also survived the Good Friday Earthquake, which dropped the narrow peninsula by 6 feet and leveled most of the buildings. By high tide, the Spit was no longer a spit but an island. Six years and almost $7 million after the earthquake, the Spit and the road to it were reconstructed.

The Spit has also survived the ravages of fire and high water, political battles over land use and the current onslaught of tourism. Nonetheless, its unique character is still intact, as is the rest of Homer.

Although the community depends on the fishing and tourism industries for its livelihood, it's still recognized around the state as the arts capital of Southcentral Alaska and remains something of a retreat for the 1960s radicals, artists and dropouts from mainstream society.

It's little wonder that the graying hippies choose Homer; the scenery is inspiring and the climate exceptionally mild. Homer is protected from the severe northern cold by the Kenai Mountains to the north and east. Winter temperatures rarely drop much below 0°F, while summer temperatures rarely rise above 70°F. The annual precipitation is only 28 inches, much of it snow.

This is a town that lures you to stay for a while. Between the several espresso shops, great scenery and interesting side trips to the other side of Kachemak Bay, you could easily spend a week here.

Information

Tourist Offices The Homer Visitor Center (☎ 235-7740, www.homeralaska.org) is at 135 Sterling Hwy, or what is usually labeled as the 'Homer Bypass.' The center has racks of information for tourists, free coffee and courtesy phones to book rooms or tours. It's open 8 am to 8 pm daily in the summer and 9 am to 5 pm weekdays the rest of the year.

You'll also find some limited tourist information at the Pratt Museum and the Alaska Maritime National Wildlife Refuge Visitor Center (see those individual sections).

Money National Bank of Alaska (☎ 235-2444) has a branch at 88 Sterling Hwy (Homer Bypass).

Post
The post office is on the Homer Bypass near Lake St.

Email & Internet Access You can access email at the Homer public library, 141 W Pioneer Ave.

Travel Agencies Homer has a handful of travel agencies, including Aurora Travel (☎ 235-2111), 158 W Pioneer Ave.

Bookstores Bagdad Books & Cafe (☎ 235-8787), inside the Kachemak Mall, is the place to go for a used paperback and an affordable lunch.

Libraries The Homer public library (☎ 235-3180), 141 W Pioneer Ave, is an excellent facility. Among other services, it often has used books for sale. It's open 10 am to 8 pm

The Literary Pride of Homer

It may be an artists' colony in Alaska, but around the country Homer is best known as the home of Tom Bodett, the folksy voice that tells millions of Americans that 'Motel 6 has the lowest rates of any national chain.'

Born in Sturgis, Michigan, Bodett dropped out of Michigan State University and followed his wanderlust first to Oregon and eventually to Homer, where he was making a living as a construction worker. His literary career started when he tried to quit smoking and wrote a humorous piece about it for the *Anchorage Daily News*. That resulted in a Sunday column and commentaries on National Public Radio.

His life really changed when a Dallas advertising executive in charge of the Motel 6 account became infatuated with Bodett's accent while listening to National Public Radio. In 1986, Bodett, then just a nervous carpenter and fledgling radio commentator, wound up in a San Francisco recording studio doing the voice-overs for the Motel 6 ads. With a couple of seconds to spare after reading the ad copy, he ad-libbed the 'We'll leave the light on for ya' tag line. It was pure heartland America and has become one of the most noted advertising slogans of its time. Thirteen years and 350 Motel 6 advertising spots later, it's still being used.

The fame allowed Bodett to begin producing his *End of the Road* variety show, in which he mixed his tales with homegrown musical talent, at his own Clearshot Studios in Homer. The show immediately drew comparisons to Garrison Keillor's *A Prairie Home Companion*, though Bodett's humor tends to be simpler and more innocent. *End of the Road* aired for three years and, at its peak in 1990, reached listeners on 150 stations across the country.

After a follow-up show, *Bodett & Co*, Bodett stepped away from the radio shows in 1993 to concentrate on his writing. His humorous tales and 'aw-shucks' stories on National Public Radio resulted in four books of short stories and his first novel, *The Free Fall of Webster Cummings*. In 1999, he released *Williwaw*, his first young-adult novel.

Tuesday and Thursday, 10 am to 6 pm Wednesday, Friday and Saturday.

Laundry You can take a shower ($3) and wash your clothes at the same time on the way to the Spit at Washboard Laundromat (☎ 235-6781), 1204 Ocean Drive.

Medical Services The South Peninsula Hospital (☎ 235-8101) is north of the Pratt Museum on Bartlett St. Next door is the Homer Medical Clinic (☎ 235-8586) for walk-in service.

Pratt Museum

The Pratt Museum (☎ 235-8635), on Bartlett St, features Native Alaskan artifacts, historical displays and exhibits on marine life in Kachemak Bay. Among the intriguing specimens kept in aquariums and tidal pool tanks are some octopuses and sea anemones.

Complete skeletons of a Bering Sea beaked whale and a beluga whale are on display.

Its best exhibit, however, is on the lower level. Entitled 'Darkened Waters,' the exhibit provides a stunning and emotional look at the Exxon oil spill, with an hour-by-hour account of the effort to save just one oil-soaked seal, the radio tapes of Capt Joseph Hazelwood contacting the Coast Guard, and displays on both protesters and 'spillionaires' – locals who made small fortunes from the spill. It is by far the best look at Alaska's worse environmental tragedy. The museum is open 10 am to 6 pm daily in summer and charges $5 for admission.

Alaska Maritime National Wildlife Refuge

More natural-history displays can be seen nearby at the Alaska Maritime National Wildlife Refuge Visitor Center, on the

Sterling Hwy just before you enter town. The center contains a small theater with regularly scheduled videos, as well as a book and map counter where you can pick up information on hiking and kayaking in Kachemak Bay. Guided bird walks and children's programs occur throughout the summer. The center (☎ 235-6961) is open 9 am to 6 pm daily.

Galleries

The beautiful scenery has inspired numerous artists to gather here, and the handful of galleries in town display more than the usual ivory carvings and gold-nugget jewelry you see everywhere else. Most of the galleries are along Pioneer Ave, including Ptarmigan Arts (☎ 235-5345), which features a variety of jewelry, pottery and weaving from more than 40 artists in the area, and Fireweed Gallery (☎ 235-7040) next door. Bunnell Street Gallery (☎ 235-8881), in the same building as the Old Town B&B and Two Sisters Bakery, features 'explorative Alaskan Art,' while the Pratt Museum also has an art gallery with work by artists from the Kenai Peninsula. You can also visit a number of artists who maintain galleries in their studios, including Ahna Iredale, whose pottery is often decorated with Alaskan landscapes or fish. Her Rare Bird Pottery Studio (☎ 235-7687) is 10 minutes from downtown on Bay Ridge Rd.

For a map and descriptions of the galleries in town, pick up the *Downtown Homer Art Galleries* from the visitor center or the *Homer Tourist Guide*, published by the *Homer News*.

Homer Spit

This long needle of land is a 5-mile sand bar that stretches into Kachemak Bay; during the summer, it's the center of activity in Homer and the heart of the local fishing industry. The Spit draws thousands of tourists and backpackers every year, making it not only a scenic spot but an interesting mecca for fishers, cannery workers, visitors and charter-boat operators.

The hub of all this activity is the **small boat harbor** at the end of the Spit, one of the best facilities in Southcentral Alaska and home to more than 700 boats. On each side of the harbor's entrance is a cannery. Nearby is the **Seafarer's Memorial**, a touching monument to the 27 residents who have been lost at sea.

The favorite activity on the Homer Spit, naturally, is beach-combing, especially at dawn or dusk while viewing the sunset or sunrise. You can stroll for miles along the beach, where the marine life is as plentiful as the driftwood, or you can go clamming at Mud Bay on the east side of the Spit. Blue mussels, an excellent shellfish overlooked by many people, are the most abundant. Locals call the clams and mussels 'Homer grown.'

Another popular activity on the Spit is a shrimp, clam or crab boil. Grab your camp stove and large metal pot, purchase some fresh seafood from the seafood markets around the small boat harbor and buy a can of beer from the general store next door to the Salty Dawg Saloon. Then head down to the beach and enjoy your Alaskan feast while watching the tide roll in and the sun set. Be aware, though, that no beach fires are allowed between Land's End and the Whitney Fidalgo Access Rd.

If you'd rather catch your dinner than shovel or buy it, try your luck at the **Fishing Hole**, on Homer Spit Rd just before the Pier One Theatre. The small lagoon is the site of a 'terminal fishery' in which salmon are planted by the state and then return three or four years later to a place where they can't spawn. From mid-May to mid-September, anglers bait their hooks with colorful spoons, salmon eggs, or herring or shrimp under bobbers and then cast into the lagoon. More than 15,000 salmon, ranging from 40lb kings to 5lb pinks and cohos, are caught here every summer.

Skyline Drive

North of town are bluffs, referred to by locals as 'the Hill,' that rise gently to 1100 feet. On a clear day, these green slopes dotted with colorful patches of wildflowers provide excellent views of the glaciers that spill out of the Harding Ice Field across the bay.

For the best view, head to Skyline Drive, which runs along the bluff above Homer.

Follow Pioneer Ave east out of town (it eventually turns into E End Rd) and then turn north onto E Hill Rd, proceeding up the bluffs to Skyline Drive. At the west end of Skyline Drive is Ohlson Mountain Rd, which ascends 1513 feet to the peak of Ohlson Mountain. Many roads, including E End Rd, are paved and ideal for cycling (see the Homer Bicycling section).

Hiking

For all its natural beauty, Homer lacks good public trails. The best hiking is along the beaches, while most trails that begin at the roadside are private paths that usually lead to somebody's homestead or cabin.

Bishop Beach Trail This hike, which begins at Bishop Park, makes either an excellent afternoon stroll or an 11-mile trek north of Homer. The views of Kachemak Bay and the Kenai Mountains are superb, while the marine life that scurries along the sand at low tide is fascinating.

Check a tide book, available from most gasoline stations or sports stores, and leave before low tide and return before high tide. High tides cover most of the sand, forcing

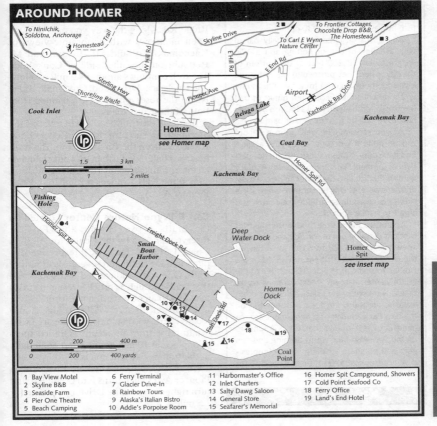

AROUND HOMER

1 Bay View Motel	6 Ferry Terminal	11 Harbormaster's Office	16 Homer Spit Campground, Showers
2 Skyline B&B	7 Glacier Drive-In	12 Inlet Charters	17 Cold Point Seafood Co
3 Seaside Farm	8 Rainbow Tours	13 Salty Dawg Saloon	18 Ferry Office
4 Pier One Theatre	9 Alaska's Italian Bistro	14 General Store	19 Land's End Hotel
5 Beach Camping	10 Addie's Porpoise Room	15 Seafarer's Memorial	

SOUTHCENTRAL

Hooking a Halibut in Homer

To thousands of tourists who come to Alaska every summer, Homer is the place where you go to catch a halibut. Halibut is a bottom-dweller that, when first born, looks like any normal fish with an eye on each side of the head. But as a halibut feeds exclusively off the bottom, it flattens out and one eye moves to the other side, which has become the 'top' of the fish.

Females are larger than males; in fact, just about every halibut weighing more than 100lb is a female. And almost without fail, a 300lb halibut is hauled out of Kachemak Bay every summer. The state-record halibut tipped the scales at almost 500lb. The average size fish, however, is closer to 30 or 40lb.

Anglers use a large hook, usually baited with a chunk of cod or herring and a 40lb weight to take it 200 feet to the bottom of the bay, where they proceed to 'jig' (raise and lower the hook slightly) for a fish. Or, as one writer described it, 'People put hunks of bait the size of footballs on hooks the size of trailer hitches to pull up fish the size of barn doors.'

As you can imagine, reeling in a halibut can be quite a workout, and many anglers find it exciting, though these fish are not battlers or jumpers like salmon or trout. Actually getting the fish into the boat can be the most dramatic part, as charter captains often use a club or even a gun to subdue their catch and a gaff to haul it aboard.

There are more than two dozen charter captains working out of the Spit and charging anywhere from $120 to $185 for a halibut trip. Just about all of them run an ad in the *Homer Tourist Guide*, handed out free at the visitor center in town. Most captains try to take advantage of two slack tides and often leave at around 6 am for a 12-hour trip on the bay. Pack a lunch or purchase one from a handful of restaurants that sell box lunches on the Spit. Also take warm clothing and rain gear and purchase a fishing license (nonresident licenses cost $20 for three days, $30 for 14 days).

you to scramble onto the base of the nearby cliffs. Within 3 miles of the park, you'll pass a sea-otter rookery a few hundred yards offshore. In 7 miles, you'll reach Diamond Creek, which will lead you up to the Sterling Hwy, 4 miles north of town. To reach Bishop Park, head south on Main St, then left on Bunnell Ave and right on Beluga Ave.

Homestead Trail This relatively new trail, developed by the Kachemak Heritage Land Trust (KHLT), is a 6.7-mile trek from Rogers Loop Rd to the City Reservoir, just off Skyline Drive on Crossman Ridge Rd. From Rogers Loop Rd, it's a 2.5-mile walk to Rucksack Drive, which crosses Diamond Ridge Rd. Along the way you pass through open meadows with panoramic views of Kachemak Bay and Mt Iliamna and Mt Redoubt on the other side of Cook Inlet. The trek continues another 4.2 miles, following Rucksack Drive and Crossman Ridge Rd to the reservoir. Cars are banned from both of these dirt roads.

To reach the trail, head out of town on the Sterling Hwy and turn right on Rogers Loop Rd across from the Bay View Inn. The trailhead is a half mile farther, on your right. For an interpretive brochure describing the trail, stop at the KHLT office (☎ 235-5263), 395 E Pioneer Ave.

Carl E Wynn Nature Center Located on the bluffs above Homer, this 126-acre reserve managed by the Center for Alaskan Coastal Studies features interpretive displays in a log cabin and several short nature trails. One is a handicapped-accessible trail that leads through a spruce forest and grassy meadow to an observation platform.

Because a 30-acre wildlife refuge is also located here, you can only visit the area with a naturalist from the center. Guided tours take place at 10 am, noon, 2 and 4 pm daily in the summer. Admission is $5.

To reach the nature center, drive east on Pioneer Ave, which turns into E Hill Rd, and turn right onto Skyline Drive, continuing for 1.5 miles.

Bicycling

The dirt roads in the hills above Homer lend themselves to some great mountain biking, especially Diamond Ridge Rd and Skyline Drive. For an easy tour, just head out E End Rd, which extends 20 miles east to the head of Kachemak Bay. Homer Saw & Cycle (☎ 235-8406), 1535 Ocean Drive on the way to the Spit, rents mountain bikes ($15 for a half day, $25 for a full day) and sells both maps of the area and a limited selection of parts.

Rocky River The best mountain-bike adventures in the area are on the south side of Kachemak Bay, where you can ride along the Jakolof-Rocky River Rd from Jakolof Bay all the way to Windy Bay. The 20-mile rough dirt road follows a riverbed that cuts across the very tip of the Kenai Peninsula. There are numerous stream crossings. Beware of loggers, and thus logging trucks, in the Windy Bay area. Cyclists in good shape can reach the end of the road and return in one day, a 30-mile ride. Otherwise, plan to camp. To reach the dock on Jakolof Bay, hop a ride on the Jakolof Ferry Service (☎ 235-2376), which departs the Spit at 10 am daily during the summer. The roundtrip fare is $45.

Viewing Brown Bears

Because of Homer's proximity to the McNeil River State Game Sanctuary and Katmai National Park, bear watching has become an increasingly popular flightseeing trip. Because it takes more than 90 minutes to reach the bear-viewing areas of the Alaska Peninsula on a floatplane, most flights are a full-day trip that include one or two landings to view bears and to eat lunch.

Among the many companies that offer such trips is Bald Mountain Air Service (☎ 235-7969, 800-478-7969, baldmt@ptialaska .net). Tours depart Beluga Lake at 8 am daily during the summer and return between 5 and 7 pm, depending on the tides. The cost is $475 per person, and if you're interested in going during the prime bear-viewing months of July and August, you should book a flight in advance.

Special Events

For birders, one of the best times to be in the area is mid-May, when shorebird migration peaks and Homer celebrates its Kachemak Bay Shorebird Festival. During the first two weeks of the month, more than 100,000 shorebirds pass through Mud Bay, making it the largest bird migration site along the Alaskan road system. The tidal flats of Homer become the staging area for thousands of birds, including one-third of the world's surfbirds.

The festival, usually held on the second weekend of the month, attracts hundreds of birders to the town for a series of workshops at the Alaska Maritime National Wildlife Refuge, guided birding tours, exhibits, and arts and crafts shows. For an update on the migration or any birding activity in the area, call the Kachemak Bay Bird Watchers Hotline (☎ 235-7337).

Other events in Homer include the almost monthlong Spring Arts Festival in May. This event began as an outlet for local artists to display their work and has since evolved into a festival with dancers, musicians and craftspeople.

The July 4th celebration is usually a three-day event that includes a parade, a footrace, a grease-pole climb, and arts and crafts booths.

Places to Stay

Camping Beach camping is allowed in designated areas on the west side of Homer Spit, a beautiful spot to pitch a tent. (Be forewarned, though, that the Spit can get rowdy at times.) The nightly fee is $3 for pitching a tent in the city-controlled sections near the end of the Spit, $7 for parking an RV. There are toilets next to the harbormaster's office. A shower costs $3 at the *Homer Spit Campground* (☎ 235-8206, 4661 Homer Spit Rd).

The *Karen Hornaday Memorial Campground* is on a wooded hill with an impressive view of the town and bay below, making it considerably more private than the Spit. This city campground, which you reach by driving north on Bartlett St and following the signs, also has a $3 nightly fee for tents and a 14-day limit.

Hostels While there's no official hostel in Homer, there is *Seaside Farm* (☎ 235-7850), 5 miles from Homer on E End Rd. This working farm has a variety of accommodations, including a backpacker hostel with bunks for $15 a night, rustic cabins for $55 and a grassy pasture where you can pitch a tent ($6) on a site overlooking Kachemak Bay. The farm has an outdoor kitchen area for campers, showers and laundry facilities. For more adventurous accommodations, try the Seaside Farm Outpost, along Swift Creek at the head of Kachemak Bay. Fifteen miles beyond the farm, the bunkroom ($15 per night) is a half-mile hike away from E End Rd.

Within downtown Homer, *Sunspin Guest House* (☎ 235-6677, 800-391-6677, sunspin@ xyz.net, 358 E Lee Drive) has bunkrooms for $28 per person, as well as private rooms for $65. The rates include pickup service from the airport or ferry terminal and breakfast.

B&Bs These places have popped up in Homer like mushrooms in the spring, and at last count there were more than 40 in the area. You can pick up brochures for most of them at the visitor center and then use the courtesy phones to book a room. There's a 5.5% tax on rooms in Homer.

In the heart of town is the *Lily Pad B&B* (☎ 235-6630, 3954 Bartlett St), with seven rooms above a beauty salon. Doubles with shared bathrooms are $75. The *Old Town B&B* (☎ 235-7558, 106 W Bunnell Ave), above Two Sisters Bakery, overlooks Bishop's Beach and has three rooms that range from $60 to $70.

In the downtown area, the *Spruce Acres Cabins* (☎ 235-8388, 910 Sterling Hwy), just before Pioneer Ave, has four cabins that sleep two people for $60 to $80. The *Brass Ring B&B* (☎ 235-5450, 987 Hillfair Court) is a log-cabin home with five rooms and an outdoor hot tub, among other amenities. Singles/doubles with shared bathrooms are $74/79. Above the city is *Skyline B&B* (☎ 235-3832, 60855 Skyline Drive), with a

beautiful view of Grewingk Glacier, four rooms for $60/65 and a bunkroom with single beds for $20.

The other option is to head out on E End Rd, where you will pass one B&B sign after another. Practically all of them have a grand view of Kachemak Bay and the surrounding mountains. *Frontier Cottages* (☎ 235-8275), 3.5 miles from Homer, features four new cabins, each with a kitchen, living room and upstairs sleeping loft. The rate is $98 for up to three people; children are free.

Head farther east still to reach the *Chocolate Drop B&B* (☎ 235-3668, 800-530-6015, chocdrop@xyz.net). More of a lodge than a B&B, the Chocolate Drop is a stunning log inn overlooking the bay, with an outdoor hot tub on the 2nd floor porch and a sauna inside. All rooms have bathrooms and private entrances and range from $109 to $119. A family suite with a kitchen costs $179 for four people.

Hotels There are almost a dozen hotels and motels in the area, with most single rooms ranging from $60 to $70. All of them are heavily booked during the summer. A delightful, small hotel is the *Driftwood Inn* (☎ 235-8019, 800-478-8019, driftinn@xyz.net), on the corner of Main St and Bunnell Ave. Rooms without a view or a bathroom are $46/56, while the 'Ship Quarters' accommodations – small rooms with a bathroom – begin at $54/74. In the lounge is a fieldstone fireplace, while overlooking the bay are a barbecue area and deck. Coffee and rolls are available in the morning.

Within walking distance of downtown Homer is the *Ocean Shores Motel* (☎ 235-7775, 800-770-7775, 3500 Crittenden Drive). Doubles begin at $95, while new bay-view rooms with kitchenettes are $140. Right on Pioneer Ave is *Heritage Hotel* (☎ 235-7787, 800-380-7787, heritage.xyz.net, 147 E Pioneer Ave); the historical log lodge has singles/ doubles for $80/90. A block down the street is *Pioneer Inn* (☎ 235-5670, 800-782-9655, 244 W Pioneer Ave), with rooms for $69/89 singles/doubles.

For something more upscale, try *Beluga Lake Lodge* (☎ 800-478-8485 in Alaska,

235-5995, 984 Ocean Drive), which overlooks its namesake lake. Double rooms with one bed begin at $88. At the end of the Spit is **Land's End Hotel** (☎ *800-478-0400 in Alaska, 235-2500)*, where rooms with an outdoor balcony and a spectacular view begin at $140.

Places to Eat

Sure, Homer has a **McDonald's** and even two **Subway** shops, but pass up the fast lane to fast food and try one of the charming and unique eateries. Spoon for spoon, no other town in Alaska has the culinary variety that Homer boasts, with the exception of the big two – Anchorage and Fairbanks.

The assortment of cafes and bakeries includes a handful of espresso shops. Amazingly, this town of 3000 supports more than a half dozen places where you can get a cup of cappuccino. The most interesting is **Cafe Cups** *(162 W Pioneer Ave)*, with its bizarre coffee-cup exterior and its pleasant interior; each wall is an art gallery. Huge sandwiches, made with thick cuts of bread, are $6 and include several veggie options, while homemade soup is $5. The cafe opens at 7 am and serves several unusual egg dishes – just what you would expect in Homer.

You can enjoy lattes, baked goods and 1960s atmosphere at **Two Sisters Bakery**, on the corner of Main St and Bunnell Ave. Inside the Old Inlet Trading Post building, the shop has a few tables inside and a few more on the porch overlooking the bay.

On Pioneer Ave as you head into town is **Espresso Express**, a small cafe with a coffee drive-thru window. It has the best prices, with a 16oz latte under $3 and bagels and cream cheese for $1.50.

Neon Coyote *(435 E Pioneer Ave)* is an interesting and affordable diner that specializes in Southwest cooking. At dinner, the grande burrito filled with chicken and black beans will fill you up for $7, or you can order shrimp enchiladas for $16.

The best vegetarian spot is **Smoky Bay Natural Foods** *(248 W Pioneer Ave)*. This co-op is Homer's health-food store, which includes a small kitchen that serves filling vegetarian dishes at lunch for under $7 and soups and sandwiches for even less. There's

limited seating inside. Carnivores in search of the best baby-back ribs should go to the nearby **Pioneer Barbecue** *(270 W Pioneer Ave)*.

Homer has two Chinese restaurants next door to each other on Pioneer Ave. It's a toss-up between the **Thai & Chinese Restaurant** *(601 E Pioneer Ave)*, in the Kachemak Mall, and **Young's Oriental** *(565 E Pioneer Ave)*, both featuring a $7 feast for lunch and an all-you-can-eat deal at dinner for just $1 more. **Pioneer Pizza** *(265 E Pioneer Ave)* offers all the pizza, salad and soda you can 'scarf' down for $8.50 from Monday to Saturday.

On the way to the Spit, you'll pass **Eagle Quality Center** *(90 Sterling Hwy)*, the best place in town for groceries, fresh baked breads, deli sandwiches and salads ($3.50 per pound). The supermarket is open 24 hours. Just after crossing Beluga Slough, you'll find **Fresh Sourdough Express** *(1316 Ocean Drive)*, a good bakery and breakfast spot. Eggs, potatoes and sourdough toast cost $5, with huge sourdough pancakes for $5.75.

Cheap eats at the end of the Spit consist of a **Subway** franchise, a fish-and-chips takeout place, **Glacier Drive-In** and a couple of vans selling espresso and fresh bagels. For something more charming, try **Whales Cove**, on the Thompson Boardwalk. You can enjoy Kachemak Bay halibut and chips or homemade chowder in a bread bowl while taking in the nice view. Nearby is **Cold Point Seafood Point Co**, offering fresh, smoked and canned salmon, halibut, prawns and other delicacies from Kachemak Bay.

A step up is **Alaska's Italian Bistro**, with an elegant dining room overlooking Kachemak Bay. A 12-inch pizza costs $13, a plate of pasta and salad $14, and most seafood dinners $18. Across the road is **Addie's Porpoise Room**, which has a dining room and bar overlooking the small boat harbor. The baked halibut dinner costs $16, and steamed tanner crab in the shell costs $20, while most hamburgers cost about $7 and a halibut burger costs $8.

Eight miles east of town is **The Homestead** (☎ *235-6723)*, E End Rd, a log lodge that houses Homer's finest restaurant. You must have a reservation, but it's worth the effort, as the food and view of the bay and mountains are excellent. Pasta dinners are $15 to $18, seafood $18 to $21, and prime rib $20.

Entertainment

Homer's most famous drinking hole is on the Spit. The *Salty Dawg Saloon*, a log-cabin bar with a lighthouse tower over it, has the same claim to fame as Juneau's Red Dog Saloon, right down to the sawdust on the floor and an amazing collection of orange life preservers on the walls, each stenciled with the name of the ship from which it came. The saloon is made up of three small log structures, including a tower that was originally a water tank but was relocated here after the Good Friday Earthquake of 1964. It's worth at least a look at the life preservers, if not a few beers while you study them.

Downtown, *Alice's Champagne Palace (195 E Pioneer Ave)* rocks with bands and live music almost nightly. Next door is the saloon of the *Heritage Hotel*. *Moby Dick's Bar & Grill (984 Ocean Drive)*, in the Beluga Lake Lodge, hosts live music throughout the summer, while the *Waterfront Bar (120 W Bunnell Ave)*, across from the Driftwood Inn, features rock-and-roll bands and a packed dance floor Wednesday through Saturday.

The Grog Shop (369 E Pioneer Ave) is the place to pick up some brew to take back to the campsite. The shop's excellent selection of beer includes most of the brands produced by the Alaskan microbreweries.

Homer is also blessed with entertainment that doesn't require a bar stool. *Pier One Theater (☎ 235-7333)* features live drama and comedy in a 'come-as-you-are' warehouse next to the Fishing Hole on the Spit. Performances start at 8:15 pm Friday and Saturday and 7:30 pm on Sunday throughout the summer. Tickets prices range from $7 to $11. The *Homer Family Theater (☎ 235-6728)*, Main St at Pioneer Ave, shows movies.

Getting There & Away

Air ERA Aviation (☎ 235-7565, 800-426-0333), the contract carrier for Alaska Air-lines, provides eight daily flights between Homer and Anchorage from Homer's airport, 1.7 miles east of town on Kachemak Drive. The one-way fare is $98; a roundtrip, advance-purchase ticket is $140. Homer Air (☎ 800-478-8591 in Alaska, 235-8591) provides an air-taxi service to Seldovia. The one-way fare is $30; roundtrip is $55.

Bus Kachemak Bay Transit (☎ 877-235-9101, 235-3795) provides service between Homer and Anchorage and points in between along the Sterling Hwy. A bus departs Homer at 9 am and arrives in Anchorage around 5 pm. The one-way fare is $45. Homer Stage Lines (☎ 235-7009) offers the same runs for the same rate.

Car To obtain an affordable rental car, stop at Polar Car Rental (☎ 235-5998, 455 Sterling Hwy) or at its desk in the airport. The small dealer has subcompacts for $60 a day, with the first 100 miles free.

Hitchhiking KBBI-AM 890 airs a 'Rideline' three times a day for people seeking either transportation out of town or passengers. Call the public radio station (☎ 235-7721) to leave a message for the show.

Boat The ferry M/V *Tustumena* provides twice-weekly service from Homer to Seldovia and thrice-weekly service to Kodiak, including one run that continues onto Seward and the rest of the Southcentral ports. The one-way fare from Homer to Seldovia is $18; from Homer to Kodiak, it's $48. The ferry terminal (☎ 235-8449) is at the end of Homer Spit.

Rainbow Tours (☎ 235-7272) departs at 11 am daily from the Spit en route to Seldovia; it returns at 4 pm. The trip takes 1.5 hours, and the fare is $25 one-way or $45 roundtrip.

KACHEMAK BAY

This beautiful body of water extends 30 miles into the Kenai Peninsula and features a coastline of steep fjords and inlets with the glacier-capped peaks of the Kenai Mountains in the background. Marine and bird life are plentiful in the bay, but it is best known for its rich fishing grounds, which boast an abundance of halibut.

A portion of the bay is preserved as Kachemak Bay State Park, a popular destination for backpackers and kayakers. A handful of small villages and wilderness lodges dot the shores near a few of the bays and long fjords.

Gull Island

For those who have no desire to hook an 80lb halibut, there's Gull Island, a group of bare rock islets halfway between the Spit and Halibut Cove. The islands attract thousands of nesting seabirds: tufted puffins, black legged kittiwakes, common murres, cormorants and many more species. If you can survive the stench, you'll enjoy plenty of opportunities to photograph the birds up close, even if you don't have a 300mm lens.

Several tour-boat operators on the Homer Spit offer a cruise to the rookery. Rainbow Tours (☎ 235-7272) departs at 9 am and 4:30 pm daily for a 1.5-hour trip. The cost is $20 per person, making it possibly the best deal on birding tours in the state.

Rainbow Tours also has a Natural History tour, a full-day trip to Kachemak Bay. In addition to wildlife viewing, groups explore tide pools during a visit to the **Center for Alaskan Coastal Studies**, a nonprofit marine center in Peterson Bay. The tours depart at 9 am daily, return at 6 pm and cost $63 per person (less for seniors and kids).

Halibut Cove

Halibut Cove, a small village of 70 people on the south shore of Kachemak Bay, makes for another interesting side trip. In the early 1920s, the cove supported 42 herring salteries and had a population of over 1000. Today, the quaint community has a pair of art galleries that produce 'octopus ink paintings,' plus the noted Saltry Restaurant, some cabins for rent and boardwalks but no roads.

The ferry *Danny J* travels to the cove from the Homer Spit daily. It departs at noon, swings past Gull Island and arrives at Halibut Cove at 1:30 pm. There, you have 2.5 hours to explore the 12 blocks of board-

walks and galleries or have lunch. The ferry returns to the Spit by 5 pm and then makes an evening run to the cove for dinner at the Saltry Restaurant, returning to Homer at 10 pm.

The noon tour of the *Danny J* costs $42 per person, while its evening trip is $21. Book the ferry through Kachemak Bay Ferry (☎ 296-2223) or Central Charter Booking Agency (☎ 235-7847, 800-478-7847), which has an office on the Spit.

Places to Stay & Eat To make Halibut Cove an even more interesting side trip, spend the night. Book one of the five cabins at *Quiet Place Lodge* (☎ 296-2212), right on the waterfront boardwalk. The cost ($185 per couple) includes a full breakfast. *Halibut Cove Cabins* (☎ 296-2214) offers a pair of cozy cabins that rent for $85 a night for two people or $135 for four (bring your own sleeping bags). At *Country Cove Cabins* (☎ 888-353-2683, 296-2257, ctjones@xyz.net), the cabins cost $95 per night for two people, but there is a discount if you arrive with a sleeping bag.

Many who come to Halibut Cove stop to dine on the outdoor deck of the *Saltry Restaurant* (☎ 296-2223), an excellent spot for seafood and vegetarian cuisine. Dinner at the Saltry starts at about $16, and it's well worth it.

Tutka Bay

North of Seldovia is remote Tutka Bay, where Jon and Nelda Osgood run their *Tutka Bay Wilderness Lodge* (☎ 235-3905, 800-606-3909). This resort is a series of chalets, cottages and rooms surrounding the lodge house, where guests enjoy their meals with a sweeping view of the inlet and Jakolof Mountain. The accommodations are very comfortable, the food is excellent and the amenities include a sauna, deepwater dock, boathouse and hiking trails. Activities range from clamming to sea kayaking.

The isolated resort always gets high marks from visitors, but it's a total vacation experience rather than just a place to stay. You have to book a room or cottage for at least two nights, and the rates begin at $600 per person, which includes all meals and transportation from Homer.

Just to the north of Tutka Bay is Sadie Cove, home of the *Sadie Cove Wilderness Lodge* (☎ 888-283-7234, 235-2350, sadiecove@ netalaska.com). This wilderness lodge offers similar amenities – cabins, sauna, outdoor hot tub, Alaskan seafood dinners – but it's not quite as elegant or pricey. Accommodations cost $175 per night per person.

Kachemak Bay State Park

This park, along with the adjoining Kachemak Bay State Wilderness Park to the south, includes 350,000 acres of mountainous and glacial wilderness that is only accessible by bush plane or boat. The most popular attraction of the park is Grewingk Glacier, which can clearly be seen across the bay from Homer. Viewing the glacier at closer range means a boat trip to the park and a one-way hike of 3.5 miles.

In recent years, a controversy has erupted between helicopter operators, who have been running an increasing number of sightseeing trips to the glacier, and hikers, who feel they are constantly being buzzed by the $300-an-hour flights.

Outside of the glacier, however, you can easily escape into the wilderness by either hiking or kayaking. Visitor facilities include almost 40 miles of trails and several rental cabins. Camping is permitted throughout Kachemak Bay State Park, and a number of free, primitive campsites have been developed in Halibut Cove and along the China Poot Lake and Moose Valley Trails. For information on the park, contact the Alaska Division of Parks & Outdoor Recreation office (☎ 235-7024), 4 miles north of Homer at Mile 168.5 of the Sterling Hwy.

Cabins

The state of Alaska rents out three cabins in Halibut Cove Lagoon. The original cabin, called *Lagoon Lookout*, was a bunkhouse for trail crews before being converted into a three-room facility in 1992. The cabin has a pair of bunk-bed sleeping platforms, as well as electricity and water. It's at the southern end of Halibut Cove and can be reached by

boat, water taxi or a hike along the Lagoon Trail. The *Lagoon East Cabin* is next door, while the *Lagoon West Cabin* is a half mile west of the public dock. Each of these three cabins costs $50.

On the south shore of Tutka Bay, 13 miles from the Homer Spit, is the *Sea Star Cove Cabin*. The Tutka Bay Taxi (☎ 235-7166, tutkataxi@yahoo.com) will drop you off there. With the same amenities as the lagoon cabins, this one also rents for $50.

As with USFS cabins, you need to reserve these state cabins in advance during the summer. Contact the Department of Natural Resources Public Information Center (☎ 762-2261), 3601 C St in the Frontier Building in Anchorage, or the Alaska Division of Parks & Outdoor Recreation (☎ 235-7024). Otherwise, stop at the Homer Ranger Station (☎ 235-5581), at Mile 168.5 of the Sterling Hwy (if it happens to be open).

Hiking

Glacier Lake Trail The most popular hike in Kachemak Bay State Park is this 3.5-mile, one-way trail that begins at the Glacier Spit trailhead, near the small Rusty Lagoon Campground. The level, easy-to-follow trek proceeds across the glacial outwash and ends at a lake with superb views of Grewingk Glacier. Camping on the lake is spectacular, and often the shoreline is littered with icebergs.

Alpine Ridge Trail At the high point of the mile-long Saddle Trail, an offshoot of Glacier Lake Trail, you'll reach the posted junction for this 2-mile climb to an alpine ridge above the glacier. The climb can be steep at times but manageable for most hikers with day packs. On a nice day, the views of the ice and Kachemak Bay are stunning.

Lagoon Trail Also departing from the Saddle Trail is this 5.5-mile route that leads to the ranger station at the head of Halibut Cove Lagoon. Along the way it passes Goat Rope Spur Trail, a steep 1-mile climb to the alpine tundra. You also pass the posted junction of Halibut Creek Trail. If Grewingk Glacier is too crowded for you, follow this trail a half mile to Halibut Creek to spend the night in a beautiful but much more remote valley.

Lagoon Trail is considered a moderately difficult hike and involves fording Halibut Creek, which should be done at low tide. At the ranger station, more trails extend south to several lakes, as well as Poot Peak and the Wosnesenki River.

Grace Ridge Trail Built in 1998, this 7-mile trail stretches from a campsite at Kayak Beach trailhead to deep inside Tutka Bay in the state park. Much of the hike runs above the tree line along the crest of Grace Ridge, where, needless to say, the views are stunning. You could hike the trail in a day, but it makes a great two-day trek with an overnight camp in the alpine. Tutka Bay Taxi (☎ 235-7166) will provide transportation from Homer to Kayak Beach and then pick you up at the South Grace Ridge trailhead for the return trip; the cost is $45 per person.

Paddling

You can also spend three or four days paddling the many fjords of the park, departing from Homer and making overnight stops at Glacier Spit or Halibut Cove. Think twice before crossing Kachemak Bay from the Spit, however. Although it's only 3.5 miles to the eastern shore, the currents and tides are strong and can cause serious problems for inexperienced paddlers.

Tour boats that run hikers across can also transport kayakers (see the Getting There & Away section). Or St Augustine's Charters (contact Inlet Charters; ☎ 235-6126, 800-770-6126) offers rentals from its Peterson Bay Kayak Center, on the east side of the bay, and a guided day trip that includes paddling around Gull Island ($125).

Farther south near Sadie Cove and Tutka Bay you can rent kayaks from True North Kayak Adventures (☎ 235-2376, 235-6384 in the summer, kayaking@jakolofferryservice .com). This small company runs trips out of Hesketh Island, which you can reach through Jakolof Ferry Service. True North also rents rigid single/double kayaks for $35/60 per day, with a $5 discount for each additional day.

For those with no paddling experience, True North leads a day trip to view the rugged coastline and wildlife of nearby Yukon Island. The cost is $125 per person and includes lunch, equipment and roundtrip water-taxi transportation. True North also offers guided overnight trips.

Getting There & Away

The state park makes an excellent side trip for anybody who has a tent, a spare day and the desire to escape the overflow of RVers on Homer Spit. A number of tour boats offer drop-off and pickup service, charging $50 to $70 for a roundtrip ticket. St Augustine's Charters will drop you off at Rusty Lagoon and pick you up at Saddle Trail so that you can avoid some backtracking. The roundtrip fare is $50. Book St Augustine's boat through Inlet Charters (☎ 235-6126, 800-770-6126) on the Spit. You can also try Homer Ocean Charters (☎ 235-6212, 800-426-6212, hoc@xyz.net) or Mako's Water Taxi (☎ 235-9055). Jakolof Ferry Service (☎ 235-2376) provides transportation to Jakolof Bay.

SELDOVIA

Across Kachemak Bay from Homer and in a world of its own is Seldovia (population 280), a small fishing village. The sleepy town lives up to its nickname, 'City of Secluded Charm.' Although tour boats have made it a regular stop in recent years, the village has managed to retain much of its old Alaskan charm and can be an interesting and inexpensive side detour from Alaska's highway system.

History

Seldovia is one of the oldest settlements along Cook Inlet and may have been the site of the first coal mine in Alaska. (The Russians began operating one in the late 1700s.) Named after the Russian word *seldevoy*, meaning herring bay, the town grew into a year-round harbor for the Russians, who gathered timber here to repair ships. By the 1890s, Seldovia was an important shipping and supply center for the region, and the town boomed right into the 1920s, with salmon canning, fur farming and

SELDOVIA

PLACES TO STAY
11 Boardwalk Hotel
18 Gerry's Place
19 Dancing Eagles B&B
20 Seldovia Row Club
21 Swan House South B&B

PLACES TO EAT
4 Seldovia Mart
12 Pumi's Seldovia Barbecue
13 Buzz Coffee House
17 The Mad Fish Restaurant

OTHER
1 Seldovia Historical Museum
2 City Office
3 Alaska Tribal Cache
5 St Nicholas Church
6 Post Office
7 Seldovia Medical Clinic
8 Library
9 Kayak'Atak
10 Rocky Raven
14 Harbormaster's Office
15 Harbor Laundromat
16 Synergy Art Works

a short-lived herring industry. After the Sterling Hwy to Homer was completed in the 1950s, Seldovia's importance as a supply center began to dwindle, along with its population, but it was the 1964 earthquake that caused the most rapid changes in the community.

The Good Friday Earthquake caused the land beneath Seldovia to settle 4 feet, allowing high tides to flood much of the original town. In the reconstruction of Seldovia, much of its waterfront and beloved boardwalk were torn out, while Cap's Hill was leveled to provide fill material.

Information

There's an information stand in Synergy Art Works, on Main St across from the boat harbor. The rustic log building is a co-op where local artists display and sell their pottery, jewelry, prints and other handcrafted items. You can also contact the Seldovia Chamber of Commerce (☎ 234-7612, www.xyz.net/~seldovia) for information.

The post office is near the corner of Main St and Anderson Way.

At Harbor Laundromat (☎ 234-7420), on Main St, you can do your laundry, take a shower, play a game of pool or have an ice cream. Owner Peggy Boscacci calls it 'diversification,' because 'when you're this small, you've got to cover your bases.'

The Seldovia Medical Clinic (☎ 234-7825) is on Anderson Way, not far off Main St.

Things to See & Do

You'll see a small remnant of the early boardwalk if you walk a short distance to the east of the ferry terminal. It stretches along Seldovia Slough, with a number of historic houses perched on pilings nearby.

On Main St, the **Alaska Tribal Cache**, operated by the Seldovia Native Association, features a small collection of Native Alaskan and Russian artifacts. It's open 10 am to 5 pm daily. To view more artifacts, go to the **Seldovia Historical Museum**, on Anderson Way, or ask for a map of the **Seldovia Outdoor Museum**. The museum is actually a walking tour, featuring 12 interpretive signs that list the town's history chronologically.

Seldovia's most popular attraction by far is **St Nicholas Church**, which overlooks the town from a hill just off Main St. Built in 1891 and restored in the early 1980s, the Russian Orthodox church is open on weekday afternoons, when you can go inside to view the icons.

Outside Beach is an excellent place for wildlife sightings and a little beach-combing. To reach it, follow Anderson Way (Jakolof Bay Rd) out of town for a mile, then head left at the first fork to reach the picnic area at Outside Beach Park. You stand a good chance of spotting eagles, seabirds and possibly even otters here. At low tide, you can explore the sea life among the rocks, and on a clear day the views of Mt Redoubt and Mt Iliamna are stunning.

Berry Picking

In Homer, Seldovia is known best for blueberries. They grow so thick just outside town that you often can rake your fingers through the bushes and fill a two-quart bucket in minutes. You'll also come across plenty of low-bush cranberries and salmonberries, a species not found around Homer. But the blueberries, which ripen from late August to mid-September, are the best. One of the best places for picking is **Blueberry Hill** between the airstrip and the slough.

Hiking

The Otterbahn is a footpath that was created by high school students who dubbed it the 'we-worked-hard-so-you-better-like-it' trail. The trailhead lies behind Susan B English School, off Anderson Way. The trail itself skirts the coastline most of the way and reaches Outside Beach in 1.5 miles. Make sure you hike it at low tide, for the last stretch runs across a slough that is only passable when the water is out.

Two trails start from Jakolof Bay Rd. You can either hike down the beach toward the head of Seldovia Bay at low tide, or you can follow a 4.5-mile logging road to reach several secluded coves. There is also Tutka/Jakolof Trail, a 2.5-mile trail to a campsite on the Tutka Lagoon, the site of a state salmon-rearing facility. The posted trail departs from Jakolof Bay Rd about 10.5 miles east of town.

Paddling

There are some excellent kayaking opportunities in the Seldovia area. To the north, or 5 miles south of the Homer Spit, is Eldred Passage and the three islands (Cohen, Yukon and Hesketh) that mark the entrance to it. All three are prime spots for viewing otters, sea lions and seals, while the northern shore of Yukon Island features caves and tunnels that can be explored at high tide. Even closer are Sadie Cove and Tutka and Jackolof Bays, where you can paddle in protected water, amid interesting geological features and near numerous camping areas along the beaches.

In town, rent kayaks through Kayak'Atak (☎ 234-7425, kayaks@alaska.net) and then contact South Shore Tours (☎ 234-8000) about transportation to Jakolof Bay dock so that you can skip the open stretch of Kachemak Bay. Single kayaks are $50 for the first day, $30 for each additional day. Doubles are $75, with a $50 charge for each extra day. Kayak'Atak also offers guided trips in the area. A six-hour day trip departs at 11 am daily and costs $110, including equipment and lunch.

SOUTHCENTRAL

Places to Stay

The best option for many is to camp on spectacular Outside Beach, where the city maintains **Seldovia Wilderness Park** (☎ 234-7643). The rustic facility has spots for both RVers ($8) and tent campers ($5). RVers have to stay in the park on the bluff, but backpackers can also pitch their tents closer to the shore at one end of Outside Beach.

If you'd like a bed in town, there are several B&Bs. **Gerry's Place** (☎ 243-7471), a block from the harbor on Fulmore Ave, has some of the best rates, with singles/doubles for $40/60. The **Seldovia Rowing Club** (☎ 234-7614) is on the old boardwalk, with a deck overlooking the water. Rooms cost $80/90. **Dancing Eagles B&B** (☎ 234-7627) is also on the old boardwalk and has rooms with shared bathrooms for $55/85, a chalet cabin for $125 per couple and, best of all, a hot tub. The upscale **Swan House South B&B** (☎ 234-8888, 800-921-1900) has five rooms for $119/129.

For something a little different, try **Across the Bay Tent & Breakfast** (☎ 235-3633 in summer, 345-2571 in winter, ecotour@ ptialaska.net), 8 miles from town on Jakolof Bay. Its cabinlike wall tents are $48, which includes a full breakfast and transportation from Seldovia. For $75, you get all your meals – and dinner could consist of fresh oysters, beach-grilled salmon or halibut stew. The offbeat resort also rents mountain bikes for $25 per day and organizes kayak trips.

At Seldovia's hotel, the **Boardwalk Hotel** (☎ 234-7816, 800-238-7862), on Main St across from the small boat harbor, doubles begin at $89; the rate increases if the room has a view of the harbor. The hotel also offers a package that includes one night's accommodations, a cruise to Seldovia and a flight back for $129 per person.

Places to Eat

A good place to start the day is the **Buzz Coffee House**, Main St. The coffee house opens at 6 am and doubles as a bakery and restaurant serving quiches, muffins, croissants and pastries – all presented in tableware produced by a local potter. Stop by at lunch for homemade soup and bread for $6.

A bowl of chowder, seafood lunch specials and a cold beer are all available at **The Mad Fish Restaurant**, on the corner of Fulmore Ave and Main St. **Pumi's Seldovia Barbecue**, Main St, is behind the Buzz Coffee House and has Oriental takeout.

The **Seldovia Mart**, on Main St, sells groceries, beer and supplies. You'll also find three bars in town.

Getting There & Away

The ferry M/V *Tustumena* travels to Seldovia twice a week from Homer. It's best to go on Tuesday, when the boat leaves Homer around noon, arrives in Seldovia at 2 pm and stays in port for four hours before returning. The other weekly trip, which alternates between Sunday and Monday, arrives in the early hours of the morning. The Seldovia ferry terminal (☎ 234-7886) is at the north end of Main St. The one-way fare from Homer to Seldovia is $18.

Several tour boats also offer trips to Seldovia and generally stay in port for two to three hours. Among them is Rainbow Tours (☎ 235-7272 in Homer), which departs at 11 am daily and swings past the Gull Island bird rookery as well. The roundtrip fare is $45. Jakolof Ferry Service (☎ 235-2376) departs Homer and swings by Halibut Cove and Sadie Cove before arriving at its dock in Jakolof Bay, 10 miles east of town. The roundtrip fare is $45.

You can also fly to Seldovia. A scenic 12-minute flight from Homer passes over the Kenai Mountains and Kachemak Bay. Homer Air (☎ 800-478-8591 in Alaska, 235-8591) offers several flights daily to Seldovia, with a one-way fare of $30 and a roundtrip fare of $55.

Getting Around

At the Buzz Coffee House, you can rent a mountain bike ($25 to $30 for the day, $30 to $35 overnight) to see the sights and surrounding area. The Rocky Raven bicycle shop (☎ 234-7816) also rents bikes in town. Check at the Buzz (☎ 234-7479) to see who, if anybody, is running a van out to the dock in Jakolof Bay. The coffeehouse often doubles as a pickup point for the vans.

Southwest Alaska

Stretching more than 1500 miles, from Kodiak to the western end of the Aleutian Islands, is Southwest Alaska, an island-studded region that can be a stormy and violent place at times. It's home of the worst weather in Alaska, with little to protect it from the high winds and storms that sweep across the North Pacific. Along Alaska's outlying arm, the Arctic waters of the Bering Sea meet the warm Japanese Current, causing considerable cloudiness, rain and fog.

The region is also the northern rim of the volcanic chain in the Pacific Ocean known as the Ring of Fire. Forty-six active volcanoes are spread along the Alaska Peninsula and the Aleutian Islands, the greatest concentration anywhere in North America. It's an unusual year when one of the volcanoes of Southwest Alaska isn't spewing ash and steam.

Despite the harsh weather and volcanic activity – or maybe because of it – Southwest Alaska is a region of diverse habitats rich in wildlife. It boasts the largest bears in the world on Kodiak Island, the richest salmon runs in Alaska at Bristol Bay and some of the biggest blueberries you'll ever pick on the windswept islands of the Aleutians. From a naturalist's point of view, few places on the earth have an abundance of wildlife comparable to that in Southwest Alaska.

In recent years, the region has become an increasingly popular destination for travelers. They arrive for the outstanding sportfishing, the opportunities to view wildlife ranging from walruses to whales or simply to experience an area not overrun by cruise ships or tour buses. In this regard, Southwest Alaska has much to offer the adventurous traveler – though budget travel is not one of benefits.

Southwest Alaska can be divided into four areas. To the east is the Kodiak Archipelago, with Kodiak Island, the largest island. Though often caught in the rainy and foggy weather created on the Gulf of Alaska, the island possesses a rugged beauty, an interesting history and a considerable amount of wilderness to explore. Kodiak Island is also the most accessible area, thanks to the Alaska Marine Ferry, which connects the city of Kodiak with Southcentral Alaska.

Just to the west of Kodiak Island is the Alaska Peninsula, which extends 550 miles from the western shore of Cook Inlet to its tip at False Pass. The rugged volcanic arm includes two major attractions of Southwest Alaska: Katmai National Park and McNeil River State Game Sanctuary. Farther north on the peninsula is Lake Clark National Park and Preserve, a destination for anglers and rafters.

Highlights

- Take a flightseeing tour in a floatplane to see the giant Kodiak brown bears

- Learn to kayak in the calm bays near Kodiak

- From an observation platform, watch brown bears catch salmon in Katmai National Park

- View the barren Valley of 10,000 Smokes on a bus tour in Katmai National Park

- Hike up Unalaska's Bunker Hill to view gun turrets, Quonset huts and other WWII military remains

- Pick Alaska's biggest blueberries in August on Unalaska Island

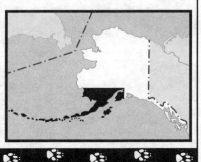

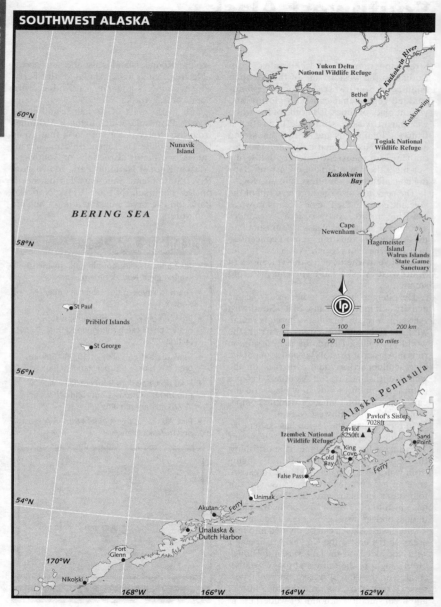

SOUTHWEST ALASKA

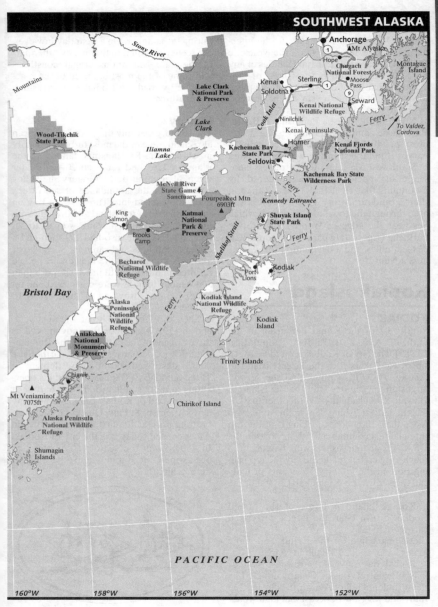

SOUTHWEST ALASKA

Stony River

Mountains

Lake Clark
National Park
& Preserve

Anchorage
①
▲Mt Alyeska
Hope
Chugach
National Forest
Montague
Island

Kenai
Sterling
Soldotna
Moose
Pass
⑨
Seward

Kenai National
Wildlife Refuge

Cook Inlet

Ninilchik

To Valdez,
Cordova

Lake
Clark

Iliamna
Lake

Wood-Tikchik
State Park

Kenai Peninsula

Homer

Kachemak Bay
State Park
Seldovia

Kachemak Bay State
Wilderness Park

McNeil River
State Game
Sanctuary

Fourpeaked Mtn
6903ft ▲

Kennedy Entrance

Dillingham

King
Salmon

Katmai
National
Park &
Preserve

Brooks
Camp

Shuyak Island
State Park

Ferry

Shelikof Strait

Becharof
National Wildlife
Refuge

Bristol Bay

Alaska
Peninsula
National
Wildlife
Refuge

Ferry

Port
Lions

Kodiak

Kodiak Island
National Wildlife
Refuge

Kodiak
Island

Aniakchak
National
Monument
& Preserve

Trinity Islands

Chignik ▲

Mt Veniaminof
7075ft

Chirikof Island

Alaska Peninsula
National Wildlife
Refuge

Shumagin
Islands

PACIFIC OCEAN

160°W   158°W   156°W   154°W   152°W

The Aleutians is a chain of more than 200 islands that curve 1100 miles west into the Pacific Ocean from False Pass to the international date line. Most of the volcanic islands are devoid of tourism facilities of any kind. The exception is the island of Unalaska, which is not only an intriguing place to visit but five times a year can be reached by the Alaska Marine Hwy ferry.

North of the Alaska Peninsula is Bristol Bay, whose commercial fishery is the state's most productive and whose red salmon harvest the largest in the world. This area of Southwest Alaska is often a treeless landscape of spacious tundra bordered by mountains that rival the Alaska Range in their grandeur. Many visitors access the area through the town of Dillingham which lies near the edge of Wood-Tikchik State Park, the largest state park in the country, at 2344 sq miles, and a destination for wilderness adventure.

Kodiak Island

KODIAK

Southwest of the Kenai Peninsula in the Gulf of Alaska is Kodiak (population 13,989). The city of Kodiak is on the eastern tip of Kodiak Island, the largest island in Alaska, at 3670 sq miles, and the second largest in the country after the Big Island of Hawaii. Kodiak claims several other firsts. It has the largest fishing fleet in the state, with more than 1000 boats, placing it in the top three largest commercial fishing ports in the USA. At one time, fishers were hauling in so much king crab it made the city the top fishing port in the country. Residents proudly call their town the 'King Crab Capital of the World.'

Kodiak Island is home of the famed Kodiak brown bear, the largest terrestrial carnivore in the world. An estimated 2400 of these bears live on the island, and some males have reached 1500lb in weight.

Kodiak has some of the foggiest weather in Southcentral Alaska. Greatly affected by the turbulent Gulf of Alaska, the city is often rainy and foggy, with occasional high winds.

The area receives 80 inches of rain per year and has an average temperature of 60°F during the summer. On a clear day, however, the scenery is equal to that in any other part of the state. Mountains, craggy coastlines and some of the most deserted beaches accessible by road are Kodiak's most distinctive features.

History

The island, especially the city of Kodiak, can also claim some of the most turbulent history in Alaska. The Russians first landed on the island in 1763 and returned 20 years later when Siberian fur trader Grigory Shelekhov heard about the abundance of sea otters. Shelekhov sailed into Three Saints Bay on the south side of the island and brought with him his wife, the first white woman to set foot in Alaska. He also had 192 men and a cache of muskets and cannons. Shelekhov's attempts to 'subdue' the indigenous people resulted in a bloodbath in which more than 500 Alutiiq Indians were massacred and an equal number drowned in their effort to escape.

Shelekhov returned home the next year, and in 1791, Aleksandr Baranov arrived as the manager of the colony and the Russian-American Company. After an earthquake nearly destroyed the infant settlement at Three Saints Bay, Baranov moved his operations to more stable ground at a harbor at the north end of Kodiak Island, naming the new settlement St Paul. Quickly, it became a bustling port, as the first capital of Russian America, and today it is the city of Kodiak. In 1804, when the sea-otter colonies had been wiped out, Baranov moved again, this time to Sitka.

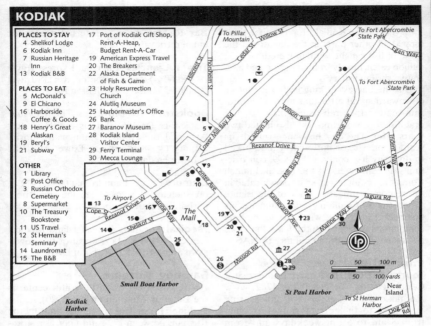

KODIAK

PLACES TO STAY
4 Shelikof Lodge
6 Kodiak Inn
7 Russian Heritage Inn
13 Kodiak B&B

PLACES TO EAT
5 McDonald's
9 El Chicano
16 Harborside Coffee & Goods
18 Henry's Great Alaskan
19 Beryl's
21 Subway

OTHER
1 Library
2 Post Office
3 Russian Orthodox Cemetery
8 Supermarket
10 The Treasury Bookstore
11 US Travel
12 St Herman's Seminary
14 Laundromat
15 The B&B

17 Port of Kodiak Gift Shop, Rent-A-Heap, Budget Rent-A-Car
19 American Express Travel
20 The Breakers
22 Alaska Department of Fish & Game
23 Holy Resurrection Church
24 Alutiiq Museum
25 Harbormaster's Office
26 Bank
27 Baranov Museum
28 Kodiak Island Visitor Center
29 Ferry Terminal
30 Mecca Lounge

Kodiak had its next disaster in 1912, when Mt Katmai on the nearby Alaska Peninsula erupted. The explosion not only created the Valley of 10,000 Smokes, now part of Katmai National Park, but the ash from the eruption blotted out the then sun for two days and blanketed the then sleepy fishing village with 18 inches of ash. It was so dark that, when a 20-room log cabin caught fire, people 200 feet away were unaware of the blaze. Kodiak's 400 residents escaped to sea briefly on a ship that was in port fueling but soon returned to find ash drifts several feet high and spawning salmon choking in ash-filled streams.

Disaster struck again in 1964. The Good Friday Earthquake shook the entire island, and the subsequent tsunami completely leveled the downtown area, destroying the boat harbor and wiping out the local fishing fleet. Processing plants, canneries and 158 homes were lost; damage was $24 million, an unheard of sum back then.

The natural disasters, however, are now part of Kodiak's turbulent history. Today, the city thrives as the fishing capital of Alaska, with 14 fish-processing plants employing thousands of people during the summer. Kodiak Island is also the site of Alaska's largest US Coast Guard station, which occupies the old US naval base. Three large Coast Guard cutters patrol out of Kodiak, seizing foreign vessels that illegally fish in US waters and assisting distressed ships caught in the violent storms of the North Pacific.

Kodiak Island was also affected by the *Exxon Valdez* oil spill, but the spill's impact on the fishing pales compared with what overharvesting did to several species, most notably the king crab.

This giant of crabs is taken from especially deep areas of the ocean and can easily exceed 10 to 15lb – enough to feed two or three people. The record king taken in Kodiak weighed a whopping 25lb and had a leg span of almost 5 feet. Kodiak began canning king crabs in 1949, and by 1966, the peak year of the catch, the town landed 90 million pounds. Two years later Kodiak, for the first time, topped all other ports in the country in the value of fish caught, with an incredible $132 million catch, mostly from king crab and a lucrative shrimp fishery.

But the harvest of king crab went into a downward spiral after that until a moratorium halted the crab fishery in 1983. The drag fishery for shrimp was also halted two years later. The city has since rebuilt its seafood industry on bottom fish and worked to diversify its economy. In 1999, construction was completed on the Kodiak Launch Complex, a commercial spaceport located in the remote southeast corner of the island. When the $40 million facility launches its first rocket in 2000, it will become the only commercial spaceport in the USA that does not share a site with the military or NASA.

Information

Tourist Offices The Kodiak Island Visitor Center (☎ 486-4782, 800-789-4782, www .kodiak.org), at Center Ave and Marine Way next to the ferry terminal, is open from 8 am to 5 pm weekdays and from 10 am to 4 pm weekends.

The Alaska Division of Parks and Outdoor Recreation maintains an office (☎ 486-6339) at Fort Abercrombie State Historical Park, 4.5 miles northeast of the city off Monashka Bay Rd. The office is open 8 am to 5 pm weekdays and is the place to go for information on hiking trails, state campgrounds or renting recreation cabins.

The Kodiak National Wildlife Refuge office (☎ 487-2600) is 4 miles southwest of the city, near the airport at 1390 Buskin River Rd. Open 8 am to 4:30 pm weekdays and from noon to 4:30 pm weekends, it has information on the public-use cabins.

Money National Bank of Alaska (☎ 486-3126) is on the corner of Mission Rd and Marine Way and features a king crab display in its lobby.

Post The post office is on Lower Mill Bay Rd, just north of the library.

Email & Internet Access The Holmes Johnson Memorial Library, 319 Lower Mill Bay Rd, can provide Internet access for email retrieval.

Travel Agencies American Express Travel (☎ 486-6084) is at 202 Center Ave; US Travel (☎ 486-3232) is at 340 Mission Rd.

Bookstores & Libraries The Treasury Bookstore (☎ 486-5001) is at 104 Center Ave, and the Holmes Johnson Memorial Library (☎ 486-8686), on Lower Mill Bay Rd, is open daily.

Laundry Ernie's Laundromat (☎ 486-4119), on Shelikof St across from the small boat harbor, has showers for $4.

Medical Services Kodiak Island Medical Center (☎ 486-3281) is north of the downtown area, at 1915 E Rezanof Drive.

Baranov Museum

Across the street from the visitor center is the Baranov Museum (☎ 486-5920), in the Erskine House. The house was built by the Russians between 1792 and 1799, as a storehouse for precious sea otter pelts. The museum contains many items from the Russian period of Kodiak's history and many fine examples of Aleut basketry. It is open 10 am to 4 pm weekdays and noon to 4 pm weekends; admission is $2.

Holy Resurrection Church

Near the museum on Mission Rd is the Holy Resurrection Church, which serves the oldest Russian Orthodox parish in the New World. Established in 1794, the parish celebrated its bicentennial in 1994 with a visit from the patriarch of the Russian Orthodox Church, Alexy II. The present church was built in 1945 and is the third one at this site.

One of the original clerics was Father Herman, who was elevated to sainthood at Kodiak in 1970, during the first canonization ever performed in the USA. His relics are kept in a carved wooden chest near the altar. Also within the church are polished brassware, several icons and rare paintings. The church doesn't keep set opening hours; inquire at the visitor center about tours. The church's blue onion domes make a great photograph, if you can squeeze out the huge gas storage tank that flanks it. A better place to photograph the church is directly above it, from Mill Bay Rd, where there is an overview of the structure.

Alutiiq Museum & Archaeological Repository

Kodiak showcases 7000 years of native culture at the Alutiiq Museum & Archaeological Repository (☎ 486-7004). The museum, just up Mission Rd from the church, opened in 1995 and features displays, galleries and exhibits in an effort to explain and preserve the Alutiiq heritage of Kodiak's indigenous people. Artifacts range from bone fishhooks and a spruce-framed kayak to a diorama of a traditional village. Hours are 9 am to 5 pm weekdays, 10 am to 4 pm Saturday and 11 am to 4 pm Sunday; admission is $2.

St Herman's Theological Seminary

More Russian Orthodox history can be explored still farther along Mission Rd at St Herman's Theological Seminary, founded in 1973. Its Veniaminov Research Institute Museum is open to the public 1 to 4:30 pm daily. On display are indigenous artifacts, icons and Bibles used by Orthodox missionaries on the Yukon River in the 1800s.

Boat Harbors

Follow Marine Way left (west) from the ferry terminal as it curves past the **small boat harbor**, the heart and soul of Kodiak. Crab boats, salmon seiners and halibut schooners cram the city docks, and more boats dock across the channel, at **St Herman Harbor** on Near Island. An afternoon on the docks can lead to friendly encounters with fishers and the chance to see catches unloaded or nets being repaired. Although no tours are available, canneries on nearby Shelikof St clatter and steam around the clock during the summer, or take the bridge across the channel to St Herman Harbor to view more boats and stop at the **Fish Industrial Technol-**

ogy Center (☎ 486-1500). Known locally as the Fish Tech Center, this extension of the University of Alaska Fairbanks provides research for the Alaskan seafood industry. Its bayside setting on Near Island is beautiful, and inside the lobby is a visitor information display. Hours are 8 am to 5 pm weekdays. Nearby is the **Kodiak Fisheries Research Center** (☎ 481-1800), open the same hours, which has aquariums, touch tanks and interpretive displays inside.

Fort Abercrombie State Historical Park

This military fort and a pair of 8-inch guns were built by the US Army during WWII, for a Japanese invasion that never came. In the end, Kodiak's lousy weather, not the army's superior firepower, kept the Japanese bombers away from the island. Today, the fort is a state historical park, sitting majestically on the cliffs over the wooded Monashka Bay coast.

A small visitor center inside the Miller Rd Bunker, within the 143-acre park, has

St Herman

natural history displays, and a self-guided tour winds through the military relics on Miller Point. At 2:30 pm on Sunday, Tuesday and Friday, the park staff give a guided historic tour, beginning at the visitor center. Just as interesting as the gun emplacements are the tidal pools found along the rocky shorelines of the park. Bring rubber boots, if you can, for an afternoon of searching for starfish and other sea creatures. The park is 4.5 miles northeast of Kodiak, off Monashka Bay Rd.

Pillar Mountain

The placement of a Distant Early Warning (DEW) Line site (a series of radar towers across Alaska and northern Canada that were built primarily to detect an air or missile attack on North America by the USSR), and later a communications saucer, on top of this 1270-foot mountain has resulted in a road that climbs to a scenic overlook behind the city and provides excellent views of the surrounding mountains, ocean, beaches and islands. One side seems to plunge straight down to the harbor below, and the other overlooks the green interior of Kodiak Island. Pick up the bumpy dirt road to Pillar Mountain by heading north up Thorsheim St and turning left on Maple Ave, which runs into Pillar Mountain Rd.

Buskin River State Recreation Site

Four miles southwest of the city on Chiniak Rd is this 90-acre state recreation area, containing 15 campsites and access to the Buskin River. Anglers flock here for the salmon fishing, the best on this part of Kodiak Island. The US Fish and Wildlife Service visitor center dedicated to Kodiak National Wildlife Refuge is nearby. The center has numerous displays and films on the island's wildlife, including brown bears. Hours are 8 am to 4:30 pm weekdays and noon to 4:30 pm weekends. The Buskin View Trail, near the center, is a short, self-guided nature trail.

Hiking

The Kodiak area has dozens of hiking trails, but unfortunately, very few are maintained and the trailheads are not always marked along the roads. Windfall can make following the track difficult or even totally conceal it. Still, hiking trails are the best avenues to the natural beauty of Kodiak Island. Before starting out, contact the Kodiak area ranger of the Alaska Division of Parks (☎ 486-6339) for the exact location and condition of trails.

Pillar Mountain Trails Two trails depart from Pillar Mountain Rd. The first begins near the KOTV satellite receiver, near the lower city reservoir, and provides an easy walk north to Monashka Bay Rd. The second begins at the communications tower at the top of the mountain and descends the southwest side. It ends at the Tie Substation, where a gravel road leads out to Chiniak Rd, about a mile northeast of the Buskin River State Recreation Site. Plan on an afternoon for either trail.

Barometer Mountain Trail This popular hiking trail is a steep climb of 5 miles to the 2452-foot summit. To reach the trailhead, follow Chiniak Rd south of the Buskin River Campground and turn right on the first road immediately after passing the end of the airport's runway. Look for a well-worn trail on the left. The trek begins in thick alder before climbing the hogback ridge of the mountain and provides spectacular views of Kodiak and the bays south of the city.

Termination Point Trail This is another popular hike, along a 5-mile trail that starts at the end of Monashka Bay Rd and branches into several trails near Termination Point. Most hiking is done in virgin spruce forest.

Bicycling

Cyclists will find Kodiak's roads interesting to ride on, especially the 12-mile Anton Larsen Bay Rd, which leads northwest from near Buskin River Campground and over the mountain pass to the west side of the island, where you will find quiet coves and shorelines to explore. Plan on two hours for the ride to Anton Larsen Bay. The ride

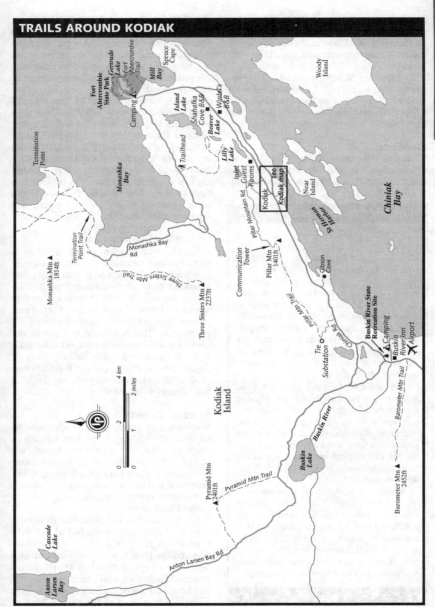

TRAILS AROUND KODIAK

down Chiniak Rd can be equally impressive, and there is now a bike trail that begins on Beaver Lake Loop and ends at the entrance of Fort Abercrombie State Historical Park.

58 Degrees North (☎ 486-6249, thowland@ptialaska.net) 1231 Mill Bay Rd, is an outdoor shop that rents mountain bikes for $35 per day and stocks spare parts and services bikes.

Paddling

With its many bays and protected inlets, scenic coastline and offshore rookeries, much of Kodiak is a kayaker's dream. Pad-

---

Hanging Ten in Alaska

Surfin' USA? Alaska may have 34,000 miles of coastline, more than any other state in the USA, but the last thing most people associate with the Frozen North is surfing. But that's slowly changing. In recent years, a growing number of hardy surfers have been showing up with their boards at a handful of beaches across the state, from Sitka to Yakutat. In 1995, *Surfer* magazine wrote a cover story on surfing in Alaska, and the state even merited a few scenes in the sequel to *Endless Summer*, the classic 1966 film about two surfers searching the world for the perfect wave.

The capital of Alaskan surfing is Kodiak. You can even buy a surfboard here, because enough locals were hitting the beaches that in 1999 the Kodiak Island Surf Shop opened in downtown Kodiak. Alaska's 'Big Island' has an almost endless number of places to surf, but the vast majority of surfers head to the beaches clustered around Pasagshak Point, 40 miles south of town.

A surfin' safari, Alaskan style, means packing as warm a wet suit as you can find and wearing a helmet. You also need to watch out for the brown bears that often roam the beaches in search of washed up crabs, salmon and other entrees. In Kodiak, surfers have been known to encounter gray whales or chunks of ice right after spring breakup.

---

dling around Near and Woody Islands (both of which have trails on them) and onto Monashka Bay is a scenic day trip from the downtown area. More extensive expeditions can be put together by flying into the long bays of Kodiak National Wildlife Refuge or Shuyak Island.

To rent a kayak, contact Mythos Expeditions (☎ 486-5536, mythosdk@ptialaska.net), which has singles/doubles for $45/65 a day. Mythos Expeditions, along with Kodiak Kayak Tours (☎ 486-2722, Fish2live@aol.com) and Wavetamer Kayaking (☎ 486-2604, wavetamer@gci.net), offers guided trips in which all equipment is provided. A two- to three-hour paddle to Near Island costs around $50 per person; a half-day outing to Monashka Bay is $90.

Organized Tours

A handful of companies provide either a city tour of Kodiak or a day-long scenery-viewing tour from the island's road system. A city tour is usually three to four hours long and includes the wildlife refuge center, Baranov Museum, Pillar Mountain and Fort Abercrombie State Historical Park for around $70 per person. The 'backcountry tour' of the island's roads often involves 4WD vans and is $100. If interested call Custom Tours of Kodiak (☎ 486-4997), Alaska Outback Tours (☎ 486-5101, aktours@ptialaska.net) or Wild Bear Tours (☎ 486-0908).

Special Events

Kodiak's best event, if you happen to be around in late May, is its Crab Festival, which was first held in 1958 to celebrate the end of crabbing season. Today the weeklong event features two parades, a blessing of the fleet, foot and kayak races, fishers'-skill contests like a survival-suit race and a lot of cooked king crab.

Kodiak also has the State Fair & Rodeo, held on Labor Day weekend at the Bell Flats rodeo grounds, a 4th of July celebration and the Bear Country Music Festival, a three-day event in mid-July that features country, bluegrass and Alaskan music.

The Chad Ogden Ultramarathon is a 43-mile race, staged at the end of May by

Kodiak Parks and Recreation (☎ 486-8665), that attracts runners from around the world. In mid-April, the city stages Whale Fest to celebrate the return of migrating gray whales.

Places to Stay
Kodiak doesn't have a hostel, and hotels are expensive, partly because the city hits you with a 6% sales tax and a 5% bed tax. On a $70 room, you add more than $7 in local taxes.

Camping There are no campgrounds in Kodiak, and camping within the city limits is illegal. The closest campground is *Buskin River State Recreation Site* (15 sites, $10), at Mile 4.4 on Chiniak Rd on the way to the airport. This is a pleasant spot to camp, with secluded tent sites, picnic shelters, pit toilets, trails and good fishing on Buskin River or surf fishing in the ocean. Nearby is the Kodiak National Wildlife Refuge headquarters and visitor center.

The most scenic campground is at *Fort Abercrombie State Historical Park* (13 sites, $10 fee), northeast of Kodiak, and *Pasagshak River State Recreation Site*, on Pasagshak Bay Rd 45 miles from town, has seven free sites.

B&Bs There are almost 20 B&Bs in Kodiak, and most have rates of $60 to $70. While not exactly budget accommodations, they provide breakfast, usually transportation from the airport and sometimes laundry service. You can get a current list of B&Bs that includes rates, facilities offered and other details through the visitor center's website (www.kodiak.org).

Kodiak B&B (☎ 486-5367, monroe@ptialaska.net, 308 Cope St), in the downtown area just up the hill from the small boat harbor, has rooms for $70/82 singles/doubles. *Inlet Guest Rooms* (☎ 486-4004, 800-423-4004, 1315 Mill Bay Rd) is 10 blocks north of the downtown area and has six rooms for $55 to $65.

Many of the B&Bs are on Mission Rd toward the Coast Guard base, but all of them provide pickup service. These include *Win-tel's B&B* (☎ 486-6935, awintel@ptialaska.net, 1723 Mission Rd), with five rooms for $55 to $90, and *Shahafka Cove B&B* (☎ 486-2409, rwoitel@ptialaska.net, 1812 Mission Rd), with four rooms for $65 to $115.

Hotels The *Russian Heritage Inn* (☎ 486-5657, niki4224@ptialaska.net, 119 Yukon St) has rooms with kitchenettes, bicycle rentals and an on-site Laundromat. Singles/doubles cost $75/85. In the same price range is *Shelikof Lodge* (☎ 486-4141, kyle@ptialaska.net, 211 Thorsheim St). More upscale is *Kodiak Inn* (☎ 888-563-4254, 486-5712, kodiakin@ptialaska.net, 236 Rezanof Drive), downtown, and *Buskin River Inn* (☎ 487-2700, 800-544-2202, 1395 Airport Way), adjacent to the airport. At either, expect to pay $130/140 during the summer.

Places to Eat
For fast food, there are *McDonald's (209 Thorsheim St)* and *Subway (326 Center)*, where small subs cost $4 and a large seafood and crab sub costs $7. There's also a *Pizza Hut (2625 Mill Bay Rd)*.

King's Diner, in Lilly Lake Plaza on Mill Bay Rd, opens daily at 5:30 am to serve sourdough pancakes. At night, it serves dinner specials and homemade pie. *El Chicano (103 Center St)*, in the mall next to the Ford dealer, serves big portions of Mexican food and 'grande' margaritas. Its License Plate Burrito costs $9 and will keep you filled all weekend.

Henry's Great Alaskan, on the mall in front of the small boat harbor, has burgers starting at $7, beer on tap and sports on 12 televisions scattered through the restaurant and bar. The best king crab dinner is at *Eagle's Nest (395 Airport Way)*, in the Buskin River Inn, but it will set you back $28.

Good coffeehouses include *Beryl's (202 Center Ave)* and *Harborside Coffee & Goods (216 Shelikof St)*. The best delicatessen, *Mimi's Deli (3420 E Rezanof Drive)*, is 3 miles north of the downtown area. Or, have a night of adventure by driving 40 miles to the end of Chiniak Rd, where you'll find *Road's End Restaurant* (☎ 486-2885). Dinners cost $10 to $20.

Entertainment

Clustered around the city waterfront and small boat harbor are a handful of bars that cater to Kodiak's fishing industry. At night, they are interesting places, overflowing with fishers, deckhands and cannery workers drinking hard and talking lively. The *B&B (326 Shelikof St)*, across from the harbor, claims to be Alaska's oldest bar, having served its first beer in 1899. The *Breakers (320 Center Ave)* is almost as colorful inside as is its mural outside. For music at night, there is *Mecca Lounge (302 Marine Way)*, with rock & roll music booming across its dance floor on most nights in the summer.

Getting There & Away

Air Both Alaska Airlines and its contract carrier ERA (☎ 800-426-0333) fly to Kodiak, for six flights daily. The regular roundtrip fare is $300 to $380, but a 14-day advance purchase ticket, with which you stay over on Sunday, is only $186 – not bad compared to $176 and 12 hours on a bus if you travel from Anchorage to Kodiak via bus to Homer and then the ferry. The airport is 5 miles south of Kodiak on Chiniak Rd; the airport shuttle will run you into town for $5.

Boat The ferry M/V *Tustumena* stops at Kodiak three times a week, coming from either Seward or Homer and stopping first at Port Lions, a nearby village on Kodiak Island. The ferry terminal (☎ 486-3800, 800-526-6731) is right downtown, where it's easy to walk around even if you're just in port for an hour or two. The one-way fare to Homer is $48 and to Seward $54.

Getting Around

A number of car rental companies in Kodiak will provide you with wheels to explore the island's outer edges. The cheapest is Rent-A-Heap, with used two-door compacts for $30 a day plus 29¢ per mile. The company has two locations: at the airport (☎ 487-4001) and at the Port of Kodiak Gift Shop (☎ 486-8550) downtown on the mall. If you're planning to drive around the island, that 29¢-a-mile rate will quickly drain your funds. In that case, rent a subcompact from Budget

Rent-A-Car (☎ 487-2220, carrent@ptialaska .net), with unlimited mileage for $45 a day.

AROUND KODIAK

More than 100 miles of paved and gravel roads head from the city into the wilderness that surrounds Kodiak. Some of the roads are rough jeep tracks, manageable only by 4WD vehicles, but many can be driven or hitched along to reach isolated stretches of beach, great fishing spots and superb coastal scenery.

To the south of Kodiak, Chiniak Rd winds 47.6 miles to Cape Greville, following the edge of three splendid bays along the way. The road provides access to some of the best coastal scenery in Alaska and opportunities to view sea lions and puffins offshore, especially at Cape Chiniak near the road's southern end.

Just past Mile 30 of Chiniak Rd, you arrive at the junction with Pasagshak Bay Rd, which winds 16.4 miles due south to the Pasagshak River State Recreation Site, near a beautiful stretch of rugged coastline. This small, riverside campground (seven sites, free) is famous for its silver and king-salmon fishing and for a river that reverses its flow four times a day with the tides. These scenic areas, not the city, are the true attractions of Kodiak Island. Anybody who has the time (and patience) to hitchhike or the money to rent a car (see the Getting Around section) should explore these roads.

Kodiak National Wildlife Refuge

This 2812-sq-mile preserve, which covers the southern two-thirds of Kodiak Island, Ban Island and a small section of Afognak Island, is the chief stronghold of the Alaska brown bear. An estimated 3000 bears reside in the refuge and the surrounding area, which is known worldwide for brown bear hunting and to a lesser degree for salmon and steelhead fishing. There are no maintained trails within the preserve. Cross-country hiking is extremely hard, due to thick bush, and the road system does not enter the refuge. Access into the park is by charter plane or boat out of Kodiak. As most of the refuge is at least 25 air miles away, either form of transportation can run you a tab.

What most people really want to see in the refuge are the massive brown bears. Just about every air charter company in town offers a brown bear-viewing flight in which you fly over remote shorelines in the refuge looking for bears. The length of flights and the number of times you land differ from one 'tour' to the next, but generally you can count on paying $200 to almost $400 per person for flights lasting from 90 minutes to half a day. That usually includes landing and photographing bears feeding on salmon. For travelers with only a day or two in Kodiak, this is really the only feasible way to see the famous bears. Among the air services that offer bear tours are Seahawk Air (☎ 486-8282, 800-770-4295), Andrew Airways (☎ 487-2566, andrewair1@aol.com) and Uyak Air Service (☎ 486-3407, 800-303-3407, uyakair@ptialaska.net).

Places to Stay The US Fish and Wildlife Service administers seven cabins in the refuge. The closest to Kodiak are *Uganik Lake Cabin* and *Veikoda Bay Cabin*, which are on the ocean and feature good beaches nearby. The rate is $20 a night, and the cabins should be reserved in advance. Write to the Kodiak National Wildlife Refuge, 1390 Buskin River Rd, Kodiak, AK 99615, about reserving a cabin. If you're already in Kodiak, call the wildlife refuge headquarters (☎ 487-2600) to check for any available cabins.

The Bears of Kodiak

The Kodiak Archipelago is home to a wide range of land mammals, including river otters, Sitka black-tailed deer, Roosevelt elk and mountain goats. But almost everybody arrives hoping to catch a glimpse of just one animal – the Kodiak bear. This subspecies of the brown bear, *Ursus arctos middendorffi*, is the largest land carnivore in the world. Males normally weigh in at more than 800lb but have been known to exceed 1500lb. Females usually weigh in at 400 to 600lb. From late April to June, the bears range from sea level to mid-elevations and are seen feeding on grasses and shrubs. In July, many are found grazing in alpine meadows. But from mid-July to mid-September, the bears congregate at streams to gorge themselves on spawning salmon. The runs are so heavy that the bears often become selective, and many feast only on females and then eat only the belly portion containing the eggs. The carcass they toss aside is immediately devoured by such scavengers-in-waiting as red foxes, bald eagles and seagulls.

Because of Kodiak bears' overwhelming size and strength and their unpredictable personalities, they are potentially very dangerous animals, but they rarely live up to their 'killer' reputations. Only seven people were mauled between 1973 and 1992, and none of them died. In fact, no one has been killed by a bear on Kodiak in more than 35 years.

Biologists estimate there are 3000 brown bears living in the archipelago, or one bear per 1.5 sq miles, with more than 2500 on Kodiak Island itself. That's more than three times the number of brown bears in the rest of the USA. But you won't see any near the city of Kodiak or even from the road system itself. Like most wild animals, Kodiak bears are often secretive around humans. They are most active in early morning and late evening hours and spend much of their time in dense alder thickets.

The best time to see the bears is during the salmon-feeding period from July to September, and the only practical way to do this is through the handful of air-charter operators who specialize in bear-sighting flights. A half-day flight usually includes 30 to 60 minutes in the air and a couple of hours on the ground watching the bears feed at a salmon stream. The cost can range anywhere from $300 to $500 a person. If the bears are not cooperating on Kodiak Island, most pilots will continue flying west to look for them in Katmai National Park and Preserve on the Alaska Peninsula. One place or the other, they can generally find you a brown bear to view.

Shuyak Island State Park

Covering almost a quarter of the most northern island in the Kodiak Archipelago, this park, 54 air miles north of Kodiak, features a unique rain forest of virgin Sitka spruce, rugged coastline, beaches and protected waterways. Wildlife includes otters, sea lions and Dall porpoises offshore and a modest population of the famous Kodiak brown bear on shore.

Shuyak is not large – the island is only 12 miles long and 11 miles wide – yet it contains more sheltered waterways than any other part of the archipelago, making it a kayaker's delight. Most of the kayaking takes place in and around Big Bay, the heart of the state park. From the bay you can paddle and portage to four public cabins and other protected bays, including Skiff Passage and Western Inlet, where there are numerous islands to explore and the opportunity to sight an occasional humpback whale.

The park's four cabins are on Big Bay, Neketa Bay and Carry Inlet. The cabins cost $50 per day and are cedar structures with bunks for eight, woodstoves, propane lights and cooking stoves but no running water. Write before your trip to Kodiak State Parks for reservations, 1400 Abercrombie Drive, Kodiak, AK 99615. You can call the Alaska Division of Parks in Kodiak (☎ 486-6339, kodsp@ptialaska.net) in advance to see what cabins are available.

Airfare to be dropped off at Big Bay in Shuyak Island is around $380 for a Cessna 206 capable of carrying four passengers. Double that to be picked up as well. For a kayak, check with Mythos Expeditions in Kodiak (☎ 486-5536), which keeps some rentals at the park.

Alaska Peninsula

Due west of Kodiak Island is the Alaska Peninsula, stretching 550 miles from Cook Inlet to its tip at False Pass. The rugged volcanic arm includes the largest lakes in Alaska – Lake Clark, Iliamna Lake and Becharof Lake – and some of the state's most active volcanoes. Birds, marine mammals,

brown bears and other wildlife are plentiful on the peninsula, and anglers from around the world come here to fish for trophy rainbow trout and five species of salmon.

The Alaska Marine Hwy does stop at four small communities along the Alaska Peninsula (see the Aleutian Islands section), but they are of little interest to tourists. The most popular attraction of the region is Katmai National Park and Preserve, which has turned King Salmon into the main access point to the Alaska Peninsula. Two other natural preserves also attract the interest of travelers: McNeil River State Game Sanctuary and Lake Clark National Park and Preserve.

KING SALMON

Located 300 air miles from Anchorage, King Salmon and its runway is the transportation hub to Katmai National Park (see Getting There & Away in the Katmai National Park section). Most people see little more than the terminal building where they pick up their luggage and the float dock where they catch a flight to Brooks Camp in the park, which is fine. King Salmon is a village of 499 residents, with most all of them employees of the National Park Service or US Fish and Wildlife Service.

Information

Tourist Offices In a joint effort, the National Park Service, US Fish and Wildlife Service and the local boroughs operate the King Salmon Visitor Center (☎ 246-4250), next door to the airport terminal, which is open 8 am to 5 pm daily during the summer.

Just up the road from the terminal, on the way to the town of Naknek, is the headquarters of Katmai National Park (☎ 246-3306), on the 2nd floor of the King Salmon Mall. It's open 8 am to 5 pm Monday to Friday and is a good place to ask questions.

Money A National Bank of Alaska (☎ 246-3306) with an ATM is in the King Salmon Mall, a short walk west of the airport.

Post King Salmon has a post office, but it is 2 miles west of the airport. You can purchase stamps and mail letters at the visitor center or the airport.

Email & Internet Access Internet access is available at Trout Net, a restaurant in the King Salmon Mall.

Laundry King Ko Inn (☎ 246-3377, 100 Airport Rd) has laundry facilities with showers ($5).

Medical Services Medical services are available at the King Salmon Health Clinic (☎ 246-3322).

Things to Do

Occasionally, you get stuck in King Salmon for a few hours or even a day. If that's the case, head to the **King Salmon Visitor Center**, next door to the terminal. The center is open daily during the summer and has an excellent selection of books and maps for sale, a growing number of displays and a small video room where you can view a variety of videos on subjects ranging from brown bears to the creation of the park. There are also interactive computers: one features a bear quiz and the other a program on Southwest Alaska.

If you are struck for a day in King Salmon, consider giving **Bristol Bay Tours** (☎ 246-4218) a call. It offers van tours of the area, including the village of Naknek, for a look at rural Alaska, a salmon cannery and a hike along the Bering Sea. The tours run three to four hours and cost $40 per person, with a minimum of two people.

Places to Stay

Most visitors try to avoid spending a night in King Salmon, but if you haven't made reservations at Katmai National Park for either the campground or the lodge, you'll have to overnight in King Salmon and visit the park as a day trip.

Camping You can camp at *R&G Boat Rental* (☎ 246-3353, 246-6571) for $8 a night. The 160-acre campground is located across the Naknek River from King Salmon, so you'll have to pony up $5 for the roundtrip

fare to ride the ferry. Or, you could just wander down the road away from town and set up camp on the banks of the river. Just remember that winds can be murderous here, the real reason for the lack of trees in the region, so you'd best have a tent that can withstand strong gusts.

Hotels The *King Ko Inn (☎ 246-3377, 100 Airport Rd)* has cabins for $170/185 singles/doubles. Better but more expensive accommodations can be found at *Quinnat Landing Hotel (☎ 246-3000, 800-770-3474)*, on Eskimo Creek Rd, where rooms cost $190/215. The best deal in lodging is across the river at *R&G Boat Rental (☎ 888-575-4249, 246-3750)*, which has four-person cabins for $80 a night plus the $5 per person ferry fare to get there.

Places to Eat

For supplies and groceries there is *City Mart*, a short walk west of the airport, which has a deli, coffee shop and camping gear for sale. Soup, sandwiches and such are available at *Trout Net*, in the King Salmon Mall, and the *Cheechako Cafe* is next door to the airport if you don't have much time to spare.

KATMAI NATIONAL PARK

In June 1912, Novarupta Volcano erupted violently and, along with the preceding earthquakes, rocked the area now known as Katmai National Park and Preserve. The wilderness was turned into a dynamic landscape of smoking valleys, ash-covered mountains and small holes and cracks fuming with steam and gas. In only one other eruption in historic times, on the Greek island of Santorini in 1500 BC, has more ash and pumice been displaced.

If the eruption had happened in New York City, people living in Chicago would have heard the explosion; the force of the eruption was 10 times greater than the 1980 eruption of Mt St Helens in the state of Washington. For two days, people in Kodiak could not see a lantern held at arm's length, and the pumice, which reached half the world, lowered the temperature in the

Northern Hemisphere that year by 2°F. In history books, 1912 will always be remembered as the year without a summer, but the most amazing aspect of this eruption, perhaps the most dramatic natural event in the 20th century, was that no one was killed.

The National Geographic Society sent Robert Grigg to explore the locality in 1916, and standing at Katmai Pass, the explorer saw for the first time the valley floor with its thousands of steam vents. He named it the Valley of 10,000 Smokes. Robert Grigg's adventures revealed the spectacular results of the eruptions to the rest of the world, and two years later, the area was turned into a national monument. In 1980, the monument was enlarged to 6094 sq miles and designated a national park and preserve.

Although the fumaroles no longer smoke and hiss, the park is still a diverse and scenic wilderness, unlike any in Alaska. It changes from glaciated volcanoes and ash-covered valleys to island-studded lakes and a coastline of bays, fjords and beaches. Wildlife is abundant, with more than 30 species of mammals, including large populations of brown bears, some over 1000lb. Katmai is also a prime habitat for moose, sea lions, arctic foxes and wolves. The many streams and lakes in the park are known around the state for providing some of the best rainbow trout and salmon fishing.

The weather in the park is best from mid-June to the end of July. Unfortunately, mosquitoes, always heavy in this part of the state, are also at their peak. The best time for hiking and backpacking trips is from mid-August to early September, when the colors of fall are brilliant, the berries ripe and juicy and the insects scarce. However, be prepared for frequent storms. In fact, be ready for rain and foul weather at any time in Katmai, and always pack warm clothing. The summer high temperatures are usually in the low 60s.

The summer headquarters for Katmai National Park is **Brooks Camp**, on the shores of Naknek Lake, 47 miles from King Salmon. The camp is best known for Brooks Falls, which thousands of red sockeye salmon attempt to jump every July, much to the interest of bears and tourists. In the middle of the wilderness, this place crawls with visitors – and bears – during July, when as many as 300 people will be in Brooks Camp and the surrounding area in a single day.

When you arrive at the camp, you are immediately given a bear orientation by a ranger, as the bruins are frequently seen – often strolling down the beach, between the lodge and cabins and the floatplanes pulled up the sand. From there you can head straight to a visitor center, open 8 am to 6 pm daily, for additional information or to fill out

Katmai National Park on the Move

Because the bears won't move from their favorite fishing grounds, Katmai National Park officials decided it was time to move. In 2000, construction began to move Brooks Camp away from the Brooks River. Since the 1950s, Brooks Camp has been the site of the park's facilities, including the lodge, restaurant, campground and ranger station. But it also lies in the middle of a 'bear corridor,' an avenue used every summer by brown bears to access the bountiful salmon runs near Brooks Falls. Visitors often landed in a floatplane and immediately saw a 600lb bear strolling the beach not more than 40 yards away. Or visitors watched from their cabin door as a bear walked through the middle of camp. Such close contact has had the park staff nervous for years.

The plan calls for relocating Brooks Camp to Beaver Pond Terrace, a low ridge a mile south of the river. The park would then use buses to shuttle visitors to trailheads for the hike to the bear viewing areas and platforms. The construction will be done in phases but should be completed by the summer of 2002. When it is finished, all facilities will be out of sight of the river, making the north bank, according the National Park Service, 'the exclusive domain of the bears and other wildlife.'

backcountry permits. Rangers run a variety of interpretive programs, including a daily walk to an Inuit pit house at 1 pm. At 8 pm nightly there are programs or slide shows at a nearby auditorium. You can also purchase books or maps at the center.

Information

Katmai is not a place to visit on a whim. Because of the cost of reaching the park, it's best to spend at least four days or more to justify the expenses. Be sure to make advance reservations, or you will have to settle for visiting the park during the day and sleeping in King Salmon. To contact the park in advance, write to Katmai National Park (☎ 246-3305, www.nps.gov/katm), PO Box 7, King Salmon, AK 99613.

In 1997, the National Park Service instituted fees for the first time at Katmai. Brooks Camp now has a $10 per person per day user fee and an additional $5 per person per night fee if you stay at the campground. The user fee is assessed only if you are at Brooks Camp and does not apply once you enter the backcountry on an extended trek or paddle.

You are also required to make camping and day-use reservations in advance through Biospherics (☎ 800-365-2267, 301-722-1257 for international calls), which the NPS has contracted to handle the reservation system. You cannot show up at the park unless you have a reservation voucher or a confirmed reservation number.

Katmailand (☎ 243-5448, 800-544-0551, katmailand@alaska.net, www.katmailand .com), 4550 Aircraft Drive, Anchorage, AK 99502, is the concessionaire that handles the lodge and bus transportation within the park. To reserve a spot in either, contact the company in advance.

If you purchase a packaged tour, especially the growing number of day tours offered out of Anchorage, Homer or King Salmon, the price will include the necessary reservation vouchers.

Bear Watching

Katmai has the largest population of protected brown bears in the world – more than 2000. At Brooks Camp, they congregate around Brooks River to take advantage of the easy fishing for salmon. Most of this takes place in July, when there can be more than 40 bears along a half mile of the Brooks River. In that month, it is almost impossible to get a campsite, a cabin or sometimes even a spot on the observation decks without planning months in advance. The bear activity then tapers off in August, when the animals follow salmon up into small streams, but it increases again in September as the bears return to congregate in the lower rivers, where they then feed on spawned-out fish. In reality, a few brown bears can be spotted in the Brooks Camp area through much of the summer; a couple younger ones always seem to be hanging around.

There are two established viewing areas. From Brooks Lodge, a dirt road leads to a bridge over the river and a large observation deck, dubbed 'Fort Stevens' by rangers for the Alaskan senator who secured the funding for it. From here you can spot the bears feeding in the mouth of the river or swimming in the bay. Continue on the road to the Valley of 10,000 Smokes, and in half a mile a marked trail winds to Brooks Falls. It's another half-mile walk to the falls, where there is a second observation deck. This is the prime viewing area. Right above the falls, you can photograph salmon making spectacular leaps or a big brownie at the top of the cascade waiting with open jaws to catch a fish.

At the peak of the salmon run, there are usually eight to 12 bears, two or three of them on the falls themselves. The observation deck was enlarged in 1999 to hold 40 people, and in July will be crammed with 50 or more photographers. You can imagine how heated it gets there, with people trying to squeeze in their open tripods for the photo of a lifetime – professionals with 2-foot-long lenses battling it out with amateurs with point-and-shoot cameras. The NPS institutes a number of rules and limits stays at the site to an hour or less. It's the only way to keep a 35mm war from breaking out on the deck.

Hiking

Hiking and backpacking are the best ways to see the park's unusual backcountry. Like Denali National Park, Katmai has few formal trails; backpackers follow river bars, lake shores, gravel ridges and other natural routes. Many hiking trips begin with a ride on the park bus along the dirt road to the Valley of 10,000 Smokes (see the Backpacking section in the Wilderness chapter). The bus will also drop off and pick up hikers along the road. One-way fare is $37.

Dumpling Mountain Trail The only developed trail from Brooks Camp is a half-day trek to the top of Dumpling Mountain, elevation 2520 feet. The trail leaves the ranger station and heads north past the campground, climbing 1.5 miles to a scenic overlook. It then continues another 2 miles to the mountain's summit, where there are superb views of the surrounding lakes.

Paddling

The area has some excellent paddling (see the Savonoski River Loop in the Paddling section of the Wilderness chapter). Lifetime Adventures (☎ 746-4644, 800-952-8624, adventures@matnet.com) rents hard-shell double kayaks for $55 a day or $275 a week and folding doubles for $65/350. You can also rent canoes at Brooks Camps but remember that the winds are strong here and the lakes big. That's okay for sea-touring kayakers but can be a dangerous combination when you're in a canoe. Lifetime Adventures also has a Katmai rental package for $755 per person, which includes a kayak for six days and roundtrip transportation from Anchorage to Katmai.

Bay of Islands A group of dozens of islands lies at the east end of Naknek Lake's North Arm, a one-way paddle of 30 miles from Brooks Camp. Kayakers can make it in a long day; canoeists should plan on two days to reach them. You'll find the islands scenic and the water exceptionally calm. The fishing for rainbow trout is also good, and at the very end of the lake is a ranger cabin. If the ranger is not in, paddlers are welcome to use the cabin. It makes a nice break from a tent. This is a good four- to five-day paddle, depending on how much time you want to spend in the islands.

Margot Creek Along the south shore of the Iliuk Arm of Naknek Lake is the mouth of Margot Creek, where you will find good fishing and lots of bear activity. It's a 10-mile paddle from Brooks Camp, and in ideal conditions, you can reach it in under five hours. But for most people it's a good overnight trip, as you can camp on islands nearby to minimize encounters with bears.

Organized Tours

The only road in Katmai is 23 miles long and ends at Overlook Cabin, where there is a sweeping view of the Valley of 10,000 Smokes. Katmailand, which runs the lodge at Brooks Camp, also has a bus that makes a daily run out to Overlook Cabin and back, usually leaving at 9 am and getting back at 4:30 pm. Each bus carries a ranger who describes what you're looking at and then leads a short hike from the cabin to the valley below. You have a three-hour layover at Overlook Cabin, more than enough time to get a close view of this barren valley and its moonlike terrain.

The fare for the tour is now $75 per person. Believe it or not, if the weather isn't too bad, most people feel it's money well spent, by the end of the day. If you want a box lunch thrown in, it's $83. Sign up for the tour at the Katmailand office across from the lodge as soon as you arrive at Brooks Camp. The bus is filled most of the summer, and you often can't get a seat without reserving one a day or two in advance.

The alternative to the bus is biking the park road. Life Time Adventures (☎ 746-4644, 800-952-8624) has mountain bikes for rent at Brooks Camp for $35 a day.

Places to Stay & Eat

You must reserve a site in the *campground*, but it might be easier winning the New York lottery. Reservations are accepted only by telephone (☎ 800-365-2267, 301-722-1257 for international calls), beginning on the first working day of January, and often the campsites for the prime bear-viewing month of July are filled within three or four days. Camping is $5 per person per night and limited to a maximum of seven nights. If you don't have a reservation, you don't get a site. Park officials no longer try to squeeze in walk-in campers.

Within Brooks Camp is **Brooks Lodge**, which offers basic cabins that hold two to four people. Cabins are rented as packaged tours that include transportation from Anchorage and park fees. A one-night package is $619 per person, and a three-night package is $991. It's best to book a cabin at least several months in advance through Katmailand (see Information).

A store at Brooks Campt sells limited supplies of freeze-dried food and campstove fuel, fishing equipment, flies and other odds and ends like beer. You can also sign up for the all-you-can-eat meals at Brooks Lodge without being a cabin renter; it's $12 for breakfast, $14 for lunch and $24 for dinner. Also in the lodge is a lounge with a huge stone fireplace, soft couches and bar service in the evening.

Getting There & Away

The vast majority of visitors to Katmai fly into King Salmon on Alaska Airlines. You can get there from Kodiak or Homer, but this would involve smaller planes and higher ticket prices. A roundtrip ticket on Alaska Airlines from Anchorage to King Salmon is generally around $400 in the summer. Also check with Peninsula Airways (☎ 800-448-4226), which offers service from Anchorage to King Salmon.

Once you're in King Salmon, a number of air taxi companies will fly out to Brooks Camp, including Katmai Air (☎ 246-3079, 800-478-3079 within Alaska), which charges $138 roundtrip. You can also take a jet boat from King Salmon to Brooks Camp on the *Katmai Lady*. The daily service is run through Quinnat Landing Hotel (☎ 246-3000), with the boat departing in the morning and making a return trip to King Salmon in late afternoon. The roundtrip fare is $125.

MCNEIL RIVER STATE GAME SANCTUARY

The McNeil River State Game Sanctuary, just north of Katmai National Park on the Alaska Peninsula, 200 miles southwest of Anchorage, is famous for its high numbers of brown bears from July to August. The majority of the bears gather a mile upstream from the mouth of the river, where falls slow down the salmon and provide an easy meal. This spot is world-renowned among wildlife photographers, and every great bear-catches-salmon shot you've ever seen has most likely taken from either here or the Brooks River. Often, 20 or more brown bears will feed together below the McNeil River Falls, and up to 80 have been seen congregated here at one time.

The Alaska Department of Fish and Game has set up a viewing area and allows 10 visitors per day for a four-day period to watch the bears feed. From a camp, park guides lead a 2-mile hike across sedge flats and through thigh-deep Mikfik Creek to the viewing area on a bluff. There you can watch the bears feed less than 20 yards away, in what is basically a series of rapids and pools where the salmon gather between leaps. Though an expensive side trip for most visitors, viewing and photographing giant brown bears this close is a once-in-a-lifetime experience.

In June, viewing is done at Mikfik Creek, a small, 20-foot-wide creek. Viewing is switched to the much bigger McNeil River in July, the prime season for bear watching. Usually more than 1200 applications are received from around the world.

Visits to the game sanctuary are on a permit basis only – by lottery – and your odds of drawing a permit from the lottery are less than one in five. Write to the Alaska Department of Fish and Game, Wildlife Conservation Division, 333 Raspberry Rd, Anchorage, AK 99518-1599, for an application, or call ☎ 907-267-2182. You can also request one via fax (☎ 267-2433). Return your application with a $25 nonrefundable fee by March 1 for the lottery drawing. Permits are drawn for 10 people a day for four-day periods, and you must be self-sufficient, with camping equipment and food. The user fee for the sanctuary is $350 for non-Alaskans. Despite the fee, if your name is drawn, by all means take advantage of this rare opportunity in wildlife photography.

Getting There & Away
Most visitors depart for McNeil River from Homer. Kachemak Air Service (☎ 235-8924), based in Homer, offers a roundtrip fare of $320 to McNeil River. It makes the trip whether the plane is filled to capacity (12 seats) or carries only one passenger. Even if you don't have a permit, check with the air service. They stay in constant touch with rangers at the state game area. On some occasions, cancellations or no-shows will lead to last-minute openings in the sanctuary's permit system.

LAKE CLARK NATIONAL PARK
Apart from backpacking enthusiasts and river runners in Southcentral Alaska, few people knew about Lake Clark National Park and Preserve, 100 miles southwest of Anchorage, until recently. Yet it offers some of the most spectacular scenery of any of the newly created parks in the state. The Alaska Range and Aleutian Range meet within this 5625-sq-mile preserve. Among the many towering peaks are Mt Iliamna and Mt Redoubt, two active volcanoes that can be clearly seen from Anchorage and the western shore of the Kenai Peninsula.

Much of the park's obscurity changed in January 1990, when Mt Redoubt erupted after 25 dormant years. The volcano roared back to life, sending ash into the air and creating a cloud that could be seen along the western shore of the Kenai Peninsula. The spreading ash closed the Anchorage International Airport and oil terminals in the area, and 10,000 face masks were distributed to the residents of central Kenai Peninsula to protect against inhaling the fine powder.

Along with its now famous volcanoes, the park also has numerous glaciers, truly spectacular turquoise lakes (including Lake Clark, the park's centerpiece) and three designated wild rivers that have long been havens for river runners.

Wildlife includes brown and black bears, moose, red foxes, wolves and Dall sheep on the alpine slopes. Caribou roam the western foothills, and the park's watershed is one of the most important producers of red salmon in the world, contributing 33% of the US catch. The weather in the western section of the preserve, where most of the rafting and backpacking takes place, is generally cool and cloudy, with light winds through much of the summer. Temperatures range from 50 to 65°F from June to August, with an occasional heat wave of 80°F.

Information
There is a summer ranger station at Port Alsworth (☎ 781-2218) that has displays and videos on the park and even a limited selection of maps and books for sale. Before arriving, contact the park headquarters (☎ 271-3751) in Anchorage regarding desirable places to hike and camp. The park also has a website (www.nps.gov/lacl), or you can write to them for information at Lake Clark National Park, 4230 University Drive, Suite 311, Anchorage, AK 99508.

Hiking
Lake Clark is another remote park exclusively for the experienced backpacker. Most extended treks take place in the western foothills north of Lake Clark, where the open and relatively dry tundra provides ideal conditions for hiking. Less experienced backpackers are content to be dropped off at the shores of the many lakes in the area to camp and undertake day hikes.

Telaquana Trail This 50-mile historic trail, first used by Dena'ina Athabascans and later by fur trappers and miners, is the best cross-country route in the park. It begins on the north shore of Lake Clark, near the Athabascan village of Kijik, and ends near Telaquana Lake. In between, you pass through boreal forests, ford glacial rivers and cross the fragile alpine tundra when the route skirts the western flank of the Alaska Range.

You need route finding and backcountry wilderness skills to follow what is basically an unmarked route. Also, the Kijik River is a difficult ford throughout the summer and at times impossible to cross. For this reason, backpackers begin or end their trip north of the river. Although a few people follow the entire route, most are satisfied with hiking just a portion of it. One of the most popular sections is from Turquoise south to Twin Lakes, where there is usually a ranger stationed. Experienced backpackers can travel between the two lakes in a day.

River Running
Float trips down any of the three designated wild rivers are spectacular and exciting, since the waterways are rated from Class III to IV. Raft rentals are usually available in Port Alsworth. Contact the ranger to ask who is providing the service.

Chilikadrotna River Beginning at Win Lakes, this river offers a good adventure for intermediate rafters. Its steady current and narrow course winds through upland spruce and hardwood forest, draining the west flank of the Alaska Range. From the lakes to a takeout on the Mulchatna River is a 60-mile, four-day float with some Class III stretches.

Tlikakila This fast but small glacial river flows from Summit Lake to upper Lake Clark through a narrow, deep valley within the Alaska Range. The 46-mile trip requires three days and hits a few stretches of Class III water. The hiking in tundra around Summit Lake is excellent, and from there, you make a portage to the river.

Mulchatna River Above Bonanza Hills, this river is a shallow, rocky channel from its headwaters at Turquoise Lake with stretches of Class III rapids. Below the hills, the Mulchatna River is an easy and leisurely float. Plan on two days to float from the lake to the end of Bonanza Hills. The entire river is a 220-mile run to the Nushagak River.

Places to Stay
Port Alsworth is on Lake Clark's southeastern shore and serves as the main entry point into the park. Along with the NPS field office, there is a cafe, a designated camping area and a couple of lodges. *The Farm* (☎ 781-2211) provides lodging and three meals for $80 per person per day, or just a bed and breakfast for $60. The inn also operates a flying service for backpacking drop-offs and river trips. Right on the airstrip is *Wilder House B&B* (☎ 781-2228), with rooms for $85 per person.

Iliamna, a small village 30 miles south of the park, is another jump-off spot for trips into Lake Clark National Park. Located at the airport is *Airport Hotel* (☎ 571-1276), which has a restaurant, taxi service and rooms for $155 per person, including all meals. There is also *Roadhouse Inn B&B* (☎ 571-1272), near downtown Iliamna, in the same price range.

Getting There & Away
Access to the Lake Clark region is by small charter plane, which makes the area tough to visit on a limited budget. The cheapest way to reach Iliamna is to book 14 days in advance through Alaska Airlines (☎ 800-426-0333). A roundtrip ticket from Anchorage is $260. ERA Aviation, a contract carrier of Alaska Airlines, makes the flight twice a day. From Iliamna, you have to charter a plane to your destination within the park through air-taxi operators such as Iliamna Air Taxi (☎ 571-1245). The alternative is to fly into Port Alsworth. Lake Clark Air (☎ 800-662-7661) offers daily flights to the village from Anchorage for a roundtrip fare of $275.

Aleutian Islands

There are two ways to see a part of the remote region of Alaska called 'the Bush' without flying. One of them is to drive the Dalton Hwy to Prudhoe Bay. The other is to hop onto the Alaska Marine Hwy ferry when it makes its special run five times each summer along the Alaska Peninsula to the eastern end of the Aleutian Islands. Once in May, June, July, August and September, the M/V *Tustumena* continues west to Chignik, Sand Point, King Cove, Cold Bay, False Pass and Dutch Harbor/Unalaska, and possibly several other small villages, before back-tracking to Kodiak.

This is truly one of the best bargains in public transportation. The scenery and wildlife are spectacular. You'll pass the perfect cones of Pavlof and Pavlof's Sister (a pair of volcanoes on the Alaska Peninsula) the treeless but lush green mountains of the Aleutians and distinctive rock formations and cliffs. Passing through Barren Islands on the way to Kodiak, passengers often spot two-dozen whales at a time. Sea lions, otters and porpoises are commonly sighted, and more than 30 species of seabirds nest in the Aleutians and 250 species of bird pass through. Diehard birders are often on board sighting albatrosses, auklets, cormorants and puffins. Even if you don't know a puffin from a kittiwake, naturalists from the US Fish and Wildlife Service ride the ferry, pointing out birds and giving programs on other aspects of the Aleutians.

All the wildlife and scenery are very dependent, however, on the weather. This can be an extremely rough trip at times, deserving its title 'the cruise through the cradle of the storms.' On the runs in fall, 40-foot waves and 80-knot winds are the norm, and no matter when you step aboard, you'll find 'barf' bags everywhere on the ship – just in case.

The smoothest runs are from June to August. A stateroom is nice but not necessary. There are no lounge chairs in the solarium, but a sleeping pad and bag work out nicely. You'll find free showers on board, and free coffee and hot water. The hot water is especially nice, allowing you to stock up on instant soup and tea to avoid spending a small fortune in the dinning room, where lunch will cost $7 and dinner $9 to $14. And bring a good book. On days when the fog surrounds the boat, there is little to look at but the waves lapping along the side.

The M/V *Tustumena*, a 290-foot vessel that holds 230 passengers, is the only ferry in the Alaska Marine Hwy fleet rated as an oceangoing ship, thus its nickname, 'Trusty Tusty.' It leaves Kodiak on Wednesday, returns early Monday morning and contin-

ues on to Seward that day. The boat docks at the villages only long enough to load and unload (from one to two hours), but in Dutch Harbor/Unalaska it stays in port five to six hours. Still, spending just an hour in most of these villages is more than enough time to get off for a quick look around.

The roundtrip fare for walk-on passengers to Dutch Harbor from Kodiak is $404; if you begin in Homer and end in Seward, it is $492. For travelers who want to spend more time in Dutch Harbor/Unalaska, Reeve Aleutian Airways (☎ 243-4700, 800-544-2248) and Peninsula Airways (☎ 243-2323, 800-448-4226) provide services to the Aleutian Islands.

The other way to spend more time on land and reduce the cost of the trip is to leave the ferry early and then wait for it on its return run. King Cove is ideally situated for this, but the place is little more than a company town. The best place by far is False Pass, a small village surrounded by snow-covered peaks. But carefully check to see if the ferry is stopping at the town both on the way out and back. If it doesn't, it could be a long wait for the next time the M/V *Tustumena* passes through.

KING COVE

This town of 700 residents, at the western end of the Alaska Peninsula near the entrance of Cold Bay, is a commercial fishing base. Surrounded by mountains, King Cove supports the *Fleet's Inn* (☎ 497-2312), a restaurant, and a busy harbor during summer, as well as a market and a Laundromat. Those wishing to step off and just pitch a tent out on the road, beware. Brown bears wander into town frequently here. Reeve Aleutian Airways charges $405 for a one-way ticket to King Cove from Anchorage, if purchased 14 days in advance.

COLD BAY

On the west shore of Cold Bay is the town of the same name. The 160 residents are mostly government workers, as the town is a major refueling stop for many flights crossing the Pacific. Russian explorers also used the bay and most likely spent the winters here on their first trips along the coast. In 1827, before they departed, Count Feodor Lutke named Izembek Lagoon after a doctor aboard one of his ships.

A huge airstrip was built in the area during WWII; today it's the third longest in the state, making the town the transport center for the entire Aleutian chain. You can still see Quonset huts and other remains from the WWII military buildup.

The town also serves as the gateway to the **Izembek National Wildlife Refuge**, which was established in 1960 to protect some 142 species of bird, primarily the black brant. Almost the entire North American population of brant, some 150,000 of them, arrives in spring and fall during the annual migration, to feed on large eelgrass beds.

A 10-mile road runs from Cold Bay to the Izembek Lagoon; otherwise, travel in the refuge is either by foot or by plane. Contact the Izembek National Wildlife Refuge office in Cold Bay, Pouch 2, Cold Bay, AK 99571, for more information. Within town, accommodations, meals and groceries are available. Reeve Aleutian Airways (☎ 532-2380, 800-544-2248, www.reeveair.com) services the community and charges $345 for a one-way, advance-purchase ticket from Anchorage.

UNALASKA & DUTCH HARBOR

Unalaska, on Unalaska Island, and its sister town Dutch Harbor, on Amaknak Island, are at the confluence of the North Pacific and the Bering Sea, one of the richest fisheries in the world. Dutch Harbor is the only natural deep-water port in the Aleutians, and more than 400 vessels call there each year from as many as 14 countries. The two towns are in Unalaska Bay and are connected to each other by the 500-foot Bridge to the Otherside.

During the summer, the area population can easily exceed 4300 due to the influx of cannery workers who process seafood, most notably crab and pollack. Dutch Harbor also serves as a transport center for much of the Bristol Bay salmon fishery. Since 1988, the towns have led the nation in both volume and value of seafood processed. There are five major seafood plants in the area, whose

2,000 workers churn out more than 800 million pounds of seafood annually for export. Offshore fishing vessels, ranging from 70-foot crab boats to 700-foot floating processors, employ even more workers.

History

Unalaska was the first permanent Russian settlement in America and a cornerstone in the lucrative sea-otter fur trade in the 1700s. It was also an important harbor for miners sailing to the golden beaches of Nome. In 1939, the USA built navy and army installations here, and at one time, 60,000 servicemen were stationed at the bases.

In June 1942, the Japanese opened their Aleutian Islands campaign by bombing Dutch Harbor and then took Attu and Kiska Islands in the only foreign invasion of US soil during WWII other than Guam. The attack on Dutch Harbor had a silver lining in it for the USA. A fallen Zero fighter plane was retrieved near the harbor, and for the first time since the war began, the Americans could closely study Japan's most devastating weapon.

The bombing also resulted in heavy fortification of the islands and areas around Kodiak and Seward, in anticipation of future attacks and to regain control of the Aleutians. The campaign to retake the two islands was a bloody one. After a 19-day battle on Attu, the US forces recaptured the plot of barren land, but only after suffering 2300 casualties and 549 deaths. The Japanese lost even more lives.

Dutch Harbor is the site of the canneries and fish-processing plants, something of an industrial park. Unalaska is where most residents live and, despite the large influx of transient workers, can be a charming and friendly town, if you have the time to enjoy it. Unfortunately, people returning on the ferry really don't. To stay longer, you can either splurge on an expensive airline ticket or be reckless and arrive hoping to pick up a cheaper one in town. Either way, a few days in Unalaska can be a refreshing cure for anybody who is suffering from an overdose of RVers and crowds of tourists and tour buses.

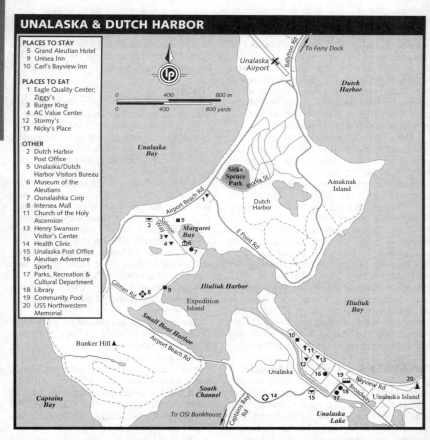

UNALASKA & DUTCH HARBOR

PLACES TO STAY
5 Grand Aleutian Hotel
9 Unisea Inn
10 Carl's Bayview Inn

PLACES TO EAT
1 Eagle Quality Center;
  Ziggy's
3 Burger King
4 AC Value Center
12 Stormy's
13 Nicky's Place

OTHER
2 Dutch Harbor
  Post Office
5 Unalaska/Dutch
  Harbor Visitors Bureau
6 Museum of the
  Aleutians
7 Ounalashka Corp
8 Intersea Mall
11 Church of the Holy
  Ascension
13 Henry Swanson
  Visitor's Center
14 Health Clinic
15 Unalaska Post Office
16 Aleutian Adventure
  Sports
17 Parks, Recreation &
  Cultural Department
18 Library
19 Community Pool
20 USS Northwestern
  Memorial

Information

The Unalaska/Dutch Harbor Visitors Bureau (☎ 581-2612, uphcvb@arctic.net, www.arctic.net/~updhcvb) is at the Grand Aleutian Hotel, on Airport Beach Rd in Dutch Harbor. Hours in the Summer are 8 am to 5 pm Monday to Saturday.

Key Bank of Alaska (☎ 581-1300) is next to AC Value Center, on Salmon Way in Dutch Harbor. There is a post office in Dutch Harbor, next to AC Value Center, and in Unalaska at 82 Airport Beach Rd.

US Travel (☎ 581-3133) is located at the Dutch Harbor Airport and is open daily

during the summer. Books and topographic maps are available at Nicky's Place (☎ 581-1570), which is located on Front Beach Rd in Unalaska.

The Iliuliuk Family and Health Clinic (☎ 581-1202), 34 LaVelle Ct just off Airport Beach Rd near the post office, has walk-in and 24-hour emergency service.

Things to See

Unalaska is dominated by the **Church of the Holy Ascension**, the oldest Russian-built church still standing in the country. It was first built in 1825 and then enlarged in 1894, when wings were attached to change its floor plan from a 'vessel' to a 'pekov,' the shape of a crucifix. On Broadway overlooking the bay, the church and its onion domes are a photographer's delight. Outside is a small graveyard, with the largest marker belonging to Baron Nicholas Zass. Born in 1825 in Archangel, Russia, he eventually became bishop of the Aleutian Islands and all of Alaska, before dying in 1882. Next door is the **Bishop's House**; both buildings are undergoing extensive renovation work to the tune of $1.5 million.

The church also contains almost 800 pieces of art, ranging from Russian Orthodox icons and books to the largest collection of 19th-century paintings in Alaska. Many of the icons are older than the building itself. To see the church's collection, call the visitor bureau (☎ 581-2612) and inquire about possible tours.

Nearby is the **Henry Swanson Visitors Center** (☎ 581-1297), on W Broadway between 2nd and 3rd Sts, the former home of one of Unalaska's most popular residents. Swanson was a fox farmer and fisherman who grew up in Unalaska and as a child watched ships depart from the harbor for the Nome gold rush. He died in 1990. His home contains books, maps, tourist information and a few displays and is open when there are volunteers. Call for hours.

In 1999, the **Museum of the Aleutians** opened on the shores of Margaret Bay. Built on the existing foundation of a WWII warehouse, the $4 million facility has exhibits on the history of Unalaska/Dutch Harbor, Native culture and art, including a 4000-year-old pumice mask, and WWII artifacts. The museum (☎ 581-5150) is open 10 am to 4 pm daily and until 7 pm on Friday; admission is a $2.

Military relics still remain around Dutch Harbor and Unalaska, though in recent years the communities have begun an effort to clean them up. On the road from the ferry terminal and airport to Unalaska, you pass one concrete pillbox after another. **Bunker Hill** is an easy place to see the remains of the Aleutian campaign. Known to the military as Hill 400, it was fortified with 155mm guns,

ammunition magazines, water tanks, 22 Quonset huts and a concrete command post at the top. You can hike to the peak of Bunker Hill along a gravel road picked up just after crossing the bridge to Amaknak Island. At the top of the hill are the gun turrets, ammunition magazines and the command post.

More war history can be found in Unalaska by following Front Beach Rd to the south end of town. There's a picturesque hillside graveyard along the bay, and in the graveyard is the **USS Northwestern Memorial**. Launched in 1889 as a passenger and freight ship for the Alaska Steamship Company, the vessel was retired in 1937, then repaired by the military in 1940 to serve as a floating bunkhouse. It was bombed during the attack on Dutch Harbor and burned for five days. In 1992, as part of the 50th anniversary of the event, the propeller was salvaged by divers and is now part of the memorial to those who died during the Aleutian campaign.

If it's raining in Unalaska, and it does more than 250 days of the year, head to the **community pool** (☎ 581-1649) in the school complex on Broadway. A number of swim periods are offered daily, and the facility also includes a sauna.

Hiking & Paddling

Sitka Spruce Park, within Dutch Harbor, is a national historical landmark where three of six trees planted by Russians in 1805 have somehow survived where all other foliage can't. Because of the treeless environment, hiking is easy here. And don't worry about bears – there aren't any.

The area has few developed trails, but an enjoyable day can be spent hiking to Uniktali Bay, a roundtrip of eight to 10 miles. From Captains Bay Rd, turn east on a gravel road just before you pass Westward Cannery. Follow the road for a mile, to where it ends and a foot trail continues along a stream. In 2 miles, the trail runs out, and you'll reach a lake in a pass between a pair of 2000-foot peaks. Continue southeast to pick up a second stream that empties into Uniktali Bay. The bay is an undeveloped stretch of

SOUTHWEST

shoreline and a great place to beach-comb. From time to time even glass floats from Japanese fishing nets wash ashore.

You can also trek to the top of 1634-foot-high Mount Ballyhoo, behind the airport, to look at more artifacts from the military buildup, including tunnels that allowed gunners to cart ammunition from one side of the mountain to the other. Views from the top include Makushin Volcano and much of Unalaska Island. Hiking is like camping away from town, as much of the land is owned by the Ounalashka (☎ 581-1276), and you need to obtain a permit before heading out. The Native corporation has an office at 400 Salmon Way near Margaret Bay, where you can pick up a permit and a brochure on hiking in the area.

The many protected harbors, bays and islands of Unalaska Island make for ideal sea kayaking conditions. The scenery is stunning and the wildlife plentiful. It is possible to encounter Steller's sea lions, sea otters and harbor porpoises. Aleutian Adventure Sports (☎ 581-4489, advsports@ansi.net), on Broadway Ave, has kayak rentals and offers guided harbor tours and day trips. Kayaks rentals are $65/85 per day for a single/double.

Places to Stay & Eat

The *Grand Aleutian Hotel* (☎ 581-3844, 800-891-1194, 980 Salmon Way), in Dutch Harbor, is the newest hotel, but unless you're willing to pay $175 a night for a double, you might want to look elsewhere for accommodations. A half mile away is *Unisea Inn* (☎ 581-3844), on Gilman Rd near the Intersea Mall. Operated by the Grand Aleutian Hotel, the Unisea has singles/doubles for $84/100. In Unalaska *Carl's Bayview Inn* (☎ 800-581-1230, 606 Bayview Rd), which has 37 rooms, with kitchenettes in a third of them. Rooms start at $90/110.

There are actually a number of lodges in the towns, most catering to the cannery workers and fishers. The best one is *OSI Bunkhouse* (☎ 581-1515), at the end of Captains Bay Rd, the first intersection after crossing the bridge to Unalaska Island. The lodge is 3 miles from Unalaska but has rooms for $72.50 per person. That price includes three meals in the restaurant, where

fishers, construction workers and others feast on an all-you-can-eat breakfasts, lunches and dinners.

Most of the land outside of town is owned by the native corporation Ounalashka (☎ 581-1276), and you need a permit before setting up a tent. The corporation office is at 400 Salmon Way, near the Grand Aleutian Hotel in Dutch Harbor.

Stormy's, at 2nd and Broadway Aves in Unalaska, serves everything from Mexican and Chinese food to pizza and sushi. You can get a latte at *Nicky's Place*, on Front Beach in Unalaska. In Dutch Harbor, *Peking Restaurant (100 Gilman Rd)* has a nice sushi bar, or head to *Ziggy's*, on Airport Beach Rd, for a good breakfast or an extensive dinner menu that includes burgers, pasta, steaks and Mexican. Finally, fast food has reached this remote corner of Alaska in the form of *Burger King*, at the AC Value Center.

Unalaska/Dutch Harbor may be the best place in Alaska to try seafood. Seriously consider splurging for the all-you-can-eat seafood buffet ($24) on Wednesday at the *Grand Aleutian Hotel (980 Salmon Way)* in Dutch Harbor. The meal is so popular you should make reservations.

For groceries, supplies, a salad bar or a deli counter, try *AC Value Center (100 Salmon Way)* or *Eagle Quality Center*, at Airport Beach Rd and E Point Rd, in Dutch Harbor. Each also has a bakery and an espresso counter.

Getting There & Around

The airport is on Amaknak Island, 3 miles from Unalaska. The ferry terminal is even farther north, on Amaknak Island off Ballyhoo Rd. The most amazing thing about this place is the number of taxi vans available. Literally dozens of them run around on the dirt and gravel roads. You can't walk more than five minutes here without a taxi driver asking if you need a ride. The basic fare is $5 per person for places around the island.

If you arrive on the ferry and are returning on it, the $10 you dish out for two taxi rides is money well spent to see as much of Unalaska as possible. If you're staying for a day or two, however, it's easy enough to hitchhike.

Another way to get around is to rent a mountain bike. The extensive, lightly used dirt roads left over from the WWII buildup make great mountain bike trails. You can rent a mountain bike from Aleutian Adventure Sports (☎ 581-4489) for $20/30 half/full day. The sport shop also maintains a rental booth at the ferry terminal for passengers who want to rent a bike during their stopover.

Other than the once-a-month ferry, the only other way of getting out of Unalaska/Dutch Harbor is flying. The town is serviced by Reeve Aleutian Airways (☎ 581-1202, 800-544-2248), Alaska Airlines (☎ 800-426-0333) and PenAir (☎ 581-1383, 800-544-2248). Reeve charges $349 for an advance purchase, one-way ticket to Anchorage and $700 to $840 for the roundtrip. If you have the time, Reeve's milk run lets you see a bit of the Alaska Peninsula on your way back to Anchorage.

Bristol Bay

The pristine lakes and rivers that empty into Bristol Bay support the world's largest run of red salmon, as well as the other four Pacific species – king, silver, chum and pink. The spawning runs have not only made Dillingham the world's salmon capital but have turned the entire region into a paradise for sportfishing. Every summer anglers from around the world shell out several thousand dollars to stay at exclusive, fly-in fishing lodges scattered throughout the region.

The top attraction is Wood-Tikchik State Park, the largest state park in the country and a destination for wilderness adventure. Equally interesting is Round Island, a remote island in Bristol Bay that is a major walrus haul-out site from April to November.

DILLINGHAM

Commercial fishing has made Dillingham (population 2302) the largest community in the Bristol Bay region. The first cannery was built in 1884, and today, more than 10,000 tons of fish, mostly salmon, crosses the city docks every summer. Roughly 55% of Dillingham's year-round residents are Native Alaskans, a mix of Eskimos, Aleuts and Athabascans, but during the summer the population doubles with a large influx of seasonal workers.

Dillingham serves as the jumping-off point for trips into Wood-Tikchik State Park, Round Island and the numerous fishing lodges in the region. The airport is 2.5 miles west of the town, and the only place you can drive to is Aleknagik Lake. The

---

Super Bowl Sunday in Dillingham

Super Bowl Sunday is virtually a national holiday in America, even in Alaska, but in Dillingham the only large-screen television in town was at the Willow Tree Bar, which by law has to be closed on Sunday. Local ordinances stipulate that the Bristol Bay town must be dry on Sunday and that bars – Dillingham has two of them – must close at midnight on Saturday. That was fine for 51 weeks of the year, but not on Super Bowl Sunday, so in 1998, residents asked the city council for a special one-time-only exemption that would allow them to gather in front of the big TV for the big game between the Denver Broncos and the Green Bay Packers.

The special ordinances passed unanimously, and for the first time, football fans in this isolated Bush town watched the Super Bowl on a large-as-life screen. Patrons showed up with potluck dishes to pass around; Budweiser sent up free T-shirts and mugs that were given away; and somebody went home with a new stereo after winning a football trivia contest.

The event was such a rousing success that now the council is asked every January to pass the special Super Bowl Sunday exemption. 'Well, you know, there's not a whole lot to do in Dillingham,' said one patron. 'We have to take advantage of every opportunity.'

most southern lake in the Wood River chain is connected to Dillingham by a 24-mile gravel road.

Information

The Dillingham Visitor Center (☎ 842-5115) is on Main St and also maintains a website (www.nushtel.com/~dlgchmbr).

The National Bank of Alaska (☎ 842-5284) is at 512 Seward St and has an ATM. The Dillingham Post Office is on D St.

World Express Travel (☎ 842-5193) is at 1190 Main St.

The Dillingham Medical Center Clinic (☎ 842-5671) is at 119 E St W and has walk-in and 24-hour emergency service.

Places to Stay & Eat

Dillingham has a number of hotels and lodges, but the price of accommodations here are on the high side, partly because of the 9% bed tax. At the top end is the *Bristol Inn* (*☎ 842-2240, 104 Main St*) at $110/135 singles/doubles. Slightly more affordable is *Dillingham Hotel* (*☎ 842-5316, 429 2nd Ave W*), in the center of town, with rooms for $109/136.

There are a half dozen restaurants in Dillingham and an AC Value Center with a deli and bakery. *Ricardo's*, on Windmill Rd, offers up pizza and Mexican dishes. *Twin Dragon*, at the airport, has Chinese food, and *Muddy Rudder* (*100 Main St*) is downtown and open for breakfast, lunch and dinner daily.

Getting There & Away

To reach Dillingham from Anchorage, try to book an air ticket 21 days in advance through Alaska Airlines (☎ 800-426-0333); a roundtrip ticket costs from $318 to $350. To reach Wood-Tikchik State Park contact any of the air charter companies in town including Fresh Water Adventures (☎ 842-5060, freshh2o@cyber-dyne.com) about chartering a float plane.

WOOD-TIKCHIK STATE PARK

At 2500 sq miles, Wood-Tikchik is the largest state park in the country. The park, 30 miles north of Dillingham, preserves two large systems of interconnecting lakes that are the important spawning grounds for Bristol Bay's salmon.

With the exception of five fishing lodges, which offer packaged stays at $2000 to $3000 a week, the park is totally undeveloped. There are no campgrounds, trails, ranger stations or shelters. In short, it is an ideal place for a wilderness canoe or kayak trip. Traditional trips include running the Tikchik or Nuyakuk Rivers or floating from lake to lake.

For park information, contact Wood-Tikchik State Park (☎ 842-2375), PO Box 3022, Dillingham, AK 99576.

Paddling

Several companies in town rent inflatable kayaks, rafts or canoes. These include Fresh Water Adventures (☎ 842-5060, freshh2o@cyber-dyne.com), which rents 20-foot inflatable kayaks for $50 a day. Robert Tours (☎ 842-5496, 842-3355, siwash@nushtel.com) will set up a kayak rental and drop-off service for you.

Wood River Lakes These lakes, in the southern half of the park, are connected to one another by shallow, swiftly moving rivers. For that reason, most parties are flown in and paddle out, returning to Dillingham via the Wood River. A popular spot to put in is at Lake Kulik. From there, the paddle is toward Dillingham, a trip of close to 140 miles requiring from seven to 10 days in a kayak or canoe. Be prepared to pay around $450 for a drop-off at Lake Kulik.

This route is attractive to many people because it eliminates the additional air time to be picked up. It is also an easy paddle for most intermediate canoeists. But keep in mind that three of the five fishing lodges are on these lakes, and they all use their powerboats extensively to get around on the water.

Tikchik Lakes In the northern half of the park, and much more remote than the Wood River lakes, are these six lakes. In the most common trip, paddlers are dropped off on Nishlik or Upnuk Lakes and travel along the Tikchik River into Tikchik Lake. You can be picked up here or continue your journey by floating the Nuyakuk River and then the Nushagak River to one of several Native Alaskan villages where air charter is available back to Dillingham. A drop-off costs around $900 for the flight at Nishlik Lake and $650 for Upnuk Lake.

Keep in mind that the Allen River, which drains from Chikuminuk Lake into Lake Chauekuktuli on another route to Tikchik Lake, requires a series of portages around Class V rapids. Likewise the upper Nuyakuk River, just below the Tikchik Lake outlet, has a white-water stretch that will require a portage. The upper lakes are more challenging and more costly to experience. But the scenery – mountains, pinnacle peaks and hanging valleys surrounding the lakes – is the most impressive in the park, and there will be far less motorboat activity, if any at all.

The paddling season is from mid-June, when the lakes are finally free of ice and snow, until early October, when they begin to freeze up again. Be prepared for cool and rainy weather and pack along plenty of mosquito repellent. On the open lakes you have to be cautious, as sudden winds can create whitecap conditions, and white water may exist on many of the streams connecting the lakes.

Highlights of any such adventure, besides the wilderness, are the possibilities of spotting brown and black bears, beavers, moose, foxes and maybe even wolves. The fishing for arctic char, rainbow trout, Dolly Varden, grayling and red salmon is excellent in late summer.

ROUND ISLAND

Southwest of Dillingham in Bristol Bay is Walrus Islands State Game Sanctuary, a seven-island preserve that includes Round Island, the largest walrus haul-out grounds in Alaska. From April to November some 15,000 Pacific walruses haul out on the beaches of Round Island to stake out their territory for the summer mating season. Other wildlife is also plentiful on this remote island, including puffins, a colony of Steller's sea lions and migrating whales off shore.

Round Island is extremely isolated and hard to reach. In the past, a permit from the Alaska Department of Fish and Game (☎ 842-2334) and a bush plane flight to Togiak Bay, where you would arrange to charter a boat from a cannery, were required. In 1999, Johnson Maritime of Dillingham began offering the first guided, regularly scheduled trips to Round Island. The Walrus Islands Expeditions are one-, three- or six-day tours in the company's *Bel Canto*, a 50-foot boat that sleeps six in three double cabins. The trips involve flying to a remote beach and then being transported to

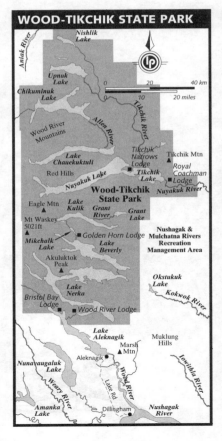

WOOD-TIKCHIK STATE PARK

the *Bel Canto* in a Zodiac. The motor yacht is used to reach walruses and sea lions at various beaches. You return to the mainland by bush plane.

Round Island offers some of the best wildlife viewing in Alaska but getting to the island is not cheap. The one-day tour costs $500 per person; a three-day tour with two nights on the boat costs $1000; and the six-day outing costs $2500. It costs another $150 per person for the roundtrip air charter out of Dillingham needed to reach the *Bel Canto*. If you are interested in a tour, contact Johnson Maritime (☎ 842-2101, walrusnt@nushtel.com), PO Box 1067, Dillingham, AK 99567.

The Interior

At the Fairview Inn in Talkeetna, the house rules are easy to understand and even easier to read. They're posted right above the hotel's horseshoe bar:

All firearms must be checked in with the bartender before drinks are ordered.

The bartender is the only one allowed to stoke the wood-burning stove.

Bury the slot machine if the Feds show up.

Welcome to Interior Alaska, that 'great, big, broad land way up yonder' between Anchorage and Fairbanks. This vast region has been searched over by miners, immortalized by poets and popularized in the quirky TV series *Northern Exposure*. Anyone who has ever seen that show can picture Alaska's heartland: dogsleds and gold pans, roadhouses and fish wheels, a moose on the side of the road and a seemingly endless stretch of pavement that disappears into the mountains.

Dramatic mountain chains surround the Interior, with the Alaska Range to the south and the Brooks Range to the north. In between is the central plateau of Alaska, a vast area of land that gently slopes to the north and contains such awesome rivers as the Yukon, Kuskokwim, Koyukuk and Tanana.

It is the home of Mt McKinley, the highest peak in North America (20,320 feet), and of Denali National Park & Preserve, Alaska's best-known spot for hiking, camping and wildlife watching. It's also the stomping grounds for brown bear, moose, caribou and Dall sheep, whose numbers here are unmatched anywhere else in the country.

The Interior can be enjoyed by even the most budget-minded traveler because it's accessible by road. The greater part of Alaska's highway system forms a triangle that includes the state's two largest cities, Anchorage and Fairbanks, and allows cheap travel by bus, train, car or hitchhiking.

The George Parks Hwy leaves Anchorage and winds 358 miles to Fairbanks, passing Denali National Park along the way. The Glenn Hwy spans 189 miles between Anchorage and Glennallen and then continues another 125 miles to Tok in a section known as the Tok Cutoff.

Beginning at Valdez, the Richardson Hwy passes Glennallen and ends at Fairbanks, 368 miles away. Dividing the triangle from east to west is the Denali Hwy, 136 miles long and at one time the only road to Denali National Park.

All four roads are called highways, though they are rarely more than two-lane roads.

Highlights

- Take a stunning flight around Mt McKinley from Talkeetna
- See brown bears, caribou and Dall sheep on the shuttle bus through Denali National Park
- Hear Robert Service's folksy poetry at the old Malemute Saloon in Ester
- Ride the rapids of the Matanuska River
- Trek across the ice of the Matanuska Glacier
- Relive Eagle's gold-mining era on a walking tour with the Eagle Historical Society

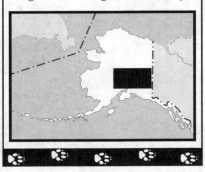

THE INTERIOR

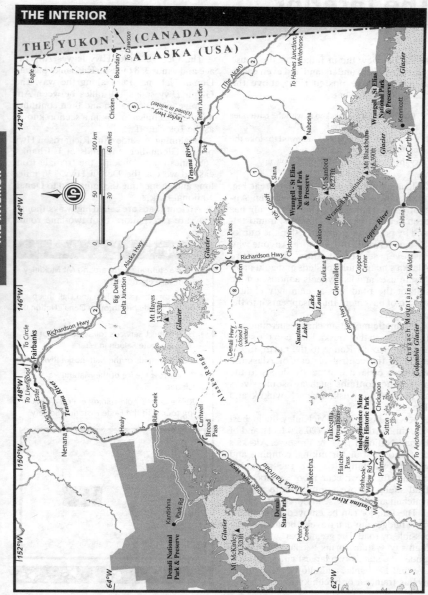

THE YUKON (CANADA)
ALASKA (USA)

To Dawson

Eagle

Boundary

Chicken

To Haines Junction,
Whitehorse

2 (The Alcan)

Taylor Hwy (closed in winter)

Tetlin Junction

Tok

Slana

Nabesna

Wrangell - St Elias
National Park
& Preserve

Glacier

Kennicott

Wrangell - St Elias
National Park & Preserve

McCarthy

Tenana River

Mt Sanford
16,237ft

Wrangell Mountains

Mt Blackburn
16,390ft

Alaska Hwy

Tok Cutoff

Chistochina

Gakona

Copper River

Chitna

Glacier

Isabel Pass

Richardson Hwy

Big Delta
Delta Junction

Paxon

Gulkana

Glennallen

Copper
Center

Churach Mountains

To Valdez

To Circle

Richardson Hwy

Fairbanks

Mt Hayes
13,832ft

Glacier

Denali Hwy
(closed in
winter)

Lake
Louise

Susitna
Lake

Glenn Hwy

Columbia Glacier

To Livengood

Ester

Parks Hwy

Tenana River

Alaska Range

Nenana

Healy

Riley Creek

Cantwell

Broad
Pass

Talkeetna
Mountains

Independence Mine
State Historic Park

Chickaloon

Sutton

To Anchorage

George Parks Hwy

Alaska Railroad

Hatcher Pass

Fishhook-
Willow Rd

Palmer

Wasilla

Denali National
Park & Preserve

Kantishna

Park Rd

Glacier

Mt McKinley
20,320ft

Denali
State Park

Talkeetna

Susitna River

Willow

Peters Creek

100 km

60 miles

0   30   50

All of the highways pass through spectacular scenery, offer good possibilities of spotting wildlife and provide access to campgrounds and hiking trails. For the most part, the towns along the highways are small, colorless service centers with gasoline stations, motels and cafes, although a few towns have managed to retain their rustic gold-rush and frontier flavor. The real attraction of the Interior is not these service centers but what lies in the hills and valleys beyond the highway.

Bus transportation is available on every highway except the Denali, and there is train service between Anchorage and Fairbanks. Bus routes and even the companies themselves change often in Alaska, so it pays to double-check bus departures with a phone call. For more information, see each separate highway section.

The hitchhiking is surprisingly good during the summer, as the highways are cluttered with a stream of RVs and summer tourists arriving from down south. Avoid backtracking if you can, even if it means going out of your way on an alternative route. All the highways offer roadside scenery that is nothing short of spectacular.

Climate

In this region of mountains and spacious valleys, the climate varies greatly and the weather can change appreciably from one day to the next. In the winter, the temperatures drop to -60°F for days at a time; in the summer, they can soar above 90°F. The norm for the summer is long days with warm temperatures of 60°F to 70°F. However, it is common for Denali National Park to experience at least one snowfall in the lowlands between June and August.

Here, more than anywhere else in the state, it's important to have warm clothes while still being able to strip down to a T-shirt and hiking shorts. Most of the area's 10 to 15 inches of annual precipitation come in the form of summer showers, with cloudy conditions common, especially north of Mt McKinley. In Denali National Park, Mt McKinley tends to be hidden by the weather for two out of every three days.

George Parks Highway

Many travelers and most overseas visitors arrive in Alaska through Anchorage and venture north along the George Parks Hwy (also known as the Parks Hwy). The road, which was opened in 1971, provides a direct route to Denali National Park while passing through some of the most rugged scenery Alaska has to offer. The road begins at a junction with the Glenn Hwy 35.3 miles north of Anchorage. Mileposts indicate distances from Anchorage and not from the junction.

WASILLA

From its junction with the Glenn Hwy, the George Parks Hwy heads west and then north. For the first 20 miles, it passes through a jungle of tacky tourist stops, strip malls and as many fast-food restaurants as you'll see in all of Southeast Alaska. At the junction with Big Lake Rd, one purveyor of discount fireworks stands has stooped to a new low, attracting tourists with huge gorilla balloons.

The reason for the development is the caravan of RVers heading north to Denali National Park – a steady stream of consumerism that everybody is trying to tap into, particularly the town of Wasilla (population 5200), just 7 miles from the junction.

History

Wasilla derives its name from Chief Wasilla, a local Dena'ina Athabascan Indian, and for most of its existence it was little more than a wide spot in the Carle Trail, which ran from the seaport of Knik to the gold mines in Hatcher Pass. It turned into a town almost overnight, after the Alaska Railroad first passed through in 1917, and remained an active mining supply center until the 1940s.

In the 1970s, Wasilla was a sleepy little town with services for local farmers. Then urban sprawl reached it. From 1980 to 1983, the population of Wasilla doubled, when Alaskans who wanted to work in Anchorage but live elsewhere began moving in. Shopping

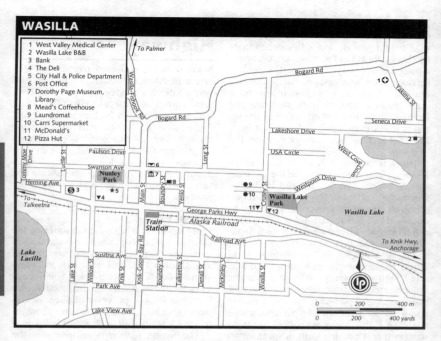

WASILLA

1 West Valley Medical Center
2 Wasilla Lake B&B
3 Bank
4 The Deli
5 City Hall & Police Department
6 Post Office
7 Dorothy Page Museum, Library
8 Mead's Coffeehouse
9 Laundromat
10 Carrs Supermarket
11 McDonald's
12 Pizza Hut

centers and businesses have mushroomed along the highway, and there was even talk of building a bridge across the Knik Arm to shorten the drive to Anchorage.

This development is all a bit ironic because many feel that Wasilla, with its strip malls and convenience stores, is now just a slice of the big city that others were trying to escape.

Information

Tourist Offices Near the junction of the George Parks Hwy and Trunk Rd is the Matanuska-Susitna Visitors Center (☎ 746-5000, www.alaskavisit.com), open 8 am to 6 pm daily during the summer. The log lodge sits on a small rise and, along with bathrooms and racks of brochures, it has an outdoor deck with a great view of the mountains surrounding Knik Inlet.

The Dorothy Page Museum (☎ 376-9071), 323 Main St, doubles as Wasilla's visitor center and is open 10 am to 6 pm daily year-round.

Money Wasilla has a half dozen banks and credit unions in town, with most of them along the George Parks Hwy. These include the National Bank of Alaska (☎ 376-5355), 581 W Parks Hwy.

Post The post office is three blocks north of the George Parks Hwy on Main St near the Dorothy Page Museum.

Email & Internet Access You can check your email or surf the Internet at Mead's Coffeehouse, 405 E Herning Ave behind the Dorothy Page Museum. The Wasilla Backpackers hostel (☎ 357-3699), 3950 Carefree Drive, also has Internet access.

Travel Agencies US Travel (☎ 373-1212) is at 1590 Financial Drive.

Libraries & Bookstores The Wasilla library, next door to the Dorothy Page Museum, is open 10 am to 8 pm Tuesday and Thursday,

10 am to 6 pm Wednesday and Friday, 1 to 5 pm Saturday. You'll find a Waldenbooks (☎ 376-1218) in the Cottonwood Creek Mall, along the George Parks Hwy on the south side of town.

Laundry There are two Laundromats in town, including Wasilla Homestyle Laundry in the Wasilla Shopping Center on the highway. It has showers as well as laundry facilities.

Medical Services The West Valley Medical Center (☎ 352-2810) is at 950 Bogard Rd, just east of Crusey St.

Dorothy Page Museum

Named after 'the Mother of the Iditarod,' this is both a museum and an interesting historical village of preserved buildings, each loaded with artifacts. The museum (☎ 376-9071), 323 Main St, displays lots of tools and other relics from the early farmers, with mining equipment in the basement. The historical village includes seven renovated buildings, mostly classic log cabins. One is Wasilla's first public sauna, which opened in 1942; men and women used it on alternate days of the week. Another is the Capital Site Cabin, first erected in Willow, a small town northwest of Wasilla, when the state debated moving its capital there in the late 1970s. In Juneau, residents feared what would become of their city while Wasilla's citizenry drooled in anticipation of all that political pork coming north. But Wasilla ended up with only this relocated cabin, a reminder of an issue that had split the state. The Dorothy Page Museum is open 10 am to 6 pm daily year-round, and admission is $3.

Museum of Alaska Transportation & Industry

What was once a Palmer attraction is now part of Wasilla, as the Museum of Alaska Transportation & Industry (☎ 376-1211) moved from the Alaska State Fairgrounds to a location off the Parks Hwy in the early 1990s. Turn off at Mile 47 and follow the signs for less than a mile to see such transportation relics as a C-123 plane, the tractors of the first Matanuska-Susitna farmers and the first

diesel locomotive used in Alaska. There is also a picnic area and a mini-steam railroad for kids. The museum is open 9 am to 6 pm daily, and admission is $5 for adults, $12 for a family.

Sled Dogs & the Iditarod

The Iditarod begins in Anchorage – but only for the sake of appearances. The event doesn't really get underway until the end of the short run in Anchorage, when the teams wave goodbye to the cameras, pack up their dogs and sleds and drive to snowier country up north for the 'restart.' Currently, Wasilla serves as the second starting point for the famous 1100-mile race to Nome, though there is talk of that changing. A lack of snow has hampered the restart, and only twice has it actually been staged in Wasilla. The rest of the time, it had to be held in Willow. Race officials are considering making Willow the permanent restart, but Wasilla residents are fighting it.

Nearby Knik also boasts a rich sled-dog history, since it's the home for many Alaskan mushers and checkpoint No 4 on the route. For more information about this uniquely Alaskan race, stop in at the **Iditarod Headquarters** (☎ 376-5155), at Mile 2.2 of the Knik Hwy (which begins in downtown Wasilla, off the Parks Hwy). The log-cabin museum has one room that's full of historical displays, photos of past champions and racks of race paraphernalia – jackets, hats and shirts for sale. The most unusual exhibit is Togo, the famous sled dog that led his team across trackless Norton Sound to deliver serum to diphtheria-threatened Nome in 1925 – a journey that gave rise to today's Iditarod. He's been stuffed and is now on display.

In another room, you can view an excellent video on sled dogs and the race itself. But almost as impressive, if it's still posted on the wall, is the checkpoint-by-checkpoint leader board of the most recent race, telling you who made it and whose team couldn't endure the challenge of 1100 miles. This is a small but interesting museum, and, best of all, it's free. It's open 8 am to 5 pm daily during the summer.

Outside, you can join a sled-dog ride with Raymie Redington, the son of Iditarod veteran Joe Redington Sr. In the summer, Red uses a wheeled dogsled and charges $5 per person.

For more information on dog mushing and racing, continue south along the Knik Hwy to the **Knik Museum & Sled Dog Musher's Hall of Fame**, at Mile 13.7. The museum, a pool hall at one time, is on the original site of Knik, which had a population of more than 500 at the turn of the 20th century, when Anchorage was nowhere to be found. First settled in the late 1800s and fueled by mining and trading, Knik was the major port for the region and even for much of the Interior. In its heyday the town boasted its own newspaper, several bars and even a movie house. But with the establish-ment of Anchorage in 1915 and the emergence of the Alaska Railroad as an overland supply link, the end for Knik came quickly.

Inside the museum you'll read about Knik's history and view artifacts from its gold rush. But most of the displays are devoted to the Iditarod Trail, early Alaskan mushers and, of course, the Canine Hall of Fame. Outside, you can easily walk a portion of the historic Iditarod Trail. The museum is open noon to 6 pm Wednesday to Sunday, and admission is $2.

Places to Stay

Camping The nearest place to camp is *Lake Lucille Park*, near the Iditarod Headquarters on the Knik Hwy, a Matanuska-Susitna

Joe Redington Sr 1917–1999

Nationally, Joe Redington Sr was not Alaska's best-known musher. Others, such as four-time Iditarod winner Susan Butcher, were better known in the outside world. But to Alaskans, no musher was better loved or more revered than Redington. In 1999, the father of the Iditarod died in his Knik home at age 82.

Redington was born in Oklahoma in 1917 and moved to Alaska in 1948 after serving in the army during WWII. He arrived with just $18 in his pocket and used $13 of it to cover a filing fee for a 101-acre homestead in Knik. By accident – or some say fate – Redington's homestead was located only a few hundred feet from the historic Iditarod Trail. By that first winter, Redington was already accumulating sled dogs and mushing. He would eventually own, train and feed 500 Alaska huskies.

Redington was always fascinated by the Iditarod Trail and the famous 'serum run' that saved Nome from diphtheria in 1925, when a dogsled raced along the trail with medical supplies. By the early 1970s, he worried that snowmobiles might soon replace sled dogs, so he proposed an Anchorage-to-Nome race along the historic trail. Redington and his wife worked tirelessly to organize and raise funds for the first Iditarod in 1973. When the race was announced, Redington was the first musher to sign up but had to bow out in order to continue raising money for the purse he guaranteed.

Redington made his Iditarod debut the following year at age 57. He completed the 1100-mile route in 23 days for 11th place, winning a $465 share of the purse. He went on to run the Iditarod 19 times. His best finish was fifth, and his best time was 12 days, two hours and 57 minutes in 1989. The most he ever won from the Iditarod was $9000. He clearly wasn't in it for the money.

Redington loved sled dogs almost as much as he loved Alaska. He helped five-time Iditarod winner Rick Swenson get into the sport, and he tutored Butcher, who lived at his homestead in the 1970s. His most noted accomplishment came in 1979, when he teamed up with Butcher and renowned mountain guide Ray Genet to drive a dog team to the summit of Mt McKinley, the highest peak in North America. But to many, his most amazing feat was his final Iditarod in 1997. At age 80, Redington completed the grueling race across the Alaska wilderness in 13 days.

Alaska is going to miss its favorite son but not forget him. Not soon after his death, Alaskans started a fundraiser to build the Joe Redington Museum at his Knik homestead.

Borough park. The park has a campground (46 sites, $8) with rest rooms, a shelter and a network of trails. You can fish in the lake, which is stocked annually with silver salmon and rainbow trout.

Hostels *Wasilla Backpackers* (☎ *357-3699, travel@wasillabackpackers.com, 3950 Carefree Drive*) is 2 miles south of Wasilla, just off the Parks Hwy at Mile 39. This pleasant home hostel has 18 bunks for $22, tent sites for $15 and mountain bikes for $20 a day. Also available are laundry facilities and Internet service.

B&Bs Still want more on mushing? Can't get that Iditarod blood out of your system? Then book a room at *Yukon Don's Bed & Breakfast* (☎ *800-478-7472, 376-7472, 2221 Yukon Circle*), 1.5 miles down Fairview Loop Rd. Within this converted barn are seven guest rooms, including the Iditarod Room, filled with memorabilia of the famous race, including a dogsled that hangs above the bed. The smaller rooms cost $75/85.

Overlooking Wasilla Lake near the downtown area is *Wasilla Lake B&B* (☎ *376-5985, wasillalake@alaskan.com, 961 North Shore Drive*). The B&B has three rooms for $65/75 and a rustic cottage that sleeps two for $95. Ten minutes north of Wasilla is *Alaska Hillside Cabins* (☎ *376-4912, goldrush@matnet.com*), with cabins in a secluded setting and an outdoor hot tub. Cabins include kitchens and are $60 for two people.

Hotels The most convenient place to stay is the *Windbreak Hotel* (☎ *376-4484*), a mile south of town on the Parks Hwy. The hotel has rooms for $65/70, a pub and a good cafe that isn't part of a national chain – a rarity in Wasilla. Also check the *Mat-Su Resort* (☎ *376-3228, 1850 Bogard Rd*), on the shores of Wasilla Lake. The resort has rooms and cabins, some with kitchenettes if you plan to stay for a while, along with a restaurant, lounge and an assortment of rowboats and paddleboats for rent on the lake. Cabins are $95 for two people, but the resort does have some basic rooms for $40.

Places to Eat

The variety of fast-food restaurants found in Wasilla is mind-boggling, and most survive on the highway trade. In this town of less than 5000 residents, you'll find a *Pizza Hut*, *Arby's*, not one but two *McDonald's*, *Burger King* and *Taco Bell*. Recently, even the Colonel joined the group.

For big portions, go to the *Windbreak Hotel*, on the George Parks Hwy as you enter town. The menu features 18 types of hamburgers and 15 chicken sandwiches, all of which you can enjoy while admiring the impressive display of trophy fish mounted on the walls. Sandwiches are $6 to $8; dinners are $9 to $15.

The Deli (*185 E Parks Hwy*) serves homemade baked goods, large sandwiches and fresh salads. Breakfasts start at $6; sandwiches range from $5 to $7. A little farther west, *Chepo's* (*731 W Parks Hwy*) serves good Mexican fare, with dinners from $8 to $12 and lunch specials for $6.

Enjoy a latte or surf the Internet at *Mead's Coffeehouse* (*405 E Henning Ave*), behind the Dorothy Page Museum. The building was Wasilla's first general store when it opened in 1917, which explains the coffeehouse's unusual split-level interior. At night the place comes alive, with local musicians on hand.

In town is a *Carrs Supermarket*, Crusey St at the Parks Hwy, with a salad bar, bakery, ready-to-eat entrees and seating inside. East on the Parks Hwy, *Fred Meyer* serves the same type of meals and also has indoor seating. At the old Wasilla town site, behind the Dorothy Page Museum, you'll find the *Wasilla Farmer's Market*, held from 4 to 7 pm every Wednesday. There, you can pick up some of those oversized local veggies.

Getting There & Away

The Alaska Railroad train from Anchorage stops at Wasilla at 9:45 am daily during the summer. The train from Fairbanks arrives at 6:20 pm. Any of the Denali van services (see the Anchorage chapter) will drop you off in town, and Parks Highway Express (☎ 888-600-6001) will even take you to the Wasilla Backpackers hostel. The one-way fare from Anchorage to Wasilla is $15.

Getting Around

The best way to see the surrounding area, especially Independence Mine State Historic Park and Hatcher Pass, is to rent a car in Wasilla. The several local agencies include Denali Car Rental (☎ 800-669-1230, 373-1230), 301 Lucas St, just off the Parks Hwy on the west side of town. Compacts are $35 per day.

BIG LAKE

From Wasilla, the George Parks Hwy continues in a westerly direction for the next 10 miles and then curves north, reaching Willow at Mile 69. Before entering the small village, you'll pass two side roads that lead west to state recreation areas with lakeside campgrounds and canoe trails.

At Mile 52.3, where the George Parks Hwy curves north, Big Lake Rd meets the highway. Head 3.3 miles down the road and turn right at the gasoline station; in half a mile, you'll reach the *Rocky Lake State Campground* (10 sites, $10). A few hundred yards farther along Big Lake Rd is a fork known as 'Fisher's Y,' where the town of Big Lake (population 2150) has sprung up. The right fork leads 1.6 miles to the *Big Lake North State Campground* (150 sites, $10), the left fork 1.7 miles to the *Big Lake South State Campground* (13 sites, $10). Keep in mind that in the mid-1990s the Big Lake area was engulfed by wildfires that burned almost 40,000 acres and since then has experienced almost uncontrolled growth along its lakes. Both the fire and the ensuing commercial and residential development have made the area less appealing from a traveler's point of view.

NANCY LAKE STATE RECREATION AREA

The George Parks Hwy continues northwest from Big Lake Rd, passes the village of Houston (population 840) and *Little Susitna River City Campground* (86 sites, $10), and reaches the junction with Nancy Lake Pkwy at Mile 67.2. The parkway leads to the northern portion of the Nancy Lake State Recreation Area, one of Alaska's few flat, lake-studded parks that offers camping, fishing, canoeing and hiking.

Although it lacks the dramatic scenery of the country to the north, the 22,685-acre state park with its 130 lakes is still a scenic spot and one worth stopping at for a couple of days if you have the time. After driving a mile or so on the parkway, you'll come to the state recreation area office (☎ 495-6273). It's unmarked from the road so most people just pass it by, but it is the place to stop for information or to reserve a cabin. Nancy Lake Parkway extends 6.6 miles to the west and ends at the South Rolly Lake Campground.

Hiking

Those travelers without a canoe can still reach the backcountry by one of two trails. The **Chicken Lake Trail** begins at Mile 5.7 of the parkway and extends 3 miles south to the lake and another 2.5 miles to the east shore of Red Shirt Lake. A roundtrip hike on the trail is an 11-mile overnight trek. Count on wet conditions from time to time.

Twin Shirt Lakes Trail, the other trail into the backcountry, begins near the campground at the end of the parkway. This trail is more popular and drier than the Chicken Lake Trail. Built in 1986, the trail leads 3.5 miles south primarily on high ground and ends at the north end of Red Shirt Lake. Along the way, you'll pass Red Shirt Overlook, with its scenic views of the surrounding lake country and the Chugach Mountains on the horizon. The trail ends at a group of backcountry campsites along the lake. There's a vault toilet here.

There are also two short hikes that allow you to stretch your legs. At Mile 2.5 of the Nancy Lake parkway is Tulik Trail, a 1-mile, self-guided nature trail that takes you past ponds and bogs via boardwalks and viewing platforms. Near South Rolly Lake Campground, a half-mile trail leads to North Rolly Lake.

Paddling

Lynx Lake Loop is the most popular canoe trail, a two-day, 16-mile trip that passes through 14 lakes and over an equal number of portages. The trail begins and ends at the posted trailhead for the Tanaina Lake Canoe Trail at Mile 4.5 of the parkway. The portages are well marked, and many of them are planked where they cross wet sections. The route includes 12 backcountry campsites, accessible only by canoe, but bring a camp stove because campfires are prohibited in the backcountry.

The largest lake on the route is Lynx Lake, and you can extend your trip by paddling south on the lake to the point where a portage leads off to six other lakes and two more primitive campsites on Skeetna Lake. You can rent canoes at Tippecanoe Rentals (☎ 495-6688, canoeak@alaska.net), which has an office on the George Parks Hwy just south of the parkway and a rental shed in South Rolly Lake Campground. Rates begin at $25 for a day or $45 for two days, $60 for three days and $70 for four to seven days. The company also provides free drop-off and pickup transportation within a 15-mile radius of Willow.

Places to Stay

Camping The *South Rolly Lake Campground* (106 sites, $10) is a rustic campground with secluded sites. It's so large that you stand a good chance of finding an open site, even on the weekend. Within the campground is a canoe-rental shed if you're interested in an easy paddle on the small lake.

The only other vehicle-accessible campground in the park is *Nancy Lake Campground* (30 sites, $10), just off the George Parks Hwy and just south of the entrance to the parkway. This is not nearly as nice as setting up your tent at South Rolly Lake, though.

Cabins The state recreation area has 12 cabins scattered along the shorelines of four lakes. They can be rented for up to three nights, and most hold six people for $35. Four of the cabins are on Nancy Lake, and three of these can be reached after a short hike from the Nancy Lake Pkwy. Four more cabins are on Red Shirt Lake, but these require a 3-mile hike in and then a short canoe paddle. Tippecanoe Rentals (see Paddling, above) keeps some canoes stashed on

the lake and rents them to cabin users. The other four cabins are on the Lynx Lake canoe route, with three on Lynx Lake and one on James Lake.

The cabins have plywood sleeping platforms, a wood stove and screens on the windows. As you can imagine, they are very popular. Try to reserve them ahead of time through the Alaska Public Lands Information Center (☎ 271-2737) in Anchorage or the Division of Parks & Outdoor Recreation office (☎ 745-3975) in Finger Lakes.

WILLOW

Willow (population 500), at Mile 69 of the George Parks Hwy, is a sleepy little village that became famous in the 1970s as the place selected for the new Alaskan capital that was to be moved from Juneau. The capital-move controversy was put on the back burner in 1982, however, when funding for the immense project was defeated in a general state election.

To many travelers heading north, Willow offers the first overwhelming view of Mt McKinley. If the day is clear, 'the Great One' dominates the Willow skyline. Actually, just about anything would dominate the skyline of this sparse little village.

More Sled Dogs

Willow, like many towns along this stretch, owes it existence to gold and the Alaska Railroad, which came through in the early 1920s to serve the Hatcher Pass mines. Today the town calls itself 'Dog Mushing Capital of the World,' though Wasilla, Tok and a few other communities would surely dispute that. The area does, however, have its share of mushers, and in the 1993 Iditarod, 13 teams from the Willow area competed, with 10 completing the 1100-mile event. Five teams even finished in the top 20 to bring home a piece of the purse.

Several of the kennels offer informal tours. Two of them also offer lodging. The **Susitna Dog Tours B&B** (☎ 495-6324, susdog@ matnet.com), Mile 91.5 of the Parks Hwy, doubles as the dog kennel of Bill Davidson and Rhodi Karella, both Iditarod finishers. Karella was a grandmother when she ran and finished the 1987 race. The rooms are in a new log lodge and cost $55/75, including breakfast and a dog tour.

Lucky Husky Racing Kennel (☎ 495-6470), at Mile 80, has a gift shop and an Iditarod Checkpoint Display. Tour the kennels here for $4, or take a short ride in a basket sled on wheels pulled by one of the teams for $12.50. To experience the dog yard fully, rent one of the cabins that sleep up to four people for $40. But be forewarned: Alaskan huskies are so friendly you might end up bringing one home.

Places to Stay & Eat

Any possible service you need is available at the *Willow Trading Post Lodge* (☎ 495-6457), just off the Parks Hwy across from the train platform. This is a classic Alaskan roadhouse, originally built for the Lucky Shot Mine and moved to Willow in 1945. You can get a shower, a sauna, a shot of whiskey and a beer to chase it down. The food is basic but plentiful, with nightly specials ($10 to $14) that include everything from coffee to dessert. Cabins without bathrooms are $60 for two people, but rooms with bathrooms are also available for $47. The lodge has a liquor store, laundry facilities and just about everything you need to recuperate from a week in the wilderness.

Two miles north of Willow is the junction with Fishhook-Willow Rd, which leads 31.6 miles to Independence Mine State Park, via Hatcher Pass, and eventually to the Glenn Hwy. By driving just 1.3 miles up this road, you'll reach the *Deception Creek State Campground* (17 sites, $10).

To spend a night in a rustic cabin or to try a great piece of homemade pie, stop at the *Sheep Creek Lodge* (☎ 495-6227, jeffnpj@sheepcreeklodge.com), Mile 88 of the Parks Hwy. The lodge has four log cabins, without plumbing, that sleep two for $40. (The outhouse is nearby.) The main lodge contains a restaurant, a lunch counter and a bar.

TALKEETNA

At Mile 98.7 of the George Parks Hwy, a side road heads 14.5 miles north to Talkeetna (population 360), the most interesting and colorful town along the highway. Located near the confluence of the Susitna, Talkeetna and Chulitna Rivers, Talkeetna gets its name from a Tanaina Native word meaning 'river of plenty.'

History

Gold brought miners to the Susitna River in 1896, and by 1901 Talkeetna was a miner's supply center and eventually a riverboat station. But its real growth came in 1915, when Talkeetna was chosen as the headquarters of the Alaska Engineering Commission, which was responsible for building the railroad north to the Tanana River at Nenana. When the railroad was finished in 1923, President Warren G Harding arrived in Alaska and rode the rails to the Nenana River, where he hammered in the golden spike. In Talkeetna, locals swear (with grins on their faces) that he stopped here on the way home, had numerous drinks in the local hotel and wound up dying in San Francisco less than a week later. For a long time, residents of this offbeat little town boasted that President Harding had been poisoned at the Fairview Inn.

Talkeetna's population peaked at 1000 residents before the mining slowed and WWI dramatically decreased its size. In 1964, new life flowed into Talkeetna when a 14-mile spur road connected the town to the George Parks Hwy, drawing the interest of anglers, hunters and others who enjoyed outdoor recreation. But the people most interested in Talkeetna were climbers, who used the town as a staging area for ascents of Mt McKinley and hired its bush pilots for transportation to the mountain.

Talkeetna has managed to retain much of its early Alaskan flavor, thanks to its narrow dirt roads lined with log cabins and clapboard businesses. Main St, the only paved road in the village, begins with a 'Welcome to beautiful downtown Talkeetna' sign at the town park and ends at the banks of the Susitna River. For fans of the *Northern Exposure* TV series, Talkeetna often becomes the mythical Cicely, Alaska, that many tourists seek. As a result, there are almost a dozen gift shops in

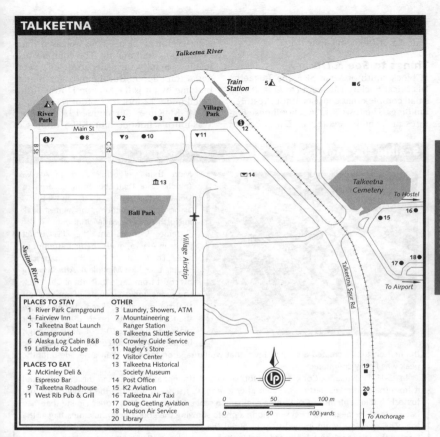

TALKEETNA

PLACES TO STAY
1 River Park Campground
4 Fairview Inn
5 Talkeetna Boat Launch
  Campground
6 Alaska Log Cabin B&B
19 Latitude 62 Lodge

PLACES TO EAT
2 McKinley Deli &
  Espresso Bar
9 Talkeetna Roadhouse
11 West Rib Pub & Grill

OTHER
3 Laundry, Showers, ATM
7 Mountaineering
  Ranger Station
8 Talkeetna Shuttle Service
10 Crowley Guide Service
11 Nagley's Store
12 Visitor Center
13 Talkeetna Historical
   Society Museum
14 Post Office
15 K2 Aviation
16 Talkeetna Air Taxi
17 Doug Geeting Aviation
18 Hudson Air Service
20 Library

this small town. What's even more amazing is that every one of them sells moose-nugget items: nugget earrings, nugget Christmas ornaments, a nugget on a stick called 'Lollipoop' and moose nugget swizzle sticks. Imagine putting that in your drink.

Information

In a small log cabin at the junction of the George Parks Hwy and Talkeetna Spur Rd is a gift shop that doubles as the Talkeetna-Denali Visitor Center (☎ 800-660-2688, 733-2688). In town, the best place for information is the Talkeetna Historical Society Museum (☎ 733-2487).

There are no banks in town, but there is an ATM at Three Rivers Tesoro (☎ 733-2620), on Main St.

The post office is just off Talkeetna Spur Rd as you enter town.

The Talkeetna library is on Talkeetna Spur Rd just south of town. It's open Tuesday to Saturday.

A Laundromat and public showers are available in the Three Rivers Tesoro on Main St.

For medical services, the Sunshine Community Health Center (☎ 733-2273) is at Mile 4.5 of Talkeetna Spur Rd.

Things to See & Do

A block south of Main St is the **Talkeetna Historical Society Museum** (☎ 733-2487), a small complex that consists of four restored buildings. The town's 1936 schoolhouse features an exhibit devoted to Don Sheldon (the bush pilot who pioneered landing climbers high on Mt McKinley's glaciers for a better shot at the peak), as well as artifacts on trapping and mining. The complex also includes a fully furnished trapper's cabin and a train depot. But the most fascinating building by far is the Section House. Inside you'll find a 12-foot by 12-foot relief model of Mt McKinley surrounded by Bradford Washburn's famous mural-like photos of

Scaling the Mountain

More than any other place in Alaska (much more than the entrance area of Denali National Park itself), Talkeetna is associated with climbing the highest peak in North America, Mt McKinley.

James Wickersham, the US District judge in Alaska, made the first attempt to scale 'The Great One' (as the Athabascan people called Mt McKinley). After moving his court from Eagle to Fairbanks in 1903, the judge took a couple of months off that summer and trekked overland more than 100 miles to reach the 7500-foot mark of the 20,320-foot peak. Though his party was unsuccessful in its bid to be the first on top, it created a summit fever that would rage on for more than a decade until the peak was finally conquered.

In 1906, Dr Frederick Cook returned for his second attempt at the peak and this time attacked it from the south. His party disbanded after a month of slogging through the heavy brush and tussock, but in September, Cook and a companion sent a telegram to New York claiming that they had reached the peak and even sent along a photo showing the good doctor holding a flag at the top. The climbing world immediately disputed the claim, and four years later Belmore Brown located the false peak and duplicated Cook's photo. Not only was the 8000-foot peak a lot shorter than Mt McKinley, but it was also more than 20 miles from the true summit. Despite all the evidence, the controversy over Cook continued right into the 1970s, when his daughter wrote to Ray Genet for his opinion on the 1906 feat and photo. Both the letter and Genet's reply are now on display at the Talkeetna Historical Society Museum.

The next serious attempt came in 1910, when four Fairbanks miners decided that Alaskans, not Outsiders, should be the first to conquer the peak. Dubbed the Sourdough Expedition, the group headed straight for the peak visible from Fairbanks. Remarkably, they climbed the final 11,000 feet and returned to their base camp in 18 hours. Even more remarkably, they carried only a thermos of hot chocolate, a bag of donuts and a 14-foot spruce pole. Imagine their shock when they reached the top of the North Peak only to realize that it was 850 feet lower than the South Peak and, thus, not the true summit.

the mountain – impressive. An exhibit devoted to the town's best-known climber, Ray 'the Pirate' Genet, is also on display.

The museum is open 10:30 am to 5:30 pm daily during the summer; admission is $2. You can also pick up a map of the town's historical walking tour here. The walk weaves you through Talkeetna, past 16 historical buildings, each featuring a plaque relating the history and stories behind the structure.

The new **Mountaineering Ranger Station** (☎ 733-2231), at the corner of 1st and B Sts, is an impressive log-and-stone building constructed in 1997. In addition to coordinating the numerous expeditions to Mt McKinley during the summer, the ranger station serves as a visitor center. Inside is a large reading room with mountain photographs, climbing club flags from around the world and signed ice axes from successful climbs. For those

Scaling the Mountain

Success finally came in 1913 when an expedition made up of Hudson Stuck, Henry Karstens, Robert Tatum and Walter Harper reached the top on June 7. The foursome would have made it in May, but they spent three weeks hewing a 3-mile staircase through a mass of jumbled ice caused by the 1912 volcanic eruption and earthquakes at Katmai 300 miles away. When they reached the top, they saw the spruce pole on the North Peak to verify the claims of the Sourdough Expedition.

The most important date to many climbers, however, is 1951. That year, Bradford Washburn, the director of the Boston Museum of Science, arrived and pioneered the West Buttress route, by far the preferred avenue to the top. Not long after that, Talkeetna's two most famous characters – Ray 'the Pirate' Genet and Don Sheldon – began to have an impact on the climbing world. Genet was an Alaskan mountain climber who made a record 25 climbs to the summit of Mt McKinley, including the first successful winter ascent. Sheldon was a bush pilot who pioneered many of the routes used to carry climbers to Mt McKinley today.

The two men worked closely together in guiding climbers to the top and, more importantly, rescuing those who failed. Their rescue attempts are legendary, and you can read about some of them in the Talkeetna Historical Society Museum. Sadly, the town unexpectedly lost both men within four years. Sheldon, the most famous of all Alaskan bush pilots, died of cancer in 1975 at age 56. Genet died at age 48 in Nepal. After reaching Mt Everest, the highest peak in the world, Genet froze to death in his sleeping bag on the descent and is still entombed on the side of that mountain today.

The colorful legends of both these men add considerably to the mountaineering atmosphere that is felt, seen and heard in Talkeetna every summer, especially during the climbing season of May and June. More than 80% of the climbers use the West Buttress route, which means flying in ski planes from Talkeetna's airstrip to a base camp on the Kahiltna Glacier. From here, at 7200 feet, they begin climbing for the South Peak, passing a medical/rescue camp maintained by mountaineering clubs and the National Park Service at 14,220 feet.

Between 1000 and 1300 climbers attempt the peak each year, spending an average of three weeks on the mountain. Expeditions carry roughly 120lb of food and gear per person for the ascent. Ironically, due to the multiple trips required to shuttle gear to higher camps, successful climbers actually climb the mountain twice.

In a good season, when storms are not constantly sweeping across the range, more than 50% of those attempting the summit will be successful, including some unlikely climbers. In 1995, for example, a 12-year-old Anchorage girl became the youngest person to scale the mountain. In a bad year, though, less than 40% of the attempts meet with success, and several people die. In 1992, the mountain claimed 11 lives, including an 18-year-old climber.

thinking of scaling the peak, the station also has an extensive mountaineering library and a special video program. It's open 8 am to 6 pm daily. At 7 pm on Wednesday and Saturday, you can see an interesting slide presentation on how the park service rescues climbers in trouble.

For a greater sense of adventure, go to the main airport, just down Talkeetna Spur Rd in East Talkeetna. During May and June, several charter operators with wheel-and-ski planes fly the climbers up to the 7000-foot level.

Perhaps the most solemn way to appreciate the effect of the mountain on this town, and to understand how the residents grieve when climbers are lost, is to visit the **Talkeetna Cemetery**, just off Talkeetna Spur Rd near the airport. Don Sheldon's grave is the most impressive, with a mounted ice axe and the epitaph 'He wagered with the wind and won.' The Mt McKinley Climber's Memorial includes a stone for Genet despite the fact that his body was never removed from the slopes of Mt Everest. The most touching sight, however, is a bulletin board that lists the names and ages of all the climbers who have died on Mt McKinley over the years. Some were as young as 18.

The town also has two privately owned museums, both attached to gift shops. The **Museum of the Northern Adventure** (☎ 733-3999), right on Main St, consists of 24 large dioramas dramatizing historical events on two floors. It's a little cheesy, but admission is only $2. It's open 10 am to 6 pm daily.

Even more interesting is the **Fairview Inn**, on Main St. It's not an official museum, but it might as well be. The hotel was built in 1923 to serve as the overnight stop between Seward and Fairbanks on the newly constructed Alaska Railroad. When it opened, it boasted Talkeetna's first bathtub (there are several now), and patrons had to ask the bartender for a towel. Unfortunately, Anchorage, not Seward, was chosen as the start of the northerly trip, so Curry, not Talkeetna, was the halfway point and overnight stop. Still, the hotel survived and today is listed on the National Register of Historic Places.

And it should be. The bar on the 1st floor is classic Alaska, with walls covered in memorabilia. (Deadman's Wall features pictures of those who have fallen victim to the mountain.) The place also contains Talkeetna's only slot machine, a corner devoted to President Harding and the ad in which Ray Genet is promoting 'Hot Tang.' Most interesting, perhaps, is a photo labeled 'The Women of Talkeetna,' which appeared in a 1985 issue of *Playboy* magazine. The story behind it is hilarious. The only way to enjoy the inn is to belly up to the bar, order a schooner of beer and take in the decor.

Nagley's Store, across the street, is another of Talkeetna's gems. Built in 1921 and listed on the National Register of Historic Places, Nagley's is an old-time store with artifacts on the walls. Stop in just to see the bear trap, large enough to catch a 800-pound grizzly if the device was still legal. If you're looking for Cicely, Alaska, of *Northern Exposure* fame, tune your radio in to KTNA (88.5 FM). Located on 2nd St, the **public radio station** is a two-room log cabin dwarfed by a satellite dish.

Bicycling

Crowley Guide Service (☎ 733-1279), on Main St, rents mountain bikes ($10 for a half day, $15 for a full day). You can rent one for several days and then hop on the train to Denali National Park and explore the park road by pedaling.

Special Events

Talkeetna's love of moose scat can be traced back to 1974, when the town first began holding its annual Moose Dropping Festival on the second weekend of July. The three-day event has the usual festivities: a parade, live entertainment and a beer tent they call a 'Tee Pee.' And then there are bizarre things you will only find in Talkeetna: a Moose Dropping Toss Game (or 'how far can you throw a moose turd?'), an opportunity to kiss a moose and the Mountain Mother Contest, in which single women compete in various skills – wood chopping, water hauling, fire building, etc – in front of a panel of eligible bachelors. If you're in the area, you should make every effort to attend. But beware – more than 8000 people now pack Talkeetna during the event.

The town's other noted event is the Talkeetna Bluegrass Festival, which began in 1982. The four-day event takes place in early August and has grown so large that it's been moved to 142 acres of forested land at Mile 102 of the George Parks Hwy. Admission is $25 whether you stay one day or all four.

Organized Tours

With Mt McKinley in Talkeetna's backyard, scenic flights have become a staple for the handful of local air-service companies. All summer, they offer scenic flights of the mountain and the Alaska Range, and on a clear day it's the best bargain in this expensive state. At times, it's even possible to see climbing parties en route to the summit.

Comparison shop, but plan on spending $80 to $150 for a flight, depending on whether you want to land on a glacier. And if it's a clear day, plan on waiting in line. The handful of operators include K2 Aviation (☎ 733-2291, 800-764-2291), Hudson Air Service (☎ 733-2321) and Doug Geeting Aviation (☎ 733-2366, 800-770-2366). Talkeetna Air Taxi (☎ 733-2218, 800-533-2219) offers the usual flights that range from $90 to $140 per person but will also add a glacier landing for an additional $35 per person.

Places to Stay

There are numerous hotels, roadhouses, B&Bs and now even a hostel in Talkeetna along with two public campgrounds. At *River Park Campground*, at the end of Main St, sites cost $8. *Talkeetna Boat Launch Campground*, east of the tracks at the end of F St, is much nicer, with sites near the Talkeetna River, covered tables and lots of privacy. Talkeetna River Guides (☎ 733-2677) manages the facility, where sites cost $12.

The new *Talkeetna Hostel International* (☎ 733-4678, heather@akhostel.com), I St, provides affordable lodging and a reason to linger longer here. The hostel, a 10-minute walk from Main St, has a kitchen, laundry, showers, free coffee in the morning and sled dogs in the backyard (usually, there's a dog in the house, too). The 14 beds cost $22, and a private double room costs $40. To reach the hostel, follow the Talkeetna Spur Road toward downtown, but take the turn for the airport. You'll pass I St on the way to the runway at the end of the road.

How about renting a log cabin? Hey, why not, this is Alaska. Call *Zeroth's Cabin Rental* (☎ 800-660-2688, 733-2499, talkaero@alaska.net) for an isolated cabin on Gold Creek in a mountainous setting north of Talkeetna. To get there, take the Alaska Railroad flag stop train. The cabin holds up to five people for $90.

For a log-cabin experience in town, try *Alaska Log Cabin B&B* (☎ 733-2584), a private cabin close to the Talkeetna River, or *Trapper John's B&B* (☎ 733-2353, 800-735-2354 in Alaska, trapperj@alaska.net), a 1920s cabin and outhouse at the south end of the Village Airstrip. A double is $85.

Also in town, the *Fairview Inn* (☎ 733-2423), Main St, has seven rooms with a shared bathroom for $53/63. Remember that on the weekends the band in the bar just below you plays until 2:30 am. The *Talkeetna Roadhouse* (☎ 733-1351, rdhouse@alaska.net), Main St, has equally small rooms with shared bathrooms for $48/63 and a bunkroom with four single beds for $21. Of the handful of motels in town, try the *Latitude 62 Lodge* ((☎ 733-2262), Mile 13.5 of Talkeetna Spur Rd, where singles/doubles with private bathrooms cost $63/73. If money is no option, stay at the luxurious *Talkeetna Lodge* (☎ 877-258-6877, 265-4500), Mile 12.5 of Talkeetna Spur Rd, which opened up in 1999. Its 99 rooms begin at $169/179.

Places to Eat

The best place for a hearty meal is the *Talkeetna Roadhouse*, Main St, where the Red House special (eggs, toast, potatoes and sausage, fresh fruit and so on) fills up climbers and other hungry folks for $8. The restaurant also doubles as a bakery, cooking up giant cinnamon rolls in the morning.

At the back of Nagley's Store is *West Rib Pub & Grill*, Main St, a good place to kick back and enjoy a draft of Alaskan beer and hamburger and fries ($6). If the sun is shining, you can sit outside. The *Fairview Inn*, Main St, erects a beer garden tent that doubles as a salmon bake and barbecue site in the summer. Steak, salmon or halibut costs $17; a half-chicken is $14. For cheap eats, there's *McKinley Deli & Espresso Bar*, where sandwiches cost $6, subs $7 and a medium pizza with one item costs $13.

Getting There & Away

Bus Any of the Denali van services (see Getting There & Away in the Anchorage chapter) will drop you off at Talkeetna Junction; Parks Highway Express (☎ 888-600-6001) is the cheapest, with a $25 one-way ticket. The problem is you're still 14 miles from town. For a little more, you can hop on the Talkeetna Shuttle Service van (☎ 888-288-6008), which departs Anchorage at 8 am daily and Talkeetna from its office on Main St at 5 pm for the return trip. One-way fare is $40.

Train The Alaska Railroad's express train stops daily in Talkeetna from late May to mid-September on both its northbound and southbound runs between Anchorage and Fairbanks. The northbound train from Anchorage, heading for Denali National Park, arrives at 11:25 am; the southbound train arrives at 4:40 pm and reaches Anchorage at 8:15 pm. The one-way fare from Anchorage is $60.

The *Hurricane*, made up of self-propelled rail diesel cars, provides local rural service on Thursday through Sunday during the summer. This flag stop train (see the boxed text 'Flagging A Train' in the Getting Around chapter) departs Talkeetna for a one-day trip to Hurricane Gulch, where it turns around and heads back. This 'milk run' takes you within view of Mt McKinley and into some remote areas and allows you to mingle with more local residents than you would on the express train. From May to October, the train departs Talkeetna at 12:15 pm, reaches Hurricane Gulch at 2:15 pm and then turns around and arrives back at Talkeetna at 5:45 pm. The one-way fare to Hurricane Gulch is $20.

DENALI STATE PARK

This 324,240-acre reserve, the fourth-largest state park in Alaska and roughly half the size of Rhode Island, begins when you cross the southern boundary at Mile 132.2 of the George Parks Hwy. The park covers the transition zone between the coastal region and the spine of the Alaska Range and provides numerous views of towering peaks, including Mt McKinley and the glaciers on its southern slopes. On a clear day, some say the panorama of Mt McKinley is the most spectacular view in North America. The park is largely undeveloped but does offer a handful of turnoffs, trails, two rental cabins and three campgrounds that can be reached from the George Parks Hwy, which runs through the park.

It may share the same name and a border with the renowned national park to the north, but Denali State Park is an entirely different experience. Because of its lack of facilities, you need to be better prepared for your hiking and backpacking adventures. But this may be the park's blessing, for this preserve also lacks the crowds, long waits and tight regulations that curse Denali National Park to the north. At the height of the summer season, experienced backpackers may want to consider the state park as a hassle-free and cheaper alternative to the national park.

South Denali Viewpoint

You'll reach this viewpoint less than 3 miles from the southern boundary of the park, at Mile 135.2 of the George Parks Hwy. Displays at the paved lookout point out Ruth Glacier, less than 5 miles to the northwest, as well as Mt McKinley, Mt Hunter, Moose Tooth and several other glaciers.

Two miles north of the viewpoint is the Lower Troublesome Creek State Recreation Site. Along with a campground, the recreation site features a day-use area with picnic shelters and a half-mile trail to the Chulitna River. The trail parallels the lower end of Troublesome Creek, where you can fish for rainbow trout, grayling and salmon.

Hiking

There are several trails and alpine routes in the park, and interested hikers should stop at the Alaska Veterans Memorial, Mile 147 of the Parks Hwy just north of Byers Lake Campground. Within the day-use area is a new state park visitor center that has free handouts, sells topographic maps and provides bear-resistant food containers at no cost. The center will also have information on Troublesome Creek Trail, which is usually closed from July to September due to high bear activity. It's open 9 am to 6 pm daily during the summer. Also keep in mind that no fires are allowed in the backcountry so you must pack a stove if you plan to camp overnight.

Troublesome Creek Trail The trailhead is posted in a parking area at Mile 137.6 of the George Parks Hwy. The trail ascends along the creek until it reaches the tree line, where you enter an open area dotted with alpine lakes and surrounded by mountain views. From here, the route is marked only by rock cairns as it heads north to Byers Lake.

Byers Lake Campground is a 15-mile backpacking trip of moderate difficulty, but if you're more adventurous, you can continue on to Little Coal Creek Trail, a 36-mile trek above the tree line. The views from the ridges are spectacular. Numerous black bears feeding on salmon gave the creek its name. Because of them, the trail is usually closed to hikers in July and August.

Byers Lake Trail This easy 4.8-mile trek around the lake begins at the Byers Lake Campground and passes six hike-in campsites on the other side of the lake. These are 1.8 miles from the posted trailhead.

Kesugi Ridge Traverse This route departs from the Byers Lake Trail and ascends its namesake ridge as a trail. Once on the ridge, you follow a route north to Little Coal Creek Trail at the north end of the park. Little Coal Creek Trail leads back to the George Parks Hwy. The 27.4-mile route is well marked with cairns and flags.

If you are contemplating this trek, remember that it is far easier for hikers to access the ridge along Little Coal Creek Trail than it is to hike from Byers Lake Trail, which is a much steeper climb.

Little Coal Creek Trail At Mile 163.9 of the George Parks Hwy, you'll arrive at a trailhead and parking area for Little Coal Creek Trail, which ascends to the alpine areas of Kesugi Ridge. From there, you continue to the summit of Indian Mountain, an elevation gain of about 3300 feet, or continue along the ridge to either Byers Lake or Troublesome Creek. Within 3 miles, Little Coal Creek Trail climbs above the tree line at a spot known as the North Fork Birdhouse, a great place to set up an alpine camp for the night. It's a 9-mile roundtrip trek to Indian Peak and 27.4 miles to Byers Lake.

Places to Stay

Lower Troublesome Creek State Recreation Site, Mile 137.3 of the George Parks Hwy, has 10 sites for $6, and *Byers Lake State Campground*, Mile 147 of the George Parks Hwy, has 66 sites for $12. Byers Lake Campground also offers access to walk-in sites along the loop trail around the lake and to two state-park rental cabins. You can drive to one; the other is a 0.3-mile hike away. Both are $35 a night and must be reserved in advance through the Department of Natural Resources Public Information Center (☎ 269-8400) in Anchorage or the state park office in Wasilla (☎ 745-3975).

At Mile 162.7 of the Parks Hwy is *Denali View North Campground*, with 20 sites for $10. With the exception of some charming walk-in sites, the campground is basically a parking lot, but the views are stunning. You overlook the Chulitna River while Mt McKinley overwhelms you from above. Interpretive displays and a spotting scope help you enjoy the panorama.

At Mile 156 is the *Chulitna River Lodge (also known as Wolf Pack Lodge;* ☎ 242-5060), the only facility within the park. The lodge has a small cafe, gas, limited supplies and log cabins for $50 to $80.

BROAD PASS TO DENALI NATIONAL PARK

The northern boundary of the Denali State Park is at Mile 168.5 of the George Parks Hwy, and 9 miles beyond that is the bridge over Honolulu Creek, where the road begins a gradual ascent to Broad Pass. Within 18 miles of the creek, you start to see the pass, but you don't actually reach it until Mile 203.6, where there is a paved parking area.

Broad Pass (elevation 2300 feet) is a dividing line; rivers to the south of the pass drain into Cook Inlet, and those rivers to the north empty into the Yukon River. The area is right at the tree line and worth stopping at for some hiking. The mountain valley, surrounded by tall white peaks, is unquestionably one of the most beautiful spots along the George Parks Hwy or the Alaska Railroad, as both use the low gap to cross the Alaska Range.

From the pass, the George Parks Hwy begins a descent and after 6.3 miles comes to the Cantwell post office just before Mile 210, at the junction with the Denali Hwy. Originally built along the Alaska Railroad line (2 miles west on the Denali Hwy), **Cantwell** (population 160) later spread to the Parks Hwy, which attracted most of the commercial district in the early 1970s. On the highway today, you'll find gas pumps, small grocery stores and accommodations, including *Lazy J Cabins & Cafe* (☎ 768-2414), which has small cabins ($70), a restaurant and a friendly bar.

At Mile 234 on the east side of the highway, another scenic spot offers fine views of **Mt Fellows**, which has an elevation of 4476 feet. The mountain is often photographed because of the constantly changing shadows on its sides. The peak is especially beautiful at sunset.

The entrance to Denali National Park and Preserve is at Mile 237.3 of the Parks Hwy, and just inside the park are two campgrounds. The next public campground is in Fairbanks. The highway before and after the park entrance has become a tourist strip of private campgrounds, lodges, restaurants and other businesses, all feeding off Alaska's most famous drawing card.

DENALI NATIONAL PARK

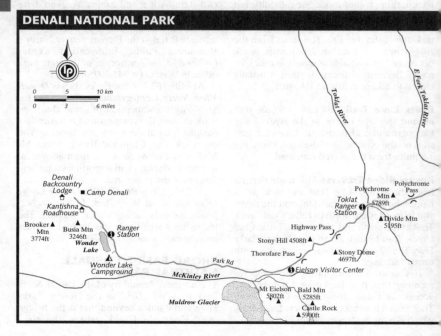

Denali National Park

Call it the Dilemma in Denali: 'We love the wilderness and its wildlife so much we were overrunning Alaska's best known attraction,' according to a park ranger. So in 1995, with the park attracting more than 300,000 visitors during the summer, the National Park Service instituted the most sweeping change in the history of its management of the wilderness by allowing a concessionaire to implement fees for the shuttle buses, along with a reservation system for seats on the buses and sites in the campgrounds.

These and Denali's carefully imposed barriers (including backcountry zones) have reduced, but probably will never eliminate, the lines at the visitor center, the crowds at the entrance area and the bizarre atmosphere of people hustling around just for an opportunity to get away from it all. Backcountry

bus fees now range as high as $31, while reserved seats take up 65% of the buses.

If you can make reservations or arrive late n the summer or summon the patience to wait for permits and bus seats on a first-come-first-served basis, Denali National Park is still the great wilderness that awed so many of us 10 or 20 years ago. The entrance has changed, but the park itself hasn't, and a brown bear meandering on a tundra ridge still provides the same quiet thrill as it did when the Denali first opened in 1917.

History

Although generations of Athabascans had wandered through the area that the national park now encompasses, they never set up permanent settlements. This changed in 1905, when gold was discovered and a miners' rush gave birth to the town of Kantishna. A year later, naturalist and noted hunter Charles Sheldon was stunned by the beauty of the land and horrified at the reckless abandon of

THE INTERIOR

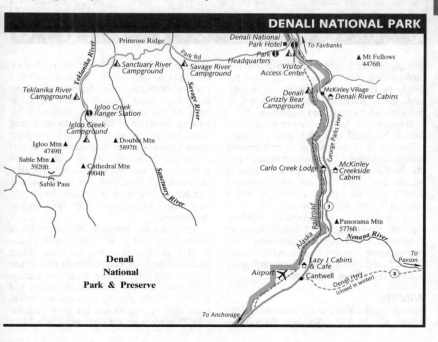

DENALI NATIONAL PARK

THE INTERIOR

Changes at Denali National Park

In 1997, the National Park Service released its Entrance Area and Road Corridor Development Concept Plan for Denali National Park & Preserve, and by the end of the century it had already begun implementing some of the recommendations. But many more changes are scheduled to take place in the near future.

The most significant one will be the closing of the Denali National Park Hotel. By 2002, a portion of the hotel will become an Environmental Education and Science Center, and the rest will turn into staff housing. After that, no accommodations other than campsites will be available inside the national park.

The plan calls for expanding the existing Visitor Access Center into an interpretive center and building a new VAC and parking lot nearby. Other changes include an additional 50 campsites at Riley Creek, new campgrounds in the Nenana River corridor and the Kantishna area, a bicycle permit system for the park road and permanent rest areas and interpretive facilities at Savage and Toklat Rivers. Eventually the park plans to develop a southern Denali entrance, which will include a visitor center and a campground.

One change that has already taken place is the construction of additional trails. As far as backpackers are concerned, Denali will remain a 'trail-less park,' but there are now a growing number of footpaths designed for the casual day hiker. The park is building interpretive loops of a mile or less at the Primrose turnoff; the Savage, Toklat and Teklanika rest areas; and the Eielson Visitor Center.

There will also be several trails near Wonder Lake Campground. The main one, McKinley Bar Trail, has already been relocated and upgraded. This 2-mile trail descends from the campground access road and heads south to the McKinley River flats. Plan on a half day for the roundtrip hike on the McKinley Bar Trail.

the miners and others who hunted the caribou and other big game. Sheldon returned in 1907 and traveled the area with guide Harry Karstens in an effort to set up boundaries for a proposed national park.

Sheldon then launched a campaign for a Denali National Park, but politics being politics and Ohio having a particularly strong delegation of senators, it emerged as Mt McKinley National Park. Karstens became the park's first superintendent, and in 1923, when the railroad arrived, 36 visitors enjoyed the splendor of Denali.

As a result of the 1980 Alaska Lands Bill, the park was enlarged by 4 million acres, redesignated and renamed. Denali now comprises an area slightly larger than the state of Massachusetts, and is generally ranked as one of Alaska's top attractions.

Wildlife

Situated on the north and south flanks of the Alaska Range, 237 miles from Anchorage

and about half that distance from Fairbanks, Denali is the nation's first subarctic national park, a wilderness that can be enjoyed by those who never sleep in a tent. Within it roam 37 species of mammals, ranging from lynx, marmots and Dall sheep to foxes and snowshoe hares, while 130 different bird species have been spotted, including the impressive golden eagle. Most visitors, however, want to see four animals in particular: the moose, caribou, wolf and brown bear. If you see all four from the shuttle bus, you'll have scored a rare 'grand slam,' according to the drivers.

There are an estimated 200 brown bears in the park and another 200 black bears, most of them west of Wonder Lake. When you're on one bus, you're almost sure to see everybody's favorite: the brown, or grizzly, bear. Since Denali's streams are mostly fed by glaciers, the fishing is poor, and bears must rely on vegetation for 85% of their diet. This accounts for their small size. Most males range from only 300 to 600lb while their cousins on the salmon-rich coasts can easily top 1000lb.

All the caribou in the park belong to the Denali herd, one of 13 herds in Alaska, which fluctuates in size between 2500 and 3000 animals. Since the park has been enlarged, the entire range of the herd, from its calving grounds to its wintering site, is now in Denali. The best time to spot caribou is often late in the summer, when the animals begin to band into groups of six to a dozen in anticipation of the fall migration. Caribou are easy to spot, as the racks of a bull often stand 4 feet high and appear to be out of proportion with the rest of his body.

Most visitors will sight their moose on the east half of the park road, especially along the first 15 miles. Moose are almost always found in stands of spruce and willow shrubs (their favorite food), and often you have a better chance of seeing a moose while you're hiking Horseshoe Lake Trail than you do in the tundra area around Eielson Visitor Center. Roughly 1500 moose roam the north side of the Alaska Range, and the most spectacular scene in Denali comes in early September, when the bulls begin to clash their immense racks over breeding rights to a cow.

The wolf is the most difficult of the 'grand slam' four to see in the park. There is a stable population of 150 wolves, and during much of the summer, when small game is plentiful, the packs often break down and wolves become solitary hunters. Then, visitors stand a chance of seeing a lone wolf crossing the park road.

Because hunting has never been allowed in the park, professional photographers refer to animals in Denali as 'approachable wildlife.' That doesn't mean you can actually approach them, though every year visitors and photographers alike try to do so in an effort to get that photo-of-a-lifetime. It means bears, moose, Dall sheep and caribou are not nearly as skittish as in other regions of the state and tend to continue their natural activities despite the sight of 40 heads with camera lenses hanging out of a bus 70 yards away on the park road. Both the animals' obliviousness and the park road,

which was built to maximize the chances of seeing wildlife by traversing high open ground, makes the national park an excellent place to view a variety of animals.

Mt McKinley

Despite the excellent wildlife-watching opportunities, the park's main attraction is still Mt McKinley – an overwhelming sight if you catch it on a clear day. At 20,316 feet, the peak of this massif is almost 4 miles high, but what makes it stunning is that it rises from an elevation of 2000 feet. What you see from the park road is 18,000 feet (more than 3 miles) of rock, snow and glaciers reaching for the sky. In contrast, Mt Everest, the highest mountain in the world at 29,028 feet, only rises 11,000 feet from the Tibetan Plateau.

When to Visit

Combine the park's easy viewing of wildlife and the grandeur of Mt McKinley with its wilderness reputation throughout the world, and suddenly the crowds start to make sense. From late June to late August, Denali National Park is a busy and popular place, despite the often cool weather, which includes long periods of overcast conditions and drizzle during the summer. Nonetheless, Riley Creek Campground overflows with camper vans, nearby Morino Campground attracts crowds of backpackers and the park's hotel bustles with large tour groups. At the height of the season, the pursuit of shuttle-bus seats, backcountry permits and campground reservations at the Visitor Access Center can involve Disney-World-like lines.

The crowds disappear once you are hiking in the backcountry and are not a factor in early June or in September. September can be particularly pleasant, for not only are the crowds thinning out but so are the bugs. This is also when the foliage changes color, and valleys go from a dull green to a fiery red while the willows turn shades of yellow and gold. Getting a campground site or backcountry permit then is not the agonizing challenge it is in July. The problem is that the shuttle buses (your ticket into the backcountry) stop running around September 10 to 14. A four-day vehicle lottery follows, as 400 private cars a day are allowed into the park, and then the road closes to all traffic until next May. By late September, the snow has usually arrived for the winter, and another backpacking season comes to an end.

Whenever you go, it's best to arrive at the park with extra days. If all you want to do is camp at the entrance and take the shuttle bus out along the road one day at the height of the tourist season, you'll need a minimum of four days to ensure that you get a seat on the bus. If you want to spend three days backpacking or stay in the interior campgrounds, set aside a week to 10 days.

Throughout much of the summer, there's no getting around long waits. Without advance reservations for campsites, you'll waste one day alone on the outside of the park waiting to get into the Riley Creek area. Another two days may go by while you wait for a campground or backcountry area to become available.

In the end, however, if you are patient and follow the system, you will get into the backcountry, and then, thanks to the rules and permit limits you were cussing just a day before, you'll enjoy a quality wilderness experience.

Information

Reservations & Fees If you can plan the exact days you'll be in the park, booking bus seats and campsites in advance saves an awful lot of hassle. The system worked so well the first year, when reservations claimed a third of the bus seats and sites, that in 1999 the park management allowed advance bookings to claim 65% of what was available. To arrange a reservation, call Denali National Park Reservation Service (☎ 272-7275, 800-622-7275 in the USA). You can also print out the reservations form from the Denali National Park website (www.nps.gov/dena) and send it in by fax (☎ 907-264-4684), but you need to have a credit card. For the buses, you can make reservations by phone beginning in late February (for the same year) or by fax beginning in December.

As of 1999, all of the sites in Riley Creek, Savage River, Teklanika and Wonder Lake Campgrounds can be reserved in advance, but sites in Sanctuary River and Igloo Creek Campgrounds are available only on a walk-in basis at the Visitor Access Center (see Tourist Offices, below). For the campgrounds, you pay a one-time $4 reservation fee.

There is also an admission fee, though it should hardly stop anybody from visiting the park. A $5-per-person or $10-per-family fee is charged to all visitors traveling beyond the checkpoint at Savage River Campground. The fee is good for seven days in the park and is collected when you obtain a shuttle bus ticket at the Visitor Access Center. This is only an entrance fee, and you still have to pay to stay in the campgrounds.

Tourist Offices The Visitor Access Center, or VAC for short, near the entrance of the park is the place to organize your trip and to pick up permits and coupons as well as purchase topographic maps and books. The center is open 7 am to 8 pm daily during the summer, and sometimes lines begin forming outside before the doors are even unlocked. At the height of the summer, there is something of a stampede at 7 am, since only 35% of the shuttle bus seats and campsites are available, while backcountry permits are only handed out one day in advance. That's why you can't arrive at the park at midday and plan your stay. It's almost imperative you be at the VAC early in the morning to be able to book anything at all.

Within the VAC you'll find a bookstore; staff counters for backcountry permits, shuttle buses and campsites; a video theater with shows 10 and 40 minutes after the hour; and rest rooms. You can also go to an area with information on other parks in Alaska in case the Denali hassle is too much for you. Outside, an information board lists all park activities, and you can stow your stuff in storage lockers that are big enough to handle a backpack. (Competition for the lockers is fierce, and if you lose out, you might try storing your luggage at the Denali National Park Hotel, though it's supposed to be for guests only.)

The VAC offers a variety of programs during the summer, all of them free. One of

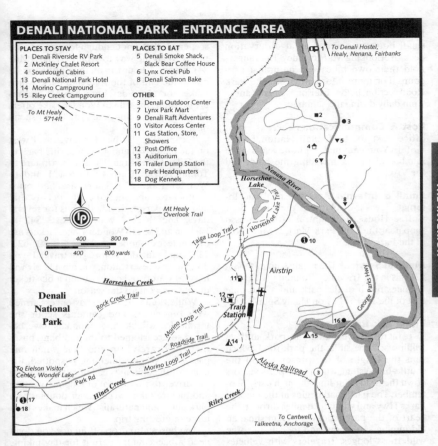

DENALI NATIONAL PARK - ENTRANCE AREA

PLACES TO STAY
1 Denali Riverside RV Park
2 McKinley Chalet Resort
4 Sourdough Cabins
13 Denali National Park Hotel
14 Morino Campground
15 Riley Creek Campground

PLACES TO EAT
5 Denali Smoke Shack,
Black Bear Coffee House
6 Lynx Creek Pub
8 Denali Salmon Bake

OTHER
3 Denali Outdoor Center
7 Lynx Park Mart
9 Denali Raft Adventures
10 Visitor Access Center
11 Gas Station, Store, Showers
12 Post Office
13 Auditorium
16 Trailer Dump Station
17 Park Headquarters
18 Dog Kennels

To Denali Hostel, Healy, Nenana, Fairbanks

To Mt Healy 5714ft

THE INTERIOR

Mt Healy Overlook Trail

Horseshoe Lake

Nenana River

Taiga Loop Trail

Horseshoe Lake Trail

0   400   800 m
0   400   800 yards

Airstrip

Horseshoe Creek

Denali National Park

Rock Creek Trail

Morino Loop Trail

Train Station

Roadside Trail

Morino Loop Trail

To Eielson Visitor Center, Wonder Lake

Park Rd

Hines Creek

George Parks Hwy

Alaska Railroad

Riley Creek

To Cantwell, Talkeetna, Anchorage

---

the most popular is the sled-dog demonstration. Denali is the only national park that keeps the sled dogs for winter maintenance, and during the summer dog handlers hold demonstrations at 10 am and 2 and 4 pm daily at the kennels, 3.5 miles west of the park entrance on the park road. A free bus leaves the VAC half an hour before each demonstration and departs from the Denali National Park Hotel 20 minutes before the show.

The VAC also offers daily nature walks and longer hikes throughout the park (see Hiking, below) while the auditorium behind the park hotel features slide or film programs at 1:30 and 8 pm daily. These cover the history, wildlife or mountaineering aspects of the park. Every night at 8 pm, campfire programs take place at Riley Creek, Savage River and Teklanika River Campgrounds; these are open to anybody.

For information in advance of arriving, call the VAC (☎ 683-2294, 683-1266 in the summer), check the park's excellent website (www.nps.gov/dena) or stop in at one of the Alaska Public Lands Information Centers in Anchorage, Tok or Fairbanks (see those individual sections of this book).

Eielson Visitor Center, a smaller center at Mile 66 of the park road, features displays, a small bookstore and a great observation deck overlooking Mt McKinley. The rangers hold their own hikes and naturalist programs. For more information, see the Park Road section, below. Eielson is open 9 am to 7 pm daily during the summer.

Post & Communications There is a post office next to the Denali National Park Hotel. You can make phone calls at a number of places, including the hotel and the VAC.

Email & Internet Access Email and Internet access is available at the Black Bear Coffee House, a delightful little espresso shop near the Lynx Park Mart, at Mile 238.5 of the Parks Hwy.

Medical Services The Healy Clinic (☎ 683-2211) is in the Tri-Valley Community Center, 13 miles north of the park and a half mile east of the Parks Hwy on Healy Spur Rd.

The Park Road

Two factors have made the park and its wildlife so accessible: the park road, which runs the length of the preserve, and the shuttle-bus system, which transports visitors down the road from June through early September. The park road begins at the George Parks Hwy and winds 91.6 miles through the heart of the park, ending at Kantishna, an old mining settlement and the site of three wilderness lodges. Travelers with vehicles can only drive to a parking area along the Savage River at Mile 14, a mile beyond the Savage River Campground, unless they have a special permit that's nearly impossible to obtain.

Park officials banned private vehicles to prevent the park road from becoming a highway of cars and RVs. The shuttle-bus service began in 1972, after the George Parks Hwy opened and attendance in the park doubled in a single season. In 1995, 25 buses were added, and buses now leave the VAC for Eielson Visitor Center (at Mile 66) every half hour from 6:30 am until 2 pm. The ride to Eielson and back is an eight-hour journey that passes spectacular mountain scenery. If that's not enough for you, several buses go all the way to Wonder Lake (Mile 84). It's an 11-hour trip on the shuttle to ride out to the end of the road and back, which makes for a long day, but when Mt McKinley is visible, the ride to Wonder Lake offers 11 of the most scenic hours you'll ever spend on a bus.

Technically, you pay for any travel west on the park road and get a free ride back to the Riley Creek area. The single-trip fare to Toklat is $12.50, to Eielson $21 and to Wonder Lake $27. There are half-price youth fares and multiple-trip tickets that allow one person to ride the bus for several days. The three-day ticket costs $42 to Eielson and $54 to Wonder Lake. Tickets are available by phone (☎ 272-7275, 800-622-7275) up to the day before you travel. If you don't have a reservation, you most likely will have to wait two days to obtain a bus ticket during the peak of the season.

While riding the buses, passengers armed with binoculars and cameras scour the terrain for wildlife; most animals have become so accustomed to the rambling buses that they rarely run and hide when one passes by. When something is spotted, the name of the animal is called out, prompting the driver to slow down or stop for viewing and picture taking. The driver doubles as a park guide and naturalist, which makes for a more interesting trip.

The buses also drop off hikers; you don't need a backcountry permit for day hiking. Once in the backcountry, you can stop a bus heading east on the park road by flagging it down for a ride back. Changing buses several times each day is a practice commonly referred to as 'shuttle bus surfing.' By all means, get off the buses, as it's the only way you will truly experience the park, but remember that you can only get back on if there is an available seat. People are never left out in the backcountry against their will, but it's not too uncommon to have to wait two or three hours at the height of the season because the first four buses that pass you are full.

The old yellow school buses were replaced with more comfortable tour buses when the fee system was implemented. Still, if you're planning just to spend the day riding the bus, pack plenty of food and drink. It can be a long, dusty ride, and there are no services in the park, not even a vending machine at Eielson Visitor Center. Also, carry a park map so you know where you are and what ridges or riverbeds appeal to you for hiking. The best seats to grab are generally at the front of the bus, but if you end up in the back, don't be shy about leaning over somebody for a view out a window.

Mt McKinley is not visible from the park entrance or the nearby campgrounds and hotel. Your first glimpse of it comes between Mile 9 and Mile 11, if you're blessed with a clear day. (The rule of thumb stressed by the National Park Service rangers is that Mt McKinley is hidden two out of every three days.) While 'the Great One' might not be visible for most of the first 15 miles, this is the best stretch to spot moose because of the proliferation of spruce and especially willow, the animal's favorite food.

From Savage River, the road dips into the Sanctuary and Teklanika River valleys, and Mt McKinley disappears behind the foothills. Both these rivers are in excellent hiking areas, and three of the five backcountry campgrounds lie along them. Sanctuary River Campground, at Mile 22, is the most scenic of the three, and it's a good base camp for hiking Primrose Ridge.

Equally scenic and just as small (seven sites) is the Igloo Creek Campground, at Mile 34 in spruce woods along the creek. From here, you can make an easy day hike into the Igloo and Cathedral Mountains to spot Dall sheep.

After passing through the canyon formed by the Igloo and Cathedral Mountains, the road ascends to **Sable Pass** (3880 feet) at Mile 38.5. The canyon and surrounding mountains are excellent places to view Dall sheep, while the pass is known as a prime habitat for Toklat brown bears. From here, the road drops to the bridge over the East Fork Toklat River at Mile 44. Hikers can trek from the bridge along the riverbanks both north and south. By hiking north, you can complete a 6-mile loop that ends at the **Polychrome Pass Overlook** at Mile 46.3.

The pass is a rest stop for the shuttle buses and a popular spot for visitors. This scenic area, at an elevation of 3500 feet, gives way to views of the Toklat River to the south. The alpine tundra above the road is good for hiking, as you can easily scramble up ridges that lead north and south of the rest-stop shelter.

The park road then crosses two single-lane, wooden bridges over the Toklat River and ascends near **Stony Hill** (4508 feet) at Mile 61. This is perhaps the finest place to view Mt McKinley along the stretch to Eielson Visitor Center. Another quarter mile down the road is a lookout where you might spot caribou. From here, a short scramble north takes you to the summit of Stony Hill.

After climbing through Thorofare Pass (3900 feet), the road descends to the **Eielson Visitor Center** at Mile 66. The center is known for its excellent views of Mt McKinley, the surrounding peaks of the Alaska Range and Muldrow Glacier. It offers a few interpretive displays and conducts a series of programs, including an hour-long tundra hike at 1:30 pm daily. Catch a shuttle bus by 9 am at Riley Creek to make it to the Eielson Visitor Center for the walk. Several day and overnight hikes are possible from the center, including one around Mt Eielson (see the Hiking section in the Wilderness chapter) and another to Muldrow Glacier.

Past the Eielson Visitor Center, the park road drops to the valley below, passing a sign for **Muldrow Glacier** at Mile 74.4. At this point, the glacier lies about a mile to the south, and the terminus of the 32-mile ice floe is clearly visible, though you might not recognize it because the ice is covered with a mat of plant life. If the weather is cloudy and Mt McKinley and the surrounding peaks are hidden, the final 20 miles of the bus trip will be a ride through rolling tundra and past numerous small lakes known as kettle ponds. Study the pools of water carefully to spot beavers or waterfowl.

Wonder Lake Campground is at Mile 84. Here, the beauty of Mt McKinley is doubled on a clear day, with the mountain's reflection in the lake's surface. Ironically, the heavy demand for the 28 sites at Wonder Lake and the numerous overcast days caused by Mt McKinley itself prevent the majority of visitors from ever seeing this remarkable panorama. If you do experience the reddish sunset on the summit reflecting off the still waters of the lake, cherish it as a priceless moment.

The campground is on a low rise above the lake's south end and is only 26 miles from the mountain. First the shuttle bus stops at a bus shelter near the campground and then drives to the edge of the lake for a half hour or so before turning around and heading back. Those who come on the early buses can gain another hour at the lake by getting off and picking up a later bus for the trip back. Keep in mind that those famous McKinley-reflected-in-the-lake photos are taken along the northeast shore, 2 miles beyond the campground, so you might want to save some time for hiking. The historic mining town of Kantishna is 6 miles from where the shuttle bus stops.

Hiking

Even for those who have neither the desire nor the equipment for an overnight trek, hiking is still the best way to enjoy the park and to see the land and its wildlife up close. To do a day hike (which doesn't require a permit), just ride the shuttle bus and get off at any valley, riverbed or ridge that grabs your fancy.

There are few trails in the park, as most hiking is done across open terrain. You can hike virtually anywhere in the park that hasn't been closed because of the impact on wildlife. Popular areas include the Teklanika River south of the park road, the Toklat River, the ridges near Polychrome Pass and the tundra areas near the Eielson Visitor Center.

There are numerous guided walks in the park for those unsure of entering the backcountry on their own. The best is the Discovery Hike, which departs at 8 am daily for a moderately strenuous, three- to four-hour hike in the park's backcountry. The location of this trail-less adventure changes daily, and you must sign up one to two days in advance. The VAC keeps a list of all ranger-led hikes. Sign up for the hikes there.

The few maintained trails in the park can be found around the main entrance area and are described below.

Horseshoe Lake Trail This trail is a leisurely 1.5-mile walk through the woods to an overlook of an oxbow lake, followed by a steep trail to the water. The trailhead is about a mile from the start of the park road, where the railroad tracks cross. Follow the tracks north a short way to the wide gravel path.

Morino Loop Trail You can begin this leisurely walk of 1.3 miles in the back of Morino Campground or at the park hotel parking lot. It offers good views of Hines and Riley Creeks.

Taiga Loop Trail This is another easy hike that begins off the parking lot of the park hotel and loops 1.3 miles through the taiga forest.

Mt Healy Overlook Trail Veering off the Taiga Loop Trail is this steep climb up Mt Healy. A roundtrip of 5 miles, the trail ascends 1700 feet and offers fine views of the Nenana Valley. Plan on three to five hours for the hike.

Rock Creek Trail This moderate 2.3-mile walk connects the hotel area with the park headquarters and dog kennels. However, it's far easier hiking the trail downhill from headquarters to the hotel rather than climbing uphill from the hotel to headquarters. The trail begins just before the park road crosses Rock Creek but doesn't stay with the stream. Instead, it climbs a gentle slope of mixed aspen and spruce forest, breaks out along a ridge with scenic views of Mt Healy and the Parks Hwy and then begins a rapid descent to the service road behind the hotel and ends on the Taiga Loop Trail.

Backpacking

For many, the reason to come to Denali and to endure the long lines at the VAC is to escape into the backcountry for a true wilderness experience. Unlike many parks in the Lower 48, Denali's rigid restrictions ensure that you can trek and camp in a piece of wilderness that you can call your own, even if it's just for a few days.

The park is divided into 43 zones, and in 41 of them only a regulated number of backpackers are allowed at a time. You have to obtain a permit for the zone where you want to stay overnight, and that usually means waiting two days or more at Riley Creek until something opens up.

Obtain permits at the VAC, where you'll find two wall maps with the zone outlines and a quota board indicating the number of vacancies in each unit. Permits are issued only a day in advance, and at first glance backpackers can be horrified to find most units full for two or three days in a row.

The first step in the permit process is to watch the Backcountry Simulator Program in a video booth in the VAC. It's an interactive video that covers such topics as dealing with bears and other challenges of backcountry travel. Then, check the quota board for an area that you can access within a day. Finally, approach the ranger behind the desk to outline your entire backcountry itinerary.

Like getting into the campgrounds, the key to obtaining a permit is first getting an open spot anywhere in the backcountry. Once you're 'in,' you can book a string of other units throughout the park for the next 14 days. Units that are easier to obtain include Nos 1, 2, 3 and 24 because they surround the park entrance and are heavily wooded. Spend a night or two here and then jump on a camper bus for a more favorable place deeper in the park. Or, try for one of the units that don't abut the park road, such as Nos 37 to 41. Reserving your first night in such a zone means you'll have to start off early in the day to reach your designated area, but at least you're in the backcountry. At the west end of the park is No 23, one of the two zones with unlimited access, located in an area of extensive tussock where the trekking is extremely difficult.

Although any regulated zone can be filled, you'll generally find the more popular ones to be Nos 12, 13 and 18 in the tundra area south of Eielson Visitor Center. In fact, in the middle of the summer it may be almost impossible to get spots here without spending a week or more elsewhere in the backcountry. You'll also find it challenging to get a permit for Nos 8, 9, 10 and 11, which include both branches of the Toklat River and tundra area south of Polychrome Pass; No 27, north of Sanctuary Campground; and No 15, just west of Wonder Lake.

For the best overview of the different units in the park, purchase the book *Backcountry Companion for Denali National Park* by Jon Nierenberg (Alaska National History Association). It's available at both the VAC and the park hotel gift shop.

Some other essential items to take along include a bear-resistant food container, which you'll receive free of charge with your permit. The containers are bulky, but they work – they've reduced bear encounters by 90% since 1986. Before you go, you'll have to purchase a camper bus ticket ($15.50) and whatever topographic maps ($4) you'll need, all available at the VAC.

It's important to realize that Denali is a trail-less park, and the key to successful backcountry travel is being able to read a topographic map. You must be able to translate the contours (elevation lines) on the map into the land formations in front of you. Riverbeds are easy to follow and make excellent avenues for the backpacker, but they always involve fording water. Pack a pair of tennis shoes or rafters' sandals for this.

Ridges are also good routes to hike if the weather is not foul. The tree line in Denali is at 2700 feet, and above that you usually will find tussock or moist tundra – humps of watery grass that make for sloppy hiking. In extensive stretches of tussock, the hiking has been best described as 'walking on basketballs.' Above 3400 feet you'll encounter alpine or dry tundra, which generally makes for excellent trekking.

Regardless of where you're headed, remember that 5 miles is a full-day trip for the average backpacker in Denali's backcountry.

Bicycling

An increasingly popular way to explore the park road is on a mountain bike. No special permit is needed to ride your bike on the road, but you're not allowed to leave the road at any time. Most bikers book a campsite at the VAC and then carry the bike on the camper bus (see Camping in the Places to Stay section) to the campsite, beginning bike trips from there. You can even book sites at a string of campgrounds and ride with your equipment from one to the next. Rental bikes at Denali Outdoor Center (☎ 683-1925, 888-303-1925, docadventure@hotmail.com) cost $40 for one day, $37 a day for two to four days and $35 a day for five days or more. The center is at Mile 238.9 of the George Parks Hwy, next to the Northern Lights Gift Shop, but it offers free shuttle transportation from the railroad depot in the park.

River Running

The Nenana River and the impressive gorge it carves is the most popular white-water rafting area in Alaska in terms of sheer numbers of river runners. The most exciting stretch of the river begins near the park entrance and ends 10 miles north near the town of Healy. Here the river is rated Class III, as rafters sweep through standing waves, rapids and holes with names like 'Coffee Grinder' in sheer-sided canyons. South of the entrance the river is much milder, but to many it's just as interesting, as it swings away from both the highway and the railroad and increases your chances of sighting wildlife.

Several rafting companies offer daily floats during the summer, and the Nenana is easily one of the most rafted rivers in Alaska. Denali Raft Adventures (☎ 888-683-2234, 683-2234, denraft@mtaonline.net) has been around the longest and seems the most organized. Its office is at Mile 238 of the George Parks Hwy, but it provides free transportation from the train station inside the park. Both the Canyon Run through the

gorge and the milder McKinley Run cost $50 per person and depart three or four times daily. The four-hour Healy Express is a combination of both for $70. It departs at 7:30 am and 12:30 pm daily.

Organized Tours

Denali Park Resorts operates two narrated, wildlife bus tours along the park road. The Tundra Wildlife tour departs from the Denali National Park Hotel twice daily. The six-hour tour, designed primarily for package-tour groups, costs $64 per person and goes to Stony Hill when the mountain is visible, to the Toklat River when it isn't. There is also a three-hour Natural History tour ($35) that departs twice daily for Primrose Ridge. Reserve a seat for either tour the night before at the Denali National Park Hotel reservation desk or by calling in advance (☎ 800-276-7234, 276-7234).

The Kantishna Roadhouse (☎ 800-942-7420) offers a one-day bus tour ($99) along the park road to the historic Kantishna district, where you enjoy an interpretive tour of the area, lunch in the dining hall and a little gold panning before returning. You stand a very good chance of seeing wildlife on this tour.

Places to Stay

Inside the Park For information on reserving campsites, see Reservations & Fees in the Information section, above. If you don't have a reservation, you'll probably have to camp outside the park for the first night or two before you can secure a campsite in the park.

The key to getting into the campground of your choice, like Wonder Lake, is just finding a spot in a campground, any campground, including either Morino or Riley Creek. Once you're 'in,' you can reserve a guaranteed site for the next 14 days wherever there is an opening. With this system, you can still end up at Wonder Lake even during the busiest time of the year if you are willing to camp elsewhere in the park for four or five days. This is especially easy for people without reservations, as they can immediately pitch a tent in Morino (a walk-in campground), then return to the VAC that afternoon to book other campgrounds for the next two weeks. The limit on staying in one campground or a combination of them is 14 days.

Due to the popularity of the shuttle buses, the Park Service also provides a handful of camper buses with a third of the seats removed to facilitate hauling backpacks and mountain bikes. These buses charge a straight $15.50 fare to any point along the park road, including Wonder Lake. Purchase your ticket at the VAC.

Riley Creek Campground, at the main entrance of the park, is the largest and nicest facility in Denali as well as the only one open year-round. A quarter-mile west of George Parks Hwy, Riley Creek has 102 sites ($12), piped-in water, flush toilets and evening interpretive programs. Its amenities make it popular with RVers – in fact, overrun by RVers.

Morino Campground, near the train station, is a walk-in campground for backpackers without vehicles. It provides piped-in water and vault toilets but only two metal caches to keep your food away from the bears, Though its capacity is around 40 sites, it has to be really crowded for anybody to be turned away. You pick out a site first and then register and pay your $6 at the VAC.

Despite its name, *Savage River Campground* is a mile short of the actual river, at Mile 13 of the park road. It's one of only two campgrounds with a view of Mt McKinley. It has 33 sites ($12) that can accommodate both RVs and tents, with such amenities as piped-in water, flush toilets and evening interpretive programs. Those with a vehicle can drive to this campground.

At Mile 23, *Sanctuary River Campground* is the next campground down the road. On the banks of a large glacial river, the seven sites ($6) here are for tents only and can't be reserved in advance. While there's no piped-in water, Sanctuary River makes a great area for day hiking. You can either head south to hike along the river or climb Mt Wright or Primrose Ridge to the north for an opportunity to photograph Dall sheep.

At Mile 29, *Teklanika River Campground* has 50 sites ($12) for either RVs or tents, piped-in water and evening programs. Since you can drive to this campground, you must book a site here for a minimum of three days. Registered campers are issued a road pass for a single trip to the facility and then must leave their vehicle parked until they are ready to return to Riley Creek.

Igloo Creek Campground, a waterless facility at Mile 34, has only seven sites ($6) limited to tents. These cannot be reserved in advance. The day hiking in this area is excellent, especially the numerous ridges around Igloo Mountain, Cathedral Mountain and Sable Pass that provide good routes into the alpine area.

Wonder Lake Campground, at Mile 85, is the jewel of Denali campgrounds, thanks to its immense views of Mt McKinley. The facility has 28 sites ($12) for tents only but does contain flush toilets and piped-in water. If you are lucky enough to reserve a site, book it for three nights and then pray that the mountain appears during one of the days you are there. Also, pack plenty of insect repellent and maybe even a head net. In midsummer, the bugs are vicious.

Those opposed to sleeping in a tent have few alternatives right now and even fewer in the future. The *Denali National Park Hotel* (☎ 279-2653 year-round, 683-2215 in the summer) is the only lodging available in the entrance area of the park, and rooms here are $159 for two people per night. By 2002, this hotel will become an Environmental Education and Science Center, and no accommodations other than campsites will be available.

At the western end of the park road are three places that are as close to wilderness lodges as you'll ever find on a road. Their rates tend to shock most budget-conscious backpackers but include roundtrip transportation from the train station, meals and guided activities.

Camp Denali (☎ 683-2290, dnpwild@ alaska.net) offers several different types of accommodation, most with fixed arrival and departure dates. The camp is more of a resort and definitely not just a place to sleep, as it offers a wide range of activities, including wildlife observation and photography,

THE INTERIOR

rafting, fishing, gold panning and, of course, hiking. Plus, the camp provides your best view of Mt McKinley.

Rooms at both Camp Denali and its North Face Lodge are $335 per person per night; you must book for three or four-day stays. The price includes all meals, most guided activities, your transportation from the Denali train station and use of recreational equipment.

Nearby is the ***Kantishna Roadhouse*** (☎ 683-1475, 800-942-7420, kantishna@polarnet .com), with 28 cabins that cost $280 per person per night. Again, this includes all meals, activities and transportation from the park entrance. The wilderness resort offers gold panning, hiking and photography activities during the day and has a hot tub and sauna to enjoy at night.

These places will most likely be booked long before you arrive in Alaska. If you want to treat yourself (and escape the crowds at Riley Creek), email or write to the lodges in advance – six months in advance is not overdoing it. Write to Camp Denali, PO Box 67, Denali National Park, AK 99755, or Kantishna Roadhouse, PO Box 81670, Fairbanks, AK 99708, for reservations.

Also at the end of the road, the ***Denali Backcountry Lodge*** (☎ 783-1342, 800-841-0692, denalibl@pobox.alaska.net) has 30 cabins for $300 per person based on double occupancy, or $249 per person for a quad.

Outside the Park For a park of 6 million acres, Denali occasionally stuns visitors who arrive late in the afternoon or the early evening expecting to find a place to stay in the park. Instead, National Park Service rangers give out the names of individuals offering private accommodations outside the park; these people make a living just from the overflow.

Included among these are several private campgrounds where you can expect to pay $15 to $20 for a campsite. Three miles north of the park is ***Denali Riverside RV Park*** (☎ 888-778-7700, rvalaska@aol.com), Mile 240 of the George Parks Hwy, with tent sites for $10 and RV sites for $25. This campground is basically a gravel parking lot squeezed in between the highway and the Nenana River.

Farther out of the park, the small town of Healy (11 miles north of the park entrance) contains ***McKinley RV & Campground*** (☎ 683-2379, 800-478-2562), Mile 248.4 of the Parks Hwy. The wooded facility offers tent sites ($18), RV sites ($20 to $28) and bus transportation to the VAC.

South of the park, your best bet is ***Denali Grizzly Bear Campground*** (☎ 683-2696), Mile 231 of the Parks Hwy. Just 6 miles from the park entrance, the campground offers wooded campsites for $17, platform tents for $23, and 20 well-spaced cabins that range from $50 for two people to $100 for four. Most cabins are $70 to $100.

If there are three or four in your party, consider booking a cabin in advance. Across the highway from Grizzly Bear Campground is ***Denali River Cabins*** (☎ 683-2500, 800-230-7275, denali@polarnet .com), Mile 231 of the Parks Hwy, with cedar cabins for two people ($99) and for four ($156). The cabins are 2 miles south of the park, but there is a free shuttle bus to the park entrance.

Farther south of the entrance, at Mile 224 of the George Parks Hwy, you'll reach ***McKinley Creekside Cabins*** (☎ 683-2277, 888-533-6254, cabins@mtaonline.net) and, across the street, ***Carlo Creek Lodge*** (☎ 683-2576). Both have cabins that sleep two for $90 to $110, but those at Carlo Creek enjoy a much nicer setting along the creek. Carlo Creek also has a wooded campground. This is a great area to spend your nights; you can escape the park crowds here, but you need a vehicle. Neither lodge supplies transportation to the park.

Some cabins closer to the entrance do offer van transportation, but space is at a premium just north of the park. Cabins here are small and usually crammed together. But if you're determined to stay near the park, try ***Sourdough Cabins*** (☎ 800-354-6020, 683-2773, denalisourdough@hotmail), Mile 238.8 of the Parks Hwy, where rates begin at $150.

Farther north, beyond Healy, ***Earthsong Lodge*** (☎ 683-2863, earthsong@mail.denali

.k12.ak.us), Stampede Rd, rents out 10 cabins above the tree line at 1900 feet. This getaway setting offers a stunning view of Mt McKinley. The cabins cost $105 to $125 for two people, including breakfast and slide programs. In the evening you can help feed the 30 sled dogs.

For budget travelers, there is an excellent backpacker's hostel just south of Healy. *Denali Hostel* (☎ 683-1295), Otter Lake Rd, has bunks ($24), kitchen facilities, showers and transportation back to the park as early as 6 am so you can catch the first shuttle bus! If you arrive on the train, look for the Denali Hostel van at the depot.

The town of Healy also contains a handful of B&Bs and motels. The best B&B in Healy is *Denali Dome Home* (☎ 683-1239, denalidome@alaskaone.com), Healy Spur Rd, a geodesic house with doubles for $90. *Totem Inn* (☎ 683-2420), Parks Hwy at Healy Spur Rd, offers economy ($74) and deluxe ($101) rooms in what is basically an elongated trailer.

Places to Eat

Inside the Park There are two restaurants and one bar in the park, all off the lobby of the Denali National Park Hotel. The *Denali Dining Room* serves full meals in pleasant surroundings but is overpriced for most budget travelers. Breakfast after 7 am, however, can be a leisurely and reasonable $6 to $8 affair. The *Whistle Stop Snack Shop*, also off the lobby, opens at 5:30 am to provide early shuttle-bus passengers with breakfast or a box lunch. Egg breakfasts start at $5, and hamburgers and sandwiches cost less than $7. Surprisingly, the shop serves garden burgers and veggie sandwiches. The *Gold Spike Saloon*, two lounge cars side by side, is the hotel's bar.

McKinley Mercantile, a block from the hotel, sells a variety of fresh and dried food, some canned goods and white gas in small quantities ($2 for a quart). The selection is limited and highly priced. Your best bet is to stock up on supplies in Fairbanks, Anchorage or Wasilla before leaving for the park. The small park grocery store is open 8 am to 11 pm daily and has showers ($5).

Outside the Park For the best pizza outside the park, try the *Lynx Creek Pub* (☎ 683-2548), Mile 238.6 of the Parks Hwy, north of the park entrance. A one-item large pizza costs $17. The log-cabin restaurant also has vegetarian specials, a lunch buffet and an impressive selection of beer. Across the highway in a log-cabin strip mall (only in Alaska!) is *Denali Smoke Shack & Whitewater Ale House*. The interior has a rafter's motif, with a collection of broken oars, life jackets and white-water photos decorating the walls. The menu includes barbecue, steaks and salads, with dinners ranging from $7 to $13. This place may offer the best deal in the morning; a full breakfast with ham is only $4.

Nearby, on the same side of the highway, is *Denali Salmon Bake*, where $20 buys you the usual Alaskan salmon dinner. You get a single serving of salmon, but everything else is all-you-can-eat. Also located here is *Lynx Creek Park Mart*, offering the best selection of groceries and liquor in the area.

South of the park entrance is *The Loose Moose*, Mile 229 of the Parks Hwy at Denali Cabins (not to be confused with the Denali River Cabins, at Mile 231). In the morning, huge pancakes with hash browns, sausage and blueberries cost $7. At night, you can feast on Moose Nachos ($9), large salads ($5 to $10) or even veggie burgers ($8).

Even farther south is *The Perch* (☎ 683-2523), Mile 224 of the Parks Hwy, the place to head for a fine dinner. Steak, pasta or seafood dinners range from $16 to $28, and all come with the lofty view enjoyed by every table. In the morning, stop by for a just-baked cinnamon roll and coffee.

Getting There & Away

Bus Both northbound and southbound bus services are available from Denali National Park. If heading south to Anchorage, try the Alaska Backpacker Shuttle (☎ 344-8775) for $40 or the Parks Highway Express (☎ 888-600-6001) for $35. Both depart the VAC at 1 pm. Their vans also leave around 3 pm for Fairbanks ($25 one-way).

Train The most enjoyable way to arrive or depart from the park is aboard the Alaska

Railroad (see the Getting Around chapter), with its viewing-dome cars that provide sweeping views of Mt McKinley and the Susitna and Nenana River valleys along the way. All trains arrive at the train station between the Riley Creek Campground and the park hotel, only staying long enough for passengers to board.

The northbound train arrives in Denali at 3:45 pm and reaches Fairbanks at 8:15 pm. The southbound train arrives in Denali at noon and in Anchorage at 8:15 pm. Tickets are not cheap; the one-way fare from Denali National Park to Anchorage is $102, from Denali to Fairbanks $54.

Getting Around

Courtesy Buses There is free transportation within the area around the park entrance. The Front-Country Shuttle Buses run every half hour, beginning at the VAC and stopping at the hotel, the train station and Riley Creek Campground. The park also runs free buses to the sled-dog demonstrations; these depart the VAC a half hour before each show. There are also courtesy buses that transport people from the hotels, lodges and campgrounds outside Denali to the park hotel, where a schedule is usually posted. If you want to go to Lynx Creek Pub, Denali Salmon Bake or anywhere north of the entrance, catch the bus to McKinley Chalets.

North of Denali National Park

Continuing north, the George Parks Hwy parallels the Nenana River for the next 50 miles. Along the way, you'll pass many viewpoints of the scenic river. One of them is the June Creek Rest Area at Mile 269, where a gravel road leads down to the small creek and a wooden staircase takes you up to fine views of the area.

NENANA

The only major town between Denali National Park and Fairbanks is Nenana (population 435), at Mile 305 of the George Parks

Hwy, before the road crosses the Tanana River. Nenana was little more than the site of a roadhouse until it was chosen as the base for building the northern portion of the Alaska Railroad in 1916. The construction camp quickly became a boomtown that made history on July 5, 1923, when President Warren G Harding arrived to hammer in the golden spike on the north side of the Tanana River.

The sickly Harding, the first president ever to visit Alaska, missed the golden spike the first two times, or so the story goes, but finally drove it in to complete the railroad. Less than a month later, the president died in San Francisco, prompting the citizens of Talkeetna to claim he was 'done in' when he stopped at their Fairview Inn for a drink on the ride home.

In preparation for the president's arrival, the Nenana train station was built in 1923 at the north end of A St. Extensively restored in 1988, it's now on the National Register of Historic Places. The impressive building includes the **Alaska State Railroad Museum** (☎ 832-5500), which houses railroad memorabilia and local artifacts. It's open 8:30 am to 6 pm daily, and admission is by donation. East of the train station, a monument commemorates the occasion when President Harding drove in the golden spike, marking the completion of the Alaska Railroad.

The **Nenana Visitor Center** (☎ 832-9953), George Parks Hwy at A St, is an equally interesting building – a log cabin with a sod roof that's planted with colorful flowers during the summer. The center features a few displays on the Nenana Ice Classic, the town's noted gambling event, as well as local information. Outside the visitor center is the *Taku Chief* river tug, which once pushed barges along the Tanana River. The center is open 8 am to 6 pm daily during the summer.

Travel down Front St, parallel to the river in town, or cross to the north side of the bridge to view **fish wheels** at work, best seen in late summer during the salmon runs. The wheels, a traditional fish trap, scoop salmon out of the water as they move upstream to spawn.

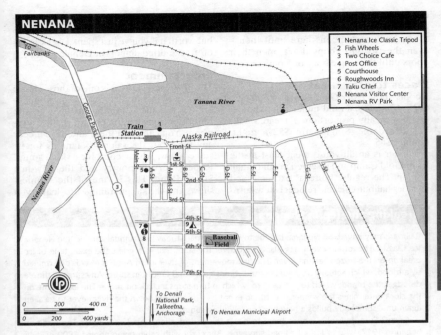

NENANA

To Fairbanks

Tanana River

Train Station

Alaska Railroad

Front St

Nenana River

George Parks Hwy

Main St

Market St

A St

B St

C St

D St

E St

F St

G St

Front St

1st St

2nd St

3rd St

4th St

5th St

6th St

7th St

Baseball Field

To Denali National Park, Talkeetna, Anchorage

To Nenana Municipal Airport

0   200   400 m
0   200   400 yards

1 Nenana Ice Classic Tripod
2 Fish Wheels
3 Two Choice Cafe
4 Post Office
5 Courthouse
6 Roughwoods Inn
7 Taku Chief
8 Nenana Visitor Center
9 Nenana RV Park

THE INTERIOR

Places to Stay & Eat

Nenana Valley RV Park (☎ 832-5230), on 4th St one block from the Parks Hwy, offers tent sites for $12, free showers, a Laundromat and bike rentals.

South of Nenana is *Finnish Alaska B&B* (☎ 832-5628), located at Mile 302 of the Parks Hwy, which has three rooms and a Finnish log sauna for guests. Rates for rooms range from $70 to $90.

In town, the *Roughwoods Inn* (☎ 832-5299), on the corner of 2nd and A Sts, rents double rooms with kitchenettes for $67. There's a cafe on the premises and a coin laundry next door.

For a bite to eat, try the *Two Choice Cafe* (711 N A St), just to the north. Breakfast items and hamburgers are available at both. For better dining, visit the *Tamarack Inn*, south of town at Mile 298 of the Parks Hwy, or *Monderosa Bar*, north of town at Mile 309 of the Parks Hwy, which features an outdoor patio.

ESTER

From Nenana, the George Parks Hwy shifts to a more easterly direction, passes a few more scenic turnoffs and arrives at the old mining town of Ester (population 240) at Mile 351.7. The town was established in 1906, when miners made a sizable gold strike at Ester Creek, and at one time Ester was a thriving community of 15,000, with three hotels and five saloons. The town came back to life in the 1920s, when the Fairbanks Exploration Company began a large-scale mining operation. Most of Ester's historical buildings date from that era and were either built by the company or moved from Fox, just a few miles north of Fairbanks.

Gold mining still takes place in the hills surrounding Ester, but the town is best known as the home of the Cripple Creek Resort and its Malemute Saloon. The restored mess hall and bunkhouse from the mining camp have become a regular stop for every tour bus out of Fairbanks. If you can hold off from rushing into Fairbanks, an evening here can be enjoyable but only after 5 pm. Nothing happens here until then – even the two gift shops don't open their doors until the magic hour of 5 pm.

Places to Stay & Eat

Rooms at the *Ester Gold Camp* (☎ 800-676-6925, 479-2500), an old miner's bunkhouse, are 'historically proportioned' (read: small) but affordable. Singles are $52 a night, doubles $65.

Dinner is an all-you-can-eat feast at the Ester Gold Camp and is served in dining-hall fashion. The regular buffet is excellent and includes halibut, chicken, reindeer stew, corn-on-the-cob and great biscuits, among other things. The price is $16, which is not cheap but worth it if you've just spent a week living off freeze-dried dinners at Denali.

Entertainment

The *Malemute Saloon* is one of those classic Alaskan bars: sawdust on the floors, junk – err, excuse me – mining artifacts in the rafters, patrons tossing peanut shells everywhere. You can go in there and have a beer any time, but the saloon is famous for its stage show, which combines skits, songs, Robert Service poetry and the Sawdust String Band. This is one of the funniest shows in Alaska, guaranteed to leave you

Breaking the Ice in Nenana

Railroads may have built Nenana, but the town's trademark today is its annual gamble, the Nenana Ice Classic. The lottery event has Alaskans all over the state trying to guess the exact time of ice breakup on the frozen Tanana River. The first movement of river ice in April or May is determined by a tripod, which actually has four legs and stands guard 300 feet from shore. Any surge in the ice dislodges the tripod, which tugs on a cord, which in turn stops a clock on shore. The exact time on the clock determines the winner. The tripod eventually disappears down the river never to be seen again until somebody builds a new one the following summer.

Crazy? Sure, but what else is there to do at the end of a long Alaskan winter? The tradition began in 1917, when Alaska Railroad surveyors, stir crazy with cabin fever, pooled $800 of their wages and made bets about when the ice would move out. That same excitement still swells in the small town, and through most of Alaska for that matter, as breakup in Nenana triggers visions of $100,000 payouts everywhere else.

When will the ice break? Your guess is as good as anybody else's. The earliest recorded break came at 3:47 pm on April 20, 1940. The latest was 11:41 am on May 20, 1964.

Tickets are $2 for each guess, and guesses must be registered by April 1. What you win is determined by how many other people had the same guess as you did. In 1998, the jackpot topped more than $300,000 for the first time. Often so many people have the same guess that the winners take home only a few hundred dollars.

The 2000 Nenana Ice Classic marked the first time tickets were sold statewide during the preceding summer. But you can enter the contest even if you're basking in the sun in southern California. Frostbitten toes are not a requirement to lay down your bets. Just send a $2 money order and include the date, hour and minute you think the ice will go out to: Ice Classic Office, PO Box 272, Nenana, AK 99760. The office will then send you a photocopy of your guess and keep the original in case you are the winner.

You can view a replica of the Ice Classic tripod and the 1974 book of guesses – a 12- by 18-inch volume that is almost 4 inches thick – at the Nenana Visitor Center. You can usually see the next Nenana Ice Classic tripod even if you're not getting off the train. During the summer, it's on the banks of the Tanana River near the depot, ready to be positioned on the ice in February during the town's Tripod Raising Festival.

rolling in the sawdust and peanut shells by the end of the night. Show time is 9 pm Monday to Saturday, while there's a second show at 7 pm Wednesday to Saturday in July. Tickets are $12.

Getting There & Away

From Ester, it is 7 miles to Fairbanks, the second-largest city in Alaska, at the end of the George Parks Hwy (see the Fairbanks chapter). A taxi will run you from Ester to the airport for $15 and to the downtown area for around $24.

The Alcan

Travelers heading north along the Alcan (also called the Alaska Hwy) from Dawson Creek in British Columbia reach the US/Canadian border at Mile 1189. The spot is marked by an observation deck and plaque; a half mile farther along the highway is the US Customs border station. On the US side of the highway, you'll notice mileposts at almost every mile. These posts were erected in the 1940s to help travelers know where they were on the new wilderness road. Today, they are a tradition throughout Alaska and are still used for mailing addresses and locations of businesses. They measure the mileage from Dawson Creek, Mile 0.

Your first opportunity to get information and free handouts comes at Mile 1229. The **Tetlin National Wildlife Refuge Visitor Center** (☎ 883-5312) is a sod-covered log cabin with a huge viewing deck overlooking the Scotty and Deeper Creek drainage areas. The Mentasta and Nutsotin Mountains loom in the distance. Inside, the cabin is packed with interpretive displays on wildlife and mountains and racks of brochures. It's open 7 am to 7 pm daily during the summer.

You also pass two US Fish & Wildlife campgrounds (free!) along the Alcan before you reach Tok. *Deadman Lake Campground*, Mile 1249.4, has 18 sites, a boat ramp on the lake and a short nature trail but no drinking water. *Lakeview Campground*, Mile 1256.7, features eight sites on beautiful Yager Lake, where you can see the St Elias Range to the south on a nice day. It also lacks piped-in water.

TOK

Although you enter Alaska just north of Beaver Creek in the Yukon, Tok serves as the gateway to the 49th state. The town of 1200 people, 125 miles beyond the US/Canadian border, is at the major junction between the Alcan, which heads 206 miles northwest to Fairbanks, and the Tok Cutoff, an extension of the Glenn Hwy that ends in Anchorage, 328 miles to the southwest.

Tok was born in 1942 as a construction camp for the Alcan. Originally, it was called Tokyo Camp near Tokyo River, but WWII sentiment caused locals to shorten it to Tok. Today, the town is a trade and service center for almost 4000 residents in the surrounding area. If you're just arriving in Alaska from Canada, this is your first chance to gather information and brochures for the entire state.

Information

If nothing else, Tok is a town full of information, maps and brochures because of its role as 'the Gateway to Alaska.' Near the corner of the Tok Cutoff (Glenn Hwy) and the Alcan is the Tok Mainstreet Visitors Center (☎ 883-5775). The center houses the Tok Chamber of Commerce visitor center, which offers regional and local travel information along with free coffee, pay phones and rest rooms. Also inside is the Alaska Public Lands Information Center (☎ 883-5667), which provides a mountain of information on the state's parks and outdoor activities. The Tok Mainstreet Visitors Center is open 8 am to 8 pm daily during the summer.

Directly across the highway from the visitor centers is the US Fish & Wildlife Service office (☎ 883-5312), which has information about various USFW refuges in northern Alaska, including Tetlin National Wildlife Refuge. It's open 8 am to 4:30 pm Monday to Friday.

The only bank in Tok is Denali State Bank (☎ 883-2265), Mile 1314 of the Alcan, in the Frontier Foods Supermarket.

The post office is on the Alcan, just west of the intersection with the Tok Cutoff.

The Tok library is in the Tok Mainstreet Visitors Center. The best place to purchase Alaska books is at the Alaska Public Lands Information Center, inside the visitor center. You can do your laundry at several places around town, including the Village Texaco (☎ 883-4660), Mile 1313.4 of the Alcan.

If you need medical care, go to the Public Health Clinic (☎ 883-4101), Mile 1314 of the Alcan, next to the Alaska State Police office.

Things to See & Do

The **Tok Mainstreet Visitors Center** is a massive log building that was built in 1992 to the tune of $450,000 to celebrate the 50th anniversary of the Alcan. Locals claim the 7000-sq-foot lodge is the largest natural log structure in Alaska. Along with racks of brochures, the center contains displays on wildlife, gold panning and the construction of the Alaska Hwy. The Alaska Public Lands Information Center, in the same building, shows videos. On a clear day the center's large picture window frames the Alaska Range.

Tok, along with a half dozen other towns, considers itself the 'Sled Dog Capital of Alaska.' It's estimated that one of every three people in the area is involved with the sport in some way – most of them raise dogs. Free sled-dog demonstrations take place at 7:30 pm daily except Sunday at the Burnt Paw Gift Shop (☎ 883-4121), next door to the post office.

Places to Stay

Camping The closest private campground is the *Golden Bear Motel* (☎ 888-252-2123, 883-2561, mbrooks@polarnet.com), a quarter mile south of town on the Tok Cutoff. The motel has tent spaces for $15, full hookups for RVs and showers. The cafe opens at 6 am. Another mile farther south is *Sourdough Campground* (☎ 883-5455), Mile 122.8 of the Tok Cutoff, with tent sites for $12.50 in a more wooded area, plus showers and a coin laundry.

Hostels Probably the most affordable place to stay in town is at the *Tok International Hostel* (☎ 883-3745), a mile south on Pringle Drive at Mile 1322.5 of the Alcan. That puts it 9 miles west of the town, but it provides 10 beds in a big army tent along with tent sites in a pleasant wooded area. (Those cycling to Alaska should note that Tok's bike trails pass near the hostel before ending at Tanacross Junction, Mile 1325.8.) The nightly rate of $10 includes a shower.

Hotels Those travelers who are bussing north from Haines or Skagway will usually find themselves stopping overnight in Tok. There are eight hotels and motels in the area; many of them are around the junction of the two highways. The cheapest motel is the *Snowshoe Motel* (☎ 883-4511, 800-478-4511 in Alaska or the Yukon), on the Alaska Hwy east of the visitor center. The motel has singles/doubles for $62/68, including a light breakfast.

Young's Motel (☎ 883-4411), Mile 1313 of the Alcan, is a large, clean modern motel with 43 rooms and private bathrooms for $68/73. The *Golden Bear Motel* (☎ 888-252-2123, 883-2561, mbrooks@polarnet.com), a quarter mile south of town on the Tok Cutoff, rents double rooms for $85.

Places to Eat

Road food rules in Tok! Cafes line the Alaska Hwy in this town. For burgers or a salad bar, there's *Fast Eddy's*, Mile 1313.3 of the Alcan, where a full dinner costs $10 to $16. *Young's Cafe*, on the Alcan across from the Tok Mainstreet Visitors Center, has ribs and chicken as well. Both serve sourdough pancakes for breakfast in the morning. In fact, everybody does in Tok, including the *Sourdough Campground*, Mile 122.8 of the Tok Cutoff, where a plate of hotcakes and reindeer sausage is $6, a bargain in Alaska. *Valley Bakery*, Main St, has good European breads and pastries prepared by the Norwegian baker, Roger Skarie. *Gateway Salmon Bake* (☎ 883-5555), Mile 1313 of the Alcan, serves up grilled salmon with chowder and salad for $12 to $18. Call for a free shuttle ride, or camp for free for the night with the purchase of dinner.

Getting There & Away

Bus If you can't score a ride, even after pleading with motorists at the visitor center, keep in mind that Alaskon Express is likely to have a bus headed where you want to go. The buses leave from the Westmark Inn (☎ 883-2291). On Sunday, Tuesday and Friday, a bus leaves at 4 pm and stops overnight in Beaver Creek, reaching Whitehorse, Haines or Skagway the next day. On Monday, Wednesday and Friday, a bus departs at 11 am and reaches Anchorage by 7:30 pm. The one-way fare from Tok to Anchorage is $108, to Fairbanks $70, to Glennallen $60, to Haines $148 and to Skagway $163.

The Alaska Direct bus (☎ 800-770-6652) passes through Tok on Sunday, Wednesday and Friday during the summer. On its way to Whitehorse and Haines, it pulls in at 2:30 pm and then continues on to Beaver Creek. Westbound buses depart at 2:30 pm, with one heading for Glennallen and then Anchorage and another going to Fairbanks. The one-way fare from Tok to Anchorage is $65, to Fairbanks $40.

Hitchhiking For many backpackers, the most important item at the Tok Mainstreet Visitors Center is the message board. Check out the board or display your own message if you're trying to hitch a ride through Canada along the Alcan. It's best to arrange a ride in Tok and not wait until you reach the international border. In recent years, the Canadian customs post at the border has developed a reputation as one of the toughest anywhere. Thanks to the new 'zero tolerance' attitude, it's not unusual to see hitchhikers, especially Americans, turned back at the border.

TOK TO DELTA JUNCTION

Ten miles west of Tok on the Alcan, you'll be greeted with views of the Alaska Range, which parallels the road to the south. *Moon Lake State Campground*, 18 miles west of Tok at Mile 1332 of the Alcan, has 15 sites ($10). This state wayside offers tables, outhouses and a swimming area, where it's pos-

sible to do the backstroke while watching a float plane land nearby.

Although there are no more public campgrounds until Delta Junction, camping is permitted at the *Gerstle River State Wayside*, a large lookout at Mile 1393 of the Alcan. The scenic spot provides covered tables and outhouses but no piped-in drinking water. Nearby is the trailhead for the **Donna Lakes Trail**, a 3.5-mile trek to Big Donna Lake and a 4.5-mile trip to Little Donna Lake. Both are stocked with rainbow trout.

DELTA JUNCTION

This town (population 890) is known as the 'End of the Alcan,' as the famous highway joins the existing Richardson Hwy here to complete the route to Fairbanks. The community began as a construction camp and picked up its name from the junction between the two highways. Delta Junction was also home to Fort Greely, which at one point

DELTA JUNCTION

1 Quartz Lake State Campground
2 Big Delta State Historic Park
3 Alaska 7 Motel
4 Delta Laundry & Thrift Shop
5 Family Medical Clinic
6 Delta State Campground
7 Post Office
8 IGA Food Cache
9 Visitor Center, Sullivan Roadhouse
10 Pizza Bella

To Fairbanks

Quartz Lake

Lost Lake

Tanana River

Big Delta

0   2 km

0   .5   1 mile

Delta River

Richardson Hwy

Trans-Alaska Pipeline

Berm Rd

Clearwater Lake

Jack Warren Rd

To Clearwater State Recreation Area, Clearwater Lodge

Delta Junction

Nistler Rd

Alaska Hwy

Jarvis Creek

Clearwater Rd

To Gulkana, Glennallen

To Alaska Homestead & Historical Museum, Tok

employed 250 civilians, but in 1996 the Army began transferring the base to Fairbanks, and now it is virtually closed. The town continues to serve as a service center not only for travelers but also for the growing agricultural community in the surrounding valleys.

Information

The Delta Junction Visitor Center (☎ 895-5068, deltacc@knix.net) offers local information, free coffee and a courtesy phone to make local calls. You'll find mounted wildlife on the 1st floor and a display of historical photos on the 2nd, while those who have just completed the journey on the Alcan from Dawson Creek can purchase an End-of-the-Highway certificate. It's open 8 am to 8 pm daily in the summer.

For cash, head to the National Bank of Alaska (☎ 895-4691) in Diehl's Shopping Center, a half mile north of the visitor center.

The post office is on the east side of the Richardson Hwy, two blocks north of the visitor center.

The public library (☎ 895-4102), behind city hall in the center of town, runs a paperback swap for travelers if you have run out of reading material after the long haul on

Highway sign near Delta Junction

the Alcan. It's open Wednesday, Thursday and Saturday in the summer.

Delta Laundry & Thrift Shop (☎ 895-4561), two blocks north of Delta State Campground on the Richardson Hwy, has showers and stays open until 7 pm daily. There is also a coin laundry at Green Acres RV Park (☎ 895-4369), 1.5 miles north of the visitor center on the Richardson Hwy.

The Family Medical Clinic (☎ 895-5100) is just north of Delta State Campground on the Richardson Hwy.

Things to See & Do

There isn't a lot to do in Delta Junction unless you wander in during the Deltana Fair (giant vegetables, livestock shows and parades) on the last weekend of July. The Delta Junction Visitor Center is in the 'Triangle,' the area where the Alcan merges with the Richardson Hwy and the town's unofficial 'downtown.' Just outside the visitor center you'll see the large white milepost for **Mile 1422 of the Alcan**, marking the end of the famous highway, and some outdoor displays on the Trans-Alaska Pipeline.

Across the parking lot from the visitors center is **Sullivan Roadhouse**. The classic log structure was built in 1906 and served travelers along the old Fairbanks-Valdez Trail until 1927. It was placed on the National Register of Historic Places in 1979 and in 1997 moved, log by log, from Fort Greely to its present location in the Triangle. Now a museum, the roadhouse displays historic photographs and excavated artifacts in several exhibits dedicated to travel in Alaska in the early 1900s, the so-called 'roadhouse era.' It's open 8 am to 5 pm daily in the summer. Admission is free.

To see a homestead farm or a large collection of early farming equipment, head to the **Alaska Homestead & Historical Museum** (☎ 895-4431), 6 miles east of town on the Alcan. It's open 10 am to 7 pm daily in the summer, but the one-hour tours ($10 per person) are by appointment only.

If you have the time, head 3 miles south of Delta Junction down the Richardson Hwy to the scenic lookout across from the FAA facility. The mountainous panorama, with the

Delta River in the foreground, is spectacular from this spot. On a clear day you can easily spot Mt Hayes (13,697 feet) in the center and Mt Moffit (13,020 feet) to the left, as well as several other peaks. At Mile 258.5 of the Richardson Hwy, you can view the Trans-Alaska Pipeline and a visit a pump station. The one-hour pump station tours begin at 9, 10 and 11 am daily in the summer and cost $5 per person.

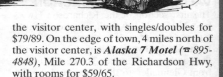

Places to Stay

There are a handful of commercial RV campgrounds and three public campgrounds in the area. The closest public facility is the ***Delta State Campground*** (also called the Delta State Recreation Site), a mile north of the visitor center at Mile 267 of the Richardson Hwy, which has 25 sites ($8), some overlooking the local airstrip.

You'll find the ***Clearwater State Recreation Area*** (18 sites, $8), 13 miles northeast of town. Follow the Richardson Hwy and turn right on Jack Warren Rd, 2.4 miles north of the visitor center. Head 10.5 miles east along the road and look for signs to the campground. Most of the wooded sites overlook Clearwater Creek, which has a good grayling fishery with special catch-and-release regulations.

Also north of town, the ***Quartz Lake State Campground***, Mile 277.7 of the Richardson Hwy, has 80 sites ($8). Turn east at the posted road and head 2.8 miles to the campground, along the shores of a scenic lake where you can fish for rainbow trout. A trail from the campground leads over to nearby Lost Lake, where there are two more campsites.

If you're really low on funds and don't have a tent, the ***Clearwater Lodge*** (☎ 895-5152), next to the Clearwater State Recreation Area on Remington Rd, has three cabins for $20 a night, but they're small and dark and lack electricity. You do get a key to the washroom at the lodge, which features a deck overlooking the Clearwater River.

Delta Junction also has several motels, including ***Kelley's Country Inn*** (☎ 895-4667, *1616 Richardson Hwy*), two blocks north of

the visitor center, with singles/doubles for $79/89. On the edge of town, 4 miles north of the visitor center, is ***Alaska 7 Motel*** (☎ 895-4848), Mile 270.3 of the Richardson Hwy, with rooms for $59/65.

Places to Eat

Delta Junction contains a handful of restaurants and an ***IGA Food Cache***, Mile 266 of the Richardson Hwy, a half mile north of the visitor center. The market features a bakery, salad bar, deli and an espresso cart, plus homemade soup and other ready-to-eat items to go. It's the place to go in the morning for coffee, a pastry and a bit of local news.

Buffalo Center Diner, Kimball Rd at the Richardson Hwy, is perhaps the best restaurant in town, with dinners ranging from $9 to $15 and breakfasts that begin at $6. Try the buffalo black-bean chili ($4). At ***Pizza Bella***, across from the visitor center, you can enjoy a pepperoni pizza for $14 or homemade lasagna for $10.

Richardson Highway

The Richardson Hwy, Alaska's first highway, begins in Valdez and extends north 266 miles to Delta Junction, where the Alcan joins it for the final 98 miles to Fairbanks. The road was originally scouted in 1919 by US Army Capt WR Abercrombie, who was looking for a way to link the gold town of Eagle with the warm-water port of Valdez. At first it was a telegraph line and footpath, but it quickly turned into a wagon trail following the turn-of-the-century gold strikes at Fairbanks.

Today, the road is a scenic wonder; it cuts through the Chugach Mountains and the Alaska Range while providing access to Wrangell-St Elias National Park. Along the way it passes waterfalls, glaciers, five major rivers and the Trans-Alaska Pipeline, which parallels the road most of the way. Many say the most scenic stretch of highway in the state is the 100-mile drive from Gulkana to Delta Junction.

VALDEZ TO DELTA JUNCTION
The first section of the Richardson Hwy – from Valdez, *Mile 0*, to the junction with the Glenn Hwy, *Mile 115* – is covered in the Richardson Hwy to Glennallen section in the Southcentral chapter. The next 14 miles – from Glennallen to the junction of the Tok Cutoff, which includes the campgrounds at the Dry Creek State Recreation Site and Gulkana – is covered in the Tok Cutoff section, later in this chapter. Mileposts along the highway show the distances from old Valdez, 4 miles from the present city, which is the new beginning of the Richardson Hwy.

Glennallen to Sourdough Creek
At Mile 112.6 of the highway, just north of Glennallen, you'll reach a turnoff with an interpretive display on the development of transportation in Alaska. Even more appealing is the view from a nearby bluff, where you can see several peaks of the Wrangell Mountains in Wrangell-St Elias National Park. The highest mountain is Mt Blackburn (16,518 feet).

At Mile 147.6, the road reaches the ***Sourdough Creek Campground*** (60 sites, free), which provides canoeists and rafters access to the Gulkana River. In 1994, this Bureau of Land Management (BLM) campground was reopened after a $2-million facelift and now includes a new boat launch and entrance, trails that lead to a river observation shelter and a fishing deck. Also in the campground, a set of interpretive panels details the history of the Sourdough Roadhouse, a colorful lodge and national historic site that burned to the ground in 1992.

Gulkana Canoe Route
This trip along the Gulkana River from Paxson Lake, Mile 175 of the Richardson Hwy, to where the highway crosses the river at Gulkana is a popular canoe, kayak and raft route of 80 miles. The first 45 miles are only for experienced white-water paddlers or rafters, as they involve several challenging rapids, including the Class IV Canyon Rapids. Although there is a short portage around Canyon Rapids, rough Class III waters follow. The final 35 miles from the Sourdough Creek Campground to Gulkana make for a pleasant one- or two-day paddle in mild water that can be enjoyed by less hard-core canoeists.

All the land from the Sourdough Creek Campground south belongs to the Ahtna Native Corporation, which charges boaters to camp. The exceptions – three single-acre sites – are sign-posted along the riverbanks and have short trails leading back to the highway. Raft rentals and shuttle service for many area rivers, including the Gulkana River, can be arranged through River Wrangellers (☎ 888-822-3967, 822-3967, raftak@alaska.net) in Gakona.

Alaska Range Foothills to Black Rapids Glacier
Ten miles north of Sourdough Creek, the Richardson Hwy enters the foothills of the Alaska Range. Gradually, sweeping views open up, showcasing not only the Alaska Range to the north but the Wrangell Mountains to the south and the Chugach Mountains to the southwest. More splendid views follow; to the west, you can see the large plateau where the headwaters of the Susitna River form, while you'll glimpse the Glennallen area to the south. At Mile 175 of the Richardson Hwy is the gravel spur that leads 1.5 miles west to the recently upgraded ***Paxson Lake BLM Campground*** (50 sites, $6). The lakeshore campground now has walk-in sites ($3) for tents only.

At the junction with the Denali Hwy, you'll find the small service center of **Paxson**. The ***Paxson Inn*** (☎ 822-3330), Mile 185.5 of the Richardson Hwy, has singles/doubles for $60/70, a cafe and a bar. Five miles north of

Paxson, on the west side of the highway, look for the parking area by the Gulkana River, where there are trash cans and picnic tables. This scenic spot provides views of Summit Lake and the Trans-Alaska Pipeline. From mid- to late summer, this is also a good spot to watch the salmon spawn.

After passing Summit Lake, the bridge over Gunn Creek at Mile 196.7 provides views of **Gulkana Glacier** to the northeast. From here, the highway begins climbing to its highest point at **Isabel Pass** (3000 feet). The pass, at Mile 197.6, is marked by a historical sign dedicated to General Wilds Richardson, after whom the highway is named. From this point you can view Gulkana Glacier to the northeast and the Isabel Pass pipeline camp below it.

Three miles north of the pass, a gravel spur leads 1.5 miles to *Fielding Lake Wayside*, where you can camp (seven sites, free) in a scenic area above the tree line at 2973 feet. This high up in the Alaska Range, the ice often remains on the lake until July. The highway and the pipeline parallel each other north from Fielding Lake, and there are several lookouts where you can view the monumental efforts to move oil. One of the best is at Mile 205.7, where the pipeline travels up a steep hill.

At Mile 225.4, you'll find a viewpoint with picnic tables and a historical marker pointing out what little ice remains of **Black Rapids Glacier** to the west. The glacier became known as the 'Galloping Glacier' after its famous 3-mile advancement in the winter of 1936, when it almost engulfed the highway. Across from the marker, the easy **Black Rapids Lake Trail**, 0.3-miles long, winds through wildflowers to Black Rapids Lake.

Donnelly Creek to Delta Junction

The last public campground before Delta Junction is just before Mile 238 of the Richardson Hwy, where a short loop road leads west of the highway to the *Donnelly Creek State Campground* (12 sites, $8). This is a great place to camp, as it is seldom crowded and is extremely scenic, with good views of the towering peaks of the Alaska Range. Occasionally, the Delta bison herd can be seen from the campground.

You'll pass two interesting turnoffs in the final 25 miles before you reach the Alcan. The first, at Mile 241.3, overlooks the calving grounds of the Delta buffalo herd to the west. In 1928, 23 bison were relocated here from Montana for the pleasure of sportsmen, and today there are more than 400 bison. The animals have established a migratory pattern that includes summering and calving along the Delta River. If you have binoculars, you can spot up to 100 animals here.

The other turnoff, just before Mile 244, offers spectacular views of the pipeline and three of the highest peaks in the Alaska Range to the southwest. From south to west, you can see Mt Deborah (12,339 feet), Hess Mountain (11,940 feet) and Mt Hayes (13,697 feet).

The highway passes Fort Greely just beyond Mile 261 and then arrives at the Delta Junction Visitor Center on the 'Triangle,' where the Alcan merges with the Richardson Hwy at Mile 266. From here, it is 98 miles to Fairbanks.

DELTA JUNCTION TO FAIRBANKS

From Delta Junction, the Richardson Hwy merges with the Alcan for the remaining 98 miles to Fairbanks and passes the most interesting attraction in the Delta Junction area at Mile 275. **Big Delta State Historic Park** (see the Delta Junction map; ☎ 895-4201), a 10-acre historical park on the Tanana River, preserves Rika's Landing, an important crossroads for travelers, miners and soldiers on the Valdez-to-Fairbanks Trail from 1909 to 1947.

The centerpiece of the park is **Rika's Roadhouse**, which has been renovated and now contains historical displays and a large gift shop. The roadhouse began as little more than a cabin in 1904, when John Hajdukovich came along and constructed most of the buildings within the park before trading them to a young Swedish woman in 1923, reportedly for $10 and her back wages. The roadhouse is named after this lucky barterer, Erika Wallen, who ran it until the late 1940s and lived there until her death in 1969.

Of the 30 roadhouses that once stretched along the rutted and muddy Valdez-to-Fairbanks Trail (now the Richardson Hwy), only three remain: Rika's, the Sullivan Roadhouse in Delta Junction and the one in Copper Center.

Today, guides in period dress lead tours through the complex, which includes a blacksmith's shop museum, Signal Corp station, and the Packhouse Pavilion, where local artisans work on spinning, weaving, quilting and willow carving. The roadhouse is open 8 am to 8 pm daily during the summer. Admission and the guided tours are free. At the *Packhouse Restaurant*, open 9 am to 5 pm, the specialty is the bear claw ($2), a sweet pastry that resembles a bear paw. It's filled with nuts and dripping in icing. Also at the Big Delta State Historic Park is a rustic *campground* (25 sites, $8).

Near the state historic park at Mile 275.3, you'll cross a bridge over the Tanana River. Look east for an impressive view of the Trans-Alaska Pipeline suspended over the water, or look west for equally impressive views of the Alaska Range. The highway then parallels the river much of the way to Fairbanks. Turnoffs allow you to search the braided channels for wildlife.

The *Quartz Lake State Campground* (see the Delta Junction map), Mile 277.7, has 80 sites ($8). For more information, see Places to Stay in the Delta Junction section, earlier in this chapter.

For the next 20 miles, the highway passes a handful of lookouts with spectacular views of both the Tanana River in the foreground and the Alaska Range behind it.

At Mile 321.5, a spur leads to *Harding Lake State Campground* (83 sites, $8). The campground, which has a ranger office near the entrance, features picnic shelters and five walk-in sites on the water, as well as swimming, canoeing and fishing (Arctic char and pike) opportunities in the lake.

From the campground, it is 43 miles to Fairbanks, with two public campgrounds along the way. At Mile 346.7, you'll reach the **Chena Lakes Recreation Area**. This facility opened in 1984 as the last phase of an Army Corps of Engineers flood-control project, which was prompted by the Chena River's flooding of Fairbanks in 1967. Two separate parks, Chena River and Chena Lakes, make up the recreational area, which is 18 miles southeast of Fairbanks off the Laurance Rd exit of the Richardson Hwy. The Chena River park contains a 2.5-mile self-guided nature trail. The Chena Lakes park offers swimming opportunities, as well as canoe, sailboat and paddleboat rentals. Between the two parks, three campground loops provide access to 78 sites. The day-use fee is $3, and overnight camping costs $8. The Richardson Hwy reaches Fairbanks at Mile 363 as a four-lane highway.

Denali Highway

With the exception of 21 miles that are paved at its east end, the Denali Hwy is a gravel road extending from Paxson on the Richardson Hwy to Cantwell on the George Parks Hwy, just south of the main entrance to Denali National Park. Since the early 1980s, though, the Alaska Department of Transportation has been pushing to pave the road, and it appears that the project might begin in 2000. Too bad. The rough nature of the road and the spectacular scenery that greeted the drivers who braved it always have made for a great Alaskan adventure.

When the 135-mile route was opened in 1957, it was called Alaska Route No 8 and was the only road to the national park. But the Denali Hwy quickly became a secondary route after the George Parks Hwy was completed in 1972, and today it's only open from mid-May to October. Most of it runs along the foothills of the Alaska Range to the north and through glacial valleys where you can see stretches of alpine tundra, enormous glaciers and braided rivers. The scenery is spectacular, but the road itself can be a disaster at times. This, say most travelers, is the worst road in Alaska. Plan on at least six hours to drive it from end to end. On the other hand, it's quickly becoming a favorite for mountain bikers.

Numerous trails lead into the surrounding backcountry, but none are marked. Also in the area are two popular canoe routes. Ask locals at the roadhouses for information and take along topographic maps that cover the areas you intend to trek or paddle.

There are no established communities along the way, but four roadhouses provide food and lodging. Two of them, at Mile 20 and Mile 81, sell gas. If you're driving, you'd better fill up with gasoline at Paxson or Cantwell.

PAXSON TO TANGLE LAKES

From Paxson, *Mile 0*, the highway heads west and passes the mile-long gravel road to Sevenmile Lake at Mile 7. From here, the terrain opens up and provides superb views of the nearby lakes and peaks of the Alaska Range. Most of the lakes – as many as 40 in the spring – can be seen from a lookout at Mile 13.

Swede Lake Trail

This trail, near Mile 15, leads south 3 miles to Swede Lake, passing Little Swede Lake at the 2-mile mark. Beyond here, it continues to the Middle Fork of the Gulkana River, but the trail is extremely wet at times and suitable only for off-road vehicles. Anglers fish the lakes for trout and grayling. Inquire at the Tangle River Inn (☎ 822-7304, tangle@alaska.net), Mile 20, for directions to the trail and an update on its condition.

Paddling

The **Delta River canoe route** is a 35-mile paddle that begins at the Tangle Lakes Campground, Mile 21.5 of the Denali Hwy, and ends a few hundred yards from Mile 212.5 of the Richardson Hwy. Begin the canoe route by crossing Round Tangle Lake and continuing to Lower Tangle Lake, where you must make a portage around a waterfall. Following the waterfall is a set of Class III rapids that you must either line for 2 miles or paddle if you have an experienced hand. Every year, numerous canoeists damage their boats beyond repair on these rapids and then must hike 15 miles back out to the

Denali Hwy. The remainder of the route is a much milder trip.

The **Upper Tangle Lakes canoe route** is easier and shorter than the Delta River route but requires four portages, which aren't marked but are easy to figure out in the low bush tundra. All paddlers attempting this route must have topographic maps. The route begins at Tangle River (where the Denali Hwy crosses the river) and passes through Upper Tangle Lake before ending at Dickey Lake, 9 miles to the south. There is a 1.2-mile portage into Dickey Lake.

From here, experienced paddlers can continue by following Dickey Lake's outlet to the southeast into the Middle Fork of the Gulkana River. For the first 3 miles, the river is shallow and mild, but then it plunges into a steep canyon where canoeists have to contend with Class III and IV rapids. Most canoeists choose to line their boats carefully or make a portage. Allow seven days for the entire 76-mile trip from Tangle Lakes to Sourdough Campground, on the Gulkana River off the Richardson Hwy.

Places to Stay

The *Tangle River Inn* (☎ 822-7304, tangle@alaska.net), Mile 20 of the Denali Hwy, contains a cafe, the Grizzly Bar, gas pumps, showers and a bunkroom with beds for $25. The inn's motel rooms range from $45 to $69 for two people. The *Tangle Lakes Lodge* (☎ 688-9173, tanglelakeslodge@corecom.net), Mile 22, has cabins that sleep up to three people for $65.

The paved portion of the Denali Hwy ends just beyond Mile 21, and in another half mile the highway reaches the BLM's *Tangle Lakes Campground* (13 sites, free) to the north, on the shores of Round Tangle Lake. It features displays explaining the archaeological digs in the area. A second BLM campground, *Upper Tangle Lakes* (seven sites, free), is a quarter mile down the road on the south side. Both campgrounds serve as the departure point for two scenic canoe routes, and the nearby Tangle River Inn rents canoes ($24 a day). You might spot some caribou in the surrounding hills.

THE INTERIOR

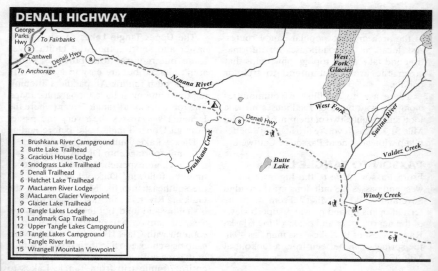

DENALI HIGHWAY

1 Brushkana River Campground
2 Butte Lake Trailhead
3 Gracious House Lodge
4 Snodgrass Lake Trailhead
5 Denali Trailhead
6 Hatchet Lake Trailhead
7 MacLaren River Lodge
8 MacLaren Glacier Viewpoint
9 Glacier Lake Trailhead
10 Tangle Lakes Lodge
11 Landmark Gap Trailhead
12 Upper Tangle Lakes Campground
13 Tangle Lakes Campground
14 Tangle River Inn
15 Wrangell Mountain Viewpoint

TANGLE LAKES TO DENALI NATIONAL PARK

At Mile 25, the Denali Hwy crosses Rock Creek Bridge, where the **Landmark Gap Trail** leads north 3 miles to Landmark Gap Lake, with an elevation of 3217 feet. You can't see the lake from the highway, but you can spot the noticeable gap between the Amphitheatre Mountains.

At Mile 32, a parking lot on the north side of the highway marks the start of the 3-mile **Glacier Lake Trail**. From here, the highway ascends **MacLaren Summit** (4086 feet), one of the highest highway passes in the state. The summit, offers views of Mt Hayes, Hess Mountain and Mt Deborah to the west and MacLaren Glacier to the north.

You'll cross the MacLaren River on a 364-foot multiple-span bridge at Mile 42 of the Denali Hwy. Nearby is the Maclaren River Lodge. Another bridge crosses Clearwater Creek at Mile 56; there are campsites and outhouses nearby. The first of many hiking trails in the area begins at Mile 69; all are unmarked, and many are nothing more than old gravel roads. Inquire at the Gracious House Lodge, a roadhouse at Mile 82, for the exact location of the trails.

Hiking

There are many hiking opportunities in the next 25 miles of the highway. The **Hatchet Lake Trail**, a 5-mile walk, begins near Raft Creek, just before Mile 69.

Denali Trail begins on the north side of the highway at Mile 79, a half mile before the road crosses the Susitna River on a multiple-span bridge. The 6-mile trail winds its way to the old mining camp of Denali, first established in 1907. A few of the old buildings still remain. Today, gold mining has resumed in the area. Several old mining trails branch off the trail, including an 18-mile route to Roosevelt Lake from Denali Camp. The area can provide enough hiking for a two- to three-day trip, but only tackle these trails with a map and compass in hand.

The **Snodgrass Lake Trail** leads 2 miles south of the highway to Snodgrass Lake, known among anglers for its good grayling fishing. The trail starts at a parking area between Mile 80 and Mile 81 of the Denali Hwy.

The **Butte Lake Trail**, an off-road-vehicle track, leads 5 miles south to Butte Lake, known for its large lake trout, which often weigh over 30lb. The trailhead is at Mile 94.

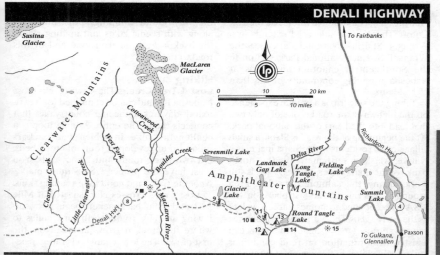

DENALI HIGHWAY

Places to Stay & Eat

The Maclaren River Lodge (☎ 822-7105), Mile 42, has campsites, 4 cabins ($150 to $250), 7 rooms ($50 to $80) and a restaurant. The *Gracious House Lodge* (☎ 877-822-7307, 333-3148, CRhoa36683@aol.com), Mile 82, offers tent sites ($5) and B&B rooms ($110 for two people). The lodge also serves food in its cafe and sells gas. At Mile 104.3 is the *Brushkana River Campground* (17 sites, free). This BLM campground has a shelter, drinking water and a meat rack for hunters, who invade the area in late summer and fall. The river, which the campground overlooks, can be fished for grayling and Dolly Varden trout.

Twenty miles from here, the Denali Hwy merges with the George Parks Hwy. The entrance to Denali National Park is 17 miles north of this junction, on the George Parks Hwy.

Tok Cutoff

The Tok Cutoff is often considered to be the northern half of the Glenn Hwy, but mileposts along the road show distances from Gakona Junction, at the southern end of the cutoff, and not from Anchorage, as they do once you pass Glennallen.

From Tok, it is 328 miles to Anchorage, or a full day's drive. You first travel 139 miles southwest along the Tok Cutoff to Glennallen, at the junction of the Richardson and Glenn Hwys, and then another 189 miles to Anchorage via the Glenn Hwy.

The first of only two public campgrounds on the Tok Cutoff pops up at Mile 109.3 as you drive south from Tok. The *Eagle Trail State Recreation Site* (40 sites, $10) is near Clearwater Creek and provides drinking water, toilets, rain shelter and fire pits. The historical **Eagle Trail**, which at one time extended to Eagle on the Yukon River, can still be hiked for a mile from the campground. Look for the posted trailhead near the covered picnic shelters.

The second campground is another 45 miles southwest along the highway. The *Porcupine Creek State Recreation Site*, Mile 64.2, has 12 wooded sites ($10) in a scenic spot along the creek. A mile north along the highway, you'll find a historical marker and splendid views of Mt Sanford (16,203 feet), a dormant volcano.

NABESNA ROAD

At Mile 59.8, Nabesna Rd intersects the Tok Cutoff. The 45-mile side road extends into Wrangell-St Elias National Park (see the Wrangell-St Elias National Park section in the Southcentral chapter) and ends at **Nabesna**, a mining community of less than 25 residents.

Taking the side trip is a unique experience off the highways; the road is one of only two that lead into the heart of the national park. At the beginning of the road is **Slana**, a small village of 50 residents or so. Slana includes a Native Alaskan settlement on the north banks of the Slana River, and fish wheels still work during the salmon runs. The area around it was one of the last places in the USA to be opened to homesteading, as late as the early 1980s. The National Park Service ranger station (☎ 822-5238) in Slana can assist with information on road conditions and possible hikes in this region of Wrangell-St Elias National Park. The station also has a few displays and sells USGS maps. It's open 8 am to 5 pm daily from June to September.

You'll find some unique accommodations near Slana. *Huck Hobbit's Homestead (☎ 822-3196)* is a wilderness retreat 4 miles off Nabesna Rd; the last half mile is accessible only by hiking or ATVs. The two cabins ($20) are relatively new and include beds, sheets, a woodstove and cooking area. Showers are available. Campsites cost $2.50, and the hosts serve home-style meals for $5 per person. Stay an extra day here – the scenery is beautiful – and splurge on a canoe trip down the Slana River for $35 per canoe (two people). Ask at the ranger station in Slana for directions to the hostel.

The first 30 miles of Nabesna Rd is a manageable gravel road, but after that the surface is extremely rough, with several streams flowing over it. The *Sportsman Paradise Lodge (☎ 822-5288)*, Mile 28.6, has accommodations and gas. *End of the Road B&B (☎ 822-5312)*, Mile 42, is as out-of-the-way lodging as you're going to find in Alaska. Beds in the bunkhouse cost $20, and two cabins sleep two for $60. Breakfast and showers are included. The lodge is packed with hunters beginning August 1.

There are no public campgrounds along the way. Good camping spots, however, along with scenic lakes and inviting ridges for backpackers, lie from one end of this road to the other.

Hiking

Lost & Trail Creeks These two creeks cross Nabesna Rd and can be combined for a two- to four-day trek to the high country pass that connects them. The entire 23-mile loop is a challenging hike in which backpackers follow an undeveloped route of creek beds, old two-track roads and game trails. You must have the proper USGS quad map – *Nabesna C-5* – and good map-reading skills.

Lost Creek crosses Nabesna Rd at Mile 31.2, and many backpackers begin here, following an ATV route north for 6 miles to where the creek narrows at a canyon, the first of two. The lower canyon is rarely passable, forcing you to climb up and around it. In roughly 8.5 miles, you'll reach the creek headwaters and then climb to a 6000-foot pass between the two stream systems. This pass allows you to follow Trail Creek south to return to Nabesna Rd at Mile 29.6. If planning this adventure, stop at the Slana ranger station to pick up a map and a set of trail notes.

Soda Lake ATV trails lead from Lost Creek east 8 miles to Soda Creek, and from there backpackers can hike another 2 miles to Soda Lake, above the tree line. At Soda Lake, a horse trail continues east 3 miles across a low pass to Totschunda Creek. The roundtrip to Soda Lake is a 20-mile trek that makes for an ideal three- or four-day outing, with a spare day spent at the lake.

Reese Field Trail At Mile 41, a mile before the state maintenance of the Nabesna Rd ends, a marked trail leads 5 miles to the Nabesna River and the site of the old Reese Filed airstrip. The landing strip was once used to fly supplies into the mining camps and to transport gold out. Devils Mountain (5335 feet), looms overhead at times, but there is very little elevation gain on this trek.

CHISTOCHINA & GAKONA JUNCTION

Halfway way between Nabesna Rd and Gakona Junction on the Tok Cutoff, you'll pass the settlement of Chistochina (population 50). The handful of businesses here include the *Chistochina Lodge & Trading Post* (☎ 822-3366), Mile 32.8 of the Tok Cutoff. Built in 1921 to service travelers along the Eagle-Valdez Trail, the lodge is a classic Alaskan roadhouse. Today, the lodge is a National Historic Place, as well as a spot to stop for a shower, gas, a sourdough pancake-and-caribou sausage breakfast, a cold beer in the saloon or a bed for the night. Rooms are $65 for two people; cabins are $75.

Officially, the Tok Cutoff ends at Gakona Junction, 125 miles southwest of Tok, where it merges with the Richardson Hwy. The village of **Gulkana** (population 90) is 2 miles to the south, and you can camp along the Gulkana River by the bridge in town. For an interesting meal, try the dining room of the *Gakona Lodge* (☎ 822-3482, gakonalg@alaska.net), Mile 2 of the Tok Cutoff. The roadhouse opened in 1905 as Doyle's Ranch near the junction of the Eagle and Fairbanks Cutoffs. In 1929, a larger lodge was added, and the original one was made into a carriage house. Today, it's listed on the National Register of Historic Places, and the carriage house has been turned into a dining room, a bar and a natural-food store. The eight double rooms rent for $80.

From Gakona Junction, the Richardson Hwy leads 14 miles south to the eastern end of the Glenn Hwy.

Glenn Highway

The Glenn Hwy runs west from Glennallen to Anchorage, with the mileposts along the road showing the distance from Anchorage, Mile 0.

GLENNALLEN

Glennallen (population 500), referred to by some as 'the Hub' of Alaska's road system, is a service center on the Glenn Hwy, 2 miles west of the junction with the Richardson Hwy. Because of its strategic location, the town provides a wide range of facilities and serves as the major departure point for those going to Wrangell-St Elias National Park. It's also the home base for many fishing and hunting guides. Otherwise, it looks like an RV park, and there's little reason to linger here.

Information

The Greater Copper River Valley Visitor Center (☎ 822-5555) is a log cabin at the junction of the Glenn and Richardson Hwys. It's open 8 am to 7 pm daily.

Glennallen has the only full-service bank in the Copper Valley region – a National Bank of Alaska (☎ 822-3214), Mile 187.5 of the Glenn Hwy.

The post office is on Aurora Drive, just off the Glenn Hwy near the bank.

The public library is on the Glenn Hwy on the west side of town. It's open 1 to 6 pm Tuesday to Saturday.

The Glennallen Laundromat (☎ 822-3999) is next to Park's Place supermarket, on the Glenn Hwy in downtown Glennallen.

The Cross Road Medical Center (☎ 822-3203), near the corner of the Glenn Hwy and Aurora Drive, is a walk-in clinic and pharmacy with 24-hour emergency service.

Places to Stay

The closest public campground is the *Dry Creek State Recreation Site* (60 sites, $10), 5 miles northeast of town on the Richardson Hwy between the junction with the Glenn Hwy and the Tok Cutoff. Within town, *Northern Nights Campground* (☎ 822-3199), Mile 188.7 of the Glenn Hwy, has tent sites ($10) but no showers. You might as well walk a half mile out of town and camp for free in the woods.

The *New Caribou Hotel* (☎ 822-3302, chotel@alaska.net), Mile 186.9 of the Glenn Hwy, is right in town, and its lack of competition shows. The rooms are nice but run a steep $130 for singles or doubles. Four miles west of Glennallen is *Brown Bear Roadhouse* (☎ 822-3663), Mile 183.6 of the Glenn Hwy, with three 'camping cabins' for $45 for two people.

Getting There & Away

Glennallen is notorious among hitchhikers as a place for getting stuck (especially at the Glenn Hwy junction) when trying to thumb a ride north to the Alcan. Luckily, a variety of buses are always passing through.

Gray Line's Alaskon Express passes through almost daily, en route to either Anchorage or Tok. On Sunday, Tuesday and Friday, a bus heads north at 12:30 pm; on Monday, Wednesday and Friday, a bus heads south at 3 pm. The one-way fare to Anchorage is $61, to Haines $176. A Parks Highway Express bus (☎ 888-600-6001) passes through at 11:30 am bound for Fairbanks ($45), at noon for Anchorage ($45) and at 2:20 pm for Valdez ($20). Backcountry Connection vans (☎ 822-5292, 800-478-5292 in Alaska) depart for McCarthy at 7 am on Monday through Saturday, reaching the historic town at noon. The one-way fare is $70.

The Caribou Cafe (☎ 822-3656), next door to the Caribou Hotel, serves as the pickup point for both Alaskon Express and Backcountry Connection. Parks Highway Express departs from the Greater Copper River Valley Visitor Center.

GLENNALLEN TO PALMER

The Glenn Hwy runs west from Glennallen through a vast plateau bordered by the Alaska Range to the north and the Chugach Mountains to the south. This is an incredibly scenic section that extends almost 150 miles west; it's a prime area for spotting wildlife. Moose and caribou roam the lowlands, and black bears and grizzlies live on the timbered ridges. On the slopes of both mountain ranges, and often visible from the highway, are Dall sheep.

Tolsona Creek to Little Nelchina River

The first campground west of Glennallen is the ***Tolsona Wilderness Campground*** (☎ 822-3865, *twcg@alaska.net*), Mile 173, a private facility with 80 sites that border the river. Sites cost $12 to $18, but that buys you access to fresh water, coin-operated showers and laundry facilities.

A lookout with trash cans marks the trailhead for the **Mae West Lake Trail**, a short hike away from Mile 169.3 of the Glenn Hwy. This mile-long trail leads to a long, narrow lake fed by Little Woods Creek. The trailhead for the **Lost Cabin Lake Trail** is on the south side of the highway at Mile 165.8, marked by a pair of trash cans. The trail winds 2 miles to the lake and is a berry-picker's delight from late summer to early fall.

The first public campground that's accessible from the highway is the ***Lake Louise State Recreation Area*** (52 sites, $10), which provides shelters, tables and drinking water. You can swim in the lake. This scenic campground is 17 miles up Lake Louise Rd, which leaves the Glenn Hwy at Mile 160. A mile up Lake Louise Rd, there's a turnoff with good views of Tazlina Glacier and Carter Lake.

At Mile 138.3 of the Glenn Hwy, the **Old Man Creek Trail** begins. This trail leads 2 miles to Old Man Creek and 9 miles to Crooked Creek, where you can fish for grayling. It ends at the old mining area of Nelchina, 14.5 miles from the highway, where it merges into the old Chickaloon-Knik-Nelchina Trail, a gold miner's route used before the Glenn Hwy was built.

The **Chickaloon-Knik-Nelchina Trail** is an extensive system of trails that extends as far as Palmer and beyond, with many posted access points along the north side of the highway. The system is not maintained regularly, and hikers attempting any part of it should have good outdoor experience and the right topographic maps. You'll have to share the trail with off-road vehicles.

The final campground on this stretch of road is the ***Little Nelchina State Recreation Site*** at Mile 137.5, just off the Glenn Hwy. Its 11 campsites are free.

Eureka Summit to Palmer

From Little Nelchina River, the Glenn Hwy begins to ascend, and views of Gunsight Mountain (you have to look hard to see the origin of its name) come into view. From Eureka Summit, you can see both Gunsight Mountain and the Chugach Mountains to the south, the Nelchina Glacier spilling down in the middle and the Talkeetna Mountains to the north. This impressive, unobstructed view extends to the west, where you can see the highway dropping into the river valleys that separates the two mountain chains. Eureka Summit (3322 feet) is at Mile 129.3 of the Glenn Hwy; it is the highway's highest point.

The trailhead for the **Belanger Pass Trail**, at Mile 123.3 on Martin Rd across from the Tahneta Lodge, is marked by a Chickaloon-Knik-Nelchina Trail sign. For the most part, miners and hunters in off-road vehicles use it to travel into the Talkeetna Mountains, and at times the mining scars are disturbing.

The views from Belanger Pass, a 3-mile hike, are excellent and well worth the climb. From the 4350-foot pass, off-road-vehicle trails continue north to Alfred Creek, another 3.5 miles away, and eventually lead around the north side of Syncline Mountain past active mining operations.

Two miles west of the Belanger Pass trailhead is **Tahneta Pass** at Mile 121. Half a mile farther, you can view the 3000-foot pass at a scenic turnoff. East of the turnoff lies Lake Liela, with Lake Tahneta beyond it.

The **Squaw Creek Trail** is another miners' and hunters' trail that begins at Mile 117.6 of the Glenn Hwy and merges into the Chickaloon-Knik-Nelchina Trail. It begins as an off-road-vehicle trail marked by a Squaw Creek Trail sign. It extends 3.5 miles to Squaw Creek and 9.5 miles to Caribou Creek after ascending a low pass between the two. Although the trail can be confusing at times, the hike is a scenic one, with the Gunsight, Sheep and Syncline Mountains as a backdrop.

From here, the Glenn Hwy begins to descend, and the scenery becomes stunning as the road heads toward the Talkeetna Mountains, passing an oddly shaped rock formation known as the Lion's Head at Mile 114. A half mile beyond it, the highway reaches the first view of Matanuska Glacier. To the north is Sheep Mountain – properly named, as you can often spot Dall sheep on its slopes.

At Mile 113.5 of the Glenn Hwy is the *Sheep Mountain Lodge (☎ 745-5121, sheepmtl@alaska.net)*. The lodge is 70 miles east of Palmer and features a cafe, bar and liquor store along with cabins that start at $95 for two people. The lodge also offers dormitory-style accommodations in two bunkrooms. Four people can share one of these rooms for $50. The lodge occasionally squeezes an extra bed into each bunkroom, but this still limits the number of available beds to 10, many of which are booked ahead (even overbooked at times). Everybody at the lodge can enjoy the sauna and hot tub, along with the great hiking nearby. The restaurant serves excellent homemade soups and sandwiches for $6 to $8.

At Mile 101, you'll reach the *Matanuska Glacier State Recreation Site* (12 sites, $10). The area has sheltered tables, drinking water, trails and viewing decks that provide good views of the glacier. It's a beautiful campground but a popular one, so there is a three-day limit here.

Matanuska Glacier is a stable ice floe that is 4 miles wide at its terminus and extends 27 miles back into the Chugach Mountains. Some 18,000 years ago, it covered the area where the city of Palmer is today. If you want to drive near the glacier's face, swing into the *Glacier Park Resort (☎ 745-2534)*, Mile 102, and pay $6.50 to follow its private road to within 400 feet of the ice. At this point some people just walk to the face, while others spend a whole day on the ice. For another $6 per person, you can camp at this 540-acre resort, which features a cafe and limited supplies. The picture windows at the *Long Rifle Lodge (☎ 800-770-5151, 745-5151)*, Mile 102.2, allow you to gaze at the glacier from the dining room while enjoying a good bowl of chili. The lodge-bar-motel sits just before the entrance to Glacier Park Resort.

The **Purinton Creek Trail** starts just before the bridge over the creek at Mile 89. A short dirt road heads north of the highway and then east, passing an off-road-vehicle trail that ascends a steep hill to the north. The Purinton Creek Trail is a 12-mile walk to the foot of Boulder Creek, though most of the final 7 miles is a trek along the gravel bars of the river. The Chugach Mountain scenery is excellent, and you'll find good camping spots along Boulder Creek.

In the next 13 miles, the Glenn Hwy passes three public campgrounds. The first is *Long Lake State Recreation Site* (nine sites, free) at Mile 85.3. Along with toilets and fire pits, the campground offers access to a grayling fishing hole that's a favorite with Anchorage residents.

Two miles west of the Long Lake State Campground is a gravel spur road that leads to the *Lower Bonnie Lake State Recreation Site* (eight sites, free), a 2-mile side trip from the highway. The third campground is the *King Mountain State Recreation Site* (22 sites, $10), Mile 76 of the Glenn Hwy. This scenic campground sits on the banks of the Matanuska River, with a view of King Mountain to the southeast. Just outside the campground is *King Mountain Lodge* (☎ 745-4280), Mile 76.2, where you can get a burger and beer along with some supplies. The lodge also rents motel rooms for $40 and rustic cabins for $35.

Across the highway is the office for Nova (☎ 745-5753, 800-746-5753, nova@alaska .net), a rafting company that runs the Matanuska River daily. The company offers a mild 3½-hour run at 10 am ($60 per person) and a wilder one, which features Class IV rapids around Lionshead Wall, at 9 am and 2 pm ($75). All this – the scenery, the rafting and the beer store – makes the state campground a good place to pull up, or stop hitching, for a day or two.

Just before passing through Sutton (population 470) at Mile 61, you'll come to **Alpine Historical Park** (☎ 745-7000). The park contains several buildings, including the Chickaloon Bunkhouse and the original Sutton post office, which now houses a museum. Inside, the displays are devoted to the Athabascan people, the 1920 coal-boom era of Sutton and the building of the Glenn Hwy. The park is open 10 am to 6 pm daily during the summer. Admission is $2.

Almost 12 miles beyond Sutton is the junction with the Fishhook-Willow Rd,

which provides access to Independence Mine State Park (see the Hatcher Pass section in the Anchorage chapter). The highway then descends into the agricultural center of Palmer.

From Palmer, the Glenn Hwy merges with the George Parks Hwy and continues south to Anchorage, 43 miles away (see the Anchorage chapter).

Taylor Highway

The scenic Taylor Hwy extends 161 miles north from Tetlin Junction, 13 miles east of Tok on the Alcan, to the historic town of Eagle on the Yukon River. It's a beautiful but rough drive as the narrow, winding road ascends Mt Fairplay, Polly Summit and American Summit, all over 3500 feet.

The highway offers access to the popular Fortymile River canoe route and much off-road hiking. As on the Denali Hwy, many of the trailheads are unmarked, making it necessary to have the proper topographic maps in hand. Many trails are off-road-vehicle tracks that hunters use heavily in late summer and fall.

By Alaskan standards, the summer traffic is light-to-moderate until you reach Jack Wade Junction, where the majority of vehicles continue east to Dawson City in the Yukon. Hitchhikers going to Eagle have to be patient in the final 65 miles north of Jack Wade Junction, but the ride will come. If you're driving, leave Tetlin Junction with a full tank of gasoline because roadside services are limited along the route.

From Tetlin Junction, *Mile 0*, the highway heads north, and within 9 miles begins to climb Mt Fairplay (5541 feet). At Mile 35, a lookout near the summit is marked by trash cans and an interpretive sign describing the history of the Taylor Hwy. From here, you should see superb views of Mt Fairplay and the valleys and forks of the Fortymile River to the north. The surrounding alpine area offers good hiking for those who need to stretch their legs.

The first state campground is at Mile 49, on the west side of the highway. *West Fork*

Campground (25 sites, free) has outhouses but no drinking water; all water taken from nearby streams should be boiled or treated first. Travelers packing along gold pans can try their luck in the West Fork River, which is the first access point for a canoe trip down the Fortymile River.

CHICKEN

After crossing a bridge over the Fortymile River's Mosquito Fork at Mile 64.4, the Taylor Hwy passes the old **Chicken post office** on a hill beside the road at Mile 66.2. The post office, still operating today, was originally established when Chicken was a thriving mining center. **Old Chicken**, the original mining camp, is now privately owned, but you can see it on a walking tour that begins at 1 pm daily at the Chicken Creek Cafe. The buildings in the complex include the schoolhouse of Ann Purdy, who later wrote the novel *Tisha*, based on her days as a schoolteacher here. You can purchase a copy of the book at the Chicken Mercantile Emporium.

The community of Chicken itself (population 40 or so) is 300 yards to the north on a spur road that leads to an airstrip, a grocery store, the *Chicken Creek Cafe* and a gas station. The town's name, according to one tale, originated at a meeting of the resident miners in the late 1800s. When trying to come up with a name for the new tent city, somebody suggested Ptarmigan, since the chicken-like bird existed in great numbers throughout the area. All the miners liked it, but none of them could spell it. The town's name has been Chicken ever since.

Just north of the spur road to the village is the Chicken Creek Bridge, built on tailing piles from the mining era. If you look back to the left, you can see the **Chicken Dredge**, which was used to extract gold from the creek between 1959 and 1965. Most of the forks of the Fortymile River are virtually covered from one end to the other by active mining claims, and often you can see suction dredging for gold from the highway. At Mile 75.3, the bridge over South Fork marks the most popular access point for the Fortymile River canoe route.

FORTYMILE RIVER CANOE ROUTE

The historic Fortymile River, designated as the Fortymile National Wild River, offers an excellent escape into scenic wilderness for paddlers experienced in lining their canoes around rapids. It is also a step back into the gold-rush era of Alaska, as the river passes abandoned mining communities, including Franklin, Steele Creek and Fortymile, as well as some present-day mining operations. The best place to start is the bridge over South Fork, because the access points south of here on the Taylor Hwy are often too shallow for an enjoyable trip.

Many canoeists paddle the 40 miles from the South Fork bridge to the bridge over O'Brien Creek, Mile 113 of the Taylor Hwy. This two- to three-day trip involves three sets of Class III rapids. For a greater adventure, continue past O'Brien Creek and paddle the Fortymile River into the Yukon River; from here, head north to Eagle at the end of the Taylor Hwy. This trip is 140 miles long and requires seven to 10 days to cover the distance. You'll need to line several sets of rapids in the Fortymile River. Such an expedition calls for careful planning before you leave for Alaska.

Eagle Canoe Rentals (☎ 547-2203) in Eagle is the closest place from which you can obtain a canoe or raft for your trip (see the Eagle section for details).

WALKER FORK TO AMERICAN CREEK

At Mile 82 of the Taylor Hwy is the *Walker Fork Campground* (18 sites, $4), which lies on both sides of the highway and has tables, firewood and a short trail to a limestone bluff overlook.

At Mile 86, a lookout offers a view of the **Jack Wade Dredge**, which operated from 1900 to 1942. For most of its working days, the dredge was powered by a wood-burning steam engine that required 10 to 12 cords of wood per day. The old Jack Wade mining camp lies 4 miles north of the dredge; after being abandoned for 30 years, the mine is now being reworked to capitalize on higher gold prices.

Panning for a Fortune

After all the gold rushes that have been staged in Alaska, can there possibly be any gold left for recreational gold panners? You bet! Although more than 30 million ounces of placer gold have been mined in Alaska since 1880, including 450,000 ounces in 1997 alone, some geologists estimate that this amount represents only 5% of what the state contains.

Suddenly interested? Alaska has more than 150 public prospecting sites where you can recreationally pan for gold without staking a claim or filing for a permit. The best ones are in the Interior region of the state. They include the Jack Wade Dredge, at Mile 86 of the Taylor Hwy, and American Creek, at Mile 151; the Petersville State Recreation Mining Area, on Petersville Rd off the George Parks Hwy at Trapper Creek; and Caribou Creek, at Mile 106.8 of the Glenn Hwy, and Nelchina River, at Mile 137.5.

When panning for gold, you must have one essential piece of equipment: a gravity-trap pan, one that measures 10 to 20 inches in diameter. It can usually be bought at any good Alaskan hardware or general store. Those who have panned for a while also show up with rubber boots and gloves to protect feet and hands from icy waters, a garden trowel to dig up loose rock, a pair of tweezers to pick up gold flakes and a small bottle to hold their find.

Panning techniques are based on the notion that gold is heavier than the gravel it lies in. Fill your pan with loose material from cracks and crevices in streams, where gold might have washed down and become lodged. Add water to the pan and rinse and discard larger rocks, keeping the rinsing in the pan. Continue to shake the contents toward the bottom by swirling the pan in a circular motion and wash off the excess sand and gravel by dipping the front into the stream.

You should be left with heavy black mud, sand and, if you are lucky, a few flakes of gold. Use tweezers or your fingernails to transfer the flakes into a bottle filled with water.

You'll reach the Jack Wade Junction at Mile 95.7, and here the Top of the World Hwy (also known as the Dawson Hwy) winds 3.5 miles to the Canadian/US border and another 75 miles east to Dawson City. The Taylor Hwy continues north from the junction and ascends **Polly Summit** (3550 feet). The summit sits at Mile 105, and 5 miles beyond it there's a scenic lookout with views of the Fortymile River.

From the summit, the Taylor Hwy begins a steep descent; drivers must take this section slowly. Along the way, you'll pass numerous lookouts with good views, as well as a variety of abandoned cabins, old gold dredges and mine tailings. Primitive camping is possible at Mile 135, on the south side of a bridge over North Fork Solomon Creek. This is a former BLM campground that has not been maintained in years. Holiday prospectors should try their luck in the nearby creek. Eagle is another 27 miles north.

EAGLE
History

The historic town of Eagle (population 150) had its beginnings in the late 1800s and today is one of the best-preserved boomtowns of the mining era in Alaska.

The original community, today called Eagle Village, was established by the Athabascan Indians long before Francois Mercier arrived in the early 1880s and built a trading post in the area. A permanent community of miners took up residence in 1898. A year later, the US Army decided to move in and build a fort as part of its effort to maintain law and order in the Alaskan Interior. Judge Wickersham established a federal court at Eagle in 1900, and the next year President Theodore Roosevelt issued a charter that made Eagle the first incorporated city of the Interior.

Eagle reached its peak at the turn of the 20th century, when it boasted a population of more than 1500 residents, some of whom went so far as to call their town the 'Paris of the North,' though that was hardly the case. The overland telegraph wire from Valdez arrived in 1903. This new technology proved particularly useful to the famous Norwegian explorer Roald Amundsen, who hiked overland to Eagle in 1905 after his ship froze in the Arctic Sea off Canada. From the town's telegraph office, he sent word to the waiting world that he had just navigated the Northwest Passage. Amundsen stayed two weeks in Eagle and then mushed back to his sloop. Nine months later, the ship reached Nome, completing the first successful voyage from the Atlantic to the Pacific Ocean across the Arctic Ocean.

Other gold strikes in the early 1900s, most notably at Fairbanks, began drawing residents away from Eagle and caused the removal of Judge Wickersham's court to the new city in the west. The army fort was abandoned in 1911, and by the 1940s Eagle's population had dwindled to 10. At one point, it is said, the population of Eagle dipped to nine residents, seven of whom served on the city council. When the Taylor Hwy was completed in the 1950s, however, the town's population increased to its present level. In the late 1970s, noted author John McPhee arrived in Eagle, rented a cabin for part of a year and worked on his bestseller *Coming Into The Country*, which immortalized life in Eagle, Alaska.

Information

The best place for information is the National Park Service Visitor Center (☎ 547-2233), which serves as the headquarters for the Yukon-Charley Rivers National Preserve. The center is a log cabin on the banks of the Yukon River, off 1st Ave beside the downtown airstrip. Inside you can buy books, use the reference library or watch a video on the 3906-sq-mile Yukon-Charley Rivers National Preserve. The visitor center is open 8 am to 5 pm daily in the summer.

THE INTERIOR

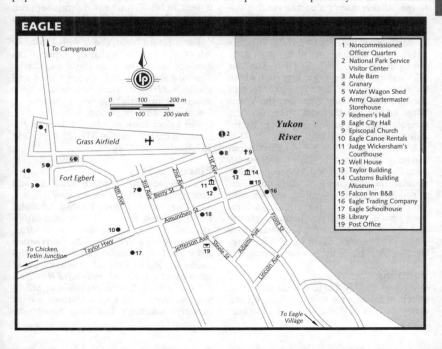

EAGLE

To Campground

Yukon River

Grass Airfield

Fort Egbert

To Chicken, Tetlin Junction

Taylor Hwy

2nd Ave

1st Ave

4th Ave

3rd Ave

Berry St

Amundsen St

Jefferson Ave

Steele St

Adams Ave

Front St

Lincoln Ave

To Eagle Village

0   100   200 m
0   100   200 yards

1 Noncommissioned Officer Quarters
2 National Park Service Visitor Center
3 Mule Barn
4 Granary
5 Water Wagon Shed
6 Army Quartermaster Storehouse
7 Redmen's Hall
8 Eagle City Hall
9 Episcopal Church
10 Eagle Canoe Rentals
11 Judge Wickersham's Courthouse
12 Well House
13 Taylor Building
14 Customs Building Museum
15 Falcon Inn B&B
16 Eagle Trading Company
17 Eagle Schoolhouse
18 Library
19 Post Office

The post office, on the corner of 2nd Ave and Jefferson Ave, also doubles as the US Customs office.

The public library (☎ 547-2334) is on Amundsen St, just east of 2nd Ave. You can purchase Alaska books in the National Parks Service Visitor Center or at the museum store in Judge Wickersham's Courthouse, on the corner of Berry St and 1st Ave.

You'll find a coin laundry in the Eagle Trading Company, at the end of Amundsen St on the banks of the Yukon River.

The Eagle Health Clinic (☎ 547-2243) is in Eagle Township, 3 miles south of town on 1st Ave.

Things to See & Do

Residents say Eagle has the state's largest 'museum system,' boasting five restored turn-of-the-century buildings.

If you're spending a day in Eagle, the best way to see the buildings and learn the town's history is to go to the upstairs courtroom of **Judge Wickersham's Courthouse**, on the corner of Berry St and 1st Ave, at 9 am. The courthouse, now a museum managed by the Eagle Historical Society (☎ 547-2325), offers a three-hour walking tour of the town daily during the summer, beginning here. The tour is $5 and includes the **Eagle City Hall**, where the city continues to hold regular meetings, the **Customs Building Museum**, the **Water Wagon Shed** and the **post office**, where a plaque commemorates explorer Roald Amundsen's visit to Eagle.

To the north of town is **Fort Egbert**, which can be reached from the Taylor Hwy via 4th Ave. The Bureau of Land Management has restored the old army fort, which once contained 37 buildings; several are now open to visitors during the summer, including the restored mule barn, carriage house, doghouse and officers' quarters, which are clustered together in one section of the fort. An interpretive display explains the renovation project.

Paddling

During its heyday, Eagle was an important riverboat landing for traffic moving up and down the Yukon River. It is still an impor-

tant departure point for the many paddlers who come to float the river through the Yukon-Charley Rivers National Preserve. The 150-mile Yukon River trip extends from Eagle to Circle, at the end of the Steese Hwy northeast of Fairbanks; most paddlers plan on six to 10 days for the float trip.

It is not a difficult paddle, but it must be planned carefully, as you'll need an air-taxi operator to shuttle boats, equipment and people from Circle. Floaters and paddlers should come prepared for insects but can usually camp on open beaches and river bars, where winds keep the bugs at bay. Paddlers also need to be prepared for extremes in weather; freezing nights can be followed by daytime temperatures of 90°F.

Eagle Canoe Rentals (☎ 547-2203), on the Taylor Hwy as you enter town, provides canoes for travel between Dawson City or Eagle and Circle. Pick up the boat at either the Dawson City River Hostel (☎ 867-993-6823) or at the shop in Eagle and then leave it in Circle. A four-day rental between Dawson City and Eagle is $110; a five-day rental between Eagle and Circle is $160.

For a return flight, check with Tatonduk Air (☎ 474-4697 in Fairbanks), which offers flag-stop service between Eagle and Circle. The cost for a flight between Circle and Eagle is $100 per person, plus a freight charge for any extra baggage beyond the allowance of 40lb per person.

For information in advance, contact the National Park Service (☎ 547-2233), PO Box 167, Eagle, AK 99738.

Places to Stay

Most people camp at the Bureau of Land Management's *Eagle Campground* (15 sites, $4). To reach it, follow 4th Ave 1.5 miles north through Fort Egbert to the campground. At Eagle's public boat landing, south of town, you'll find *Yukon Adventure B&B* (☎ 547-2249, 404 Golden Ave), with rooms for $60 to $80 and spaces outside to pitch a tent. At the *Falcon Inn B&B* (☎ 547-2254, 220 Front St), rooms begin at $65/75 singles/doubles.. This spot features a deck that overlooks the Yukon River. Nearby, the

The USS *Northwestern* Memorial, Unalaska

Fishing trawler in Dutch Harbor

Church of the Holy Ascension, Unalaska

Kayakers in Katmai National Park

LEE FOSTER

Mt. McKinley, Denali National Park

DEANNA SWANEY

Nancy Lake State Recreation Area

Eagle Trading Company (☎ *547-2220, 3 Front St*) has rooms for $50/60 singles/doubles, along with groceries, a cafe and public showers.

Getting There & Away

There are no buses in or out of Eagle, but there is the *Yukon Queen*, operated by

Gray Line (☎ 867-993-5599 in Dawson City, the Yukon Territory). The 130-seat tour boat makes the trip from Dawson City as part of a package tour, but the operators will also sell roundtrip and one-way tickets to fill up the empty seats. The roundtrip fare between Eagle and Dawson City is $140; one-way is $90.

Fairbanks

Fairbanks goes by a lot of names and descriptions. It's often referred to as the Golden Heart City, because of its location in the center of the state and, I suspect, the willingness of the residents to help each other out during long, cold winters. It's also been labeled the Hub of the Interior for the role it plays as the transportation center for the Bush. But perhaps the best description for Fairbanks was a slogan its visitor bureau came up with one summer. Fairbanks, according to the ad campaign, was 'extremely Alaska.' Oh, is it ever. Extremes are a way of life in the state's second largest city.

At first glance, Fairbanks appears to be a spread out, low-rise city with the usual hotels, shopping malls, fast-food chains and a university tucked away on the outskirts of town. A second look reveals that this community is different, that the people and the place are one of a kind, even for Alaska. Fairbanks has log cabins, lots of them, in the heart of town and hidden among the trees on the back roads. It has a semiprofessional baseball team that plays games at midnight without the aid of artificial lights. It also has a golf course that claims to be the 'world's most northernmost,' a college campus where, if the day is clear, students can view the highest mountain in North America and more sled dogs than there are horses in the bluegrass state of Kentucky.

'Extremely Alaska' is the only way to describe Fairbanks' weather. During the summer, it is pleasantly warm, with an average temperature of 70°F and an occasional hot spell in August when the temperature breaks 90°F. The days are long, with more than 20 hours of light from June to August, peaking at almost 23 hours on June 21. In the winter, however, Fairbanks is cold. The temperature often drops to -60°F, or even lower, for days at a time.

History

Consider the city's boom-or-bust economy for extremes. Fairbanks was founded in 1901, when ET Barnette was heading up the Tanana River on the SS *Lavelle Young* with 130 tons of supplies for the Tanacross goldfields. When the river became too shallow to travel, he convinced the riverboat captain to try the Chena. When that river was also too shallow, the captain set Barnette, his wife and his supplies ashore at what is now the corner of 1st Ave and Cushman St. Barnette could have been just another failed trading post merchant in the Great White North, but the following year an Italian prospector named Felix Pedro struck gold 12 miles north of Barnette's trading post. A large boomtown sprang to life amid the hordes of miners stampeding into the area, and by

Highlights

- Gaze at Mt McKinley from the University of Alaska Fairbanks campus

- Enjoy an afternoon wandering through century-old cabins at Alaskaland

- Rent a canoe and paddle the Chena River

- Near the summer solstice of June 21, view the midnight sun from Eagle Summit

- Marvel at the gold nugget collection at the Circle District Historical Society Museum

- Soak in the hot tubs and pools at Chena Hot Springs

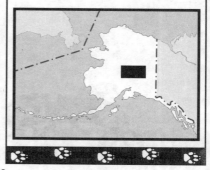

FAIRBANKS & VICINITY

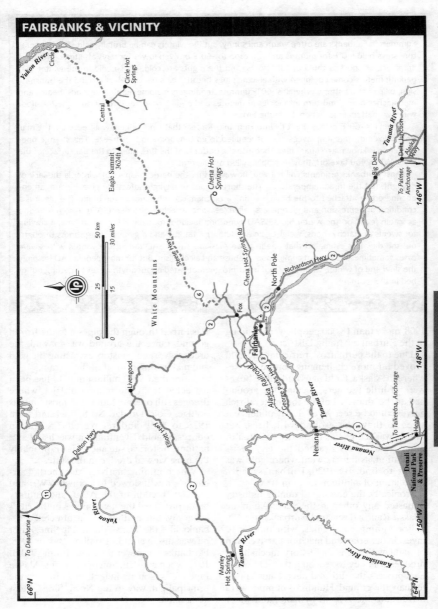

Winter in Fairbanks

Summers in Fairbanks are often warm and sunny, but the winters can be brutally cold. The temperature stays below 0°F for months and can drop to -60°F or even lower for days at a time. The days are short, as short as three or four hours, and the nights are cold. It's so cold in the winter that parking meters come equipped with electric plugs because cars have heaters around the transmission, oil pan and battery. When it's -60°F unprotected fingers become numb in seconds, beards and moustaches freeze and turn into icicles in minutes and a glass of water thrown out of a 2nd-floor window shatters as ice when it hits the ground.

When it's -60°F, planes don't fly into Fairbanks for fear that landing gear will freeze up; the mail isn't delivered; state employees are not required to go to work; and tires freeze. This strange phenomenon is known as 'square tires,' because the bottoms of the tires mold to the flat surface of the road. When you take off, they're simply pulled off the rims.

Most Fairbanks residents will tell you, however, that the hardest aspect of winter is the lack of daylight, not the frigid temperatures. The short periods of daylight affect the pineal gland, an endocrine organ attached to the brain, causing a biochemical imbalance in the brain. The result is a condition of depression and gloominess called 'seasonal affective disorder' (SAD). Also referred to as 'cabin fever' or 'the winter blues,' SAD symptoms include trouble waking up on time, a craving for sweets or starchy foods, weight gain and lethargy, fatigue and a general sluggishness throughout the day. It is estimated that one in three Alaskans suffer SAD during the winter, with severe cases sometimes resulting in crime, spousal abuse and alcoholism. But for most people SAD is simply the slow end of winter, when they find it hard to get motivated about anything, even getting out of bed in the morning.

1908, more than 18,000 people were residing in the Fairbanks Mining District.

Due to the permafrost, retrieving the gold proved far more challenging here than elsewhere in Alaska. Gold pans and sluice boxes were of little use here, because the ground had to be thawed before the mineral-rich gravel could be recovered. Early miners cut trees to thaw the ground with fires, but timber was scarce this far north. Eventually, other gold rushes drained the city of its population, as miners went where gold was easier to find. By 1920, Fairbanks had a population of a little more than 1000.

Ironically, the city's gold mining industry outlasted any other in the state. After the Alaska Railroad reached Fairbanks in 1923, major mining companies, with money to invest in materials and machines, arrived and brought with them three-story mechanized dredges. The key to reaching the gold was a new process that utilized needle-nose pipes to thaw the ground. Hundreds of pipes were driven into the ground by hand, and water was forced through the pipes into the frozen ground. Once the ground was thawed, the dredges worked nonstop, extracting the gold and making mincemeat of the terrain.

More than $200 million in gold has been extracted from the mining district, where dredges still operate today. The most famous dredge, Gold Dredge No 8, operated from 1928 to 1959 and recovered 7.5 million ounces of gold. Eventually it was listed as a national historical site and today is probably the most viewed dredge in the state.

When mining activity declined, Fairbanks' growth slowed to a crawl. WWII and the construction of the Alcan and military bases produced the next booms in the city's economy, but neither boom affected Fairbanks like the Trans-Alaska Pipeline. After oil was discovered in Prudhoe Bay in 1968, Fairbanks was never the same. From 1973 to 1977, when construction of the Trans-Alaska Pipeline was at its height, the town, as the principal gateway to the North Slope, burst at its seams.

FAIRBANKS

The aftermath of the pipeline construction was just as extreme. The city's population shrank and unemployment crept towards 25% through much of 1979. The oil industry bottomed out in 1986 with the declining price of crude, and Fairbanks, like Anchorage, suffered through more hard times.

By the late 1990s, however, the city was on the rebound thanks to tourists and gold. Just north of the city is the Fort Knox Gold Mine, the largest in Alaska. In 1998, Fort Knox produced 365,000oz of gold (worth $170 million), employed 260 workers and contributed more than $4 million in taxes to the city. Despite the price of gold tumbling to below $300 an ounce, the mine is still acquiring prospects in the region in an attempt to expand its operation.

Whether gold is a lasting economic benefit for Fairbanks or just another boom-and-bust industry remains to be seen. Either way, Fairbanks' residents will endure. They are a hardy and independent breed because they have to be. That endurance, more than the log cabins or the midnight sun, is the city's trademark. The residents tend to be more colorful than most Alaskans, maybe a bit louder and a degree more boastful. They exemplify the Alaskan theme of 'work hard, play hard, drink hard.'

Whether you enjoy Fairbanks or not depends on where you're coming from and your perceptions. If you've just spent 10 days paddling along the Noatak River in the Brooks Range, Fairbanks can be an extremely hospitable place to recuperate – and an affordable one at that. Generally, you'll find tourist-related businesses – hotels, taxis, restaurants, etc – to be much more reasonably priced than in Anchorage. If, however, you've just arrived from Homer or Juneau, the charming aspects of these towns surrounded by mountains, glaciers and the sea might blind you to what is so unique – and so extreme – about Fairbanks.

Orientation

Fairbanks, the transportation center for much of the Interior, is spread out over an area of 31 sq miles. 'Downtown' is hard to describe and even harder to recognize. It is generally considered to be centered around Golden Heart Plaza, on the corner of 1st Ave and Cushman St, and spreads west to Cowles St, east to Noble St, north across the Chena River to the railroad depot and south along Cushman St as far as you want to walk. Cushman St is the closest thing Fairbanks has to a main street.

Several miles to the northwest is the university area, which sprawls from the hilltop campus of UA Fairbanks to the bars, restaurants and other businesses along University Ave and College Rd that make a living serving the college crowd. The city's other major commercial district is along Airport Way, between University Ave and Cushman St, where you'll find most of the fast-food chains, malls, and many motels.

If you arrive by train, motels, B&Bs and restaurants in the downtown area are only a 15-minute walk away. If you arrive by bus, you can usually get dropped off either along the Airport Way stretch or downtown. If you fly in, the only way to get out of the airport (see Getting Around) is by taxi. The downtown area is an $8 fare away.

Information

Tourist Offices The main source of information is the Fairbanks Convention and Visitors Bureau log cabin (☎ 456-5774, 800-327-5774, fcvb@polarnet.com, www.explorefairbanks.com), which overlooks the Chena River near the corner of 1st Ave and Cushman St. The many services offered include a recorded telephone message (☎ 456-4630) that lists the daily events and attractions in town, racks of brochures and information, courtesy phones to call up motels and B&Bs, and a fairly knowledgeable staff. The log cabin is open 8 am to 8 pm daily during the summer.

Other visitor centers are in the railroad depot (open before and after each train arrival) and Alaskaland, and there's a limited visitor center near the baggage claim of the Fairbanks International Airport.

Head to the Alaska Public Lands Information Center (☎ 456-0527), on Cushman St two blocks south of the Chena River, for brochures, maps and information on state and national parks, wildlife refuges and

FAIRBANKS

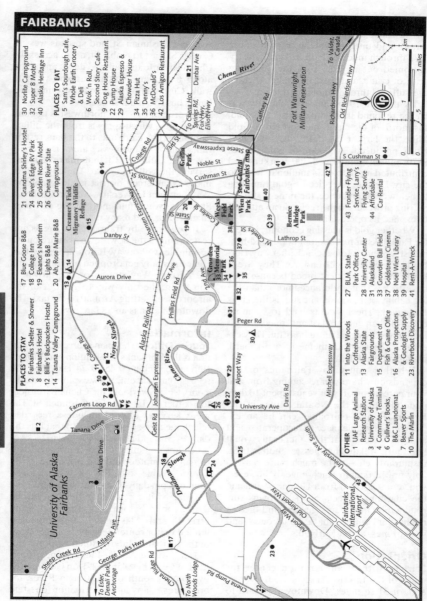

PLACES TO STAY
2 Fairbanks Shelter & Shower
8 Fairbanks Hostel
12 Billie's Backpackers Hostel
14 Tanana Valley Campground

17 Blue Goose B&B
18 College Inn
19 Eleanor's Northern Lights B&B
20 Ah, Rose Marie B&B

21 Grandma Shirley's Hostel
24 River's Edge RV Park
25 Golden North Motel
26 Chena River State Campground

30 Norlite Campground
32 Super 8 Motel
40 Alaska Heritage Inn

PLACES TO EAT
5 Sam's Sourdough Cafe, Whole Earth Grocery & Deli
6 Wok 'n Roll, Second Story Cafe
9 Dog House Restaurant
22 Pump House
29 Alaska Espresso & Chowder House
34 Pizza Hut
35 Denny's
36 McDonald's
42 Los Amigos Restaurant

OTHER
1 UAF Large Animal Research Station
3 University of Alaska
4 Commuter Terminal
6 Gulliver's Books, B&C Laundromat
7 Beaver Sports
10 The Marlin
11 Into the Woods Coffeehouse
13 Alaska State Fairgrounds
15 Department of Fish & Game Office
16 Alaska Prospectors & Geologist Supply
23 Riverboat Discovery

27 BLM, State Park Offices
28 University Center
31 Alaskaland
33 Growden Ball Field
37 Goldstream Cinema
38 Noel Wien Library
39 Hospital
41 Rent-A-Wreck
43 Frontier Flying Service, Larry's Flying Service
44 Affordable Car Rental

Chena River
Fort Wainwright Military Reservation
To Valdez, Canada
Richardson Hwy
Old Richardson Hwy
Gaffney Rd
Dunbar Ave
S Cushman St
To Chena Hot Springs Rd, Fox Hwy, Elliott Hwy
Steese Expressway
Griffin Park
Noble St
Cushman St
See Central Fairbanks map
College Rd
Illinois St
Johansen Expressway
Creamer's Field Migratory Wildlife Refuge
Danby St
Weeks Field Park
State St
Cowles St
Wien Park
Bernice Altride Park
Lathrop St
W Cowles St
Growden Memorial Park
2nd Ave
Fox Ave
Aurora Drive
Phillips Field Rd
Peger Rd
College Rd
Noyes Slough
Alaska Railroad
Chena River
Johansen Expressway
Farmers Loop Rd
Geist Rd
Tanana Drive
Yukon Drive
University of Alaska Fairbanks
Atlanta Ave
Sheep Creek Rd
George Parks Hwy
Chena Ridge Rd
To Ester, Denali Park, Anchorage
To North Woods Lodge
Chena Pump Rd
Deadman Slough
Airport Way
Davis Rd
Mitchell Expressway
University Ave
University Ave South
Old Airport Way
Airport Way
Fairbanks International Airport

0   .5   1 miles
0   .5   1   2 km

recreation areas. The center has exhibits and video programs on a variety of topics and a small theater that shows nature films at 10 am, noon, 2 pm and 4 pm and interpretive programs at 3 pm daily. Hours are 9 am to 6 pm daily during the summer.

Money Banks and ATMs are scattered all over the city. Downtown, the Key Bank of Alaska (☎ 452-2146) is at Cushman St and 1st Ave. The bank has an impressive gold nugget display. Nearby, at 613 Cushman St, you will find the National Bank of Alaska (☎ 459-4343).

Post The main post office is downtown, on 4th Ave between Barnette and Cushman Sts.

Email & Internet Access Cybercafes in Fairbanks include Cafe Latte, at 6th Ave and Lacy St downtown, and Second Story Cafe, above Gulliver's Books in the Campus Corner Mall, on College Rd and University Ave. The Noel Wien Library and many hostels also provide Internet access.

Travel Agencies Vista Travel (☎ 456-7888) is at 1211 Cushman St, and US Travel (☎ 452-8992) is at 609 2nd Ave.

Bookstores Gulliver's Books (☎ 474-9574) sells new and used books and Alaskan titles at its shop in Campus Corner Mall, near UAF. The Alaska Public Lands Information Center, downtown, and the UAF Bookstore, on campus, also have good selections of books.

Libraries The excellent Noel Wien Library (☎ 459-1020), on the corner of Airport Way and Cowles St, is a long walk from the log cabin visitor center (take the MACS Blue Line bus). Along with a large Alaskan section, the library has a selection of more than 50 paintings and prints, many by Alaskan artists, and a stone fireplace, so it can be a warm place to be on a rainy day. Hours are 10 am to 9 pm Monday to Thursday, 10 am to 6 pm on Friday and 10 am to 5 pm on Saturday. The library is closed on Sunday in the summer.

Laundry & Showers If you need a shower and some clean clothes, there's B&C Laundromat (☎ 479-2696) in the Campus Corner Mall. It's open to 10:30 pm daily, and showers cost $3. In the downtown area, head north of the Chena River to B&L Laundromat (☎ 452-1355), in the Eagle Plaza on 3rd St, a block east of Steese Hwy.

Medical Services Fairbanks Memorial Hospital (☎ 452-8181) is at the corner of W Cowles St and 14th Ave, on the south side of Airport Way.

Downtown

Next to the log cabin visitor center is the **Golden Heart Plaza**, a pleasant riverside park that is truly the center of the city. In the middle of the plaza is an impressive bronze statue, *The Unknown First Family,* which was dedicated in 1986 and depicts an Athabascan family braving the elements.

Head west along 1st Ave to view old Fairbanks, the city of log cabins. Within a half mile are a half-dozen log homes and several historical buildings, including **St Matthew's Episcopal Church**, a log church that was built in 1905 and rebuilt in 1948 after it burned down. The **Immaculate Conception Church**, just across the Chena River Bridge from Golden Heart Plaza, was built in 1904 and moved to its present location in 1911. The church is a national historic monument and features beautiful stained-glass windows.

At the corner of Fifth Ave and Cushman St, in the old city hall, is the **Fairbanks Community Museum** (☎ 452-8671). Opened in 1996, the museum features displays, exhibits and artifacts tracing the 200-year history of the Golden Heart City. Hours are 11 am to 3 pm Monday to Saturday in the summer; admission is $1.

Alaskaland

The city's largest attraction is this 44-acre pioneer theme park created in 1967 to commemorate the 100th year of the US possession of Alaska. Inside are such historical displays as the *Nenana,* a former sternwheeler of the Yukon River fleet, the railroad car that carried President Warren Harding

CENTRAL FAIRBANKS

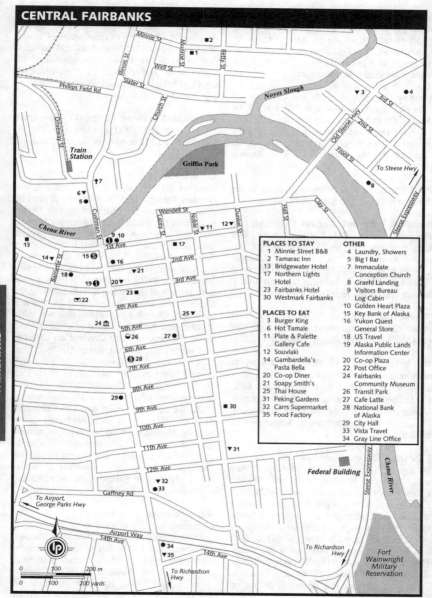

PLACES TO STAY
1 Minnie Street B&B
2 Tamarac Inn
13 Bridgewater Hotel
17 Northern Lights Hotel
23 Fairbanks Hotel
30 Westmark Fairbanks

PLACES TO EAT
3 Burger King
6 Hot Tamale
11 Plate & Palette Gallery Cafe
12 Souvlaki
14 Gambardella's Pasta Bella
20 Co-op Diner
21 Soapy Smith's
25 Thai House
31 Peking Gardens
32 Carrs Supermarket
35 Food Factory

OTHER
4 Laundry, Showers
5 Big I Bar
7 Immaculate Conception Church
8 Graehl Landing
9 Visitors Bureau Log Cabin
10 Golden Heart Plaza
15 Key Bank of Alaska
16 Yukon Quest General Store
18 US Travel
19 Alaska Public Lands Information Center
20 Co-op Plaza
22 Post Office
24 Fairbanks Community Museum
26 Transit Park
27 Cafe Latte
28 National Bank of Alaska
29 City Hall
33 Vista Travel
34 Gray Line Office

FAIRBANKS

to the golden spike ceremony in 1923, the home of Judge James Wickersham and a century-old carousel that still offers rides to the young and young-at-heart. You'll also find Gold Rush Town here, a street of relocated log cabins, many converted into gift shops; the Pioneer Air Museum; and the Pioneers Museum, which depicts the settlement of Alaska.

At the back of the park, you'll find the Native Village Museum, a look at traditional Athabascan life, and the Mining Valley, which has displays of gold-mining equipment. A miniature 30-gauge train, the Crooked Creek & Whiskey Island Railroad, will take the kids around the park, and at night there are entertainment at the Palace Saloon and one of the best salmon bakes in the state.

The entrance to Alaskaland is off Airport Way near Peger Rd. A free shuttle bus, made to look like a train, makes hourly runs each day between the visitor center and major hotels to the park from 4 am to 9 pm. You can also reach the park on a MACS Blue Line bus. Alaskaland (☎ 459-1087) is open 11 am to 7 pm daily. A theme park in Alaska may sound a little corny, but Alaskaland makes for a very enjoyable afternoon, allowing you to take a step back into Alaska's history. You can't beat the price. A few of the museums inside charge a $2 admission, but otherwise the park is free.

University of Alaska Fairbanks

The University of Alaska Fairbanks (UAF) is the original and main campus of the statewide college and an interesting place to wander around for an afternoon. It was incorporated in 1917 as the Alaska Agricultural College and School of Mines and began its first year with six students. Today, it has more than 8,000 students and 70 degree programs, despite the cold winters. The school is 4 miles west from the center of Fairbanks, in a beautiful and unusual setting for a college; it is on a hill that overlooks the surrounding area, and on a clear day it is possible to view Mt McKinley from marked vantage points.

Stop first at the Wood Center, in the middle of campus, to pick up a map of the college. The building is the student center and general meeting place on campus; it provides a cafeteria, pizza parlor, games rooms, outdoor patio, and an information desk for all activities on the campus. Nearby is Constitution Hall, where territorial delegates drafted a constitution for statehood. Now it's the site of, among other things, the University Bookstore, where UAF and Nanook (school mascot) sweatshirts can be purchased.

The main tourist attraction of UAF is the excellent University of Alaska Museum, which sits splendidly on top of a grassy ridge overlooking the Tanana Valley. The museum is generally regarded as one of the best in the state, rivaling the state museum in Juneau, and definitely the best attraction in Fairbanks. Inside, the museum is divided into regions of the state, with each section examining the geology, history and unusual aspects of that area.

The most famous exhibit is Blue Babe, a fully restored 36,000-year-old bison that was found preserved intact, thanks to the permafrost, by Fairbanks-area miners. Even more impressive, however, is the state's largest public gold display, with nuggets large enough to make you run out and buy a gold pan. The museum is open 9 am to 7 pm daily in the summer and to 5 pm in May and September. The admission is $5 – well worth it if you have the better part of an afternoon to thoroughly enjoy each exhibit.

There are free guided tours of UA Fairbanks at 10 am Monday to Friday (meet at the museum), and at 2 pm on Thursday there are tours of the school's premier research facility, the Geophysical Institute (☎ 474-7558), on the West Ridge of the campus.

On the outskirts of the campus is the Agricultural Experiment Farm (☎ 474-7627), where the university dabbles in growing vegetables of mythical proportions and small grains, like barley, wheat and oats, that seem best suited for the short Alaskan growing seasons.

Ironically, the station's grain fields are ideal places spot sandhill cranes, an endangered species in the rest of the country. The station is open for self-guided tours 8 am to

The Northern Lights

Fairbanks' best attraction is also its highest one: the aurora borealis, better known as the northern lights. The aurora is a phenomenon of physics that takes place 50 to 200 miles above the earth's surface. As solar winds flow across the earth's upper atmosphere, they hit gas molecules, which light up much like the high-vacuum electrical discharge of a neon sign. What you end up with is a solar-powered light show of waving, curtainlike light streaming across the night sky. In the dead of winter, the aurora often fills the sky with the dancing light for hours. Other nights, 'the event,' as many call it, lasts less than 10 minutes, with the aurora spinning into a giant green ball and then quickly fading. Milky green and white are the most common colors; red auroras are the rarest. In 1958, the northern sky was so bloody with brilliant red auroras that fire trucks rushed out to the hills surrounding Fairbanks, only to discover the expected massive forest fires were just the northern lights.

This polar phenomenon has been seen as far south as Mexico, but Fairbanks is the undisputed aurora capital. Somebody in upper Minnesota might witness less than 20 events a year and in Anchorage around 150, but in Fairbanks you can see the lights on an average of 240 nights a year. North of Fairbanks, the number begins to decrease. At the North Pole, somebody would see the lights less than 100 nights a year.

From May to mid-August, there is too much daylight in Alaska to see an 'event,' but generally, by the second week of August, the aurora begins to appear in the Interior and can be enjoyed if you're willing to be awake at 2 am. By mid-September the lights are knocking your socks off, and people are already asking, 'did you see the lights last night?'

The best viewing in Fairbanks is in the outlying hills, away from the city lights. University of Alaska Fairbanks is also a good spot to view the lights, and you'll find a permanent aurora exhibit in the University of Alaska Museum. Its Geophysical Institute sells an informative booklet, *Understanding the Aurora*.

If you're passing through Fairbanks during June or July, you're out of luck. In that case, you might want to head to Ester, where Leroy Zimmerman presents his *The Crown of Lights*. The show features panoramic slides of the northern lights projected on a 30-foot screen and accompanied by classical music. It's the best view of the aurora you can get indoors. Shows are at 6:45 and 7:45 pm daily at the Firehouse Theater (☎ 479-2500); admission is $6.

8 pm Monday to Friday, and guided tours are offered at 2 pm on Friday. To reach the station take Tanana Drive west from the lower campus, bear left at the fork and continue for a mile on Sheep Creek Rd.

The UAF's Large Animal Research Station, which focuses on unique adaptations of animals to a sub-Arctic climate, is off Farmers Loop Rd. Best known as a musk ox farm, the station also features colonies of reindeer, caribou and experimental hybrids of the two called 'reinbou' and 'carideer.' Platforms outside the fenced pastures provide visitors with a place to view the herds, but bring binoculars, as the animals aren't always cooperatively grazing nearby. View-ing is free, and a gift shop sells, among other things, raw qiviut (wool from the musk ox). Guided walking tours are $5. To reach the station, head north from the campus on Farmers Loop Rd, turn left on Ballaine Rd and then left again on Yanovich Rd.

Because of its lofty perch, the campus is the best place in Fairbanks to view Mt McKinley on a clear day. A turnoff and marker defining the mountainous horizon is at the south end of Yukon Drive. Call the UAF Relations office (☎ 474-7581) for more information on any UAF tour or attraction. Reach the campus by taking MACS Red or Blue Line buses right to Wood Center. There is also a museum shuttle that departs from the log cabin visitor center at 1:30 am and the campus at 4:15 pm. The fare is $3/5 one-way/roundtrip.

Trans-Alaska Pipeline

The closest spot to view the Trans-Alaska Pipeline, where some 1.5 million barrels of oil flow daily on their way to Valdez, is at the Alyeska Pipeline Visitor Center, 8 miles north of the city on the Steese Hwy. The center, basically a gift shop selling pipeline T-shirts, is open 8 am to 6 pm daily from Memorial Day to Labor Day. The outdoor displays are interesting, and the pipeline is so close they had to hang a sign on it asking people not climb on it. Tourists – they'll do anything for a photo.

Dog Mushing

Like a handful of other towns in Alaska, Fairbanks bills itself as the dog mushing capital of the world. It's hard to argue with the claim. Snow and temperatures begin dropping in early October, and sled dog racers enjoy a season that often exceeds five months. The city even has Jeff Studdert Racegrounds, a 'musher's race track.' At Mile 4 on Farmers Loop Rd, the track is a system of groomed trails ranging in length from three to more than 20 miles.

Fairbanks is the home of the North America Sled Dog Championships, a three-day event in which mushers, some with teams as large as 20 dogs, compete in a series of races. This is not the Iditarod. Speed, not endurance, is the key, as the races range from 20 to 30 miles long. The Alaska Dog Mushers Association, which hosts the championships, also operates the Dog Mushing Museum (☎ 456-6874) at the racegrounds. Open 10 am to 6 pm daily during the summer, the museum has a few exhibits on sled dog racing, of course, and videos of races and dogs in training. Among the equipment on display are the sleds used by Susan Butcher and Martin Buser to win the Iditarod.

Though the Iditarod is the best-known dogsled event in Alaska, it's only one of two long-distance races. The other is the Yukon Quest, a 1023-mile run between Fairbanks and Whitehorse that was organized in 1983 along many of the early trails used by trappers, miners and the postal service. Many mushers will argue that the Quest is by far the tougher of the two races. Mushers climb four mountains over 3000 feet in elevation and run along 200 miles of the frozen Yukon River. While the Iditarod has 25 checkpoints at which racers must stop, the Quest has only six.

The race headquarters is at the Yukon Quest General Store (☎ 451-8985), on the corner of Cushman St and 2nd Ave. The store is open 10 am to 6 pm Monday to Saturday and noon to 4 pm Sunday. Inside you'll find race memorabilia, a few displays and lots of sled dog souvenirs for sale.

Gold Panning

Travelers inspired by the huge gold nuggets at the University of Alaska Museum can try their hands at panning in the Fairbanks area. If you're serious about panning, start out at Alaskan Prospectors & Geologists Supply (☎ 452-7398), 504 College Rd, which stocks and sells all the necessary equipment for recreational prospecting. The store also has books, pamphlets and videos to help you strike it rich. It even offers panning instructions. Hours are 10 am to 5 pm Monday to Friday.

The next stop should be the Alaska Public Lands Information Center, to research where you can pan. Popular places in the area include Pedro Creek, off the Elliott Hwy near the Felix Pedro monument, and the Chatanika River, off the Steese Hwy.

For people less serious about panning, there are two gold-mining attractions that include a little panning as part of the tour. At Mile 9 of Old Steese Hwy is Gold Dredge No 8 (☎ 457-6058), which includes gold panning as part of its $20 tour. Tours are held 9 am to 6 pm daily. The El Dorado Gold Mine (☎ 479-7613) has a two-hour train tour on a mile-long narrow-gauge track that winds through a reconstructed mining camp and culminates with visitors panning gold-laden dirt. The train departs daily from Mile 1 of the Elliott Hwy, and tickets are $25. Gold Dredge No 8 is the less touristy attraction of the two.

Hiking

Unlike Anchorage or Juneau, Fairbanks does not have outstanding hiking on its doorstep. The best trail for an extended backpacking trip is the impressive **Pinnell Mountain Trail** at Mile 85.5 and Mile 107.3 of Steese Hwy (see the Backpacking section in the Wilderness chapter). For a variety of long and short hikes, head to Chena River State Recreation Area. The recreation area is served by public transportation, and hitching Chena Hot Springs Rd would be fairly easy.

For information on Pinnell Mountain Trail or Summit Trail, part of the White Mountains Trail system (see the Backpacking section in the Wilderness chapter), stop at the Public Lands Information Center (☎ 456-0527) or the Bureau of Land Management office (☎ 474-2200), on the corner of Airport Way and University Ave. Practically next door to the BLM office is the Division of Parks office of Alaska Natural Resources (☎ 451-2695), which has information on Chena River State Recreation Area.

The Public Lands Information Center sells USGS topographic maps for the Fairbanks region. You can pick up topo maps for anywhere in Alaska at the Geophysical Institute Map Office (☎ 474-6960) on the UAF campus. Hours are 8 am to 5 pm Monday to Friday.

Creamer's Field Trail This is a self-guided, 2-mile nature trail that winds through Creamer's Field Migratory Wildlife Refuge, an old dairy farm that has since become an bird lover's paradise, as more than 100 species of bird pass through each year. The refuge is at 1300 College Rd (MACS Red Line bus), and the trailhead is in the parking lot adjacent to the Alaska Department of Fish and Game office (☎ 452-1531), where trail guides are available. The trail is mostly boardwalk, with an observation tower along the way and lots of bugs.

Granite Tors Trail Along with the Chena Dome Trail, a 29-mile backpacking adventure (see the Wilderness chapter), there are several other good treks in Chena River State Recreation Area. The Granite Tors Trail is a 15-mile loop that provides access into the alpine area and to the unusual tors. Tors are isolated pinnacles of granite popping out of the tundra. The first set of tors is 6 miles from the trailhead; the best group lies 2 miles farther along the trail. The entire hike is a five- to eight-hour trek, with a free-use shelter halfway along the way. The trailhead is in Tors Trail State Campground, at Mile 39 of the Chena Hot Springs Rd. Chena Hot Springs Resort (☎ 369-4111) will provide roundtrip van transportation for $30 per person.

Angel Rocks Trail This 3.5-mile loop trail leads to Angel Rocks, large granite outcroppings near the north boundary of Chena River State Recreation Area. It's a moderate day hike; the rocks are less than 2 miles from the road. The trail is also the first leg of the Angel Rocks-Chena Hot Springs Traverse, a more difficult 8.3-mile trek that ends at the famous Chena Hot Springs Resort, at the end of the Chena Hot Springs Rd. Roughly halfway along the traverse is a free-use shelter. The posted trailhead for Angel Rocks is just south of a rest area at Mile 49 of the Chena Hot Springs Rd. The southern trailhead for the Chena Dome Trail is practically across the street.

Paddling

Fairbanks offers a wide variety of canoeing opportunities, both leisurely afternoon paddles and overnight trips, into the surrounding area. There are also several places to rent boats. The most convenient is 7 Bridges Boats & Bikes (☎ 479-0751) at 7 Gables Inn, just off the river at 4312 Birch Lane. It provides canoes and a pickup and drop-off service. Canoes are $30 a day, and transportation costs $1.50 a mile, with a $15 minimum. You can even arrange to paddle down the Chena River and bike back to the downtown area.

Check the Guide Companies section of the Wilderness chapter for a list of the Fairbanks-based outfitters that raft in the Brooks Range and Arctic National Wildlife Refuge. For a milder float, CanoeAlaska (☎ 479-5183) offers a full-day float on the

Upper Chena River, which includes equipment, transport and lunch, for $99 per person.

Around Town An afternoon can be spent paddling the Chena River; its mild currents let you paddle upstream as well as down. You can launch a canoe from almost any bridge crossing the river, including the Graehl landing, near the north side of Steese Hwy, where locals like to paddle upstream and then float back down.

From 7 Bridges Boats & Bikes, you can drop a canoe in the Chena River, head downstream and into the quiet Noyes Slough and complete the loop by paddling east back into the river, a 13-mile roundtrip journey.

Chena & Tanana Rivers Those looking for an overnight – or even longer – paddle should try a float down the Chena River from the Chena Hot Springs Rd east of Fairbanks (see the Paddling section in the Wilderness chapter) or a pleasant two-day trip down the Tanana River. The popular Tanana River trip usually begins from the end of Chena Pump Rd and finishes in the town of Nenana, where you can return with your canoe to Fairbanks on the Alaska Railroad. This 60-mile trip can be done in a single day but would require 10 to 12 hours of paddling.

Chatanika River The Chatanika River can be paddled for 28 miles, west from Cripple Creek Campground at Mile 60 of Steese Hwy. The river runs parallel to the highway until Chatanika River State Campground,

at Mile 39. From here, the trip can be extended another 17 miles to a bridge at Mile 11 of Elliott Hwy. The river is not a difficult paddle, but the trip requires considerable driving because you must shuttle boats and people between Fairbanks and the two highways. Many locals get around this by only paddling the upper portion of the river and leaving a bicycle chained at the end of the route, so they can get back to their car. You can also call Chandalar River Outfitters (☎ 451-6587), which rents canoes ($50 per day) and will provide drop-off and pickup service for an additional fee.

Organized Tours

GO Shuttles & Tours (☎ 474-3847, 800-478-3847) and Alaska Sightseeing offer three-hour city tours that include the university, UAF's Large Animal Research Station and the Trans-Alaska Pipeline. Go Shuttle & Tours departs five times a day from the log cabin visitor center and charges $25 per person. Alaska Sightseeing departs from the Bridgewater Hotel (☎ 452-8518) only at 9 pm, and the fare is $23.

Gray Line (☎ 451-6835), 1980 S Cushman St, has a gold tour that departs at 9 am and noon and includes Gold Dredge No 8, the Trans-Alaska Pipeline and lunch, for $57.

You can travel the Chena River on the historic sternwheeler *Riverboat Discovery* (☎ 479-6673), if you're up to parting with $40 for the four-hour trip. Along the way, the boat stops at a replica of an Athabascan village and the riverfront home and kennels of Susan Butcher, the noted four-time winner of the Iditarod. The boat departs at

8:45 am and 2 pm daily in the summer from Discovery Landing, off the Dale Rd exit at Mile 4.5 of Airport Way.

The Arctic Circle may be an imaginary line, but it's fast becoming one of Fairbanks' biggest draws. Small air-charter companies are now doing booming business flying travelers across the Arctic Circle, landing in a small village for an hour or two and then heading back. Larry's Flying Service (☎ 474-9169) offers a four-hour air tour that includes an hour with a local guide in Fort Yukon before heading back. The cost is $200, and the plane departs at 9 pm daily. Arctic Circle Air Adventures (☎ 474-8600, 800-474-1986) does the same but flies to Bettles instead.

Chena Hot Springs Resort (☎ 369-4111) also has a fun and affordable one-day tour, which includes roundtrip transportation out to the resort, lunch and a pass to the hot spring pools and hot tubs, for $33 per person. The van leaves Fairbanks at 8 am and returns around 7 pm.

Special Events

Golden Days has grown to be Fairbanks' largest celebration of the summer. Staged during the third week of July, the festival commemorates Felix Pedro's discovery of gold with parades, games, booths, a boat parade on the Chena River and numerous special events, such as the hairy legs contest and locking up unsuspecting visitors in the Golden Days Jail. The summer solstice is also well celebrated, on June 21, when the sun shines for almost 23 hours. Events include footraces, speedboat races, art and craft booths and the traditional midnight sun baseball game, which pits the Alaska Goldpanners against another Alaskan rival in a night game in which no artificial lights are used.

Around the second week in August, the Tanana Valley Fair is held at the fairgrounds on College Rd. Alaska's oldest fair features sideshows, a rodeo, entertainment, livestock shows and large produce.

Places to Stay

Camping The only public campground in the Fairbanks area is the *Chena River State Campground*, on University Ave just north of Airport Way, which has 57 sites for $15 a night. The campground has tables, toilets, fireplaces and water and, being right on the river, a boat launch. It can be reached by MACS Blue Line bus.

If you just want to park the van or RV and don't need facilities or a hookup, you can spend the night in the *Alaskaland* (☎ 459-1087) parking lot, at Airport Way and Peger Rd, for $12. Even better is the *Fred Meyers*, just west on Airport Way. It's become a common practice since the store arrived for RVers and others to just spend the night in the parking lot. The store is open to 10 pm daily for restocking your supplies, and spending the night is free.

The other campgrounds in the city are private and charge $15 to $25 per night to camp when you have a vehicle. They include

Hitting the Links at Two in the Morning

If you get the urge to tee up at 3 am, Fairbanks is the place you want to be. From June through July, the Fairbanks Golf & Country Club is open 24 hours a day. Built in 1946, the nine-hole course is the 'Farthest North Golf Course in the World' (so claim club officials) and one of the oldest in Alaska. Due to that northerly latitude, the course manager decided in 1997 to take advantage of the near-constant daylight in June and July and offer 24-hour tee times. Golfers are able to play around the clock, even when the sun sets for a few hours, because dusk – not darkness – replaces daylight. The course is on Farmers Loop Rd and features three par-three holes, three par-four holes and three par-five holes; a clubhouse, a driving range; and a pro shop with club rentals. To reserve a tee time call ☎ 479-6555. Schedule it between 10 pm and 6 am, and they'll knock $3 off a nine-hole round. Hey, what else are you doing then?

the **Norlite Campground** (☎ 474-0206, 800-478-0206 in Alaska), on Peger Rd just south of Airport Way and the entrance to Alaskaland. Norlite has showers, laundry facilities, a small store and tent sites for $9 for two people with no vehicle, but its sites are close together and have little privacy. **River's Edge RV Park** (☎ 474-0286, 800-770-3343, 4140 Boat St), near the corner of Airport Way and University Ave, charges $16 for tents and $25 for hookups. The campground is on the Chena River and has showers, laundry facilities, shuttle service and access to the city's bike trail system. Finally, **Tanana Valley Campground** (☎ 452-3750, tvfa@polarnet.com, 1800 College Rd), near the Alaska State Fairgrounds, has $8 tent sites and $15 RV sites with electricity.

Cabins Off Mile 62 of Elliott Hwy, 10 miles before the junction with Dalton Hwy, a short spur leads from the road to **Fred Blixt Cabin**. This public-use cabin should be reserved in advance through the BLM office (☎ 474-2200) in Fairbanks. The rental fee is $20 per night.

An old trapper's cabin, **Cripple Creek Cabin**, was renovated by the BLM in 1972. The cabin is between the Steese Hwy (Mile 60.5) and the Chatanika River and is reached by a short trail. The cabin, available only from mid-August to mid-May, does not offer a truly isolated setting, because Cripple Creek Campground and a YCC Camp are nearby. Still, the surrounding area is scenic. The rental fee is $20, and the cabin should be reserved in advance through the Fairbanks BLM office.

In the White Mountains National Recreation Area, **Lee's Cabin** is accessed from the Wickersham Creek Trail at Mile 28 of the Elliott Hwy. It's a 7-mile hike to the cabin, which has a large picture window overlooking the White Mountains and a loft that comfortably sleeps eight. Rental is $25, and the BLM is the place to reserve it in advance.

Chena River State Recreation Area has five rental cabins. The **North Fork Cabin** ($35 per night) is at Mile 47.7 of Chena Hot springs Rd and can be reached by vehicle.

The rest can only be accessed on foot or by mountain bike and ATV. The closest is **Lower Angel Creek Cabin** ($25 per night), which is 3.6 miles along an ATV trail from Mile 50.5 of Chena Hot Springs Rd. Stop at the state park office (☎ 451-2705), 3700 Airport Way, to check availability.

Hostels One of the best things to happen to Fairbanks is the arrival of backpackers' hostels that offer inexpensive, bunkroom lodging. There is no official international hostel, but there are five other ones, all charging $12 to $18 for a bunk. One of the best is **Billie's Backpackers Hostel** (☎ 479-2034, akbillie@aol.com, 2895 Mack Rd), which can be reached from the MAC Red Line. This hostel has a common kitchen, lounge area, a sundeck and an optional $7 breakfast that includes homemade sourdough bread or pancakes.

The **Fairbanks Hostel** (☎ 479-0099, 3412 College Rd) is next door to UAF and has showers and kitchen facilities. Rates are $15 if you have your own sleeping bag. **Fairbanks Shelter & Shower** (☎ 479-5016, brob@alaska.net, 248 Madcap Lane) is just north of UAF and has tent space, bunks and rooms. A tent space is $10, a dorm room $15, and a private room is $18.

Alaska Heritage Inn (☎ 451-6587, 1018 22nd Ave), off South Cushman St, is an ex-bordello, formerly known as Ruthie's Place, in the south Fairbanks area. The inn has seven bunks ($15 a night) and rooms that begin at $40. **North Woods Lodge** (☎ 479-5300, 800-478-5305), on Chena Hills Drive northwest of the city, has a hostel-style sleeping loft for $15. **Grandma Shirley's Hostel** (☎ 451-9816, 510 Dunbar), 1.5 miles northeast from the log cabin visitor center and a block from the MACS Purple Line, has bunks for $16 a night and free bicycles for guests.

B&Bs Fairbanks has more than 100 B&Bs, and most of them have brochures in the visitor center downtown. A courtesy phone there lets you check who has a room and who's filled for the night. The Fairbanks Association of Bed & Breakfasts also publishes a brochure with more than 50 members listed in it and a map showing their locations. Pick it up at the visitor center.

If you're arriving by train or bus, *Ah, Rose Marie* (☎ 456-2040), at Cowles St and 3rd Ave within easy walking distance of the depot, has singles/doubles starting at $50/75. Even closer is *Minnie Street B&B* (☎ 888-456-1849, 456-1802, minniebb@mosquitonet .com, 345 Minnie St), on the same side of the river as the depot. Double rooms with shared baths are $85 to $105. A 10-minute walk from the visitor center is *Eleanor's Northern Lights B&B* (☎ 452-2598, nlightsb@eagle .ptialaska.net), at State St and 4th Ave, with five rooms for $50 (single with shared bath) to $75 (double with private bath).

If you have a vehicle, try the *North Woods Lodge* (☎ 479-5300, 800-478-5305), on Chena Hills Drive. You can reach it from Chena Ridge Rd by turning south on Chena Pump Rd then turning west on Roland Rd to Chena Hills Drive. Cabins and rooms are $35/45, and the lodge has laundry facilities, a common kitchen, a large outdoor hot tub and bike rentals. Nearby is the *Blue Goose B&B* (☎ 479-6973, 800-478-6973, blugoose@ mosquitonet.com, 4466 Dartmouth St), off Chena Pump Rd. The B&B has three rooms for $55 to $75 for two. The price includes a piece of Alaskan rhubarb pie with breakfast.

Hotels Most hotel and motel rooms in Fairbanks are not as expensive as those in Anchorage, but be prepared to pay $80 per night during the summer, especially when you add the 8% city bed tax. The few hotels with reasonable rates are less than desirable or are a considerable distance from the city center.

Of the places clustered downtown on the east side of Cushman St, check out the room before handing over your money. The exception is the *Fairbanks Hotel* (☎ 888-329-4685, fbxhotl@alaska.net, 517 3rd Ave). A flophouse in the 1980s, the hotel was extensively renovated in 1996 and now has rooms with a shared bath for $55/85. It also offers free transportation from the airport or train station. Nearby, the *Northern Lights Hotel*

(☎ 452-4456, 427 1st Ave) is clean and has rooms for $80/90.

The *Tamarac Inn* (☎ 456-6406, 252 Minnie St), on the north side of the Chena River, is within easy walking distance from the railroad depot. Rooms are $74/86; some units have cooking facilities.

By heading away from the city center, you can find better rates and cleaner rooms. Try *College Inn* (☎ 474-3666, 700 Fairbanks St), reached by heading west on Geist Rd from University Ave or taking the MACS Blue Line. Rooms are small but cost $59/69. The inn has a kitchen, a coin-operated laundry and Internet access. The *Golden North Motel* (☎ 479-6201, 800-447-1910, 4888 Airport Way) has rooms with cable TV, rolls and coffee in the office and free van service within the city. Rooms tend to be on the small side and begin at $69. Closer to the downtown area is *Super 8 Motel* (☎ 451-8888, 1909 Airport Way), with clean, big rooms that cost $97/106.

Finally, if you've just spent 10 days in the Bush and want to splurge, check into the *Bridgewater Hotel* (☎ 452-6661, 800-528-4916, 723 1st Ave) downtown. The hotel is one of the nicest in Fairbanks and certainly has the best location, overlooking the Chena River. Singles/doubles cost $140/150 a night.

Places to Eat

Downtown A relatively inexpensive breakfast of two eggs and toast ($4.25) is available at *Co-op Diner*, in the Co-op Plaza at 3rd Ave and Cushman St. The 1950ish diner also has hamburgers and sandwiches ($6 to $7) and Thai specials that begin at $7.

A few blocks east is *Souvlaki*, at 1st Ave and Dunkel St, for gyros, spinach and cheese pie, stuffed grape leaves and lunch specials for under $6. For affordable Mexican food, try *Hot Tamale* (112 N Turner St), across the Chena River from the log cabin visitor center. Dinners with rice and beans cost $8 to $9.

Soapy Smith's (543 2nd Ave) is an interesting restaurant with a saloon atmosphere. Despite the fact that Smith is a Skagway character and never set foot in Fairbanks, the restaurant has good hamburgers, including a half-pounder for $7, deli sandwiches, salads and clam chowder. Next door to the Bridgewater Hotel is *Gambardella's Pasta Bella (706 2nd Ave)*, for homemade pasta dinners for $10 to $17 and some of the best pizza in the Interior ($10 to $12). Its outdoor cafe is a delight during Fairbanks' long summer days. *Plate & Palette Gallery Cafe*, at 1st Ave and Noble St, has vegetarian dishes on the menu and local artwork on the walls. Sandwiches are $4 to $7, dinners can range from $13 to $18.

By walking south on Cushman St, you'll reach several more restaurants. *Thai House (526 5th Ave)* has some of the best Thai dishes in town. Most dinners cost around $9, but don't order anything 'blistering hot' unless you have a cast-iron stomach. Nearby is *Cafe Latte*, at 6th Ave and Lacy St, with good espresso drinks, bagels, Internet access and outdoor seating. *Peking Gardens*, at 12th Ave and Noble St, has a daily lunch buffet special for $7; dinners cost $8 to $12. *Carrs (526 Gaffney Rd)*, nearby just off Cushman St, is the city's best 24-hour supermarket. Besides produce and groceries, you'll find an excellent salad bar ($3.50 a pound), homemade soups ($3 a pound), a deli, a bakery and the 'Orient Express' counter. The store also has seating inside and outside on an enclosed deck.

Airport Way This area is Fairbanks' answer to your craving for fast food just like you eat at home. Between Cushman St and University Ave, there are a *McDonald's*, a *Pizza Hut* with a lunch buffet, *Burger King* and a *Denny's* that will even give you a souvenir card saying you ate in the 'Farthest North Denny's in the World.' Hungry souls should take in the *Alaskaland Salmon Bake* (free shuttle bus from major hotels, including the Bridgewater), where, for $20, you not only get grilled salmon but halibut, spareribs and salad.

Just south of Airport Way is *Food Factory (1707 S Cushman)*, which has large subs for $8, wraps for $6 to $7, chicken wings and good burgers that can be enjoyed with a wide selection of beers (there is another outlet on College Rd). Good soup, sandwiches and espresso drinks are available at *Alaska*

Espresso & Chowder House (3226 Airport Way), east of University Center. The best Mexican restaurant is *Los Amigos*, at 28th Ave and Cushman St, south of Airport Way, where dinners cost $9 to $11.

University Area At Campus Corner Mall, *Wok 'n Roll (3535 College Rd)* is good for quick and cheap Chinese, and next door *Second Story Cafe*, above Gulliver's Books, has sandwiches, lattes and used books. Several blocks south is *Whole Earth Grocery & Deli (1157 Deborah St)* for natural foods, organic produce and a lunch menu of veggie sandwiches, meatless hamburgers, tortilla wraps and salads that cost $5 to $6. You can have good sourdough pancakes ($4.25) any time of the day next door at *Sam's Sourdough Cafe*, as well as sourdough omelettes, sourdough sandwiches or a bowl of soup and a mini loaf of sourdough bread ($4.75).

To the east along College Rd are more eateries. *Dog House (3400 College Rd)* is a small restaurant and pub with an outdoor patio. Hamburgers and sandwiches cost $5 to $7. At the fairgrounds, the *Tanana Valley Farmers' Market*, at College Rd and Aurora Drive, is held throughout much of the summer 11 am to 4 pm Wednesday and 9 am to 4 pm Saturday. Come in late August and you can buy a 20lb cabbage, enough for a month's supply of coleslaw.

Fine Dining The best place around town to turn dinner into an evening is the *Pump House* (☎ 479-8452, *796 Chena Pump Rd*), 2 miles from downtown. The Pump House, once used in the gold-mining era, is now a national historical site that houses a restaurant and saloon. The atmosphere is classic gold rush; inside and out there are artifacts and relics from the city's mining era. The bar in the saloon is solid mahogany and nearby is an antique Brunswick pool table. Dinners cost $18 to $26. You can also enjoy a drink on the outdoor deck while watching the boat traffic on the Chena River. The MACS Blue Line bus includes the restaurant in its run.

Another enjoyable spot for fine dining is *Two Rivers Lodge* (☎ 488-6815), 16 miles out on Chena Hot Springs Rd. The lodge offers rustic decor, complete with bear skin rugs, in a natural setting away from town. The drive out is almost as pleasant as the meal itself. The *Turtle Club* (☎ 457-3883), on Old Steese Hwy in Fox, also gets high marks for its seafood and salad bar. Plan on $15 to $25 for a dinner.

Entertainment

Cinemas Fairbanks' largest movie house is *Goldstream Cinema* (☎ 456-5113), at Airport Way and Lathrop St, which has 10 screens. Shows that start before 6 pm are only $4.50, after 6 pm $7.50.

Theater Interested in a little culture in the Far North? Then check out the *Fairbanks Shakespeare Theatre* (☎ 457-7038). During July the group performs a Shakespeare classic at the Birch Hill Ski Area, north of Fairbanks. They call it 'Shakespeare amongst the aspens.' Performances are staged on various days throughout the month and begin at 7:30 pm. Tickets are $15. Bring a lawn chair, blanket or sleeping bag to sit on.

Saloons Rowdy saloons that are throwbacks from the mining days are the area's specialty. The *Palace Saloon* (☎ 456-5960), at Alaskaland, is alive at night with honky-tonk piano, turn-of-the-century can-can dancers and other acts in the *Golden Heart Revue*, which is performed on its large stage. Show time is at 8:15 pm nightly, and admission is $12. The *Malamute Saloon*, 7 miles west of Fairbanks in Ester, also offers music, skits and vaudeville and its ritual of reading Robert Service poetry. The bar is a classic, and the show is perhaps one of the best locally produced acts in Alaska. They'll have you laughing in the sawdust by the end of the evening. Show time is at 9 pm nightly, and in July a show is added at 7 pm. Admission is $11. There's free bus transportation from Fairbanks that stops at major hotels, including the Bridgewater. Or you can make it an evening by booking a room or a tent site at Ester Gold Camp (see Ester in the Interior chapter).

Music The *Marlin* (3412 College Rd) hops with live music six nights a week, including jazz on two nights and blues on two others. Live jazz can also be enjoyed nearby at *Into the Woods Coffeehouse* (3560 College Rd). The liveliest establishment is the *Howling Dog Saloon*, at the intersection of the Steese and Elliott Hwys in Fox, 12 miles north of the city center; across the street is the *Fox Roadhouse*. The Howling Dog has rock & roll bands and volleyball games and horseshoes played out back under the midnight sun. Fox Roadhouse is home of Silver Gulch Brewing and Bottling Co, one of Alaska's better microbrews. Glasses of the home brew only cost $2.

Bars Bars are the best places to meet locals in Fairbanks, and it seems you never have to travel far to find one. If you're here in September, live music and a college atmosphere are found at the *University Pub*, in the Wood Center at UAF, once classes are in session. In the city center, try the *Big I Bar*, the local hangout for city workers and reporters from the *Daily News-Miner*. The bar is north of the Chena River, near the railroad depot on N Turner Rd. Another spot to meet locals is *LA*, at 28th Ave and Cushman St south of Airport Way, the bar downstairs from Los Amigos restaurant.

Spectator Sports

The Goldpanners baseball team is Fairbanks' entry in a semipro league of teams of top college and amateur players from around the country. More than 80 professionals, including Tom Seaver, Dave Winfield and Barry Bonds, have played in what began as an all-Alaska baseball league but now includes teams from Hawaii, Nevada and other states as well. Games are played at Growden Memorial Park, on the corner of Wilbur St and 2nd Ave. Games start at 7:30 pm, and admission is $5.

Getting There & Away

Air Fairbanks International Airport serves as the gateway for supplies and travelers heading into the Brooks Range and Arctic Alaska. The airport is almost 4 miles southwest of the city, off Airport Way. Alaska Airlines (☎ 474-0481) provides eight daily flights to Anchorage, where there are connections to the rest of the state, and a direct flight from Fairbanks to Seattle. The one-way standard fare to Anchorage is normally around $100 to $150, but airfare wars have pushed it to as low as $50 at times, making it cheaper than taking the train or bus. Delta Air Lines (☎ 800-221-1212) also offers a handful of flights between the two cities, and Air North Canada (☎ 867-668-2228, 800-764-0407 in Alaska) provides service to Dawson City, with a connecting flight to Whitehorse. Roundtrip advance-purchase tickets are $160 to Dawson City and $270 to Whitehorse.

For travel into Arctic Alaska, try Larry's Flying Service (☎ 474-9169) and Frontier Flying Service (☎ 474-0014, info@frontierflying .com) with offices/terminals next door to each other off University Ave, on the east side of the airport. There are regularly scheduled flights to more than 30 villages, including Nome, Kotzebue and Galena. The roundtrip fare to Bettles, to access Gates of the Arctic National Park, is $248 and to Fort Yukon $172. Frontier Flying also flies daily to Anchorage for $80/120 one-way/roundtrip.

Bus From Fairbanks, Alaskon Express (☎ 451-6835) stops at Delta Junction, Tok and then overnights at Beaver Creek in the Yukon. The next day you can make connections to Haines or Whitehorse. Buses depart from the Westmark Fairbanks, 820 Noble St, in the city center at 8 am Sunday, Tuesday and Friday during the summer. The one-way fare from Fairbanks to Tok is $70 and to Haines $182 (lodging at Beaver Creek is not included). Alaska Direct Busline (☎ 800-770-6652) makes the Fairbanks-Whitehorse run at 9 am on Sunday, Wednesday and Friday, charging a one-way fare of $120.

Van service is the cheapest way to reach Denali National Park, other than hitching. Parks Highway Express (☎ 888-600-6001) departs the log cabin visitor center in Fairbanks at 9 am daily and arrives at the park's Visitor Access Center at 1 pm and Anchorage at 6:30 pm. A one-way fare to Denali is $20, Anchorage $55. Alaska Backpacker Shuttle (☎ 344-8775) departs the Fairbanks Railroad Depot at 8:30 am for the same run.

Parks Highway Express also provides bus transportation down the Richardson Hwy to Valdez and points in between. The bus departs the Fairbanks visitor center at 9 am on Wednesday, Friday and Sunday and reaches Valdez at 5 pm. A one-way fare is $59.

Train The Alaska Railroad (☎ 456-4155) has an express train that departs Fairbanks daily at 8:15 am from late May to mid-September. The train reaches Denali National Park around noon and Anchorage at 8:15 pm. The railroad depot is at 280 North Cushman St, a short walk from the Chena River. The one-way fare to Denali National Park is $54 and to Anchorage $154. If you plan to take the train, arrive at the depot a few minutes early to take in the model train that is maintained by the Tanana Valley Railroad Club. It's as extensive a model train as you'll see, complete with mountains, tunnels, entire towns and, this being Alaska, a glacier. The display fills a room of its own at the depot.

Hitchhiking Thumbing is made much easier by jumping on a MACS bus first (see Getting Around). Hitchhikers heading towards Denali National Park and Anchorage on George Parks Hwy should take the Blue Line bus and get off on the corner of Geist St and the George Parks Hwy. To head down Richardson Hwy towards Delta Junction and the Alcan, jump on the Green Line Bus for the Santa Claus House on Richardson Hwy in North Pole.

Getting Around
To/From the Airport There's no Metropolitan Area Commuter Service (MACS) bus to the airport; the closest stop is a 1.5-mile hike from the airport at the University Center on the corner of Airport Way and University Ave. A taxi from the airport to downtown costs around $10. GO Shuttle & Tours (☎ 474-3847, 800-478-3847) or Airlink shuttle (☎ 452-3337) will provide transportation to the airport for $7 per person.

Bus Metropolitan Area Commuter Service (MACS) provides local bus transportation in the Fairbanks area from 6:25 am to 7:45 pm

Monday to Friday, with limited services on Saturday and none on Sunday. Transit Park, on the corner of Cushman St and 5th Ave, is the central terminal for the system. All buses pass through here. There are now six runs. The Green Line heads from Transit Park downtown out to North Pole on the Richardson Hwy. The Blue Line runs from Transit Park west via Airport Way and the university. The Red Line goes from the hospital on the south side of Airport Way, through the city and to the university via College Rd.

The fare is $1.50, or you can purchase an unlimited day pass for $3. For more information call the Transit Hot Line (☎ 459-1011), which gives daily bus information.

There is also the Alaskaland Tram, which runs daily from 11:30 am to 9 pm and passes the log cabin visitor center and a few of the major hotels (Westmark Inn, Golden Nugget) every hour. It heads west along 1st Ave to Alaskaland before heading back to the city center along Airport Way and Cushman St. It's limited transportation, but it's free.

Car For two or three travelers, a used-car rental is the cheapest way of getting around the city and outlying areas such as Chena Hot Springs. What many car rental agencies won't let you do, however, is drive the rough Steese, Elliott or Dalton Hwys to visit such places as the Circle or Manley Hot Springs. If that's your destination, look around for an agency that lists 'gravel road permission,' such as Aurora Rental Car (☎ 459-7033, 800-653-3300), 1000 Cadillac Court.

If you can drive a stick, Rent-A-Wreck (☎ 452-1606, 800-478-1606), at 2105 Cushman St, has compacts for $37 per day with the first 100 miles free and every mile after that 30¢ (ouch!). Affordable Car Rental (☎ 800-471-3101), at 3101 Cushman St, south of Airport Way, has some small compacts for $40 a day with unlimited mileage. Also check with Arctic Rent-A-Car (☎ 479-8044), at the airport, which offers one-way rental between Anchorage and Fairbanks.

Bicycle Like so many other towns, Fairbanks is well on its way to putting together a fine network of bike routes in and around the city. Bike paths begin at 1st Ave and Cushman St and extend all the way past Alaskaland, across the Chena River and to UAF and Parks Hwy. Shoulder bikeways lead you out of town.

You can pick up a free *Fairbanks Bikeways* map at the visitor center and then rent a road bike for $10 a day or a mountain bike for $15 a day from 7 Bridges Boats & Bikes (☎ 479-0751) at 7 Gables Inn, 4312 Birch Lane. The best bikes, including tandems, are rented from Beaver Sports, 3480 College Rd. Rates are $16 for six hours or $94 for a week. One of the more popular rides is to head north on Illinois St and then loop around on College Rd and Farmers Loop Rd for a ride of 17 miles.

Around Fairbanks

NORTH POLE

Back in the 1940s, a group of people was kicking around names for their crossroad hamlet southeast of Fairbanks, and somehow Mosquito Junction just wasn't very appealing. So they settled on North Pole, Alaska. While the name hasn't brought in any Fortune 500 companies, a steady stream of camera-toting tourists has been wandering through ever since. Today the funky little town (population 1600) keeps up the Christmas theme year-round, with holiday decorations and trimmings even if it's 80°F in July. You can wander down streets named Kris Kringle Drive and Mistletoe Lane or do your wash at Santa's Suds Laundromat. The town comes alive in December, when radio stations from around the world call City Hall with disc jockeys asking what the temperature is or if 'Santa Claus really lives there?' And at the North Pole Post Office, 325 S Santa Claus Lane, more than 400,000 pieces of mail arrive annually simply addressed to 'Santa Claus, North Pole, Alaska.'

The biggest attraction in town is **Santa Claus House**, a sprawling barnlike store that claims to be the 'largest theme gift shop in Alaska.' Outside, there is a giant statue of Santa Claus; inside you'll find endless aisles

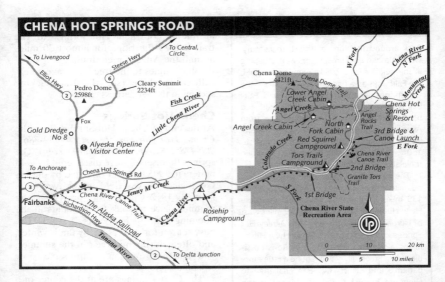

CHENA HOT SPRINGS ROAD

of Christmas ornaments and toys, a live Santa to listen to your Christmas wishes and the 'North Pole,' a candy-striped post. Santa Claus House is on the Richardson Hwy between the North Pole exits and is open until 8 pm daily. There's also **Jesus Town**, a sod-roofed log cabin community that surrounds KJNP, the 'Gospel Station at the Top of the Nation,' across the Richardson Hwy off Mission Rd. A half mile to the north is the Chamber of Commerce Log Cabin (☎ 488-2242) for information, and free tent camping is available at the **North Pole Public Park**, on 5th Ave. Right at the Santa Claus Lane exit there is a **Carrs** and a half dozen restaurants, including such fast food chains as **Taco Bell** and **Wendy's**.

The town is about 15 minutes south of Fairbanks and can be reached on the MACS Green Line or via the free Santa Claus House Shuttle (☎ 488-2200) that picks up from major hotels and RV parks. Gimmicky? Sure, but if you have nothing else to do on an afternoon in Fairbanks, why not?

CHENA HOT SPRINGS ROAD

Chena Hot Springs Rd extends 56 miles east off Steese Hwy to the hot springs of the same name. The road is paved and in good condition. The resort, the closest hot-spring resort to Fairbanks, is also the most developed. It has been turned into a year-round facility offering downhill skiing in the winter.

From Mile 26 to Mile 51, Chena Hot Springs Rd passes through the middle of the **Chena River State Recreation Area**, a 397-sq-mile preserve containing the river valley and the surrounding alpine areas. This scenic park offers good hiking (see the Fairbanks Hiking section), fishing and three public campgrounds.

The first is **Rosehip State Campground**, Mile 27 Chena Hot Springs Rd, whose large, flat gravel pads make it a favorite with RVers. There are 37 sites for $8 a night. Farther to the east is **Tors Trails State Campground**, Mile 39.5 Chena Hot Springs Rd, with 24 sites ($8). The large sites are in a stand of spruce with a canoe launch on the Chena River. Across the highway is the trailhead for the Granite Tors Trail (see the Fairbanks Hiking section). The last is **Red Squirrel Campground**, Mile 42.8 Chena Hot Springs Rd, with 12 sites ($8). All three campgrounds tend to be popular during the summer, but there are many gravel turnoffs

Hot Springs near Fairbanks

Back around the turn of the 19th century, when Alaskan gold prospectors were stooping in the near-freezing creeks panning for gold, the Fairbanks area had one saving grace – the hot springs. There are several around Fairbanks, and all were quickly discovered and used by the miners as a brief escape from Alaska's ice and cold. Today, the same mineral water, ranging in temperature from 120° to 150°F, soothes the aches and pains of frigid travelers passing through.

The hot springs include Chena Hot Springs, 56 miles east of Fairbanks; Circle Hot Springs, 135 miles northeast of Fairbanks on Steese Hwy; Hutlinana Warm Springs 129 miles west of Fairbanks on Elliott Hwy; and Manley Hot Springs at the end of the Elliott Hwy. Hitchhiking along Chena Hot Springs Rd is possible, while Steese Hwy will require a little more patience and Elliott Hwy is a challenge to even the hottest thumb. Hutlinana Warm Springs, an undeveloped thermal area, is an eight-mile hike in from the Elliott Hwy.

There is shuttle service to Chena and Circle Hot Springs, or you can rent a car (see the Fairbanks Getting Around section). If you are driving, you'll find Chena Hot Springs Rd a paved and pleasant drive. Steese Hwy is paved for about the first 40 miles and is a well-maintained gravel road beyond that, but Elliott Hwy is a long dusty haul like the Denali Hwy or the road to McCarthy.

Other thermal areas in Alaska include Chief Shakes Hot Springs (near Wrangell), Tenakee Springs (near Juneau) and White Sulphur Springs (near Sitka) in the Southeast and Pilgrim Hot Springs and Serpentine Hot Springs outside of Nome on the Seward Peninsula.

along the road for the nights when the campgrounds are full.

Just before the fifth bridge over the Chena River, at Mile 49 of Chena Hot Springs Rd, is the turnoff for the 3.5-mile Angel Rocks Trail (see the Fairbanks Hiking section).

The trailhead for the **Chena Dome Trail** is at Mile 50.5 of Chena Hot Springs Rd. The trail follows the ridge for almost 30 miles around the Angel Creek drainage area, but the first 3 miles to the tree line make an excellent day hike (see the Backpacking section in the Wilderness chapter).

Chena Hot Springs

At the end of Chena Hot Springs Rd is the *Chena Hot Springs Resort* (☎ 452-7867, 800-478-4681, vhenahs@polarnet.com). The springs themselves were discovered by gold miners in 1905 and first reported by the US Geological Survey field teams two years later. By 1912, Chena Hot Springs was the premier place to soak for residents in the booming town of Fairbanks. It still is. The busy season for this resort, by far, is winter, and often, during midweek in the summer, you can score on some impressive 'slow season discounts.'

The Chena springs are at the center of a 40-sq-mile geothermal area and produce a steady stream of water that's so hot, at 156°F, it must be cooled before you can even think about a soak. The most popular activity is hot-tub soaking, done both outdoors and indoors, where there are three Jacuzzis, a pool and a hot (very hot) tub. Other activities include mountain biking ($7.50 an hour), hiking, horseback riding ($60 an hour) and fishing the local streams for grayling.

The resort has a fine restaurant where full dinners cost $15 to $24 and a bar that is decorated in Yukon Quest memorabilia. Hotel rooms are $105 per couple per night, rustic cabins begin at $65. Large cabins with sleeping lofts that hold six cost $110.

If there are only one or two of you, head for the campground, where a wooded site along a stream costs $15 per night. The use of the hot tubs is extra for campers: $8 for unlimited day use, $6 after 7 pm.

Getting There & Away

Call the Chena Hot Springs Resort to book shuttle-van service. Roundtrip transportation is $30 per person. Hitchhiking is not the grand effort it is on the Elliott Hwy, because of the heavy summer usage of the Chena River State Recreation Area.

STEESE HIGHWAY

Circle Hot Springs lies off the 162-mile-long Steese Hwy, which was once a miners' trail. You can still see the signs of old mining camps and new ones. The road is paved for the first 44 miles and then has a good gravel base to Central. In the final 30 miles, the highway narrows and becomes considerably rougher. The excellent scenery along the highway and the good accommodations at Circle Hot Springs make this side trip well worth the time and money.

The Steese Hwy starts in Fairbanks, Mile 0, at the junction of Airport Way and Richardson Hwy. From there, it passes the beginning of Chena Hot Springs Rd at Mile 4.6 and then Elliott Hwy at Mile 11 near Fox, a small service center and your last opportunity to purchase beer, other supplies and gas at a reasonable price. Steese Hwy's golden past can first be seen at Mile 9.5, where it passes the Goldstream Rd exit to **Gold Dredge No 8**, a five-deck, 250-foot dredge built in 1928 and named a national historical site in 1984. The dredge operated until 1959

and had displaced 1065 tons of pay dirt from Pedro, Engineer and Goldstream Creeks before it was closed. No 8 is still making money; it's probably the most visited dredge in Alaska (see Gold Panning in the Fairbanks section).

At Mile 16.6, on the east side of the highway, is the **Felix Pedro Monument**, commemorating Felix Pedro, whose discovery of gold nearby resulted in the boomtown that was to become Fairbanks. Amateur gold panners are often in the nearby stream 'looking for color,' or you can go another 10 miles to see a much more serious attempt at obtaining the metal. At Mile 27.9 you take a sharp turn up a hill to reach the old gold camp of **Chatanika**. The support center was built in 1925 for the gold dredging that went on from 1927 to 1957 and removed an estimated $70 million in gold at yesterday's prices.

Chatanika Lodge (☎ 389-2164), Mile 28.6 Steese Hwy, is a log lodge with moose heads, bear skins and mining artifacts hanging all over the walls of the dining room and saloon. Single/double rooms cost $50/60.

The first public campground along the Steese Hwy is the ***Upper Chatanika River***

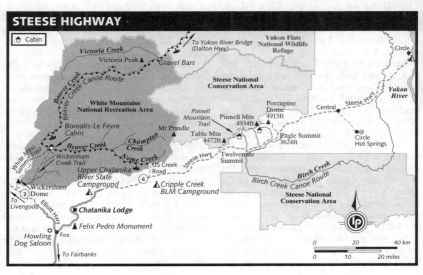

State Recreation Site, Mile 39, which has 25 sites on the river ($8). Water and firewood are usually available, but have your bug dope handy – this is mosquito country. People with canoes can launch their boats here, and the fishing for grayling is generally good. The next campground is the *Cripple Creek BLM Campground*, Mile 60, with 21 sites ($10). The campground has tables, water and a nature trail nearby and is the site of the uppermost access point to the Chatanika River canoe route (see the Fairbanks Paddling section).

Access points for the **Pinnell Mountain Trail** (see the Backpacking section in the Wilderness chapter) are at Mile 85.6 and Mile 107 of the Steese Hwy. The first trailhead is Twelvemile Summit, and even if you have no desire to undertake the three-day trek, the first 2 miles is an easy climb to spectacular views of the alpine area and past some unusual rock formations.

The **Birch Creek canoe route** begins at Mile 94 of the Steese Hwy, where a short road leads down to a canoe launch on the creek. The wilderness trip is a 140-mile paddle to the exit point, at Mile 147 of the highway. The overall rating of the river is Class II, but there are some Class III and Class IV parts that require lining your canoe. More details on the trip can be obtained from the Fairbanks BLM office (☎ 474-2200).

Eagle Summit (3624 feet) is at Mile 107, where you'll find a parking area and a display for the second trailhead of the Pinnell Mountain Trail. A climb of less than a mile leads to the top of Eagle Summit, the highest point along the Steese Hwy and a place where the midnight sun can be observed skimming the horizon around the summer solstice on June 21. The summit is also near a caribou migration route. The next 20 miles, from Eagle Summit to the town of Central, is a scenic stretch of the Steese Mountains. Practically every one of these mountains has been marred and eroded to piles of rubble and tailings due to gold mining. Most of the operations are small and involve sluicing the rock with water from the creek. It's amazing how

much of a creek bed or hillside the miners will chew up in their quest to find the precious metal. To environmentalists and others unaccustomed to active mining, it's repulsive, but it's still pretty wild country, despite the mining activity.

Central

At Mile 127.5, the highway reaches Central (population 400 in the summer), where the road's briefly paved and there are gas and groceries, a post office and various places to stay, including a motel and cabins for rent.

History Originally referred to on maps as Central House, the town began as a supply stop on the trail from Circle City to the surrounding creeks of the Circle Mining District. Central became a town in the 1930s, thanks largely to the Steese Hwy, which was built in 1927. Then in the late-1970s and early 1980s, the town experienced something of a second gold rush.

With the price of the metal bouncing between $300 and $400 an ounce, miners were suddenly making a fortune sluicing the streams. One miner alone, Jim Regan, recovered 26,000oz of gold from the Crooked Creek area between 1979 and 1986. Even more interesting was a diamond that was recovered by gold miners in 1982. Nicknamed Arctic Ice, it was the first diamond ever recovered from Alaska.

Although mining activity has dwindled in recent years and most efforts are now small family operations, the miners' distrust of anybody or any agency threatening their right to make a living still looms throughout the town, especially at the bars.

Things to See & Do One of the best museums of any small Alaskan town is the Circle District Historical Society Museum, on the Steese Hwy in Central. Established in 1984, the main portion of the museum is a large log lodge that houses a miner's cabin, exhibits on early mining equipment and dog-team freight and mail hauling and the Yukon Press, the first printing press north of Juneau, which produced Interior Alaska's first newspaper.

The most interesting display is the museum's collection of gold nuggets and gold flakes recovered and donated by local miners. This, more than anything else, will help you understand why they continue to tear away at the hills and streams in an effort to find the precious metal.

Outside in a large barn is a collection of dog sleds and other large artifacts, including an unusual covered wagon – covered with metal, not cloth. The museum also has a small video area with tapes on mining and a variety of topics, a gift shop, and a visitor information area. Most amazing, the museum is open and staffed noon to 5 pm daily during the summer; admission is $1.

The museum sells gold pans, but before you go splashing around in the local creeks trying to find nuggets of your own, be aware that most streams are staked. To wander un-invited onto somebody's claim is asking for a nasty encounter with a miner or even worse – having a few potshots aimed at your head. If you are swept up by the gold fever of this town, the safest place to pan is wherever the Steese Hwy crosses a creek or stream, since the road is public land.

Places to Stay & Eat In town is the *Central Motor Inn* (☎ 520-5228), which has it all – rooms, campsites, showers, cafe, gas, you name it. Double rooms cost $50/60 for shared/private bath. Tent sites cost $11 for two people, and a shower costs $3. The cafe is perhaps the best place to eat anywhere on the Steese Hwy. Three eggs with toast and potatoes are less than $6, and at night it often has specials for around $10. If the bugs are not too vicious, you can enjoy the meal on an outdoor deck under the midnight sun.

Groceries and other supplies can be purchased at *Crab's Corners*, which also has a cafe and Laundromat.

Circle Hot Springs

Just beyond Central, Circle Hot Springs Rd heads south, and in 6 miles, it passes the site of a former BLM campground along Ketchem Creek. There are no facilities here, but it's still the best place to pitch a tent in the area. Two miles beyond the creek is

Circle Hot Springs Resort (☎ 520-5113), a popular spot with Fairbanks residents. The springs were first used by Kutchin Indians, and then miners began soaking in the naturally hot water in the 1900s. The resort followed 30 years later, when Frank Leach arrived and made the development of the springs his lifelong obsession. Leach started by building Alaska's first runway specifically designed for airplanes in 1924 and then followed this by building his impressive four-story hotel in the early 1930s, hauling most of the materials down the Yukon River to Circle City and then overland by wagon to the springs.

Now listed on the National Register of Historical Sites, the hotel is a classic. Inside the lobby and lounge there are artifacts everywhere, including a safe where gold was once stored, photos and clippings on the wall illustrating the early mining era, and a poker table that looks as natural here as it would in Las Vegas. Outside is a string of small log cabins, each with some old mining equipment out in front and a moose rack over the doorway.

The water from the hot springs is 139°F but piped into an Olympic-sized pool at

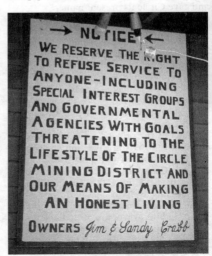

The independent spirit in Central

103°F at a rate of 231 gallons a minute. Spend 20 or 30 minutes soaking here, and you won't have sore muscles or a care in the world. There are also a restaurant and miner's saloon on site. The hotel rooms with shared baths begin at $100 for doubles. Five sleeping cubbyholes on the 3rd floor are $20/35 singles/doubles, but you need your own sleeping bag and pad. The rustic cabins, some with no running water, and other more deluxe cabins with kitchens and hot tubs, go for around $110 for two people. If you're camping down the road, it costs $5 to soak in the pool, which is open until midnight.

Circle

Beyond Central, the Steese Hwy passes the exit point of the Birch Creek canoe route at Mile 147 and ends at Circle (population 100) at *Mile 162*. Circle is an interesting little wilderness town that lies on the banks of the Yukon River and was the northernmost point you could drive to before the Dalton Hwy was opened up. A large sign in the center of town still proclaims this fact. The town is 50 miles south of the Arctic Circle, but miners who established it in 1896 thought they were near the imaginary line and gave Circle its present name.

After gold was discovered in Birch Creek, Circle was a bustling log-cabin city of 1200 with two theaters, a music hall, eight dance halls and 28 saloons. It was known as the 'largest log-cabin city in the world' until the Klondike gold rush reduced the town significantly and the Steese Hwy reduced its importance even more. For the most part, Central has now replaced Circle City as the supply center for area miners.

Much of the original town has been devoured by the Yukon River, but you can get a feeling for the town's history by walking to **Pioneer Cemetery**, which has headstones dating back to the 1800s. To find it, head upriver along the gravel road. Beyond a barricade is a trail that leads into dense underbrush, and the graves are off to the left.

A city-operated *campground* at the end of Steese Hwy consists of tables, outhouses and a grassy area along the banks of the Yukon River where you can pitch your tent.

Nearby is the *Yukon Trading Post* (☎ 773-1217), which includes a general store with Arctic Alaska prices, a cafe, bar and a free campground. The bar is an especially important spot because this is the only place you can go to at night (other than your car) to escape the maddening wave of mosquitoes.

Getting There & Away

Needless to say, hitchhiking is more difficult on Steese Hwy than on Chena Hot Springs Rd, but it's not as difficult as it might appear. A fair amount of traffic moves between the communities and Fairbanks, and people this far north are good about stopping. Still, you have to consider your time schedule and patience level before attempting this road.

In 1999, bus service was resurrected to Central, Circle Hot Springs and Circle. Steese Highway Stage Lines (☎ 520-5610, loki@xyz.net) departs Circle Hot Springs (although the bus company calls it 'Arctic Circle Hot Springs') for Fairbanks at 9 am on Monday, Wednesday and Friday and then leaves Fairbanks at 2 pm for the return trip. Circle is driven to on request, and the van company will drop off canoeists and backpackers along the way. The roundtrip fare to Circle Hot Springs is $100, to Circle $145. This is a great service, and hopefully there is sufficient demand to keep the company in business.

You can also reach the area by renting a vehicle in Fairbanks, but you will have to look around. Most car-rental companies, including the discount ones like Rent-A-Wreck, do not allow their vehicles to be driven on the Steese Hwy. Look for those that advertise 'gravel road permission.' Flying into Circle Hot Springs is not that expensive, and the area is well worth it. Warbelo Air (☎ 474-0518), in Fairbanks, has regular flights to the hot springs airstrip Monday to Friday for $150 roundtrip.

ELLIOTT HIGHWAY

From the crossroad with the Steese Hwy, at Fox north of Fairbanks, the Elliott Hwy extends 152 miles north and then west to

Manley Hot Springs, a small settlement near the Tanana River. This is by far the roughest road out of Fairbanks. The first 28 miles of the highway are paved, and the rest is gravel; sections past the junction with Dalton Hwy are so narrow and steep you could get stuck behind an RV for days. At Mile 28 of Elliott Hwy is the trailhead, parking lot and information box for the White Mountain Trail to Borealis-Le Fevre and Lee's cabins (see the Backpacking section in the Wilderness chapter, and Cabins in the Fairbanks Places to Stay section). Lee's is a 7-mile hike in, and Borealis-Le Fevre is a hike of 19 miles over the Summit Trail.

An old Bureau of Land Management (BLM) campground, no longer maintained, is passed at Mile 57 of Elliott Hwy, where a bridge crosses the Tolovana River. There is still a turnoff here. The fishing is good for grayling and northern pike, but the mosquitoes are of legendary proportions. Nearby is the start of the **Colorado Creek Trail** to Windy Gap BLM Cabin. Check with the BLM office (☎ 474-2200) in Fairbanks about use of the cabin during the summer.

At Mile 71 is the service center of **Livengood**, where you will find a small general store. At this point, Elliott Hwy swings more to the west and, in 2 miles, passes the junction of the Dalton Hwy (see the Dalton Hwy section in the Bush chapter).

Hutlinana Creek is reached at Mile 129.3, and a quarter mile east of the one-lane bridge is a well-defined trail that heads north along the creek. The trail extends to **Hutlinana Warm Springs**, an undeveloped thermal area. It's an 8-mile trek to the springs, which have been dammed up into a 3-foot-deep pool. Carry in a tent and spend the night soaking away your worries. From

Hutlinana Creek, it is another 23 miles southwest to Manley Hot Springs.

Manley Hot Springs

Manley Hot springs was first homesteaded in 1902 by JF Karshner, just as the US Army Signal Corps arrived to put in a telegraph station. Frank Manley arrived a few years later and built a four-story hotel at the trading center, which was booming with miners from the nearby Eureka and Tofly mining areas. Most of the miners are gone now, but Manley left his name on the village. Today it's a quiet but friendly spot known for its lush gardens, a rare sight this far north.

Just before entering the village, you pass the **Manley Hot Springs** (☎ 672-3171), up on a hill, where most of the serious bathing is done. Once a resort that included a restaurant and a bar, the mineral hot springs are now privately owned but still available for bathing. The springs themselves are three concrete baths in a cement pool building with a plastic roof. It costs $5 for a soak.

Places to Stay & Eat The town, which has a summer population of 150 or so, is on the west side of Hot Springs Slough and provides a *public campground* (near the bridge that crosses the slough) for $5 a night. In town is the *Manley Roadhouse* (☎ 672-3161), offering singles/doubles for $65/90 and cabins that sleep up to four people for $95. This classic Alaskan roadhouse was built in 1906 and features antiques in its restaurant, bar and lounge. You will find groceries, gas, liquor and the post office at the *Manley Trading Post*, or you can wander around town and usually purchase vegetables from some of the residents. The produce here is unbelievable.

The Bush

The Bush, the wide rim of wilderness that encircles Anchorage, Fairbanks and all the roads between the two, constitutes a vast majority of the state's area, yet only a trickle of tourists ventures into the region for a firsthand look at rural Alaska. Cost, more than mountains or rivers, is the barrier that isolates the Bush. For budget-minded travelers who reach the 'Great White North,' what lies out in the Bush is usually beyond the reach of their wallets. Apart from a few exceptions, flying is the only way to reach many areas. Once you're out there, facilities can be sparse and very expensive, especially if you don't arrive with a tent and back-packer's stove.

Those people who do endure the high expense and extra travel are blessed with a land and people that have changed far less than the rest of the state. The most pristine wilderness lies in the many newly created national parks and preserves found away from the road system – parks without visitor centers, campgrounds or shuttle buses running trips into the backcountry. Only nature in all its grandeur is encountered. Traditional villages, where subsistence is still the means of survival, and hearty home-steaders, as independent and ingenious as they come, lie hidden throughout rural Alaska.

There are three general areas in Bush Alaska: Southwest Alaska, Western Alaska and Arctic Alaska. The Southwest – the Alaska Peninsula, the Aleutian Islands and the rich salmon grounds of Bristol Bay – is covered in the Southwest Alaska chapter, because it is the most developed area for travel.

Western Alaska is a flat, treeless plain that borders the Bering Sea north of the Alaska Peninsula to Kotzebue above the Arctic Circle. This flatland is broken up by millions of lakes and slow-moving rivers such as the Yukon. The weather in the summer is cool and cloudy, with consider-able fog and drizzle. The most visited parts of this region are the towns of Nome and Kotzebue and the Pribilof Islands, which are north of the Aleutian Islands in the Bering Sea and are the location of seal-breeding grounds and bird rookeries.

Arctic Alaska, often referred to as the North Slope, is that region that lies north of the Arctic Circle. Here the Brooks Range slopes gradually to the north and is eventually replaced by tundra plains that end at the Arctic Ocean. The harsh climate and short summers produce 400 species of plants in the treeless tundra, often dwarfed versions of those farther south. Wildlife in the

Highlights

- See more than a million fur seals gather at the Pribilof Islands
- Camp and pan for gold on the beaches of Nome
- Rent a truck and see historic gold dredges along the Seward Peninsula road system
- Pitch a tent and spend a night at the Arctic Circle along the Dalton Hwy
- Take a bus tour through the Brooks Range to Prudhoe Bay
- Stroll the beach and stick your toes in the Arctic Ocean at Barrow

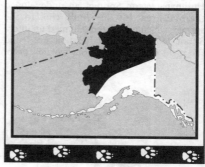

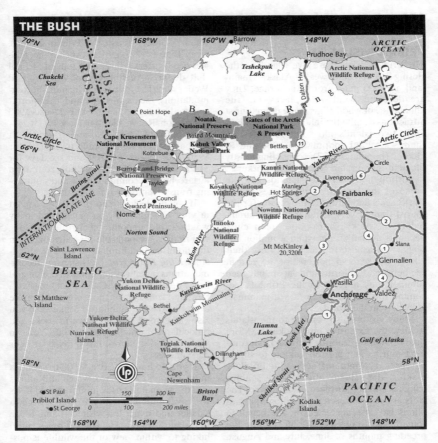

THE BUSH

form of polar bears, caribou, wolves and brown bears have adapted amazingly well to the rough conditions.

Arctic Alaska is characterized by nightless summers and dayless winters. In Barrow, Alaska's northernmost village, the midnight sun doesn't set from May to August. Surprisingly, the Arctic Alaska winters are often milder than those in the Interior. The summers, however, are cool at best, and temperatures are rarely warmer than 45°F. Barrow attracts a small number of tourists each summer, and backpackers have discovered

that the Gates of the Arctic National Park and Preserve, an intriguing place for a wilderness adventure, is becoming more accessible and more affordable with every passing summer.

Don't just pick out a village and fly to it. It is wise to either have a contact there (someone you know, a guide company or a wilderness lodge) or to travel with somebody who does. The indigenous people, especially the Inuit, are very hospitable, but there can be much tension and suspicion of strangers in small, isolated rural communities.

Western Alaska

PRIBILOF ISLANDS

The Pribilof Islands are five islands in the Bering Sea, 300 miles west of Alaska's mainland and 900 miles from Anchorage. They are desolate, windswept places, but the abundance of wildlife has made them tourist attractions despite the inhospitable weather. Only two islands have communities on them – St Paul (population 673) and St George (population 173) – consisting mostly of Aleut Indians and government workers.

Although the Pribilof Islands are the home of the largest Aleut villages in the world, seals and birds are the reason for the tourist trade. Every summer the tiny archipelago of rocky shores and steep cliffs becomes a mad scene, when a million fur seals swim ashore to breed and raise their young. The seals spend most of the year at sea between California and Japan, but each summer they migrate to the Pribilofs, becoming the largest group of sea mammals anywhere in the world.

Many visitors also venture to the islands to view the extensive bird rookeries. More than 2.5 million seabirds, ranging from common murres and crested auklets to tufted puffins and cormorants, nest at the Pribilofs, making the islands the largest seabird colonies in the Northern Hemisphere. The cliffs are easy to reach and photograph, and blinds have been erected on the beach in some places to observe wildlife. During the breeding months of June, July and August, more than 230 species of birds have been sighted, the reason many hard-core birders say the Pribilofs are one of the most spectacular bird-watching locations in the world.

Roughly 1000 people visit St Paul every summer, the largest island, with a length of 14 miles and a width of 8 miles at its widest point. A road circles the island, though much of it is impassable, and the community has a hotel and a store, but not much else. A fish processor runs a cafeteria, but there are no other restaurants or accommodations in town, and camping is not permitted on the island.

Because of strict regulations and limited facilities, most travelers choose package tours in order to visit the Pribilof Islands. Gray Line (☎ 277-5581 in Anchorage, 800-478-6388) offers a three-day tour of St Paul that departs Anchorage on Monday and Wednesday. The tour, which includes accommodations, meals, airfares and transportation to the beaches and rookeries, costs $900 per person. Reeve Aleutian Airways (☎ 243-4700, 800-544-2248) also runs tours to St Paul and offers longer stays: three days for $950, four days for $1100 and six days for $1400. These packages include roundtrip airfare, hotel accommodations and sightseeing transportation, but not meals.

If you do decide to go, read the fine print in your brochure. If you get socked in by weather, not uncommon in the Pribilofs, you're often responsible for extra nights in the hotel and additional meals. The three-story *King Eider Hotel* has spartan accommodations but always has pots of coffee and hot water in the lobby. Consider taking extra food and trail snacks; the store is expensive even by Alaskan standards. Make sure you also pack good rain gear, warm socks and binoculars for watching the wildlife. You can leave behind the mosquito spray, bear bells and sunglasses.

If you do have an extra $1000 to spend, a more unique experience, which still allows you to see an immense amount of wildlife, is to travel independently to St George, a smaller and much less visited island. Since the island isn't that big (only 5 miles wide) hiking to within view of the wildlife is possible. You can stay at the *St George Hotel*, a designated national historical landmark, where rooms are $99 a person per night and you can cook your own meals in the kitchen downstairs. Call St George Tanaq Corp (☎ 272-9886) in Anchorage to reserve a room at the hotel. Then contact Peninsula Airways (☎ 243-2323, 800-448-4426) to book a flight to St George; the return fare is around $900.

NOME

Nome (population 3615) serves as the transportation center for much of Western Alaska,

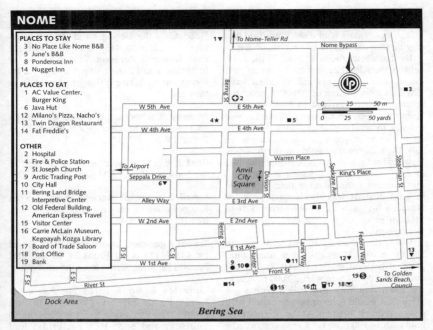

NOME

PLACES TO STAY
3 No Place Like Nome B&B
5 June's B&B
8 Ponderosa Inn
14 Nugget Inn

PLACES TO EAT
1 AC Value Center,
   Burger King
6 Java Hut
12 Milano's Pizza, Nacho's
13 Twin Dragon Restaurant
14 Fat Freddie's

OTHER
2 Hospital
4 Fire & Police Station
7 St Joseph Church
9 Arctic Trading Post
10 City Hall
11 Bering Land Bridge
   Interpretive Center
12 Old Federal Building,
   American Express Travel
15 Visitor Center
16 Carrie McLain Museum,
   Kegoayah Kozga Library
17 Board of Trade Saloon
18 Post Office
19 Bank

and during summer, oceangoing barges unloading offshore are a common sight. A surge in gold prices in the late 1980s gave new life to the mining industry, and the lure of gold still draws people to Nome, but summer tourists, rather than miners, are the real contributors to Nome's economy these days, especially with the price of gold dropping below $300 per ounce in recent years.

Of the three major towns in Bush Alaska – Nome, Kotzebue and Barrow – Nome is the most affordable and best set up for travelers. It has a wide range of accommodations, from top-of-the-line hotels to free camping on the beach, a fine visitor center and plenty of friendly bars in which to meet the locals. Nome has a low percentage of Native Alaskan residents and is not a showcase for Native culture like Kotzebue and Barrow, but this former boomtown does have something the other two don't – roads. No trip to Nome would be complete without renting a pickup truck and exploring the outlying areas.

Some tourists mistakenly see Nome as a grimy, treeless town of unpainted houses with forsaken refrigerators and broken-down snowmobiles in the front yards. True, very few roads in Nome are paved and a grassy lawn is unheard of here, but you'll find the town's colorful history intriguing, the residents extremely friendly and the gold fever contagious. From the prospectors on the beach to the weather-beaten sourdoughs in the saloons, this place on the edge of the continent is as Alaskan as a town can get.

History
In September 1898, only two years after the strike on Bonanza Creek set off the great Klondike gold rush, Jafet Lindeberg, Erik Lindblom and John Brynteson found gold in Anvil Creek outside of Nome. They became known as the 'Three Lucky Swedes,' even though one was Norwegian, because they were new to the area and had only eight weeks of mining experience between them.

THE BUSH

They managed to stake one of the richest sources of gold ever found in Alaska and set off the 'poor man's gold rush'; it was said that digging for gold was easier than stealing it.

By that winter the news reached the gold-fields of the Klondike, and the following year the tent city that miners initially called Anvil City had a population of 10,000. One of the stampeders who arrived in 1899 was John Hummel, a prospector from Idaho. He was too sick to head inland to search the tundra creeks, so he stayed near the ocean and, in July 1899, discovered gold on the beaches. News of the 'golden sands of Nome' resulted in 2,000 stampeders working the beaches that summer, panning more than $1 million in gold dust. It was the banner year for Nome, with each man recovering $20 to $100 of gold per day on the edge of the Bering Sea.

When the news finally made its way to Seattle in 1900, it set off yet another stampede of hopeful miners to Alaska. By the end of that year, there were 20,000 people in the town that was now called Nome – a place that would forever be associated with gold and quick fortunes. At the height of the gold rush, in 1900, the US Census recorded a permanent population of 12,488 and listed one-third of all non-Native Alaskan residents as living in the city, making Nome Alaska's largest city.

Like much of Alaska, Nome has had its fair share of natural disasters. Fires all but destroyed the town in 1905 and 1934, and a violent Bering Sea storm overpowered the sea walls in 1974. Even more disheartening to many Nome residents was the drop in the price of gold to $254 an ounce in 1999, forcing the Alaska Gold Company, Nome's largest private-sector employer, to reduce its workforce by 65%. Though little of Nome's gold-rush architecture remains and the future of gold mining is uncertain, the character of the city has survived, and today Nome is as colorful as any town in Alaska.

Information

Tourist Offices The Nome Visitor Center (☎ 443-5535, www.nomealaska.org) is on Front St across from the city hall and is open

9 am to 7 pm daily. Practically across the street, in the Sitnasuak Native Corporation Building, is the Bering Land Bridge Interpretive Center (☎ 443-2522). This National Park Service center is open to 6 pm Monday to Saturday and is the best place to go for information on hiking, fishing and wildlife in the area.

Money The National Bank of Alaska (☎ 443-2223) is at the corner of Front St and Federal Way.

Post The post office is on Front St, next to the National Bank of Alaska.

Email & Internet Access The Kegoayah Kozga Public Library, on Front St, provides free Internet access.

Travel Agencies American Express Travel (☎ 443-2211) is on Front St, in the Old Federal Building across from the post office.

Libraries & Bookstores The Kegoayah Kozga Public Library (☎ 443-5133), on Front St, is open noon to 8 pm Monday to Thursday and noon to 6 pm Friday and Saturday. The library has been in operation since 1902 and includes a section of rare and first-edition books. It also has a used book exchange. The Arctic Trading Post, 67 Front St, has a good selection of books on local topics.

Laundry Nome does not have a commercial Laundromat, but you can take showers ($5) at the Nome Recreation Center (☎ 443-5431), at D St and 6th Ave.

Medical Services Norton Sound Hospital (☎ 443-3311), a 19-bed facility with 24-hour emergency medical service, is at the corner of 5th Ave and Bering St.

Things to See & Do

Begin at the **Nome Visitor Center** at the corner of Front and Hunter Sts and pick up a copy of its walking tour brochure. Also inside are a dozen albums with historic photos covering everything from the gold rush to Balto,

The Unknown First Family, Fairbanks

Preserving salmon, Fairbanks

Panning for gold in Fairbanks

The Last Train to Nowhere, near Solomon on the Seward Peninsula

Native whaling umiaks on the frozen Arctic Ocean, Barrow

Cabin on the Seward Peninsula, outside of Nome

the famous sled dog, and a few exhibits, including a mounted musk ox. Outside, overlooking the seawall, is the **Donald Perkins Memorial Plaza**, featuring a collection of old mining equipment, including dredge buckets. During Nome's golden heyday there were more than 100 gold dredges in the area, and each one had hundreds of these buckets to scoop up gravel and dirt. Today, you'll see the buckets all over town, often used as giant flowerpots. Near the plaza is a wooden platform on the seawall that provides views of the Bering Sea and Sledge Island.

Across the street is the **Bering Land Bridge Interpretive Center**, in the Sitnasuak Native Corporation Building. The center is dedicated to Beringia, the 1000-mile-wide landmass that linked Alaska and Siberia until about 10,000 years ago. Archaeologists believe that the first people to arrive in Alaska, along with a variety of animals, used this land bridge. The center also has displays on mammoths, early Native culture and reindeer herding and a collection of short videos that are shown on request. Hours are 8 am to 6 pm Monday to Friday and 10 am to 6 pm Saturday.

To the east of the visitor center on Front St is the **Carrie McLain Museum** (☎ 443-2566), which is in the basement of the Kegoayah Kozga Library. The museum also features exhibits on the Bering Land Bridge and Inuit culture but focuses on gold-rush history and Nome in the early 20th century. Along with exhibits and artifacts on display, there are boxes of historic photos, from the more than 12,000 in the museum collection. The museum is open 10 am to 6 pm Monday to Friday and noon to 8 pm on Saturday and Sunday; admission is free.

In a lot next to the city hall is the **Iditarod finish-line arch**. The huge wooden structure, a distinctly bent pine with burls, is raised above Front St every March in anticipation of the mushers and their dogsled teams ending the 1049-mile race here. The original arch fell apart after the 1999 race, and Nome, being in a basically treeless region, sent out a call for help throughout the state to find a new one. The next pine was located near Hope.

Among the historic buildings listed in the walking tour is **Saint Joseph Church**, which overlooks Anvil City Square at Bering St and 3rd Ave. Built in 1901, when there were 30,000 people living in Nome, this huge church was originally located on Front St, and the electrically lit cross at the top of the building was used as a beacon for seamen. By the 1920s, the population of the city had plummeted to less than 900, and the Jesuits abandoned the structure. At one time, Saint Joseph was used for storage by a mining company, before the city purchased the church in 1996, moved it to its present location and restored it as a multipurpose building. Also in the square are statues of the Three Lucky Swedes, dozens of dredge buckets, the 'world's largest gold pan' and about the only grass you'll see in Nome.

A very interesting afternoon can be spent at Nome's **Golden Sands Beach**, a mile east of town along Front St. At the height of summer, a few local children may be seen playing in the 45°F water, and on Memorial Day (in May), more than 100 residents participate in the annual Polar Bear Swim by plunging into the ice-choked waters.

More numerous than swimmers here are gold prospectors, as the beach is open to recreational mining. Miners will set up camp along the shore and work the sands throughout the summer. The serious miners will rig their sluice and dredging equipment on a small pontoon boat and anchor it 100 yards offshore to suck up the more productive sand along the bottom. Others will set up sluice boxes at the edge of the water. On a calm day at the peak of the summer, more than a dozen pontoons will be humming offshore, and an equal number of operations will be on the beach. Miners are generally friendly, and occasionally you can even coax one to show you his gold dust and nuggets. If you catch the fever, practically every gift shop and hardware store in town sells black plastic gold pans (see 'Striking It Rich in Nome' boxed text). As you're panning, think about the visitor who was simply beachcombing in 1984. He found a 3.5-inch nugget that weighed 1.29oz, at the east end of the seawall.

THE BUSH

A Day at the Beach in Nome

Sure there are Polar Bear Swims in other parts of the USA, but few are as old as the one in Nome, and probably none are as cold.

Nome's annual event dates back to the early 1970s, when a resident decided the Bush community needed a Memorial Day event to kick off the summer. That's summer in technical terms only, because on most Memorial Days in Nome, the temperature rarely breaks out of the 30s and freezing rain, snow or both are likely to be falling.

Still, more than 100 brave souls troop down to the beach, disrobe to swimsuits and sandals and take a plunge into a sea clogged with icebergs, some the size of small cars. A few of the veterans actually spend some time bobbing between bergs, but most of the swimmers rush in and then rush out of the 32°F water.

The atmosphere on the beach, however, is a festive one. Hundreds of spectators cheer on the swimmers; a huge bonfire is lit to warm up everybody; and vendors sell hot dogs and other refreshments. Also on hand is the Nome Volunteer Ambulance – for obvious reasons – and the local Rotary Club. The Rotarians stage the event and afterwards award a certificate to anybody who kicks off another Arctic summer by nearly freezing to death in the Bering Sea.

After walking along the beach to Fort Davis Roadhouse (nice place to have a beer), return along Front St to see **Swanberg's Gold Dredge**, near the Homer Bypass junction. The dredge was in operation until the 1950s, before being passed on to the city for its historic value. Near the dredge is a rusty collection of other mining equipment. By 1912, almost 40 gold dredges were scattered throughout the Seward Peninsula. Other dredges close to Nome include the huge **Alaska Gold Co dredge**, which operated until the mid-1990s, just north of town on the Nome-Teller Rd.

Organized Tours

City Tours Nome Tour and Marketing uses large vans to visit such sights as the golden beaches of Nome, the camp of Howard Farley, an original Iditarod musher, and Little Creek Mine. The price is $52 per person. Tours are booked and begin at the Nugget Inn (☎ 443-2651) on Front St.

Nome Discovery Tours (☎ 443-2814) also offers a city tour ($45 for half day) or a full-day tour that includes a portion of the road system that extends from Nome. The longer tour includes a picnic at Salmon Lake, seeing the 'Last Train to Nowhere' on the way to Council and possibly even stream fishing. The cost is $85.

Russian Far East Tours In 1988, Bering Air (☎ 443-5464) was the first commercial carrier to be granted permission for flights across the Bering Straits to the Russian city of Provideniya and today, through Circumpolar Expeditions (☎ 272-9299), offers tours to the Chukchi region. The tour is a three-day and two-night stay with a host family in Chukchi and includes a hike on the tundra, cultural entertainment and a visit to an abandoned Inuit village. The cost for the tour is $999 per person for the flight, lodging, meals and ground transportation.

Places to Stay

Camping Camping is permitted on the beach a mile east of Nome to the Fort Davis Roadhouse. There aren't facilities such as drinking water, but camping is free. By camping toward the west end of the beach, you can run across the road and use the outhouse and pavilion in a small public park at Homer Bypass.

B&Bs There are a handful of B&Bs in Nome, and they are often the best and most affordable accommodations. *No Place Like Nome B&B* (☎ 443-2451), at Steadman St and 5th Ave, is a large home with five bedrooms for $70/80 singles/doubles. *Betty's Igloo* (☎ 443-2419), at 3rd Ave and K St, has three bedrooms for $55/70, and *June's B&B* (☎ 443-5984, 800-494-6994, june@gold-digger.com, E 4th Ave) has three rooms for $65/75, which includes a sourdough pancake breakfast and even a little sourdough starter to take home.

Hotels There are four hotels in town, but avoid the seedy Polaris Hotel. *Nugget Inn* (☎ 443-4189), at Front St and Bering St, is right downtown. It is full of gold-rush artifacts and has singles/doubles for $92/100. The *Ponderosa Inn* (☎ 443-5737), at 3rd Ave and Spokane, is clean and has rooms that begin at $75/85. The newest hotel is the *Aurora Inn* (☎ 443-3838, 800-354-4606), at Front St and Moore Way. Built in 1999, the hotel overlooks the Bering Sea and has some small doubles for $90.

Places to Eat

The local cafe is at *Fat Freddie's*, attached to the Nugget Inn. Tables overlook the Bering Sea, and the menu includes two-egg breakfasts ($6), hamburgers and fries ($7) and dinners that cost $12 to $18. Good Chinese food is found at *Twin Dragon*, at Front and Steadman Sts. Most lunches cost around $8, and there is a two-person dinner special for $19 that may be the best priced meal in town.

For Mexican food, there is *Nacho's*, in the Old Federal Building on Front St, which also serves Chinese. In the same building is *Milano's Pizzeria*, which also serves Japanese dinners. You figure it out. Mexican dinners at Nacho's cost $12 to $14; a medium pizza with one item at Milano's is $14. For a good latte, go to *Java Hut*, at Bering St and Seppala Drive, a coffeehouse where they don't mind if you spend a rainy afternoon reading.

The best dinners in town are at the *Fort Davis Roadhouse*, 2 miles east of town on Front St, where dinner for two is a $50 affair. On the weekends there are seafood and prime rib buffets for $30 per person. For cheap eats, head to *AC Value Center*, at Bering St and Homer Bypass. The supermarket has a bakery, espresso counter, a deli with ready-to-eat items and even a Burger King outlet that will sell you a Whopper for $4. There is seating inside.

Entertainment

Even by Alaskan standards, drinking in Nome is legendary. Among the early bar owners in Nome was Wyatt Earp, the noted gunslinger at the OK Corral (see the boxed text 'Wyatt Earp in Alaska'). All but two of the bars are clustered around one another on Front St. The *Board of Trade Saloon*, dating back to 1900, claims to be the oldest bar on the Bering Sea. It is also the most colorful, with live music nightly, arm-wrestling tournaments and disco on Sundays

---

Striking It Rich in Nome

Recreational mining is allowed along a mile of Nome's east beach, from the seawall to the Fort Davis Roadhouse. You don't need a permit or to stake a claim to use a gold pan, small rocker box or portable dredge with an intake of less than 2 inches. But before you sell your return ticket home to make your fortune on the beaches of Nome consider this: the amount of gold in a cubic yard is small, and the amount of gravel that must be washed out to make a living is extremely large.

Before 1961, the average gold-bearing gravel mined in Alaska yielded 35¢ to 75¢ per cubic yard. Today, because of the higher prices of gold, that value ranges up to $12 per cubic yard, the reason you will see a couple dozen recreational miners on the Nome beach every summer. But a cubic yard of gravel is 180 large panfuls, and even for a sourdough miner, it usually takes five minutes of steady, careful panning to work down the concentration of gold in a pan without losing the gold.

Still want to sell the farm? Try this first: Take a No 2 round-pointed shovel generously filled with fine gravel or sand and place it in your pan. Stir in some iron filings or small buckshot to simulate gold. Start separating it. How long did it take you to reach the buckshot? Now multiply that by 180, and you've just earned $10 or $15 on the beaches of Nome. You'll probably make more flipping burgers at McDonald's.

THE BUSH

Wyatt Earp in Alaska

A bit of the Old West found its way to Nome when Wyatt Earp and his wife arrived at the boomtown in 1899. Earp was a former marshal and noted gunslinger who teamed up with Doc Holliday to win the famous shootout at the OK Corral in Tombstone, Arizona. When Earp heard about the Klondike gold rush, he packed his bags and left Arizona to seek his fortune, but not as a prospector. Earp was above working a rocker box or getting his suits dirty. Rather he headed to Alaska, as one friend suggested to him, 'to mine the miners.'

While on the road, Earp read about Alaska's newest boomtown. Quickly, he switched his destination and, after the spring thaw of 1899, arrived at Nome on a steamer with his wife, Josie. Teaming up with a partner, Earp immediately built the Dexter, the first two-story, wooden structure in what was basically still a tent city full of prospectors. It was Nome's largest and most luxurious saloon, with a 12-foot ceiling and 12 plush club rooms upstairs, and was located only a block from 'the Stockade,' the city's red-light district.

Earp's timing was amazing. By July of that year, gold was discovered on the beaches of Nome. More than 2,000 men stampeded to the city that summer, and by early fall, they had recovered $1 million in gold dust and nuggets. Earp managed to get his share of the gold. By October of 1901, having already endured two winters on the Bering Sea, the Earps left Nome. Legend has it they departed with $80,000 in their bags, a fortune at that time.

You can see pictures of Earp on the streets of Nome and some of the turn-of-the-century gambling devices used in Nome at the Carrie McLain Museum on Front St.

(honest to God, Saturday Night Fever on Sunday evenings in Nome, Alaska). For a quieter place where you can sit and chat with locals, try **Anchor Tavern**, on Front St, which has a nice selection of beer on tap.

Getting There & Away

Air Nome is serviced by Alaska Airlines (☎ 800-468-2248), which offers two daily flights from Anchorage and a nonstop flight four days a week. A roundtrip ticket, booked two weeks in advance, costs $350. The daily Alaska Airlines flights also fly from Nome to Kotzebue. A roundtrip, advance-purchase ticket from Anchorage that includes both Bush communities is only $462.

The airport is a little more than a mile from town. If the day is nice, it's a nice walk. If not, then any taxi will give you a ride for $5 per person.

Organized Tours Many people visit Nome and Kotzebue on package tours, which, depending on the airfare, may not be as cheap as purchasing your ticket and lodging separately. Gray Line (☎ 277-5581 in Anchorage) offers a two-day package tour that begins in Anchorage, spends a day in Kotzebue and then overnights in Nome for $520. Alaska Airlines (☎ 800-468-2248) has the identical trip for $576, plus a tour with a night each in Nome and Kotzebue for $672.

Getting Around

Only two places in Nome rent cars, both offering unlimited mileage in an area of the state where there is very limited mileage. Stampede Rent-A-Car (☎ 443-3838) is in the Aurora Inn on Front St and has pickups, vans and campers for rent. A two-wheel-drive pickup is $65 a day. Alaska Cab Garage (☎ 443-2939), at 4th Ave and Steadman St, has pickups, 4WD pickups and Suburbans for $75 to $85 a day. When budgeting for a rental, keep in mind that gas in Nome often costs $1.85 to $2 a gallon. You burn up around $20 in gas for every day driving.

Hitchhiking is possible, and locals are really good about picking people up. But you must be patient and willing to sit in the back of an open pickup truck on a very dusty road.

AROUND NOME

Extending from Nome are three major roads that are maintained by the state and well traveled during the summer. Each is an adventure in itself, but they offer absolutely no roadside services whatsoever, not even gas stations. While Nome itself can appear dusty and rundown at times, the surrounding country is beautiful, a blend of treeless tundra, crystal-clear rivers and the rugged Kigluaik Mountains. Once you've come all the way to Nome, don't leave without splurging on a car rental, at least for one day. This is the best that Nome has to offer tourists.

Nome-Council Road

This 73-mile route heads northeast to the old mining village of Council and is perhaps the most interesting of the three drives. For the first 30 miles, the road follows the coast, where you pass a string of huts of summer fish camps. During the salmon season, you will see fish drying near the huts, on drift-wood racks. At Mile 22, the road crosses Safety Sound, a prime area for birding, and then 10 miles later reaches Bonanza Crossing. On the other side of this bridge is the **Last Train to Nowhere**, a series of locomotives that were abandoned in the tundra in 1907 by the Council City and Solomon River Railroad and have been rusting away ever since. Just to the north is the ghost town of Solomon, which was originally established in 1900 and once boasted a population of 1000, seven saloons, a post office and a ferry dock. The town was destroyed by a storm in 1913, and although it was relocated to higher ground, it was further decimated by the 1918 flu epidemic. Today, only four families remain.

Near Mile 40, you pass the first of two **gold dredges** within a couple of miles of each other. By 1912, almost 40 dredges worked Seward Peninsula, and today many are still visible from the Nome road system. These two are in the best shape and are the most picturesque. Nome-Council Rd begins

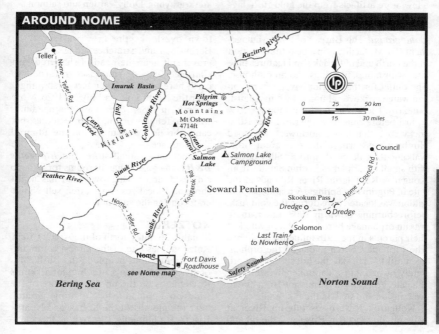

AROUND NOME

climbing after passing the second dredge and reaches **Skookum Pass** at Mile 53. There is a parking area at the pass, so you can pull off and admire the views or take a hike on the nearby ridges.

The road ends at Mile 73 at **Council**. Actually, the road ends at the banks of the Niukluk River, and most of Council is on the other side. The houses you see are second homes and weekend getaways for people living in Nome. There are very few, if any, year-round residents in Council. Locals drive across the river – with the water often reaching their running boards – to reach their houses. Tourists with rental vehicles should stay put. There are no services or shops in Council, but the Niukluk River is an excellent place to fish for grayling.

Kougarok Road

Also known as Nome-Taylor Rd, Kougarok Rd leads 86 miles north, through the heart of the Kigluaik Mountains, allowing you to see a few more artifacts from the gold-rush days and the best mountain scenery in the Nome area. At Mile 40, you pass *Salmon Lake Campground*. This Bureau of Land Management (BLM) facility is in a beautiful location at the north end of the lake and features nine sites with tables, fire rings and an outhouse. The outlet for the Pilgrim River, where you can watch sockeye salmon spawn in August, is nearby. There is no fee for camping.

Just before Mile 54 is Pilgrim River Rd, a rocky road that heads northwest. The road climbs a pass, where there is great ridge walking, then descends into a valley dotted with small tundra lakes. Within 8 miles from Kougarok Rd, Pilgrim River Rd ends at the gate of **Pilgrim Hot Springs**. A roadhouse and saloon was located here during the gold rush, before burning down in 1908. Later, there was an orphanage here for children who lost their parents in the 1918 influenza epidemic. The Catholic Church managed the orphanage until 1942. Today, the hot springs are privately owned, but a caretaker lives outside the gate. You can get permission from him to walk inside and soak in the hot ponds.

Kougarok Rd crosses Pilgrim River at Mile 60, the Kuzitrin River at Mile 68 and

the Kougarok Bridge at Mile 86. This is one of the best areas to look for herds of musk oxen. At all three bridges, you can fish for a variety of fish species, including grayling, Dolly Varden and salmon. After the Kougarok Bridge, the road becomes a very rough track, suitable only for ATVs.

Nome-Teller Road

This road leads 73 miles, a one-way drive of two hours, to Teller, a year-round, subsistence Inuit village of 247. The scenery is rugged, with steep climbs and spectacular rolling tundra. Musk oxen can sometimes be spotted on this drive, as can a portion of the reindeer herd that is owned by families in Teller. Nome-Teller Rd also crosses a number of rivers that drain the south side of the Kigluaik Mountains, all of them offering fishing opportunities. The Snake River, crossed near Mile 8; the Sinuk River, crossed at Mile 26.7; and the Feather River, crossed at Mile 37.4, are three of the more productive rivers for arctic grayling, Dolly Varden and salmon.

Teller lies at the westernmost end of the westernmost road in North America. The town overlooks the gray waters of the Bering Sea and stretches along a tapering gravel spit near the head of sheltered Port Clarence. Roald Amundsen returned to earth here after his legendary airship flight over the North Pole on May 14, 1926. More recently, in 1985, Teller made the headlines when a Teller woman, Libby Riddles, became the first woman to win the Iditarod sled dog race.

Teller has a small store, and *Blodgett's B&B* (☎ 642-3333) has 10 rooms for $87/120 singles/doubles. The town also has a gift shop, and local residents often sell Native crafts during the summer.

KOTZEBUE

Situated 26 miles north of the Arctic Circle, Kotzebue has one of the largest communities of indigenous people in the Bush; 90% of its 3600 residents are Inupiat Eskimo. Kotzebue is on the northwest shore of the Baldwin Peninsula in Kotzebue Sound, near the mouths of the Kobuk and Noatak Rivers. Traditionally, it serves as the trans-

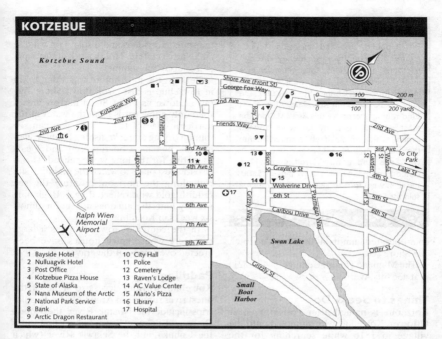

KOTZEBUE

Kotzebue Sound

1 Bayside Hotel
2 Nulluagvik Hotel
3 Post Office
4 Kotzebue Pizza House
5 State of Alaska
6 Nana Museum of the Arctic
7 National Park Service
8 Bank
9 Arctic Dragon Restaurant
10 City Hall
11 Police
12 Cemetery
13 Raven's Lodge
14 AC Value Center
15 Mario's Pizza
16 Library
17 Hospital

portation and commerce center for Northwest Alaska.

The city also enjoys a steady flow of tourists in the summer, mostly through the efforts of NANA (Northwest Alaska Native Association), a Native corporation, and as the departure point into the national preserves and parks nearby. NANA also manages a reindeer herd, numbering over 6000 head, on the Baldwin Peninsula and is half owner of the Red Dog zinc mine. Many residents still depend on subsistence hunting and fishing to survive.

Kotzebue has received a boost from the Red Dog Mine, the largest economic project in northwest Alaska, located 90 miles north of the city. Red Dog Mine holds some of the richest zinc deposits in North America, and at peak production it is expected to produce 5% of the world's supply of zinc and provide 360 direct jobs.

Most travelers to Kotzebue are either part of a tour group or are just passing through on their way to a wilderness expedition in the surrounding parks. The community is extremely difficult to visit for an independent traveler on a limited budget.

Information

Kotzebue doesn't have a visitor center or tourist office. The best place to call for advance information is the city hall (☎ 442-3401). The National Park Service maintains the Western Arctic National Parklands Visitors Center (☎ 442 3890), near the corner of 2nd Ave and Lake St. The center has information about the town and the surrounding national parks and sells books and videos of local interest.

The National Bank of Alaska (☎ 442-3258) is on the corner of 2nd Ave and Lagoon St and has an ATM. The post office is on Shore Ave, next to the First Baptist church.

Within Chukchi College, 604 3rd Ave, is the Chukchi Consortium Library (☎ 442-2410), which is open to the public. There is a

THE BUSH

Arctic Fund-Raising

When public radio and television stations around the country raise money through telethons and auctions, they generally give away T-shirts, coffee mugs, wildlife prints or lunch with local celebrities, but not KOTZ, the public radio station in Kotzebue. At a recent fund-raising auction for this Arctic station, the most popular items by far were a dead caribou with a couple of whitefish tucked into the carcass, 10lb of *muktuk* (whale blubber), two seals and a husky-wolf puppy. The caribou and puppy each drew bids of $200; the seals went for $100 each; and the *muktuk* sold for $175.

coin-operated laundry at the Bayside Hotel, 303 Shore Ave.

The Maniilaq Health Center (☎ 442-3321) is at 436 5th Ave.

Things to See & Do

Kotzebue is named after Polish explorer Otto von Kotzebue, who stumbled onto the village in 1816 while searching for the Northwest Passage for the Russians. Much of the town's history and culture can be viewed at the **Museum of the Arctic** (☎ 442-3747), where 2nd and 3rd Aves meet at the western end of town. The center is owned and operated by NANA, which offers a two-hour program at 3:15 pm daily of indigenous culture, demonstrations of Inupiat handicrafts, and a *nalukataq*, the traditional blanket toss. The program is scheduled to accommodate day tours from Anchorage, but walk-ins are welcomed. Admission is $26.50. Tour Arctic also offers a day tour to the Inupiat village of Kiana ($227, including a bush flight) and a day or evening tour of Kotzebue ($85). The **town museum**, Ootukahkuktuvik, or 'the place of old things,' lies beneath the Yogi and Boo-Boo sign in the town center, but it may be visited only by prior arrangement with the city hall.

At the corner of Lake St and 2nd Ave, the National Park Service maintains the **Western Arctic National Parklands Visitors Center.**

The visitor center has information on the large tracts of public land in this corner of the state and videos and displays on wildlife and Native culture. Hours are 8 am to 7 pm daily during the summer.

Perhaps the most interesting thing to do in Kotzebue is just stroll down **Shore Ave** (also known as Front St), a narrow gravel road only a few yards from the water at the northern edge of town. Here you can see salmon drying on racks, fishing boats crowding the beach to be repaired and locals preparing for the long winter ahead. This is also the best place to watch the midnight sun roll along the horizon, painting the sea reddish gold with reflected light. Beginning in early June, the sun does not set for almost six weeks in Kotzebue.

In the center of town, there is a large **cemetery** where spirit houses have been erected over many of the graves.

Paddling

Kotzebue provides access to some of the finest river running in Arctic Alaska. Popular trips include the Noatak River, the Kobuk River and Salmon River (which flows into the Kobuk) and the Selawik River (which originates in the Kobuk lowlands and flows west into Selawik Lake). Trips along the Kobuk National Wild River consist of floats from Walker Lake 140 miles downstream to the villages of Kobuk or Ambler, where there are scheduled flights to both Kotzebue and Bettles, another departure point for this river. Bering Air Service (☎ 442-3943) charges $120 for a one-way flight from either Kobuk or Ambler to Kotzebue. Most of the river is rated Class I, but some lining of boats may be required just below Walker Lake and for a mile through Lower Kobuk Canyon. Paddlers usually plan on six to eight days for the float.

The Noatak National Wild River is a 16-day float of 350 miles from Lake Matcharak to the village of Noatak, where Bering Air has scheduled flights to Kotzebue for $70 per person one way. However, the numerous access lakes on the river allow it to be broken down into shorter paddles. The entire river is rated from Class I to II. The upper portion, in the Brooks Range, offers much more dramatic scenery and is usually accessed from Bettles (see the Gates of the Arctic section in this chapter). The lower half, accessed through Kotzebue, flows through a broad, gently sloping valley where hills replace the sharp peaks of the Brooks Range. The most common trip here is to put in at Nimiuktuk River where, within an hour of paddling, you enter the 65-mile-long Grand Canyon of the Noatak, followed by the 7-mile-long Noatak Canyon. Most paddlers pull out at Kelly River, where there is a ranger station with a radio. Below the confluence with the Kelly River, the Noatak becomes heavily braided.

For more information contact the National Park Service office (☎ 442-3890), PO Box 1029, Kotzebue, AK 99752, before you depart for Alaska.

Canoes can be rented in Kotzebue through Arctic Air Guides Flying Service (☎ 442-3030) for $40 a day or in Ambler from Ambler Air Service (☎ 445-2121), which can also supply transportation up the Kobuk River. It is possible to book a roundtrip supersaver flight from Anchorage to Ambler, stopping at Kotzebue ($670), and from there rent boats from Ambler Air Service. See the list of guide companies at the end of the Wilderness chapter.

Places to Stay & Eat

Kotzebue does not have a public campground or hostel. The *Nullagvik Hotel* (☎ *442-3331, 308 Shore Ave)* is built on pilings to keep the heat and weight of the three-story building from melting the permafrost. The modern rooms, complete with cable TV, are $150 for a double during the summer. Two doors down is *Bayside Hotel* (☎ *442-3600, 303 Shore Ave)*, a cheaper hotel with doubles for $100. The more basic *Raven's Lodge* (☎ *442 3544)*, on 3rd Ave, charges $55/70 for rooms with a shared bath. It is common practice among backpackers, however, to hike south of town (a quarter mile past the airport) and pitch a tent on the beach. Much of the beach around Kotzebue, however, is difficult to camp on because it is narrow and sloping or privately owned.

For a meal there's *Mario's Pizza*, at 3rd Ave and Bison St, a pizza-Chinese-burger-Japanese place with sushi. A hamburger is $6; dinners are around $10 to $15; and pizzas $10 to $20. The best hamburgers are at *Kotzebue Pizza House*, at 2nd Ave and Bison St. *Arctic Dragon* has Chinese food, and the restaurant at *Nullagvik Hotel* has specialties like reindeer and arctic char.

Getting There & Away

Alaska Airlines (☎ 800-426-0333) offers a roundtrip ticket to Kotzebue for $350 from Anchorage, if booked two weeks in advance. You can also purchase a roundtrip ticket from Anchorage with stopovers in both Nome and Kotzebue for $462. See Getting There & Away in Nome for the tours offered by Gray Line and Alaska Airlines.

Arctic Alaska

DALTON HIGHWAY

Although officially called the Dalton Hwy, for years this road was best known simply as the 'haul road,' because of its origins as a rough truck supply route during the construction of the Trans-Alaska Pipeline. This stretch of gravel winds 416 miles north from the Elliott Hwy to Deadhorse at Prudhoe Bay, the community that houses the workers of what was once the largest oil reserve in the USA. Prudhoe Bay is the start of the pipeline that carries oil 800 miles to the ice-free port of Valdez on Prince William Sound.

After the road was completed in 1978, all but the first 56 miles of the highway, which leads to the Yukon River, was kept closed to the public. In 1981, after a bitter battle in the state legislature, the public was allowed to drive 211 miles to Disaster Creek, along a section of the highway that goes into the Brooks Range and near the border of the Gates of the Arctic National Park and Preserve. In 1994, the entire road was opened, and the required permit from the Department of Transportation was dropped.

The Dalton Hwy is the northernmost extension of the US highway system, but it is definitely not a trip for the misinformed or

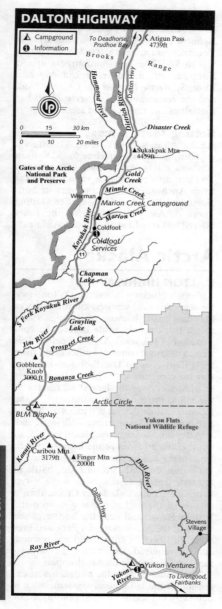

DALTON HIGHWAY

△ Campground
ⓘ Information

To Deadhorse,
Prudhoe Bay
Atigun Pass
4739ft

Brooks   Range

Hammond River

Dietrich River

Dalton Hwy

0   15   30 km
0   10   20 miles

Disaster Creek

▲ Sukakpak Mtn
4459ft

**Gates of the Arctic
National Park
and Preserve**

Gold
Creek

Minnie Creek

Wiseman

Marion Creek Campground

△ *Marion Creek*

● Coldfoot

ⓘ Coldfoot
Services

11

*Chapman
Lake*

S Fork Koyukuk River

Koyukuk River

*Grayling
Lake*

Jim River

Prospect Creek

Gobblers
Knob
3000ft *Bonanza Creek*

Arctic Circle

BLM Display

**Yukon Flats
National Wildlife Refuge**

Kanuti River

▲ Caribou Mtn
3179ft ▲ Finger Mtn
2000ft

Dall River

Dalton Hwy

Stevens
Village

Ray River

△ ⓘ Yukon Ventures

Yukon
River

To Livengood,
Fairbanks

---

ill-prepared. In the summer, the 28-foot-wide truck route of coarse gravel is dusty, punctuated with potholes and littered with the carcasses of blown tires. It's not a question of whether your car will get paint scratches or window chips but how many, the main reason rental car companies in Fairbanks don't allow their vehicles on the highway. There are few services, such as telephones, tire repair, fuel and restaurants on the road, and none for the final 225 miles from Wiseman to Deadhorse. A tow back to Fairbanks can cost $2000. Beyond the BLM campground near Wiseman, there are only undeveloped campsites and turnouts, some with outhouses and picnic tables.

The road is open year- round, but travelers should only drive it between late May and early September, when there is virtually endless light and the road is usually free of ice. Few people except truckers manage to exceed 55mph on the road. Expect a 40mph average and two hard days to reach Deadhorse. Better yet, turn around at Wiseman or the Atigun Pass, where the most dramatic scenery is. Beyond the pass is the flat, treeless coastal plain known as the North Slope.

Mile 0 of Dalton Hwy is at the junction with Elliott Hwy, 84 miles north of Fairbanks. The beginning is marked by an information center that covers the route north. At Mile 25, there is a lookout with good views of the pipeline crossing Hess Creek. There are campsites in the trees near the Hess Creek Bridge.

The highway begins to descend to the Yukon River at Mile 47, providing views of miles of pipeline. The **Yukon River Bridge** is at Mile 56. The wooden-decked bridge, the only one to cross the Yukon in Alaska, was completed in 1975 and is 2290 feet long. On the north side of the bridge is *Yukon Ventures Alaska* (☎ 655-9001), which includes a motel, restaurant, tire repair facilities and a phone. Also located here is the **Yukon Crossing Visitor Center**, which is managed by the BLM and has interpretive displays on the pipeline and the terrain you're about to enter. On the east side of the highway are some rustic campsites, and 4 miles north of the Yukon River, an old pipeline camp work

THE BUSH

pad is slated to become a BLM campground. The site is open to camping now and is already equipped with an outhouse and well.

At Mile 86.5, there is a lookout with a scenic view of granite tors to the northeast and Fort Hamlin Hills to the southeast. In the next 10 miles, the highway ascends above the tree line into an alpine area where there is good hiking and berry picking. The road stays in this alpine section for another 5 miles before the terrain turns rugged.

The **Arctic Circle**, near Mile 115 of Dalton Hwy, is the site of an impressive BLM display that was installed in 1992. The exhibit includes a large, brightly colored circumpolar map of the imaginary line and four information panels explaining the basis for the seasons and what it means to Arctic plants and animals. There are also a viewing deck, picnic tables and a road leading a half mile to rustic campsites.

Keep in mind, however, that you can't really see the midnight sun here, because it ducks behind the mountains on the northern horizon at that magical moment. To view the sun all night long (having driven this far north you might as well do it) continue on to **Gobbler's Knob**, a hilltop viewpoint at Mile 132, where there is a pullover with an outhouse.

From this turnoff, the road passes six streams and small Grayling Lake in the next 50 miles, all of which offer superb grayling fishing. **Coldfoot** is at Mile 175. Originally named Slate Creek, the area was first settled by miners in 1898. When a group of green stampeders got 'cold feet' at the thought of wintering in the district, they headed south, but the new name remained. In 1981, Iditarod musher Dick Mackey set up an old school bus at Coldfoot and began selling hamburgers to truck drivers servicing Prudhoe Bay. The truckers liked the location so much they helped Mackey build the present truck stop, including raising the center pole, which many of them engraved their names on, next to the cash register.

The **Coldfoot Interagency Visitor Center**, located here, is manned by the National Park Service, BLM and US Fish and Wildlife Service and can supply information on fishing, backpacking, gold panning and camping in the surrounding wilderness areas. There are also exhibits on Coldfoot's gold rush and slide programs most evenings. Hours during the summer are 10 am to 7 pm daily.

Services at Coldfoot include gas, tire repair, a Laundromat where a shower costis $6, and the 'farthest north saloon in North America.' The restaurant is open 24 hours, and its photo collection of jackknifed and overturned semi trucks will make you think twice about driving the road any farther. The food is surprisingly good. The *Slate Creek Inn* (☎ 678-5224, 678-5201) has singles/doubles for $100/130. There is also a private campground in Coldfoot now, but for a more pleasant spot, head another 5 miles north to *Marion Creek Campground*, at Mile 180. This 27-site campground is situated in an open spruce forest with stunning views of the Brooks Range. There is a fee for camping.

The road is near the boundary of Gates of the Arctic National Park at this point, and the scenery is at its best. Wildlife is plentiful, especially Dall sheep high on the mountain slopes. After you pass Mile 186, there is a lookout where you can view the historical mining community of **Wiseman**, west of the highway across the Koyukuk River, which can now be reached by an improved road at Mile 188.6. The town's heyday was in 1910, when it replaced Coldfoot as a service center for gold miners. Many buildings from that era still stand, including the **Wiseman Trading Company**. It doubles as the general store and the town's museum, with historic photos and mining equipment. Wiseman also has a public phone and a *campground*. You can also secure lodging at *Igloo No 8 B&B* (☎ 678-4456), which has a cabin for $90 a night.

More spectacular mountain scenery begins around Mile 194 of the Dalton Hwy, with the first views of Sukakpak Mountain to the north and Wiehl Mountain to the east, both over 4000 feet in elevation. Poss Mountain (6189 feet) comes into view to the east after another 2.5 miles, and the Koyukuk River, a heavily braided stream, is seen near Mile 201.

Just before Mile 204 is a lookout with a half-mile trail leading to Sukakpak Mountain.

THE BUSH

The mounds between the road and the mountain were formed by ice pushing up the soil and vegetation.

Another lookout is passed after Mile 206, where there are good views of Snowden Mountain (5775 feet), 10 miles to the northwest. Six miles north of the lookout is Disaster Creek and the point where people were forced to turn around before the road was opened to the public.

You are now allowed to drive the remaining 208 miles to Deadhorse. Even if you have no desire to see the North Slope, continue another 40 miles to **Atigun Pass**. At an elevation of 4739 feet, this is the highest highway pass in Alaska and marks the continental divide. The steep climb to the pass begins at Mile 242.5, and the pass is reached within 2 miles. There is a pullover at the top. To the east are the Phillip Smith Mountains, to the west the Endicott Mountains. Straight ahead is the descent into the North Slope, the arctic plains beyond the tree line (trees won't grow north of the tree line).

A campground is slated to be built on an old pipeline camp work pad at **Galbraith Lake** (Mile 275), where both the BLM and US Fish and Wildlife Service maintain field stations. Until the campground is completed, there are rustic campsites for travelers and an outhouse. Three more scenic overlooks are passed on the way to Deadhorse, the last being the **Coastal Plain Overlook** at Mile 365.

Deadhorse, at Mile 414, is the end of the highway, a few miles short of the Prudhoe Bay oil fields and the Arctic Ocean. Surprisingly, the town has a population that ranges from 3000 to more than 8000, and three motels, including the *Arctic Caribou Inn* (☎ 659-2840), where rooms are $85 to $175 a night. There are also restaurants, fuel, supplies and a post office. Send mom a post card from the top of the world! For security reasons, you can't drive into the massive oil complex but must join a commercial tour through *Prudhoe Bay Hotel* (☎ 659-2449). What disappoints most people, however, is to discover that, after driving 400 miles north, they can't camp on the shores of the Arctic Ocean.

Organized Tours

A number of tours are now available in Fairbanks for a trip up the highway. Northern Alaska Tour Company (☎ 474-8600, adventure@alaskasarctic.com) offers three, including a daily bus tour to the Arctic Circle and back for $109 and a three-day trip to Prudhoe Bay for $599 that includes lodging at Wiseman and Deadhorse, some meals and a flight back. Trans Arctic Circle Treks (☎ 479-5451, arctictk@ptialaska.net) has similar tours, and All Points Alaska Tours (☎ 458-8971, apatours@mosquitonet .com) has a two-day trip to the Arctic Circle that includes camping in the Arctic tundra for $139 per person.

Getting There & Away

Bus There is now scheduled van service between Fairbanks and Prudhoe Bay that, among other things, will drop off campers and backpackers along the way. Dalton Highway Express (☎ 452-2031) makes the run twice a week during the summer, depending on the demand, overnighting at Deadhorse. The roundtrip fare to the Arctic Circle is $100, Wiseman $130, Galbraith Lake $180 and Deadhorse $250. The run to Deadhorse includes a trip out to the Arctic Ocean but not lodging.

Car Finding somebody to rent you a car in Fairbanks for travel on the Dalton Hwy is a major challenge if not an impossible one. Don't even bother with the used-car rentals (see the Getting Around section in the Fairbanks chapter). If you're driving, remember that the road is used by tractor-trailer rigs driving at high speeds. Never stop in the middle of the road to observe wildlife or scenery, as trucks have limited braking ability. Gasoline at about $2 a gallon, tire-repair services and limited food supplies are available where the road crosses the Yukon River and at Coldfoot, and Deadhorse.

GATES OF THE ARCTIC NATIONAL PARK

The Gates of the Arctic National Park and Preserve, one of the finest wilderness areas in the world, straddles the Arctic Divide (the point where rivers either flow north to the Arctic Ocean or south to drain into the Yukon) in the Brooks Range, 200 miles northwest of Fairbanks.

The entire park covers 13,125 sq miles, extends 200 miles from east to west and is completely north of the Arctic Circle. The park extends from the southern foothills of the Brooks Range, across the range's ragged peaks and down onto the North Slope. Most of the park is vegetated with shrubs or is tundra. It is a habitat for grizzly bears, wolves, Dall sheep, moose, caribou and wolverines. Fishing is considered superb for grayling and arctic char in the clear streams and for lake trout in the larger, deeper lakes.

Within this preserve, there are dozens of rivers to run, miles of valleys and tundra slopes to hike and, of course, the Gates themselves. Mt Boreal and Frigid Crags are the gates that flank the north fork of the Koyukuk River. In 1929, Robert Marshall found an unobstructed path northward to the Arctic coast of Alaska through these landmark mountains. Marshall's name for the two mountains has remained ever since.

Hiking in the Arctic

The park is a vast wilderness containing no National Park Service facilities, campgrounds or trails. Many backpackers follow the long, open valleys for extended treks or work their way to higher elevations where open tundra and sparse shrubs provide good hiking terrain. Regardless of where you hike, trekking in the Arctic is a challenge and not for people who are only used to the posted trails in the Lower 48. Hiking across boggy ground and tussock, inevitable on any trip in the Gates of the Arctic, has been described by one guide as 'walking on basketballs.' A good day's travel in the Arctic is covering 5 or 6 miles.

The Arctic ecosystem is very fragile. Its delicate balance of tundra, tussock plains and spruce boreal forests can be easily damaged by the most sensitive backpackers and require years to regenerate because of the permafrost and the short growing season. For these reasons the NPS puts a six-person limit on trekking parties. Travel in a fan pattern whenever possible, to avoid forming trails, and never mark routes.

Campsite selection is your most important decision when trying to minimize impact. Gravel bars along rivers and creeks are the best choice due to their durable and well-drained nature. If you must choose a vegetated site, select one with a hardier species, such as moss or heath, rather than the more fragile lichens. And avoid building fires at all costs. Tree growth in the Arctic is extremely slow. A spruce only inches in diameter may be several hundred years old.

Many backpackers enter the park by way of charter air taxi out of Bettles, which can land on lakes, rivers or river bars. Extended treks across the park require outdoor experience and good map and compass skills. One of the more popular treks is the four- to five-day hike from Summit Lake through the Gates to Redstar Lake.

Less-experienced backpackers often choose to be dropped off and picked up at one lake and from there explore the surrounding region on day hikes. Lakes ideal for this include Summit Lake, the Karupa lakes region, Redstar Lake, Hunt Fork Lake or Chimney Lake.

The exception to chartering a plane is the trek beginning from the Dalton Hwy into several different areas along the eastern border of the park. First stop at the Coldfoot Interagency Visitor Center for advice and assistance in trip planning. Then drive north to your access point into the park. The farther north you travel on the highway, the quicker you will get into the tundra and the truly spectacular scenery. Many backpackers stop at Wiseman, which provides access to several routes, including the following.

Nolan/Wiseman Creek Area Just before Mile 189 of the Dalton Hwy, head west at the Wiseman exit and continue hiking along the Nolan Rd, which passes through Nolan, a hamlet of a few families, and ends at Nolan Creek. This will provide access to Wiseman Creek and Nolan Creek Lake, which lies in the valley of Wiseman and Nolan Creeks at the foot of three passes: Glacier, Pasco and Snowshoes.

Any of these passes provides a route to Glacier River, which can be followed to the north fork of the Koyukuk for a more extensive hike. The USGS topographic maps that cover this area are Wiseman B-1, B-2, C-1 and C-2.

Lower Hammond River Area From Wiseman, continue north by hiking along the Hammond Rd, which can be followed for quite a way along the Hammond River. By following the river, you can further explore the park by following one of several drainage areas, including Vermont and Canyon Creeks and Jenny Creek, which heads east to Jenny Creek Lake. The USGS maps that cover this area are Chandlar C-6 and B-6 and Wiseman C-1 and B-1.

Paddling

Floatable rivers in the park include the John, the north fork of the Koyukuk, the Tinayguk, the Alatna and the middle fork of the Koyukuk River from Wiseman to Bettles. The headwaters for the Noatak and Kobuk Rivers are in the park.

The waterways range from Class I to III in difficulty. Of the various rivers, the north fork of the Koyukuk River is one of the most popular, because the float begins in the shadow of the Gates and continues downstream 100 miles to Bettles through Class I and II waters. Canoes and rafts can be rented in Bettles and then floated downstream back to the village.

Upper Noatak The best-known river and the most popular for paddlers is the upper portion of the Noatak, because of the excellent scenery as you float through the sharp peaks of the Brooks Range and also because it is a relatively mild river that can be handled by many canoeists on an unguided trip.

The most common trip is a 60-mile float that begins with a put-in near Portage Creek and ends at a riverside lake near Kacachurak Creek, just outside the park boundary. This float is often covered in five to seven days but does involve some Class II and possible Class III stretches of rapids toward the end. During the summer you will most likely see other canoeing or rafting parties on the water.

Guide Companies A number of guide companies run trips through the Gates of the Arctic National Park, including Sourdough Outfitters (☎ 692-5252, info@sourdoughoutfitters.com), which charges $1540 for a six-day canoeing expedition on the north fork of the Koyukuk River and $2000 for a 10-day paddle on the headwaters of the Noatak River. Para Tours (☎ 479-7272, para@alaska.net) of Fairbanks offers a guided trip along the Koyukuk River that begins with a flight from Fairbanks to Coldfoot, a four-day float to Bettles and a return flight the next day. The cost is $1315 per person and includes lodging in Bettles. Check the Wilderness chapter for other Fairbanks outfitters that offer trips in the Brooks Range region.

Canoes and rafts can be rented from Sourdough Outfitters, which offers unguided expeditions with arranged drop-off and pickup air services for independent backpackers. A six-day backpacking adventure from Summit Lake to Chimney Lake is $487 per person for a party of two; a seven-day combination of backpacking and canoeing the North Fork of the Koyukuk is $686 per person. The company has a wide range of other unguided trips and rents canoes for $25 a day and rafts for $35 to $50, depending on their size. Bettles Lodge (☎ 692-5111, bttlodge@alaska.net) also runs float trips and rents rafts and inflatable canoes for $45/35 a day.

Getting There & Away

Access to the park's backcountry is usually accomplished in two steps, with the first being a scheduled flight from Fairbanks to Bettles. Check out Frontier Flying Service (☎ 474-0014), or Larry's Flying Service (☎ 800-478-5169) in Fairbanks, which makes regular flights to Bettles for $248 roundtrip.

The second step is to charter an air taxi from Bettles to your destination within the park. A Cessna 185 on floats holds three passengers and costs around $225 per hour. Most areas in the park can be reached in under two hours. If you're in Bettles, check with Brooks

Range Aviation (☎ 692-5444) or Bettles Air Service (☎ 692-5111) for air charters.

The alternative to expensive air chartering is to begin your trip from the Dalton Hwy. Twice a week Dalton Highway Express (☎ 452-2031) makes a run from Fairbanks to Prudhoe Bay and will drop off backpackers along the way. Roundtrip fare to Wiseman, the most popular place to begin trekking from the highway, is $130.

BETTLES

This small village of 50 residents serves as the major departure point to the Gates of the Arctic National Park. Founded by Gordon C Bettles in 1900 as a trading post, Bettles was originally 6 miles down the middle fork of the Koyukuk River. Riverboats would work their way up the Koyukuk and unload their supplies in Bettles, which were then transported to smaller scows and horse-drawn barges. The smaller boats would then take the cargo to the mining country farther upriver.

WWII brought a need for a major airstrip in Arctic Alaska, and the Civil Aviation Agency (now the Federal Aviation Administration) chose to construct one on better ground upriver. Eventually the entire village moved to the airstrip. Today, Bettles has the distinction of being the smallest incorporated city in Alaska.

Information

The National Park Service maintains a ranger station (☎ 692-5494) at Bettles, just beyond the airstrip, next door to Sourdough Outfitters. During the summer the station is open 8 am to 5 pm daily, and inside there are a stack of handouts and a small library of books and videos relating to the park.

Hiking

If you find yourself with an unexpected day in Bettles, something that can easily happen in August, take a hike up to Birch Hill Lake. The trailhead is unmarked but can be located by first heading to the Evansville Health Clinic. Next to it is a small brown house, and the trail can be found just to the right of the house. The trail is a 3-mile trek

to the lake and can get swampy. Wear rubber boots.

Places to Stay & Eat

Camping is allowed behind the Bettles Flight Service building, off the runway and at the north edge of the aircraft parking area, where you'll find barbecue grills. It would be just as easy to pitch a tent on the gravel bars along the middle fork of the Koyukuk River.

A variety of accommodations are available at **Bettles Lodge** (☎ 692-5111, bttlodge@ alaska.net), just off the runway. Actually everything in Bettles is just off the runway. The original inn is a classic Alaskan log lodge with a restaurant, a small tavern and bush pilots constantly wandering through in their hip boots. Singles/doubles with a shared bath cost $95/115 a night. The lodge's new Aurora Lodge has eight rooms with private baths for $115/140, and there is a bunkhouse hostel where a bed costs $15.

Sourdough Outfitters (☎ 692-5252, info@ sourdoughoutfitters.com) also has a bunkroom ($15), showers ($4) and two cabins. The cabins sleep up to four people and are $80 a night for two people.

The **Bettles Lodge Restaurant** is open 8 am to 8 pm and has breakfasts for $8 to $10, hamburgers for $7 and the single main course at dinner for $12 to $15. Sign up for dinner if you plan to eat there. The other option for food is the **Bettles Trading Post**, which is run by Sourdough Outfitters and has the usual Bush Alaska selection and prices to match.

Getting There & Away

See Getting There & Away in the earlier Gates of the Arctic section

BARROW

Barrow (population 4380) is the largest Inupiat community in Alaska and one of the largest in North America. It is the seat for the North Slope Borough, a countylike government that oversees an area larger than Nebraska. Although residents enjoy such modern-day conveniences as a local bus system, satellite dishes for their televisions,

THE BUSH

softball leagues in the summer and gas heating in their homes courtesy of the nearby oil fields, they remain traditional in their outlook. This is best symbolized by the spring whale hunts and seen during the Nalukataq Festival staged in June to celebrate a successful hunt.

The town, the northernmost community in the USA, is 330 miles north of the Arctic Circle and less than 1300 miles from the North Pole. Once known as a commercial whaling center for European and American ships, Barrow is now famous for being the destination of US humorist Will Rogers when he died in 1935. The plane carrying Rogers and Wiley Post stalled and crashed into a river 15 miles south of Barrow during their Fairbanks-to-Siberia trip.

The main reason most people visit Barrow is not so much for its Inupiat culture but its latitude. They want to see the midnight sun, which never sets for 82 days from May to early August, and say they've been at the top of the world. Beyond dipping a toe in the Arctic Ocean or watching the sun skim the horizon at 2 am, there is very little to see in Barrow.

The vast majority of the 8,000 tourists who arrive every summer are part of a package tour. Barrow is not geared for tourism like Nome, making it an expensive side trip for independent travelers. The roundtrip airfare from Fairbanks can be as low as $360 if you book it 14 days in advance on Alaska Airlines, but rooms here can easily exceed $140 a night during the summer.

Information

The Barrow Visitors Information Center is at Momegana and Ahkovak Sts, near the airport, and is open only during the summer, 2 to 4 pm Monday to Friday. You can also contact the North Slope Borough Public Information Office (☎ 852-0215), PO Box 60,

Baseball in Barrow

To the surprise of many tourists, the rage in Barrow during the summer is softball. This community of 4000 residents boasts 18 locally sponsored teams and produced four Alaska state champion squads in the 1990s. Barrow is so softball crazy that in 1995 the city spent almost $1 million to build Piuraagvik Park, its softball field. The construction included laying down a thick Styrofoam pad over the permafrost, to keep the infield from turning into a quagmire.

Not that softball is an easy game at the top of the world. They can't grow grass, so they play on gravel. Games, especially early or late in the season, might include 0°F weather, 30mph winds or fogs so thick that outfielders can hardly see the batters, much less the ball. Players will often wear two or three sweatshirts and reek of Ben-Gay, in an attempt to stay warm and prevent pulled muscles.

Then there is the possibility of a polar bear wandering near the field. 'You have to be careful when you chase foul balls,' one player told the *Wall Street Journal* in a 1998 interview. 'Up here, you're not at the top of the food chain.'

The idea of Arctic softball was so unusual that the *Wall Street Journal* piece put Barrow in the spotlight. Later that summer, players were interviewed on National Public Radio's *All Things Considered*, and NBC's *Today Show* followed up by sending a film crew to the Bush community.

THE BUSH

Barrow, AK 99723, for information in advance of your trip.

The National Bank of Alaska (☎ 852-6200) is at Agvik and Kiogak Sts, and there is an ATM at the Alaska Commercial Co (Stuaqpak) on Agvik St. The post office is at Cunningham and Kongosak Sts.

The Tuzzy Library (☎ 852-0246) is on Nachik and Stevenson Sts.

Samuel Simmonds Memorial Hospital (☎ 852-4611) is on Agvik St.

Things to See & Do

The main thing to do at the top of the world is to stand on the shore of the **Arctic Ocean** and look toward the North Pole. You can stroll the gravel road that parallels the sea to view *umiaks* (Inupiat skin boats), giant jawbones of bowhead whales, fish-drying racks and the jumbled Arctic pack ice that still litters the sandy shoreline in June and can be seen stretched across the horizon even in July.

Within town, there is the **Inupiat Heritage Center** on Ahkovak St. Dedicated in 1999, the 24,000-sq-foot center houses a museum, library and a large room designed for traditional dance performances. The museum features exhibits on the Inupiat culture and commercial whaling, as well as displays on ice-age animals – mammoths, ancient horses and lions and giant bears – that inhabited the area of Alaska and Siberia known as Beringia. Each afternoon, local people present a cultural program that features traditional singing, dancing and drumming. Hours are 8.30 am to 5 pm Monday to Friday; admission is free.

More Inupiat culture and art is on display in the lobby of the **North Slope Borough Building** on Agvik St. A gift shop here has such items as baleen baskets, sealskin bags and Native ivory carvings for sale. At the airport there is a small **Will Rogers and Wiley Post Monument**.

Perhaps the biggest attraction in the area is **Point Barrow**, a narrow spit of land about 12 miles northeast of the city. The spit is the northernmost point of land in North America, dividing the Chukchi Sea to the west from Beaufort Sea to the east. In the winter and spring, Point Barrow is where

polar bears den; in the summer, it's the featured stop of organized tours. The buses never actually reach the tip of the point, as the road ends several miles short of it. To continue on, you must walk or rent an ATV.

Native-owned Tundra Tours (☎ 852-3900, 800-882-8478), part of the Top of the World Hotel, uses small buses to show visitors the town, the Arctic Ocean and the surrounding tundra. During the short summers, a variety of birds and other wildlife can often be spotted. A blanket toss and Native drumming and dance performance is also included in the six-hour tour. The tour costs $58 per person and includes lunch.

Special Events

The Nalukataq Festival is held in late June, after the spring whaling hunt has been completed. Depending on how successful the whaling captains have been, the event can last from a few days to more than a week. The festival is a rare cultural experience if you are lucky enough to be in Barrow during it. One Inupiat tradition calls for the whaling crews to share their bounty with the village, and during the festival, you can watch families carry off platters and plastic bags full of raw whale meat. Dishes served include *muktuk*, the pink blubbery part of the whale, which is boiled, pickled or even eaten raw with hot mustard or soy sauce. It is an acquired taste, to say the least, and usually too tough and chewy for Outsiders.

The main event of the festival is the blanket toss, in which locals gather around a sealskin tarp and pull it tight to toss people into the air, much like a trampoline. The object is to jump as high as is possible and inevitably there are a number of sprains and fractures at every Nalukataq.

Places to Stay & Eat

There are three hotels in Barrow. The ***Top of the World Hotel*** (☎ 852-3900, 800-882-8478, *1200 Agvik St*) is the largest and most modern hotel in Barrow, where most of the package tours stay. Double rooms are $179 per night. Near the airport is ***Barrow Airport Inn*** (☎ 852-2525, 800-375-2527, *1815 Momegana St*), with 14 rooms that include refrigerators,

THE BUSH

microwaves and the use of kitchenettes. Rooms begin at $120/130. The cheapest place to stay is the *UIC-NARL Hostel (☎ 852-7800 at NARL)*, at the former Naval Arctic Research Lab east of town, which was transferred to Ukpeagvik Inupiat Corp in the 1980s and is mainly used for the local community college now. Rooms with shared facilities cost $65 per person.

Barrow's top restaurant is *Pepe's North of the Border*, next to the Top of the World Hotel on Agvik St, where dinners cost $16 to $20. Pepe's, the 'northernmost Mexican restaurant in the world,' has good food and Mexican decor that will make you forget you're in Barrow. *Arctic Pizza (125 Upper Apayauk St)* is a pizzeria on the 1st floor and an Italian restaurant upstairs, where you can dine with a view of the Arctic Ocean. A medium pizza with one item costs $15. The quirky *Ken's*, above the Cape Smythe Air office, has $10 lunch specials.

Another interesting restaurant is *Brower's Cafe*, in the Browerville section of town. The building was built in the late 19th century by Charles Brower, an American whaler who settled here in 1882, to house stranded whalers. The cafe is something of a museum, as well as a restaurant. Outside, there are arched whale jawbones and a traditional whaling boat. Inside are oil paintings of Brower and early whaling crews. Sandwiches, pizza, pasta, seafood and beef dishes cost $7 to $15. On weekends, they serve breakfast from 10 am.

Getting There & Away

The only way to reach Barrow is to fly. A roundtrip, advance-purchase ticket from Fairbanks to Barrow through Alaska Airlines is $356 and from Anchorage $420.

Such fares make package tours the most affordable way to see Barrow. A one-day

Barrow on the Tonight Show

Barrow's best-known restaurant, Pepe's North of the Border, was opened in 1978 by Fran Tate, a tireless promoter of the city and Arctic Alaska. That effort led to her 1984 appearance on the *Tonight Show* with Johnny Carson. She first presented the famous talk-show host with some bowhead whale *muktuk*. 'No thanks,' quipped Carson while looking at the raw blubber. 'I just had whale for lunch.' The audience roared with laughter.

Tate, however, had the last laugh. When she presented Carson with an *oosik*, he held the 2-foot-long bone, studied it closely and asked, 'What's an *oosik*?'

'Let's just say every male walrus has one,' Fran replied with a smile.

tour, which includes airfare from Fairbanks and a village tour, but not meals, is $395. Throw in a night at the Top of the World Hotel, and it's $438 per person, based on double occupancy. Companies offering Barrow tours include Gray Line (☎ 456-5816), Alaska Airlines (☎ 800-468-2248) and Northern Alaska Tour Company (☎ 474-8600). Alaska Airlines also offers the tour out of Anchorage, for an extra $170.

Getting Around

During the day, city buses ($1) run every 20 minutes between Barrow, Browerville and NARL. You can rent ATVs from North Slope Auto & Rental (☎ 852-7325) or cars from UIC Auto Rental (☎ 852-2700) and Arctic Airport Truck Rentals (☎ 852-3342).

For a taxi, phone Arctic Cab (☎ 852-2227), Quilamik (☎ 852-2020) or City Cab (☎ 852-5050).

Glossary

Alcan or **Alaska Hwy** – The main overland route into Alaska. Although the highway is almost completely paved now, completing a journey across this legendary road is still a special accomplishment that will earn you a slash mark on the side of your pickup truck. The Alcan begins at the Mile 0 milepost, in Dawson Creek in northeastern British Columbia, Canada. It heads northwest through Whitehorse, the capital of the Yukon Territory, and officially ends at Delta Junction (Mile 1422), 101 miles southeast of Fairbanks.

aurora borealis or **northern lights** – The mystical snakes of light that weave across the sky from the northern horizon, a spectacular show on clear nights, possible at almost any time of the year. The lights are the result of gas particles colliding with solar electrons. The northern lights are best viewed from the Interior, away from city lights, between late summer and winter.

bidarka – A skin-covered sea kayak used by the Aleuts

blanket toss – An activity originating with the Inuit, in which a large animal skin is used to toss a person into the air

blue cloud – What Southeasterners call a break in the clouds

breakup – When the ice on rivers suddenly begins to melt, breaks up and flows downstream. Many residents also use this term to describe spring in Alaska, when the rain begins, the snow melts and everything turns to mud and slush.

bunny boots – Large, oversized and usually white plastic boots used extensively in subzero weather to prevent the feet from freezing. Much to the horror of many Alaskans, the company that manufactured the boot announced in 1995 it would discontinue the style.

Bush, the – Any area in the state that is not connected by road to Anchorage or is not part of the Alaska Marine Hwy

cabin fever – A winter condition in which cross-eyed Alaskans go stir-crazy in their one-room cabins because of too little sunlight and too much time spent indoors

cache – A small hut or storage room built high off the ground to keep supplies and spare food away from roaming bears and wolves. The term, however, has found its way onto the neon signs of everything from liquor stores to pizza parlors in the cities.

capital move – The political issue that raged in the early 1980s, concerning moving the state capital from Juneau closer to Anchorage. Although residents rejected funding the move north in a 1982 state election, the issue continues to divide Alaska.

cheechako – Tenderfoot, greenhorn or somebody trying to survive their first year in Alaska

chum – Not your mate or good buddy but a nickname for the dog salmon

clear-cut – A hated sight for environmentalists, an area where loggers have cut every tree, large and small, leaving nothing standing. The first view of a clear-cut in Alaska, often from a ferry, is a shocking sight for a traveler.

d-2 – A phrase that covers the lands issue of the late 1970s, pitting environmentalists against developers over the federal government's preservation of 156,250 sq miles of Alaskan wilderness as wildlife reserves, forests and national parks

Eskimo ice cream – A traditional Inuit food made of whipped animal fat, berries, seal oil and sometimes shredded caribou meat

fish wheel – A wooden trap that scoops salmon or other large fish out of a river into a holding tank, using the current as power

freeze-up – That point in November or December when most rivers and lakes ice over, signaling to Alaskans that their long winter has started in earnest

glacier fishing – Practiced by both bears and people, picking up flopping salmon along the Copper River in Cordova after a large calving from the Childs Glacier strands the fish during the August spawning run

humpie – A nickname for the humpback or pink salmon, the mainstay of the fishing industry in the Southeast

ice worm – A small, thin black worm that thrives in glacial ice and was made famous by a Robert Service poem

Iditarod – The 1049-mile sled-dog race run every March from Anchorage to Nome. The winner usually completes the course in under 14 days and takes home $50,000.

Lower 48 – An Alaskan term for the continental USA

moose nuggets – Hard, smooth little objects dropped by moose after a good meal. Some enterprising resident in Homer has capitalized on them by baking, varnishing and trimming them with evergreen leaves to sell during Christmas as Moostletoe.

mukluks – Lightweight boots of sealskin trimmed with fur, made by the Inuit

muktuk – Whale skin and blubber. Also known as *maktak,* it is delicacy among Inuit and is eaten in a variety of ways, including raw, pickled and boiled.

muskeg – The bogs in Alaska, where layers of matted plant life float on top of stagnant water. These are bad areas in which to hike.

no-see-um – Nickname for the tiny gnats found throughout much of the Alaskan wilderness, especially in the Interior and parts of the Brooks Range

Outside – To residents, any place that isn't Alaska

Outsider – To residents, anyone who isn't an Alaskan

permafrost – Permanently frozen subsoil that covers two-thirds of the state

petroglyphs – Ancient rock carvings

potlatch – A traditional gathering of indigenous people held to commemorate any memorable occasion

qiviut – The wool of the musk ox, often woven into garments

scat – Animal droppings; however, the term is usually used to describe bear droppings. If the scat is dark brown or bluish and somewhat square in shape, a bear has passed by. If it is steaming, the bear is eating blueberries around the next bend.

solstice – The first day of summer on June 21 and the first day of winter on December 21. In Alaska, however, solstice is synonymous with the longest day of the year and is celebrated in most towns.

sourdough – Any old-timer in the state who, it is said, is 'sour on the country but without enough dough to get out.' Newer residents believe the term applies to anybody who has survived an Alaskan winter. The term also applies to a 'yeasty' mixture used to make bread or pancakes.

stinkhead – An Inuit 'treat' made by burying a salmon head in the sand. Leave the head to ferment for up to 10 days then dig it up, wash off the sand and enjoy.

Southeast sneakers – The tall, reddish-brown rubber boots that Southeast residents wear when it rains, and often when it doesn't, also known as 'Ketchikan tennis shoes,' 'Sitka slippers,' 'Petersburg pumps' and a variety of other names

taku wind – Juneau's sudden gusts of wind, which may exceed 100mph in the spring and fall. Often, the winds cause horizontal rain, which, as the name indicates, comes straight at you instead of falling on you. In Anchorage and throughout the Interior, these sudden rushes of air over or through mountain gaps are called 'williwaws.'

tundra – Often used to refer to the vast, treeless Arctic plains

ulu – A fan-shaped knife that indigenous people traditionally used to chop and scrape meat; now used by gift shops to lure tourists

Acknowledgments

THANKS

Thanks to the following travelers, who read the last edition of this book and wrote to us about their experiences in Alaska:

A Chan, Abraham Blum, Adriana Gardella, Alex Carter, Alfred and Ilana Drukker, Amrita Alberti, Andrew Firman, Andrew Reback, Angela Riley, Barbara Lashbrook, Belinda Johnson, Bernard Blanch, Bob Hook, Brian and Helen Phillips, Bronwyn Siviour, Bruce Gareth Chen, Bruce Reznick, Candace Ward, Carolyn McLeod, Catalina Hall, Catherine Allcock, Cheryl van der Eerden, Chris Garthee, Chris S Stevens, Chris Whitelaw, Claudia Egelhoff, Constance Frey, Corinna Thiemann, Cormiac Willis, Dominique Bachelet, Don Howe, Douglas Fischer, Elad Benjamin and Or Kirsch, Elaine Slaybaugh, Elisabeth Taylor, Eric Venot, Eva Blackwell Fain, Eyal and Lisbeth CB Biger, Fred Klingener, Gabrielle and Anthony McCann, Gavin Hardy, Geoff Caflisch, Gerald Boyle, Gerry Ostrow, Gianmario Casalis-Cavalchini, Guy Hefetz, Hamutal Davidi, Heather Tregoning, Helene and David Eichholz, Hermann Koerbel, Ian Harrison, Ingela Jansson, J M MacPherson, Jan Harrison, Jane Dunn, Jane Kelly, Janice and Malcolm Pinchstone, Jasper van de Hoef, Jean Albrecht Lucken, Jennifer Craig, Jennifer Gunter, Jennifer L Capuano, Jenny Wise, Jillian L Wallace, Jimmy Barnes, John K Ling, John Stedman, Jorge H Tolaba, Julie Halligan, Julie Pappas, Karen Ambrose Hickey, Karin Satter, Katja Muggler, KC Hughes, Kelly Jamail, Kim Senger, KL Dayes, Kristina Peterson, Kurt Simeck, L Hunter, Lea Zore, Lim Regina, Linda Greenfield, Lorraine Grave, Lorraine Hart, Mandy Mulvey, Marcia Smith, Margaret Macpherson, Margot S Weston, Marie Helmold, Martha Bowen, Matt Harcombe, Michael Livni, Mike Hoogkamp, MML Nieste, Mogens Holm, Nate Reynolds, Nicole Kinson, Nina Mckenna, Noreen Campbell, Ori Aphek, Pancras Van der Laan, Pat Ashwell, Patricia P Hunt, Paul Carter, Peter van As, Phyl Shimeld, PW Heaven, Rachel Yee Quill, Randeep Jawa, Ray Fort, Rebekka Chaplin, Renate and Bernhard Linke, Rene Gayhart, RG Spencer-Jones, Rhonda Cooper, Robert Fliegler, Roland Spencer-Jones, Ron Margolis, Ron Phillips, Sandy Horrocks, Sarah Fleming, Sarah Heck, Sean Burns, Sharon Gilkey, Stan Malcolm, Stanley F Rose, Steffanie Grundman, Sylvie Desilets and Ajit, Ted Masur, Tim Hildebrandt, Timothy J Schaefer, Tony Wills, Tyler K Lee, Vel Natarajan, Wendy Bell, Wiebke Hagele, William Maloney, Wilma E Leslie, Yvonne Lentwyler, Zane Miller

LONELY PLANET

You already know that Lonely Planet produces more than this one guidebook, but you might not be aware of the other products we have on this region. Here is a selection of titles which you may want to check out as well:

Hiking in Alaska
ISBN 1 86450 038 7
US$19.99 • UK£12.99 • 149FF

Pacific Northwest USA
ISBN 0 86442 534 1
US$24.95 • UK£14.99 • 180FF

The Arctic
ISBN 0 86442 665 8
US$19.95 • UK£12.99 • 160FF

Canada
ISBN 0 86442 752 2
US$24.95 • UK£14.99 • 180FF

Available wherever books are sold.

LONELY PLANET

Guides by Region

onely Planet is known worldwide for publishing practical, reliable and no-nonsense travel information in our guides and on our web site. The Lonely Planet list covers just about every accessible part of the world. Currently there are fifteen series: travel guides, Shoestrings, Condensed, Phrasebooks, Read This First, Healthy Travel, Walking guides, Cycling guides, Pisces Diving & Snorkeling guides, City Maps, Travel Atlases, Out to Eat, World Food, Journeys travel literature and Pictorials.

AFRICA Africa on a shoestring • Africa – the South • Arabic (Egyptian) phrasebook • Arabic (Moroccan) phrasebook • Cairo • Cape Town • Cape Town city map • Central Africa • East Africa • Egypt • Egypt travel atlas • Ethiopian (Amharic) phrasebook • The Gambia & Senegal • Healthy Travel Africa • Kenya • Kenya travel atlas • Malawi, Mozambique & Zambia • Morocco • North Africa • Read This First Africa • South Africa, Lesotho & Swaziland • South Africa, Lesotho & Swaziland travel atlas • Swahili phrasebook • Tanzania, Zanzibar & Pemba • Trekking in East Africa • Tunisia • West Africa • Zimbabwe, Botswana & Namibia • Zimbabwe, Botswana & Namibia travel atlas • World Food Morocco
Travel Literature: The Rainbird: A Central African Journey • Songs to an African Sunset: A Zimbabwean Story • Mali Blues: Traveling to an African Beat

AUSTRALIA & THE PACIFIC Auckland • Australia • Australian phrasebook • Bushwalking in Australia • Bushwalking in Papua New Guinea • Fiji • Fijian phrasebook • Healthy Travel Australia, NZ and the Pacific • Islands of Australia's Great Barrier Reef • Melbourne • Melbourne city map • Micronesia • New Caledonia • New South Wales & the ACT • New Zealand • Northern Territory • Outback Australia • Out to Eat – Melbourne • Out to Eat – Sydney • Papua New Guinea • Pidgin phrasebook • Queensland • Rarotonga & the Cook Islands • Samoa • Solomon Islands • South Australia • South Pacific • South Pacific Languages phrasebook • Sydney • Sydney city map • Sydney condensed • Tahiti & French Polynesia • Tasmania • Tonga • Tramping in New Zealand • Vanuatu • Victoria • Western Australia
Travel Literature: Islands in the Clouds • Kiwi Tracks: A New Zealand Journey • Sean & David's Long Drive

CENTRAL AMERICA & THE CARIBBEAN Bahamas, Turks & Caicos • Bermuda • Central America on a shoestring • Costa Rica • Cuba • Dominican Republic & Haiti • Eastern Caribbean • Guatemala, Belize & Yucatán: La Ruta Maya • Jamaica • Mexico • Mexico City • Panama • Puerto Rico • Read This First Central & South America • World Food Mexico • Yucatán
Travel Literature: Green Dreams: Travels in Central America

EUROPE Amsterdam • Amsterdam city map • Andalucía • Austria • Baltic States phrasebook • Barcelona • Berlin • Berlin city map • Britain • British phrasebook • Brussels, Bruges & Antwerp • Budapest city map • Canary Islands • Central Europe • Central Europe phrasebook • Corfu & Ionians • Corsica • Crete • Crete condensed • Croatia • Cyprus • Czech & Slovak Republics • Denmark • Dublin • Eastern Europe • Eastern Europe phrasebook • Edinburgh • Estonia, Latvia & Lithuania • Europe on a shoestring • Finland • Florence • France • French phrasebook • Germany • German phrasebook • Greece • Greek Islands • Greek phrasebook • Hungary • Iceland, Greenland & the Faroe Islands • Istanbul city map • Ireland • Italian phrasebook • Italy • Krakow • Lisbon • London • London city map • London condensed • Mediterranean Europe • Mediterranean Europe phrasebook • Munich • Norway • Paris • Paris city map • Paris condensed • Poland • Portugal • Portugese phrasebook • Portugal travel atlas • Prague • Prague city map • Provence & the Côte d'Azur • Read This First Europe • Romania & Moldova • Rome • Russia, Ukraine & Belarus • Russian phrasebook • Scandinavian & Baltic Europe • Scandinavian Europe phrasebook • Scotland • Slovenia • Spain • Spanish phrasebook • St Petersburg • Switzerland • Trekking in Spain • Ukrainian phrasebook • Venice • Vienna • Walking in Britain • Walking in Ireland • Walking in Italy • Walking in Spain • Walking in Switzerland • Western Europe • Western Europe phrasebook • World Food Italy • World Food Spain
Travel Literature: The Olive Grove: Travels in Greece

LONELY PLANET

ON THE ROAD

Travel Guides explore cities, regions and countries and supply information on transport, restaurants and accommodations, regardless of your budget. They come with reliable, easy-to-use maps, practical advice, cultural and historical facts and a run down on attractions both on and off the beaten track. There are over 200 titles in this classic series, covering nearly every country in the world.

Lonely Planet Upgrades extend the shelf lives of existing travel guides by detailing any changes that may affect travel in a region since the book has been published. Upgrades can be downloaded for free on **www.lonelyplanet.com/upgrades**.

For travelers with more time than money, **Shoestring** guides offer dependable, firsthand information with hundreds of detailed maps, plus insider tips for stretching money as far as possible. Covering entire continents in most cases, the six-volume shoestring guides have been known as 'backpackers' bibles' for over 25 years.

For the discerning short-term visitor, **Condensed** guides highlight the best a destination has to offer in a full-color, pocket-sized format designed for quick access. From top sights and walking tours to opinionated reviews of where to eat, stay, shop and have fun.

CitySync lets travelers use their Palm™ or Visor™ handheld computers to guide them through a city's highlights with quick tips on transport, history, cultural life, major sights and shopping and entertainment options. It can also quickly search and sort hundreds of reviews of hotels, restaurants and attractions and pinpoint the place on scrollable street maps. CitySync can be downloaded from **www.citysync.com**.

MAPS & ATLASES

Lonely Planet's **City Maps** feature downtown and metropolitan maps as well as transit routes and walking tours. The maps come complete with an index of streets, a listing of sights and a plastic coat for extra durability.

Road Atlases are an essential navigation tool for serious travelers. Cross-referenced with the guidebooks, they also feature distance and climate charts and a complete site index.

LONELY PLANET

ESSENTIALS

Read This First books help new travelers to hit the road with confidence. These invaluable predeparture guides give step-by-step advice on preparing for a trip, budgeting, arranging a visa, planning an itinerary and staying safe while still getting off the beaten track.

Healthy Travel pocket guides offer a regional run down on disease hot spots and practical advice on predeparture health measures, staying well on the road and what to do in emergency situations. The guides come with a user-friendly design and helpful diagrams and tables.

Lonely Planet's **Phrasebooks** cover the essential words and phrases travelers may need when they're strangers in a strange land. It comes in a pocket-sized format with color tabs for quick reference, extensive vocabulary lists, easy-to-follow pronunciation keys and two-way dictionaries.

Lonely Planet's **Travel Journal** is a lightweight but sturdy travel diary for jotting down all those on the road observations and significant travel moments. It comes with a handy time zone wheel, world maps and useful travel information.

Lonely Planet's eKno is an all-in-one communication service developed especially for travelers, with low-cost international calls, free email and voicemail so that you can keep in touch while on the road. Check it out on **www.ekno.lonelyplanet.com**.

FOOD & RESTAURANT GUIDES

Lonely Planet's **Out to Eat** guides recommend the brightest and best places to eat and drink in the top international cities. These gourmet companions are arranged by neighborhood, packed with dependable maps, garnished with scene-setting photos and served with quirky features.

For people who live to eat, drink and travel, **World Food** guides are full of lavish photos good enough to eat. They come packed with details on regional cuisine, guides to local markets and produce, sumptuous recipes, useful phrases for shopping and dining, and a comprehensive culinary dictionary.

LONELY PLANET

OUTDOOR GUIDES

For those who believe the best way to see the world is on foot, Lonely Planet's **Walking Guides** detail everything from family strolls to difficult treks, with 'when to go and how to do it' advice supplemented by reliable maps and essential travel information.

Cycling Guides map a destination's best bike tours, long and short, in day-by-day detail. They contain all the information a cyclist needs, including advice on bike maintenance, places to eat and stay, innovative maps with detailed cues to the rides and elevation charts.

The **Watching Wildlife** series is perfect for travelers who want authoritative information but don't want to tote a field guide. Packed with advice on where, when and how to view a region's wildlife, each title features photos of over 300 species and contains engaging comments and insights into local flora and fauna.

With underwater color photos throughout, **Pisces Books** explore the world's best diving and snorkeling areas. Each book contains listings of diving services and dive resorts and detailed information on depth, visibility, difficulty of dives and a round up of the marine life you're likely to see through your mask.

LONELY PLANET

OFF THE ROAD

Journeys, the travel literature series written by renowned travel authors, capture the spirit of a place or illuminate a culture with a journalist's attention to detail and a novelistic flair for words. These are tales to soak up while you're actually on the road or dip into as an at-home armchair indulgence.

The new range of lavishly illustrated **Pictorial** books is just the ticket for both travelers and dreamers. Offbeat tales and vivid photographs bring the adventure of travel to your doorstep long before the journey begins and long after it is over.

The Lonely Planet **Videos** encourage the same independent tough-minded approach as the guideboks. Currently airing throughout the world, this award-winning series features innovative footage and an all-original soundtrack.

Yes, we know, work is tough, so do a little bit of desk side-dreaming with the spiral bound Lonely Planet **Diary,** the tear away page-a-day **Day to Day Calendar** or any Lonely Planet **Wall Calendar,** filled with great photos from around the world.

TRAVELERS NETWORK

Lonely Planet online, Lonely Planet's award-winning Web site has insider information on hundreds of destinations from Amsterdam to Zimbabwe, complete with interactive maps and relevant links. The site also offers the latest travel news, recent reports from travelers on the road, guidebook upgrades, a travel links site, an online book buying option and a lively traveler's bulletin board. It can be viewed at **www.lonelyplanet.com** or AOL keyword: **lp**.

Planet Talk is the quarterly print newsletter full of gossip, advice, anecdotes and author articles. It provides an antidote to the being-at-home blues and lets you plan and dream for the next trip. Contact the nearest Lonely Planet office for you free copy.

Comet, the free Lonely Planet newsletter, comes via email once a month. It's loaded with travel news, advice, dispatches from authors, travel competitions and letters from readers. To subscribe, click on the Comet subscription link on the front page of the Web site.

Index

A

Abercrombie, William 300, 433
accommodations 65–8. *See also individual locations*
  B&Bs 67–8
  cabins 65–7
  camping 65, 100, 105–6
  costs 44, 45
  hostels 41, 67
  hotels & motels 68
  roadhouses 68
  wilderness lodges 68
acute mountain sickness (AMS) 56
Admiralty Island 223–5
Aialik Bay 333
AIDS 57
air travel 72–8, 88–90
  bush planes 89–90
  flightseeing 263–4
  glossary 74–5
  tickets 73–4
airports 72–3. *See also individual locations*
  security 53–4
Alaska Aviation Heritage Museum 260
Alaska Center for the Performing Arts 255
Alaska Chilkat Bald Eagle Preserve 236–7
Alaska Direct Bus Line 79, 91
Alaska Division of Parks 104
Alaska Homestead & Historical Museum 432
Alaska Hwy. *See* Alcan
Alaska Lands Bill 20
Alaska Marine Hwy 98, 99, 385–6
Alaska Maritime National Wildlife Refuge 351–2
Alaska Museum of Natural History 282

Alaska National Interest Lands Conservation Act 32
Alaska Native Claims Settlement Act 18, 20, 27, 31–2
Alaska Native Heritage Center 258
Alaska Natural History Association (ANHA) 59
Alaska Peninsula 378–85
Alaska Pioneers Home 193
Alaska Public Lands Information Center 253, 254
Alaska Railroad 92–5, 251, 254, 274, 426, **93**
Alaska Range 23, 434
Alaska Raptor Rehabilitation Center 195
Alaska SeaLife Center 326
Alaska State Museum 210
Alaska State Railroad Museum 426
Alaska Wilderness Recreation & Tourism Association (AWRTA) 58–9
Alaska Wilderness Studies (AWS) 63
Alaska Zoo 259
Alaskaland 455, 457
AlaskaPass 82
Alaskon Express 79, 90–1
Alcan 17, 31, 36, 78, 80–1, 88, 429–33
alcohol 61, 69. *See also* bars; breweries
alder 150
Aleutian Islands 385–91
Aleutian Range 23
Aleuts 14, 31, 33, 292
Alsek River 234
altitude sickness 56
Alutiiq Museum & Archaeological Repository 371
Alyeska Glacier 279
Alyeska Ski Area 277–8
American Bald Eagle Foundation 232

American Sightseeing 86
AMS. *See* acute mountain sickness
Anan Bear Observatory 181
Anchor Point 348–9
Anchorage 249–89, **250, 252, 256–7**
  accommodations 265–7
  activities 260–3
  climate 24
  entertainment 270–2
  history 249, 251
  north of 281–9
  organized tours 263–5
  restaurants 267–70
  shopping 272–3
  south of 275–81
  transportation 273–5
  walking tour 254
Anchorage Coastal Wildlife Refuge 275
Anchorage Museum of History & Art 255
Angoon 223–4
ANHA. *See* Alaska Natural History Association
Aniakchak National Monument & Preserve 26
ANWR. *See* Arctic National Wildlife Refuge
Arctic Alaska 476–7, 489–98
Arctic Bicycle Club 59
arctic char 146
Arctic Circle 491
Arctic National Wildlife Refuge (ANWR) 20, 25, 28
Arctic Ocean 497
Arctic opal 70
artists 255, 352
arts & crafts 33–4, 70–1, 232
Athabascans 14, 31, 33, 446
Atigun Pass 492
ATMs 43
Auke Bay 215
aurora borealis 458

AWS. *See* Alaska Wilderness Studies
AWRTA. *See* Alaska Wilderness Recreation & Tourism Association

B

backcountry. *See* wilderness
backpacking. *See* hiking & backpacking
bald eagles 157, 215, 232, 236–7
B&Bs. *See* accommodations
bank accounts 43
Baranov, Aleksandr 15, 191, 368
Baranov Museum 370
Barnette, ET 450
Barrow 495–8
bars 69–70. *See also* breweries
Bartlett Cove 228–9
baseball 70, 466, 496
basket weaving 33
Bear River Glacier 173
Beardslee Islands 228–9
bears
    avoiding 60–1
    species of 151–3, 377
    watching 181, 223, 224, 355, 377, 380, 381, 383–4
Beaver Creek canoe route 144, **121**
Begich-Boggs Visitor Center 281
Bellingham, Washington 84
belugas 156, 276, 340
Bering, Vitus 14, 191, 292
Bering Land Bridge 26, 481
Bering Strait 17
Berners Bay 215
berries 150–1, 363
Bettles 495
bicycles
    air shipping 76
    rental & purchase 98

bicycling 96–8. *See also* mountain biking
    Anchorage area 260–1
    club 59
    guidebooks 97
    The Interior 422
    routes 97–8
    Southcentral Alaska 335, 355
    Southeast Alaska 165
    Southwest Alaska 372, 374
    tours 100
Big Delta State Historic Park 435
Big Lake 402
birch 150
Birch Creek canoe route 472
birds. *See also* bald eagles
    rehabilitation center 195
    species of 50, 157–8
    watching 59, 158, 280, 355, 359, 386, 478
black bears 152
black cottonwood 150
Black Rapids Glacier 435
black spruce 149
Blackstone Bay 318–9
blanket toss 34
BLM. *See* Bureau of Land Management
boats. *See* cruises; ferries
Bodett, Tom 351
Bonanza Mine 314
books 48–51
breweries 272
Bristol Bay 391–4
Broad Pass 412
Brooks Range 23
brown bears 152, 355, 377, 383, 414–5
Bunker Hill 389
Bureau of Land Management (BLM) 67, 103–4
buses 78–80, 90–1
The Bush 476–98, **477**
bush planes 89–90
business hours 61
Buskin River State Recreation Site 372

Butcher, Susan 400
Byron Glacier 281

C

cabins. *See* accommodations
Caines Head State Recreation Area 328
camping. *See* accommodations
Canadian border 30, 173
canoeing. *See* paddling & river running
Cantwell 412
Cape Krusenstern National Monument 26
Captain Cook State Recreation Area 341
caribou 25, 153–4, 415
Carl E Wynn Nature Center 354
Carroll Inlet 166
cars 80–1, 95–6
    drinking & driving 61
    driver's license 41
    purchasing 96
    renting 36, 95–6
carvings 70–1
Cavern Lake Cave 177
caves 177
Central 472–3
Chatanika 471
Chatanika River 461
Chena Dome Trail 117–9, **118**
Chena Hot Springs 470
Chena Hot Springs Rd 469–71, **469**
Chena Lakes Recreation Area 436
Chena River 143, 461, 469
Chichagof Island 197
Chicken 445
Chief Shakes Island 180
children, traveling with 58
Childs Glacier 299
Chilikadrotna River 385
Chilkat River 234
Chilkoot Trail 110–2, **111**
Chistochina 441
Chitina 310–1

Chugach Heritage Center
326
Chugach State Park 261
Church of the Holy Ascension
388–9
Circle 474
Circle District Historical
Society Museum 472–3
Circle Hot Springs 473–4
Clam Gulch 345
clams 347
Clausen Memorial Museum
187
climate 24–5
climbing 59, 406–7. *See also*
rock climbing
clothes 38
Coast Range 23
Coastal Trail 116–7, **117**
coffee 69
Cold Bay 386–7
Coldfoot 491
Columbia Glacier 292, 304–5,
308
consulates 41–2
Cook, Frederick 406
Cook, Captain James 14, 15,
249, 254, 348
Cooper Landing 336–7
copper 313
Copper Center 309
Copper River 299
Copper River Delta 298
Cordova 292–300, **293**
Cordova Library & Museum
294
costs 44–5
cottonwood 150
courses 63
crabs 369–70
Craig 176
credit cards 43
crime 44
Cross Admiralty Island canoe
route 137–8, **136–7**
Crow Creek Mine 277
Crow Pass Trail 279
cruises 85–6, 99–100
currency 42
customs 42

cutthroat trout 145–6
cycling. *See* bicycling

D

Dall sheep 155
Dalton, Jack 230–1, 232
Dalton Hwy 489–92, **490**
Dan Moller Trail 126–7, **127**
daylight 24–5
Deadhorse 492
deer 154
Deer Mountain Trail 124–5,
124
Deer Mountain Tribal Hatchery & Eagle Center 164
Delta Junction 431–3, 435,
431
Delta River 437
Denali Hwy 436–9, **438–9**
Denali National Park 26,
413–26, **412–3, 417**
accommodations 422–5
bicycling 422
hiking & backpacking
121–3, 420–2
history 413–4
park road 418–20
restaurants 425
river running 422
transportation 91, 425–6
when to visit 415–6
Denali State Park 410–1
Denver Glacier 243
Dillingham 391–2
disabled travelers 57–8
Dixie Pass Route 129–30,
129
documents 40–1
dogsleds 70, 107, 399–400,
403–4, 430, 459, 481
Dolly Varden 146
dolphins 156
Donnelly Creek 435
Dorothy Page Museum 399
drinks
alcohol 61, 69
coffee 69
driver's license 41
drownings 130
drugs 61

d-2 20
Dutch Harbor 387–91,
388
Dyea 238, 241, 242

E

Eagle 446–9, **447**
Eagle River 282–3
Eagle Summit 472
eagles 157, 215, 232, 236–7
Earp, Wyatt 484
earthquakes 18, 23, 251, 258,
300
economy 28–30
Edgecumbe, Mt 196–7
education 33, 63
Eklutna 283–4
El Capitan Cave 177
Elderhostel 63
Eldred Passage 363
electricity 54
Elliott Hwy 474–5
Elmendorf AFB Wildlife
Museum 259
email 46–7
embassies 41
employment 63–5
entertainment 69–70. *See also
individual locations*
environmental issues & groups
20, 25–6, 59
Eskimos. *See* Inuit; Inupiat
Ester 427–9
etiquette 35
exchange rates 42–3
Exit Glacier 332
Exxon Valdez oil spill 19, 20,
294, 302, 351
Eyak, Mt 294–5
Eyak 292

F

Fairbanks 450–75, **451, 454,
456**
accommodations 462–4
activities 459–61
climate 24, 452
entertainment 466
history 450, 452–3
restaurants 464–6

transportation 466–8
Fairbanks Community
    Museum 455
Fairview Inn 408, 409–10
Far North Bicentennial Park
    259, 261
farming 30, 285, 286
fauna. See wildlife
fax 46
Fellows, Mt 412
ferries 36, 82–5, 98–9, 385–6
films 51
fish. See also halibut; salmon
    hatcheries 164, 190–1,
        221, 307
    species of 145–6
Fish Industrial Technology
    Center 371
fishing, recreational 144–6
    The Bush 493
    contests 62
    guidebooks 145
    Southcentral Alaska 298,
        336, 343, 348, 352,
        354
    Southeast Alaska 190
fishing industry 28–9, 30,
    295, 387
Flattop Mountain 262
flightseeing 263–4
flora. See plants
Fonte, Bartholeme de 14
food 68
    berries 150–1, 363
    clams 347
    paralytic shellfish poisoning
        (PSP) 59
    Spam & pilot bread 18
Fords Terror 134
Fort Abercrombie State
    Historical Park 371–2
Fort Egbert 448
Fort Knox Gold Mine 453
Fort Seward 231, 232
Fortymile River canoe route
    445
fur industry 14–5

G

Gakona Junction 441
Galaup, Jean-Françoise 15
Galbraith Lake 492
garnets 182
Gastineau Salmon Hatchery
    Visitor Center 221
Gates of the Arctic National
    Park 26, 492–5
Gavan Hill Trail 196
gay & lesbian travelers 57
Genet, Ray 406, 407, 408
geography 20–3, **21**
geology 23–4, 50
George Ashby Museum 309
George Inlet 166
George Parks Hwy 397–412
giardia 55, 106
Girdwood 277–80, **278**
Glacier Bay National Park 26,
    139–40, 225–9, **226**
Glacier Gardens 221
glaciers 23–4, 211–2, 225
    Alyeska Glacier 279
    Bear River Glacier 173
    Black Rapids Glacier 435
    Byron Glacier 281
    Childs Glacier 299
    Columbia Glacier 292,
        304–5, 308
    dangerous 299
    Denver Glacier 243
    Exit Glacier 332
    Grewingk Glacier 360
    Gulkana Glacier 435
    Hubbard Glacier 248
    Laughton Glacier 243
    Le Conte Glacier 188
    Malaspina Glacier 247
    Mendenhall Glacier 211–2
    Miles Glacier 299
    Muldrow Glacier 419
    Portage Glacier 280–1
    Root Glacier 314
    Saddlebag Glacier 296
    Sheridan Glacier 296, 298
    Sherman Glacier 296
    Shoup Glacier 304
    Taku Glacier 215

Valdez Glacier 300
    Worthington Glacier 309
Glenn Hwy 281–4, 441–4
Glennallen 441–2
goats, mountain 154–5
Gobbler's Knob 491
gold. See also Klondike gold
    rush; mining
    history 16, 29, 205, 210–1,
        450, 452–3, 472, 479–80
    panning 334–5, 446, 459,
        473, 481, 483
Gold Rush Cemetery 241
Golden Circle Route 246–7
Golden Sands Beach 481
golf 462
Good Friday Earthquake of
    1964 18, 251, 258, 300
government 28
Governor's Mansion 210
Gray Line 86
grayling 146
Green Tortoise 86–7
Grewingk Glacier 360
Greyhound 78–9
guide companies 106–9
guidebooks 48–9
Gulf Coast region. See South-
    central Alaska
Gulkana 441
Gulkana Glacier 435
Gulkana River 434
Gull Island 359
Gustavus 227–8, **227**

H

Haida 14, 31, 33, 177
Haines 229–37, **230, 233**
Haines Hwy 231
halibut 354
Halibut Cove 359
Hammond River 494
Harding, Warren G 17, 404,
    408, 426, 455
Harding Ice Field 332, 333
Harper, Walter 407
Hatcher Pass 288–9
health issues 54–7. See also
    safety issues
    altitude sickness 56

giardia 55, 106
HIV & AIDS 57
hypothermia 55–6
insurance 54
medical kit 55
motion sickness 56
paralytic shellfish poisoning
    (PSP) 59
rabies 56–7
sunburn & windburn 55
water purification 54–5
hemlock, western 149
Henry, Michael J 292
Heritage Library Museum
    255, 258
highways **90**. See also indi-
    vidual highways
hiking & backpacking. See
    also wilderness; individual
    trails
Anchorage area 261–3,
    278–9, 282, 284, 286–7,
    289
bears 60–1
The Bush 493–4, 495
equipment 39
Fairbanks area 460, 472
guide companies 106–9
guidebooks 49
hostels 67
The Interior 403, 410–1,
    420–2, 438, 440, 442–4
maps 38
popular routes 110–30
Southcentral Alaska 295–6,
    303–4, 313–4, 318,
    321–3, 327–8, 332–3,
    335, 338, 353–4, 360–1,
    363, **322**
Southeast Alaska 165, 181,
    187–8, 195–7, 203–4,
    212–5, 228, 232–3,
    242–3, **233, 245**
Southwest Alaska 372,
    382, 389–90, **373**
water purification 54–5,
    106
Historic Alaska Heritage
    Center 307
history 14–20, 50

hitchhiking 81–2
HIV 57
holidays 61–2
Holy Resurrection Church
    370–1
Homer 349–58, **349, 353**
Homer Spit 352
Hoonah 203–4
Hoonah-Tenakee kayak route
    138–9, **139**
Hope Hwy 334–5
Hope-Sunrise Mining
    Museum 334
hostels. See accommodations
hot springs 201, 470, 473–4,
    475, 486
hotels. See accommodations
Hubbard Glacier 248
humpbacks 225
hunting 32, 42, 337
Hutlinana Warm Springs 475
Hydaburg 177
Hyder 85, 172–4
hypothermia 55–6

I

Iditarod 70, 399, 400, 481
Iditarod Trail 282, 323, 327,
    400
Imaginarium 255
Independence Mine State
    Historical Park 288–9
indigenous peoples. See
    Native Alaskans
insects 59–60
Inside Passage waterway 20,
    82, 185
insurance 40–1, 54
The Interior 395–449, **396**
international transfers 43
Internet
    access 46–7
    resources 47–8
Inuit 14, 31, 33, 35, 154
Inupiat 495, 497
Inupiat Heritage Center 495
Isabel Pass 435
itineraries, suggested 36
Izembek National Wildlife
    Refuge 387

J

Jesus Town 469
Johnson Pass Trail 115–6, **116**
Juneau 205–22, **206, 222**
    accommodations 216–8
    activities 212–6
    climate 24
    entertainment 219–20
    history 205, 207–8
    restaurants 218–9
    transportation 220–1
Juneau, Mt 212
Juneau-Douglas City Museum
    209–10

K

Kachemak Bay 358–61
Kachemak Bay State Park 360
Kachemak Bay Transit 91
Kake 188, 201
Karstens, Henry 407
Kasilof 344–5
Katlian Bay 197
Katmai National Park 26–7,
    379–83
    hiking & backpacking
        127–8
    paddling 142
kayaking. See paddling & river
    running
Kenai 339–41, **340**
Kenai Fjords National Park 27,
    331–4
Kenai National Wildlife
    Refuge 104, 337–9
Kenai Peninsula 320–64, **322**
Kenai River 343
Kennicott 313
Kennicott River 314–5
Ketchikan 161–74, **162, 170**
    accommodations 167–8
    activities 165–6
    entertainment 168
    history 161
    restaurants 168
    transportation 169
Keystone Canyon 308
killer whales. See orcas
King Cove 386

king crab 369–70
King Salmon 378–9
Klawock 176–7
Klondike gold rush 16, 110, 238, 242, 300
Klondike Gold Rush National Historical Park 27, 240
Kluane National Park 237
Knightly Tours 86
Knik Museum & Sled Dog Musher's Hall of Fame 400
Knowles, Tony 19, 28, 32
Kobuk National Wild River 488
Kobuk Valley National Park 27
Kodiak 368–76, **369, 373**
Kodiak bears 377
Kodiak Island 368–78
Kodiak National Wildlife Refuge 104, 376–7
Kotzebue 24, 486–9, **487**
Kougarok Rd 486
Koyukuk River 494
Kuskulana River Bridge 312

L

Lake Clark National Park 27, 384–5
Lake Hood Air Harbor 260
land ownership 27
languages, Native 34, 35, 292
Last Chance Mining Museum 210–1
Laughton Glacier 243
laundry 54
Laurence, Sydney 255
Lazy Mountain 286
Le Conte Glacier 188
legal matters 61
lesbians. See gay & lesbian travelers
Livengood 475
logging 25, 30, 203
Lowe River 304
Lynx Lake 402–3

Bold indicates maps.

M

MacLaren Summit 438
magazines 52
mail 45–6
Malaspina Glacier 247
Manley Hot Springs 475
maps 37–8, 105
Marathon, Mt 327
marijuana 61
Marine Science Education Center 326
Matanuska Valley 281, 285, **283**
Matanuska Valley Agricultural Showcase 285
McCarthy 312
McCarthy Rd 310–2, **311**
McKinley, Mt 50, 122, 255, 395, 406–7, 415, 419
McNeil River State Game Sanctuary 383–4
measurements 54
medical kit 55
medical problems 55–7
Mendenhall Glacier 211–2
Mendenhall Valley 208, **208**
Metlakatla 171–2
Miles Glacier 299
Million Dollar Bridge 299
mining 29, 207, 210–1, 288–9, 309, 313. See also gold
Misty Fjords National Monument 132–4, 171, **133**
money 42–5
moose 153, 415
mosquitoes 60
motels. See accommodations
motion sickness 56
motorhomes 96
mountain biking 146
mountain goats 154–5
Mountaineering Club of Alaska 59
mountains 23
    Eagle Summit 472
    Edgecumbe 196–7
    Eielson 122
    Eyak 294–5
    Fellows 412
    Flattop 262
    Juneau 212
    Lazy 286
    Marathon 327
    McKinley 50, 122, 255, 395, 406–7, 415, 419
    Rendezvous Peak 263
    Ripinsky 232
    Roberts 210, 212
    Verstovia 196
    Williwaw 262–3
    Wolverine Peak 262
mud flats 279
Muir, John 178, 181, 225
Muir Inlet 139–40
Mulchatna River 385
Muldrow Glacier 419
museums
    Alaska Aviation Heritage Museum 260
    Alaska Homestead & Historical Museum 432
    Alaska Museum of Natural History 282
    Alaska State Museum 210
    Alaska State Railroad Museum 426
    Alutiiq Museum & Archaeological Repository 371
    Anchorage Museum of History & Art 255
    Baranov Museum 370
    Circle District Historical Society Museum 472–3
    Clausen Memorial Museum 187
    Cordova Library & Museum 294
    Dorothy Page Museum 399
    Elmendorf AFB Wildlife Museum 259
    Fairbanks Community Museum 455
    George Ashby Museum 309
    Heritage Library Museum 255, 258
    Hope-Sunrise Mining Museum 334
    Imaginarium 255

Juneau-Douglas City
    Museum 209–10
Knik Museum & Sled Dog
    Musher's Hall of Fame
    400
Last Chance Mining
    Museum 210–1
Museum of Alaska Trans-
    portation & Industry 399
Museum of the Aleutians
    389
Museum of the Arctic 488
Oscar Anderson House 254
Potter Section House
    275–6
Pratt Museum 351
Resurrection Bay Historical
    Museum 326
Sheldon Jackson Museum
    194
Sheldon Museum 232
Sullivan Roadhouse 432
Talkeetna Historical Society
    Museum 406–7
Trail of '98 Museum 241
Valdez Museum 303
Wrangell Museum 180
Musk Ox Farm 286

N

Nabesna Rd 440
Nagley's Store 408
Naha River Trail 166
Naknek Lake 382
Nancy Lake State Recreation
    Area 402
National Audubon Society 59
National Park Service 103
national parks 26–7. *See also*
    individual parks
Native Alaskans 31–3. *See
    also* Alaska Native Claims
    Settlement Act
    Aleuts 14, 31, 33, 292
    arts & crafts 33–4, 70–1,
        232
    Athabascans 14, 31, 33, 446
    culture 34–5, 258
    Eyak 292
    Haida 14, 31, 33, 177

Inuit 14, 31, 33, 35, 154
    Inupiat 495, 497
    languages 34, 35, 292
    petroglyphs 180
    Tlingit 14, 15, 31, 33, 191,
        194, 223
    writers 50
Nenana 426–7, 428, **427**
Nenana River 422
newspapers 52
Ninilchik 345–6, 348, **346**
Nizina River 315
Noatak National Preserve 27
Noatak River 488–9, 494
Nome 478–86, **479, 485**
Nome-Council Rd 485–6
Nome-Teller Rd 486
Norline Coaches 79–80
North Pole 468–9
North Slope 20, 23, 28
North Star bicycle route 98
northern lights 458
Northwestern Lagoon 333
Novarupta Volcano 379–80

O

oil industry 18–20, 28, 251,
    302. *See also* Trans-Alaska
    Pipeline
oil spill 19, 20, 294, 302, 351
Oliver Inlet 215
orcas 156
Oscar Anderson House 254

P

packing 38–9
paddling & river running
    blue-water 130–1
    The Bush 488–9, 494
    Fairbanks area 460–1, 472
    guide companies 106–9
    guidebooks 49–50
    The Interior 402–3, 422,
        434, 437, 445, 448
    popular routes 132–44
    safety 130
    Southcentral Alaska
        299–300, 304–5, 314–5,
        318–9, 328, 333, 361,
        363

Southeast Alaska 165–6,
        181–2, 188, 197, 201,
        202, 204, 215, 223,
        228–9, 234, 248
    Southwest Alaska 374,
        378, 382, 385, 390,
        392–3
    white-water 131–2
Palmer 284–8, **285**
paper birch 150
paralytic shellfish poisoning
    (PSP) 59
Park Creek 224–5
Parks Hwy. *See* George Parks
    Hwy
Parks Hwy Express 91
passports 40
Paxson 437
Pedro, Felix 16, 450, 459,
    462, 471
Pelican 204–5
Permanent Fund 28, 29
Perseverance Theater 34, 220
Perseverance Trail 212, **213**
personal ads 52
Petersburg 185–91, **184, 186**
Petersburg Lake Trail 125–6,
    126
petroglyphs 180
phones 46
photography 52–4
Pilgrim Hot Springs 486
Pillar Mountain 372
pilot bread 18
Pilz, George 205
Pinnell Mountain Trail
    119–20, **119**
pipeline. *See* Trans-Alaska
    Pipeline
planning 36–9
plants 50–1, 148–51. *See also*
    individual species
Point Barrow 25, 497
Point Bridget State Park 222
Polar Bear Swims 482
polar bears 153
politics 28
population 30–3
porpoises 156
Portage 280

Portage Glacier 280–1
Portage Pass Trail 318
postal services 45–6
potlatch 34
Potter Section House 275–6
Pratt Museum 351
Pribilof Islands 478
Prince of Wales Island 174–7, **175**
Prince Rupert, British Columbia 84–5
Prince William Sound 290–320
Prudhoe Bay 18, 19, 28, 29, 251
PSP. *See* paralytic shellfish poisoning
ptarmigan 157

R

rabies 56–7
radio 52
rainbow trout 145
Redington, Joe, Sr 400
Reid, Frank 238, 241
Reindeer Farm 286
religion 35
Rendezvous Peak 263
restaurants 45, 69. *See also individual locations*
Resurrection Bay 333
Resurrection Bay Historical Museum 326
Resurrection Pass Trail 112–4, **113**
Resurrection River 327
Richardson Hwy 308–10, 433–6
Richardson Wildlife Center 259
Rika's Roadhouse 435–6
Ring of Fire 22, 23, 365
Ripinsky, Mt 232
river running. *See* paddling & river running
roadhouses. *See* accommodations

Roberts, Mt 210, 212
rock climbing 147, 261
Rogers, Will 496, 497
Root Glacier 314
Round Island 393–4
Round-the-World tickets 73
Russell Fjord 23–4
Russian Bishop's House 194
Russian Lakes Trail 114–5, **115**
Russian Orthodox Church 35, 370, 371
Russian-American Company 15, 368
RVs 96

S

Saddlebag Glacier 296
safety issues. *See also* health issues
  bears 60–1
  crime 44
  drownings 130
salmon 28–9, 30, 157, 161, 164, 221, 343, 391
Santa Claus House 468–9
Savonoski River 142, **143**
Saxman Totem Park 169–70
SEACC. *See* Southeast Alaska Conservation Council
seals 156, 478
seasonal affective disorder (SAD) 452
Seldovia 361–4, **362**
senior travelers 41, 58, 63
Seward 323–31, **324**
Seward, William H 15–6
Seward Bus Lines 91
Seward Hwy 275–7, 321, 323
Shakes, Chief 180
sheep 155
Sheldon, Don 406, 407, 408
Sheldon Jackson Museum 194
Sheldon Museum 232
Shelekhov, Grigory 368
Shelikof Bay 197
Sheridan Glacier 296, 298
Sherman Glacier 296
shopping 70–1
Shoup Bay 304
Shoup Glacier 304

Shrine of St Terese 221
Shuyak Island State Park 378
Sierra Club 59
Sitka 191–201, **192, 195**
Sitka National Historic Park 27, 194–5
Sitka spruce 149
Skagway 238–47, **239, 245**
skiing 277–8
Slana 440
Smith, Soapy 238, 241, 243, 245
softball 496
Soldotna 341–4, **342**
Solomon Gulch 304, 307
Sourdough Creek 434
Sourdough Expedition 406–7
Southcentral Alaska 290–364, **291**
Southeast Alaska 159–248, **160**
Southeast Alaska Conservation Council (SEACC) 59
Southwest Alaska 365–94, **366–7**
Spam 18
special events 62–3
sports 70. *See also individual sports*
spruce 149
St George 478
St Herman's Theological Seminary 371
St Joseph Church 481
St Michael's Cathedral 193
St Nicholas Russian Orthodox Church 209
St Paul 478
Stan Price State Wildlife Sanctuary 224
state capitol 209
state fair 62, 234, 286, 287
statehood 16–7
Steese Hwy 471–4, **471**
Sterling Hwy 336, 344
Stevens, Ted 25–6
Stikine River 181–2
Stuck, Hudson 407
students 41, 65
subsistence rights 32

Sullivan Roadhouse 432
summer solstice 61–2
sunburn 55
surfing 374
Swanson Lake canoe route
    140, 142, **141**
Swanson River canoe route
    140, 142
Swenson, Rick 400

T

Taku Glacier 215
Taku Inlet 215
Talkeetna 404–10, **405**
Talkeetna Cemetery 408
Talkeetna Historical Society
    Museum 406–7
Tanana River 461
Tangle Lakes 437, 438
Tatshenshinin River 234
Tatum, Robert 407
taxes 45
Taylor Hwy 444–9
Tebenkof Bay Wilderness 201
telephones 46
Teller 486
Tenakee Springs 201–3
Tetlin National Wildlife Refuge
    Visitor Center 429
theater 34, 69, 220
Thomas Bay 188
Thorne Bay 177
tidal bores 277
tides 279
Tikchik Lakes 392–3
time zone 54
tipping 45
Tlikakila 385
Tlingit 14, 15, 31, 33, 191,
    194, 223
Tok 429–30
Tok Cutoff 439–41
Totem Bight State Park 171
totems 31, 33–4, 164, 165,
    169–70, 171
tourism 29, 202
tourist offices 39–40
tours, organized 86–7,
    99–100. *See also individual
    locations*

Tracy Arm 134–5, 215–6,
    135
Trail of '98 Museum 241
trains 36, 92–5, 110, 274, **93**
Trans-Alaska Pipeline 18–9,
    302, 307, 308, 452–3, 459
transportation
    air travel 72–8, 88–90
    bicycles 96–8
    buses 78–80, 90–1
    cars 36, 80–1, 95–6
    cruises 85–6, 99–100
    ferries 36, 82–5, 98–9,
        385–6
    hitchhiking 81–2
    local 99
    trains 36, 92–5, 274, **93**
travel insurance 40–1, 54
traveler's checks 43
Treadwell Mine 211
trees 149–50
trekking. *See* hiking & back-
    packing
tsunamis 18, 23
tundra 149, 476
Turnagain Arm 276–7
Tutka Bay 359–60
TV 51, 52

U

Unalaska 387–91, **388**
University of Alaska 33, 63,
    221
    Anchorage 260
    Fairbanks 457–9
Upper Tangle Lakes 437
US Fish & Wildlife Service
    104
US Forest Service (USFS)
    65–6, 103

V

Valdez 300–7, **301**
Valdez Glacier 300
Valdez Museum 303
Valley of 10,000 Smokes
    127–8, 380, **128**
Vancouver, George 15, 225,
    254
Verstovia, Mt 196

video 52–4
visas 40
visitor guides 51
volcanoes 22, 23, 365,
    379–80
volunteer work 64–5

W

walruses 393
Washburn, Bradford 407
Wasilla 397–402, **398**
water purification 54–5, 106
websites 47–8
weights 54
West Chichagof 197
Westchester Lagoon Sanctuary
    259
Western Alaska 476, 478–89
whale watching 157
    Anchorage area 276, 277
    Southcentral Alaska 340
    Southeast Alaska 188–9,
        198, 225
whales 156–7
    belugas 156, 276, 340
    humpbacks 225
White Mountains Summit Trail
    120–1, **121**
White Pass & Yukon Route
    railroad 110, 238, 240,
    243
white-water paddling. *See*
    paddling
Whittier 316–20, **317**
Wickersham, Judge James
    210, 406, 447, 448, 457
Wickersham State Historical
    Site 210
wilderness 101–9, **102**. *See
    also individual activities*
    camping 105–6
    conduct 105
    essentials 104–5
    governmental control of
        103–4
    guide companies 106–9
    lodges 68
    maps 105
Wilderness Society 59
wildflowers 50, 151

wildlife 148, 151–8. *See also individual species*
  centers 259
  dangerous 59–61
  guidebooks 50–1, 148
  refuges 20, 224, 275, 337–9, 351–2, 376–7, 387
  tracks 147
wildlife watching 147
  The Bush 478
  The Interior 414–5
  Southcentral Alaska 298, 310, 337
  Southwest Alaska 386, 393–4
  tours 100

Williwaw, Mt 262–3
Willow (town) 403–4
willow (tree) 150
windburn 55
Wiseman 491
Wolf Creek 166
Wolf Song of Alaska 259
Wolverine Peak 262
wolves 25, 154, 155–6, 259, 415
women travelers 57
Wood River 392
Wood-Tikchik State Park 392–3, **393**
work 63–5
World Eskimo-Indian Olympics 34–5

World War II 387, 389
Worthington Glacier 309
Wrangell 178–85, **179, 184**
Wrangell Museum 180
Wrangell–St Elias National Park 27, 129–30, 310–6

Yakutat 247–8
Yukon Quest 459
Yukon River 448, 490
Yukon-Charley Rivers National Preserve 27, 448

zoo 259

Boxed Text

Air Shipping a Bicycle 76
Air Travel Glossary 74–5
Alaska by Dogsled 107
Alaska in April 37
Alaskan Cuisine: Spam & Pilot Bread 18
Alaska's Permanent Fund 29
Arctic Fund-Raising 488
The Art of Sydney Laurence 255
Barrow on the Tonight Show 498
Baseball in Barrow 496
The Bears of Kodiak 377
The Border Patrol at Hyder 173
Breaking the Ice in Nenana 428
Brewing Beer in Anchorage 272
A Bridge to Dyea 242
The Business of Ferrying 99
Canaries of the Sea 276
Changes at Denali National Park 414
A Day at the Beach in Nome 482
Deadly Glaciers 299
Death by Drowning 130
Death in the Mud Flats 279
Digging for Clams 347
Everyday Health 57
Flagging a Train 94
Garnet Sellers of Wrangell 182
The Great Salmon War 30
Hanging Ten in Alaska 374

Hitting the Links at Two in the Morning 462
Hooking a Halibut in Homer 354
Hot Springs near Fairbanks 470
The Inuit Culture of Snow 35
Joe Redington Sr 1917–1999 400
Katmai National Park on the Move 380
The Largest King of Them All 343
The Literary Pride of Homer 351
Looking for Love in Alaska 52
Love Boat Go Home 202
Medical Kit 55
Native Alaskan Culture in Anchorage 258
The Northern Lights 458
Panning for a Fortune 446
A Presidential Visit to Alaska 17
The Right to Subsist 32
The Rise & Fall of Totems 165
A Road to Somewhere Else 207
A Road to Whittier 319
Scaling the Mountain 406–7
Skipping the Alcan 88
Striking It Rich in Nome 483
Super Bowl Sunday in Dillingham 391
Ten Years after the Spill 302
Who Owns the Land? 27
Winter in Fairbanks 452
Wyatt Earp in Alaska 484

MAP LEGEND

BOUNDARIES

- ·‒·‒·‒·‒·‒ International
- ·········· State, Province
- ‒‒‒‒‒ County

HYDROGRAPHY

Water
Reef
Coastline
Beach
River, Waterfall
Swamp, Spring

ROUTES & TRANSPORT

Freeway
Toll Freeway
Primary Road
Secondary Road
Tertiary Road
Unpaved Road
Pedestrian Mall
Trail
Chair Lift
Ferry Route
Railway, Train Station
Mass Transit Line & Station

ROUTE SHIELDS

1 Highway
10 State Highway

AREA FEATURES

Cemetery
Ecological Reserve
Glacier
Golf Course
Mud
Park

MAP SYMBOLS

- ✪ NATIONAL CAPITAL
- ◉ State, Provincial Capital
- ● LARGE CITY
- ● Medium City
- ● Small City
- ● Town, Village
- ○ Point of Interest

- ■ Place to Stay
- ▲ Campground
- ⛏ RV Park

- ▼ Place to Eat
- ⊌ Bar (Place to Drink)

- ✚ Airfield
- ✈ Airport
- ∴ Archaeological Site, Ruins
- ⑤ Bank
- ⌂ Baseball Diamond
- ⏚ Beach
- ⤧ Border Crossing
- ⊖ Bus Depot, Bus Stop
- ⊞ Cathedral
- ⛟ Canoe
- ⌁ Cave
- ✝ Church
- ⊙ Embassy
- ⤫ Footbridge
- ⤚ Fish Hatchery
- ✿ Garden
- ⛽ Gas Station
- ✛ Hospital, Clinic
- ⓘ Information
- 🗼 Lighthouse
- ✳ Lookout

- 🞂 Mine
- Å Monument
- ▲ Mountain
- 🏛 Museum
- 🜨 Observatory
- ← One-Way Street
- ♣ Park
- P Parking
-)(Pass
- 🎋 Picnic Area
- ★ Police Station
- 🏊 Pool
- ✉ Post Office
- ❖ Shopping Mall
- ⛷ Skiing (Alpine)
- 🎿 Skiing (Nordic)
- 🏛 Stately Home
- ✡ Synagogue
- 🚶 Trailhead
- 🍷 Winery
- 🐘 Zoo

Note: Not all symbols displayed above appear in this book.

LONELY PLANET OFFICES

Australia
PO Box 617, Hawthorn 3122, Victoria
☎ 03 9819 1877 fax 03 9819 6459
email talk2us@lonelyplanet.com.au

USA
150 Linden Street, Oakland, California 94607
☎ 510 893 8555, TOLL FREE 800 275 8555
fax 510 893 8572
email info@lonelyplanet.com

UK
10A Spring Place, London NW5 3BH
☎ 020 7428 4800 fax 020 7428 4828
email go@lonelyplanet.co.uk

France
1 rue du Dahomey, 75011 Paris
☎ 01 55 25 33 00 fax 01 55 25 33 01
www.lonelyplanet.fr

World Wide Web: www.lonelyplanet.com *or* AOL keyword: lp
Lonely Planet Images: lpi@lonelyplanet.com.au

520